★★★★★★★★★

The Brief
American Pageant

VOLUME II

★★★★★★★★★

The Brief
American Pageant

A HISTORY OF THE REPUBLIC

Fifth Edition

★★★★★★★★★

David M. Kennedy
Stanford University

Lizabeth Cohen
Harvard University

Thomas A. Bailey
Valparaiso University

Mel Piehl
Valparaiso University

HOUGHTON MIFFLIN COMPANY
Boston   New York

★★★★★★★★★

Sponsoring Editor: Colleen Shanley Kyle
Senior Project Editor: Rosemary R. Jaffe
Senior Production/Design Coordinator: Jill Haber
Senior Cover Design Coordinator: Deborah Azerrad Savona
Senior Manufacturing Coordinator: Marie Barnes
Senior Marketing Manager: Sandra McGuire

Cover image: *Parade, Washington Square, 1912,* by William J. Glackens.
Collection of the Whitney Museum of American Art, New York.

Printed in the U.S.A.

Library of Congress Catalog Card Number: 99-71963

ISBN: 0-395-97867-X

1 2 3 4 5 6 7 8 9-QF-03 02 01 00 99

Contents

Maps, Graphs, and Tables

Sail, sail thy best, ship of Democracy,
Of value is thy freight, 'tis not the Present only,
The Past is also stored in thee,
Thou holdest not the venture of thyself alone, not of
　　the Western continent alone,
Earth's résumé entire floats on thy keel,
　　O ship, is steadied by thy spars,
With thee Time voyages in trust, the antecedent
　　nations sink or swim with thee,
With all their ancient struggles, martyrs, heroes,
　　epics, wars, thou bear'st the other continents,
Theirs, theirs as much as thine, the destination-port
　　triumphant. . . .

WALT WHITMAN

Thou Mother with Thy Equal Brood, 1872

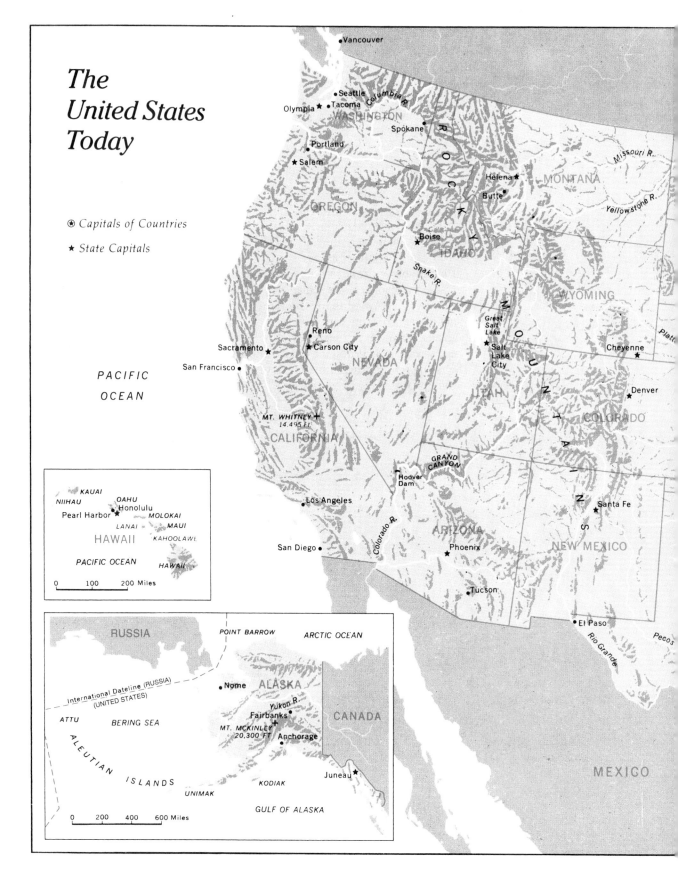

The United States Today

⊛ Capitals of Countries
★ State Capitals

PACIFIC OCEAN

Vancouver

Seattle
Olympia ★ ★ Tacoma
WASHINGTON
Spokane

Portland
Salem ★
OREGON

R
O
C
K
Y

Helena ★
MONTANA
Butte

Boise ★
IDAHO

Snake R.

WYOMING

Missouri R.
Yellowstone R.

Reno
Sacramento ★ ★ Carson City
San Francisco
NEVADA

Great Salt Lake
Salt ★ Lake City
UTAH

Platt

Cheyenne ★

Denver ★
COLORADO

MT. WHITNEY
14,495 Ft.
CALIFORNIA

M
O
U
N
T
A
I
N
S

GRAND CANYON
Hoover Dam

Los Angeles

Colorado R.

San Diego

ARIZONA
Phoenix ★

Tucson

Santa Fe ★

NEW MEXICO

El Paso
Rio Grande
Pecos

MEXICO

KAUAI
NIIHAU   OAHU
Pearl Harbor ★ Honolulu
LANAI   MOLOKAI
HAWAII   MAUI
KAHOOLAWE
PACIFIC OCEAN
HAWAII

0   100   200 Miles

RUSSIA
POINT BARROW   ARCTIC OCEAN

International Dateline (RUSSIA)
(UNITED STATES)

Nome   ALASKA

Yukon R.
Fairbanks
MT. MCKINLEY
20,300 FT.   Anchorage

CANADA

ATTU   BERING SEA

A L E U T I A N   I S L A N D S

UNIMAK   KODIAK

Juneau ★

GULF OF ALASKA

0   200   400   600 Miles

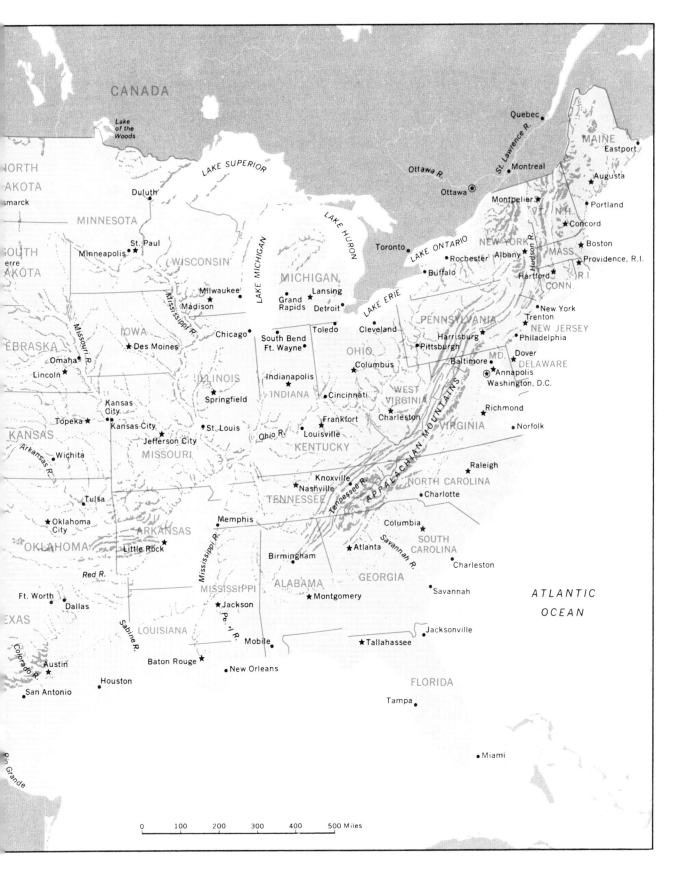

CANADA

Lake of the Woods

LAKE SUPERIOR

NORTH DAKOTA
Bismarck

SOUTH DAKOTA
Pierre

MINNESOTA
Duluth

Ottawa R.
Ottawa

Quebec
St. Lawrence R.
Montreal

MAINE
Eastport
Augusta

Montpelier
VT. N.H.
Portland
Concord

St. Paul
Minneapolis

WISCONSIN

LAKE MICHIGAN

LAKE HURON

Toronto

LAKE ONTARIO
Rochester
Buffalo

NEW YORK
Albany
Hartford

MASS.
Boston
Providence, R.I.
R.I.
CONN.

Hudson R.

NEBRASKA

Omaha
Lincoln

Missouri R.

Milwaukee
Madison

Mississippi R.

IOWA
Des Moines

MICHIGAN
Grand Rapids
Lansing
Detroit

LAKE ERIE

Cleveland

New York
Trenton
NEW JERSEY
Philadelphia

Chicago

South Bend
Ft. Wayne

Toledo

OHIO
Columbus

PENNSYLVANIA
Harrisburg
Pittsburgh

Baltimore
MD.
Dover
DELAWARE
Annapolis
Washington, D.C.

ILLINOIS

INDIANA
Indianapolis

Springfield

Cincinnati

WEST VIRGINIA

Richmond

KANSAS
Topeka
Wichita

Kansas City
Kansas City

Jefferson City

St. Louis

MISSOURI

Ohio R.

Frankfort
Louisville

KENTUCKY

Charleston

VIRGINIA

Norfolk

Arkansas R.

Tulsa

Oklahoma City

OKLAHOMA

Memphis

ARKANSAS
Little Rock

Knoxville
Nashville

TENNESSEE

Tennessee R.

APPALACHIAN MOUNTAINS

NORTH CAROLINA

Raleigh

Charlotte

Columbia

SOUTH CAROLINA

Charleston

Red R.

Mississippi R.

Birmingham

Atlanta

Savannah R.

GEORGIA

Savannah

MISSISSIPPI

ALABAMA

Montgomery

ATLANTIC OCEAN

Ft. Worth
Dallas

TEXAS

Colorado R.

Austin

San Antonio

Houston

Sabine R.

LOUISIANA

Jackson

Pearl R.

Mobile

Baton Rouge

New Orleans

Tallahassee

Jacksonville

FLORIDA

Tampa

Miami

Rio Grande

0   100   200   300   400   500 Miles

Preface

The American Pageant has long enjoyed a reputation as one of the most accessible, popular, and effective textbooks in the field of American history. Its authors, Thomas A. Bailey and David M. Kennedy, now joined by Lizabeth Cohen, have sustained and enhanced the key features that strongly distinguish the *Pageant* from other American history textbooks and make it both appealing and useful to countless students: clarity, concreteness, a consistent chronological narrative, strong emphasis on major themes, avoidance of clutter, access to a variety of interpretive perspectives, and a colorful writing style leavened, as appropriate, with wit.

Mel Piehl has seen to it that *The Brief American Pageant*, Fifth Edition, maintains these outstanding attributes of the parent text in a format suitable for one-semester courses in American history, as well as for courses that rely heavily on supplementary readings in secondary historical works or primary sources. Like the longer Eleventh Edition from which it is drawn, *The Brief American Pageant* incorporates its authors' combined strengths in political, economic, social, and cultural history. This edition is especially concerned with integrating the rich recent scholarship in social history into *The Brief American Pageant*'s core political narrative. It maintains a commitment to telling the story of the American past as vividly and clearly as possible, without sacrificing a sense of the often-sobering seriousness of history, and of its sometimes challenging complexity.

To help students come to grips with that complexity, the book has been divided into six sections and organized around sets of major issues that shaped successive stages of American history. Each section begins with an essay that establishes the basic thematic contours of the group of chapters that follow. The essay on "Founding the New Nation," for example, introduces the chapters dealing with the settlement and colonial periods. It emphasizes the themes of racial, ethnic, religious, and regional diver-

sity in Britain's North American colonies, and the slow emergence of an "American" national identity, culminating in the Revolution of 1776. To take another example, the essay on "Making Modern America" highlights the role of World War II both in propelling the phenomenal wave of postwar prosperity at home and setting the stage for the Cold War that dominated both the domestic and international scenes for nearly half a century thereafter.

These six essays, then, are intended to guide readers into unfamiliar material, to serve as reference points with which to make sense of the material as they work through it, and as tools for reviewing their understanding of the larger structures and deeper dynamics of history that are often obscured by a preoccupation with discrete facts. The essays reflect the authors' conviction that historical study should strive for synthesis and informed interpretation. Students should not merely seek to memorize mountains of data, but to identify patterns in the often baffling welter of factual detail, and to appreciate complex chains of cause and consequence.

Readers will find other new features in this edition of *The Brief American Pageant* as well: a number of substantially revised and expanded "Varying Viewpoints" essays; enriched discussion at many points of the contributions of women; expanded treatment of working-class life; extensive analysis of the concept of republicanism; a thoroughly updated account of Reconstruction; substantial attention to African-American and Native American history; and careful integration of social, political, and cultural themes in the post–World War II period. The material concerning the period from 1800 to 1824 has been reorganized into two chapters that cover the Jefferson and Madison presidencies (Chapter 11) and the War of 1812 through the Monroe Doctrine (Chapter 12). In addition, this Fifth Edition features a new design, many revised maps and charts, and several entirely new maps and photographs.

Supplements Available with *The Brief American Pageant,* Fifth Edition

A complete supplementary program accompanies the fifth edition of *The Brief American Pageant,* comprised of the following items:

A revised **Instructor's Resource Guide** is available with this edition, featuring summaries of chapter themes; chapter outlines; suggestions and resources for lectures; and chapter sketches. It also includes identification, multiple choice, and essay questions for the instructor's use.

The test questions found in the **Instructor's Resource Guide** can also be accessed through the Computerized Test Bank for Windows computers. Adopters of the text can add to and customize their own testing materials with this program.

The **Student Guidebook** assists students by focusing their attention on the central themes and major historical developments of each chapter, while presenting a variety of exercises, a glossary of key historical terms, and numerous study review questions designed to reinforce comprehension of the text.

@history: an interactive American history source is a multimedia teaching/learning package that combines a variety of material on a cross-platformed CD-ROM—primary sources (text and graphic), video, and audio—with activities that can be used to analyze, interpret, and discuss primary sources; to enhance collaborative learning; and to create multimedia lecture presentations. **@history** also has an accompanying web site, where on-line resources for *The American Pageant* and links to relevant sites can be found.

There is also a set of over one hundred fifty full-color **American History Map Transparencies**, available in two volume sets upon adoption.

A variety of **videos**, documentaries and docudramas by major film producers, is available for use with *The Brief American Pageant.*

Please contact your local Houghton Mifflin representative, or visit Houghton Mifflin's web site at http://www.hmco.com/college for more information about the ancillary items or to obtain desk copies.

Acknowledgments

Many people have contributed to this and past editions of *The Brief American Pageant.* We would especially like to thank the following colleagues who reviewed the manuscript and offered several useful suggestions for improvement: Douglas E. Kupel, Gateway Community College; Sandra K. Matthews-Lamb, Nebraska Wesleyan University; Margaret Rung, Roosevelt University; Thomas R. Turner, Bridgewater State University; Stephen Wiesner, Springfield Technical Community College.

Brevity, Shakespeare noted, is the soul of wit. Though condensed, this edition seeks to preserve the bright personality that has led generations of students to learn from *The American Pageant* that the pages of history need not be dull. We hope that readers will take pleasure in learning American history from this briefer book, and gain from it both a fresh appreciation of what has gone before and a seasoned perspective on what is to come.

D.M.K.
L.C.
M.P.

★★★★★★★★★

The Brief
American Pageant

23

****

The Ordeal of Reconstruction,

1865–1877

*****

With malice toward none, with charity for all, with firmness in the right as God gives us to see the right, let us strive on to finish the work we are in, to bind up the nation's wounds, to care for him who shall have borne the battle and for his widow and orphan, to do all which may achieve and cherish a just and lasting peace among ourselves and with all nations.

*****

ABRAHAM LINCOLN, SECOND INAUGURAL ADDRESS, MARCH 4, 1865

The Problems of Peace

The battle was done; the buglers were silent. Bone-weary and bloodied, the American people, North and South, faced the staggering challenges of peace. Four questions loomed large. How would the South, physically devastated by war and socially revolutionized by emancipation, be rebuilt? How would the liberated blacks fare as free men and women? How would the

Southern states be reintegrated into the Union? And who would direct the process of Reconstruction—the Southern states themselves, the president, or Congress?

Other questions also clamored for answers. What should be done with the captured Confederate ringleaders? During the war a popular Northern song had been "Hang Jeff Davis to a Sour Apple Tree."

Davis was clapped into prison for two years, but no treason trials were ever held. President Andrew Johnson pardoned all "rebel" leaders as a sort of Christmas present in 1868. Congress removed their civil disabilities thirty years later.

Dismal indeed was the picture presented by the war-wracked South when the rattle of musketry faded. Not only had an age perished, but a civilization had collapsed, in both its economic and its social structure. The moonlight-and-magnolia Old South, largely imaginary in any case, had forever gone with the wind.

Handsome cities of yesteryear, like Charleston and Richmond, were rubble strewn and weed choked. An Atlantan returned to his once-fair hometown and remarked, "Hell has laid her egg, and right here it hatched." Economic life had creaked to a halt. Banks and business houses had locked their doors, ruined by runaway inflation. Factories were smokeless, silent, dismantled. The transportation system had broken down completely. Efforts to untwist the rails corkscrewed by Sherman's soldiers proved bumpily unsatisfactory.

Agriculture—the economic lifeblood of the South—was almost hopelessly crippled. Once-white cotton fields yielded a lush harvest of nothing but green weeds. The slave-labor system had collapsed, seed was scarce, and livestock had been driven off by plundering Yankees. Pathetic instances were reported of men hitching themselves to plows, while women and children gripped the handles.

The princely planter aristocrats were humbled by the war—at least temporarily. Reduced to proud poverty, they faced charred and gutted mansions, lost investments, and almost worthless land. Their investment of more than $2 billion in slaves, their primary form of wealth, had evaporated with emancipation.

Beaten but unbent, many high-spirited white Southerners remained dangerously defiant. They cursed the "damnyankees" and spoke of "your government" in Washington instead of "our government." Conscious of no crime, these former Confederates continued to believe that their view of secession was correct and that the "lost cause" was still a just war. One popular anti-Union song ran:

> I'm glad I fought agin her, I only wish we'd won,
> And I ain't axed any pardon for anything I've done.

Such attitudes boded ill for the prospects of painlessly binding up the Republic's wounds.

Freedmen Define Freedom

Confusion abounded in the still-smoldering South about the precise meaning of "freedom" for blacks. Emancipation took effect haltingly and unevenly in different parts of the conquered Confederacy, and in some regions planters stubbornly protested that slavery was legal until state legislatures or the Supreme Court might act. For many slaves, the shackles of bondage were not struck off in a single mighty blow; long-suffering blacks often had to struggle out of their chains link by link.

Richmond Devastated *Charleston, Atlanta, and other Southern cities looked much the same, resembling bombed-out Berlin and Dresden in 1945.*

The variety of responses to emancipation, by whites as well as blacks, illustrated the sometimes startling complexity of the master-slave relationship. Loyalty to the plantation master prompted some slaves to resist the liberating Union armies. Other slaves' pent-up bitterness burst violently forth on the day of liberation. In one instance, a group of Virginia slaves laid twenty lashes on the back of their former master—a painful dose of his own favorite medicine.

Prodded by the bayonets of Yankee armies of occupation, all masters were eventually forced to recognize their slaves' permanent freedom. The once-commanding planter would assemble his former human chattels in front of the porch of the "big house" and announce their liberty. Though some blacks initially responded to news of their emancipation with suspicion and uncertainty, they soon celebrated their new-found freedom. Many took new names in place of the ones given by their masters and demanded that whites formally address them as "Mr." or "Mrs."

Tens of thousands of emancipated blacks took to the roads, some to test their freedom, others to search for long-lost spouses, parents, and children. Emancipation thus strengthened the black family, and many newly freed men and women formalized "slave marriages" for personal and pragmatic reasons, including the desire to make their children legal heirs.

Whole communities sometimes moved together in search of opportunity. From 1878 to 1880, some twenty-five thousand blacks from Louisiana, Texas, and Mississippi surged in a mass exodus to Kansas. The westward flood of these "Exodusters" was stemmed only when steamboat captains refused to transport more black migrants across the Mississippi River.

The church became the focus of black community life in the years following emancipation. As slaves, blacks had worshiped alongside whites, but now they formed their own churches pastored by their own ministers. The black churches grew robustly. The 150,000-member black Baptist church of 1850 reached 500,000 by 1870, while the African Methodist Episcopal church quadrupled in size from 100,000 to 400,000 in the first decade after emancipation. These churches formed the bedrock of black community life, and they soon gave rise to other benevolent, fraternal, and mutual aid societies. All these organizations helped blacks protect their newly won freedom.

Emancipation also meant education for many blacks. Learning to read and write had been a privilege generally denied to them under slavery. Freedmen wasted no time establishing societies for self-improvement, which undertook to raise funds to purchase land, build schoolhouses, and hire teachers. With black teachers in short supply, they turned to white women sent by the American Missionary Association for help, and to the federal government.

The Freedmen's Bureau

Abolitionists had long preached that slavery was a degrading institution. Now the emancipators had to face the brutal truth that the former slaves were overwhelmingly unskilled, unlettered, without property or money, and with scant knowledge of how to survive as free people. To cope with this problem throughout the conquered South, Congress created the Freedmen's Bureau in 1865.

On paper at least, the bureau was intended to be a kind of primitive welfare agency. It was to provide food, clothing, and education both to freedmen and to white refugees. It was also authorized to distribute up to forty acres of abandoned or confiscated land to black settlers. Headed by General O. O. Howard, who later founded Howard University, the bureau achieved its greatest successes in education. It taught an estimated 200,000 blacks how to read. Many former slaves had a passion for learning, partly because they wanted to close the gap between themselves and the whites and partly because they longed to read the Word of God.

But in other areas the bureau's accomplishments were meager—or even mischievous. Little confiscated Confederate land actually passed into black hands, as had been promised. Instead, local administrators often collaborated with planters in expelling blacks from towns and cajoling them into signing labor contracts to work for their former masters. Still, the white South resented the bureau as a meddlesome federal interloper that threatened to upset white racial dominance. President Andrew Johnson, who shared the white-supremacist views of most white Southerners, repeatedly tried to kill it, and it expired in 1872.

Primary School for Freedmen in Vicksburg, Mississippi, 1866   Top: *Outdoor recess at school.* Bottom: *Teaching the pupils; notice the wide range of ages.*

Johnson: The Tailor President

Few presidents have ever been faced with a more perplexing sea of troubles than that confronting Andrew Johnson. What manner of man was this medium-built, dark-eyed, black-haired Tennessean, chief executive by virtue of the bullet that killed Lincoln?

No citizen, not even Lincoln, ever reached the White House from humbler beginnings. Born to impoverished parents in North Carolina and early orphaned, Johnson never attended school but was apprenticed to a tailor at age ten. Ambitious to get ahead, he taught himself to read, and later his wife taught him to write and do simple arithmetic. Like many a self-made man, he was inclined to overpraise his maker.

Johnson early became active in politics in Tennessee, where he had moved when seventeen years

old. He shone as an impassioned champion of the poor whites against the planter aristocrats, and as a two-fisted stump speaker before angry and heckling crowds. Elected to Congress, he refused to secede with his own state and was then appointed war governor after Tennessee was partially "redeemed" by Union armies.

Political exigency next thrust Johnson into the vice presidency. Lincoln's Union party in 1864 needed to attract support from the War Democrats and other pro-Southern elements, and Johnson, a Democrat, seemed to be the ideal man.

"Old Andy" Johnson was no doubt a man of parts—unpolished parts. He was intelligent, able, forceful, and steadfastly devoted to duty and the Constitution. Yet the man who had raised himself from the tailor's bench to the president's chair was a misfit. A Southerner who did not understand the North, a Tennessean who had earned the distrust of the South, a Democrat who had never been accepted by the Republicans, a president who had never been elected to the office, he was not at home in a Republican White House. Hotheaded, contentious, and stubborn, he was the wrong man in the wrong place at the wrong time. A Reconstruction policy devised by the angels might well have failed in his tactless hands.

Presidential Reconstruction

Even before the shooting war had ended, the political war over Reconstruction had begun. Abraham Lincoln believed that the Southern states had never legally withdrawn from the Union. Their formal restoration to the Union would therefore be relatively simple. Accordingly, Lincoln in 1863 proclaimed his "10 percent" Reconstruction plan. It decreed that a state could be reintegrated into the Union when 10 percent of its voters in the presidential election of 1860 had taken an oath of allegiance to the United States and pledged to abide by emancipation. The next step would be formal erection of a state government. Lincoln would then recognize the purified regime.

Lincoln's proclamation provoked a sharp reaction in Congress, where Republicans feared the restoration of the planter aristocracy to power and the possible re-enslavement of the blacks. Republicans therefore rammed through Congress in 1864 the Wade-Davis Bill. It required that 50 percent of a state's voters take the oath of allegiance and demanded stronger safeguards for emancipation than Lincoln's as the price of readmission. Republicans were outraged when Lincoln "pocket-vetoed" this bill by refusing to sign it after Congress had adjourned.

The controversy surrounding the Wade-Davis Bill revealed deep differences between the president and Congress. Unlike Lincoln, many in Congress insisted that the seceders had indeed left the Union—had "committed suicide" as republican states—and had therefore forfeited all their rights. They could be readmitted only as "conquered provinces" on such conditions as Congress should decree.

The episode further revealed differences among two emerging Republican factions, moderates and radicals. The majority moderate group tended to agree with Lincoln that the seceded states should be restored to the Union as simply and swiftly as reasonable—though on Congress's terms, not the president's. The minority radical group believed that before the South could be restored its social structure should be uprooted, the haughty planters punished, and the newly emancipated blacks protected by federal power.

After the assassination of President Lincoln in April 1865, some radicals hoped that spiteful Andy Johnson, who shared their hatred for the planter aristocracy, would also share their desire to reconstruct the South with a rod of iron. But Johnson soon disillusioned them. He quickly recognized several of Lincoln's 10 percent governments, and on May 29, 1865, he issued his own Reconstruction proclamation. It disfranchised certain leading Confederates and called for special state conventions, which were required to repeal secession, repudiate all Confederate debts, and ratify the slave-freeing Thirteenth Amendment.

Johnson, savoring his dominance over the high-toned aristocrats who now begged his favor, granted pardons in abundance. Bolstered by the political resurrection of the planter elite, the recently rebellious states moved rapidly in the second half of 1865 to organize governments. But as the pattern of the new governments became clear, Republicans of all stripes grew furious.

The Baleful Black Codes

Among the first acts of the new Southern regimes sanctioned by Johnson was the passage of the iron-toothed Black Codes. These laws were designed to regulate the affairs of the emancipated blacks, much as the slave statutes had done in pre–Civil War days. The Black Codes aimed, first of all, to ensure a stable and subservient labor force. Dire penalties were therefore imposed on blacks who "jumped" their labor contracts, which usually committed them to work for the same employer for one year, generally at pittance wages.

The codes also sought to restore as nearly as possible the pre-emancipation system of race relations. Freedom was legally recognized, as were some other privileges, such as the right to marry. But all the codes forbade a black to serve on a jury or vote, and some even barred blacks from renting or leasing land.

These oppressive laws mocked the ideal of freedom, so recently purchased by buckets of blood. The Black Codes imposed terrible burdens on the unfettered blacks, struggling against mistreatment and poverty to make their way as free people. Thousands of impoverished former slaves slipped into virtual peonage as sharecropper farmers, as did many landless whites.

The Black Codes made an ugly impression in the North. If the former slaves were being re-enslaved, people asked one another, had not the Boys in Blue spilled their blood in vain? Had the North really won the war?

Congressional Reconstruction

These questions grew more insistent when the congressional delegations from the newly reconstituted Southern states presented themselves in the Capitol in December 1865. To the shock and disgust of the Republicans, many former Confederate leaders were on hand to claim their seats.

The appearance of these ex-rebels was a natural but costly blunder. Voters of the South, seeking able representatives, had turned instinctively to their experienced statesmen. But most of the Southern leaders were tainted by active association with the "lost cause." Among them were four former Confederate generals, five colonels, and various members of the Richmond cabinet and Congress. Worst of all, there was the shrimpy but brainy Alexander Stephens, ex–vice president of the Confederacy, still under indictment for treason.

The presence of these "whitewashed rebels" infuriated the Republicans in Congress. The war had been fought to restore the Union, but not on these kinds of terms. Most Republicans balked at giving up the political advantage they had enjoyed while the South had been "out" from 1861 to 1865. On the first day of the congressional session, December 4, 1865, they banged shut the door in the face of the newly elected Southern delegations.

Looking to the future, the Republicans were alarmed to realize that a restored South would be stronger than ever in national politics. Before the war a black slave had counted as three-fifths of a person in apportioning congressional representation. But now, owing to full counting of free blacks, the eleven rebel states were entitled to twelve more votes in Congress, and twelve more presidential electoral votes, than they had previously enjoyed. Again, angry voices in the North raised the cry, Who won the war?

Republicans had good reason to fear that ultimately they might be elbowed aside. Southerners might join hands with Democrats in the North and win control of Congress or maybe even the White House. If this happened, they could perpetuate the Black Codes, virtually re-enslaving the blacks. They could dismantle the economic program of the Republican party and possibly even repudiate the national debt. President Johnson thus deeply disturbed the congressional Republicans when he announced on December 6, 1865, that the recently rebellious states had satisfied his conditions and that in his view the Union was now restored.

Johnson Clashes with Congress

A clash between president and Congress was now inevitable. It exploded into the open in February 1866, when the president vetoed a bill (later repassed) extending the life of the controversial Freedmen's Bureau.

Aroused, the Republicans swiftly struck back. In March 1866 they passed the Civil Rights Bill, which conferred on the blacks the privileges of American citizenship and struck at the Black Codes. President Johnson resolutely vetoed this forward-looking measure, but in April congressmen steam-rolled it over his veto—something they repeatedly did henceforth. The hapless president, dubbed "Sir Veto" and "Andy Veto," had his presidential wings clipped short, as Congress increasingly assumed the dominant role in running the government.

The Republicans undertook to rivet the principles of the Civil Rights Bill into the Constitution as the Fourteenth Amendment. The proposed amendment, as approved by Congress and sent to the states in June 1866, was sweeping. It (1) conferred civil rights, including citizenship but excluding the franchise, on the freedmen; (2) reduced proportionately the representation of a state in Congress and in the Electoral College if it denied blacks the ballot; (3) disqualified from federal and state office former Confederates who as federal officeholders had once sworn to "support the Constitution of the United States"; and (4) guaranteed the federal debt, while repudiating all Confederate debts. (See text of the Fourteenth Amendment in the Appendix.)

The radical faction was disappointed that the Fourteenth Amendment did not grant the right to vote, but all Republicans agreed that no state should be welcomed back into the Union fold without first ratifying the Fourteenth Amendment. Yet President Johnson advised the Southern states to reject it, and all of the "sinful eleven," except Tennessee, defiantly spurned the amendment.

Swinging 'Round the Circle with Johnson

As 1866 lengthened, the battle grew between Congress and the president. Now the issue was whether Reconstruction was to be carried on with or without the drastic Fourteenth Amendment. The Republicans would settle for nothing less.

The crucial congressional elections of 1866—more crucial than some presidential elections—were fast approaching. Johnson was naturally eager to escape from the clutch of Congress by securing a majority favorable to his soft-on-the-South policy. Invited to dedicate a Chicago monument to Stephen A. Douglas, he undertook to speak at various cities en route in support of his views.

Johnson's famous "swing around the circle," beginning in the late summer of 1866, was a serio-comedy of errors. The president delivered a series of "give 'em hell" speeches, in which he accused the radicals in Congress of having planned large-scale antiblack riots and murder in the South. As he spoke, hecklers hurled insults at him. Reverting to his stump-speaking days in Tennessee, he shouted back angry retorts, amid cries of "You be damned" and "Don't get mad, Andy." The dignity of his high office sank to a new low.

As a vote-getter, Johnson was highly successful—for the opposition. His inept speechmaking heightened the cry "Stand by Congress" against the "Tailor of the Potomac." When the ballots were counted, the Republicans had rolled up more than a two-thirds majority in both houses of Congress.

Republican Reconstruction

The Republicans had a veto-proof Congress and virtually unlimited control of Reconstruction policy. But moderates and radicals still disagreed over the best course to pursue in the South.

The radicals in the Senate were led by courtly and principled Charles Sumner, and in the House by crusty and vindictive Thaddeus Stevens, both devoted not only to black freedom but to racial equality. Still opposed to rapid restoration of the Southern states, the radicals wanted to keep them out as long as possible, and to apply federal power to bring about a drastic social and economic transformation in the South.

But moderate Republicans, more attuned to time-honored Republican principles of states' rights and self-government, preferred policies that restrained the states from abridging citizens' rights, rather than policies that directly involved the federal government in individual lives. The actual policies adopted by Congress showed the influence of both these schools of thought, though the moderates, as the majority faction, had the upper hand. And one thing both groups had come to agree on by 1867 was the necessity to enfranchise black voters, even if it took federal troops to do it.

Against a backdrop of vicious and bloody race riots that had erupted in several Southern cities, Congress passed the Reconstruction Act on March 2, 1867. This drastic legislation divided the South into five military districts, each commanded by a Union general and policed by blue-clad soldiers, about twenty thousand all told.

Congress additionally laid down stringent requirements for the readmission of the seceded states. The wayward states were required to ratify the Fourteenth Amendment, giving the former slaves their rights as citizens, and to guarantee in their state constitutions full suffrage for their former adult male slaves. Yet the act, reflecting moderate sentiment, stopped short of giving the freedmen land or education at federal expense. The overriding purpose of the moderates was to create an electorate in Southern states that would vote those states back into the Union on acceptable terms and thus free the federal government from direct responsibility for the protection of black rights. As later events would demonstrate, this approach proved woefully inadequate to the cause of justice for the blacks.

The radical Republicans still worried that once the unrepentant states were readmitted, they would amend their constitutions to withdraw the ballot from the blacks. They therefore sought the ironclad safeguard of black suffrage in the federal Constitution. This goal was finally achieved by the Fifteenth Amendment, passed by Congress in 1869 and ratified by the required number of states in 1870. (For text, see the Appendix.)

Military Reconstruction of the South not only usurped certain functions of the president as commander in chief but set up a martial regime of dubious legality. The Supreme Court had already ruled, in the case *Ex parte Milligan* (1866), that military tribunals could not try civilians, even during wartime, in areas where the civil courts were open. Peacetime military rule seemed starkly contrary to the spirit of the Constitution, but for the time being the Supreme Court avoided offending the Republican Congress.

Prodded into line by federal bayonets, the Southern states got on with the task of constitution making. By 1870 all of them had reorganized their governments and had been accorded full rights. The hated "bluebellies" remained until the new regimes—usually called "radical" regimes—appeared to be firmly entrenched. Yet when the last federal muskets were removed from state politics in 1877, the white "redeemer" governments swiftly returned to power, and the "solid" Democratic South congealed.

The passage of the three Reconstruction Amendments—the Thirteenth, Fourteenth, and Fifteenth—delighted former abolitionists but deeply disappointed advocates of women's rights. Women had played a prominent part in the prewar abolitionist movement, and in the eyes of many women the struggle for black freedom and the crusade for

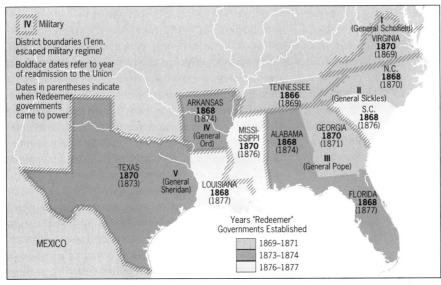

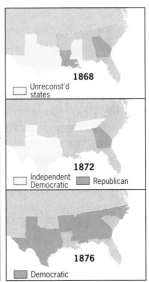

Military Reconstruction, 1867 (five districts and commanding generals)   *For many white Southerners, military Reconstruction amounted to turning the knife in the wound of defeat. An often-repeated story of later years had a Southerner remark, "I was sixteen years old before I discovered that* damnyankee *was two words."*

Presidential Electoral Vote by Party

women's rights were one and the same. Now, feminist leaders reeled with shock when the Fourteenth Amendment, which defined equal national citizenship, for the first time inserted the word *male* into the Constitution in referring to a citizen's right to vote. When the Fifteenth Amendment proposed to prohibit denial of the vote on the basis of "race, color, or previous condition of servitude," women's rights leaders Susan B. Anthony and Elizabeth Cady Stanton wanted the word *sex* added to the list. They lost this battle, too. Fifty years would pass before the Constitution granted women the right to vote.

The Realities of Radical Reconstruction in the South

Blacks now had freedom, of a sort. By 1867 Republican hesitation over black voting had given way to a hard determination to enfranchise the former slaves wholesale and immediately, while thousands of white Southerners were being denied the right to vote. By glaring contrast most of the Northern states, before ratification of the Fifteenth Amendment in 1870, withheld the ballot from their tiny black minorities. White Southerners naturally concluded that the

Republicans were hypocritical in insisting that blacks in the South be allowed to vote.

Having gained their right to suffrage, Southern black men seized the initiative and began to organize politically. Their primary vehicle became the Union League, originally a pro-Union organization based in the North. Assisted by Northern blacks, freedmen turned the League into a network of political clubs that educated members in their civic duties and campaigned for Republican candidates. The League's mission soon expanded to include building black churches and schools, representing black grievances before local employers and government, and recruiting militias to protect black communities from white retaliation.

Though African-American women did not obtain the right to vote, they too assumed new political roles. Black women faithfully attended the parades and rallies common in black communities during the early years of Reconstruction and helped assemble mass meetings in the newly constructed black churches. They even showed up at the constitutional conventions held throughout the South in 1867, monitoring the proceedings and participating in informal votes outside the convention halls.

But black men elected as delegates to the state constitutional conventions held the greater political authority. They formed the backbone of the black political community. At the conventions, they sat down with whites to hammer out new state constitutions, which most importantly provided for universal male suffrage.

The sight of former slaves holding office deeply offended their onetime masters, who lashed out with fury at the freedmen's white allies, labeling them "scalawags" and "carpetbaggers." The so-called scalawags were Southerners, often former Unionists, whom former Confederates wildly accused of plundering the treasuries of the Southern states through their political influence in the radical governments. The carpetbaggers were supposedly sleazy Northerners who had packed all their worldly goods into a carpetbag suitcase at war's end and come south to seek personal power and profit. In fact, most were former Union soldiers and Northern businessmen and professionals who wanted to play a role in modernizing the "New South."

How well did the radical regimes rule? Black voters made up a majority of the electorate in five states, but only in South Carolina did blacks predominate in the lower house of the legislature. Many of the newly elected black legislators were literate and able; more than a few came from the ranks of the pre-war free blacks who had acquired considerable education. More than a dozen black congressmen and two black United States senators, Hiram Revels and Blanche K. Bruce, both of Mississippi, did creditable work in the national capital.

In some radical regimes, there was truth to the charges of graft and corruption. This was especially true in South Carolina and Louisiana, where conscienceless promoters and other pocket-padders used politically inexperienced blacks as cat's-paws. The worst "black-and-white" legislatures purchased as "legislative supplies" such "stationery" items as hams, perfumes, suspenders, bonnets, corsets, champagne, and a coffin. Yet this kind of corruption was no more outrageous than the scams and felonies being perpetrated in the North at the same time, especially in Boss Tweed's New York.

The radical legislatures also passed much desirable legislation. For the first time in Southern history, steps were taken toward establishing adequate public schools. Tax systems were streamlined; public works were launched; and property rights were guaranteed to women. Many of these reforms were so welcome that they were retained by the all-white "redeemer" governments that later returned to power.

Freedmen Voting, Richmond, Virginia, 1871 *The exercise of democratic rights by former slaves constituted a political and social revolution in the South, and was bitterly resented by whites.*

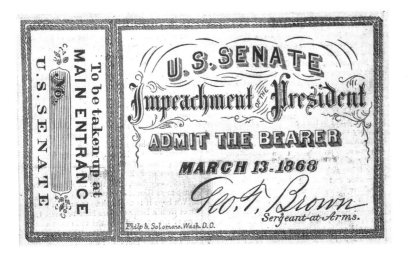

Impeachment Drama   *The impeachment proceedings against President Andrew Johnson, among the most severe constitutional crises in the Republic's history, were high political theater, and tickets were in sharp demand.*

The Ku Klux Klan

Deeply embittered, some Southern whites resorted to savage measures against "radical rule." Many whites resented the success and ability of black legislators as much as they resented alleged "corruption." A number of secret organizations mushroomed forth, the most notorious of which was the "Invisible Empire of the South," or Ku Klux Klan, founded in Tennessee in 1866. Besheeted nightriders, their horses' hoofs muffled, would approach the cabin of an "upstart" black and hammer on the door. In ghoulish tones one thirsty horseman would demand a bucket of water. Then, under pretense of drinking, he would pour the whole bucket into a rubber attachment concealed beneath his mask and gown, smack his lips, and declare that this was the first water he had tasted since he was killed at the Battle of Shiloh. If fright did not produce the desired effect of intimidating black voters, force was employed. Such terror tactics proved partially effective. Many ex-bondsmen and white "carpetbaggers," quick to take a hint, shunned the polls. Those stubborn souls who persisted in their "upstart" ways were flogged, mutilated, or even murdered.

Congress, outraged by this night-riding lawlessness, passed the harsh Force Acts of 1870 and 1871. Federal troops were able to stamp out much of the "lash law," but by this time the Invisible Empire had already done its work of intimidation.

White resistance undermined attempts to empower the blacks politically. The white South for many decades openly flouted the Fourteenth and Fifteenth Amendments. Wholesale disfranchisement of the blacks, starting conspicuously about 1890, was achieved by intimidation, fraud, and trickery. Among various underhanded schemes were the literacy tests, unfairly administered by whites to the advantage of illiterate whites. In the eyes of white Southerners, the goal of white supremacy fully justified these dishonorable devices.

Johnson Walks the Impeachment Plank

Radicals meanwhile had been sharpening their hatchets for President Johnson. Not content with curbing his authority, they decided to remove him altogether by constitutional processes.*

As an initial step, Congress in 1867 passed the Tenure of Office Act—as usual over Johnson's veto. Contrary to precedent, the new law required the president to secure the consent of the Senate before he could remove his appointees, once they had been approved by that body. One purpose was to freeze into the cabinet the secretary of war, Edwin M. Stanton, a holdover from the Lincoln administration. Although outwardly loyal to Johnson, he was secretly serving as a spy and informer for the radicals.

Johnson provided the radicals with a pretext to begin impeachment proceedings when he abruptly

---

* For impeachment, see Art. I, Sec. II, para. 5; Art. I, Sec. II, paras. 6, 7; Art. II, Sec. IV, in the Appendix.

dismissed Stanton early in 1868. The House of Representatives immediately voted 126 to 47 to impeach Andrew Johnson for "high crimes and misdemeanors," as provided for by the Constitution. They charged him with various violations of the Tenure of Office Act. Two additional articles related to Johnson's verbal assaults on the Congress, involving "disgrace, ridicule, hatred, contempt, and reproach."

A Not-Guilty Verdict for Johnson

With evident zeal, the radical-led Senate sat as a court to try Johnson on the dubious impeachment charges. The House conducted the prosecution. The trial aroused intense public interest and, with one thousand tickets printed, proved to be the biggest show of 1868. Johnson kept his dignity and maintained a discreet silence. His able battery of attorneys argued that the president had merely fired Stanton in order to test the Tenure of Office Act before the Supreme Court. The House prosecutors, including oily-tongued Benjamin F. Butler and embittered Thaddeus Stevens, had a harder time building a case for impeachment.

On May 16, 1868, the day for the first voting in the Senate, the tension was electric, and heavy breathing could be heard in the galleries. By a margin of only one vote, the radicals failed to muster the two-thirds majority for Johnson's removal.

Die-hard radicals were infuriated. "The Country is going to the Devil!" cried the crippled Stevens as he was carried from the hall. But the nation, though violently aroused, accepted the verdict with a good temper that did credit to its political maturity. In a less stable republic, an armed uprising might have erupted against the president.

The nation thus narrowly avoided a bad precedent that would have gravely weakened one of the three branches of the federal government. Johnson was clearly guilty of bad speeches, bad judgment, and bad temper, but not of "high crimes and misdemeanors." From the standpoint of the radicals, his greatest crime had been to stand inflexibly in their path.

The Purchase of Alaska

Johnson's administration, though largely reduced to a figurehead, achieved its most enduring success in the field of foreign relations. The Russians by 1867 were in a mood to sell the vast and chilly expanse of land now known as Alaska. The region had been ruthlessly "furred out" and was a growing economic liability. The Russians were therefore eager to unload their "frozen asset" on the Americans, primarily because they wanted to strengthen further the Republic as a barrier against their ancient enemy, Britain.

In 1867 Secretary of State William Seward, an ardent expansionist, signed a treaty with Russia that

THIS LITTLE BOY WOULD PERSIST IN HANDLING BOOKS ABOVE HIS CAPACITY.

AND THIS WAS THE DISASTROUS RESULT.

Crushed by the Constitution
President Andrew Johnson revered the U.S. Constitution, but eventually felt its awesome weight in his impeachment trial.

transferred Alaska to the United States for the bargain price of $7.2 million. But Seward's enthusiasm for these frigid wastes was not shared by his ignorant or uninformed countrymen, who jeered at "Seward's Folly," "Seward's Icebox," "Frigidia," and "Walrussia." The American people, still preoccupied with Reconstruction and other internal vexations, were economy minded and anti-expansionist.

Then why did Congress and the American public sanction the purchase? For one thing Russia, alone among the powers, had been conspicuously friendly to the North during the recent Civil War. Americans did not feel that they could offend their great and good friend the tsar by hurling his walrus-covered icebergs back into his face. Besides, the territory was rumored to be teeming with furs, fish, and gold, and it might yet "pan out" profitably—as it later did, with natural resources, including oil and gas.

The Heritage of Reconstruction

Many white Southerners regarded Reconstruction as a more grievous wound than the war itself. It left a festering scar that would take generations to heal. They resented the upending of their social and racial system, the political empowerment of blacks, and the insult of federal intervention in their local affairs. Yet given the explosiveness of the issues that had caused the war, and the bitterness of the fighting, the wonder is that Reconstruction was not far harsher than it was. Northern policymakers groped for the right policies, influenced as much by Southern responses to defeat and emancipation as by any specific plans of their own.

The Republicans acted from a mixture of idealism and political expediency. They wanted both to protect the freed slaves and to promote the fortunes of the Republican party. In the end their efforts backfired badly. Reconstruction conferred only fleeting benefits on the blacks, and it virtually extinguished the Republican party in the South for nearly one hundred years.

Moderate Republicans never fully appreciated the efforts necessary to make the freed slaves completely independent citizens, or the lengths to which Southern whites would go to preserve their system of racial dominance. Had Thaddeus Stevens's radical program of drastic economic reforms and heftier protection of political rights been enacted, things might well have been different. But deep-seated racism, ingrained American resistance to tampering with property rights, and rigid loyalty to the principle of local self-government, combined with spreading indifference in the North to the plight of the blacks, formed too formidable an obstacle. Despite good intentions by Republicans, the Old South was in many ways more resurrected than reconstructed.

Chronology

1863	Lincoln announces "10 percent" Reconstruction plan.
1864	Lincoln vetoes Wade-Davis Bill.
1865	Lincoln assassinated. Johnson issues Reconstruction proclamation. Congress refuses to seat Southern congressmen. Freedmen's Bureau established. Southern states pass Black Codes.
1866	Congress passes Civil Rights Bill over Johnson's veto. Congress passes Fourteenth Amendment. Johnson-backed candidates lose congressional election. *Ex parte Milligan* case. Ku Klux Klan founded.
1867	Reconstruction Act. Tenure of Office Act. United States purchases Alaska from Russia.
1868	Johnson impeached and acquitted. Johnson pardons Confederate leaders.
1870	Fifteenth Amendment ratified.
1870– 1871	Force Acts.
1872	Freedmen's Bureau ended.
1877	Reconstruction ends.

varying

viewpoints

How Radical Was Reconstruction?

Few topics have triggered as much intellectual warfare as the "dark and bloody ground" of Reconstruction. The period provoked questions—sectional, racial, and constitutional—about which people felt deeply and remain deeply divided even today. Scholarly argument goes back to a Columbia University historian, William A. Dunning, who wrote about Reconstruction as a kind of national disgrace, foisted on a prostrate region by vindictive and self-seeking radical Republican politicians.

In the 1920s, widespread suspicion that the Civil War itself had been a tragic and unnecessary blunder shifted attention to Northern politicians. Scholars like Howard Beale argued that the radical Republicans had masked a ruthless desire to exploit Southern resources and expand Republican power in the South behind a false "front" of concern for the freed slaves.

After World War II, Kenneth Stampp, among others, turned this view on its head. Influenced by the modern civil rights movement, he argued that Reconstruction was a noble attempt to extend American principles of equity and justice. By the early 1970s, this view had become orthodoxy, and it generally holds sway today. Yet some scholars such as Michael Benedict and Leon Litwack claimed to discover that Reconstruction was never really very radical, and they argued that the Freedmen's Bureau and other agencies merely allowed white planters to maintain local political and economic control.

More recently, Eric Foner has powerfully reasserted the argument that Reconstruction was a truly radical and noble attempt to establish an interracial democracy. Drawing on the work of black scholar W. E. B. Du Bois, Foner emphasizes that Reconstruction allowed blacks to form political organizations and churches and to establish some measure of economic independence. Many of the benefits of Reconstruction were erased by white Southerners during the Gilded Age, but in the twentieth century, constitutional principles and organizations developed during Reconstruction provided the foundation for the modern civil rights movement—which some have called the Second Reconstruction.

SUGGESTED READINGS

Primary Source Documents

Booker T. Washington's classic autobiography *Up from Slavery** (1901) records one freedman's experiences. Contemporary comments on Reconstruction include the laments of editor Edwin L. Godkin, *The Nation* (December 7, 1871, p. 364),* and Frederick Douglass, *Life and Times of Frederick Douglass** (1882), as well as the debates in the *Congressional Globe** (1867–1868) between radicals such as Thaddeus Stevens and moderates like Lyman Trumbull.

Secondary Sources

Eric Foner, *Reconstruction: America's Unfinished Revolution, 1863–1877* (1988), is a superb synthesis of current scholarship. Overall accounts may be found in James G. Randall and David Donald, *The Civil War and Reconstruction* (rev. ed., 1969), and James McPherson, *Ordeal by Fire: The Civil War and Reconstruction* (1981), perhaps the best brief introduction. Conditions in the South are analyzed in W. E. B. Du Bois's controversial classic *Black Reconstruction* (1935) and in Leon F. Litwack's brilliantly evocative *Been in the Storm So Long* (1979), a revealing study of the initial responses, by both blacks and whites, to emancipation. An excellent account of the Southern economy after the war is Gavin Wright, *Old South, New South: Revolutions in the Southern Economy Since the Civil War* (1986). See also James Roark, *Masters Without Slaves: Southern Planters in the Civil War and Reconstruction* (1977). Barbara Fields looks at the Border State of Maryland in *Slavery and Freedom on the Middle Ground* (1985). William McFeely offers an excellent biography of *Frederick Douglass* (1991). On the political economy of the postbellum South see Dewey W. Grantham, *Life and Death of the Solid South* (1988), and Edward L. Ayers, *The Promise of a New South: Life After Reconstruction* (1992). C. Vann Woodward, *The Strange Career of Jim Crow* (rev. ed., 1974), is a classic study of the origins of segregation. His views have drawn criticism in Harold O. Rabinowitz, *Race Relations in the Urban South, 1865–1890* (1977). See also Rabinowitz's *Southern Black Leaders of the Reconstruction Era* (1982). The Freedmen's Bureau has been the subject of several studies, including Peter Kolchin, *First Freedom* (1972); Claude Oubré, *Forty Acres and a Mule: The Freedmen's Bureau and Black Land Ownership* (1978); and Donald

Nieman, *To Set the Law in Motion: The Freedmen's Bureau and the Legal Rights of Blacks, 1865–1868* (1979). Nell Irvin Painter follows African-Americans who chose to leave the South altogether in *Exodusters: Black Migration to Kansas After Reconstruction* (1976). Richard N. Current rehabilitates the maligned carpetbaggers in *Those Terrible Carpetbaggers* (1988). A broad range of Reconstruction scholarship is presented in Kenneth M. Stampp and Leon Litwack, eds., *Reconstruction: An Anthology of Revisionist Writings* (1969), and Robert P. Swierenga, ed., *Beyond the Civil War Synthesis* (1975). J. Morgan Kousser and James M. McPherson, eds., *Region, Race, and Reconstruction: Essays in Honor of C. Vann Woodward* (1982), contains some intriguing essays. Eric Foner looks at emancipation in a comparative perspective in *Nothing but Freedom* (1983).

---

* An asterisk indicates that the document, or an excerpt from it, can be found in Thomas A. Bailey and David M. Kennedy, eds., *The American Spirit: United States History as Seen by Contemporaries*, 9th ed. (Boston: Houghton Mifflin, 1998).

PART FOUR

✱✱✱✱✱✱✱✱✱✱

Forging an Industrial Society

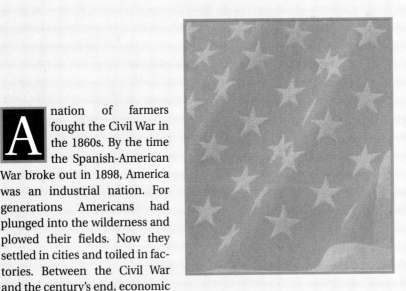

A nation of farmers fought the Civil War in the 1860s. By the time the Spanish-American War broke out in 1898, America was an industrial nation. For generations Americans had plunged into the wilderness and plowed their fields. Now they settled in cities and toiled in factories. Between the Civil War and the century's end, economic and technological change came so swiftly and massively that it seemed to many Americans that a whole new civilization had emerged.

In some ways it had. The sheer scale of the new industrial civilization was dazzling. Transcontinental railroads knit the country together from sea to sea. New industries like oil and steel grew to staggering size—and made megamillionaires out of entrepreneurs like oilman John D. Rockefeller and steelmaker Andrew Carnegie.

Drawn by the allure of industrial employment, Americans moved to the city. In 1860 only about 20 percent of the population were city dwellers. By 1900 that proportion doubled, as rural Americans and European immigrants alike flocked to mill town and metropolis in search of steady jobs.

These sweeping changes challenged the spirit of individualism that Americans had celebrated since the seventeenth century. Even on the western frontier, that historic bastion of rugged loners, the hand of government was increasingly felt, as large armies were dispatched to subdue the Plains Indians and federal authority was invoked to regulate the use of natural resources. The rise of powerful monopolies called into question the government's traditional hands-off policy toward business, and a growing band of reformers increasingly clamored for government regulation of private enterprise. The mushrooming cities, with their needs for transport systems, schools, hospitals, sanitation, and fire and police protection, required bigger governments and budgets than an earlier generation could have imagined. As never before, Americans struggled to adapt old ideals of private autonomy to the new realities of industrial civilization.

With economic change came social and political turmoil. Labor violence brought bloodshed to places such as Chicago and Homestead, Pennsylvania. Small farmers, squeezed by debt and foreign competition, rallied behind the People's, or "Populist," party, a radical movement of the 1880s and 1890s that attacked the power of Wall Street, big business, and the banks. Anti-immigrant sentiment swelled. Bitter disputes over tariffs and monetary policy deeply divided the country, setting debtors against lenders, farmers against manufacturers, the West and South against the Northeast. And in this unfamiliar era of big money and expanding government, corruption flourished, from town hall to Congress, fueling loud cries for political reform.

The bloodiest conflict of all pitted Plains Indians against the relentless push of westward expansion. As railroads drove their iron arrows through the heart of the West, the Indians lost their land and life-sustaining buffalo herds. By the 1890s, after three decades of fierce fighting with the U.S. Army, the Indians who had once roamed across the vast rolling prairies were confined to the open-air prisons called reservations.

The South remained the one region largely untouched by the industrial revolution sweeping the rest of America. A few sleepy southern hamlets did become boomtowns; but for the most part, the South's rural way of life, and its peculiar system of race relations, were largely unperturbed by the changes happening elsewhere. On African-Americans, the vast majority of whom continued to live in the Old South, the post-emancipation era inflicted new forms of racial injustice. State legislatures systematically deprived black Americans of their political rights, including the right to vote. Segregation of schools, housing, and all kinds of public facilities made a mockery of African-Americans' Reconstruction-era hopes for equality before the law.

The new wealth and power of industrial America nurtured a growing sense of national self-confidence. Literature flowered, and a golden age of philanthropy dawned. The reform spirit spread. So did a restless appetite for overseas expansion. In a brief war against Spain in 1898, the United States, born in a revolutionary war of independence and long the champion of colonial peoples yearning to breathe free, seized control of the Philippines and itself became an imperial power. Uncle Sam's venture into empire touched off a bitter national debate about America's role in the world and ushered in a long period of argument over the responsibilities, at home as well as abroad, of a modern industrial state.

24

****

Politics in the Gilded Age,

1869–1896

******

Grant . . . had no right to exist. He should have been extinct for ages. . . . That, two thousand years after Alexander the Great and Julius Caesar, a man like Grant should be called— and should actually and truly be—the highest product of the most advanced evolution, made evolution ludicrous. . . . The progress of evolution, from President Washington to President Grant, was alone evidence enough to upset Darwin. . . . Grant . . . should have lived in a cave and worn skins.

******

HENRY ADAMS, *THE EDUCATION OF HENRY ADAMS*, 1907

The "Bloody Shirt" Elects Grant

Disillusionment ran deep among idealistic Americans in the era after the Civil War. They had spilled their blood for Union, emancipation, and Abraham Lincoln, who had promised "a new birth of freedom." Instead, they got a bitter dose of corruption, petty politics, and Ulysses S. Grant, a great soldier but an inept politician.

Wrangling between Congress and Andrew Johnson had soured the people on professional politicians, and the notion still prevailed that a good general was bound to make a good president. Stubbly bearded General Grant, with his slightly stooped body measuring a shade over 5 feet, 8 inches, was by far the most popular northern hero to emerge from the war. Unfortunately, this hard-riding soldier was a greenhorn in the political arena. He had almost no political experience, and his one presidential vote had been cast for the Democratic ticket in 1856.

The Republicans, freed from the Union party coalition of war days, enthusiastically nominated Grant for the presidency in 1868. The party's platform sounded a clarion call for continued Reconstruction of the South under the glinting steel of federal bayonets.

Expectant Democrats, meeting in their own nominating convention, denounced military Reconstruction but could agree on little else. Wealthy eastern delegates demanded that federal war bonds be redeemed in gold, while the poorer midwesterners backed the "Ohio Idea" calling for redemption in greenbacks. Agrarian Democrats thus hoped to make loans less costly by keeping more money in circulation.

Midwestern delegates got the pro-Greenback platform but not the candidate. The nominee, former New York governor Horatio Seymour, sank the Democrats' scant hopes for success by repudiating the Ohio Idea plank. Republicans whipped up enthusiasm for Grant by energetically "waving the bloody shirt"—that is, reviving gory memories of the Civil War—which became for the first time a prominent feature of a presidential campaign. "Vote as You Shot" was a powerful Republican slogan aimed at Union army veterans.

Grant won, with 214 electoral votes to 80 for Seymour. But despite his great popularity, the former general scored a majority of only 300,000 in the popular vote (3,013,421 to 2,706,829). Most white voters apparently supported Seymour, and the ballots of three still-unreconstructed southern states (Mississippi, Texas, and Virginia) were not counted. An estimated 500,000 former slaves gave Grant his margin of victory. To remain in power, the Republican party had to continue to control the South—and to keep the ballot in the hands of the grateful freedmen. Republicans could not take future victories "for Granted."

The Era of Good Stealings

The population of the Republic continued to vault upward by vigorous leaps, despite the awful bloodletting of the Civil War. Census takers reported over 39 million people in 1870, a gain of 26.6 percent over the previous decade, as the immigrant tide surged again. The United States was now the third-largest nation of the Western world, ranking behind Russia and France.

But the moral stature of the Republic fell regrettably short of its physical stature. The war and its aftermath bred waste, extravagance, speculation, and graft. The whole atmosphere was fetid. The Man in the Moon, it was said, had to hold his nose when passing over America. Railroad promoters sometimes left gullible bond buyers with only "two streaks of rust and a right of way." Unscrupulous stock-market manipulators were a cinder in the public eye. Too many judges and legislators put their power up for hire. Cynics defined an honest politician as one who, when bought, would stay bought.

Notorious in the financial world were two millionaires, "Jubilee Jim" Fisk and Jay Gould. This crafty pair concocted a plot in 1869 to corner the gold market. Their slippery game would work only if the federal Treasury refrained from selling gold. The conspirators worked on President Grant directly, and also through his brother-in-law, who received $25,000 for his complicity. On "Black Friday" (September 24, 1869), Fisk and Gould madly bid the price of gold skyward, while scores of honest businesspeople were driven against a wall. The bubble finally broke when the Treasury, contrary to Grant's supposed assurances, was compelled to release gold. A congressional probe concluded that Grant had done nothing crooked, though he had acted stupidly and indiscreetly.

The infamous Tweed Ring in New York City vividly displayed the ethics (or lack of ethics) typical of the age. Burly "Boss" Tweed—240 pounds of rascality—employed bribery, graft, and fraudulent elections to milk the metropolis of as much as $200 million.

Tweed's luck finally ran out. The *New York Times* secured damning evidence in 1871 and courageously published it, though offered $5 million not to do so. Gifted cartoonist Thomas Nast pilloried Tweed mercilessly, after spurning a heavy bribe to desist. A New York attorney, Samuel J. Tilden, headed the prosecution and gained fame that later paved the path to his presidential nomination. Unbailed and unwept, Tweed died behind bars.

A Carnival of Corruption

More serious than Boss Tweed's sticky fingers was the corrupt atmosphere in the federal government. President Grant's cabinet was a nest of grafters and incompetents, and favor seekers even haunted the White House, plying Grant himself with cigars, wine, and horses.

The easygoing Grant was first tarred by the Crédit Mobilier scandal. Union Pacific Railway insiders had formed the Crédit Mobilier construction company and then cleverly hired themselves at inflated prices to build rail lines, thereby earning dividends of 348 percent in one year. Fearing that Congress might blow the whistle, the company furtively distributed shares of its valuable stock to key congressmen. A newspaper exposé and congressional investigation of the scandal in 1872 led to the censure of two congressmen and the revelation that the vice president of the United States had also accepted Crédit Mobilier stock and dividends.

The breath of scandal in Washington also reeked of alcohol. In 1874–1875 a sprawling Whiskey Ring robbed the Treasury of millions in excise tax revenues, and when President Grant's private secretary turned up among the culprits, the president volunteered a written statement to a jury that helped the thief escape. Further rottenness in the Grant administration turned up in 1876, when Secretary of War William Belknap resigned after impeachment by the House for pocketing bribes from Indian suppliers. Grant, ever loyal to his crooked cronies, accepted Belknap's resignation "with great regret."

The Liberal Republican Revolt of 1872

By 1872 a powerful wave of disgust with Grantism was beginning to build up throughout the nation, even before some of the worst scandals had been exposed. Reform-minded citizens banded together in the Liberal Republican party. Voicing the slogan "Turn the Rascals Out," they urged purification of the Washington administration and an end to military Reconstruction.

The Liberal Republicans muffed their chance when their Cincinnati nominating convention astounded the country by nominating the brilliant but erratic Horace Greeley for the presidency. Although Greeley was a fearless editor of the *New York Tribune*, he was dogmatic, emotional, petulant, and notoriously unsound in his political judgments.

More astonishing still was the action of the office-hungry Democrats, who endorsed Greeley's candidacy. In swallowing Greeley the Democrats "ate crow" in large gulps, for the eccentric editor had long blasted them as traitors, slave whippers, saloon keepers, horse thieves, and idiots. Yet Greeley pleased the Democrats, North and South, when he pleaded

Can the Law Reach Him? 1872 *Cartoonist Thomas Nast attacked "Boss" Tweed in a series of cartoons like this one that appeared in* Harper's Weekly *in 1872. Here Nast depicts the corrupt Tweed as a powerful giant, towering over a puny law force.*

for a clasping of hands across "the bloody chasm." The Republicans dutifully renominated Grant, and the voters were thus presented with a choice between two candidates who had made their careers in fields other than politics and who were both eminently unqualified, by temperament and lifelong training, for high political office. In the mud-spattered campaign, Greeley was denounced as an atheist, a free-lover, and a vegetarian, while Democrats derided Grant as a drunken swindler. But the regular Republicans, chanting "Grant us another term," pulled the president through. The count in the electoral column was 286 to 66, in the popular column 3,596,745 to 2,843,446.

Liberal Republican agitation frightened the regular Republicans into cleaning their own house before they were thrown out of it. The Republican Congress in 1872 passed a general amnesty act, removing political disabilities from all but some five hundred former Confederate leaders. Congress also moved to reduce high Civil War tariffs and to fumigate the Grant administration with mild civil-service reform. Like many American third parties, the Liberal Republicans left some enduring footprints, even in defeat.

Depression and Demands for Inflation

The evil repute of the scandal-scarred Grant years was worsened by the paralyzing panic that broke in 1873. Bursting with startling rapidity, the crash was one of those periodic plummets that roller-coastered the economy in this age of unbridled capitalist expansion. Boom times became gloom times as more than fifteen thousand businesses went bankrupt; and in New York City an army of unemployed riotously battled the police.

Hard times were especially distressing to debtors, who began to clamor for inflationary policies. Proponents of inflation breathed new life into the issue of greenbacks. During the war $450 million of the "folding money" had been issued, but it had depreciated under a cloud of popular mistrust and dubious legality.* By 1868 the Treasury had already withdrawn $100 million of the "battle-born currency" from circulation, and "hard-money" people everywhere looked forward to its complete disappearance.

But now afflicted agrarian and debtor groups—"cheap-money" supporters—clamored for a reissuance of the greenbacks. They reasoned correctly that more money meant cheaper money and, hence, rising prices and easier-to-pay debts. Creditors, of course, reasoning from the same premises, advocated precisely the opposite policy.

The "hard-money" advocates carried the day in 1874 when they persuaded the confused Grant to veto a bill to print more paper money. They scored another victory in the Resumption Act of 1875, which pledged the government to the further withdrawal of greenbacks from circulation, and to the redemption of all paper currency in gold at face value, beginning in 1879.

Down but not out, debtors looked for relief to another precious metal, silver. The "sacred white metal," they claimed, had received a raw deal. In the early 1870s, the Treasury stubbornly and unrealistically maintained that an ounce of silver was worth only one-sixteenth as much as an ounce of gold, though open-market prices for silver were higher. Silver miners thus stopped offering their shiny product for sale to the federal mints. With no silver flowing into the federal coffers, Congress formally dropped the coinage of silver dollars in 1873. Fate then played a sly joke when new silver discoveries later in the 1870s shot production up and forced silver prices down. Westerners from silver-mining states joined with debtors in assailing the "Crime of '73," demanding a return to the "Dollar of Our Daddies." This demand, like the demand for more greenbacks, was essentially a call for inflation.

Republicans resisted this call and counted on Grant to hold the line against it. The Treasury began to accumulate gold stocks against the appointed day for resumption of metallic-money payments. Coupled with the reduction of greenbacks, this policy was called "contraction." It had a noticeable deflationary effect—the amount of money per capita in

---

* The Supreme Court in 1870 declared the Civil War Legal Tender Act unconstitutional. With the concurrence of the Senate, Grant thereupon added to the bench two justices who could be counted on to help reverse that decision, which happened in 1871. This is how the Court grew to its current size of nine justices.

circulation actually *decreased* between 1870 and 1880, from $19.42 to $19.37. Contraction probably worsened the impact of the depression. But the new policy did restore the government's credit rating, and it brought the embattled greenbacks up to their full face value. When Redemption Day came in 1879, few greenback holders bothered to exchange the lighter and more convenient bills for gold.

Republican hard-money policy had a political backlash. It helped elect a Democratic House of Representatives in 1874, and in 1878 it spawned the Greenback Labor party, which polled over a million votes and elected fourteen members of Congress.

Pallid Politics in the Gilded Age

The political see-saw was delicately balanced throughout most of the Gilded Age (a sarcastic name given to the post–Civil War era by Mark Twain in 1873). Even a slight nudge could tip the teeter-totter to the advantage of the opposition party. Every presidential election was a squeaker, and the majority party in the House of Representatives switched six times in the eleven sessions between 1869 and 1891. Wobbling in such shaky equilibrium, politicians tiptoed timidly, producing a political record that was often trivial and petty.

Few significant economic issues separated the major parties. Democrats and Republicans saw very nearly eye-to-eye on major questions such as the tariff, currency, and civil-service reform. Yet despite their rough agreement on these national matters, the two parties were ferociously competitive with each other. They were tightly and efficiently organized, and they commanded fierce loyalty from their members. Voter turnouts reached heights of nearly 80 percent in the three decades after the Civil War, a figure unmatched before or since. On election day, droves of the party faithful tramped behind marching bands to the polling places, and "ticket splitting," or failing to vote the straight party line, was as rare as a silver dollar.

How can this apparent paradox of political consensus and partisan fervor be explained? The answer lies in the sharp ethnic and cultural differences in the membership of the two parties—in distinctions of style and tone, and especially of religious sentiment.

Republican voters tended to adhere to those creeds that traced their lineage to Puritanism. They stressed strict codes of personal morality and believed that government should play a role in regulating both the economic and the moral affairs of the community as a whole. Democrats, among whom immigrant Lutherans and Roman Catholics figured heavily, were likely to adhere to faiths that took a less stern view of human weakness. Their religions professed toleration of differences in an imperfect world, and they spurned government efforts to impose a single moral standard on the entire society. These differences in temperament and religious values often produced raucous political contests at the local level, where issues such as prohibition and education loomed large.

Democrats had a solid electoral base in the South and in the northern industrial cities, which were packed with immigrants and controlled by well-oiled political machines. Republicans could usually count on winning the Midwest and the rural and small-town Northeast. Grateful freedmen in the South contributed significant numbers of votes to the Republicans. Another important bloc of Republican ballots came from the members of the Grand Army of the Republic (GAR)—a politically potent Union veterans' organization. The lifeblood of both parties was patronage—disbursing jobs by the bucketful in return for votes, kickbacks, and party service.

Boisterous infighting beset the Republican party in the 1870s and 1880s. A "Stalwart" faction, led by handsome and imperious Senator Roscoe ("Lord Roscoe") Conkling of New York, unblushingly embraced the time-honored system of swapping civil-service jobs for votes. Opposed to the Conklingites were the so-called Half-Breeds, who flirted coyly with civil-service reform, but whose real quarrel with the Stalwarts was over who should grasp the ladle that dished out the spoils. The champion of the Half-Breeds was James G. Blaine, a radiantly personable congressman from Maine with a fine physical presence, a thrilling speaking voice, and an elastic conscience. A perennial contender for the presidency, Blaine was inclined to demagoguery in his pursuit of the office. But despite all the color of their personalities, Conkling and Blaine succeeded only in stalemating each other and deadlocking their party.

The Hayes-Tilden Standoff, 1876

Hangers-on around Grant, like fleas urging their ailing dog to live, begged the "Old Man" to try for a third term in 1876. The general, blind to his own ineptitudes, showed a disquieting willingness. But the House, by a lopsided bipartisan vote of 233 to 18, spiked the third-term boom. It passed a resolution that sternly reminded the country—and Grant—of the antidictator implications of the two-term tradition.

With Grant out of the running, and with the Conklingites and Blaineites neutralizing each other, the Republicans turned to a compromise candidate, Rutherford B. Hayes, who was obscure enough to be dubbed "the Great Unknown." His foremost qualification was the fact that he hailed from the electorally doubtful but potent state of Ohio, where he had served three terms as governor.

Pitted against the humdrum Hayes was the Democratic nominee Samuel J. Tilden, who had risen to fame as the man who bagged Boss Tweed in New York. Campaigning against Republican scandal, Tilden racked up 184 electoral votes of the needed 185, with 20 votes in four states doubtful because of irregular returns. Surely Tilden could pick up at least one of these, especially in view of the fact that he had polled 247,448 more popular votes than Hayes, 4,284,020 to 4,036,572.

Both parties scurried to send "visiting statesmen" to the contested southern states of Louisiana, South Carolina, and Florida. All three disputed states submitted two sets of returns, one Democratic and one Republican. As the weeks drifted by, the paralysis tightened. Here were the makings of a major constitutional crisis. The Constitution merely specifies that the electoral returns from the states shall be sent to Congress, and in the presence of the House and Senate they shall be *opened* by the president of the Senate (see the Twelfth Amendment). But who should *count* them? On this point the Constitution was silent. If counted by the president of the Senate (a Republican), the Republican returns would be selected. If counted by the Speaker of the House (a Democrat), the Democratic returns would be chosen.

The Compromise of 1877 and the End of Reconstruction

Clash or compromise was the stark choice. The danger loomed that there would be no president on inauguration day, March 4, 1877. "Tilden or Blood!" cried Democratic hotheads, and some of their "Minute

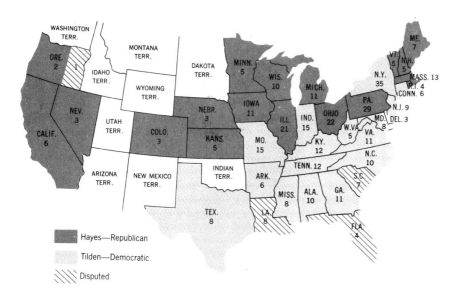

Hayes-Tilden Disputed Election of 1876 (with electoral vote by state) *Nineteen of the twenty disputed votes composed the total electoral count of Louisiana, South Carolina, and Florida. The twentieth was one of Oregon's three votes, cast by an elector who turned out to be ineligible because he was a federal officeholder (a postmaster), contrary to the Constitution (see Art. II, Sec. I, para. 2).*

Men" began to drill with arms. But behind the scenes frantically laboring statesmen gradually hammered out an agreement in the Henry Clay tradition—the Compromise of 1877.

The election deadlock itself was to be broken by the Electoral Count Act, which passed Congress early in 1877. It set up an electoral commission consisting of fifteen men selected from the Senate, the House, and the Supreme Court.

In February 1877, about a month before inauguration day, the Senate and House met together in an electric atmosphere to settle the dispute. The roll of the states was tolled off alphabetically. When Florida was reached—the first of the three southern states with two sets of returns—the disputed documents were referred to the electoral commission, which sat in a nearby chamber. After prolonged discussion the members agreed, by the partisan vote of eight Republicans to seven Democrats, to accept the Republican returns. Outraged Democrats in Congress, smelling defeat, undertook to launch a filibuster "until hell froze over."

Renewed deadlock was avoided by the rest of the complex Compromise of 1877, already partially concluded behind closed doors. The Democrats reluctantly agreed that Hayes might take office in return for his withdrawing intimidating federal troops from the two states in which they remained, Louisiana and South Carolina. Among various concessions, the Republicans assured the Democrats a place at the presidential patronage trough and support for a bill subsidizing the Texas and Pacific Railroad's construction of a southern transcontinental line. Not all of these promises were kept in later years, including the Texas and Pacific subsidy. But the deal held together long enough to break the dangerous electoral standoff.

The compromise bought peace at a price. Violence was averted by sacrificing the black freedmen in the South. With the Hayes-Tilden deal, the Republican party quietly abandoned its commitment to black equality. That commitment had been weakening, in any case. The Civil Rights Act of 1875 was in a sense the last feeble gasp of the congressional radical Republicans. The act supposedly guaranteed equal accommodations in public places and prohibited racial discrimination in jury selection, but the law

was born toothless and stayed that way for nearly a century. The Supreme Court pronounced much of the act unconstitutional in the *Civil Rights Cases* (1883), declaring that the Fourteenth Amendment prohibited only *government* violations of civil rights, not the denial of civil rights by *individuals*. Hayes clinched the bargain by withdrawing the last federal troops that were propping up carpetbag governments, and the bayonet-backed Republican regimes collapsed as the blue-clad soldiers departed.

The Democratic South speedily solidified and swiftly suppressed the now friendless blacks. For generations to come, southern blacks were condemned to eke out a threadbare living under conditions scarcely better than slavery. They were forced into woefully inferior schools, denied the ballot by fraud and intimidation, and legally separated from whites in virtually all public facilities, including segregated "Jim Crow" railroad cars and even restrooms.

The Supreme Court validated the South's strictly segregationist social order in the case of *Plessy v. Ferguson* (1896). It ruled that "separate but equal" facilities were constitutional under the "equal protection" clause of the Fourteenth Amendment. But in reality the quality of African-American life was grotesquely unequal to that of whites. In the 1890s a record number of lynchings occurred, often against blacks who dared to assert themselves as equals. It would take a second Reconstruction, nearly a century later, to redress the racist imbalance of southern society.

Class Conflicts and Ethnic Clashes

The year 1877 marked more than the end of Reconstruction. As the curtains officially closed on regional warfare, they opened on scenes of class warfare. The explosive atmosphere was largely a by-product of the long years of depression and deflation following the panic of 1873. Railroad workers faced particularly hard times. When the presidents of the nation's four largest railroads collectively decided in 1877 to cut employees' wages by 10 percent, the workers struck back. President Hayes's decision to call in federal troops to quell the unrest brought the striking laborers an outpouring of working-class support. Work stoppages spread like wildfire in cities from Baltimore

The First Blow at the Chinese Question, 1877 *Caucasian workers, seething with economic anxiety and ethnic prejudice, savagely mistreated the Chinese in California in the 1870s.*

to St. Louis. When the battling between workers and soldiers ended after several weeks, over one hundred people had died.

The failure of the great railroad strike exposed the weakness of the labor movement. Racial and ethnic fissures among workers fractured labor unity and were particularly acute between the Irish and Chinese in California. By 1880 the Golden State counted seventy-five thousand Asian newcomers, about 9 percent of its entire population.

Many Chinese were recruited to build the transcontinental railroad or labor in the California gold mines. They later worked at the most menial jobs, often as cooks, laundrymen, or domestic servants. Without women or families, the Chinese male laborers lived lonely lives, bereft of the children who

in other communities eased their parents' assimilation into the United States through their exposure to the English language and American customs in school (see "Makers of America: The Chinese," pp. 340–341).

In San Francisco, Irish-born demagogue Denis Kearney incited his followers, many of them recently arrived European immigrants, to violent abuse of the hapless Chinese. Taking to the streets, gangs of Kearneyites terrorized the Asians by shearing off precious pigtails. Some victims were murdered outright.

Congress finally responded to all this uproar in 1879, when it passed a bill severely restricting the influx of Chinese immigrants. But Hayes, who had accomplished little except writing "finished" to Reconstruction, angered Californians by vetoing this discriminatory measure. But once Hayes was out of the way, in 1882, Congress slammed the door on Chinese laborers with the enactment of the Chinese Exclusion Act, and the door stayed closed until 1943.

Garfield and Arthur

Having freed itself of "Granny" Hayes, the Republican party sought a new standard-bearer for 1880. The deadlocked convention finally nominated a dark-horse candidate, James A. Garfield of Ohio. His vice-presidential running mate was a notorious spoilsman and Stalwart henchman, Chester A. Arthur of New York.

Energetically waving the bloody shirt, and ignoring Democratic candidate General Winfield Hancock's charges of corruption, Garfield barely squeaked out a victory. He polled only 39,213 more votes than Hancock—4,453,295 to 4,414,082—but his margin in the electoral column was a comfortable 214 to 155.

The new president was an energetic and able man, but was immediately besieged by patronage-hungry Republicans and by political conflict between his new secretary of state, James G. Blaine, and Blaine's Stalwart nemesis, Senator Roscoe Conkling. As this battle was raging, one disappointed and mentally deranged office-seeker, Charles J. Guiteau, shot President Garfield in the back in a Washington railroad station. Garfield died eleven weeks later, on September 19, 1881, and Chester Arthur assumed the

MAKERS OF AMERICA

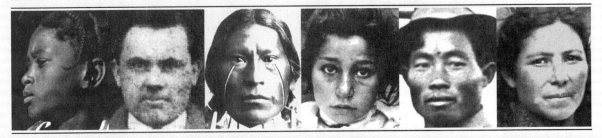

The Chinese

In the late nineteenth century the burgeoning industries and booming frontier towns of the United States' Pacific Coast hungered for laborers. In faraway Asia the Chinese answered the call. Contributing their muscle to the building of the West, they dug in the gold mines and helped to lay the transcontinental railroads that stitched together the American nation.

The first major wave of Chinese came in response to the discovery of gold in California in 1848. The fortune-hungry immigrants who sailed into San Francisco named the city the "golden mountain."

The California boom coincided with the culmination of years of tumult and suffering in China. As the once-great Chinese Empire disintegrated, the European imperial powers forced their way into the unstable country. Faced with economic hardship and political turmoil, more than 2 million Chinese left their homeland between 1840 and 1900, for destinations as diverse as Southeast Asia, Peru, Hawaii, and Cuba. More than three hundred thousand entered the United States. Although their numbers included a few merchants and artisans, most were unskilled country folk.

The Chinese-America of the late-nineteenth-century West was overwhelmingly a bachelor society.

Chinese Butcher Shop, San Francisco, California, c. 1890

Women of good repute rarely made the passage. Of the very few Chinese women who did venture to California at this time, most became prostitutes.

Although a stream of workers returned to China, many Chinese stayed. "Chinatowns" sprang up wherever economic opportunities presented themselves. Chinese in these settlements spoke their own language, enjoyed the fellowship of their own compatriots, and sought safety from prejudice and violence. Many immigrant clubs and associations were American adaptations of Chinese traditions of loyalty to clan. The poorest and most alienated immigrants also established *tongs*—literally, "meeting halls"—secret societies that acquired a sinister reputation among non-Chinese.

After 1882 the Chinese Exclusion Act barred nearly all Chinese from the United States for six decades. Many of the bachelors died or returned home. Slowly, however, those men and the few women who remained raised families and reared a new generation of Chinese-Americans. Like their immigrant parents, this second generation suffered from discrimination. They had to eke out a living in jobs despised by Caucasian laborers or take daunting risks in small entrepreneurial ventures. Yet many hard-working Chinese did manage to open their own restaurants, laundries, and other small businesses. Such enterprises formed a solid economic foundation for their small community and remain a source of livelihood for many Chinese-Americans even today.

presidency. Garfield's tragic death did have one positive outcome: it shocked politicians and the public into reforming the shameful spoils system.

The instrument of reform was Garfield's successor, "Prince" Chester Arthur. Arthur's past cronyism and his love of fine wines and elegant clothes (including eighty pairs of trousers) made him an unlikely candidate for improving the political process. But Arthur surprised his critics by prosecuting post office frauds and giving his former Conklingite pals the cold shoulder.

Disgust with Garfield's murder propelled the Republican party itself into a previously undetected willingness to reform. The medicine finally applied to the long-suffering federal government was the Pendleton Act of 1883—the so-called Magna Carta of civil-service reform. It prohibited, at least on paper, compulsory campaign payments from federal employees, and it established a Civil Service Commission charged with making appointments to office on the basis of competitive examinations rather than "pull."

Although at first covering only about 10 percent of federal offices, civil service did erode the most blatant political abuses. Yet like many well-intentioned reforms, it bred unintended problems of its own. With the cream of federal offices increasingly beyond

their control, politicians were forced to look elsewhere for money, the "mother's milk of politics."

Increasingly, they turned to the bulging coffers of the big corporations. A new breed of boss emerged—less skilled at mobilizing small armies of immigrants and other voters on election day, but more adept at milking dollars from manufacturers and lobbyists. The Pendleton Act partially divorced politics from patronage, but it helped drive politicians into "marriages of convenience" with big-business leaders.

President Arthur's surprising display of integrity unfortunately offended too many powerful Republicans. His ungrateful party turned him out to pasture, and in 1886 he died of a cerebral hemorrhage.

The Blaine-Cleveland Mudslingers of 1884

James G. Blaine's persistence in pursuit of the presidential nomination finally paid off in 1884. The dashing Maine politician, blessed with almost every asset except a reputation for honesty, was clearly the choice of the Republican convention in Chicago. But many reform-minded Republicans gagged on Blaine's candidacy.

Blaine's enemies publicized the fishy-smelling "Mulligan letters," written by Blaine to a Boston businessman and linking the powerful politician to a corrupt deal involving federal favors to a southern railroad. At least one of the damning documents ended with the furtive warning "Burn this letter." Some reformers, unable to swallow Blaine, bolted to the Democrats. They were sneeringly dubbed *Mugwumps*, a word of Indian derivation apparently meaning "holier than thou."

Victory-starved Democrats turned enthusiastically to a noted reformer, Grover Cleveland. A burly bachelor with a soup-straining mustache and a taste for chewing tobacco, Cleveland was a solid but not brilliant lawyer of forty-seven. He had rocketed from the Buffalo mayor's office to the governorship of New York and the presidential nomination in three short years. He enjoyed a well-deserved reputation for probity in office.

Unfortunately, Cleveland's admirers soon got a shock. Resolute Republicans, digging for dirt in the past of bachelor Cleveland, unearthed the report that he had been involved in an amorous affair with a Buffalo widow, to whom an illegitimate son, now eight years old, had been born. Democratic elders, who had launched the campaign on a high ethical plane, were demoralized. They hurried to Cleveland and urged him to lie like a gentleman, but their ruggedly honest candidate insisted, "Tell the truth."

The campaign of 1884 sank to perhaps the lowest level in American experience, as the two parties grunted and shoved for the hog trough of office. Few fundamental differences separated them. Even the bloody shirt had faded to pale pink.* Personalities, not principles, claimed the headlines. Enormous crowds of Democrats surged through city streets, chanting—to the rhythm of left, left, left, right, left—"Burn, burn, burn this letter!" Republicans taunted in return, "Ma, ma, where's my pa?" Defiant Democrats shouted back, "Gone to the White House, ha, ha, ha!"

"I Want My Pa!"   *Malicious anti-Cleveland cartoon.*

The contest hinged on the state of New York, where Blaine blundered badly in the closing days of the campaign. A witless Republican clergyman damned the Democrats as the party of "rum, Romanism, and rebellion"—insulting at one swift stroke the national origin, faith, and patriotism of New York's numerous Irish-Americans. Blaine was present but lacked the presence of mind to repudiate the statement immediately. The pungent phrase, shortened to "RRR," stung and stuck. Blaine's silence seemed to give consent, and the wavering Irishmen who deserted his camp helped to account for Cleveland's paper-thin plurality of about a thousand votes in New York State. Cleveland swept the solid South and squeaked into office with 219 to 182 electoral votes and 4,879,507 to 4,850,293 popular votes.

"Old Grover" Takes Over

Bull-necked Cleveland in 1885 was the first Democrat to take the oath of presidential office since Buchanan, twenty-eight years earlier. Huge question marks hung over his portly frame (5 feet, 11 inches, 250 pounds). Could the "party of disunion" be trusted to govern the Union? Would desperate Democrats, ravenously hungry after twenty-four years of exile, trample the frail

---

* Neither candidate had served in the Civil War. Cleveland had hired a substitute to go in his stead while he supported his widowed mother and two sisters. Blaine was the only candidate nominated by the Republicans from Grant through McKinley (1868–1900) who had not been a Civil War officer.

sprouts of civil-service reform in a stampede to the patronage trough? Could Cleveland restore a measure of respect and power to the maligned and enfeebled presidency?

Cleveland was not a suave or skillful political leader. A staunch apostle of the hands-off creed of laissez-faire, the new president summed up his political philosophy in 1887 when he vetoed a bill to provide seeds for drought-ravaged Texas farmers. "Though the people support the government," he declared, "the government should not support the people." As tactless as a mirror and as direct as a bulldozer, Cleveland was outspoken, unbending, and profanely hot tempered.

At the outset Cleveland narrowed the North-South chasm by naming to the cabinet two former Confederates. As for the civil service, Cleveland was whipsawed between the demands of the Democratic faithful for jobs and the demands of the Mugwumps, who had helped elect him, for reform. Believing in the merit system, Cleveland at first favored the cause of the reformers; but he eventually caved in to the carpings of Democratic bosses and fired almost two-thirds of the 120,000 federal employees, including 40,000 incumbent (Republican) postmasters.

Military pensions, with their easy access to the federal Treasury, gave Cleveland painful political headaches. The politically potent GAR regularly lobbied hundreds of dubious private pension bills through a compliant Congress. Cleveland carefully read and vetoed many of these bills and in 1887 courageously risked the retribution of the GAR by refusing to add several hundred thousand new pensioners to the rolls.

Cleveland also risked his political welfare by prodding the hornet's nest of the tariff issue. Rejecting the advice of Democratic politicians, he devoted his annual message in 1887 to an appeal for lower tariffs. The response was electric. Republicans rejoiced at his apparent recklessness and marched into the 1888 presidential campaign in high spirits. "There's one more president for us in [tariff] reduction," gloated the old warrior James Blaine.

Dismayed Democrats reluctantly renominated Cleveland at their St. Louis convention, while Republicans turned to Benjamin Harrison of Indiana, the grandson of former president William Henry

("Tippecanoe") Harrison. The tariff was the prime issue, and the two parties flooded the country with some 10 million pamphlets on the subject. Republicans raised an unprecedented $3 million war chest, largely by "frying the fat" out of nervous industrialists. The money was widely used to line up corrupt "voting cattle" known as "repeaters" or "floaters."

On election day, Harrison nosed out Cleveland, 233 to 168 electoral votes. A change of about 7,000 ballots in New York would have reversed the outcome. Cleveland actually polled more popular votes, 5,537,857 to 5,447,129. Such are the curiosities of the Electoral College.

Republicans Return Under Harrison

The incoming president, stocky, heavily bearded Benjamin Harrison, was an honest and earnest party man, but he was also personally brusque and abrupt. He could charm a crowd of ten thousand with his oratory, but "the White House Ice Chest" would chill them individually with a clammy handshake.

After its four-year fast, the GOP ("Grand Old Party," the Republicans' nickname) licked its lips hungrily for the bounty of federal office. Republicans in the House of Representatives were eager to get on with squandering the surplus dollars produced by the high tariffs. But they had only three votes more than the necessary quorum of 163 members, and the Democrats were preparing to continue their obstructive practices of refusing to answer roll calls, demanding roll calls to determine the presence of a quorum, and making numerous delaying motions.

Into this explosive cockpit stepped the new Republican Speaker of the House, Thomas B. Reed of Maine. A hulking figure who towered 6 feet, 3 inches, he had already made his mark as a masterful debater. Cool and collected, he spoke with a harsh nasal drawl and wielded a verbal harpoon of sarcasm. One congressman who had declaimed that he would "rather be right than president," like Henry Clay, was silenced by Reed's rasping sneer that he would "never be either." Opponents cringed at "the crack of his quip."

Believing that the majority should legislate and not be crippled by a filibustering minority, Reed single-handedly changed the House rules early in 1890. He ignored Democratic speakers who demanded quorum counts, and counted as present Democrats who had not answered the roll call. With "Czar" Reed and his iron gavel firmly in charge, the Fifty-first, or "Billion-Dollar," Congress—the first in history to appropriate that sum—gave birth to a bumper crop of expensive legislative babies.

With the backing of President Harrison, a Civil War general, Congress opened wide the federal purse in the Pension Act of 1890. It showered pensions on Union Civil War veterans, raising the number of pensioners from 676,000 in 1891 to 970,000 in 1895, and the cost from $81 million to $135 million in 1893. "Czar" Reed's imperious gavel drove additional bills through Congress. The pioneering Sherman Anti-Trust Act of 1890, though a feeble bludgeon, helped to quiet the mounting uproar against bloated corporations.

The Sherman Silver Purchase Act of 1890 arose from the acute unhappiness of western miners over the limited silver-purchase program under the Bland-Allison Law of 1878. Debt-burdened farmers were also clamoring for the unlimited coinage of silver in order to inflate the currency, thus making for higher prices and easier debt payments. The "gold bug" East looked with conservative horror on any such tampering with the money supply but hungered for the profits that might be reaped from a boost in the tariff schedules. In a huge logrolling operation, eastern protectionists agreed to support a silver bill in exchange for western backing for a higher protectionist tariff. The Sherman Silver Purchase Act provided for the Treasury to buy 4.5 million ounces of silver monthly with notes redeemable in either silver or gold.

High-tariff Republicans reaped their political reward with the McKinley Tariff Bill of 1890, which boosted rates to their highest peacetime level yet—an average of 48.4 percent on dutiable goods. Sponsored in the House by William McKinley of Ohio, the "high priest of high protection," the bill also gave a bounty of two cents a pound to American sugar producers and raised tariffs on agricultural products—a hollow gesture to farmers because foreign growers could never compete with soil-rich Americans.

With some eastern manufacturers raising prices even before the law went into effect, the sweeping McKinley Act brought new woes to the farmer. Mounting discontent against "Bill" McKinley and his McKinley Bill caused voters to rise in wrath, especially in the midwestern farm belt. The congressional landslide of 1890 reduced the Republican membership of the House from 166 to a scant 88 members, as compared with 235 Democrats. Ominously for conservatives, the new Congress also included nine members of the Farmers' Alliance, a militant organization of southern and western farmers.

Popular Revolts in 1892

Discontent over Republican high-tariff policies gave the Democrats high hopes as the presidential election of 1892 approached. Their man of destiny was portly but energetic former president Grover Cleveland. He had built up a profitable law practice in New York City and, after hobnobbing with his wealthy clientele, had become increasingly conservative. Yet such was his reputation that he was nominated at Chicago on the first ballot.

Gathering in Minneapolis, the Republicans renominated cold-fish President Harrison, even though he was cordially disliked by party bosses. Their platform championed the protective tariff.

The campaign of 1892 also featured the new People's party (Populists), which represented frustrated farmers in the West and South. Meeting in Omaha, the Populists adopted a platform that denounced the "prolific womb of governmental injustice." It demanded free and unlimited coinage of silver at the ratio of 16 ounces of silver to 1 ounce of gold, a graduated income tax, and government ownership of the telephone, telegraph, and railroads.

An epidemic of nationwide strikes in the summer of 1892 raised the prospect that the Populists could bring aggrieved workers together with indebted farmers in a revolutionary joint assault on the capitalist order. At Andrew Carnegie's Homestead steel plant near Pittsburgh, company officials called in three hundred armed Pinkerton detectives in July to crush a strike by steelworkers angry over pay cuts. Defiant strikers, armed with rifles and dynamite, forced their assailants to surrender after a vicious battle in which ten people were killed and some sixty wounded. Troops were eventually summoned, and both the strike and the union were broken. That same month, federal troops had to be dispatched to crush a strike among silver miners in Idaho's Coeur d'Alene district.

The Populists made a remarkable showing in the 1892 presidential election. Singing "Good-by, Party Bosses," they rolled up 1,029,846 popular votes and 22 electoral votes for General James B. Weaver. They thus became one of the few third parties in U.S. history to break into the electoral column. But they fell far short of an electoral majority. Industrial laborers, especially in the urban East, did not rally to the Populist banner in appreciable numbers. Populist electoral votes came from six midwestern and western states, four of which (Kansas, Colorado, Idaho, and Nevada) fell completely into the Populist basket.

The South, although a hotbed of agrarian agitation, proved especially unwilling to throw in its lot with a new party. Race was the reason. The more than 1 million southern black farmers now organized in the Colored Farmers' National Alliance shared a host of complaints with poor white farmers, and for a time their common economic goals promised to overcome their racial differences. Recognizing the crucial edge that black votes could give them in the South, Populist leaders like Georgia's Tom Watson reached out to the black community; this wiry redhead who could "talk like the thrust of a Bowie knife" declared, "There is no reason why the black man should not understand that the law that hurts me, as a farmer, hurts him, as a farmer." Many blacks were disillusioned enough with the Republican party to respond. Alarmed, the conservative white "Bourbon" elite in the South played cynically upon historic racial antagonisms to counter the Populists' appeal for interracial solidarity and woo back poor whites.

Southern blacks were heavy losers. The Populist-inspired reminder of potential black political strength led to the near-total extinction of what little African-American suffrage remained in the South. Literacy tests and poll taxes were used to deny blacks the ballot. The notorious "grandfather clause" exempted from those requirements anyone whose forebear had voted in 1860—when, of course, black slaves had not voted at all. More than half a century would pass before southern blacks could again vote in considerable numbers. Accompanying this

disfranchisement were more severe Jim Crow laws, designed to enforce racial segregation in public places, including hotels and restaurants, and backed up by atrocious lynchings and other forms of intimidation.

The conservative crusade to eliminate the black vote also had dire consequences for the Populist party itself. Even Tom Watson abandoned his interracial appeals and, in time, became a vociferous racist himself. After 1896 the Populist party lapsed increasingly into vile racism and staunchly advocated black disfranchisement. Such were the bitterly ironic fruits of the Populist campaign in the South.

Grover, Grim Times, and Gold

With the Populists divided and the Republicans discredited, Grover Cleveland took office once again in 1893, the only president ever reelected after defeat. He was the same old bull-necked and bull-headed Cleveland, with a little more weight, polish, conservatism, and self-assertiveness.

But if it was the same old Grover, it was not the same old country. Hardly had Cleveland seated himself in the presidential chair when the devastating panic of 1893 burst about his burly frame. Lasting for about four years, it was in some respects the worst depression of the nineteenth century. Contributing causes were no doubt the splurge of overspeculation, labor disorders, and the current agricultural depression. Free-silver agitation had also damaged American credit abroad, and the usual pinch on American finances had come when European banking houses began to call in loans from the United States.

Distress was acute and widespread. About eight thousand American businesses collapsed in six months, and dozens of railroad lines went into the hands of receivers. Business executives "died like flies under the strain," wrote Henry Adams. Soup kitchens were set up for the unemployed, while gangs of hoboes wandered aimlessly about the country. Local charities did their feeble best, but the federal government, bound by the let-nature-take-its-course philosophy of the times, saw no legitimate way to relieve the suffering masses.

Cleveland, who had earlier been bothered by a surplus, now faced a growing deficit. Owners of the paper currency issued under the Sherman Silver Purchase Act were presenting the notes for gold, and by law the notes had to be reissued. New holders would then repeat the process, thus draining away gold in an "endless chain" operation.

Alarmingly, the gold reserve in the Treasury dropped below $100 million, which was popularly regarded as the safe minimum for supporting about $350 million in outstanding paper money. Cleveland saw no alternative but to halt the bleeding away of gold by engineering a repeal of the Sherman Silver Purchase Act of 1890. For this purpose he summoned Congress into an extra session in the summer of 1893.

In Congress debate over the repeal of the silver act was heated. A silver-tongued young congressman from Nebraska, the thirty-three-year-old William Jennings Bryan, held the galleries spellbound for three hours as he championed the cause of free silver. The friends of silver announced that "hell would freeze over" before Congress passed the repeal measure. But an angered Cleveland used his office-giving power to break the filibuster in the Senate. He thus alienated the Democratic silverites and disrupted his party at the very outset of his administration.

Furthermore, the repeal of the Sherman Silver Purchase Act failed to stop the hemorrhaging of gold from the Treasury. The gold reserve sank to a dismaying $41 million in February 1894. The United States was now in grave danger of going off the gold standard—a move that would render the nation's currency volatile and unreliable as a measure of value and that could mortally cripple America's international trade. Two Treasury bond issues totaling over $100 million were floated in 1894, but the gold drain continued relentlessly.

Early in 1895 Cleveland turned in desperation to J. P. Morgan, "the banker's banker," and a Wall Street syndicate. After tense negotiations at the White House, the bankers agreed to lend the government $65 million in gold. They were obviously in business for profit, so they charged a commission amounting to about $7 million. But they did make a significant concession when they agreed to obtain one-half of the gold abroad and take the necessary steps to dam it up in the leaky Treasury. The loan, at least temporarily, helped restore confidence in the nation's finances.

But the bond deal stirred up a storm. The Wall Street ogre, especially in the eyes of the silverites and

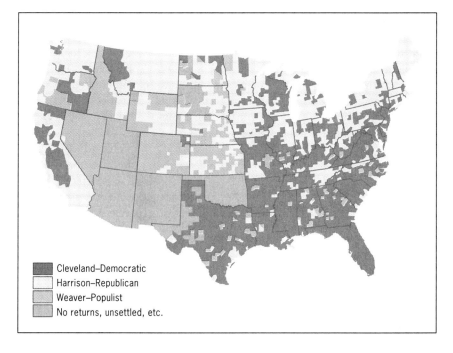

Presidential Election of 1892 (showing vote by county) *Notice the concentration of Populist strength in the semiarid farming regions of the western half of the country. People living in territories (unsettled areas—see key) could not vote.*

Cleveland–Democratic
Harrison–Republican
Weaver–Populist
No returns, unsettled, etc.

other debtors, symbolized all that was wicked and grasping. Cleveland's secretive dealings with mighty "Jupiter" Morgan were savagely condemned as a "sellout" of the national government. But Cleveland was certain that he had done no wrong. Sarcastically denying that he was "Morgan's errand boy," he asserted: "Without shame and without repentance I confess my share of the guilt."

Cleveland suffered further embarrassment with the passage of the Wilson-Gorman Tariff in 1894. The Democrats had pledged to lower tariffs, but by the time the measure got through Congress, it had been so loaded with special-interest protection that it lowered rates only slightly below those of the McKinley Tariff. An outraged Cleveland grudgingly let the bill, which also contained a 2 percent tax on incomes over $4,000, become law without his signature. When the income-tax provision was struck down by a five-to-four Supreme Court decision in 1895,* the Populists and other impoverished groups found further proof that the courts were only the tools of the plutocrats.

Democratic political fortunes naturally suffered. The tariff dynamite that had blasted the Republicans

---

* It violated the "direct tax" clause. See Art. I, Sec. IX, para. 4, in the Appendix. The Sixteenth Amendment to the Constitution, adopted in 1913, permitted an income tax.

Chronology

1868	Grant defeats Seymour for presidency.
1869	Fisk and Gould corner the gold market.
1871	Tweed scandal in New York.
1872	Crédit Mobilier scandal. Liberal Republicans break with Grant. Grant defeats Greeley for presidency.
1873	Panic of 1873.
1874–1875	Whiskey Ring scandal.
1875	Civil Rights Act of 1875. Resumption Act passed.
1876	Hayes-Tilden election standoff and crisis.
1877	Compromise of 1877. Reconstruction ends. Railroad strikes paralyze nation.
1880	Garfield defeats Hancock for presidency.
1881	Garfield assassinated; Arthur assumes presidency.
1882	Chinese Exclusion Act.
1883	*Civil Rights Cases.* Pendleton Act sets up Civil Service Commission.
1884	Cleveland defeats Blaine for presidency.
1888	Harrison defeats Cleveland for presidency.
1890	"Billion Dollar" Congress. Sherman Silver Purchase Act of 1890. McKinley Tariff Bill.
1892	Cleveland defeats Harrison and Weaver for presidency.
1893	Depression of 1893 begins.
1894	Wilson-Gorman Tariff.
1895	Morgan loans $65 million in gold to federal government. Supreme Court declares income tax unconstitutional.
1896	*Plessy* v. *Ferguson* decision upholds racial segregation.

out of the House in 1890 now dislodged the Democrats, with a strong helping hand from the depression. Revitalized Republicans, singing "The Soup House" and "Times Are Mighty Hard," won the congressional elections of 1894 in a landslide and now had 244 votes to 105 for the Democrats. Republicans looked forward to the 1896 presidential elections with glee.

Despite his gruff integrity and occasional courage, Grover Cleveland failed utterly to cope with the serious economic crisis that hit the nation in 1893. He was tied down in office by the same threads that held all the presidents of the day to Lilliputian levels. Grant, Hayes, Garfield, Arthur, and Harrison are often referred to as the "forgettable presidents." Bewhiskered and bland in person, they left mostly blanks—or blots—on the nation's political record. What little political vitality existed was to be found in local settings, or in Congress, which overshadowed the White House during most of the Gilded Age.

As the nineteenth century drew to a close, observers were asking, "Why are the 'best men' not in politics?" One answer was that they had been lured away from public life by the lusty attractions of the booming industrial economy. Talented men ached for profits, not the presidency; they dreamed of controlling corporations, not Congress. What the nation lost in political leadership, it gained in an astounding surge of economic growth. Although still in many ways a political dwarf, the United States was about to stand up before the world as an industrial colossus.

SUGGESTED READINGS

Primary Source Documents

Henry Adams penned some perceptive and sour observations on the era in his autobiographical *Education of Henry Adams* (1907) and in his novel *Democracy* (1880). See also the classic satire by Mark Twain and Charles Dudley Warner, *The Gilded Age* (1873).

Secondary Sources

The scandal-rocked Grant era is treated with brevity in James G. Randall and David Donald, *The Civil War and Reconstruction* (rev. ed., 1969), and at greater length in William Gillette, *Retreat from Reconstruction* (1979), and James M. McPherson, *Ordeal by Fire* (1981). Southern politics is detailed in J. Morgan Kousser, *The Shaping of Southern Politics* (1974), whereas William Gillette, *The Right to Vote* (1965), discusses the North. On the party systems see Paul Kleppner, *The Third Electoral System, 1835–1892* (1979); Morton Keller, *Affairs of State: Public Life in Nineteenth-Century America* (1977); and Richard Jensen, *The Winning of the Mid-West* (1971). Mark W. Summers analyzes *Railroads, Reconstruction, and the Gospel of Prosperity* (1984). Money questions are treated in Irwin Unger, *The Greenback Era* (1964); Walter T. K. Nugent, *Money and American Society, 1865–1880* (1968); and Allen Weinstein's account of the "Crime of '73," *Prelude to Populism* (1970). C. Vann Woodward sharply analyzes the Compromise of 1877 in *Reunion and Reaction* (rev. ed., 1956). California receives special attention in Alexander Saxton, *The Indispensable Enemy: Labor and the Anti-Chinese Movement in California* (1975).

25

Industry Comes of Age,
1865–1900

*The railroads are not run for the benefit of the dear public.
That cry is all nonsense. They are built for men who invest
their money and expect to get a fair percentage on the same.*

WILLIAM H. VANDERBILT, 1882

The Iron Colt Becomes an Iron Horse

The government-business entanglements that increasingly shaped politics after the Civil War also undergirded the industrial development of the nation. The unparalleled outburst of railroad construction was a crucial case. When Lincoln was shot in 1865, there were only 35,000 miles of steam railways in the United States, mostly east of the Mississippi. By 1900 the figure had spurted up to 192,556 miles, or more than that for all Europe combined.

Transcontinental railroad building was so costly and risky as to require governmental subsidies. Congress began to advance liberal money loans to two favored cross-continent companies in 1862 and added enormous donations of acreage paralleling the tracks. Granting land was a "cheap" way to subsidize a much-desired transportation system, because it

avoided new taxes for direct cash grants. All told, Washington rewarded the railroads with 155,504,994 acres, and the western states contributed 49 million more—a total area larger than Texas.

Deadlock in the 1850s over the location of the proposed transcontinental railroad was broken when the South seceded, leaving the field to the North. In 1862, the year after the guns first spoke at Fort Sumter, Congress made provision for starting the long-awaited line. One weighty argument for action was the urgency of bolstering the Union, already disrupted, by binding the Pacific Coast more securely to the rest of the Republic.

The Union Pacific Railroad—note the word *Union*—was thus commissioned by Congress to thrust westward from Omaha, Nebraska. The laying of rails began in earnest after the Civil War ended in 1865; and with juicy loans and land grants available, the "groundhog" promoters made all possible haste.

Sweaty construction gangs, containing many Irish "Paddies" (Patricks), worked at a frantic pace. On one record-breaking day, a sledge-and-shovel army of some five thousand men laid ten miles of track. A favorite song was:

> Then drill, my Paddies, drill;
> Drill, my heroes, drill;
> Drill all day,
> No sugar in your tay,
> Workin' on the U.P. Railway.

When hostile Indians attacked, the laborers would drop their picks and seize their rifles. At rail's end, workers tried to find relaxation and conviviality in tented towns known as "hells on wheels," sometimes numbering as many as ten thousand men and a sprinkling of painted prostitutes.

Rail laying at the California end was undertaken by the Central Pacific Railroad. This line pushed boldly eastward from boomtown Sacra-

mento, over and through the towering, snow-clogged Sierra Nevada. Four farseeing men—the so-called Big Four—were the chief financial backers of the enterprise. The quartet included the heavyset, enterprising ex-governor Leland Stanford of California, who had useful political connections, and the burly, energetic Collis P. Huntington, an adept lobbyist.

The Central Pacific, which was granted the same princely subsidies as the Union Pacific, had the same incentive to haste. Some ten thousand Chinese laborers sweated from dawn to dusk under their basket hats. Hundreds lost their lives in premature explosions and other mishaps. The towering Sierra Nevada presented a formidable barrier; and the nerves of the Big Four were strained when their workers could chip only a few inches a day through solid rock, while the Union Pacific was sledgehammering westward across the plains.

A "wedding of the rails" was finally consummated near Ogden, Utah, in 1869, as the cowcatchers of two locomotives gently kissed. The colorful ceremony included the breaking of champagne bottles and the driving of a last ceremonial (golden) spike, with ex-governor Stanford clumsily wielding a silver

Snow Sheds on the Central Pacific Railroad in the Sierra Nevada Mountains, by Joseph H. Becker, c. 1869
Formidable obstacles of climate and terrain confronted the builders of the Central Pacific Railroad in the mountainous heights of California. Note the Chinese laborers in the foreground.

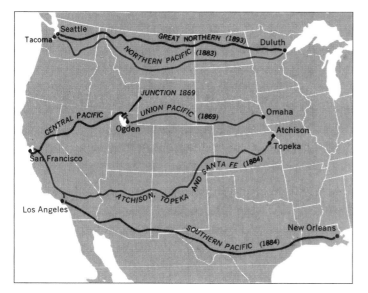

Early Pacific Railway Lines (with completion dates)   *The Great Northern line claimed several distinctions: it was the last-built of the major transcontinental roads, the only one constructed without lavish federal subsidies, and the most northerly. Its larger-than-life promoter, James J. Hill, once declared: "You can't interest me in any proposition in any place where it doesn't snow.... No man on whom the snow does not fall ever amounts to a tinker's dam."*

sledgehammer.* In all, the Union Pacific built 1,086 miles, and the Central Pacific 689 miles.

Completion of the transcontinental line welded the West Coast more firmly to the Union and facilitated a flourishing trade with Asia. It penetrated the arid barrier of the deserts, paving the way for the phenomenal growth of the Great West. Americans compared this great achievement with the Declaration of Independence and the emancipation of the slaves; jubilant Philadelphians again rang the cracked bell of Independence Hall.

Binding the Country with Railroad Ties

With the westward trail now blazed, four other transcontinental lines were completed before the century's end. None of them secured monetary loans from the federal government, as did the Union Pacific and the Central Pacific. But all of them except the Great Northern received generous grants of land.

The Northern Pacific Railroad, stretching from Lake Superior to Puget Sound, reached its terminus in 1883. The Atchison, Topeka, and Santa Fe, stretching through the southwestern deserts to California,

was completed in 1884. The Southern Pacific ribboned from New Orleans to Los Angeles and was consolidated in the same year.

The last of the five nineteenth-century transcontinental railroads, the Great Northern, ran north of the Northern Pacific from Duluth to Seattle. Its creator was James J. Hill, a far-visioned Canadian-American who perceived that the prosperity of his railroad depended on the prosperity of the area that it served. Hill's sound organization enabled his railroad to ride through later financial storms with flying colors.

Yet the romance of the rails was not without its sordid side. Pioneer builders were often guilty of gross overoptimism, laying down rails that went "from nowhere to nothing" in order to get the lavish federal land bounties. When prosperity failed to smile, they went into bankruptcy, carrying down with them the savings of trusting investors. Many of the large railroads in the post–Civil War decades passed through seemingly endless bankruptcies, mergers, or reorganizations.

Revolution by Railways

The metallic fingers of the railroads intimately touched countless phases of American life. For the

---

* The spike was promptly removed and is now exhibited at the Stanford University Museum.

first time, a sprawling nation became united in a physical sense, bound with ribs of iron and steel. By stitching North America together from sea to sea, the transcontinental lines created an enormous market for American raw materials and manufactured goods—a huge empire of commerce that beckoned to foreign and domestic investors alike.

More than any other single factor, the railroad network spurred the amazing industrialization of the post–Civil War years. The puffing locomotives opened up fresh markets for manufactured goods and sped raw materials to the factory. The forging of the rails themselves provided the largest single backlog for the adolescent steel industry.

The screeching iron horse likewise stimulated mining and agriculture, especially in the West. It took farmers out to their land, carried the fruits of their toil to market, and brought them their manufactured necessities. Clusters of farm settlements paralleled the railroads, just as earlier they had followed the rivers.

Railways were a boon for cities and played a leading role in the great cityward movement of the last decades of the century. The iron monsters could carry food to enormous concentrations of people and at the same time ensure them a livelihood by providing both raw materials and markets.

Railroad companies also stimulated the mighty stream of immigration. Seeking settlers to whom their land grants might be sold at a profit, they advertised seductively in Europe and sometimes offered to transplant the newcomers free to their farms.

The land also felt the impact of the railroad—especially the broad, ecologically fragile midsection of the continent. Settlers following the railroads plowed up the tallgrass prairies of Iowa, Illinois, Kansas, and Nebraska and planted well-drained, rectangular cornfields. On the shortgrass prairies of the high plains in the Dakotas and Montana, range-fed cattle rapidly displaced the buffalo, which were hunted to near-extinction. The white pine forests of Michigan, Wisconsin, and Minnesota disappeared into lumber that was rushed by rail to prairie farmers who used it to build houses and fences.

Time itself was bent to the railroads' needs. Until the 1880s every town in the United States had its own "local" time, dictated by the sun's position. When it was noon in Chicago, it was 11:50 A.M. in St. Louis

and 12:18 P.M. in Detroit. For railroad operators worried about keeping schedules and avoiding wrecks, this patchwork of local times was a nightmare. Thus on November 18, 1883, the major rail lines decreed that the continent would henceforth be divided into four "time zones." Most communities quickly adopted railroad "standard" time.

Finally, the railroad, more than any other single factor, was the maker of millionaires. A raw new aristocracy, consisting of "lords of the rail" like Cornelius Vanderbilt and "palace car" inventor George Pullman, replaced the old southern "lords of the lash." The multi-webbed lines became the playthings of Wall Street; and colossal wealth was amassed by stock speculators and railroad wreckers.

Wrongdoing in Railroading

Corruption lurks nearby when fabulous fortunes can materialize overnight. The fleecings administered by the railroad construction companies, such as the Crédit Mobilier, were but the first of the bunco games that the railroad promoters learned to play. Methods soon became more refined, as fast-fingered financiers executed multimillion-dollar maneuvers beneath the noses of a bedazzled public. Jay Gould was the most adept of these ringmasters of rapacity. For nearly thirty years he boomed and busted the stocks of the Erie, the Kansas Pacific, the Union Pacific, and the Texas and Pacific in an incredible circus of speculative skullduggery.

One of the favorite devices of the moguls of manipulation was "stock watering." The term originally referred to the practice of making cattle thirsty by feeding them salt, and then having them bloat themselves with water before they were weighed in for sale. Using a variation of this technique, railroad stock promoters grossly inflated their claims about a given line's assets and profitability and sold stocks and bonds far in excess of the railroad's actual value. "Promoters' profits" were often the tail that wagged the iron horse itself. Railroad managers were forced to charge extortionate rates and wage ruthless competitive battles in order to pay off the exaggerated financial obligations with which they were saddled.

The public interest was frequently trampled underfoot as the railroad titans waged their brutal wars. Crusty old Cornelius Vanderbilt, when told that the law stood in his way, reportedly exclaimed: "Law! What do I care about the law? Hain't I got the power?" His son, William H. Vanderbilt, when asked in 1883 about the discontinuance of a fast mail train, reportedly snorted, "The public be damned!"

While abusing the public, the railroaders blandly bought and sold people in public life. They bribed judges and legislatures, elected their own agents to high office, and showered free passes on journalists and politicians.

Railroad kings were, for a time, virtual industrial monarchs. As manipulators of a huge natural monopoly, they exercised more direct control over the lives of more people than did the president of the United States—and their terms were not limited to four years. They increasingly shunned the crude bloodletting of cutthroat competition and began to cooperate with one another to rule the railroad dominion. Sorely pressed to show at least some returns on their bloated investments, they entered into defensive alliances to protect precious profits.

The earliest form of combination was the "pool"—an agreement to divide the business in a given area and share the profits. Other rail barons granted secret rebates or kickbacks to powerful shippers in return for steady and assured traffic. Often they slashed their rates on competing lines, but they more than made up the difference on noncompeting ones, where they might actually charge more for a short haul than for a long one.

Government Bridles the Iron Horse

It was neither healthy nor politically acceptable that so many people should be at the mercy of so few. Impoverished farmers, especially in the Midwest, began to wonder if the nation had not escaped from the slavery power only to fall into the hands of the money power, as represented by the railroad plutocracy.

But the American people, though quick to respond to political injustice, were slow to combat economic injustice. Dedicated to free enterprise and to the principle that competition is the soul of trade, they remembered that Jefferson's ideals were hostile to governmental interference with business. Above all, there shimmered the "American dream": the hope that in a catch-as-catch-can economic system, anyone might become a millionaire.

The depression of the 1870s finally goaded the farmers into protesting against being "railroaded" into bankruptcy. Under pressure from organized agrarian groups like the Grange (see p. 395), many midwestern legislatures tried to regulate the railroad monopoly. The scattered state efforts screeched to a halt in 1886. The Supreme Court, in the *Wabash* case, decreed that individual states had no power to regulate *inter*state commerce. If the mechanical monster were to be corralled, the federal government would have to do the job.

Congress ignored President Cleveland's grumbling indifference to the problem and passed the Interstate Commerce Act in 1887. It prohibited rebates and pools and required the railroads to publish their rates openly. It also forbade unfair discrimination against shippers and outlawed charging more for a short haul than for a long one over the same line. Most important, it set up the Interstate Commerce Commission (ICC) to enforce and administer the new legislation.

Despite acclaim, the Interstate Commerce Act emphatically did not represent a popular victory over corporate wealth. One of the leading corporation lawyers of the day, Richard Olney, shrewdly noted that the new commission "can be made of great use to the railroads. It satisfies the popular clamor for a government supervision of railroads, at the same time that such supervision is almost entirely nominal. . . . The part of wisdom is not to destroy the Commission, but to utilize it."

What the new legislation did do was provide an orderly forum where competing business interests could resolve their conflicts in peaceable ways. The country could now avoid ruinous rate wars among the railroads, and outraged, "confiscatory" attacks on the lines by pitchfork-prodded state legislatures. This was a modest accomplishment but by no means an unimportant one. The Interstate Commerce Act tended to stabilize, not revolutionize, the existing business system.

Yet the act still ranks as a red-letter law. It was the first large-scale attempt by Washington to regulate business in the interest of society at large. It foreshadowed the doom of freewheeling, buccaneering business practices and served full notice that there was a public interest in private enterprise that the government was bound to protect.

Miracles of Mechanization

Postwar industrial expansion, partly a result of the railroad network, rapidly began to assume mammoth proportions. When Lincoln was elected in 1860, the Republic ranked only fourth among the manufacturing nations of the world. By 1894 it had bounded into first place. Why the sudden upsurge?

The Modern Colossus of Railroads, 1879   *William H. Vanderbilt, flanked by Cyrus Field (left) and Jay Gould (right), towers over the scene. With the Interstate Commerce Act in 1887, the government began to weaken the magnates' grip over the nation's transportation system.*

Liquid capital, previously scarce, was becoming abundant. The word *millionaire* had not been coined until the 1840s, and in 1861 only a handful of individuals composed this class. But the Civil War, partly through profiteering, created immense fortunes; and these accumulations could now be combined with the customary borrowings from foreign capitalists.

The amazing natural resources of the nation were about to be fully exploited, including coal, oil, and iron. Massive immigration helped make unskilled labor cheap and plentiful. Steel, the keystone industry, built its strength largely on the sweat of low-priced immigrant labor, working in two twelve-hour shifts, seven days a week.

American ingenuity at the same time played a vital role in the second American Industrial Revolution. American inventiveness flowered luxuriantly in the postwar years: between 1860 and 1890 some 440,000 patents were issued. Business operations were facilitated by the cash register, the stock ticker, and the typewriter ("literary piano"), which attracted women to industry. Urbanization was speeded by the refrigerator car, the electric dynamo, and the electric railway, which displaced animal-drawn cars.

The ingenious telephone was introduced in 1876 by Alexander Graham Bell, a teacher of the deaf who said that if he could make the mute talk, he could make iron speak. His invention had a great social impact on the nation, especially when it attracted many women from the home to become the "number please" operators in the gigantic communications network.

The most versatile inventor of all was Thomas A. Edison, who ran a veritable invention factory in New Jersey. He is perhaps best known for his perfection in 1879 of the electric light, which he unveiled after trying some six thousand filaments. He invented, perfected, or did useful exploratory work on the phonograph, the mimeograph, the dictaphone, and the moving picture. "Genius," he said, "is one percent inspiration and ninety-nine percent perspiration."

The Trust Titan Emerges

Despite pious protests to the contrary, competition was the bugbear of most business leaders of the day.

Tycoons such as Andrew Carnegie, the steel king, John D. Rockefeller, the oil baron, and J. Pierpont Morgan, the bankers' banker, exercised their genius in devising ways to circumvent competition. Carnegie developed the "vertical integration" of production by directly controlling every phase of his steel-making operation. His miners scratched ore from the earth in Minnesota's Mesabi range; Carnegie ships floated it across the Great Lakes; Carnegie railroads delivered it to blast furnaces at Pittsburgh. When the molten metal finally poured from the glowing crucibles into the waiting ingot molds, no other hands but those in Carnegie's employ had touched the product.

Rockefeller pursued the less economically justifiable technique of "horizontal integration," which simply meant consolidating with competitors to monopolize a given market. He perfected a device for controlling bothersome rivals—the "trust." Stockholders in various smaller oil companies assigned their stock to the board of directors of Rockefeller's Standard Oil Company. It then consolidated and concerted the operations of the previously competing enterprises. "Let us prey" was said to be Rockefeller's unwritten motto. Ruthlessly wielding vast power, Standard Oil soon cornered virtually the entire world petroleum market. Weaker competitors, left out of the trust agreement, were forced to the wall. Rockefeller's stunning success inspired many imitators, and the word *trust* came to be generally used to describe any large-scale business combination.

The imperial Morgan devised still other schemes for eliminating "wasteful" competition. The depression of the 1890s drove into his welcoming arms many bleeding businesspeople, wounded by cutthroat competition. His prescribed remedy was to consolidate rival enterprises and to ensure future harmony by placing officers of his own banking syndicate on their various boards of directors. These came to be known as "interlocking directorates."

The Supremacy of Steel

"Steel is king!" might well have been the exultant war cry of the new industrialized generation. The mighty metal ultimately held together the new civilization, from skyscrapers to coal scuttles, while providing it with food, shelter, and transportation. Steel making, notably rails for railroads, typified the dominance of heavy industry, which concentrated on making "capital goods," as distinct from the production of "consumer goods" such as clothes and shoes.

Today taken for granted, steel was a scarce commodity in the wood-and-brick America of Abraham Lincoln. Yet within an amazing twenty years after 1870 the United States outdistanced all foreign competitors and was pouring out more than one-third of the world's supply of steel. By 1900 the Americans were producing as much as Britain and Germany combined.

What wrought the transformation? Chiefly the invention in the 1850s of a method of making cheap steel—the Bessemer process. It was named after a derided British inventor, although an American had stumbled on it a few years earlier. William Kelly, a Kentucky manufacturer of iron kettles, discovered that cold air blown on red-hot iron caused the metal to become white-hot by igniting the carbon and thus eliminating impurities.

Kingpin among steelmasters was Andrew Carnegie, an undersized, charming Scotsman. As a towheaded lad, he was brought to America by his impoverished parents in 1848 and got a job as a bobbin boy at $1.20 a week. Mounting the ladder of success so fast that he was said to have scorched the rungs, he forged ahead by working hard, doing extra chores, cheerfully assuming responsibility, and smoothly cultivating influential people.

After accumulating some capital, Carnegie entered the steel business in the Pittsburgh area. By 1900 he was producing one-fourth of the nation's Bessemer steel, and his partners were dividing the profits of $40 million a year, with the "Napoleon of the Smokestacks" himself receiving a cool $25 million. These were the pre-income-tax days, when millionaires were really rich and profits represented take-home pay.

Into the picture now stepped the financial giant of the age, J. Pierpont Morgan. "Jupiter" Morgan had made a legendary reputation for himself and his Wall Street banking house by financing the reorganization of railroads, insurance companies, and banks. An impressive figure of a man, with massive shoulders, shaggy brows, piercing eyes, and a bulbous, acne-cursed red nose, he had established an enviable reputation for integrity. He did not believe that "money power" was dangerous, except when in dangerous hands—and he did not regard his own hands as dangerous.

The force of circumstances brought Morgan and Carnegie into collision. By 1900 the canny little Scotsman, weary of turning steel into gold, was eager to sell his holdings. Morgan had meanwhile plunged heavily into the manufacture of steel pipe tubing. Carnegie, cleverly threatening to invade the same business, was ready to ruin his rival if he did not receive his price. The steelmaster's agents haggled with the imperious Morgan for eight agonizing hours, and the financier finally agreed to buy out Carnegie for over $400 million. Fearing that he would die "disgraced" with so much wealth, Carnegie dedicated the remaining years of his life to giving it away for public libraries, pensions for professors, and other such philanthropic purposes—in all disposing of about $350 million.

Morgan moved rapidly to expand his new industrial empire. He took the Carnegie holdings, added others, "watered" the stock liberally, and in 1901 launched the enlarged United States Steel Corporation. Capitalized at $1.4 billion, it became America's first billion-dollar corporation—a larger sum than the total estimated wealth of the nation in 1800. The industrial revolution, with its hot Bessemer breath, had come into its own.

Rockefeller Grows an American Beauty Rose

Another new industry was born almost overnight when in 1859 the first oil well—"Drake's Folly" in Pennsylvania—poured out its liquid "black gold." Kerosene, derived from petroleum, was the first major product of the infant oil industry. Replacing whale oil as the fuel for America's lamps, kerosene became the country's fourth most valuable export by the 1870s.

But what technology gives, technology takes away. By 1885 Thomas Edison's new electric light bulbs had rendered kerosene largely obsolete. Oil might thus have remained a modest, even a shrinking industry but for yet another turn of the technological tide—the invention of the automobile. By 1900 the gasoline-burning internal combustion engine had clearly bested its rivals, steam and electricity, and the oil business got a new, long-lasting, and hugely profitable lease on life.

John D. Rockefeller—lanky, shrewd, ambitious, abstemious (he neither drank, smoked, nor swore)—came to dominate the oil industry. Born to a family of precarious income, he became a successful businessman at age nineteen. One upward stride led to another, and in 1870 he organized the Standard Oil Company of Ohio, nucleus of the great trust formed in 1882. Locating his refineries in Cleveland, he sought to eliminate the middlemen and squeeze out competitors.

Pious and parsimonious, Rockefeller flourished in an era of completely free enterprise. Operating "just to the windward of the law," he pursued a policy of rule or ruin. By 1877 Rockefeller controlled 95 percent of all the oil refineries in the country.

Rockefeller—"Reckafellow," as Carnegie once called him—showed little mercy. A kind of primitive savagery prevailed in the jungle world of big business, where only the fittest survived. Or so Rockefeller believed. His son later explained that the giant American Beauty rose could be produced "only by sacrificing the early buds that grew up around it." His father pinched off the small buds with complete ruthlessness. Employing spies and extorting secret rebates from the railroads, he even forced the lines to pay him rebates on the freight bills of his competitors!

Rockefeller thought he was simply obeying a law of nature. "The time was ripe" for aggressive consolidation, he later reflected. "It had to come, though all we saw at the moment was the need to save ourselves from wasteful conditions. . . . The day of combination is here to stay. Individualism has gone, never to return."

On the other side of the ledger, Rockefeller's oil monopoly did turn out a superior product at a relatively cheap price. It achieved important economies, both at home and abroad, by its large-scale methods of production and distribution. This, in truth, was the tale of the other trusts as well. The efficient use of expensive machinery called for bigness, and consolidation proved more profitable than ruinous price wars.

Other trusts blossomed along with the American Beauty of oil. These included the sugar trust, the tobacco trust, the leather trust, and the harvester trust, which amalgamated some two hundred competitors. The meat industry arose on the backs of bawling western herds, and meat kings like Gustavus F. Swift and Philip Armour took their place among the new royalty. Wealth was coming to dominate the commonwealth.

These untrustworthy trusts, and the "pirates" who captained them, were disturbingly new. They eclipsed an older American aristocracy of modestly successful merchants and professionals. An arrogant class of "new rich" was now elbowing aside the patrician families in the mad scramble for power and prestige. Not surprisingly, the ranks of the antitrust crusaders were frequently spearheaded by the "best men"—genteel old-family do-gooders who were not radicals but conservative defenders of their own vanishing influence.

The Gospel of Wealth

Monarchs of yore invoked the divine right of kings, and America's industrial plutocrats took a somewhat similar stance. Some candidly credited heavenly help and justified their social position with what came to be known as the "Gospel of Wealth." "Godliness is in league with riches," preached the Episcopal bishop of Massachusetts, and hard-fisted John D. Rockefeller piously acknowledged that "the good Lord gave me my money." But most defenders of wide-open capitalism relied more heavily on the survival-of-the-fittest theories of Charles Darwin. "The millionaires are a product of natural selection," concluded Yale professor William Graham Sumner. "They get high wages and live in luxury, but the bargain is a good one for society." Despite plutocracy and deepening class divisions, the captains of industry provided material progress.

Self-justification by the wealthy inevitably involved contempt for the poor. Many of the rich, especially the newly rich, had pulled themselves up by their own bootstraps; hence they concluded that those who stayed poor must be lazy and lacking in enterprise. The Reverend Russell Conwell of Philadelphia became rich by delivering his lecture "Acres of Diamonds" thousands of times. In it he said, "There is not a poor person in the United States who was not made poor by his own shortcomings." Such attitudes were a formidable roadblock to social reform.

Plutocracy, like the earlier slavocracy, took its stand firmly on the Constitution. The clause that gave Congress sole jurisdiction over interstate commerce was a godsend to the monopolists; their high-priced lawyers used it time and again to thwart controls by the state legislatures. Giant trusts likewise sought refuge behind the Fourteenth Amendment, which had been originally designed to protect the rights of ex-slaves as persons. The courts ingeniously interpreted a corporation to be a legal "person" and decreed that, as such, it could not be deprived of its property by a state without "due process of law" (see Art. XIV, para. 1).

Great industrialists likewise sought to incorporate in "easy states," like New Jersey, where the restrictions on big business were mild or nonexistent. For example, the Southern Pacific Railroad, with much of its trackage in California, was incorporated in Kentucky.

Government Tackles the Trust Evil

At long last the masses of the people began to mobilize against monopoly. They first tried to control the trusts through state legislation, as they had earlier attempted to curb the railroads. Failing here, as before, they were forced to appeal to Congress. After prolonged pulling and hauling, the Sherman Anti-Trust Act of 1890 was finally signed into law.

The Sherman Act flatly forbade combinations in restraint of trade, without making any distinction between "good" trusts and "bad" trusts. Bigness, not badness, was the sin. The law proved ineffective, largely because it had only baby teeth or no teeth at all, and because it contained legal loopholes through which clever corporation lawyers could wriggle. But it was unexpectedly effective in one respect. Contrary to its original intent, it was used to curb labor unions or labor combinations that were deemed to be restraining trade.

Early prosecutions of the trusts by the Justice Department under the Sherman Act of 1890, as it

Washington as Seen by the Trusts, 1900 *"What a funny little government," John D. Rockefeller observes in this satirical cartoon. His own wealth and power are presumed to dwarf the resources of the federal government.*

turned out, were neither vigorous nor successful. Not until 1914 were the paper jaws of the Sherman Act fitted with reasonably sharp teeth. Until then, there was some question as to whether the government would control the trusts or the trusts the government.

But the iron grip of monopolistic corporations was being threatened. A revolutionary new principle had been written into the law books by the Sherman Anti-Trust Act of 1890, as well as by the Interstate Commerce Act of 1887. Private greed must henceforth be subordinated to public need.

The South in the Age of Industry

The industrial tidal wave that washed over the North after the Civil War caused only feeble ripples in the backwater of the South. The plantation system had degenerated into a pattern of absentee landownership. White and black sharecroppers tilled the soil for a share of the crop, or they became tenants, in bondage to landlords who controlled needed credit and supplies.

Southern agriculture received a welcome boost in the 1880s, when machine-made cigarettes replaced the roll-your-own variety and tobacco consumption shot up. James Buchanan Duke took full advantage of the new technology to mass-produce the dainty "coffin nails." In 1890, in what was becoming a familiar pattern, he absorbed his main competitors into the American Tobacco Company. The cigarette czar later showed

such generosity to Trinity College, near his birthplace in Durham, North Carolina, that the trustees gratefully changed its name to Duke University.

Industrialists tried to coax the agricultural South out of the fields and into the factories, but with only modest success. The region remained overwhelmingly rural. Prominent among the boosters of a "new South" was silver-tongued Henry W. Grady, editor of the Atlanta *Constitution.* He tirelessly exhorted the ex-Confederates to become "Georgia Yankees" and outplay the North at the commercial and industrial game.

Yet formidable obstacles lay in the path of southern industrialization. One was the paper barrier of regional rate-setting systems imposed by the northern-dominated railroad interests. Railroads gave preferential rates to manufactured goods moving southward from the North, but in the opposite direction they discriminated in favor of southern raw materials. The net effect was to keep the South in a kind of "Third World" servitude to the Northeast—as a supplier of raw materials to the manufacturing metropolis, unable to develop a substantial industrial base of its own.

A bitter example of this economic discrimination against the South was the "Pittsburgh plus" pricing system in the steel industry. Rich deposits of coal and iron ore near Birmingham, Alabama, worked by low-wage southern labor, should have given steel manufacturers there a competitive edge, especially in southern markets. But the steel lords of Pittsburgh brought pressure to bear on the compliant railroads. As a result, Birmingham steel, no matter where it was delivered, was charged a fictional fee, as if it had been shipped from Pittsburgh. This stunting of the South's natural economic advantages throttled the growth of the Birmingham steel industry.

In manufacturing cotton textiles, the South fared considerably better. Southerners had long resented shipping their fiber to New England, and now their cry was, "Bring the mills to the cotton." Beginning about 1880, northern capital began to erect cotton mills in the South, largely in response to tax benefits and the prospect of cheap and nonunionized labor.

The textile mills proved a mixed blessing to the economically blighted South. Cheap labor was the South's major attraction for potential investors, and keeping labor cheap became almost a religion among southern industrialists. Mills took root in the chronically depressed piedmont region, where poor rural dwellers derided as "hillbillies"—virtually all of them white, for blacks were excluded from employment in the mills—worked from dawn to dusk amid the whirring spindles. Paid at half the rate of their northern counterparts, they were often habitually in debt to the company store. But despite their depressed working conditions and poor pay, many southerners saw employment in the mills as their salvation.

The Impact of the New Industrial Revolution on America

Economic miracles wrought during the decades after the Civil War enormously increased the wealth of the Republic. The standard of living rose sharply, and well-fed American workers enjoyed more physical comforts than their counterparts in any other powerful nation. Urban centers mushroomed as the insatiable factories demanded more American labor, and as immigrants swarmed like honeybees to the new jobs.

Early Jeffersonian ideals were withering before the smudgy blasts from the smokestacks. As agriculture declined in relation to manufacturing, America could no longer aspire to be a nation of small freehold farms. Jefferson's concepts of free enterprise, with neither help nor hindrance by Washington, were being thrown out the factory window.

Older ways of life also wilted in the heat of the factory furnaces. The very concept of time was revolutionized. Rural American migrants and peasant European immigrants, used to living by the languid clock of nature, had to regiment their lives by the factory whistle. The seemingly arbitrary discipline of industrial labor did not come easily and sometimes was forcibly taught by corporate managers.

Probably no single group was more profoundly affected by the new industrial age than women. Propelled into industry by recent inventions, chiefly the typewriter and the telephone switchboard, millions of stenographers and "hello girls" discovered new economic and social opportunities. The "Gibson Girl," a magazine image of an independent and athletic "new woman" created in the 1890s by Charles Dana Gibson, became the romantic ideal of the age. For these middle-class women, careers often meant delayed marriages and smaller families. Most women workers, however, toiled neither for independence nor for glamour but out of economic necessity. They faced the same long hours and dangerous working conditions as did their mates and brothers, and they earned less, because wages for "women's jobs" were usually set below men's.

The clattering machine age likewise accentuated class division. "Industrial buccaneers" flaunted bloated fortunes, and their rags-to-riches spouses displayed glittering diamonds. Such extravagances evoked bitter criticism. Some of it was envious, but much of it rose from the small and increasingly vocal group of socialists and other radicals, many of whom were recent European immigrants. The existence of an oligarchy of money was amply demonstrated by the fact that by 1900 about one-tenth of the people owned and controlled nine-tenths of the nation's wealth.

Finally, strong pressures for foreign trade developed as the tireless industrial machine threatened to flood the domestic market. American products radiated out all over the world—notably the five-gallon kerosene can of the Standard Oil Company. The flag follows trade, and empire tends to follow the flag—a harsh lesson that America was soon to learn.

In Unions There Is Strength

Sweat of the laborer lubricated the vast new industrial machine. Yet wage workers did not share proportionately with their employers the benefits of the age of big business.

The worker, suggestive of the Roman galley slave, was becoming a lever-puller in a giant mechanism. Individual originality and creativity were being stifled, and less value than ever before was being placed on manual skills. Before the Civil War, the worker might have toiled in a small plant whose owner hailed the employee in the morning by first name and inquired after the family's health. But now the factory hand was employed by a corporation—depersonalized, bodiless, soulless, and often conscienceless. The vast new railroad network could bring unemployed workers, including blacks and immigrants, into areas where wages were high and thus beat down wage levels. During the 1880s and 1890s and later, the labor market also had to absorb the several hundred thousand unskilled immigrant workers who poured in from Europe each year.

Individual workers were powerless to battle single-handedly against giant industry. The corporation could dispense with the individual worker much more easily than the worker could dispense with the corporation. Employers could pool vast wealth through thousands of stockholders, import strike-breakers ("scabs"), and employ thugs to beat up labor organizers. In 1886 Jay Gould reputedly boasted, "I can hire one-half of the working class to kill the other half."

Corporations had still other weapons in their arsenals. They could call upon conservative federal judges to issue injunctions against strikers, and then request state or federal authorities to send in troops if defiance continued. Employers could lock the doors of their plants—a procedure called the "lockout"—and starve rebellious workers into submission. They could compel them to sign "ironclad oaths" or "yel-

The Strike, by Robert Koehler, 1886   *Scenes like this were becoming more typical of American life in the late nineteenth century as industrialism advanced spectacularly and sometimes ruthlessly. Here Koehler (1850–1917) shows an entire community of men, women, and children—many of them apparently immigrant newcomers—challenging the power of the "boss." The scene is tense but orderly, though violence seems to be imminent as one striker reaches for a rock.*

low dog contracts," both of which were solemn agreements not to join a labor union, as a condition of employment. They could put the names of labor agitators on a "black list" and circulate it among fellow employers. A corporation might even own the "company town," which often sank workers into perpetual debt—a status that strongly resembled serfdom.

The public, annoyed by recurrent strikes, grew deaf to the outcry of the worker. Carnegie and Rockefeller had battled their way to the top, and the view was common that the laborer could do likewise. Somehow the strike seemed like a foreign importation—socialistic and hence unpatriotic. Big business might combine into trusts to raise prices, but the worker must not combine into unions to raise wages. Unemployment seemed to be an act of God, who somehow would take care of the laborer.

Labor Limps Along

Labor unions, which had been few and disorganized in 1861, were given a strong boost by the Civil War. By 1872 there were several hundred thousand organized workers and thirty-two national unions, representing such crafts as the bricklayers, typesetters, and shoemakers.

The National Labor Union, organized in 1866, represented a giant bootstride by the workers. The union lasted six years and attracted the impressive total of some 600,000 members, including the skilled, unskilled, and farmers, though it excluded the Chinese and made only nominal efforts to include women and blacks. Black workers organized their own Colored National Labor Union, but persistent white racism prevented the two national unions from working together. The National Labor Union agitated for the eight-hour day and the arbitration of industrial disputes. It finally succeeded in winning an eight-hour day for government workers, but the devastating depression of the 1870s dealt it a knockout blow. Wage reductions in 1877 touched off such disruptive strikes on the railroads that nothing short of federal troops could restore order.

A new organization—the Knights of Labor—seized the torch dropped by the defunct National Labor Union. Officially known as the Noble and Holy Order of the Knights of Labor, it began inauspiciously in 1869 as a secret society, with a private ritual, passwords, and a secret grip.

The Knights of Labor, like the National Labor Union, sought to include all workers in "one big union." Their slogan was "An injury to one is the concern of all." A welcome mat was rolled out for the skilled and unskilled, for men and women, for whites and underprivileged blacks, some ninety thousand of whom joined. The Knights barred only liquor dealers, professional gamblers, lawyers, bankers, and stockbrokers.

Setting up broad goals, the embattled Knights campaigned for economic and social reform, including producers' cooperatives and codes for safety and health. The ordinary workday was then ten hours or more, and the Knights waged a determined campaign for the eight-hour stint.

Under the eloquent but often erratic leadership of Terence V. Powderly, an Irish-American of nimble wit and fluent tongue, the Knights won a number of strikes for the eight-hour day. When the Knights staged a successful strike against Jay Gould's Wabash Railroad in 1885, membership mushroomed to about three-quarters of a million workers.

Unhorsing the Knights of Labor

Despite their outward success, the Knights were riding for a fall. They became involved in a number of May Day strikes in 1886, about half of which failed. A focal point was Chicago, home to about eighty thousand Knights. The city was also honeycombed with a few hundred anarchists, many of them foreign-born, who were advocating a violent overthrow of the American government.

Tensions rapidly built up to the bloody Haymarket Square episode. Labor disorders had broken out, and on May 4, 1886, the Chicago police advanced on a meeting called to protest alleged brutalities by the authorities. Suddenly a dynamite bomb was thrown that killed or injured several dozen persons, including police.

Hysteria swept the Windy City. Eight anarchists were rounded up. Although nobody proved that they had anything to do directly with the bomb, a judge and jury held that since they had preached incendiary doctrines, they could be charged with conspiracy.

Five were sentenced to death, one of whom committed suicide, and the other three were given stiff prison terms. They were eventually pardoned in 1892 by Illinois governor John P. Altgeld, a German-born Democrat of strong liberal tendencies.

The Haymarket Square bomb helped blow the props from under the Knights of Labor. They were associated in the public mind, though mistakenly, with the anarchists. The eight-hour movement suffered correspondingly, and subsequent strikes by the Knights met with scant success. By the 1890s the Knights had melted away to 100,000 members, and these gradually fused with other protest groups of that decade.

The AF of L to the Fore

The elitist American Federation of Labor, born in 1886, was largely the brainchild of squat, square-jawed Samuel Gompers. This colorful Jewish cigar maker, born in a London tenement and removed from school at age ten, was brought to America when thirteen. Taking his turn at reading informative literature to his fellow cigar makers in New York, he was pressed into overtime service because of his strong voice. Rising spectacularly in the labor ranks, he was elected president of the American Federation of Labor every year except one from 1886 to 1924.

Gompers adopted a down-to-earth approach, soft-pedaling attempts to engineer sweeping social reform. A bitter foe of socialism, he shunned politics for economic strategies and goals. Gompers had no quarrel with capitalism, but he demanded a fairer share for labor. All he wanted, he said simply, was "more." Promoting what he called "pure and simple" unionism, he sought better wages, hours, and working conditions.

The AF of L thus established itself on solid but narrow foundations. Although attempting to speak for all workers, it fell far short of being representative of them. Composed of skilled craftsmen, like the carpenters and bricklayers, it was willing to let unskilled laborers, including women and especially blacks, fend for themselves. The AF of L weathered the panic of 1893 reasonably well, and by 1900 it could boast a membership of 500,000.

Labor disorders continued, peppering the years from 1881 to 1900 with an alarming total of over 23,000 strikes. These disturbances involved 6,610,000 workers, with a total loss to both employers and employees of $450 million. The strikers lost about half their strikes and won or compromised the remainder. Perhaps the gravest weakness of organized labor was that it still embraced only a small minority of all working people—about 3 percent in 1900.

But attitudes toward labor had begun to change perceptibly by 1900. The public was beginning to concede the right of workers to organize, to bargain collectively, and to strike. As a sign of the times, Labor Day was made a legal holiday by act of Congress in 1894. A few enlightened industrialists had come to perceive the wisdom of avoiding costly economic warfare by bargaining with the unions and signing agreements. But the vast majority of employers continued to fight organized labor, which achieved its grudging gains only after recurrent strikes and frequent reverses. Several trouble-fraught decades were to pass before labor was to gain a position of relative equality with capital. If the age of big business had dawned, the age of big labor was still some distance over the horizon.

Chronology

1862	Congress authorizes a transcontinental railroad.
1866	National Labor Union organized.
1869	Transcontinental railroad joined near Ogden, Utah. Knights of Labor organized.
1870	Standard Oil Company organized.
1876	Bell invents the telephone.
1879	Edison invents the electric light.
1886	Haymarket Square bombing. *Wabash* case. American Federation of Labor formed.
1887	Interstate Commerce Act.
1890	Sherman Anti-Trust Act.
1901	United States Steel Corporation formed.

varying

viewpoints

Industrialization: Boon or Blight?

The capitalists who forged an industrial America in the late nineteenth century were once called "captains of industry"—a respectful title that bespoke the awe inspired by their wondrous material accomplishments. But these economic innovators have never been universally admired. During the Great Depression of the 1930s, when the entire industrial order they had created seemed to have collapsed utterly, it was fashionable to speak of them as "robber barons"—a term implying scorn for their high-handed methods. This sneer often issued from the lips and pens of leftist critics like Matthew Josephson, who sympathized with the working classes that allegedly were brutalized by the factory system.

Criticism has also come from writers nostalgic for the preindustrial past. These critics believe that industrialization stripped away the traditions, values, and pride of native farmers and immigrant craftspeople. Conceding that economic development elevated the material standard of living for working Americans, this interpretation contends that the industrial revolution diminished their spiritual "quality of life." Accordingly, historians like Herbert Gutman and David Montgomery por-

tray labor's struggle for control of the workplace as the central drama of industrial expansion.

In the 1960s, historians led by Stephan Thernstrom began to test this long-standing belief. Looking at such factors as occupation, wealth, and geographic mobility, they tried to gauge the nature and extent of social mobility in the United States. Most of these historians concluded that although relatively few Americans made rags-to-riches leaps, large numbers experienced small improvements in their economic and social status. Few sons of laborers became corporate tycoons, but many more became line bosses and white-collar clerks.

In recent years such studies have been criticized by historians who point out the difficulties involved in defining "social status." For instance, some white-collar clerical workers received lower wages than manual laborers did. But were they higher or lower on the social scale? Furthermore, as James Henretta points out, different groups defined success differently: whereas Jewish immigrants often struggled to give their sons professional educations, the Irish put more emphasis on acquiring land, and the Italians, on building small family-run businesses.

Meanwhile, leftist historians such as Michael Katz maintain that the degree of social mobility in America has been overrated. These historians argue that industrial capitalism created two classes: a working class that sold its labor, and a business class that controlled resources and bought labor. Although most Americans took small steps upward, they generally remained within the class in which they began. Thus, say these historians, the inequality of a capitalistic class system persisted in America's seemingly fluid society.

SUGGESTED READINGS

Primary Source Documents

Andrew Carnegie, "Wealth,"* *North American Review* (June 1889), gives the philosophy of the Gilded Age's greatest entrepreneur. Henry Grady's Boston speech (1889), in Joel C. Harris, *Life of Henry W. Grady** (1890), dramatizes the plight of the South. Samuel Gompers penned his "Letter on Labor in Industrial Society," an open letter to Judge Peter Grossup, in 1894 (in Richard Hofstadter, *Great Issues in American History*, 1958). William Dean Howells's novel *The Rise of Silas Lapham*

(1885) treats the moral impact of the new business culture on one New England businessman and his family.

Secondary Sources

A useful survey is Samuel P. Hays's penetrating study, *The Response to Industrialism, 1885–1914* (1957). Stuart Bruchey puts the period in context in *The Growth of the Modern Economy* (1975). Business is the subject of Alfred D. Chandler, Jr., *The Visible Hand: The Managerial Revolution in American Business* (1978); Saul Engelbourg, *Power and Morality: American Business Ethics, 1840–1914* (1980); and Naomi R. Lamoreaux, *The Great Merger Movement in American Business, 1895–1904* (1985). Olivier Zunz surveys the development of corporate culture in *Making America Corporate, 1870–1920* (1990), while Scott M. Cutlip examines *The Unseen Power: Public Relations, a History* (1994). The thought and attitudes characteristic of the new industrial age are examined by Richard Hofstadter, *Social Darwinism in American Thought* (rev. ed., 1955), and Daniel T. Rodgers, *The Work Ethic in Industrial America, 1850–1920* (1978).

On race relations in the post-Reconstruction South, see Joel Williamson, *The Crucible of Race* (1984); Howard Rabinowitz, *Race Relations in the Urban South, 1865–1890* (1978); and Neil R. McMillen, *Dark Journey: Black Mississippians in the Age of Jim Crow* (1989). Labor is the subject of Gerald Grob, *Workers and Utopia* (1961), and David Montgomery's innovative *Workers' Control in America: Studies in the History of Work, Technology, and Labor Struggles* (1979). Especially stimulating are two volumes by Herbert Gutman, *Work, Culture, and Society in Industrializing America* (1976) and *Power and Culture: Essays on the American Working Class* (1987). On female workers see David Katzman, *Seven Days a Week: Women and Domestic Service in Industrializing America* (1978); Philip Foner, *Women and the American Labor Movement* (1979); and Alice Kessler-Harris, *Out to Work: A History of Wage-Earning Women in the United States* (1982).

---

* An asterisk indicates that the document, or an excerpt from it, can be found in Thomas A. Bailey and David M. Kennedy, eds., *The American Spirit: United States History as Seen by Contemporaries*, 9th ed. (Boston: Houghton Mifflin, 1998).

26

★★★★★★★★★

America Moves to the City,

1865–1900

★★★★★★

*What shall we do with our great cities? What will our great
cities do with us . . . ? [T]he question . . . does not concern the
city alone. The whole country is affected . . . by the condition
of its great cities.*

★★★★★★

LYMAN ABBOT, 1891

The Urban Frontier

Born in the country, America moved to the city in the
decades following the Civil War. By the year 1900 the
United States' upsurging population nearly doubled
from its level of some 40 million people enumerated
in the census of 1870. Yet in the very same period the
population of American cities *tripled*. By the end of
the nineteenth century, four out of ten Americans
were city dwellers.

This cityward drift affected not only the United
States but most of the Western world. European peasants, pushed off the land in part by competition from
cheap American foodstuffs, were pulled into cities—
in both Europe and America—by the new lure of
industrial jobs. A revolution in agriculture thus fed
the industrial and urban revolutions.

The growth of American metropolises was spectacular. In 1860 no city in the United States could boast
a million inhabitants; by 1890 New York, Chicago, and
Philadelphia had spurted past the million mark. By 1900
New York, with some 3.5 million people, was the second
largest city in the world, outranked only by London.

Cities grew both up and out. Cloud-brushing
skyscrapers allowed more people and workplaces to
be packed onto a parcel of land. Appearing first as a
ten-story building in Chicago in 1885, the skyscraper
was made usable by the perfecting of the electric elevator. An opinionated Chicago architect, Louis Sullivan (1856–1924), contributed formidably to the
further development of the skyscraper with his
famous principle that "form follows function."

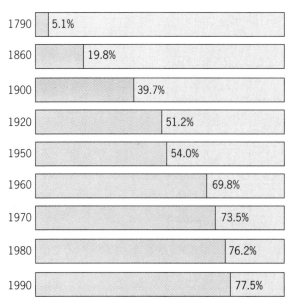

1790	5.1%
1860	19.8%
1900	39.7%
1920	51.2%
1950	54.0%
1960	69.8%
1970	73.5%
1980	76.2%
1990	77.5%

The Shift to the City   *Percentage of total population living in cities of twenty-five hundred or more. Notice the slowing of the cityward trend in the 1970s.*

Cities also spread out, turning many Americans into commuters who were carted daily by mass-transit electric trolleys between urban job and suburban home. The compact and communal "walking city" gave way to the immense and impersonal megalopolis, carved into distinctly different districts for business, industry, and residential neighborhoods—which in turn were segregated by race, ethnicity, and social class.

Rural America could not compete with the siren song of the city. Industrial jobs, above all, drew country folks off the farms and into factory centers. But the urban lifestyle also held powerful attractions. The predawn milking of cows had little appeal when compared with the late-night glitter of city lights. Electricity, indoor plumbing, and telephones all made life in the big city more alluring. Engineering marvels like the skyscraper and New York's awesome Brooklyn Bridge, a harplike suspension span dedicated in 1883, further added to the seductive glamour of the gleaming cities.

Cavernous department stores such as Macy's in New York and Marshall Field's in Chicago attracted urban shoppers and heralded the dawning era of consumerism. They also accentuated widening class divisions. When Carrie Meeker, novelist Theodore Dreiser's fictional heroine in *Sister Carrie* (1900), escapes from rural boredom to Chicago, the city's dazzling department stores awaken her to a richer, more elegant way of life.

The move to the city also introduced Americans to new ways of life. Household products sold in bulk at the local store, without wrapping, gave way to city goods that came in throwaway bottles, boxes, bags, and cans. Apartment houses had no adjoining barnyards where residents might toss garbage to the hogs. Waste disposal, in short, was an issue new to the urban age.

The jagged skyline of America's perpendicular civilization could not fully conceal the canker sores of feverish growth. Criminals flourished like lice in the teeming asphalt jungles. Impure water, uncollected garbage, unwashed bodies, and droppings from draft animals enveloped many cities in a satanic stench.

The cities were monuments of contradiction. They represented "humanity compressed," remarked one observer, "the best and the worst combined, in a strangely composite community." They harbored merchant princes and miserable paupers, stately banks and sooty factories, green-grassed suburbs and stinking tenements. The glaring contrasts that assaulted the eye in New York reminded one visitor of "a lady in ball costume, with diamonds in her ears, and her toes out at the boots."

Worst of all were the human pigsties known as slums. They seemed to grow ever more crowded, more filthy, and more rat infested, especially after the perfection in 1879 of the "dumbbell" tenement. So named because of the outline of its floor plan, the dumbbell was usually seven or eight stories high, with shallow, sunless, and ill-smelling air shafts providing minimal ventilation. Several families were sardined onto each floor of the barrackslike structures, and they shared a malodorous toilet in the hall. Small wonder that slum dwellers strove mightily to escape their wretched surroundings—as many of them did. The slums remained foul places, inhabited by successive waves of newcomers, but to a remarkable degree hard-working people moved up and out of them. The wealthiest left the cities altogether and headed for the semirural suburbs. These leafy "bedroom communi-

New York's Mulberry Street, 1904 *Outside the teeming tenement buildings, crowded city streets became places of work, play, and rough-and-tumble Americanization for many of the nation's recent immigrants.*

ties" eventually ringed the brick-and-concrete cities with a greenbelt of affluence.

The New Immigration

The powerful pull of the American urban magnet was felt even in faraway Europe. A brightly colored stream of immigrants continued to pour in from the old "mother continent." In each of the three decades from the 1850s through the 1870s, more than 2 million migrants had stepped onto America's shores. By the 1880s the stream had swelled to a rushing torrent, as more than 5 million cascaded into the country.

Until the 1880s, most immigrants had come from the British Isles and western Europe, chiefly Germany and Scandinavia. They were usually Protestant, except for the Catholic Irish and many Catholic Germans. They boasted a comparatively high rate of literacy and fitted relatively easily into American society.

But in the 1880s the character of the immigrant stream changed drastically. The so-called New Immigrants—Italians, Croats, Slovaks, Greeks, Poles—came from southern and eastern Europe. Many of them worshiped in Roman Catholic or Eastern Orthodox churches or in Jewish synagogues. Largely illiterate and impoverished, most New Immigrants hived together in the "Little Italys" and "Little Polands" of the jam-packed cities. These new peoples totaled only 19 percent of newcomers in the 1880s; but by the first decade of the twentieth century, they constituted an astonishing 66 percent of the total inflow. (See "Makers of America: The Italians," p. 368.)

Why were these bright-shawled and quaint-jacketed strangers hammering on the gates? In part, they left their old countries because Europe seemed to have no room for them. Rapid population growth, American food imports, and European industrialization shook the peasantry loose from its ancient habitats and customary occupations, creating a vast, footloose army of the unemployed. Europeans by the millions drained out of the countryside and into European cities. Most stayed there, but some kept moving and left Europe altogether. About 60 million Europeans abandoned the old continent in the nineteenth and early twentieth centuries. More than half

MAKERS OF AMERICA

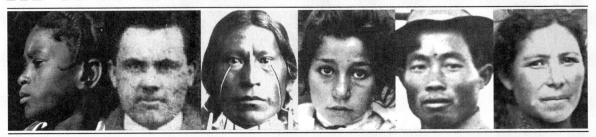

The Italians

Who were the "New Immigrants"? Who were these southern and eastern European birds of passage that flocked to the United States between 1880 and 1920? Prominent and typical among them were Italians, some 4 million of whom sailed to the United States during the four decades of the New Immigration.

They came from the southern provinces of their native land, the heel and toe of the Italian boot. These areas had lagged behind the prosperous, industrial region of northern Italy. Unification had raised hopes of similar progress in the downtrodden south, but it was slow in coming. Southern peasants tilled their fields without fertilizer or machinery, using hand plows and rickety hoes that had been passed down for generations.

From such disappointing and demeaned conditions, southern Italians set out for the New World. Almost all of them were young men who intended to spend only a few months in America, stuff their pockets with dollars, and return home. Almost half of Italian immigrants did indeed repatriate—as did comparable numbers of the other New Immigrants, with the conspicuous exception of the Jews, who had fled their native lands to escape religious persecution. Almost all Italian immigrants sailed through New York harbor, sighting the Statue of Liberty as they debarked from crowded ships. Many soon moved on to other large cities, but so many remained that, in the early years of the twentieth century, more Italians resided in New York than in Florence, Venice, and Genoa combined.

Although Italian immigrants huddled in the cities, they did not abandon their rural upbringings entirely. Much to their neighbors' consternation, they often kept chickens in vacant lots and raised vegetables in small garden plots nestled between decaying tenement houses.

Those who bade a permanent farewell to Italy clustered in tightly knit communities that boasted opera clubs, Italian-language newspapers, and courts for playing bocci—a version of lawn bowling imported from the Old Country. Pizza emerged from the hot wood-burning ovens of these Little Italys, its aroma and flavor wafting its way into the hearts and stomachs of all Americans.

Italians typically earned their daily bread as industrial laborers—most famously as longshoremen and construction workers. They owed their prominence in the building trades to the "padrone system." The *padrone,* or labor boss, met immigrants upon arrival and secured jobs for them in New York, Chicago, or wherever there was an immediate demand for industrial labor.

Lacking education, the Italians, as a group, remained in blue-collar jobs longer than some of their fellow New Immigrants. Many of them, valuing vocation over schooling, sent their children off to work as early in their young lives as possible. Before World War I, less than 1 percent of Italian children were enrolled in high school. Over the next fifty years, Italian-Americans and their offspring gradually prospered, moving out of the cities into the more affluent suburbs. Many served heroically in World War II and availed themselves of the GI Bill to finance the college educations and professional training their immigrant forebears had lacked.

of them moved to the United States. But that striking fact should not obscure the important truth that masses of people were already in motion in Europe before they felt the tug of the American magnet. Immigration to America was, in many ways, a by-product of the urbanization of Europe.

"America fever" proved highly contagious in Europe. The United States was often painted as a land of fabulous opportunity in the "America letters" sent by friends and relatives already transplanted.

The land of the free was also blessed with freedom from military conscription and religious persecution. Beginning in the 1880s, savage treatment of minorities in Europe, especially Russian Jews, drove tens of thousands of battered refugees to American shores. Virtually unique among the New Immigrants, Jews had experienced city life in Europe, and many of them brought their urban skills of tailoring and shopkeeping to American cities.

The New Immigrants struggled heroically to preserve their traditional culture. Catholics expanded their parochial school system and Jews established Hebrew schools. Foreign-language newspapers, parishes, theaters, restaurants, and social clubs all attested to the desire to keep old ways alive. Yet time took its toll on these efforts to conserve the customs of the Old World in the New. The children of the immigrants grew up speaking fluent English, sometimes mocking the broken grammar of their parents. They often rejected the Old Country manners of their mothers and fathers in their desire to plunge headlong into the mainstream of American life.

Reactions to the New Immigration

America's government system, nurtured in wide-open spaces, was ill suited to the cement forests of the great cities. Beyond minimal checking to weed out criminals and the insane, the federal government did virtually nothing to ease the assimilation of immigrants into American society. State governments, usually dominated by rural representatives, did even less. City governments, overwhelmed by the sheer scale of rampant urban growth, proved woefully inadequate to the task. By default, the business of ministering to the immigrants' needs fell to the unofficial "governments" of the urban political machines, led by "bosses" such as New York's notorious Boss Tweed.

Taking care of the immigrants was big business, indeed. Trading jobs and services for votes, a powerful boss might claim the loyalty of thousands of followers. In return for their support at the polls, the boss provided employment on the city's payroll, found housing for new arrivals, tided over the needy with gifts of food and clothing, patched up minor scrapes with the law, and helped get schools, parks, and hospitals built in immigrant neighborhoods. Reformers gagged at this cynical exploitation of the immigrant vote, but the political boss gave valuable assistance that was forthcoming from no other source.

The nation's social conscience gradually awakened to the plight of the cities and their immigrant masses. Prominent in this awakening were Protestant clergymen such as Walter Rauschenbusch of New York City and Washington Gladden of Columbus, Ohio, both of whom sought to apply the lessons of Christianity to the slums and factories. Preaching the "social gospel," they insisted that churches tackle the burning social issues of the day.

One middle-class woman who was deeply dedicated to uplifting the urban masses was Jane Addams (1860–1935). Born into a prosperous Illinois family, Addams was one of the first generation of college-educated women and sought suitable outlets for her large talents. Inspired by a visit to England, in 1889 she established Hull House in Chicago as the most prominent American settlement house. Located in a poor immigrant neighborhood of Greeks, Italians, Russians, and Germans, Hull House offered instruction in English, counseling to help newcomers cope with American big-city life, child care for working mothers, and cultural activities of all kinds for neighborhood residents.

Following Jane Addams's lead, women founded settlement houses in other cities as well—notably Lillian Wald's Henry Street Settlement in New York, which opened its doors in 1893. The settlement houses became centers of women's activism and social reform on behalf of women, children, blacks, and consumers. The women of Hull House, for example, successfully lobbied in 1893 for an Illinois anti-sweatshop law that protected women workers and prohibited child labor. They were led by Florence Kelley, a guerrilla warrior in the urban jungle who battled for decades on behalf of the underprivileged at both Hull House and Henry Street Settlement.

The pioneering work of Addams, Wald, and Kelley vividly demonstrated that the city was the frontier of opportunity for women, just as the wilderness had been for men. The urban frontier opened new possibilities for women—as social workers and secretaries, store clerks and seamstresses, telephone operators and bookkeepers. More than a million women joined the work force in the single decade of the 1890s. As America moved to the city, women moved nearer to economic and social independence.

Narrowing the Welcome Mat

Antiforeignism, or "nativism," earlier touched off by the Irish and German arrivals in the 1840s and 1850s, bared its ugly face in the 1880s with fresh ferocity. The so-called New Immigrants had come for much the same reasons as the Old—to escape the poverty and squalor of Europe and to seek new opportunities in America. But "nativists" viewed the eastern and southern Europeans as culturally and religiously

exotic hordes and often gave them a rude reception. The newest newcomers aroused widespread alarm. Their high birthrate, common among people with a low standard of living and sufficient youth and vigor to pull up stakes, raised worries that the original Anglo-Saxon stock would soon be outbred and outvoted. Still more horrifying was the prospect that it would be mongrelized by a mixture of "inferior" southern European blood and that the fairer Anglo-Saxon types would disappear. One New England writer cried out in anguish:

O Liberty, white Goddess! is it well
To leave the gates unguarded?

"Native" Americans voiced additional fears. They blamed the immigrants for the degradation of urban government. Trade unionists assailed the alien arrivals for their willingness to work for "starvation" wages, which seemed like princely sums to the immigrants themselves, and for importing in their intellectual baggage such dangerous doctrines as socialism, communism, and anarchism. Many business leaders had welcomed the flood of cheap manual labor but now began to fear that they had embraced a Frankenstein's monster.

Looking Backward
Older immigrants, trying to keep their own humble arrival in America "in the shadows," sought to close the bridge that had carried them and their ancestors across the Atlantic.

Antiforeign organizations, reminiscent of the "Know-Nothings" of antebellum days, were revived in a different guise. Notorious among them was the American Protective Association (APA), which was created in 1887 and soon claimed a million members. In pursuing its nativist goals, the APA urged voting against Roman Catholic candidates for office and sponsored the publication of lustful fantasies about runaway nuns.

Organized labor was quick to throw its growing weight behind the move to choke off the rising tide of foreigners. Frequently used as strikebreakers, the wage-depressing immigrants were hard to unionize because of the language barrier. Labor leaders argued, not illogically, that if American industry was entitled to protection from foreign goods, the American worker was entitled to protection from foreign laborers.

Congress finally nailed up partial bars against the inpouring immigrants. The first restrictive law, in 1882, banged the gate shut in the faces of paupers, criminals, and convicts, all of whom had to be returned at the expense of the greedy or careless shipper. Congress further responded to pained outcries from organized labor when in 1885 it prohibited the importation of workers under contract—usually for substandard wages.

In later years other federal laws lengthened the list of undesirables to include the insane, polygamists, prostitutes, alcoholics, anarchists, and persons carrying contagious diseases. A proposed literacy test, long a favorite of "nativists" because it favored the Old Immigrants over the New, met vigorous opposition. It was not enacted until 1917, after three presidents had vetoed it on the grounds that literacy was more a measure of opportunity than of intelligence.

The year 1882, in addition to the first federal restrictions on immigration, brought forth a law to bar completely one ethnic group—the Chinese (see "Makers of America: The Chinese," pp. 340–341). Previously America had embraced the oppressed and underprivileged of all races and creeds. Now the gates were padlocked against defective undesirables—plus the Chinese.

Four years later, in 1886, the Statue of Liberty arose in New York harbor, a gift from the people of France. On its base were inscribed the words of Emma Lazarus:

> Give me your tired, your poor,
> Your huddled masses yearning to breathe free,
> The wretched refuse of your teeming shore.

To many "nativists," those noble words described only too accurately the "scum" washed up by the New Immigrant tides. Yet the uprooted immigrants, unlike "natives" lucky enough to have had parents who caught an earlier ship, became American citizens the hard way. These new immigrants stepped off the boat ready to put their shoulders to the nation's industrial wheels. The Republic owes much to these latecomers—for their brawn, their brains, their courage, and the diversity they brought to American society.

Churches Confront the Urban Challenge

The swelling size and changing character of the urban population posed sharp challenges to American churches, which, like other national institutions, had grown up in the countryside. Protestant churches in particular suffered heavily from the shift to the city, where many of their traditional doctrines and pastoral approaches seemed irrelevant.

As they lost their bearings in the new urban world, some churches were tending to become merely sacred diversions or amusements. Reflecting the wealth of their prosperous parishioners, many of the old-line churches were distressingly slow to raise their voices against social and economic vices. John D. Rockefeller was a pillar of the Baptist church; J. Pierpont Morgan, of the Episcopal church. Cynics remarked that the Episcopal church had become "the Republican party at prayer." The mounting emphasis was on materialism; too many devotees worshiped at the altar of avarice. Money was the accepted measure of achievement, and the new "Gospel of Wealth" proclaimed that God caused the righteous to prosper.

Into this spreading moral vacuum stepped a new generation of urban revivalists. Most conspicuous was a former Chicago shoe salesman, Dwight Lyman Moody. Proclaiming a gospel of kindness and forgiveness, Moody was a modern urban circuit rider who took his message to countless American cities in the 1870s and 1880s. Clad in a dark business suit, the bearded and rotund Moody held huge audiences spellbound. He contributed powerfully to adapting the old-time religion to the realities of city life. The Moody Bible Institute, founded in Chicago in 1889, carried on his work after his death in 1899.

Simultaneously, the Roman Catholic and Jewish faiths were gaining enormous strength from the New Immigration. By 1900 the Roman Catholics had increased their lead as the largest single denomination, numbering nearly 9 million communicants. Roman Catholics and Jewish groups kept the common touch better than many of the leading Protestant churches. Cardinal James Gibbons (1834–1921) of Baltimore, an urban Catholic leader devoted to American unity, was immensely popular with Roman Catholics and Protestants alike. Acquainted with every president from Andrew Johnson to Warren Harding, he employed his liberal sympathies to assist the American labor movement.

By 1890 the variety-loving American could choose from 150 religious denominations, 2 of them newcomers. One was the band-playing Salvation Army, whose soldiers without swords invaded America from England in 1879 and established a beachhead on the street corners. Appealing frankly to the down-and-outers, the boldly named Salvation Army did much practical good, especially with free soup.

The other important new faith was the Church of Christ, Scientist (Christian Science), founded by Mary Baker Eddy in 1879, after she had suffered much ill health. Preaching that the true practice of Christianity heals sickness, she set forth her views in a book entitled *Science and Health with Key to the Scriptures* (1875), which sold an amazing 400,000 copies before her death. Appealing especially to America's hurried, nerve-wracked urban residents, Christian Science embraced several hundred thousand worshipers in the early twentieth century.

Although immigrant churches and new faiths managed to grow, traditional religion received serious blows from modern books on comparative religion and historical criticism of the Bible. Most unsettling of all was *On the Origin of Species* (1859), in which the English naturalist Charles Darwin set forth the sensational theory that humans had slowly evolved from lower forms of life. Evolution cast serious doubt on a literal interpretation of the Bible,

which relates how God created the heavens and the earth in six days.

Darwinism eventually created rifts in the churches and colleges of the post–Civil War era. Conservative believers, or "Fundamentalists," stood firmly on the Scripture as the inspired and infallible Word of God, whereas "Modernists" refused to accept the Bible as either history or science. "Modernist" clergymen were removed from their pulpits; teachers of biology who embraced evolution were dismissed from their chairs. As time wore on, an increasing number of liberal thinkers were able to reconcile Darwinism with Christianity by interpreting evolution as a newer and grander revelation of the ways of the Almighty. But Darwinism undoubtedly did much to loosen religious moorings and promote unbelief.

The Lust for Learning

Public education continued its upward climb. The ideal of tax-supported elementary schools was still gathering strength. Beginning about 1870, more and more states were making at least a grade-school education compulsory, and this gain, incidentally, helped check the frightening abuses of child labor.

Spectacular indeed was the spread of the high schools, especially by the 1880s and 1890s. By 1900 there were some six thousand high schools. In addition, the taxpayers of the states were providing free textbooks in increasing numbers during the last two decades of the century.

Other trends were noteworthy. Teacher training schools, then called "normal schools," experienced a striking expansion after the Civil War. In 1860 there were only twelve of them; in 1910, over three hundred. Kindergartens, earlier borrowed from Germany, also began to gain strong support. The New Immigration in the 1880s and 1890s brought vast new strength to the private Catholic parochial schools, which were fast becoming a major pillar of the nation's educational structure.

Public schools, though showering benefits on children, excluded millions of adults. This deficiency was partially remedied by the Chautauqua movement, launched in 1874 on the shores of Lake Chautauqua in New York. The organizers achieved gratifying success through nationwide public lec-

Booker T. Washington in His Office at Tuskegee Institute, c. 1902   *In a famous speech in Atlanta, Washington accepted social separateness for blacks: "In all things that are purely social, we can be as separate as the fingers, yet one as the hand in all things essential to mutual progress."*

W. E. B. Du Bois   *At the end of a long lifetime of struggle for racial justice in the United States, Du Bois renounced his American citizenship in 1961, at the age of 93, and took up residence in the newly independent African state of Ghana.*

tures, often held in tents and featuring such well-known speakers as Mark Twain. In addition, there were extensive Chautauqua courses of home study, for which 100,000 people enrolled in 1892 alone.

Crowded cities, despite their drawbacks, generally provided better educational facilities than the old one-room, one-teacher red schoolhouse. The success of the public schools is confirmed by the falling of the illiteracy rate from 20 percent in 1870 to 10.7 percent in 1900. Americans were developing a profound faith, often misplaced, in formal education as the sovereign remedy for their ills.

Booker T. Washington and Education for Black People

War-torn and impoverished, the South lagged far behind other regions in public education, and African-Americans suffered most severely. A stagger-

ing 44 percent of nonwhites were illiterate in 1900. Some help came from northern philanthropists, but the foremost champion of black education was an ex-slave, Booker T. Washington, who had slept under a board sidewalk to save pennies for his schooling. Called in 1881 to head the black normal and industrial school at Tuskegee, Alabama, he began with forty students in a tumbledown shanty. Undaunted, he taught black students useful trades so that they could gain self-respect and economic security. But he stopped short of advocating *social* equality with whites.

Washington's commitment to training young blacks in agriculture and the trades guided the curriculum at Tuskegee Institute and made it an ideal place for slave-born George Washington Carver to teach and research. After Carver joined the faculty in 1896, he became an internationally famous agricultural chemist who helped the economy of the South by discovering hundreds of new uses for the lowly peanut (shampoo, axle grease), sweet potato (vinegar), and soybean (paints).

Other black leaders, notably Dr. W. E. B. Du Bois, assailed Booker T. Washington as an "Uncle Tom," who was condemning their race to manual labor and perpetual inferiority. Born in Massachusetts, Du Bois was a mixture of African, French, Dutch, and Indian blood ("Thank God, no Anglo-Saxon," he would add). After a determined struggle, he earned a Ph.D. at Harvard, the first of his race to achieve this goal. He demanded complete equality for blacks, social as well as economic, and helped to found the National Association for the Advancement of Colored People (NAACP) in 1910. Rejecting Washington's gradualism and separatism, he demanded that the "talented tenth" of the black community be given full and immediate access to the mainstream of American life. An exceptionally skilled historian, sociologist, and poet, he died as a self-exile in Africa in 1963, at the age of ninety-five.

The Hallowed Halls of Ivy

Colleges and universities also shot up like lusty young saplings in the decades after the Civil War. The educational battle for women, only partially won before the war, turned into a rout of masculine die-hards. Women's colleges, such as Vassar, were gaining ground; and universities open to both genders were blossoming forth, notably in the Midwest. By 1900 every fourth college graduate was a woman. By the turn of the century as well the black institutes and academies planted during Reconstruction had blossomed into a crop of southern black colleges. Howard University in Washington, D.C., Hampton Institute in Virginia, Atlanta University, and numerous others nurtured higher education for blacks until the civil rights movement of the 1960s made attendance at white institutions possible.

The truly phenomenal growth of higher education owed much to the Morrill Act of 1862. This enlightened law, passed after the South had seceded,

Educational Levels, 1870–1990

Year	Number Graduating from High School	Number Graduating from College	Median School Years Completed Completed (Years)*	High School Graduates as a Percentage of 17-Year-Old Population
1870	16,000	9,371		2.0%
1880	24,000	12,896		2.5
1890	44,000	15,539		3.5
1900	95,000	27,410		6.4
1910	156,000	37,199	8.1†	8.8
1920	311,000	48,622	8.2†	16.8
1930	667,000	122,484	8.4†	29.0
1940	1,221,000	186,500	8.6	50.8
1950	1,199,700	432,058	9.3	59.0
1960	1,858,000	392,440	10.5	69.5
1970	2,889,000	792,656	12.2	76.9
1980	3,043,000	929,417	12.5	71.4
1990	2,587,000	1,049,657 (est.)	12.7	74.2

* People twenty-five years and over.

† 1910–1930 based on retrogressions of 1940 data; 1940 was the first year measured. (Folger and Nam, *Education of the American Population*, a 1960 Census Monograph.)

(Sources: *Digest of Education Statistics*, 1992, a publication of the National Center for Education Statistics; and *Statistical Abstract of the United States*, relevant years.)

provided a generous grant of the public lands to the states for support of education. "Land-grant colleges," most of which became state universities, in turn bound themselves to provide certain services, such as military training. The Hatch Act of 1887, extending the Morrill Act, provided federal funds for the establishment of agricultural experiment stations in connection with the land-grant colleges.

Private philanthropy richly supplemented federal grants to higher education. Many of the new industrial millionaires, developing tender social consciences, donated immense fortunes to educational enterprises. In the twenty years from 1878 to 1898 these money barons gave away about $150 million. Noteworthy among the new private universities of high quality to open their doors were Cornell (1865) and Leland Stanford Junior (1891), the latter founded in memory of the deceased fifteen-year-old only child of a builder of the Central Pacific Railroad. The University of Chicago, opened in 1892, speedily forged into a front-rank position, owing largely to the lubricant of Rockefeller's oil millions.

Towering among the new professionalized institutions of higher education was Johns Hopkins University, opened in 1876, which developed the nation's first high-grade graduate school. Several generations of American scholars, repelled by snobbish English cousins and attracted by painstaking European methods, had attended German universities. Now reputable scholars no longer had to go abroad for a gilt-edged graduate degree; Dr. Woodrow Wilson, among others, received his Ph.D. from Johns Hopkins.

The old cut-and-dried classical curriculum in the colleges was on the way out, as the new industrialization brought insistent demands for "practical" courses and specialized training in the sciences. The elective system, which permitted students to choose more courses in cafeteria fashion, was gaining popularity. It received a powerful boost in the 1870s, when Dr. Charles W. Eliot, a vigorous young chemist, became president of Harvard College and embarked on a lengthy career of educational statesmanship.

One of America's most brilliant intellectuals, the slight and sickly William James (1842–1910), served for thirty-five years on Eliot's Harvard faculty. Through his numerous writings he made a deep mark on many fields. His *Principles of Psychology* (1890) helped to establish the modern discipline of psychology. In *The Will to Believe* (1897) and *Varieties of Religious Experience* (1902), he explored the philosophy and psychology of religion. In his most famous work, *Pragmatism* (1907), he colorfully described America's greatest contribution to the history of philosophy. The concept of pragmatism held that truth was to be tested, above all, by the practical consequences of an idea, by action rather than theories. This kind of reasoning aptly expressed the philosophical temperament of a nation of doers.

The Appeal of the Press

Well-stocked public libraries—the poor people's university—were making encouraging progress, especially in Boston and New York. The magnificent Library of Congress building, which opened its doors in 1897, provided thirteen acres of floor space in the largest and costliest edifice of its kind in the world. A new era was inaugurated by the generous gifts of Andrew Carnegie. This open-handed Scotsman, book-starved in his youth, contributed $60 million for the construction of public libraries all over the country. By 1900 there were about nine thousand free circulating libraries in America, each with at least three hundred books.

Roaring newspaper presses, spurred by the invention of the Linotype in 1885, more than kept pace with the demands of a word-hungry public. But the heavy investment in machinery and plant was accompanied by a growing fear of offending advertisers and subscribers. Bare-knuckle editorials were, to an increasing degree, being supplanted by feature articles and noncontroversial syndicated material. The day of slashing journalistic giants like Horace Greeley was passing.

Sensationalism, at the same time, was beginning to debase the public taste. The semiliterate immigrants, combined with straphanging urban commuters, created a profitable market for news that was simply and punchily written. Sex, scandal, and other human-interest stories burst into the headlines as a vulgarization of the press accompanied the growth of circulation. Critics complained in vain about these "presstitutes."

Two new journalistic tycoons emerged. Joseph Pulitzer, Hungarian-born and near-blind, was a leader in the techniques of sensationalism in St. Louis and especially with the New York *World*. His use of the colored comic supplements, featuring the "Yellow Kid," gave the name "yellow journalism" to his lurid sheets. A close and ruthless competitor was youthful William Randolph Hearst, who had been expelled from Harvard College for a crude prank. Able to draw on his California father's mining millions, he built up a powerful chain of newspapers, beginning with the San Francisco *Examiner* in 1887.

Unfortunately, the influence of Pulitzer and Hearst was not altogether wholesome. Although both championed many worthy causes, both prostituted the press in their struggle for increased circulation; both "stooped, snooped, and scooped to conquer."

Apostles of Reform

Magazines partly satisfied the public appetite for good reading, notably old standbys like *Harper's*, the *Atlantic Monthly*, and *Scribner's Monthly*. Possibly the most influential journal was the liberal and highly intellectual *Nation*, which was read by its small (10,000 circulation) readership of professors, preachers, and publicists as "the weekly Day of Judgment." Launched in 1865 by the Irish-born Edwin L. Godkin, a merciless critic, it crusaded for civil-service reform, honesty in government, and a moderate tariff.

Another journalist-author, Henry George, was an original thinker who left an enduring mark. Poor in formal schooling, he was rich in idealism and in the milk of human kindness. After seeing poverty at its worst in India, and land grabbing at its greediest in California, he took pen in hand. His classic treatise, *Progress and Poverty* (1879), undertook to solve "the great enigma of our times"—"the association of progress with poverty." According to George, property owners unjustifiably profited from the pressure of growing population on a fixed supply of land. A single 100 percent tax on these windfall profits would eliminate unfair inequalities and stimulate economic growth.

George soon became a most controversial figure. His book broke into the bestseller lists and ultimately sold some 3 million copies. George also lectured widely in America, where he influenced

thinking about the maldistribution of wealth, and in Britain, where he left an indelible mark on Fabian socialism.

Edward Bellamy, a quiet Massachusetts Yankee, was another journalist-reformer of remarkable power. In 1888 he published a socialistic novel, *Looking Backward*, in which the hero, falling into a hypnotic sleep, awakens in the year 2000. He "looks backward" and finds that the social and economic injustices of 1887 have melted away under an idyllic government, which has nationalized big business to serve the public interest. To a nation already alarmed by the trust evil, the book had a magnetic appeal and sold over a million copies. Scores of Bellamy Clubs sprang up to discuss this mild utopian socialism, and they heavily influenced American reform movements near the end of the century.

Postwar Writing

As literacy increased, so did book reading. Post–Civil War Americans devoured millions of "dime novels," usually depicting the wilds of the West. Paint-bedaubed Indians and quick-triggered gunmen like "Deadwood Dick" shot off vast quantities of gunpowder, and virtue invariably triumphed. These lurid "paperbacks" were frowned on by parents, but goggle-eyed youths read them in haylofts or in schools behind the broad covers of geography books. The king of dime novelists was Harlan F. Halsey, who made a fortune by dashing off about 650 novels, often one in a day.

General Lewis Wallace—lawyer, soldier, and author—was a colorful figure. Having fought with distinction in the Civil War, he sought to combat the prevailing wave of Darwinian skepticism with his novel *Ben Hur: A Tale of the Christ* (1880). A phenomenal success, the book sold an estimated 2 million copies in many languages, including Arabic and Chinese, and later appeared on stage and screen. It was the *Uncle Tom's Cabin* of the anti-Darwinists, who found in it support for the Holy Scriptures.

An even more popular writer was Horatio ("Holy Horatio") Alger, a Puritan-reared New Englander, who in 1866 forsook the pulpit for the pen. He wrote more than a hundred volumes of juvenile fiction that sold over 100 million copies.

In poetry Walt Whitman was one of the few luminaries of yesteryear who remained active. Although shattered in health by service as a Civil War nurse, he brought out successive—and purified—revisions of his hardy perennial, *Leaves of Grass*. The assassination of Lincoln inspired him to write two of the most moving poems in American literature, "O Captain! My Captain!" and "When Lilacs Last in the Dooryard Bloom'd."

The curious figure of Emily Dickinson, one of America's most gifted lyric poets, did not emerge until 1886, when she died and her poems were discovered. A Massachusetts recluse, she wrote over a thousand short lyrics on odd scraps of paper. Only two were published during her lifetime, and those without her consent. As she wrote:

> How dreary to be somebody!
> How public, like a frog
> To tell your name the livelong day
> To an admiring bog!

Literary Landmarks

In novel writing, the romantic sentimentality of a youthful era was giving way to a rugged realism that reflected more faithfully the materialism of an industrial society. American authors turned increasingly to the coarse human comedy and tragedy of the world around them to find their subjects.

Two Missouri-born authors with deep connections to the South brought altogether new voices to the late-nineteenth-century literary scene. The daring feminist author Kate Chopin (1851–1904) wrote candidly about adultery, suicide, and women's ambitions in *The Awakening* (1899). Largely ignored in her own day, Chopin was rediscovered by later readers who cited her work as suggestive of the feminist yearnings that stirred beneath the surface of "respectability" in the Gilded Age.

Mustachioed Mark Twain (1835–1910) had leapt to fame with *The Celebrated Jumping Frog of Calaveras County* (1867) and *The Innocents Abroad* (1869). He teamed up with Charles Dudley Warner in 1873 to write *The Gilded Age*. An acid satire on post–Civil War politicians and speculators, the book gave a name to an era. With his scanty formal school-ing in frontier Missouri, Twain typified a new breed of American authors in revolt against the elegant refinements of the old New England school of writing. Christened Samuel Langhorne Clemens, he had served for a time as a Mississippi riverboat pilot and later took his pen name, Mark Twain, from the boatman's cry that meant "two fathoms." After a brief stint in the armed forces, Twain journeyed to California, a trip he described, with a mixture of truth and tall tales, in *Roughing It* (1872).

Many other books flowed from Twain's busy pen. His *The Adventures of Tom Sawyer* (1876) and *The Adventures of Huckleberry Finn* (1884) rank among American masterpieces. His later years were soured by bankruptcy growing out of unwise investments, and he was forced to take to the lecture platform and amuse what he called "the damned human race." Twain made his most enduring contribution in recapturing frontier realism and humor in the authentic American dialect.

William Dean Howells (1837–1920), a printer's son from Ohio, could boast of little schoolhouse education, but his busy pen carried him high into the literary circles of the East. In 1871 he became the editor of the prestigious Boston-based *Atlantic Monthly* and was subsequently presented with honorary degrees from six universities, including Oxford. He wrote about ordinary people and about contemporary and sometimes controversial social themes. *A Modern Instance* (1882) deals with the once-taboo subject of divorce; *The Rise of Silas Lapham* (1885) describes the trials of a newly rich paint manufacturer caught up in the caste system of Brahmin Boston. *A Hazard of New Fortunes* (1890) portrays the reformers, strikers, and Socialists in Gilded Age New York.

Stephen Crane (1871–1900), the fourteenth son of a Methodist minister, also wrote about the seamy underside of life in urban, industrial America. His *Maggie: A Girl of the Streets* (1893), a brutal tale about a poor prostitute driven to suicide, was too grim to find a publisher. Crane had to have it printed privately. He rose quickly to prominence with *The Red Badge of Courage* (1895), the stirring story of a bloodied young Civil War recruit under fire. Crane himself had never seen a battle and wrote entirely from the printed Civil War records. He died of tuberculosis in 1900, when only twenty-nine.

Henry James (1843–1916), brother of Harvard philosopher William James, was a New Yorker who turned from law to literature. Taking as his dominant theme the confrontation of innocent Americans with subtle Europeans, James penned a remarkable number of brilliant novels, including *Daisy Miller* (1879), *The Portrait of a Lady* (1881), and *The Wings of the Dove* (1902). In *The Bostonians* (1886) he wrote one of the first novels about the rising feminist movement. James frequently made women his central characters, exploring their inner reactions to complex situations with a deftness that marked him as a master of "psychological realism." Long resident in England, he became a British subject shortly before his death.

Candid portrayals of contemporary life and social problems were the literary order of the day by the turn of the century. Jack London (1876–1916), famous as a nature writer of such books as *The Call of the Wild* (1903), turned to depicting a possible fascistic revolution in *The Iron Heel* (1907). Frank Norris (1870–1902), like London a Californian, wrote *The Octopus* (1901), an earthy saga of the stranglehold of the railroad and corrupt politicians on California wheat ranchers.

Conspicuous among the new "social novelists" rising in the literary firmament was Theodore Dreiser (1871–1945), a homely, gangling writer from Indiana. He burst on the literary scene in 1900 with *Sister Carrie*, a graphically realistic narrative of a poor working girl in Chicago and New York. She becomes one man's mistress, then elopes with another, and finally strikes out on her own to make a career on the stage. The fictional Carrie's disregard for prevailing moral standards so offended Dreiser's publisher that the book was soon withdrawn from circulation.

The New Morality

Victoria Woodhull, who was real flesh and blood, also shook the pillars of conventional morality when she publicly proclaimed her belief in free love in 1871. Woodhull was a beautiful and eloquent divorcée, sometime stockbroker, and tireless feminist propagandist. Together with her sister Tennessee Claflin she published a far-out periodical, *Woodhull and Claflin's Weekly*. The sisters again shocked "respectable" society in 1872 when their journal struck a blow for the new morality by charging that Henry Ward Beecher, the most famous preacher of his day, had for years been carrying on an adulterous affair.

Pure-minded Americans sternly resisted these affronts to their moral principles. Their foremost champion was a portly crusader, Anthony Comstock, who made lifelong war on the "immoral." Armed after 1873 with a federal statute—the notorious Comstock Law—this self-appointed defender of sexual purity boasted that he had confiscated no fewer than 202,679 "obscene pictures and photos"; 4,185 "boxes of pills, powders, etc., used by abortionists"; and 26 "obscene pictures, framed on walls of saloons."

The antics of the Woodhull sisters and Anthony Comstock exposed to daylight the battle going on in late-nineteenth-century America over sexual attitudes and the place of women. Switchboards and typewriters in the booming cities became increasingly the tools of women's liberation. Economic freedom encouraged sexual freedom, and the "new morality" began to be reflected in soaring divorce rates, the spreading practice of birth control, and increasingly frank discussion of sexual topics. By 1913, said one popular magazine, the chimes had struck "sex o'clock in America."

Families and Women in the City

The new urban environment was hard on families. Paradoxically, the crowded cities were emotionally isolating places. Urban families had to go it alone, separated from clan, kin, and village. Many families cracked under the strain of providing the virtually exclusive arena for intimate companionship and emotional satisfaction. The late-nineteenth-century urban era launched the "divorce revolution" that transformed the United States' social landscape in the twentieth century.

Urban life also dictated changes in work habits and even in family size. Not only fathers but mothers and even children as young as ten years old often worked, and usually in widely scattered locations. In the city more children meant more mouths to feed, more crowding in sardine-tin tenements, and more human baggage to carry in the uphill struggle for social mobility. Not surprisingly, birthrates were still dropping and family size continued to shrink as the nineteenth century lengthened. Marriages were being delayed, and more couples learned the techniques of birth control.

Women were growing more independent in the urban environment, and in 1898 they heard the voice of a major feminist prophet, Charlotte Perkins Gilman. In that year the freethinking and original-minded Gilman published *Women and Economics*. In this classic of feminist literature, Gilman called on women to abandon their dependent status and contribute to the larger life of the community through productive involvement in the economy. Rejecting all claims that biology gave women a fundamentally different character from men, she argued that "our highly specialized motherhood is not so advantageous as believed." She advocated centralized nurseries and cooperative kitchens to facilitate women's participation in the work force—anticipating by more than half a century the day-care centers and convenience-food services of a later day.

Fiery feminists also continued to insist on the ballot. They had been demanding the vote since before the Civil War, but many high-minded female reformers had temporarily shelved the cause of women to battle for the rights of blacks. In 1890 militant suffragists formed the National American Women's Suffrage Association. Its founders included aging pioneers like Elizabeth Cady Stanton, who had helped organize the first women's rights convention in 1848, and her long-time comrade Susan B. Anthony, the radical Quaker who had courted jail by trying to cast a ballot in the 1872 presidential election.

By 1900 a new generation of women had taken command of the suffrage battle. Their most effective leader was Carrie Chapman Catt, a pragmatic and businesslike reformer of relentless dedication. Significantly, under Catt the suffragists deemphasized the argument that women deserved the vote as a matter of right, because they were in all respects the equals of men. Instead Catt stressed the desirability of giving women the vote if they were to continue to discharge their traditional duties as homemakers and mothers in the increasingly public world of the city.

By thus linking the ballot to a traditional definition of women's role, suffragists registered encouraging gains as the new century opened, despite continuing showers of rotten eggs and the jeers of male critics. Women were increasingly permitted to vote in local elections, particularly on issues related to the schools. Wyoming Territory—later called "the Equality State"—granted the first unrestricted suffrage to women in 1869. This important breach in the dike once made, many states followed Wyoming's example. Paralleling these triumphs, most of the states by 1890 had passed laws to permit wives to own or control their property after marriage.

The reborn suffrage movement and other women's organizations excluded black women from their ranks. Fearful that an integrated campaign would compromise its efforts to get the vote, the National American Women's Suffrage Association limited membership to whites. Black women, however, created their own associations. Journalist and teacher Ida B. Wells inspired black women to mount a nationwide antilynching crusade. She also helped launch the black women's club movement, which culminated in the establishment of the National Association of Colored Women in 1896.

Artistic Triumphs

John Adams had anticipated that his generation's preoccupation with nation-building would allow art to flourish in the future, but the results long proved unspectacular. Portrait painting continued to appeal, as it had since the colonial era, but many of America's finest painters made their livings abroad. James Whistler (1834–1903) did much of his work, including the celebrated portrait of his mother, in England. This eccentric and quarrelsome Massachusetts Yankee had earlier been dropped from West Point after failing chemistry. "Had silicon been a gas," he later jested, "I would have been a major general." Another gifted portrait painter, likewise self-exiled in England, was John Singer Sargent (1856–1925). His flattering but somewhat superficial likenesses of the British nobility were highly prized. Mary Cassatt, an American-in-exile in Paris, painted sensitive portrayals of women and children that earned her a place in the pantheon of the French impressionist painters.

Other brush wielders, no less talented, brightened the artistic horizon. Self-taught George Inness

(1825–1894), who looked like a fanatic with his long hair and piercing gaze, became America's leading landscapist. Thomas Eakins (1844–1916) attained a high degree of realism in his paintings, a quality not appreciated by portrait sitters who wanted their moles overlooked. Boston-born Winslow Homer (1836–1910), who as a youth had secretly drawn sketches in school, was perhaps the greatest painter of the group. Earthily American and largely resistant to foreign influences, he revealed rugged realism and boldness of conception. His canvases of the sea and of fisherfolk were masterly, and probably no American artist has excelled him in portraying the awesome power of the ocean.

Probably the most gifted sculptor yet produced by America was Augustus Saint-Gaudens (1848–1907). Born in Ireland of an Irish mother and a French father, he became an adopted American. Among his most moving works is the Robert Gould Shaw memorial, erected in Boston in 1897. It depicts Colonel Shaw, a young white "Boston Brahmin" officer, leading his black troops into battle in the Civil War.

Music, too, was gaining popularity. America of the 1880s and 1890s was assembling high-quality symphony orchestras, notably in Boston and Chicago. The famed Metropolitan Opera House of New York was erected in 1883. In its fabled "Diamond Horseshoe" the newly rich, often under the pretense of enjoying the imported singers, would flaunt their jewels, gowns, and furs. While symphonies and operas were devoted to bringing European music to elite American audiences, new strains of homegrown American music were sprouting in the South. Black folk traditions like spirituals and "ragged music" were evolving into the blues, ragtime, and jazz that would transform American popular music in the twentieth century.

A marvelous discovery was the reproduction of music by mechanical means. The phonograph, though a squeakily imperfect instrument when invented by the deaf Edison, had by 1900 reached over 150,000 homes. Americans were rapidly being dosed with "canned music," as the "sitting room" piano increasingly gathered dust.

In addition to skyscraper builder Louis Sullivan, a famous American architect of the age was Henry H. Richardson. Born in Louisiana and educated at Harvard and in Paris, Richardson settled in Boston and from there spread his immense influence throughout the eastern half of the United States. He popularized a distinctive, ornamental style that came to be known as "Richardsonian." High-vaulted arches, like those on Gothic churches, were his trademark. His masterpiece and most famous work was the Marshall Field Building (1885) in Chicago.

The Business of Amusement

Fun and frolic were not neglected by the workaday American. The legitimate stage still flourished, as appreciative audiences responded to the lure of the footlights. Vaudeville, with its coarse jokes and graceful acrobats, continued to be immensely popular during the 1880s and 1890s.

The circus—high-tented and multiringed—finally emerged full-blown. Phineas T. Barnum, the master showman who had early discovered that "the public likes to be humbugged," joined hands with James A. Bailey in 1881 to stage the "Greatest Show on Earth."

Colorful "Wild West" shows, first performed in 1883, were even more distinctively American. Headed by the knightly, goateed, and free-drinking William F. ("Buffalo Bill") Cody, the troupe included war-whooping Indians, live buffalo, and deadeye sharpshooters. Among them was the girlish Annie Oakley. Rifle in hand, at thirty paces she could perforate a tossed-up card half a dozen times before it fluttered to the ground.

Baseball, already widely played before the Civil War, was clearly emerging as the national pastime, if not a national mania. A league of professional players was formed in the 1870s, and in 1888 an all-star baseball team toured the world, using the pyramids as a backstop while in Egypt. The trend toward spectator sports was well exemplified by football, a rugged game that used the dangerous flying wedge formation. The Yale-Princeton game of 1893 drew fifty thousand cheering fans, while foreigners jeered that the nation was getting "sports on the brain."

Even boxing, with its long background of bareknuckle brutality, gained a new and gloved respectability in 1892. Agile "Gentleman Jim" Corbett wrested the

Buffalo Bill's Wild West Show, c. 1907   *By the late 1800s, the "wild" West was already passing into the realm of myth—and popular entertainment. Famed frontiersman William F. ("Buffalo Bill") Cody made his fortune showing off his tame cowboys and Indians to urban audiences.*

world championship from the aging and alcoholic John L. Sullivan, the fabulous "Boston Strong Boy."

Two crazes swept the country in the closing decades of the century. Croquet became enormously popular, though condemned by moralists of the "naughty nineties" because it exposed feminine ankles and promoted flirtation. The low-framed "safety" bicycle replaced the high-seated model. By 1893 a million bicycles were in use.

Basketball was invented in 1891 by James Naismith, a YMCA instructor in Springfield, Massa-chusetts. Designed as an active indoor sport that could be played during the winter months, it spread rapidly and enjoyed enormous popularity in the next century.

The land of the skyscraper was plainly becoming more standardized, owing largely to the new industrialization. To an increasing degree, Americans shared a common culture—playing, reading, shopping, and talking alike. As the century drew to a close, the explosion of cities paradoxically made Americans more diverse and more similar at the same time.

Chronology

1859	Charles Darwin publishes *On the Origin of Species.*
1862	Morrill Act provides public land for higher education.
1869	Wyoming Territory grants women the right to vote.
1871	*Woodhull and Claflin's Weekly* published.
1873	Comstock Law passed.
1876	Johns Hopkins University graduate school established.
1879	Henry George publishes *Progress and Poverty.* "Dumbbell" tenement introduced. Mary Baker Eddy establishes Christian Science. Salvation Army begins work in America.
1881	Booker T. Washington becomes head of Tuskegee Institute.
1882	First immigration-restriction laws passed.
1883	Brooklyn Bridge completed.
1884	Mark Twain publishes *The Adventures of Huckleberry Finn.*
1885	Louis Sullivan builds the first skyscraper, in Chicago.
1886	Statue of Liberty erected in New York harbor.
1887	American Protective Association (APA) formed.
1888	Edward Bellamy publishes *Looking Backward.*
1889	Jane Addams founds Hull House in Chicago. Moody Bible Institute established in Chicago.
1890	National American Women's Suffrage Association formed.
1891	Basketball invented.
1893	Lillian Wald opens Henry Street Settlement in New York.
1897	Library of Congress opens.
1898	Charlotte Perkins Gilman publishes *Women and Economics.*
1899	Kate Chopin publishes *The Awakening.*
1900	Theodore Dreiser publishes *Sister Carrie.*
1910	National Association for the Advancement of Colored People (NAACP) founded.

SUGGESTED READINGS

Primary Source Documents

Jacob Riis, *How the Other Half Lives** (1890), is a vivid account of life in America's slums. In *A Hazard of New Fortunes* (1890), William Dean Howells penned one of the first "urban novels" in American literature. Victoria Woodhull, *The Scarecrows of Sexual Slavery** (1874), provocatively illustrates some changing ideas about women's roles. Henry James's novel *The Bostonians* (1886) vividly portrays feminists and suffragists.

Secondary Sources

The Rise of the City, 1878–1898 (1933) is a classic study by Arthur M. Schlesinger. More recent are Gunther Barth, *City People: The Rise of Modern City Culture in Nineteenth-Century America* (1980); Howard Chudacoff, *The Evolution of American Urban Society* (1975); the opening chapters of Kenneth T. Jackson, *Crabgrass Frontier: The Suburbanization of America* (1985); and Eric H. Monkkonen, *America Becomes Urban: The Development of Cities and Towns, 1780–1980* (1988). On new urban spaces and their use by city dwellers see Roy Rosenzweig and Elizabeth Blackmar, *The Park and The People: A History of Central Park* (1992); Kathy Peiss, *Cheap Amusements: Working Women and Leisure in Turn-of-the-Century New York* (1986); and David Nasaw, *Going Out: The Rise and Fall of Public Amusements* (1993). Oscar Handlin introduced the study of immigrant communities in American cities with his *Boston's Immigrants* (rev. ed., 1959). More recent studies of the same topic include John Bodnar, *The Transplanted: A History of Immigrants in Urban America* (1985); Jon Gjerde, *From Peasants to Farmers: The Migration from Norway to the Upper Middle West* (1985); Kerby A. Miller, *Emigrants and Exile: Ireland and the Irish Exodus to North America* (1985); Donna Gabaccia, *From the Other Side: Women, Gender, and Immigrant Life in the U.S., 1820–1990* (1994); Thomas Kessner, *The Golden Door: Italian and Jewish Mobility in New York City, 1880–1915* (1977); Ronald Takaki, *Strangers from a Different Shore: A History of Asian-Americans* (1989); and Irving Howe's monumental and moving account of Jewish immigration, *World of Our Fathers* (1976). Black thought for this period is illuminated by three studies: August Meier, *Negro Thought in America, 1880–1915* (1963); Louis R. Harlan, *Booker T. Washington: The Making of a Black Leader, 1865–1901* (1972); and David Levering Lewis, *W. E. B. Du Bois: Biography of a Race, 1868–1919* (1993). For blacks in northern cities before World War I see Allan H. Spear, *Black Chicago: The Making of a Negro Ghetto, 1890–1920* (1967), and James Borchert, *Alley Life in Washington: Family, Community, Religion, and Folklife in the City* (1980). On religion see Susan Curtis, *A Consuming Faith: The Social Gospel and Modern American Culture* (1991). On women and the family consult Carl Degler, *At Odds: Women and the Family from the Revolution to the Present* (1980); Steven Mintz, *A Prison of Expectations: The Family in Victorian Culture* (1983); Mari Jo Buhle, *Women and American Socialism, 1870–1920* (1981); Margaret W. Rossiter, *Women Scientists in America* (1982); and Rosalind Rosenberg, *Beyond Separate Spheres* (1982) and *Divided Lives* (1992). James Turner probes one aspect of the conflict between science and religion in *Without God, Without Creed: The Origins of Unbelief in America* (1985). Three fascinating studies document the rise of a "new" middle-class mentality: Burton J. Bledstein, *The Culture of Professionalism* (1976); Thomas Haskell, *The Emergence of Professional Social Science* (1977); and Stuart M. Blumin, *The Emergence of the Middle Class: Social Experience in the American City, 1760–1900* (1989).

---

* An asterisk indicates that the document, or an excerpt from it, can be found in Thomas A. Bailey and David M. Kennedy, eds., *The American Spirit: United States History as Seen by Contemporaries*, 9th ed. (Boston: Houghton Mifflin, 1998).

27

★★★★★★★★★

The Great West and the Agricultural Revolt,

1865–1900

★★★★★★

Up to our own day American history has been in a large degree the history of the colonization of the Great West. The existence of an area of free land, its continuous recession, and the advance of American settlement westward, explain American development.

★★★★★★

FREDERICK JACKSON TURNER, 1893

Indians Embattled in the West

When the Civil War crashed to a close, the frontier line was still wavering westward. A long fringe of settlement, bulging outward here and there, ran roughly north through central Texas and onward to the Canadian border. Between this jagged line and the settled areas on the Pacific slope, there were virtually no white people. The few exceptions were the islands of Mormons in Utah, occasional trading posts and gold camps, and several scattered Spanish-Mexican settlements throughout the Southwest.

Sprawling in expanse, the Great West was a rough square that measured about a thousand miles on each side. Embracing mountains, plateaus, deserts, and plains, it was the habitat of the Indian, the buffalo, the wild horse, the prairie dog, and the coyote. Twenty-five years later—that is, by 1890—the entire domain had been carved into states and the three territories of Arizona, New Mexico, and the "Indian Territory," or Oklahoma. Pioneers flung themselves greedily on this enormous prize, as if to ravish it.

Native Americans, to their misfortune, stood in the path of the advancing white settlers. Diverse tribes of buffalo-hunting Indians roamed the spacious western plains in 1860. In three centuries the Spanish-introduced horse had transformed the culture of the Plains Indians, causing the tribes to become more nomadic and more warlike. The Plains Indians had become skilled riders and fighters.

When white soldiers and settlers had edged onto the plains in the two or three decades before the Civil War, they triggered an environmental cycle that set the Indian tribes against one another and ultimately undermined the foundations of Native American culture. White intruders unwittingly spread cholera, typhoid, and smallpox among the native peoples of the plains, with devastating results. By hunting and by grazing their own livestock on the prairie grasses, whites steadily shrank the Great Plains bison population. As the mammoth buffalo herds dwindled, competition and warfare among Indian peoples intensified. Pushed off their own traditional lands in the late eighteenth century, the Sioux were aggressively expanding at the expense of other Plains peoples like the Crows, Kiowas, and Pawnees.

The federal government tried to sign treaties with the "chiefs" of various tribes at Fort Laramie in 1851, but the white treaty makers misunderstood both Indian government and Indian society. Living in scattered bands, Native Americans usually recognized no authority outside their immediate family, or perhaps a village elder, and resisted white attempts to confine them to a defined territory. In the 1860s the federal government tried to herd the Plains Indians onto smaller confines like the "Great Sioux Reservation" in the Dakotas and the Indian Territory of present-day Oklahoma.

From 1868 to about 1890, almost incessant warfare between Indians and whites raged in the various parts of the West. The fighting was fierce and harrowing, especially the winter campaigning in subzero weather. Regular army troops, mostly Civil War veterans led by generals such as Sherman, Sheridan, and Custer, met formidable adversaries in the well-armed Plains Indians, who rode swift ponies and enjoyed baffling mobility. The army's ranks included four crack black units—about one-fifth of all soldiers assigned to the frontier during these years.

The Indian wars in the West were often brutal affairs. Aggressive whites sometimes shot peaceful Indians on sight. At Sand Creek, Colorado, in 1864, Colonel J. M. Chivington's militia massacred in cold blood some four hundred Indians who apparently thought they had been promised immunity. Women were shot praying for mercy, children had their brains dashed out, and braves were tortured, scalped, and mutilated.

Cruelty begot cruelty. In 1866 a Sioux war party ambushed Captain William Fetterman's command of eighty-one soldiers and civilians in Wyoming's Big Horn Mountains, killing every man and mutilating the corpses. The cycle of ferocious warfare intensified. As a result, the federal government in 1868 abandoned its attempt to construct the Bozeman Trail through Montana. The sprawling "Great Sioux Reservation" was guaranteed to the Sioux tribes.

But in 1874, a new round of warfare with the Plains Indians began when Colonel George Armstrong Custer led a "scientific" expedition into the Black Hills of South Dakota (part of the Sioux reservation) and announced that he had discovered gold. Hordes of greedy gold seekers rushed to the Dakota Territory. The aggrieved Sioux took to the warpath, led by the influential and wily Sitting Bull.

Colonel Custer's Seventh Cavalry set out to suppress the Indians and force them into the reservation. Attacking what turned out to be a superior force of some 2,500 well-armed warriors camped near the Little Big Horn River in present-day Montana, the "White Chief with Yellow Hair" and his 264 officers and men were completely wiped out in 1876 when two supporting columns failed to come to their rescue. White military reinforcements later arrived, and the Indians who defeated Custer were relentlessly crushed in a series of battles across the northern plains.

The Nez Percé Indians of Idaho were likewise goaded into warfare in 1877, when gold discoveries on their reservation prompted the federal government to shrink its size by 90 percent. Chief Joseph finally surrendered his band after a tortuous, 1,700-mile three-month trek across the Continental Divide toward Canada, where he had hoped to join forces with Sitting Bull. Betrayed into believing they would be returned to their ancestral lands in Idaho, the Nez

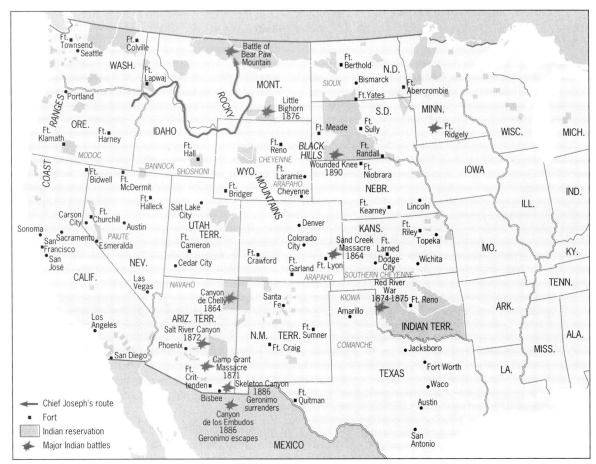

Indian Wars, 1860–1890   *Surrendering in 1877, Chief Joseph of the Nez Percés declared: "Our chiefs are killed. . . . The old men are all dead. . . . The little children are freezing to death. . . . I want to have time to look for my children. . . . Hear me, my chiefs. My heart is sick and sad. From where the sun now stands I will fight no more forever."*

Percés instead were sent to a dusty reservation in Kansas, where 40 percent of them perished from disease. The survivors eventually returned to Idaho.

Fierce Apache tribes of Arizona and New Mexico were the most difficult to subdue. Led by Geronimo, whose eyes blazed hatred of the whites, they were pursued into Mexico by federal troops. Scattered remnants of the warriors were finally persuaded to surrender after the Apache women had been exiled to Florida. The Apaches ultimately became successful farmers in Oklahoma.

This relentless fire-and-sword policy of the whites at last shattered the spirit of the Indians. The vanquished Native Americans were finally ghettoized in reservations, there to eke out an existence as wards of the government.

The defeat of the Indians was engineered by a number of factors. Of cardinal importance was the railroad, which shot an iron arrow through the heart of the West. The Indians were also ravaged by the white people's diseases and liquor, to which they showed little resistance. Above all, the virtual

Geronimo (c. 1829–1909) *He was the most famous Apache leader.*

extermination of the buffalo resulted in the near-extermination of the Plains Indians.

Bellowing Herds of Bison

Tens of millions of buffalo blackened the western prairies when the white Americans first arrived. These shaggy, lumbering animals were the staff of life for the Native Americans (see "Makers of America: The Plains Indians," pp. 388–389). Their flesh provided food; their dried dung provided fuel ("buffalo chips"); their hides provided clothing, lariats, and harnesses.

When the Civil War closed, some 15 million of these meaty beasts were still grazing on the western plains. In 1868 a Kansas Pacific locomotive had to wait eight hours for a herd to amble across the tracks. William "Buffalo Bill" Cody killed over four thousand animals in eighteen months while employed by the Kansas Pacific.

With the building of the railroad, the massacre of the herds began in deadly earnest. The creatures were slain for their hides, for a few choice cuts of meat, or simply for amusement. "Sportsmen" on lurching railroad trains leaned out the windows and blazed away at the animals to satisfy their lust for slaughter or excitement. With such wholesale butchery, fewer than a thousand buffalo were left by 1885, and the once-numerous beasts were barely saved from extinction. The whole story is a shocking example of the greed and waste that accompanied the conquest of the North American continent.

The End of the Trail

By the 1880s the national conscience began to stir uneasily over the plight of the Indians. Helen Hunt Jackson, a Massachusetts writer of children's literature, pricked the moral sense of Americans in 1881 when she published *A Century of Dishonor*. The book chronicled the sorry record of governmental ruthlessness and chicanery in dealing with the Indians. Her later novel *Ramona* (1884), a story of injustice to the California Indians, sold some 600,000 copies and further inspired sympathy for the Indians.

Debate seesawed. Humanitarians wanted to treat the Indians kindly and persuade them thereby to "walk the white man's road." Yet hard-liners insisted on the current policy of forced containment and brutal punishment. Neither side showed much respect for traditional Native American culture. Christian reformers, who often administered educational facilities on the reservations, sometimes withheld food to force the Indians to give up their tribal religion and assimilate to white society. In 1884 these zealous white souls joined with military men in successfully persuading the federal government to outlaw the sacred Sun Dance. When the "Ghost Dance" cult later spread to the Dakota Sioux, the army bloodily stamped it out in 1890 at the so-called Battle of Wounded Knee. In the fighting thus provoked, an estimated two hundred Indian men, women, and children were killed, as well as twenty-nine invading soldiers.

The misbegotten offspring of the movement to reform Indian policy was the Dawes Severalty Act of 1887. Reflecting the forced-civilization views of the

The Plains Indians

The last of the native peoples of North America to bow before the military might of the whites, the Indians of the northern Great Plains long defended their lands and their ways of life against the American cavalry. After the end of the Indian wars, toward the close of the nineteenth century, the Plains tribes struggled on, jealously guarding their communities against white encroachment.

Before Europeans first appeared in North America in the sixteenth century, the vast plain from northern Texas to Saskatchewan was home to some thirty different tribes. There was no typical Plains Indian; each tribe spoke a distinct language, practiced its own religion, and formed its own government.

Indians had first trod the arid plains to pursue sprawling herds of antelope, elk, and especially buffalo, but they were not exclusively hunters. The women were expert farmers, coaxing lush gardens of pumpkins, squash, corn, and beans from the dry but fertile soil. Still, the shaggy pelt and heavy flesh of the buffalo constituted the staff of life on the plains. Hunted by men, the great bison were butchered by women, who made use of every part of the beast.

The nomadic Plains Indians roamed the countryside in small bands throughout the winter, gathering together in the summer for religious ceremonies, socializing, and communal buffalo hunts. Then in the sixteenth century, the mounted Spanish *conquistadores* ventured into the New World, and their steeds quickly spread over the plains. The horse revolutionized Indian societies, turning the Plains tribes into

Arapaho Chief Hail Wearing Ghost Dance Shirt, c. 1890
The Ghost Dance cult originated among the Paiute Indians in the 1870s, and spread swiftly throughout the western tribes. It held out the promise of a revival of traditional Indian culture and revenge on the invading whites, but it was ruthlessly suppressed by the U.S. authorities. Ghost Dance shirts like this one were thought by their wearers to be impermeable to bullets.

efficient hunting machines that promised to banish hunger from the prairies. But the plains pony also ignited a furious competition for grazing land and for ever more horses, so that wars became increasingly bitter and frequent.

The European invasion soon eclipsed the short-lived era of the horse. After many battles the Plains Indians found themselves crammed together on tiny reservations, clinging with tired but determined fingers to their traditions. Although much of

Plains Indian culture persists to this day, the Indians' free-ranging way of life passed into memory. As Black Elk, an Ogalala Sioux, put it, "Once we were happy in our own country and we were seldom hungry, for then the two-leggeds and the four-leggeds lived together like relatives, and there was plenty for them and for us. But then the Wasichus [white people] came, and they made little islands for us . . . and always these islands are becoming smaller, for around them surges the gnawing flood of Wasichus."

reformers, the act dissolved many tribes as legal entities, wiped out tribal ownership of land, and set up individual Indian family heads with 160 free acres. If the Indians behaved themselves like "good white settlers," they would get full title to their holdings, as well as citizenship, in twenty-five years. The probationary period was later extended, but full citizenship was granted to all Indians in 1924.

The federal efforts at forced assimilation included boarding schools for Indian children, beginning in 1879 with the Carlisle Indian School in Pennsylvania. "Kill the Indian and save the man" was the motto for these schools, where Native American children, separated from their tribe, were taught English and inculcated with white values and customs. The government also sent "field matrons" to the reservations to teach Native American women the art of sewing and to preach the virtues of chastity and hygiene.

The Dawes Act struck directly at tribal organization and tried to make rugged individualists out of the Indians. This legislation ignored the inherent reliance of traditional Indian culture on tribally held land. The Dawes Act remained the cornerstone of the government's official Indian policy until 1934, when the Indian Reorganization Act ("the Indian New Deal") reversed the individualistic approach and belatedly tried to restore the tribal basis of Indian life (see p. 503).

Under these new federal policies, defective though they were, the Indian population started to mount slowly. The total number had been reduced by

1887 to about 243,000—the result of bullets, bottles, and bacteria—but the census of 1990 counted some 1.5 million Native Americans, urban and rural.

Mining: From Dishpan to Ore-Breaker

The conquest of the Indians and the coming of the railroad were life-giving boons to the mining frontier. The golden gravel of California continued to yield "pay dirt," and in 1858 an electrifying discovery convulsed Colorado. Avid "fifty-niners" or "Pike's Peakers" rushed west to rip at the ramparts of the Rockies. Many miners failed and returned "busted" and weary to the East. But bearded fortune seekers stayed on in Colorado to strip silver or develop nonmetallic wealth in the form of golden grain.

"Fifty-niners" also poured feverishly into Nevada in 1859, after the fabulous Comstock lode had been uncovered. A fantastic amount of gold and silver, worth more than $340 million, was mined by the "Kings of the Comstock" from 1860 to 1890. The scantily populated state of Nevada, "child of the Comstock lode," was prematurely railroaded into the Union in 1864, partly to provide three electoral votes for President Lincoln.

Smaller "lucky strikes" drew frantic gold and silver seekers into Montana, Idaho, and other western states. Boomtowns, known as "Helldorados," sprouted from the desert sands like magic. Every third cabin was a saloon, where sweat-stained miners drank adulterated liquor ("rotgut") in the company of accommodating women. Lynch law and vigilante

Dance-Hall Girl, Virginia City, Nevada, c. 1890 *Women as well as men sought their fortunes in the frontier West— especially in wide-open mining towns like Virginia City.*

justice, as in early California, preserved a crude semblance of order. And when the "diggings" petered out, the gold seekers decamped, leaving picturesque "ghost towns," such as Virginia City, Nevada, silhouetted in the desert. Begun with a boom, these towns ended with a whimper.

Once the loose surface gold was gobbled up, ore-breaking machinery was imported to smash the gold-bearing quartz. This operation was so expensive that it could ordinarily be undertaken only by corporations pooling the wealth of stockholders. Gradually the age of big business came to the mining industry. Dusty, bewhiskered miners, dishpans in hand, were replaced by impersonal corporations with their costly machinery and trained engineers.

Yet the mining frontier had played a vital role in subduing the continent. Magnetlike, it attracted population and wealth while advertising the wonders of the Wild West. The amassing of precious metals helped finance the Civil War, facilitated the building of railroads, enabled the Treasury to resume specie payments in 1879, and injected the silver issue into American politics. "Silver senators," representing the thinly peopled "acreage states" of the West, used their disproportionate influence to promote the interests of the silver miners. Finally, the mining frontier added to American folklore and literature, as the writings of Mark Twain so colorfully attest.

Beef Bonanzas and the Long Drive

When the Civil War ended, the grassy plains of Texas supported several million tough, longhorn cattle. These scrawny beasts were killed primarily for their hides. There was no way to get their meat profitably to market.

The problem of marketing was neatly solved when the transcontinental railroads thrust their iron fingers into the West. Cattle could now be shipped bodily to the stockyards and, under "beef barons" like the Swifts and Armours, the highly industrialized meatpacking business sprang into existence as a main pillar of the economy. Drawing on the gigantic stockyards at Kansas City and Chicago, the packers could ship their fresh products to the East Coast in the newly perfected refrigerator cars.

A spectacular feeder of the new slaughterhouses was the "Long Drive." Texas cowboys—black, white, and Mexican—drove herds numbering from one thousand to ten thousand head slowly over the unfenced and unpeopled plains until they reached a railroad terminal. The bawling beasts grazed en route on the free government grass. Favorite terminal points were fly-specked "cow towns" like Dodge City and Abilene (Kansas), Ogallala (Nebraska), and Cheyenne (Wyoming). From 1866 to 1888, bellowing herds totaling over 4 million steers were driven northward from the beef bowl of Texas.

What the Lord giveth, the Lord also can take away. The railroad made the Long Drive; and the railroad unmade the Long Drive, primarily because the locomotives ran both ways. The same rails that bore

the cattle from the open range to the kitchen range brought out the homesteader and the sheepherder. Both of these intruders, amid flying bullets, built barbed-wire fences that were too numerous to be cut down by the cowboys. Furthermore, the terrible winter of 1886–1887, with blinding blizzards reaching 68° below zero, left thousands of dazed cattle starving and freezing. Overexpansion and overgrazing likewise took their toll, as the cowboys slowly gave way to plowboys.

The only escape for the stockman was to make cattle-raising a big business and avoid the perils of overproduction. Breeders learned to fence their ranches, lay in winter feed, import blooded bulls, and produce fewer and meatier animals. They also learned to organize. The Wyoming Stock-Growers' Association, especially in the 1880s, virtually controlled the territory and its legislature.

This was the heyday of the cowboy. The equipment of the lone cowhand—from "shooting irons" and ten-gallon hat to chaps and high-heeled boots—served a useful, not an ornamental, function. A "genuwine" gun-toting cowpuncher, riding where men were men and smelled like horses, could justifiably boast of his toughness.

These bowlegged Knights of the Saddle, with colorful trappings and cattle-lulling songs, became an authentic part of American folklore. Many of them, perhaps five thousand, were blacks, who especially enjoyed the newfound freedom of the open range.

The Farmer's Frontier

The miners and cattlemen created the romantic legend of the West, but it was the sober sodbuster who wrote the final chapter of frontier history. A new day dawned for western farmers with the Homestead Act of 1862. The law provided that a settler could acquire as much as 160 acres of land (a quarter section) by living on it for five years, improving it, and paying a nominal fee averaging about $30.

The Homestead Act marked a drastic departure from previous policy. Before the act, public land had been sold primarily for revenue; now it was to be given away to encourage a rapid filling of empty spaces and to provide a stimulus to the family farm—

"the backbone of democracy." During the forty years after its passage, about half a million families took advantage of the Homestead Act to carve out new homes in the vast open stretches. Yet five times that many families *purchased* their land from the railroads, land companies, or the states.

The Homestead Act often turned out to be a cruel hoax. The standard 160 acres, quite adequate in the well-watered Mississippi basin, frequently proved pitifully inadequate on the rain-scarce Great Plains. Thousands of homesteaders, perhaps two out of three, were forced to give up the one-sided struggle against drought.

Naked fraud was spawned by the Homestead Act and similar laws. Perhaps ten times more of the public domain wound up in the clutches of land-grabbing promoters than in the hands of bona fide farmers. Unscrupulous corporations would use "dummy" homesteaders—often immigrants bribed with cash or beer—to grab the best properties, containing timber, minerals, and oil. Settlers would later swear that they had "improved" the property by erecting a "twelve-by-fourteen" dwelling, which turned out to measure twelve by fourteen *inches.*

The railways also played a major role in developing the agricultural West, largely through the profitable marketing of crops. Some railroad companies induced Americans and European immigrants to buy the cheap lands earlier granted by the government. The Northern Pacific Railroad at one time had nearly a thousand paid agents in Europe distributing leaflets in various languages.

Agriculture expanded once the myth of the Great American Desert was shattered. Pioneer explorers had assumed that the soil must be barren, simply because it was not heavily watered and did not support immense forests. But once the prairie sod was broken with heavy iron plows pulled by four yokes of oxen, the earth proved astonishingly fruitful.

Lured by higher wheat prices resulting from crop failures elsewhere in the world, settlers in the 1870s rashly pushed still farther west, onto the poor, marginal lands beyond the 100th meridian. Geologist John Wesley Powell, explorer of the Colorado River's Grand Canyon, warned in 1874 that beyond the 100th meridian so little rain fell that agriculture was impossible without massive irrigation. Ignoring Powell's advice, farmers heedlessly chewed up the crusty earth in western Kansas, eastern Colorado, and Montana. They quickly went broke as a six-year drought in the 1880s further desiccated the already dusty region. In the wake of the drought, some pioneers tried the "dry farming" technique of frequent shallow cultivation. But over time this practice pulverized the surface soil and contributed to the "Dust Bowl" several decades later (see p. 502).

Other adaptations to the western environment were more successful. Tough strains of wheat, resistant to cold and drought, were imported from Russia and blossomed into billowing yellow carpets. Barbed wire, perfected by Joseph F. Glidden in 1874, solved the problem of how to build fences on the treeless prairies. Eventually, federally financed irrigation projects on a colossal scale caused the Great American Desert to bloom. In the long run, hydraulic engineers had more to do with shaping the modern West than all the trappers, miners, cavalrymen, and cowboys there ever were.

The Great West experienced a fantastic growth in population from the 1870s to the 1890s. A parade of new western states proudly joined their eastern sisters. Boomtown Colorado, offspring of the Pike's Peak gold rush, was greeted in 1876 as the "Centennial State." In 1889–1890 a Republican Congress, eagerly seeking more Republican electoral and congressional votes, admitted in a wholesale lot six new states: North Dakota, South Dakota, Montana, Washington, Idaho, and Wyoming. The Mormon church formally banned polygamy in 1890, but not until 1896 was Utah deemed worthy of admission. Only Oklahoma, New Mexico, and Arizona remained to be formed into states from contiguous territory on the mainland of North America.

In a last gaudy fling, the federal government made available to settlers vast stretches of fertile plains formerly occupied by the Indians in the district of Oklahoma ("the beautiful land"). Scores of overeager and well-armed "sooners," illegally jumping the gun, had entered Oklahoma Territory. They had to be evicted repeatedly by federal troops, who on occasion would shoot the intruders' horses. On April 22, 1889, all was in readiness for the legal opening, and some 50,000 "boomers" were poised expectantly on the boundary line. At high noon the bugle shrilled, and a horde of "eighty-niners" poured in on lathered horses or careening vehicles. That night a lonely spot on the prairie had mushroomed into the tented city of Guthrie, with over 10,000 people. By the end of the year Oklahoma boasted 60,000 inhabitants, and Congress made it a territory. In 1907 it became the "Sooner State."

The Folding Frontier

In 1890—a watershed date—the superintendent of the census announced that for the first time in America's experience a frontier line was no longer discernible. All the unsettled areas had been invaded by isolated bodies of settlement. The "closing" of the frontier inspired one of the most influential essays ever written about American history—Frederick Jackson Turner's "The Significance of the Frontier in American History," in 1893. As the nineteenth century neared its sunset, the westward-tramping American people were disturbed to find that their fabled free land was going or had gone. The secretary of war had prophesied in 1827 that five hundred years would be needed to fill the West. But as the nation learned that its land was not inexhaustible, seeds were planted to preserve the vanishing resource. The government set aside lands for national parks—first Yellowstone in 1872 and Sequoia in 1890.

The frontier was more than a place: it was also a state of mind and a symbol of opportunity. Its passing ended a romantic phase of the nation's internal development and created new economic and psychological problems. Traditionally footloose, Americans were notorious for their mobility. The nation's farmers, unlike the peasants of Europe, seldom remained rooted to their soil. The land, sold for a profit as settlement closed in, was often the settler's most profitable crop.

Much has been said about the frontier as a "safety valve." The theory is that when hard times came, the unemployed who cluttered the city pavements merely moved west, took up farming, and prospered. In truth, relatively few city dwellers, at least in the populous eastern centers, migrated to the frontier during depressions. Most of them did not know how to farm; few of them could raise enough money to transport themselves west and then pay for livestock and expensive machinery.

But the safety valve theory does have some validity. Free acreage did lure to the West a host of immigrants, who otherwise might have remained in the eastern cities to clog the job markets. And the very *possibility* of westward migration may have induced urban employers to maintain wage rates high enough to discourage workers from leaving. Ironically, however, the real safety valve by the late nineteenth century was in cities like Chicago and San Francisco, where failed farmers, busted miners, and erstwhile easterners found a better place to seek their fortunes.

United States history cannot be properly understood unless it is viewed in light of the westward-moving experience. As Frederick Jackson Turner wrote, "American history has been in a large degree the history of the colonization of the Great West." The story of settling and taming the trans-Mississippi West in the late nineteenth century was but the last chapter in the saga of the colonizing of various American "wests" since Columbus.

Yet the trans-Mississippi West formed a distinct chapter in that saga and retains its uniqueness today. There the Native American peoples made their last struggle against colonization, and there most Native Americans live today. There "Anglo" culture collided most directly with Hispanic culture, and the Southwest remains the most Hispanicized region in America. There America faced Asia across the Pacific, and there most Asian-Americans dwell today. There the scale and severity of the environment posed their largest challenges to human ambitions, and there the environment continues to mold social and political life, as well as the American imagination, as in no other part of the nation.

The westward-moving pioneers and the country they confronted have assumed mythic proportions in the American mind. For better or worse, those pioneers planted the seeds of civilization in the immense western wilderness. The life we live, they dreamed of; the life they lived, we can only dream.

The Farm Becomes a Factory

The situation of American farmers, once Jacks-and-Jills-of-all-trades, was rapidly changing. They had once raised their own food, fashioned their own clothing, and bartered for other necessities with neighbors.

Now high prices persuaded farmers to concentrate on growing single "cash" crops, such as wheat or corn, and use their profits to buy foodstuffs at the general store and manufactured goods in town or by mail order. The Chicago firm of Aaron Montgomery Ward sent out its first catalogue—a single sheet—in 1872.

Large-scale farmers were now both specialists and businesspeople. As cogs in the vast industrial machine, they were intimately tied in with banking, railroading, and manufacturing. They had to buy expensive machinery to plant and to harvest their crops. A powerful steam engine could drag behind it simultaneously the plow, seeder, and harrow. The speed of harvesting wheat was immensely increased in the 1870s by the twine binder and then in the 1880s by the "combine"—the combined reaper-thresher, which was drawn by twenty to forty horses and both reaped and bagged the grain.

This amazing mechanization of agriculture in the postwar years was almost as striking as the mechanization of industry. As the rural population steadily decreased, those who remained achieved miracles of production, making America the world's breadbasket and butcher shop. The farm was attaining the status of a factory—an outdoor grain factory. Bonanza wheat farms of the Minnesota–North Dakota area, for example, were enormous. By 1890 at least a half-dozen of them were larger than fifteen thousand acres, with communication by telephone from one part to another. These bonanza farms foreshadowed the gigantic agribusinesses of the next century.

Agriculture was a big business from the outset in California's phenomenally productive (and phenomenally irrigated) Central Valley. California farms, carved out of giant Spanish-Mexican land grants and the railroads' huge holdings, were from the outset more than three times larger than the national average. With the advent of the railroad refrigerator car in the 1880s, California fruits and vegetable crops, raised on sprawling tracts by ill-paid Mexican and Chinese farmhands, sold at a handsome profit in the rich urban markets of the East.

Deflation Dooms the Debtor

Once the grain farmers became chained to a one-crop economy—wheat or corn—they were in the

Nebraska Homesteaders in Front of Their Sod House, 1887 *These two brothers and their families had escaped to Canada from the slave South during the Civil War. Returning to the United States in the 1880s, they took advantage of the Homestead Act to stake out farms in Custer County, Nebraska.*

same leaky boat as southern cotton growers. They were no longer the masters of their own destinies. American grain growers found themselves engaged in one of the most fiercely competitive businesses because the price of their product was determined in a world market by the world output. If the wheat fields of Argentina, Russia, and other foreign countries smiled, the price of the farmers' grain would fall and American sodbusters would face ruin, as they did in the 1880s and 1890s.

Low prices and a deflated currency were the chief worries of the frustrated farmers—North, South, and West. If a family had borrowed $1,000 in 1855, when wheat was worth about a dollar a bushel, they expected to pay back the equivalent of 1,000 bushels, plus interest, when the mortgage fell due. But if they let their debt run to 1890, when wheat had fallen to about fifty cents a bushel, they would have to pay back the price of 2,000 bushels for the $1,000 they had borrowed, plus interest. This unexpected burden struck them as unjust, though their steely-eyed creditors often branded the complaining farmers as slippery and dishonest rascals.

The deflationary pinch on the debtor flowed partly from the static money supply. There were simply not enough dollars to go around, and as a result,

prices were forced down. In 1870 the currency in circulation for each person was $19.42; in 1890 it was only $22.67. Yet during these twenty years, business and industrial activity, increasing manyfold, had intensified the scramble for available currency.

The forgotten farmers were caught on a treadmill. Despite unremitting toil, they operated year after year at a loss. In a vicious circle, their farm machinery increased their output of grain, lowered the price, and drove them even deeper into debt. Mortgages engulfed homesteads at an alarming rate; by 1890 Nebraska alone reported more than 100,000 farms blanketed with mortgages. The repeated crash of the sheriff-auctioneer's hammer kept announcing to the world that another sturdy American farmer had become landless in a landed nation.

Ruinous rates of interest, running from 8 to 40 percent, were charged on mortgages, largely by agents of eastern loan companies. The windburned sons and daughters of the sod, who felt that they deserved praise for developing the country, cried out in despair against the loan sharks and the Wall Street octopus.

Farm tenancy rather than farm ownership was spreading like stinkweed. The trend was especially marked in the sharecropping South, where cotton prices also sank dismayingly. By 1880 one-fourth of all American farms were operated by tenants. The United States was ready to feed the world, but under the new industrial feudalism the farmers were sinking into a status suggesting Old World serfdom.

Unhappy Farmers

Even Mother Nature ceased smiling as her powerful forces conspired against agriculture. Mile-wide clouds of grasshoppers, leaving "nothing but the mortgage," periodically ravaged prairie farms. The terrible cotton-boll weevil was also wreaking havoc by the early 1890s.

The good earth was going sour. Floods added to the waste of erosion, which had already washed the topsoil off millions of once-lush southern acres. A long succession of droughts seared the trans-Mississippi West, beginning in the summer of 1887. Whole towns were abandoned. "Going home to the wife's folks" and "in God we trusted, in Kansas we busted" were typical laments of many impoverished farmers as they fled their weather-beaten shacks and sun-baked sod houses.

To add to their miseries, the farmers were also "farmed" by the corporations, processors, and railroads. Trusts raised prices on farmers' supplies to extortionate levels, while storage rates for their grain at warehouses and elevators were pushed up by the operators. The railroad octopus often pushed freight rates so high that the farmers sometimes lost less if they burned their corn for fuel than if they shipped it. High government tariffs in these years poured profits into the pockets of manufacturers, while farmers were forced to sell in competitive, unprotected world markets.

Farmers still made up nearly one-half of the population in 1890, but they were hopelessly disorganized. The manufacturers and the railroad barons knew how to combine to promote their own interests, and so, increasingly, did industrial workers. But the farmers were by nature independent and individualistic—dead set against consolidation or regimentation. They never did organize successfully to restrict production until forced to by the federal government nearly half a century later, in Franklin Roosevelt's New Deal days. What they did manage to organize was a monumental political uprising.

The Farmers Take Their Stand

Agrarian unrest had flared forth earlier, in the Greenback movement shortly after the Civil War. Prices sagged in 1868, and a host of farmers unsuccessfully sought relief from low prices and high indebtedness by demanding an inflation of the currency with paper money.

The National Grange of the Patrons of Husbandry—better known as the Grange—was organized in 1867. Its leading spirit was Oliver H. Kelley, a shrewd and energetic Minnesota farmer then working as a clerk in Washington. Kelley's first objective was to enhance the lives of isolated farmers through social, educational, and fraternal activities. Bursting out like prairie flowers after a rain, the Grangers gradually raised their goals from self-improvement to improvement of the farmers' collective plight. In a determined effort to escape the clutches of the trusts, they established cooperatives for both consumers and producers.

Embattled Grangers also went into politics, enjoying their most gratifying success in the grain-growing regions of the upper Mississippi Valley, chiefly in Illinois, Wisconsin, Iowa, and Minnesota. There, through state legislation, they strove to regulate railway rates and the storage fees charged by railroads and by the operators of warehouses and grain elevators. Many of the state courts, notably in Illinois, were disposed to recognize the principle of public control of private business for the general welfare. A number of the so-called Granger Laws, however, were badly drawn, and they were bitterly fought through the high courts by the well-paid lawyers of the "interests." Following judicial reverses, most severely at the hands of the Supreme Court in the *Wabash* decision of 1886 (see p. 353), the Grangers' influence faded.

Farmers' grievances likewise found a vent in the Greenback Labor party, which combined the inflationary appeal of earlier greenbackers with a program for improving the lot of labor. In 1878, the high-water mark of the movement, the Greenback-Laborites polled over a million votes and elected fourteen members of Congress. In the presidential election of 1880 the Greenbackers ran General James B. Weaver, an old Granger who spoke to perhaps a half-million citizens but polled only 3 percent of the popular vote.

The Background of Populism

A striking manifestation of rural discontent came through the Farmers' Alliance, founded in Texas in the late 1870s. Farmers came together in the Alliance to socialize, but more importantly to break the strangling grip of the railroads and manufacturers through cooperative buying and selling. Local chapters spread throughout the South and the Great Plains during the 1880s, until by 1890 members numbered more than a million hard-bitten rural folks.

Unfortunately, the Alliance weakened itself by ignoring the plight of landless tenant farmers, sharecroppers, and farmworkers. Even more debilitating was the Alliance's exclusion of blacks, who counted for nearly half the agricultural population of the South. In the 1880s a separate Colored Farmers' National Alliance emerged to attract black farmers, and by 1890 membership numbered more than 250,000. The long history of racial division in the South, however, made it difficult for white and black farmers to work together in the same organization.

A new grouping—the People's party—began to emerge spectacularly in the early 1890s. Better known as the Populists, these zealous folk attracted countless recruits from the Farmers' Alliances. The higher the foreclosure rate on mortgages, the deeper was the anger of the farmers. Numerous fiery prophets sprang forward to lead the Populists. Among these assorted characters loomed an eloquent red-haired "spellbinder," Ignatius Donnelly of Minnesota, who was three times elected to Congress.

The queen of the "calamity howlers" was undeniably Mary Elizabeth ("Mary Yellin' ") Lease, a tall, athletically built woman who was called "the Kansas Pythoness." In 1890 she made an estimated 160 speeches denouncing Wall Street and reportedly cried that Kansans should raise "less corn and more hell." The big-city New York *Evening Post* snarled, "We don't want any more states until we can civilize Kansas." To many easterners, complaint, not corn, was the westerners' chief crop.

Yet the Populists, despite their peculiarities, were not to be laughed aside. In deadly earnest, they were leading an impassioned crusade to relieve the misfortunes of the farmer. Smiles faded from Republican and Democratic faces alike as countless thousands of Populists began to sing, "Good-bye, My Party, Good-bye."

Populists burst dramatically onto the political scene in the campaign of 1892. Rooted in the Farmers' Alliances of the West and South, the Populists adopted a scorching platform at their wildly enthusiastic convention in Omaha. It demanded the unlimited coinage of silver, a graduated income tax, and government ownership of the telephone, telegraph, and railroads.

The Populists gathered in Omaha also chose the eloquent old Greenbacker, General James B. Weaver, as their presidential candidate in 1892. Campaigning vigorously, Weaver remarkably garnered over a million votes and 22 electoral votes. The new party's strength came primarily from six states in the Midwest and West. Although they attempted to reach a national audience concerned about the trusts, the Populists proved unable to reach beyond their rural and regional base.

Coxey's Army and the Pullman Strike

The panic of 1893 and the long, severe depression that followed strengthened the arguments of Populists and other reformers that farmers and laborers were being ground under by an oppressive economic and political system. Ragged armies of the unemployed, victims of the depression, began demonstrating to protest their grievances and demand help.

The most famous of these marches was that of "General" Jacob S. Coxey, a wealthy Ohio quarry owner, who started for Washington in 1894 with several score of supporters. His platform included a demand that the government relieve unemployment by an inflationary public works program, supported by some $500 million in legal tender notes, to be issued by the Treasury. Coxey himself rode in a carriage with his wife and infant son, while his tiny "army" tramped along behind, singing:

> We're coming, Grover Cleveland,
>   500,000 strong,
> We're marching on to Washington
>   to right the nation's wrong.

The "Commonweal Army" of Coxeyites finally straggled into the nation's capital. But the "invasion" took on the aspects of a comic opera when "General" Coxey and his "lieutenants" were arrested for walking on the grass.

Violent flare-ups accompanied labor protests, notably in Chicago. Most frightening was the crippling Pullman strike of 1894 in Chicago. Eugene V. Debs, an impetuous but personally lovable labor leader, had helped organize the American Railway Union of about 150,000 members. The Pullman Palace Car Company, which maintained a model town near Chicago for its employees, was hit hard by the depression and cut wages about one-third, while holding the line on rent for company houses. The workers finally struck—in some places overturning Pullman cars—and paralyzed railway traffic from Chicago to the Pacific Coast.

The turmoil in Chicago was serious but not completely out of hand. At least this was the judgment of Governor Altgeld of Illinois, a friend of the downtrodden who had pardoned the Haymarket Square anarchists the year before (see p. 361). But Attorney General Richard Olney, an arch-conservative and an ex-railroad attorney, urged the dispatch of federal troops on the legal grounds that the strikers were interfering with the transit of the United States mail. Cleveland supported Olney, with the ringing declaration, "If it takes the entire army and navy to deliver a postal card in Chicago, that card will be delivered."

To the delight of conservatives, the Pullman strike was crushed by bayonet-supported intervention from Washington. Debs and his leading associates, who had defied a federal court injunction to cease striking, were sentenced to six months' imprisonment for contempt of court. The lean labor agitator spent much of his enforced leisure reading radical literature, which had much to do with his later leadership of the Socialist movement in America.

Embittered cries of "government by injunction" now burst from organized labor. This was the first time that such a legal weapon had been used conspicuously by Washington to break a strike, and it was all the more distasteful because defiant laborites who were held in contempt could be imprisoned without jury trial. Signs multiplied that employers were striving to smash labor unions by court action. Nonlabor elements of the country, including the Populists and

other debtors, were likewise incensed. They saw in the brutal Pullman episode further proof of an unholy alliance between big business and the courts.

Golden McKinley and Silver Bryan

The long-standing grievances of the farmers and laborers, aggravated by the immediate sufferings of depression, gave ominous significance to the election of 1896. Discontented, indebted farmers and unemployed workers looked for political salvation, while defenders of the status quo feared upheaval.

The leading candidate for the Republican presidential nomination was former Congressman William McKinley of Ohio, sponsor of the ill-starred tariff bill of 1890 (see p. 344). He had established a creditable Civil War record, having risen to the rank of major; he hailed from the electorally potent state of Ohio; and he could point to long years of honorable service in Congress, where he had made a great many friends by his kindly and conciliatory manner.

As a presidential candidate, McKinley was the creation of a fellow Ohioan, Marcus Alonzo Hanna. The latter had made his fortune in the iron business and now coveted the role of president-maker. As a wholehearted Hamiltonian, Hanna believed that a prime function of government was to aid business. As a conservative in business, he was a confirmed "standpatter," content not to rock the boat. He believed that in some measure prosperity "trickled down" to the laborer, whose dinner pail was full when business flourished. Critics assailed this idea as equivalent to feeding the horses in order to feed the sparrows.

The hardheaded Hanna, although something of a novice in politics, organized his preconvention campaign for McKinley with consummate skill and with a liberal outpouring of his own money. The convention steamroller, well lubricated with Hanna's dollars, nominated McKinley on the first ballot at St. Louis in June 1896. The Republican platform declared for the gold standard, even though McKinley's voting record in Congress had been embarrassingly friendly to silver.

Dissension riddled the Democratic camp. Cleveland no longer led his party; dubbed "the Stuffed Prophet," he was undeniably the most unpopular man in the country. Labor-debtor groups remembered too vividly the silver-purchase repeal, the Pullman strike, and the backstairs Morgan bond deal. Ultraconservative in finance, Cleveland was now more a Republican than a Democrat on the silver issue.

Rudderless, the Democratic convention met in Chicago in July 1896, with the silverites in command. Shouting insults at the absent Cleveland, they refused even to endorse their own administration. They had the enthusiasm and the numbers; all they lacked was a leader.

A new Moses suddenly appeared in the person of William Jennings Bryan of Nebraska. Then only thirty-six years of age and known as "the Boy Orator of the Platte,"* he stepped confidently onto the platform before fifteen thousand people. His masterful presence was set off by handsome features, a smooth-shaven jaw, and raven-black hair. He radiated honesty, sincerity, and energy. He had a good mind but not a brilliant one; he was less a student of books than of human nature; and he possessed broad human sympathies.

In Chicago the setting was made to order for a magnificent oratorical effort. A hush fell over the convention as Bryan stood before it. With an organlike voice that rolled into the outer corners of the huge hall, he delivered a fervent plea for silver. Rising to supreme heights of eloquence, he thundered, "We will answer their demands for a gold standard by saying to them: 'You shall not press down upon the brow of labor this crown of thorns, you shall not crucify mankind upon a cross of gold.' "

The Cross of Gold speech was a sensation. Swept off its feet in a tumultuous scene, the Democratic convention nominated Bryan the next day on the fifth ballot. The platform declared for the unlimited coinage of silver at the ratio of 16 ounces of silver to 1 ounce of gold, though the market ratio was about 32 to 1. This meant that the silver in a dollar would be worth about fifty cents.

Democratic "Gold Bugs," unable to swallow Bryan, bolted their party over the silver issue. A conservative senator from New York, when asked if he was a Democrat still, reportedly replied, "Yes, I am a Democrat still—*very* still." The Democratic minority, including Cleveland, charged that the Populist-silverites had stolen both the name and the clothes of their party. They nominated a lost-cause ticket of their own, and many of them, including Cleveland, hoped for a McKinley victory.

Populists were left out in the cold, for the Democratic majority had appropriated their main plank—"16 to 1," that "heaven-born ratio." The bulk of the Populists, fearing a hard-money McKinley victory, endorsed Bryan for president, sacrificing their identity in the process. Singing "The Jolly Silver Dollar of the Dads," they became in effect the "Demo-Pop" party. But many of the original Populists refused to support Bryan and went down with their colors nailed to the mast.

The Sacrilegious Candidate *A hostile cartoonist makes sport of Bryan's notorious Cross of Gold speech in 1896.*

---

* One contemporary sneered that Bryan, like the Platte River, was "six inches deep and six miles wide at the mouth."

William Jennings Bryan, 1896   *The premier orator of his day, the spellbinding speaker was the presidential candidate of both the Democratic and Populist parties in 1896.*

Class Conflict: Plowholders Versus Bondholders

Mark Hanna smugly assumed that he could make the tariff the focus of the campaign. But Bryan, a dynamo of energy, forced the free-trade issue into a back seat when he took to the stump in behalf of free silver. Sweeping through twenty-seven states and traveling 18,000 miles, he made between five and six hundred speeches—thirty-six in one day—and even invaded the East, "the enemy's country." Vachel Lindsay caught the spirit of his oratorical orgy:

Prairie avenger, mountain lion,
Bryan, Bryan, Bryan, Bryan,
Gigantic troubadour, speaking like a siege gun,
Smashing Plymouth rock with his boulders
    from the West.*

William Jennings Bryan created panic among eastern conservatives with his threat of converting their holdings overnight into fifty-cent dollars. "In God we trust, with Bryan we bust," the Republicans sneered. Widespread fear of Bryan and the "silver lunacy" enabled "Dollar Mark" Hanna, now chairman of the Republican National Committee, to shine as a money-raiser. He "shook down" the trusts and plutocrats, and piled up an enormous "slush fund" for a "campaign of education"—or of propaganda, depending on one's point of view. The Republicans amassed the most formidable political campaign chest thus far in American history. At all levels—national, state, and local—it amounted to about $16 million, as contrasted with about $1 million for the poorer Democrats (roughly "16 to 1"). With some justification, the Bryanites accused Hanna of "buying" the election and of floating McKinley into the White House on a tidal wave of greenbacks. The Republicans definitely had the edge in money and mud.

Bryan's cyclonic campaign, launched with irresistible enthusiasm, began to lose steam as the weeks passed. Fear was probably the strongest ally of Hanna, and the worst enemy of Bryan, who allegedly had "silver on the brain." Some Republican businesspeople threatened layoffs or wage reductions if Bryan triumphed. Such were some of the "dirty tricks" of the "Stop Bryan, Save America" crusade.

Hanna's campaign methods paid off, for on election day McKinley triumphed decisively. The vote was 271 to 176 in the Electoral College, and 7,102,246 to 6,492,559 in the popular column. Driven by fear, hope, and excitement, an unprecedented outpouring of voters flocked to the polls. McKinley ran strongly in the populous East, where he carried every county of New England, and in the upper

---

* Reprinted with permission of Macmillan Publishing Company, Inc., from *Collected Poems*, by Vachel Lindsay. Copyright 1920 by Macmillan Publishing Company, Inc., renewed 1948 by Elizabeth C. Lindsay.

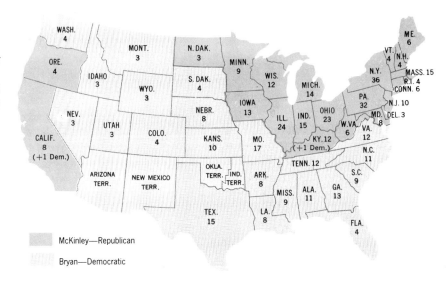

Presidential Election of 1896 (with electoral vote by state) *This election tolled the death knell of the Gilded Age political system, with its razor-close elections, strong party loyalties, and high voter turnouts. For years after 1896, Republicans predominated, and citizens showed declining interest in either joining parties or voting.*

McKinley—Republican

Bryan—Democratic

Mississippi Valley. Bryan's states, concentrated in the debt-burdened South and the trans-Mississippi West, involved more acreage than McKinley's but less population.

The free-silver election of 1896 was probably the most significant since Lincoln's victories in 1860 and 1864. Despite Bryan's strength in the South and West, the results vividly demonstrated his lack of appeal to the unmortgaged farmer and especially the eastern urban laborer. Many wage earners in the East voted for their jobs and full dinner pails, threatened as they were by free silver, free trade, and fireless factories. Living precariously on a fixed wage, the factory workers had no reason to favor inflation, which was the heart of the Bryanites' program.

The Bryan-McKinley battle heralded the advent of a new era in American politics. The outcome was a resounding victory for big business, the big cities, middle-class values, and financial conservatism. Bryan's defeat marked the last serious effort to win the White House with mostly agrarian votes. The future of presidential politics lay not on the farms, with their dwindling population, but in the mushrooming cities.

The smashing Republican victory of 1896 also heralded a Republican grip on the White House for sixteen consecutive years—indeed, for all but eight of the next thirty-six years. McKinley's election thus imparted new character to the American political system. The reign of Republican political dominance that it

ushered in was accompanied by diminishing voter participation in elections, a weakening of party organizations, and the fading away of issues like the money question and civil-service reform, which came to be replaced by concern for industrial regulation and the welfare of labor. Scholars have dubbed this new political era the period of the "fourth party system."*

Republican Standpattism Enthroned

An eminently "safe" McKinley took the inaugural oath in 1897. Though a man of considerable ability, he was an ear-to-the-ground politician who seldom got far out of line with majority opinion. His cautious, conservative nature caused him to shy away from the flaming banner of reform. Business was given a free

---

*The first party system, marked by doubts about the very legitimacy of parties, embraced the Federalist-Republican clashes of the 1790s and early 1800s. The second party system took shape with the emergence of mass-based politics in the Jacksonian era, pitting Democrats against Whigs. The third party system was characterized by the precarious equilibrium between Republicans and Democrats, as well as the high electoral participation, that lasted from the end of the Civil War to McKinley's election. The fourth party system is described above. The fifth party system emerged in Franklin Roosevelt's New Deal, which initiated a long period of Democratic ascendancy. Each "system," except the fifth, lasted about forty years. Debate continues as to whether the nation has entered or is about to enter the era of the sixth party system.

rein, and the trusts, which had trusted him in 1896, were allowed to develop more mighty muscles without serious restraints.

As soon as McKinley took office, the tariff issue, which had played second fiddle to silver in the "Battle of '96," quickly forced itself to the fore. In due course the Dingley Tariff Bill was jammed through the House in 1897. The proposed new rates were high, but not enough to satisfy the paunchy lobbyists, who once again descended on the Senate. Over 850 amendments were tacked onto the overburdened bill. The resulting piece of patchwork finally established the average rates at 46.5 percent, substantially higher than the Democratic Wilson-Gorman Act of 1894. (See the chart in the Appendix.)

With the return of prosperity under McKinley in 1897, the money issue that had dominated politics and economics since the Civil War gradually faded.

The Gold Standard Act of 1900, passed over last-ditch silverite opposition, provided that paper currency was to be freely redeemed in gold. Electrifying discoveries of new gold deposits in Canada (Klondike), Alaska, South Africa, and Australia, along with new gold-extracting processes, created moderate inflation and finally took care of the currency needs of an explosively expanding nation.

In retrospect, a controlled expansion of American currency in the 1880s and 1890s was clearly desirable. Agrarian debtors had a good cause: relief from social and economic hardship through an inflation of the dollar supply. But the free-silver fixation not only discredited the case for needed currency expansion but seriously set back the movement for agrarian reform. The tide of "silver heresy" rapidly receded, and the "Popocratic" fish were left gasping high and dry on a golden-sanded beach.

Chronology

1858	Pike's Peak gold rush.
1859	Nevada Comstock lode discovered.
1862	Homestead Act.
1864	Sand Creek massacre. Nevada admitted to the Union.
1867	National Grange organized.
1876	Battle of Little Big Horn. Colorado admitted to the Union.
1877	Nez Percé Indian war.
1881	Helen Hunt Jackson publishes *A Century of Dishonor*.
1884	Federal government outlaws Indian Sun Dance.
1885–1890	Farmers' Alliances formed.
1887	Dawes Severalty Act.
1889	Oklahoma opened to settlement.
1889–1890	North Dakota, South Dakota, Montana, Washington, Idaho, and Wyoming admitted to the Union.
1890	Census Bureau declares frontier line ended. Emergence of People's party (Populists). Battle of Wounded Knee.
1893	Frederick Jackson Turner publishes "The Significance of the Frontier in American History."
1894	Coxey's "Commonweal Army" marches on Washington. Pullman strike.
1896	McKinley defeats Bryan for presidency. Utah admitted to the Union.
1907	Oklahoma admitted to the Union.
1924	Indians granted U.S. citizenship.
1934	Indian Reorganization Act.

Was the West Really "Won"?

For more than half a century, the Turner thesis dominated historical writing about the West. In his essay, "The Significance of the Frontier in American History," historian Frederick Jackson Turner argued that the American national character had been uniquely shaped by the westward movement. The struggle to overcome the hazards of the western wilderness had transformed Europeans into tough, inventive, and self-reliant Americans.

Written just three years after the superintendent of the census declared the frontier closed, Turner's hypothesis is surely among the most provocative statements ever made about formative influences on the nation's development and character. But as the frontier era recedes ever further into the past, scholars are less persuaded that Turner's thesis adequately explains the character of American society and its differences from Europe.

Modern scholars like historian David Weber suggest that the line of the frontier did not define the quavering edge of "civilization," but rather marked the boundary between diverse and equally legitimate cultures. The frontier should therefore be understood as the principal site of the interaction between those cultures.

Several so-called New Western historians take this argument still further. Scholars such as Patricia Nelson Limerick, Richard White, and Donald Worster suggest that the cultural and ecological damage inflicted by advancing "civilization" must be reckoned with in any final accounting of what these pioneers accomplished. These same scholars insist that the West did not lose its regional identity after 1890 and is still a unique part of the national mosaic, a region whose history, culture, and identity remain every bit as distinctive as those of New England or the Old South.

But where Turner saw the frontier as the principal shaper of the region's character, the New Western historians emphasize the effects of ethnic and racial confrontation, topography, climate, and the roles of government and big business as the factors that have made the modern West. The pioneer "conquests" of Native Americans and Hispanics were less than complete, they contend, and the West therefore remains, uniquely among American regions, an unsettled arena of commingling and competition among these groups. Moreover, in these accounts the West's distinctively challenging climate and geography yielded to human habitation not through the efforts of heroic individual pioneers, but only through massive corporate—and especially federal government—investments in projects like the transcontinental railroads and irrigation systems.

SUGGESTED READINGS

Primary Source Documents

Black Elk Speaks, edited by John G. Neihardt (1932), is an eloquent Indian statement about the Sioux experience. Indian perspectives on the westward movement can be found in Jerome A. Greene, ed., *Lakota and Cheyenne: Indian Views of the Great Sioux Wars, 1876–1877** (1994). ˙eodore Roosevelt, *Hunting Trips of a Ranchman**

(1885), offers the future president's views on the Indian question. Mary Lease's famous call to arms is recorded in William E. Connelley, ed., *History of Kansas, State and People** (1928).

Secondary Sources

Vivacious chapters appear in Ray A. Billington, *Westward Expansion* (rev. ed., 1974). Walter Prescott Webb, *The Great Plains* (1931), is a classic. Robert V. Hine, *The Amer-*

ican West (2nd ed., 1984), is a useful survey. Patricia Nelson Limerick traces regional themes across time in *Legacy of Conquest: The Unbroken Past of the American West* (1987). Richard White's fresh account, *"It's Your Misfortune and None of My Own": A New History of the American West* (1991), emphasizes the role of the federal government, corporations, and the market economy in the region's development and pays special attention to the twentieth century. Women in the West are discussed in Glenda Riley, *The Female Frontier: A Comparative View of Women on the Prairie and Plains* (1988), and Beverly Beeton, *Women Vote in the West: The Woman Suffrage Movement, 1869–1896* (1986). Native Americans are discussed in Robert Utley, *The Indian Frontier of the American West, 1846–1890* (1984), and in Dee Brown's *Bury My Heart at Wounded Knee: An Indian History of the American West* (1970). Two intriguing studies of cross-cultural perception are Robert F. Berkhofer, Jr., *The White Man's Indian* (1978), and Richard Drinnon, *Facing West: The Metaphysics of Indian Hating and Empire Building* (1980). A sweeping look at Chicano history is Juan Gómez-Quiñones, *Roots of Chicano Politics, 1600–1940* (1994). David Alan Johnson explores *Founding the Far West: California, Oregon, and Nevada, 1840–1890* (1992). William Cronon explores the relationship between Chicago and the development of the "Great West" in *Nature's Metropolis* (1991), a book nicely complemented by John C. Hudson, *Making the Corn Belt* (1994). For Hispanics in the West see David J. Weber, *The Spanish Frontier in North America* (1992). Kevin Starr probes the cultural history of California in both *Americans and the California Dream, 1850–1915* (1973) and *Inventing the Dream: California Through the Progressive Era* (1985). A powerful work on the farmers' protest is Lawrence Goodwyn, *Democratic Promise* (1976), abridged as *The Populist Moment* (1978). See also Bruce Palmer, *"Man over Money": The Southern Populist Critique of American Capitalism* (1980). The election of 1896 is examined in Robert F. Durden, *The Climax of Populism: The Election of 1896* (1965), and Stanley L. Jones, *The Presidential Election of 1896* (1964). Also informative are Paul W. Glad, *McKinley, Bryan and the People* (1964), and H. Wayne Morgan, *William McKinley and His America* (1963). Three intriguing cultural histories of the period are Alan Trachtenberg, *The Incorporation of America: Culture and Society in the Gilded Age* (1982); Richard Slotkin, *The Fatal Environment: The Myth of the Frontier in American History, 1800–1890* (1985); and Lawrence Levine, *Highbrow/Lowbrow: The Emergence of Cultural Hierarchy in America* (1988).

---

* An asterisk indicates that the document, or an excerpt from it, can be found in Thomas A. Bailey and David M. Kennedy, eds., *The American Spirit: United States History as Seen by Contemporaries*, 9th ed. (Boston: Houghton Mifflin, 1998).

PART FIVE

Struggling for Justice at Home and Abroad

The new century brought astonishing changes to America. Victory in the Spanish-American War made it clear that the United States was a world power. Industrialization ushered in giant corporations, sprawling factories, sweatshop labor, and the ubiquitous automobile. A huge wave of immigration was altering the face of the nation, especially the cities, where a majority of Americans lived by 1920. With bigger cities came bigger fears—of crime, vice, poverty, and disease.

Changes of such magnitude raised vexing questions. What role should the United States play in the world? How could the enormous power of industry be controlled? How would the millions of new immigrants make their way in America? What should the country do about poverty, disease, and the continuing plague of racial inequality? All these issues turned on a fundamental point: should government remain narrowly limited in its powers, or did the times require a more potent government that would actively shape society and secure American interests abroad?

The progressive movement represented the first attempt to answer those questions. Reform-minded men and women from all walks of life and from both major parties shared in the progressive crusade for greater government activism. Buoyed by this outlook, Presidents Theodore Roosevelt, William Howard Taft, and Woodrow Wilson enlarged the capacity of government to fight graft, "bust" business trusts, regulate corporations, and promote fair labor practices, child welfare, conservation, and consumer protection. Progressive reformers, convinced that women would bring greater morality to politics, bolstered the decades-long struggle for female suffrage. Women finally secured the vote in 1920 with the ratification of the Nineteenth Amendment.

Progressive-era presidents also challenged America's tradition of isolationism in foreign policy. They felt the country had a moral obligation to spread democracy and an economic opportunity to reap profits in foreign markets. Roosevelt and Taft launched diplomatic initiatives in the Caribbean, Central America, and East Asia. Wilson aspired to "make the world safe for democracy" by rallying support for American intervention in the First World War.

The progressive spirit waned, however, as the United States retreated during the 1920s into what President Harding called "normalcy." Isolationist sentiment revived with a vengeance. Blessed with a booming economy, Americans turned their gaze inward to baseball heroes, radio, jazz, movies, and the first mass-produced American automobile, the Model T Ford. Presidents Harding, Coolidge, and Hoover backed off from the economic regulatory zeal of their predecessors.

"Normalcy" also had a brutal side. Thousands of suspected radicals were jailed or deported in the red scare of 1919 and 1920. Anti-immigrant passions flared until immigration quotas in 1924 squeezed the flow of newcomers to a trickle. Race riots scorched several northern cities in the summer of 1919, a sign of how embittered race relations had become in the wake of the "great migration" of southern blacks to wartime jobs in northern industry. A reborn Ku Klux Klan staged a comeback, not just in the South but in the North and West as well.

"Normalcy" itself soon proved short-lived, a casualty of the stock-market crash of 1929 and the Great Depression that followed. As Americans watched banks fail, businesses collapse, and millions of people lose their jobs, they asked with renewed urgency what role the government should play in res-

cuing the nation. President Franklin D. Roosevelt's answer was the "New Deal"—an ambitious array of relief programs, public works, and economic regulations that failed to cure the Depression but furnished an impressive legacy of social reforms.

Most Americans came to accept an expanded federal governmental role at home under FDR's leadership in the 1930s, but they still clung stubbornly to isolationism. The United States did little in the 1930s to check the rising military aggression of Japan and Germany. By the early 1940s events forced Americans to reconsider. Once Hitler's Germany had seized control of most of Europe, Roosevelt, who had long opposed the isolationists, found ways to aid a beleaguered Britain. When Japan attacked the American naval base at Pearl Harbor in December 1941, isolationists at last fell silent. Roosevelt led a stunned but determined nation into the Second World War, and victory in 1945 positioned the United States to assume a commanding position in the postwar world order.

The Great Depression and the Second World War brought to a head a half-century of debate over the role of government and the place of the United States in the world. In the name of a struggle for justice, FDR established a new era of government activism at home and internationalism abroad. The New Deal's legacy set the terms of debate in American political life for the rest of the century.

28

****

The Path of Empire,
1890–1909

******

We assert that no nation can long endure half republic and half empire, and we warn the American people that imperialism abroad will lead quickly and inevitably to despotism at home.

******

DEMOCRATIC NATIONAL PLATFORM, 1900

Imperialist Stirrings

From the end of the Civil War to the 1880s, the indifference of most Americans to the outside world was almost unbelievable. But then in the sunset decades of the nineteenth century, a momentous shift occurred in U.S. foreign policy. The new diplomacy mirrored the far-reaching changes that were reshaping industry, agriculture, and the social structure.

The Republic was becoming increasingly outward looking as exports of both manufactured goods and agricultural products shot up. Many Americans believed the United States had to expand or explode. Their country was bursting with a new sense of power generated by the booming increase in population, wealth, and industrial production—and it was trembling from the hammer blows of labor violence and agrarian unrest. Overseas markets might provide a safety valve to relieve such pressures.

Other forces also stimulated overseas expansion. The lurid "yellow press" of Joseph Pulitzer and William Randolph Hearst whetted the popular taste for excitement abroad. Missionaries, inspired by books like the Reverend Josiah Strong's *Our Country: Its Possible Future and Its Present Crisis,* looked overseas for new fields to till. Strong trumpeted the superiority of Anglo-Saxon civilization and summoned Americans to spread their religion and their civilization to "backward" peoples. At the same time, aggressive Americans like Theodore Roosevelt and

The Imperial Menu *A pleased Uncle Sam gets ready to place his order with headwaiter William McKinley. Swallowing some of these possessions eventually produced political indigestion.*

Congressman Henry Cabot Lodge were interpreting Darwinism to mean that the earth belonged to the strong and fit—that is, to Uncle Sam. This view was strengthened as latecomers to the colonial scramble scooped up leavings from the banquet table of earlier diners. If America was to survive in the competition of modern nation-states, perhaps it, too, would have to become an imperial power.

The development of a new steel navy also focused attention overseas. Captain Alfred Thayer Mahan's book of 1890, *The Influence of Sea Power upon History, 1660–1783*, argued that control of the sea was the key to world dominance. Mahan helped stimulate the naval race among the great powers that gained momentum around the turn of the century. Red-blooded Americans joined in the demands for a mightier navy and for an American-built isthmian canal between the Atlantic and the Pacific.

America's new international interest manifested itself in a number of diplomatic crises or near-wars in the late 1880s and early 1890s. The American and German navies nearly came to blows in 1889 over the faraway Samoan Islands in the South Pacific. The lynching of eleven Italians in New Orleans in 1891 brought America and Italy to the brink of war, until the United States agreed to pay compensation. In the ugliest affair, American demands on Chile after the deaths of two American sailors in the port of Valparaiso in 1892 made hostilities between the two countries seem inevitable. The threat of attack by Chile's modern navy spread alarm on the Pacific Coast, until American power finally forced the Chileans to pay an indemnity. A simmering argument between the United States and Canada over seal hunting near the Pribilof Islands off the coast of Alaska was resolved by arbitration in 1893. The willingness of Americans to risk war over such distant and minor disputes demonstrated the aggressive new national mood.

This new American belligerence combined with old-time anti-British feeling to create a serious crisis between the United States and Britain in 1895–1896. The jungle boundary between British Guiana and Venezuela had long been in dispute, but the discovery of gold in the contested area brought the conflict to a head. President Cleveland and his pugnacious secretary of state, Richard Olney, stepped into the affair with a smashing note to Britain that invoked the Monroe Doctrine.

British officials, unimpressed, shrugged off Olney's lengthy salvo as just another twist of the lion's tail and declared that the affair was none of America's business. President Cleveland—"mad clear through," as he put it—sent a bristling special message to Congress that called for a U.S. commission to determine where the line ought to go. Then, he implied, if the British would not accept the rightful boundary, the United States would fight for it. The entire country, irrespective of political party, was swept off its feet in an outburst of hysteria.

Fortunately, sober second thoughts prevailed on both sides of the Atlantic. Shifts in the European balance of power had left Britain in a state of insecure isolation, and an American war would be a disaster. London backed off and consented to arbitrate the Venezuelan dispute. The chastened British, their eyes wide open to the European peril, inaugurated an era of "patting the Eagle's head," which replaced a century or so of America's "twisting the lion's tail." Sometimes called the Great Rapprochement—or reconciliation—between the United States and Britain, the new Anglo-American cordiality became a cornerstone of both nations' foreign policies as the twentieth century opened.

Spurning the Hawaiian Pear

Enchanted Hawaii had early attracted the attention of Americans. In the morning years of the nineteenth century, the breeze-brushed islands were a way station and provisioning point for Yankee shippers, sailors, and whalers. In 1820 came the first New England missionaries, who preached the twin blessings of Protestant Christianity and protective calico. Americans gradually came to regard the Hawaiian Islands as a virtual extension of their own coastline. The State Department, beginning in the 1840s, sternly warned other powers to keep their hands off the islands. America's grip was further tightened in 1887 by a treaty with the native government guaranteeing priceless naval-base rights at spacious Pearl Harbor.

But trouble, both economic and political, was brewing in the languid insular paradise. Sugar cultivation went sour in 1890 when the McKinley Tariff ~cted barriers against the Hawaiian product. White planters' ambitions were blocked by the strong-willed Queen Liliuokalani, who insisted that native Hawaiians should control the islands. Desperate whites, though only a tiny minority, organized a successful revolt early in 1893. It was openly assisted by American troops, who landed under the unauthorized orders of the expansionist American minister in Honolulu. "The Hawaiian pear is now fully ripe," he wrote exultantly to his superiors in Washington, "and this is the golden hour for the United States to pluck it."

A treaty of annexation was rushed to Washington, but before it could be railroaded through the Senate, Republican President Harrison's term expired and Democratic President Cleveland came in. Suspecting that his powerful nation had gravely wronged the deposed Queen Liliuokalani, "Old Grover" abruptly withdrew the treaty. When the subsequent probe revealed the damning fact that a majority of the Hawaiian natives did not favor annexation at all, the sugarcoated move for annexation had to be abandoned. The Hawaiian pear continued to ripen until 1898.

War with Spain over Cuba

Cuba's masses, frightfully misgoverned, again rose against their Spanish oppressors in 1895. The roots of their revolt were partly economic. Sugar production—the backbone of the island's prosperity—was crippled when the American tariff of 1894 restored high duties on the toothsome product.

Driven to desperation, the insurgents adopted a scorched-earth policy, torching cane fields and sugar mills and even dynamiting passenger trains. American sympathies went out to the Cuban underdogs. Aside from pure sentiment, the United States had an investment stake of about $50 million in Cuba and an annual trade stake of about $100 million.

Fuel was added to the Cuban conflagration in 1896 with the coming of the Spanish General ("Butcher") Weyler. He undertook to crush the rebellion by herding many civilians into barbed-wire reconcentration camps, where they could not give assistance to the armed *insurrectos*. Lacking proper sanitation, these enclosures turned into deadly pestholes; the victims died like dogs.

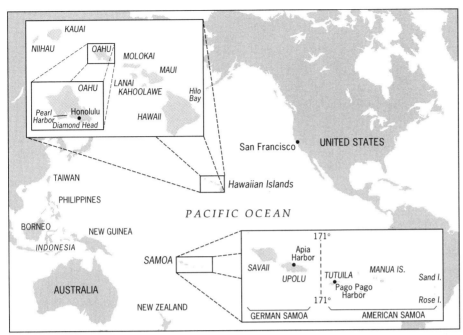

The Pacific   *The enlargements show the Hawaiian Islands and the Samoas, both areas of American imperialistic activity in the late nineteenth century.*

The atrocities in Cuba were made to order for the sensational new yellow journalism. William R. Hearst and Joseph Pulitzer, then engaged in a titanic duel for circulation, attempted to outdo each other with screeching headlines and hair-raising "scoops." Lesser competitors zestfully followed suit.

Where atrocity stories did not exist, they were invented. Hearst sent the gifted artist Frederic Remington to Cuba to draw sketches, and when the latter reported that conditions were not bad enough to warrant hostilities, Hearst is alleged to have replied, "You furnish the pictures and I'll furnish the war." Among other outrages, Remington depicted Spanish customs officials brutally disrobing and searching an American woman. Most readers of Hearst's *Journal*, their indignation soaring, had no way of knowing that such tasks were performed by female attendants.

Early in 1898 Washington sent the battleship *Maine* to Cuba, ostensibly for a "friendly visit" but actually to protect and evacuate Americans if a dangerous flare-up should again occur. Tragedy struck on February 15, 1898, when the *Maine* mysteriously blew up in Havana harbor, with a loss of 260 officers and men.

Two investigations of the iron coffin were undertaken, one by U.S. naval officers, the other by Spanish officials. The Spanish commission stated that the explosion had been internal and presumably accidental; the American commission reported that the blast had been caused by a submarine mine. Not until 1976 did Admiral Hyman G. Rickover, under U.S. Navy auspices, present overwhelming evidence that the initial explosion had resulted from spontaneous combustion in one of the coal bunkers adjacent to a powder magazine. Ironically, this is essentially what the Spanish commission had deduced in 1898.

But Americans in 1898, now war-mad, blindly accepted the unlikely explanation of Spanish government treachery. The battle cry of the hour became:

> Remember the *Maine!*
> To hell with Spain!

Nothing would do but to hurl the "dirty" Spanish flag from the hemisphere.

The Explosion of the *Maine*, February 15, 1898   *Encouraged and amplified by the "yellow press," the outcry over the tragedy of the* Maine *helped drive the country into an impulsive war against Spain.*

The national war fever burned higher, even though American diplomats had already gained Madrid's agreement to Washington's two basic demands: a revocation of reconcentration and an armistice with the Cuban rebels. The cautious McKinley did not want hostilities. Neither did Mark Hanna and Wall Street, for war might unsettle business. As "Wobbly Willy" McKinley hesitated, the jingoistic yellow press and the frenzied public denounced him. Fight-hungry Theodore Roosevelt snarled that the "white-livered" occupant of the White House did not have "the backbone of a chocolate eclair."

The president, recognizing the inevitable, finally yielded and gave the people what they wanted.

McKinley also perceived that the Democrats would make political capital out of his resistance to war, and it seemed to him better to break up the remnants of Spain's empire than to break up the Grand Old Party. On April 11, 1898, McKinley sent his war message to Congress, urging armed intervention to free the oppressed Cubans. The legislators responded uproariously with what was essentially a declaration of war. In a burst of self-righteousness, they likewise adopted the hand-tying Teller Amendment. This proviso proclaimed to the world that when America had overthrown Spanish misrule, it would give the Cubans their freedom—a declaration that caused imperialistic Europeans to smile skeptically.

Dewey's May Day Victory at Manila

The American people plunged into the war light-heartedly, like schoolchildren off to a picnic. Bands blared incessantly "There'll Be a Hot Time in the Old Town Tonight" and "Hail, Hail, the Gang's All Here," thus leading foreigners to believe that those were the national anthems.

But such jubilation seemed premature to European observers. Except for ally-seeking Britain, the Old World powers generally favored Spain in the war, and they looked with skepticism on America's unprepared army and small navy. But the new American steel navy, now fifteen years old and ranking fifth among the fleets of the world, was in fairly good trim, though the war was to lay bare serious defects.

The war got off to a splendid start for American forces. On February 25, 1898, while navy secretary John Long was away for a weekend, assistant secretary of the navy Theodore Roosevelt cabled Commodore George Dewey to send the American Asian squadron to Spain's Philippines in the event of war. Dewey carried out his orders magnificently on May 1, 1898. Sailing boldly with his six warships at night into the fortified harbor of Manila, he trained his guns the next morning on the Spanish fleet. The entire collection of antiquated and overmatched vessels was quickly destroyed, with a loss of nearly four hundred Spaniards killed and wounded and without the loss of a single life in Dewey's fleet.

Taciturn George Dewey became a national hero overnight. An amateur poet blossomed forth with

> Oh, dewy was the morning
> Upon the first of May,
> And Dewey was the Admiral
> Down in Manila Bay,
> And dewy were the Spaniards' eyes,
> Them orbs of black and blue;
> And dew we feel discouraged?
> I dew not think we dew!

Yet Dewey was in a perilous position. He had destroyed the enemy fleet, but he could not storm the forts of Manila with his sailors. His nerves frayed, he was forced to wait in the steaming-hot bay while troop reinforcements were slowly assembled in America. The appearance of German warships in Manila harbor added to the tension.

Long-awaited American troops, finally arriving in force, captured Manila on August 13, 1898. They collaborated with the Filipino insurgents, commanded by their well-educated leader, Emilio Aguinaldo. Dewey, to his later regret, had brought this shrewd and magnetic revolutionist from exile in Asia so that he might weaken Spanish resistance.

These thrilling events in the Philippines had meanwhile focused attention on Hawaii. An impression spread that America needed the archipelago as a coaling and provisioning way station in order to send supplies and reinforcements to Dewey. A joint resolution of annexation was rushed through Congress and approved by McKinley on July 7, 1898.

The Confused Invasion of Cuba

Shortly after the outbreak of war, the Spanish government ordered a fleet of warships to Cuba. Panic seized the eastern seaboard of the United States. American vacationers abandoned their seaside cottages, while nervous investors moved their securities to inland depositories. The Spanish commander, Admiral Cervera, was soon forced into Santiago harbor, where he was blockaded by the much more powerful American fleet.

Sound strategy seemed to dictate that an American army be sent in from the rear to drive out Cervera. Leading the invading force was the grossly overweight General William R. Shafter, a leader so blubbery that he had to be carried about on a door.

The "Rough Riders," a part of the invading army, now charged onto the stage of history. This colorful regiment of volunteers, short on discipline but long on dash, consisted largely of western cowboys and other hardy characters, with a sprinkling of ex–polo players and ex-convicts. Commanded by Colonel Leonard Wood, the group was organized principally by the glory-hungry Theodore Roosevelt, who had resigned from the Navy Department to serve as a lieutenant colonel.

About the middle of June a bewildered American army of seventeen thousand men finally embarked at Tampa, Florida, amid scenes of inde-scribable confusion. Shafter's landing near Santiago, Cuba, was made without serious opposition. Brisk fighting broke out on July 1 at El Caney and San Juan Hill, up which Colonel Roosevelt and his Rough Riders charged, with strong support from two crack black regiments. They suffered heavy casualties, but the colorful colonel, having the time of his life, shot a Spaniard with his revolver and rejoiced to see his victim double up like a jackrabbit. He later wrote a book on his exploits, which, humorist Finley Peter Dunne's fictional "Mr. Dooley" remarked, ought to have been entitled *Alone in Cubia* [*sic*].

The American army, fast closing in on Santiago, spelled doom for the Spanish fleet. After a running chase, on July 3, the Spanish fleet was entirely destroyed as wooden decks caught fire and the blazing infernos were beached. About five hundred Spaniards were killed, as compared with one American. "Don't cheer, men," admonished Captain Philip of the *Texas*, "the poor devils are dying." Shortly thereafter Santiago surrendered.

Hasty preparations were then made for a descent on Puerto Rico before the war ended. The American army there met little resistance. By this time Spain had satisfied its honor and on August 12, 1898, signed an armistice.

If the Spaniards had held out a few months longer in Cuba, the American army might have melted away. The inroads of malaria, typhoid, dysentery, and yellow fever became so severe that hundreds were incapacitated—"an army of convalescents." Others suffered from eating spoiled canned meat known as "embalmed beef."

One of the war's worst scandals was the high death rate from sickness, especially typhoid fever. This disease was rampant in the unsanitary training camps located in the United States. All told, nearly four hundred men lost their lives to bullets, and over five thousand succumbed to bacteria and other causes.

America's Course (Curse?) of Empire

Late in 1898 Spanish and American negotiators met in Paris. War-racked Cuba, as expected, was freed from its Spanish overlords. The Americans had little difficulty in securing the remote Pacific island of Guam, which they had captured early in the conflict. They also picked up Puerto Rico, the last remnant of what had been Spain's vast New World empire. In the decades to come, American investment in the island and Puerto Rican immigration to the United States would make this acquisition one of the weightier consequences of this somewhat carefree war (see "Makers of America: The Puerto Ricans," pp. 414–415).

Knottiest of all was the problem of the Philippines, a veritable apple of discord. These lush islands not only embraced an area larger than the British Isles but contained a completely alien population of some 7 million souls. McKinley was confronted with a devil's dilemma. He did not feel that America could honorably give the islands back to Spanish misrule, especially after it had fought a war to free Cuba. And America would be turning its back on its responsibilities, he believed, if it simply pulled up anchor and sailed away.

McKinley viewed other alternatives open to him as trouble-fraught. The Filipinos, if left to govern themselves, might fall into anarchy. One of the major powers, possibly aggressive Germany, might seize them, and the result might be a world war into which the United States would be sucked. Seemingly the least of the evils consistent with national honor and safety was to acquire all the Philippines and then perhaps give the Filipinos their freedom later.

President McKinley, ever sensitive to public opinion, kept a carefully attuned ear to the ground. The rumble that he heard seemed to call for the entire group of islands. Zealous Protestant missionaries were eager for new converts from Spanish Catholicism.* Wall Street had generally opposed the war; but awakened by the booming of Dewey's guns, it was clamoring for profits in the Philippines.

A tormented McKinley, so he was later reported as saying, finally went down on his knees seeking divine guidance. An inner voice seemed to tell him to take all the Philippines and Christianize and civilize them. Accordingly, he decided for outright annexation of the islands. The deed was accomplished by negotiators in Paris after the Americans agreed to pay

---

* The Philippines had been substantially Christianized by Catholics before the founding of Jamestown in 1607.

Spain $20 million for the Philippine Islands—the last great Spanish haul from the New World.

The signing of the pact of Paris touched off one of the most impassioned debates of American history. Except for glacial Alaska, coral-reefed Hawaii, and a handful of Pacific atolls, the Republic had hitherto acquired only contiguous territory on the continent. All previous acquisitions had been thinly peopled and capable of ultimate statehood. But in the Philippines the nation had on its hands a distant tropical area, thickly populated by Asians of a different race, tongue, and government institutions.

An Anti-Imperialist League sprang into being to fight the McKinley administration's expansionist moves. The organization counted among its members some of the most prominent people in the United States, including the presidents of Stanford and Harvard universities, the philosopher William James, and the novelist Mark Twain. The anti-imperialist blanket even stretched over such strange bedfellows as labor leader Samuel Gompers and steel titan Andrew Carnegie. "Goddamn the United States for its vile conduct in the Philippine Isles!" burst out the usually mild-mannered Professor James. The Harvard philosopher could not believe that the United States could "puke up its ancient soul in five minutes without a wink of squeamishness."

Anti-imperialists had still other arrows in their quiver. The Filipinos panted for freedom; and to annex them would violate the "consent of the governed" philosophy of the Declaration of Independence. Finally, annexation would propel the United States into the political and military cauldron of East Asia.

Yet the expansionists or imperialists could sing a seductive song. They appealed to patriotism and played up possible trade profits. Manila, in fact, might become another Hong Kong. Rudyard Kipling, the British poet laureate of imperialism, urged America down the slippery path:

> Take up the White Man's burden—
> Ye dare not stoop to less—
> Nor call too loud on Freedom
> To cloak your weariness.

In short, the wealthy Americans must help to uplift (and exploit) the underprivileged, underfed, and underclad of the world.

In the Senate the Spanish treaty ran into such heated opposition that it seemed doomed to defeat. But it received last-minute support from a surprising source—William Jennings Bryan. Bryan argued that the war would not officially end until America ratified the pact, and the sooner it accepted the document, the sooner it could give the Filipinos their independence. After Bryan had used his personal influence with certain Democratic senators, the treaty was approved, on February 6, 1899, with only one vote to spare. But the responsibility, as Bryan had foreseen, rested primarily with the Republicans.

Perplexities in Puerto Rico and Cuba

Many of Puerto Rico's 1 million inhabitants lived in poverty. The island's population grew faster than its economy. By the Foraker Act of 1900, Congress accorded the Puerto Ricans a limited degree of popular government, and in 1917 granted them U.S. citizenship. Although the American regime worked wonders in education, sanitation, good roads, and other tangible improvements, many of the inhabitants still aspired to independence. Great numbers of Puerto Ricans moved to New York City, where they added to the complexity of the melting pot.

A thorny legal problem was posed by the question: did the Constitution follow the flag? Did American laws, including tariff laws, apply with full force to the newly acquired possessions, chiefly the Philippines and Puerto Rico? Beginning in 1901 with the *Insular Cases*, a badly divided Supreme Court decreed, in effect, that the flag outran the Constitution and that the outdistanced document did not necessarily extend with full force to the new windfalls.

Cuba, scorched and chaotic, presented another headache. An American military government, set up under the administrative genius of General Leonard Wood of Rough Rider fame, wrought miracles in government, finance, education, agriculture, and public health. Under his leadership and that of Colonel William C. Gorgas, a frontal attack was launched on yellow fever. Spectacular experiments were performed by Dr. Walter Reed and others upon American soldiers, who volunteered as human guinea pigs; and the stegomyia mosquito was proved to be the lethal carrier.

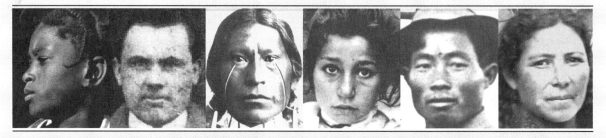

The Puerto Ricans

At dawn on July 26, 1898, the U.S. warship *Gloucester* steamed into Puerto Rico's Guánica harbor, fired at the Spanish blockhouse, and landed some thirty-three hundred troops. Within days, the Americans had taken possession of the militarily strategic Caribbean island a thousand miles southeast of Florida. In so doing they set in motion changes on the island that ultimately brought a new wave of immigrants to U.S. shores.

Puerto Rico had been a Spanish possession since Christopher Columbus claimed it for Castile in 1493. The Spaniards enslaved many of the island's forty thousand Taino Indians and set them to work on farms and in mines. Many Tainos died of exhaustion and disease, and in 1511 the Indians rebelled. The Spaniards crushed the uprising, killed thousands of Indians, and began importing African slaves—thus establishing the basis for Puerto Rico's multiracial society.

The first Puerto Rican immigrants to the United States arrived as political exiles in the nineteenth century. From their haven in America, they agitated for the island's independence from Spain. In 1897 Spain finally granted the island local autonomy; ironically, however, the Spanish-American War the following year placed it in American hands. Puerto Rican political émigrés in the United States returned home, but they were soon replaced by poor islanders looking for work.

When Congress granted Puerto Ricans U.S. citizenship in 1917, thereby eliminating immigration hurdles, many islanders hurried north to find jobs. Over the ensuing decades, Puerto Ricans went to work in Arizona cotton fields, New Jersey soup factories, and Utah mines. The majority, however, clustered in New York City and found work in the city's cigar factories, shipyards, and garment industry. Migration slowed somewhat after the 1920s as the Great Depression shrank the job market on the mainland and as World War II made travel hazardous.

When World War II ended in 1945, the sudden advent of cheap air travel sparked an immigration

The First Puerto Ricans *The Spanish* conquistadores *treated the native Taino Indian peoples in Puerto Rico with extreme cruelty, and the Indians were virtually extinct by the mid-1500s.*

explosion. As late as the 1930s, the tab for a boat trip to the mainland exceeded the average Puerto Rican's yearly earnings. But with an airplane surplus after World War II, the six-hour flight from Puerto Rico to New York cost under fifty dollars. The Puerto Rican population on the mainland quadrupled between 1940 and 1950 and tripled again by 1960. In 1970, 1.5 million Puerto Ricans lived in the United States, one-third of the island's total population.

U.S. citizenship and affordable air travel made it easy for Puerto Ricans to return home. Thus to a far greater degree than most immigrant groups, Puerto Ricans kept one foot in the United States and the other on their native island. By some estimates, 2 million people a year journeyed to and from the island during the postwar period. Puerto Rico's gubernatorial candidates sometimes campaigned in New York for the thousands of voters who were expected to return to the island in time for the election.

Puerto Ricans have fared better economically in the United States than on the island, where, in 1970, 60 percent of all inhabitants lived below the poverty line. In recent years Puerto Ricans have attained more schooling, and many have attended college. Invigorated by the civil rights movement of the 1960s, Puerto Ricans also have become more politically active, electing growing numbers of congressmen and state and city officials.

The United States, honoring its self-denying Teller Amendment of 1898, withdrew from Cuba in 1902. Old World imperialists could scarcely believe their eyes. But the Washington government could not turn this rich and strategic island completely loose on the international sea; a grasping power like Germany might secure dangerous lodgment near America's soft underbelly. The Cubans were therefore forced to write into their own Constitution of 1901 the so-called Platt Amendment.

The hated restriction severely hobbled the Cubans. They reluctantly bound themselves not to impair their independence by treaty or by contracting a debt beyond their resources. They further agreed that the United States might intervene with troops to restore order and to provide mutual protection. Finally, the Cubans promised to sell or lease needed coaling or naval stations, ultimately two and then only one (Guantánamo), to their powerful "benefactor." The United States still occupies the base under an agreement that can be revoked only by the consent of both parties.

New Horizons in Two Hemispheres

In essence the Spanish-American War was a kind of gigantic coming-out party. Dewey's thundering guns merely advertised the fact that the nation was already a world power. The war itself was short (113 days), spectacular, low in casualties, and successful—despite the bungling. American prestige rose sharply, and the European powers grudgingly accorded the Republic more respect.

An exhilarating new spirit thrilled America. National pride was touched and cockiness was increased by what John Hay called a "splendid little war."[*] America did not start the war with imperialistic motives, but after falling through the cellar door of imperialism in a drunken fit of idealism, it wound up with imperialistic and colonial fruits in its grasp.

By taking on the Philippine Islands, the United States became a full-fledged East Asian power. Hereafter these distant islands were to be a "heel of Achilles"—a kind of indefensible hostage given to Japan, as events proved in 1941. With singular short-sightedness, the Americans assumed dangerous commitments that they were later unwilling to defend by proper naval and military outlays.

But the lessons of unpreparedness were not altogether lost. Captain Mahan's big-navyism seemed vindicated, and popular support grew for more and better

---

[*] Anti-imperialist William James called it "our squalid war with Spain."

battleships. A masterly organizer, Elihu Root, took over the reins at the War Department. He established a general staff and founded the War College in Washington.

One of the happiest results of the conflict was the further closing of the "bloody chasm" between North and South. Thousands of patriotic southerners had flocked to the Stars and Stripes, and gray-bearded General Joseph ("Fighting Joe") Wheeler—a Confederate cavalry hero—was given a command in Cuba. He allegedly cried, in the heat of battle, "To hell with the Yankees! Dammit, I mean the Spaniards."

"Little Brown Brothers" in the Philippines

Unhappily, the liberty-loving Filipinos were tragically deceived. They had assumed that they, like the Cubans, would be granted their freedom after the war. Bitterness toward the American troops erupted into open insurrection on February 4, 1899, under Emilio Aguinaldo.

The war with the Filipinos, unlike the "splendid" little set-to with Spain, was sordid and prolonged. It involved more savage fighting, more soldiers killed, and far more scandal. Anti-imperialists redoubled their protests. In their view the United States, having plunged into war with Spain to free Cuba, was now fighting ten thousand miles away to rivet shackles on a people who asked for nothing but liberty—in the American tradition.

As the ill-equipped Filipino armies were defeated, they melted into the jungle to wage a vicious guerrilla warfare. Many of the outgunned Filipinos used barbarous methods, and the infuriated American troops responded in kind.

Atrocity tales shocked and rocked the United States, for such methods did not reflect America's better self. Uncle Sam's soldiers resorted to such extremes as the painful "water cure"—that is, forcing water down victims' throats until they yielded information or died. Reconcentration camps were even established that strongly suggested those of "Butcher" Weyler in Cuba. America, having begun the Spanish war with noble ideals, now dirtied its hands. One New York newspaper published a reply to Rudyard Kipling's famous poem:

> We've taken up the white man's burden
>   Of ebony and brown;
> Now will you kindly tell us, Rudyard,
>   How we may put it down?

The backbone of the Filipino insurrection was finally broken in 1901, when Aguinaldo was captured. But sporadic fighting dragged on for many dreary months.

McKinley's "benevolent assimilation" of the Philippines proceeded with painful slowness. Millions of American dollars were poured into the islands to improve roads, sanitation, and public health. Important economic ties, including trade in sugar, developed between the two peoples. American teachers—"pioneers of the blackboard"—set up an unusually good school system and helped make English a second language. But all this vast expenditure, which profited America little, was ill received. The Filipinos, who hated compulsory civilization, preferred less sanitation and more liberty. Like caged hawks, they beat against their gilded bars until they finally got their freedom, on the Fourth of July, 1946. In the meantime, thousands of Filipinos emigrated to the United States (see "Makers of America: The Filipinos," p. 418).

Hinging the Open Door in China

Exciting events had meanwhile been brewing in China. After its defeat by Japan in 1894–1895, the imperialistic European powers, notably Russia and Germany, moved in. Like vultures descending on a wounded whale, they began to tear away valuable leaseholds and economic spheres of influence from the Manchu government.

A growing group of Americans viewed the vivisection of China with alarm. Churches were worried about their missionary strongholds; manufacturers and exporters feared that Chinese markets would be monopolized by Europeans. An alarmed American public, prodded by the press and by certain free-trade Britons, demanded that Washington do something. Secretary of State John Hay finally decided on a dramatic move.

In the summer of 1899, Hay dispatched to all the great powers a communication soon known as the Open Door note. He urged them to announce that in their leaseholds or spheres of influence they would respect certain Chinese rights and the ideal of fair competition. Hay's proposal caused much squirming in the leading world capitals, but all the great powers eventually accepted it, though subject to the condition that the others acquiesce unconditionally.

Open door or not, patriotic Chinese did not care to be used as a doormat by the Europeans. In 1900 a superpatriotic group known as the "Boxers" broke loose with the cry "Kill Foreign Devils." Over two hundred missionaries and other ill-fated whites were murdered, and a number of foreign diplomats were besieged in the capital, Beijing (Peking).

A multinational rescue force of some eighteen thousand soldiers, including some twenty-five hundred Americans, arrived in the nick of time and quelled the rebellion. Such participation in a joint military operation, especially in Asia, was plainly contrary to the nation's time-honored principles of nonentanglement and noninvolvement.

The victorious allied invaders acted angrily and vindictively. They assessed prostrate China an excessive indemnity of $333 million, of which America's share was to be $24.5 million. When Washington discovered that this sum was much more than enough to pay damages and expenses, it remitted about $18 million. The Beijing government, appreciating this gesture of goodwill, set aside the money to educate a selected group of Chinese students in the United States. These bright young people later played a significant role in the westernization of Asia.

Secretary Hay let fly another paper broadside in 1900, announcing that henceforth the Open Door would embrace the territorial integrity of China. Defenseless China was spared partition during these troubled years. But its salvation was probably due not to Hay's fine phrases but to the strength of the competing powers.

Imperialism or Bryanism in 1900?

President McKinley's renomination by the Republicans in 1900 was a foregone conclusion. He had piloted the country through a victorious war; he had acquired rich, though burdensome, real estate; he

had established the gold standard; and he had brought the promised prosperity of the full dinner pail.

An irresistible vice-presidential boom had developed for "Teddy" Roosevelt (TR), the cowboy-hero of San Juan Hill. Capitalizing on his war-born popularity, he had been elected governor of New York, where the local political bosses had found him headstrong and difficult to manage. They therefore devised a scheme to kick the colorful colonel upstairs into the vice presidency.

This plot to railroad Roosevelt worked beautifully. Gesticulating wildly, he attended the nominating convention, where his western-style cowboy hat made him stand out like a white crow. Yielding to the cries of "We Want Teddy!" he received a unanimous vote, except for his own. A frantic Hanna reportedly moaned that there would be only one heartbeat between "that damned cowboy" and the presidency of the United States.

William Jennings Bryan was the odds-on choice of the Democrats, meeting at Kansas City. The Democratic platform proclaimed, as did Bryan, that the "paramount" issue was Republican overseas imperialism.

McKinley, the soul of dignity, sat safely on his front porch during the campaign of 1900. As before, Bryan took to the stump in a cyclonic campaign, assailing both imperialism and Republican-fostered trusts. Lincoln, he charged, had abolished slavery for 3.5 million Africans; McKinley had reestablished it for 7 million Filipinos.

Republicans responded by charging that "Bryanism," not imperialism, was the paramount issue. By this accusation they meant that Bryan would rock the boat of prosperity once he got into office with his free-silver lunacy and other dangerous ideas. The voters were much less concerned about imperialism than about "Four Years More of the Full Dinner Pail."

McKinley triumphed by a much wider margin than in 1896: 7,218,491 to 6,356,734 popular votes, and 292 to 155 electoral votes. Victory for the Republicans was not a mandate for or against imperialism. If there was any mandate at all it was for the two *P*s: prosperity and protection.

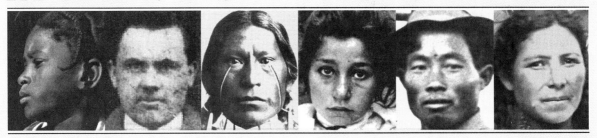

The Filipinos

At the beginning of the twentieth century, the United States, its imperial muscles just flexed in the war with Spain, found itself in possession of the Philippines. Uncertain of how to manage this empire, which seethed resentfully against its new masters, the United States promised to build democracy in the Philippines and to ready the islanders for home rule. Almost immediately after annexation, the American governor of the archipelago sent a corps of Filipino students to the United States, hoping to forge future leaders steeped in American ways who would some-day govern an independent Philippines. Yet this small student group found little favor in their adopted country, although in their native land many went on to become respected citizens and leaders.

Most Filipino immigrants to the United States in these years, however, came not to study but to toil. With Chinese immigration banned, Hawaii and the Pacific coast states turned to the Philippines for cheap agricultural labor. Beginning in 1906, the Hawaiian Sugar Planters Association aggressively recruited Filipino workers. Enlistments grew slowly at first, but by the 1920s thousands of young Filipino men had reached the Hawaiian Islands and been assigned to sugar plantations or pineapple fields.

Those Filipinos venturing as far as the American mainland found work less arduous but also less certain than did their countrymen on Hawaiian plantations. Many mainlanders worked seasonally—in winter as domestic servants, busboys, or bellhops; in summer journeying to the fields to harvest lettuce, strawberries, sugar beets, and potatoes. Eventually, Filipinos, along with Mexican immigrants, shared the dubious honor of making up California's agricultural work force.

By 1930, with Filipino male immigrants out-numbering women by fourteen to one, the issue of intermarriage became acutely sensitive. In California and many other states, demeaning laws that remained on the books until 1948 prohibited the marriage of Asians and Caucasians. Undeterred by hostility and the vigilante violence sometimes directed at them, especially in Washington and California, Filipinos continued to challenge restrictive state laws even though they did not attain U.S. citizenship until 1946.

After World War II, Filipino immigration accelerated. Between 1950 and 1970, the number of Filipinos in the United States nearly doubled. Many of these recent arrivals were solidly middle class and sought in America a better life for their children. Today, the perpetually depressed and politically unstable Philippine archipelago sends more immigrants to American shores than does any other Asian nation.

TR: Brandisher of the Big Stick

Kindly William McKinley had scarcely served another six months when, in September 1901, he was murdered by a deranged anarchist. Roosevelt became president at age forty-two, the youngest thus far in American history.

What manner of man was Theodore Roosevelt, the red-blooded blueblood? Born into a wealthy and distinguished New York family, he had fiercely built up his spindly, asthmatic body by a stern and self-imposed routine of exercise. Graduating from Harvard with Phi Beta Kappa honors, he published at the age of twenty-four the first of some thirty volumes of muscular prose. Then came busy years, which involved duties as a ranch owner and bespectacled cowboy ("Four Eyes") in the Dakotas, followed by various political posts. When fully developed, he was a barrel-chested 5 feet, 10 inches, with prominent teeth, squinty eyes, droopy mustache, and piercing voice.

The Rough Rider's high-voltage energy was electrifying. Believing that it was better to wear out than to rust out, he would shake the hands of some six thousand people at one stretch or ride horseback many miles in a day as an example for portly cavalry officers. Incurably boyish and bellicose, Roosevelt never ceased to preach the virile virtues and to denounce civilized softness, with its pacifists and other "flubdubs" and "mollycoddles." An ardent champion of military and naval preparedness, he adopted as his pet proverb, "Speak softly and carry a big stick, [and] you will go far."

Wherever Roosevelt went, there was a great stir. At a wedding he eclipsed the bride; at a funeral, the corpse. Shockingly unconventional, he loved to break hoary precedents—the hoarier the better. He loved people and mingled with those of all ranks—from Catholic cardinals to professional prizefighters, one of whom blinded a Rooseveltian eye in a White House bout.

An outspoken moralizer and reformer, Roosevelt preached virtue from the White House pulpit. Yet he was an opportunist who would compromise rather than butt his head against a stone wall. He was, in reality, much less radical than his blustery actions would indicate. A middle-of-the-roader, he stood just a little left of center and bared his mulelike molars at liberals and reactionaries alike.

Roosevelt rapidly developed into a master politician with an idolatrous personal following. A magnificent showman, he was always front-page copy; and his cowboyism, his bear shooting, his outsize teeth, and his pince-nez glasses were ever the delight of cartoonists.

Above all, Roosevelt was a direct-actionist. He believed that the president should lead. He had no real respect for the delicate checks and balances among the three branches of government. The president, he felt, may take any action in the general interest that is not specifically forbidden by the laws or the Constitution.

Building the Panama Canal

Foreign affairs absorbed much of Roosevelt's bullish energy. Having traveled extensively in Europe, he enjoyed a far more intimate knowledge of the outside world than most of his predecessors.

The Spanish-American War had emphasized the need for the long-talked-about canal across the Central American isthmus. An isthmian canal would plainly augment the strength of the navy by increasing its mobility. Such a waterway would also make easier the defense of such recent acquisitions as Puerto Rico, Hawaii, and the Philippines, while facilitating the operations of the American merchant marine.

Initial obstacles in the path of the canal builders were legal rather than geographical. By the terms of the ancient Clayton-Bulwer Treaty, concluded with Britain in 1850, the United States could not secure exclusive control over such a route. But by 1901 America's British cousins were willing to yield ground. Confronted with an unfriendly Europe and bogged down in the South African Boer War, they consented to the Hay-Pauncefote Treaty in 1901. It not only gave the United States a free hand to build the canal but conceded the right to fortify it as well.

Legal barriers now removed, the next question was, where should the canal be dug? Many American experts favored the Nicaraguan route, but agents of an old French canal company were eager to salvage something from their costly failure at S-shaped

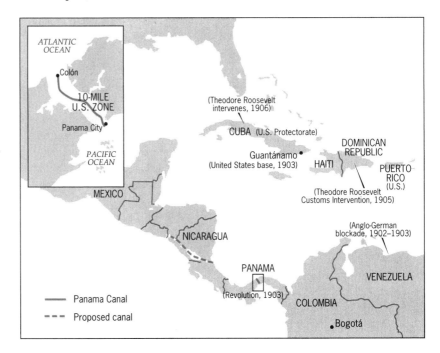

Big Stick in the Caribbean *In 1901 Roosevelt declared: "If a man continually blusters . . . a big stick will not save him from trouble; and neither will speaking softly avail, if back of the softness there does not lie strength, power. . . . If the boaster is not prepared to back up his words his position becomes absolutely contemptible."*

Panama. Represented by a young, energetic, and unscrupulous engineer, Philippe Bunau-Varilla, the New Panama Canal Company suddenly dropped the price of its holdings from $109 million to the fire sale price of $40 million.

After much debate, Congress in June 1902 finally decided on the Panama route. The scene then shifted to Colombia, of which Panama was an unwilling part. A treaty highly favorable to the United States was negotiated with the agent of the Bogotá government, but it was unanimously rejected by the Colombian senate. Impatient Panamanians, who had rebelled numerous times, were ripe for another revolt. They had counted on a wave of prosperity to follow construction of the canal, and they feared that the United States would now turn to the Nicaraguan route. Scheming Bunau-Varilla was no less disturbed by the prospect of losing the company's $40 million. Working hand in glove with the Panama revolutionists, he helped incite a rebellion on November 3, 1903. Colombian troops were gathered to crush the uprising, but U.S. naval forces would not let them cross the isthmus.

Roosevelt moved rapidly to make steamy Panama a virtual outpost of the United States. Three days after the uprising, he hastily extended the right hand of recognition. Fifteen days later, Bunau-Varilla, who was now the Panamanian minister despite his French citizenship, signed the Hay–Bunau-Varilla Treaty in Washington. The price of the canal strip was left the same, but the zone was widened from six to ten miles. The French company gladly pocketed its $40 million from the U.S. Treasury.

Critics charged that Roosevelt's "cowboy diplomacy" represented thinly disguised imperialism. European imperialists, who were old hands at this kind of thing, could now raise their eyebrows in scorn at America's superior moral pretensions—and they did. But Roosevelt heatedly defended himself against charges of evildoing. He claimed that he had received a "mandate from civilization" to start the canal and that Colombia had wronged the United States by not permitting itself to be thus benefited.

Active work was begun on "making the dirt fly" in 1904, but grave difficulties were encountered, ranging from labor troubles to landslides. The organization was finally perfected under an energetic but autocratic West Point engineer, Colonel George Washington Goethals. At the outset, sanitation proved to be more important than excavation. Colonel William C. Gorgas, the quiet and determined exterminator of yellow fever in Havana, ultimately made the Canal Zone "as safe as a health resort."

Americans finally succeeded where Frenchmen had failed. In 1914 the colossal canal project was completed at an initial cost of about $400 million.

TR's Perversion of Monroe's Doctrine

Latin American debt defaults created the conditions for further Rooseveltian involvement in affairs south of the border. Nations such as Venezuela and the Dominican Republic were chronically in arrears in their payments to European creditors, particularly Britain and Germany. Roosevelt feared that if the Germans or British got their feet in the door as bill collectors, they might remain in Latin America. He therefore devised a devious policy of "preventive intervention," better known as the Roosevelt Corol-

lary to the Monroe Doctrine. In 1904 he declared that in the event of future financial malfeasance by the Latin American nations, the United States itself would intervene, take over the customshouses, pay off the debts, and keep the troublesome powers on the other side of the Atlantic. In short, no outsiders could push the Latin nations around except Uncle Sam, Policeman of the Caribbean.

This new brandishing of the Big Stick in the Caribbean became effective in 1905. It was formalized in a treaty with the Dominican Republic two years later giving the United States supervisory powers over Dominican tariff collections.

Roosevelt's rewriting of Monroe's doctrine did more than any other single step to promote the "Bad Neighbor" policy begun in these years. As time wore on, the new corollary was used to justify wholesale interventions and repeated landings of the U.S. Marines, all of which helped turn the Caribbean into a "Yankee pond." To Latin Americans it seemed as though the Monroe Doctrine, far from providing a shield, was a cloak behind which the United States sought to strangle them.

Theodore Roosevelt and His Big Stick in the Caribbean, 1904 *Roosevelt's policies seemed to be turning the Caribbean into a Yankee pond.*

Roosevelt on the World Stage

Booted and spurred, Roosevelt charged into international affairs far beyond Latin America. The outbreak of war between Russia and Japan in 1904 gave him a chance to perform as a global statesman. With the Russians threatening permanent occupation of China's Manchuria, the Japanese suddenly began a war in 1904 with a devastating surprise attack on the Russian fleet at Port Arthur. They proceeded to administer a humiliating series of beatings to the inept Russians. But as the war dragged on, Japan began to run short of men and yen—a weakness it did not want to betray to the enemy. Tokyo officials therefore approached Roosevelt in the deepest secrecy and asked him to help sponsor peace negotiations.

Roosevelt agreed and shepherded the delegates of the two sides together at Portsmouth, New Hampshire, in 1905. The Japanese presented stern demands for a huge indemnity and the entire strategic island of Sakhalin, while the Russians stubbornly refused to admit the depths of their defeat. Blustering at both sides behind the scenes, Roosevelt forced through an accord in which the Japanese received no indemnity and only the southern half of Sakhalin.

For achieving this agreement, as well as for helping arrange an international conference at Algeciras, Spain, in 1906 to mediate North African disputes, Roosevelt received the Nobel Peace Prize in 1906. But the price of TR's diplomatic glory was high for U.S. foreign relations. Two historic friendships withered on the windswept plains of Manchuria. America's relations with Russia, once friendly, soured as the Russians implausibly accused Roosevelt of robbing them of military victory. Japan, once America's protégé, felt robbed of its due compensation. Both newly powerful, Japan and America now became rivals in Asia, as fear and jealousy between them grew.

Japanese Laborers in California

The population of America's Pacific Coast was directly affected by the Russo-Japanese War. A new restlessness swept over the rice paddies of Japan, largely as a result of the dislocation and tax burdens caused by the recent conflict. Numerous Japanese laborers, with their wives and children, began to pour into the spacious valleys of California. By 1906 approximately seventy thousand Japanese dwelt along the Pacific Coast. Nervous Californians, confronted by another "yellow peril," were fearful of being drowned in an Asian sea.

A showdown on the Japanese influx came in 1906. Following the frightful earthquake and fire of that year in San Francisco, the local school authorities, pressed for space, decreed that Japanese children should attend a special school. Instantly, the Japanese school incident brewed an international crisis. The people of Japan, highly sensitive on questions of race, regarded this discrimination as an insult to them and their beloved children. On both sides of the Pacific, irresponsible war talk sizzled in the yellow press—the real "yellow peril." Roosevelt, who as a Rough Rider had relished shooting, was less happy over the prospect that California might stir up a war that all the other states would have to fight. He therefore invited the entire San Francisco Board of Education to come to the White House.

TR finally broke the deadlock, but not until he had brandished his big stick and bared his teeth. The Californians were induced to repeal the offensive school order and to accept what came to be known as the "Gentlemen's Agreement." This secret understanding was worked out during 1907–1908 by an exchange of diplomatic notes between Washington and Tokyo. The Japanese agreed to stop the flow of laborers to the American mainland by withholding passports. Caucasian Californians, their anxiety allayed, henceforth slept more easily.

Roosevelt worried that his intercession between California and Japan might be interpreted in Tokyo as prompted by fear of the Japanese. Accordingly, he hit upon a dramatic scheme to impress the Japanese with the heft of his big stick. He daringly decided to send the entire U.S. battleship fleet on a highly visible voyage around the world.

Late in 1907, sixteen smoke-belching battleships started from Virginia waters. Their commander pointedly declared that he was ready for "a feast, a frolic, or a fight." The Great White Fleet—saluted by cannonading champagne corks—received tumultuous welcomes in Latin America, Hawaii, New Zealand, and Australia. As events turned out, an overwhelming reception in Japan was the high point of the trip. Tens of thousands of kimonoed schoolchildren waved tiny American flags and sang "The Star Spangled Banner."

In the warm diplomatic atmosphere created by the visit of the fleet, the Root-Takahira agreement of 1908 was reached with Japan. The United States and Japan solemnly pledged themselves to respect each other's territorial possessions in the Pacific and to uphold the Open Door in China. The once fight-thirsty Theodore Roosevelt, who thus went out of his way to avoid a war with Japan, regarded the battleship cruise as his most important contribution to peace.

Chronology

1820	New England missionaries arrive in Hawaii.
1889	Samoa crisis with Germany.
1890	Mahan publishes *The Influence of Sea Power upon History*.
1891	New Orleans crisis with Italy.
1892	Valparaiso crisis with Chile.
1893	White planter revolt in Hawaii. Cleveland refuses Hawaii annexation.
1895	Cubans revolt against Spain.
1895– 1896	Venezuelan boundary crisis with Britain.
1898	*Maine* explosion in Havana harbor. Spanish-American War. Teller Amendment. Dewey's victory at Manila Bay. Hawaii annexed.
1899	Senate ratifies treaty acquiring the Philippines. Aguinaldo launches rebellion against United States. First American Open Door note.
1900	Boxer Rebellion and U.S. expedition to China. Second Open Door note. McKinley defeats Bryan for presidency.
1901	McKinley assassinated; Roosevelt assumes presidency. Filipino rebellion defeated. Hay-Pauncefote Treaty. Supreme Court *Insular Cases*. Platt Amendment.
1902	Colombian senate rejects canal treaty. U.S. troops leave Cuba.
1903	Panamanian revolution against Colombia. Hay–Bunau-Varilla Treaty.
1904	Roosevelt Corollary to the Monroe Doctrine.
1904– 1914	Construction of the Panama Canal.
1905	Roosevelt mediates Russo-Japanese peace treaty.
1906	San Francisco Japanese education crisis. Roosevelt arranges Algeciras conference.
1906– 1909	U.S. Marines occupy Cuba.
1907	Great White Fleet. United States assumes legal control of Dominican Republic customs.
1907– 1908	"Gentlemen's Agreement" with Japan.
1908	Root-Takahira agreement.
1917	Puerto Ricans granted U.S. citizenship.

varying

viewpoints

Why Did America Become a World Power?

American imperialism has long been an embarrassing topic for students of American history who remember the Republic's own revolutionary origins and anticolonial tradition. Perhaps for that reason, many historians have tried to explain the dramatic overseas expansionism of the 1890s as some kind of aberration—a sudden, singular, and short-lived departure from time-honored American principles and practices. Various explanations have been offered to account for this spasmodic lapse. Scholars such as Julius Pratt pointed to the irresponsible behavior of the yellow press. Richard Hofstadter ascribed America's imperial fling to the "psychic crisis of the 1890s," a crisis brought on, he argued, by the strains of the decade's economic depression and the Populist upheaval. Howard K. Beale emphasized the contagious scramble for imperial possessions by the European powers, as well as Japan, in these years.

In Beale's argument, the United States—and Theodore Roosevelt in particular—succumbed to a kind of international peer pressure: if other countries were expanding their international roles and even establishing colonies around the globe, could the United States safely refrain from doing the same?

Perhaps the most controversial interpretation of American imperialism has come from the so-called New Left school of writers, inspired by William Appleman Williams (and before him by V. I. Lenin's 1916 book *Imperialism: The Highest Stage of Capitalism*). Historians such as Williams and Walter LaFeber argue that the explanation for political and military expansion abroad is to be found in economic expansion at home. These scholars try to link the two most striking developments of the age: the amazing industrialization of the United States in the half-century after the Civil War and the Republic's sudden emergence as a world power. Increasing industrial output, so the argument goes, required ever more raw materials and, especially, overseas markets. To meet those needs, the nation adopted a strategy of "informal empire," shunning formal territorial possessions (with the conspicuous exception of the Philippines), but seeking economic dominance over foreign markets, materials, and investment outlets.

That "revisionist" interpretation, in turn, has been sharply criticized by scholars who point out that foreign trade, especially in this period, accounted for only a tiny share of American output. Critics of the New Left view also insist that the exceedingly complex diplomacy of the period was far too diverse in its motives, methods, and goals to be reduced to the elementary explanation of "economic need."

SUGGESTED READINGS

Primary Source Documents

Examples of yellow journalism include Joseph Pulitzer's New York *World* and William R. Hearst's New York *Journal*. Particularly interesting is the editorial in the *World* of February 13, 1897,* and the article by Charles Duval in the *Journal* of October 10, 1897.* McKinley's war message,* in James D. Richardson, ed., *Messages and Papers of the Presidents* (1899), vol. X, pp. 139ff., outlines the American rationale for intervention. The anti-imperialist answer can be found in Charles E. Norton's article in *Public Opinion*, June 23, 1898, pp. 775–776.* For the intrigue surrounding the independence of Panama and the building of the canal, see *Foreign Relations of the United States** (1903) and Theodore Roosevelt to Albert

Shaw, October 10, 1903,* in *The Letters of Theodore Roosevelt*, edited by Elting E. Morison (1951), vol. 3, p. 628.

Secondary Sources

Main outlines are sketched in Foster Rhea Dulles, *America's Rise to World Power, 1898–1954* (1955), and in Thomas G. Paterson, *American Foreign Policy: A Brief History* (3rd ed., 1988). Two general (and quite contrasting) interpretations of modern American foreign policy are George F. Kennan, *American Diplomacy* (1951), and William Appleman Williams, *The Tragedy of American Diplomacy* (1959). Consult also Williams's *The Roots of the Modern American Empire* (1961); Ernest R. May, *Imperial Democracy* (1961); and Walter LaFeber, *The New Empire* (1963). On the Spanish-American War itself see Frank Freidel, *The Splendid Little War* (1958), and David F. Trask, *The War with Spain in 1898* (1981). David F. Healey examines *The United States in Cuba, 1898–1902* (1963), and Leon Wolff paints a grim picture of American involvement in the Philippines in *Little Brown Brother* (1961). For more on the Philippine imbroglio see Stuart C. Miller, *"Benevolent Assimilation": The American Conquest of the Philippines, 1899–1903* (1982), and Stanley Karnow, *In Our Image: America's Empire in the Philippines* (1989). See also H. W. Brands, *Bound to Empire: The United States and the Philippines* (1992). For the Open Door, consult A. Whitney Griswold, *The Far Eastern Policy of the United States* (1938), and Marilyn B. Young, *The Rhetoric of Empire: America's China Policy, 1895–1901* (1968). On relations with Japan see Charles E. Neu, *An Uncertain Friendship: Theodore Roosevelt and Japan,* *1906–1909* (1967) and *The Troubled Encounter: The United States and Japan* (1975). Also valuable are two books by Akira Iriye, *Across the Pacific* (1967) and *Pacific Estrangement: Japanese and American Expansion, 1897–1911* (1972). James Reed discusses *The Missionary Mind and American East Asian Policy, 1911–1915* (1983). Also see William R. Hutchinson, *Errand to the World: American Protestant Thought and Foreign Missions* (1987). On the treatment of the Japanese in the United States see Ronald Takaki, *Strangers from a Different Shore* (1989). The canal issue is analyzed in David McCullough, *The Path Between the Seas* (1977); Walter LaFeber, *The Panama Canal* (1978); and Richard H. Collin, *Theodore Roosevelt's Caribbean: The Panama Canal, the Monroe Doctrine, and the Latin American Context* (1990). For Roosevelt himself see Howard K. Beale, *Theodore Roosevelt and the Rise of America to World Power* (1956); John M. Blum, *The Republican Roosevelt* (new ed., 1977); Lewis H. Gould, *The Presidency of Theodore Roosevelt* (1991); and William H. Harbaugh, *Power and Responsibility* (1975). Especially good on the youthful TR are Edmund Morris, *The Rise of Theodore Roosevelt* (1979), and David McCullough, *Mornings on Horseback* (1981).

---

* An asterisk indicates that the document, or an excerpt from it, can be found in Thomas A. Bailey and David M. Kennedy, eds., *The American Spirit: United States History as Seen by Contemporaries*, 9th ed. (Boston: Houghton Mifflin, 1998).

29

✷✷✷✷✷✷✷✷✷

Progressivism and the Republican Roosevelt,

1901–1912

★★★★★★

When I say I believe in a square deal I do not mean . . . to give every man the best hand. If the cards do not come to any man, or if they do come, and he has not got the power to play them, that is his affair. All I mean is that there shall be no crookedness in the dealing.

★★★★★★

THEODORE ROOSEVELT, 1905

Progressive Roots

Nearly 76 million Americans greeted the new century in 1900. Of them, almost one in seven was foreign-born. In the fourteen years of peace that remained before the Great War of 1914 engulfed the globe, 13 million more migrants would carry their bundles down the gangplanks to the land of promise.

Hardly had the twentieth century dawned on the ethnically and racially mixed American people than they were convulsed by a reform movement, the like of which the nation had not seen since the 1840s.

The new crusaders, who called themselves "progressives," waged war on many evils, notably monopoly, corruption, inefficiency, and social injustice. The progressive army was large, diverse, and widely deployed, but the real heart of the movement, explained one progressive reformer, was to "use the government as an agency of human welfare."

The groundswell of the new reformist wave went far back—to the Greenback Labor party of the 1870s and the Populists of the 1890s, to the mounting unrest throughout the land as grasping industrialists concentrated more and more power in fewer and fewer hands. An outworn philosophy of hands-off individualism seemed increasingly out of place in the modern machine age. Progressive theorists were insisting that society could no longer afford the luxury of a limitless "let-alone" policy (laissez-faire). The people, through government, must substitute mastery for drift.

Well before 1900, perceptive politicians and writers had begun to pinpoint targets for the progressive attack. Bryan, Altgeld, and the Populists loudly branded the "bloated trusts" with the stigma of corruption and wrongdoing. In 1894 Henry Demarest Lloyd charged headlong into the Standard Oil Company with his book entitled *Wealth Against Commonwealth*. Eccentric Thorstein Veblen assailed the new rich with his prickly pen in *The Theory of the Leisure Class* (1899), a savage attack on "predatory wealth" and "conspicuous consumption."

Other pen-wielding knights likewise entered the fray. The keen-eyed and keen-nosed Danish immigrant Jacob A. Riis, a reporter for the *New York Sun*, shocked middle-class Americans in 1890 with *How the Other Half Lives*. His account was a damning indictment of the dirt, disease, vice, and misery of those rat-gnawed human rookeries known as the New York slums. Novelist Theodore Dreiser used his blunt prose to batter promoters and profiteers in *The Financier* (1912) and *The Titan* (1914).

Socialists, many of whom were European immigrants, began to register appreciable strength at the ballot box. High-minded messengers of the social gospel used Christian teachings to demand better housing and living conditions for the poor. Feminists in multiplying numbers added social justice to suffrage on their list of needed reforms. With urban pioneers like Jane Addams blazing the way, women entered the fight to clean up corrupt city governments, to protect women on the hazardous factory

Child Workers *Two young girls tend a thread-winding machine. The boy is already a veteran coal miner.*

floor, to keep children out of the smudgy mills and sooty mines, and to ensure that only safe food products found their way to the family table. Much of progressivism reflected the new public commitment of women, born of their changing role in the still-stretching cities.

Raking Muck with the Muckrakers

Beginning about 1902 the exposing of evil became a flourishing industry among American publishers. A group of aggressive ten- and fifteen-cent popular magazines surged to the front, notably *McClure's, Cosmopolitan, Collier's,* and *Everybody's.* Waging fierce circulation wars, they dug deep for the dirt that the public loved to hate. Enterprising editors financed extensive research and encouraged pugnacious writing by their bright young reporters, whom President Roosevelt branded as "muckrakers" in 1906.

In 1902 a brilliant New York reporter, Lincoln Steffens, launched a series of articles in *McClure's* entitled "The Shame of the Cities." He fearlessly unmasked the corrupt alliance between big business and municipal government. Steffens was followed in the same magazine by Ida M. Tarbell, a pioneering woman journalist who published a devastating factual exposé of the Standard Oil Company.

Muckrakers fearlessly assailed the malpractices of life insurance companies and tariff lobbies. They roasted the beef trust, the "money trust," the railroad barons, and the corrupt amassing of American fortunes. David G. Phillips shocked an already startled nation by his series in *Cosmopolitan* entitled "The Treason of the Senate" (1906). He boldly charged that seventy-five of the ninety senators did not represent the people at all but the railroads and trusts.

Some of the most effective fire of the muckrakers was directed at social evils. The ugly list included the immoral "white slave" traffic in women, the rickety slums, and the appalling number of industrial accidents. The sorry subjugation of America's 9 million blacks was spotlighted in Ray Stannard Baker's *Following the Color Line* (1908). The abuses of child labor were brought luridly to light by John Spargo's *The Bitter Cry of the Children* (1906).

Vendors of potent patent medicines (often heavily spiked with alcohol) likewise came in for bit-

ter criticism. These conscienceless vultures sold incredible quantities of adulterated or habit-forming drugs. Muckraking attacks in *Collier's* were reinforced by Dr. Harvey W. Wiley, chief chemist of the Department of Agriculture, who even performed experiments on himself.

Full of sound and fury, the muckrakers signified much about the nature of the progressive reform movement. They were long on lamentation and short on sweeping remedies. To right social wrongs they counted on publicity and an aroused public conscience, not drastic political change. They sought not to overthrow capitalism but to cleanse it. The cure for the ills of American democracy, they earnestly believed, was more democracy.

Political Progressivism

Progressive reformers were mainly middle-class men and women who felt themselves squeezed from above and below. They sensed pressure from the new giant corporations, the restless immigrant hordes, and the aggressive labor unions. The progressives simultaneously sought two goals: to use state power to curb the trusts, and to stem the Socialist threat by generally improving the common person's conditions of life and labor. Progressives emerged in both major parties, in all regions, and at all levels of government. The truth is that progressivism was less a minority movement and more a majority mood.

One of the first objectives of progressives was to regain the power that had slipped from the hands of the people into those of the "interests." These ardent reformers pushed for direct primary elections so as to undercut power-hungry party bosses. They favored the "initiative" so that voters could directly propose legislation themselves, thus bypassing the boss-bought state legislatures. Progressives also agitated for the "referendum." This device would place laws on the ballot for final approval by the people, especially laws that had been railroaded through a compliant legislature by free-spending agents of big business. The "recall" would enable the voters to remove faithless elected officials, particularly those who had been bribed by bosses or lobbyists. The secret Australian ballot was likewise being introduced more widely in the states to counteract boss rule.

Direct election of U.S. senators became a favorite goal of progressives, especially after muckrakers had exposed the scandalous intimacy between greedy corporations and Congress. Direct election was finally achieved by the Seventeenth Amendment to the Constitution, approved in 1913 (see the Appendix). But the expected improvement in caliber was slow in coming.

Woman suffrage, the goal of feminists for many decades, likewise received powerful new support from the progressives early in the 1900s. The political reformers believed that women's votes would elevate the political tone, and the foes of the saloon felt that they could count on the support of enfranchised females. Many of the states, especially the more liberal ones in the West, gradually extended the vote to women. But by 1910 nationwide female suffrage was still a decade away.

Progressivism in the Cities and States

Progressives scored some of their most impressive gains in the cities. Frustrated by the inefficiency and corruption of machine-oiled city government, many localities followed the pioneering example of Galveston, Texas. In 1901 it had appointed expert-staffed commissions to manage urban affairs. Other communities adopted the city manager system, also designed to take politics out of municipal administration. Some of these "reforms" obviously valued efficiency more highly than democracy, as control of civic affairs was further removed from the people's hands.

Suffragists Put the Pressure on Washington   *Success finally crowned their effort with the ratification of the Nineteenth Amendment in 1920.*

Urban reformers likewise attacked "slumlords," juvenile delinquency, and wide-open prostitution (vice-at-a-price), which flourished in red-light districts unchallenged by bribed police. Public-spirited city dwellers also moved to halt the corrupt sale of franchises for streetcars and other public utilities.

Progressivism naturally bubbled up to the state level, notably in Wisconsin, which became a yeasty laboratory of reform. Pompadoured Governor Robert M. ("Fighting Bob") La Follette was an undersized but over-engined crusader who emerged as the most militant of the progressive Republican leaders. Elected governor in 1901 after a desperate fight with the railroad and timber interests, he perfected a scheme for regulating public utilities while laboring in close association with experts on the faculty of the University of Wisconsin at Madison.

Other states marched steadily toward the progressive camp, as they undertook to regulate railroads and trusts, chiefly through public utilities commissions. Oregon was not far behind Wisconsin, and California made giant bootstrides under the stocky Hiram W. Johnson. Elected Republican governor in 1910, this dynamic prosecutor of grafters helped break the dominant grip of the Southern Pacific Railroad on California politics and then, like La Follette, set up a political machine of his own.

In these and other states, fired-up progressives tackled head-on a whole array of social problems. One of the most remarkable features of this era was the energy and confidence with which reformers did battle with a host of evils. They finally secured the enactment of safety and sanitation codes for industry and closed certain harmful trades to juveniles. Progressives further protected the toiler with workmen's compensation laws protecting injured laborers and laws setting maximum hours and minimum wages.

Steaming and unsanitary sweatshops were a public scandal in many cities. The issue was thrust into the public eye in 1911, when a fire at the Triangle Shirtwaist Company in New York City incinerated 146 women workers, most of them young women. Lashed by the public outcry, the legislature of New York and later other legislatures passed laws regulating the hours and conditions of toil in such firetraps. In the landmark case of *Muller* v. *Oregon* (1908), crusading attorney Louis D. Brandeis persuaded the Supreme Court to accept the constitutionality of laws protecting women workers by presenting evidence of the harmful effects of factory labor on women's bodies. Although this argument seems discriminatory by later standards, progressives at the time hailed Brandeis's achievement as a triumph.

But crusaders for these humane measures did not always have smooth sailing. One dismaying setback came in 1905, when the Supreme Court in *Lochner* v. *New York* invalidated a New York law establishing a ten-hour day for bakers. Yet the reformist progressive wave finally washed up into the judiciary, and in 1917 the Court upheld a ten-hour law for factory workers. Gradually, the concept of the employer's responsibility to society was replacing the old dog-eat-dog philosophy of unregulated free enterprise.

Corner saloons, with their shutter doors, naturally attracted the ire and reforming zeal of progressives. By 1900 cities such as New York and San Francisco had one saloon for about every two hundred people. Antiliquor campaigners received powerful support from several militant organizations, notably the Woman's Christian Temperance Union (WCTU). Founder Frances E. Willard, who would fall on her knees in prayer on saloon floors, mobilized nearly a million women to "make the world homelike" and built the WCTU into the largest organization of women in the world. She found a vigorous ally in the Anti-Saloon League, which was aggressive, well organized, and well financed.

Caught up in the crusade, some states and numerous counties passed "dry" laws that controlled, restricted, or abolished alcohol. The big cities were generally "wet," for they had a large immigrant vote accustomed to the free flow of wine and beer in the Old Country. When World War I erupted in 1914, nearly one-half of the population lived in "dry" territory. Demon Rum was groggy and was to be floored—temporarily—by the Eighteenth Amendment in 1919.

TR's Square Deal for Labor

Theodore Roosevelt, although something of an imperialistic busybody abroad, was touched by the progressive wave at home. Like other reformers, he feared that the "public interest" was being submerged in the drifting seas of indifference. Everybody's interest was nobody's interest. Roosevelt decided to make it his. His sportsman's instincts spurred him into demanding a "square deal" for capital, labor, and the public at large. Broadly speaking, his program embraced three *C*s: control of the corporations, consumer protection, and conservation of natural resources.

The Square Deal for labor received its acid test in 1902, when a crippling strike broke out in the anthracite coal mines of Pennsylvania. Some 140,000 besooted workers, many of them illiterate immigrants, had long been frightfully exploited and accident plagued. They demanded, among other improvements, a 20 percent increase in pay and a reduction in the workday from ten to nine hours.

Unsympathetic mine owners, confident that a chilled public would react against the miners, refused to arbitrate or even negotiate. One of their spokesmen, multimillionaire George F. Baer, wrote that workers would be cared for "not by the labor agitators, but by the Christian men to whom God in his infinite wisdom has given the control of the property interests of this country."

As coal supplies dwindled, factories and schools were forced to shut down, and even hospitals felt the icy grip of winter. Desperately seeking a solution, Roosevelt threatened to seize the mines and operate them with federal troops. Faced with this first-time-ever threat to use federal bayonets against capital, rather than labor, the owners grudgingly consented to arbitration. A compromise decision ultimately gave the miners a 10 percent pay boost and a workday of nine hours. But their union was not officially recognized as a bargaining agent.

Keenly aware of the mounting antagonisms between capital and labor, Roosevelt urged Congress to create a new Department of Commerce and Labor. This goal was achieved in 1903. (Ten years later the agency was split into two.) An important arm of the newly born Department of Commerce and Labor was the Bureau of Corporations, which was authorized to probe businesses engaged in interstate commerce. The bureau was highly useful in helping to break the stranglehold of monopoly and in clearing the road for the era of "trustbusting."

TR Corrals the Corporations

The sprawling railroad octopus sorely needed restraint. The Interstate Commerce Commission, created in 1887 as a feeble sop to the public, had proved woefully inadequate. Railroad barons could simply appeal the commission's decisions on rates to the federal courts—a process that might take ten years.

Spurred by the former-cowboy president, Congress passed effective railroad legislation, beginning with the Elkins Act of 1903. This curb was aimed primarily at the rebate evil. Heavy fines could now be imposed both on the railroads that gave rebates and on the shippers that accepted them.

Still more effective was the Hepburn Act of 1906. Free passes, with their hint of bribery, were severely restricted. The once-infantile Interstate Commerce Commission was expanded, and its reach was extended to include express companies, sleeping-car companies, and pipelines. For the first time, the commission was given real molars when it was authorized, on complaint of shippers, to nullify existing rates and stipulate maximum rates.

Roosevelt, as a trustbuster, first burst into the headlines in 1902 with an attack on the Northern Securities Company, a railroad holding company organized by financial titan J. P. Morgan and empire builder James J. Hill. These moguls of money sought to achieve a virtual monopoly of the railroads in the Northwest. Roosevelt was therefore challenging the most regal potentates of the industrial aristocracy.

The railway promoters appealed to the Supreme Court, which in 1904 upheld Roosevelt's antitrust suit and ordered the Northern Securities Company to be dissolved. The *Northern Securities* decision jolted Wall Street and angered big business but greatly enhanced Roosevelt's reputation as a trust smasher. Roosevelt's big stick crashed down on other giant monopolies, as he initiated over forty legal proceedings against the beef, sugar, fertilizer, harvester, and other monopolies.

Much mythology, however, has inflated Roosevelt's reputation as a trustbuster. The Rough Rider understood the political popularity of monopoly smashing, but he did not consider it sound economic policy. Combination and integration, he felt, were the hallmarks of the age, and to try to stem the tide of economic progress by political means he considered the rankest folly. Bigness was not necessarily badness; so why punish success? Roosevelt's real purpose in assaulting the Goliaths of industry was symbolic: to prove conclusively that the government, not private business, ruled the country. He believed in regulating, not fragmenting, the big business combines. The threat of dissolution, he felt, might make the sultans of the smokestacks more amenable to federal regulation—and it did.

In truth, Roosevelt never swung his trust-crushing stick with maximum force. His successor, William Howard Taft, actually "busted" more trusts than TR did. In one celebrated instance in 1907, Roosevelt even gave his personal blessing to J. P. Morgan's plan to have United States Steel Corporation absorb the Tennessee Coal and Iron Company, without fear of antitrust reprisals. When Taft then launched a suit against United States Steel in 1911, the political reaction from TR was explosive (see p. 436).

Caring for the Consumer

Roosevelt backed a noteworthy measure in 1906 that benefited both corporations and consumers. Big meatpackers were being shut out of certain European markets because some American meat—from the small packinghouses, claimed the giants—had been found to be tainted. Foreign governments were even threatening to ban all American meat imports by throwing out the good beef with the bad botulism.

At the same time, American consumers hungered for safer canned products. Their appetite for reform was whetted by Upton Sinclair's sensational novel *The Jungle*, published in 1906. Sinclair intended his revolting tract to focus attention on the plight of the workers in the big canning factories, but instead he appalled the public with his description of disgustingly unsanitary food products. (As he put it, he aimed for the nation's heart but hit its stomach.) The book described in noxious detail the filth, disease, and putrefaction in Chicago's damp, ill-ventilated slaughterhouses. A cynical jingle of the time ran

Mary had a little lamb,
　And when she saw it sicken,
　She shipped it off to Packingtown,
　And now it's labeled chicken.

Backed by a nauseated public, Roosevelt induced Congress to pass the Meat Inspection Act of 1906. It decreed that the preparation of meat shipped over state lines would be subject to federal inspection from corral to can. Although the largest packers resisted certain features of the act, they grudgingly accepted it as an opportunity to drive their smaller, fly-by-night competitors out of business. At the same time, they could receive the government's seal of approval on their exports. As a companion to the Meat Inspection Act, the Pure Food and Drug Act of 1906 was designed to prevent the adulteration and mislabeling of foods and pharmaceuticals.

Earth Control

Wasteful Americans, assuming that their natural resources were inexhaustible, had looted and polluted their incomparable domain with unparalleled speed and greed. Westerners were especially eager to accelerate the destructive process, for they panted to build up the country, and the environmental consequences be hanged. But even before the end of the nineteenth century, far-visioned leaders saw that such a squandering of the nation's birthright would have to be halted or America would sink from resource richness to despoiled squalor.

A first feeble step toward conservation was the Desert Land Act of 1877. More successful was the Forest Reserve Act of 1891, authorizing the president to set aside public forest land as national forests and other reserves. Under this statute some 46 million acres of magnificent trees were rescued from the lumberman's saw in the 1890s and preserved for posterity.

A new day in the history of conservation dawned with the advent of Roosevelt. Huntsman, naturalist, rancher, lover of the great outdoors, he was appalled by the pillaging of timber and other natural resources. Other dedicated conservationists, notably Gifford Pinchot, head of the federal Division

High Point for Conservation   *Conservationist Roosevelt and famed naturalist-conservationist John Muir visit Glacier Point, on the rim of Yosemite Valley, California. In the distance is Yosemite Falls; a few feet behind Roosevelt is a sheer drop of 3,254 feet (992 meters).*

of Forestry, had broken important ground before him. But Roosevelt seized the banner of leadership and charged into the fray with all the weight of his prestige, his energy, his firsthand knowledge, and his slashing invective.

The thirst of the desert still unslaked, Congress responded to the whip of the Rough Rider by passing the landmark Newlands Act of 1902. Washington was authorized to collect money from the sale of public lands in the sun-baked western states and then use these funds for the development of irrigation projects. Settlers repaid the cost of reclamation from their now-productive soil, and the money was put into a fund to finance more such enterprises.

Roosevelt pined to preserve the nation's shrinking forests. By 1900 only about a quarter of the once-vast virgin timberlands remained standing.

Lumbermen had already logged off most of the virgin timber from Maine to Michigan, and the sharp thud of their axes was beginning to split the silence in the great fir forests of the Pacific slope. Roosevelt proceeded to set aside in federal reserves some 125 million acres, or almost three times the acreage thus saved from the saw by his three predecessors. He similarly earmarked millions of acres of coal deposits, as well as water resources useful for irrigation and power.

Conservation, including reclamation, may have been Roosevelt's most enduring tangible achievement. The superactive president took conservation out of the conversation stage, threw the force of his colorful personality behind it, dramatized it, and aroused public opinion to a constructive crusade. He was buoyed in this effort by an upwelling national mood of concern about the disappearance of the frontier. City dwellers snapped up Jack London's *Call of the Wild* (1903) and other books about nature. Groups like the outdoor-oriented Boy Scouts of America and the Sierra Club, founded in 1892, dedicated themselves to preserving the wildness of the western landscape.

Conservationist forces were not all of one mind. The building of a dam in the Hetch Hetchy Valley in Yosemite National Park in 1913 laid bare a deep division that persists to this day. To the preservationists of the Sierra Club, including famed naturalist John Muir, Hetch Hetchy was a "temple" of nature that should be held inviolable by the civilizing hand of humanity. But other conservationists, among them President Roosevelt's chief forester, Gifford Pinchot, believed that "wilderness was waste." Pinchot and Roosevelt wanted to *use* their nation's natural endowment intelligently. They sought to combine recreation, sustained-yield logging, watershed protection, and summer stock grazing on the same expanse of federal land.

Rational use of resources meant large-scale and long-term planning as well as efficient administrative techniques. Roosevelt's conservation policies, like many of his business policies, meant working hand in glove with the biggest resource users. The one-man-and-a-mule logger and the one-man-and-a-dog sheepherder were inevitably shouldered aside by the combined bulk of big business and big government.

The "Roosevelt Panic" of 1907

Roosevelt was handily elected president in his own right in 1904 and entered his new term buoyed up by his enormous personal popularity. Yet the conservative Republican bosses grew increasingly restive as Roosevelt in his second term called ever more loudly for regulating the corporations, taxing incomes, and protecting workers. Roosevelt, meanwhile, had partly defanged himself after his election in 1904 by announcing that under no circumstances would he be a candidate for a third term.

Roosevelt suffered a sharp setback in 1907, when a short but punishing panic descended on Wall Street. The financial flurry featured frightened "runs" on banks, suicides, and criminal indictments against speculators. The financial world hastened to blame Roosevelt for the storm. It cried that this "quack" had unsettled industry with his boat-rocking tactics, and branded the current distress the "Roosevelt panic." The hot-tempered president angrily lashed back at his critics when he accused "certain malefactors of great wealth" of having deliberately engineered the monetary crisis to force the government to relax its assaults on trusts.

Baby, Kiss Papa Good-bye *Theodore Roosevelt leaves his baby, "My Policies," in the hands of his chosen successor, William Howard Taft. Friction between Taft and Roosevelt would soon erupt, however, prompting Roosevelt to return to politics and challenge Taft for the presidency.*

The Rough Rider Thunders Out

Still warmly popular in 1908, Roosevelt could easily have won a second presidential nomination and almost certainly the election. But he felt bound by his impulsive postelection promise after his victory in 1904. The departing president thus naturally sought a successor who would carry out "my policies." The man of his choice was amiable, ample-girthed, and huge-framed William Howard Taft, secretary of war and a mild progressive.

As heir apparent, Taft had often been called upon in Roosevelt's absence to "sit on the lid"—all 350 pounds of him. At the Republican convention of 1908 in Chicago, Roosevelt used his control of the party machinery—the "steamroller"—to push through Taft's nomination on the first ballot. Three

weeks later, in mile-high Denver, in the heart of silver country, the Democrats nominated twice-beaten William Jennings Bryan.

The dull campaign of 1908 featured the rotund Taft and the now-balding "Boy Orator" trying to claim the progressive Roosevelt mantle. The solid Judge Taft read cut-and-dried speeches while Bryan griped that Roosevelt had stolen his policies from the Bryanite camp. A majority of voters chose stability with Roosevelt-endorsed Taft, who polled 321 electoral votes to 162 for Bryan. The victor's popular count was 7,675,320 to 6,412,294. The election's only surprise came from the Socialists, who amassed 420,793 votes for Eugene V. Debs, the hero of the Pullman strike of 1894.

Roosevelt, ever in the limelight, left soon after the election for a lion hunt in Africa. His numerous enemies clinked glasses while toasting "Health to the lions," and a few irreverently prayed that some big cat would "do its duty." But TR survived, still bursting with energy at the age of fifty-one in 1909.

Roosevelt was branded by his adversaries as a wild-eyed radical, but his reputation as an eater of errant industrialists now seems inflated. He fought many a sham battle, and the number of laws that he inspired was certainly not in proportion to the amount of noise he emitted. He was often under attack from the reigning business lords, but the more enlightened of them knew that they had a friend in the White House. Roosevelt should be remembered first and foremost as the cowboy who started to tame the bucking bronco of adolescent capitalism, thus ensuring it a long adult life.

TR's enthusiasm and perpetual youthfulness, like an overgrown Boy Scout's, appealed to the young of all ages. "You must always remember," a British diplomat cautioned his colleagues, "that the president is about six." He served as a political lightning rod to protect capitalists against popular indignation—and against socialism, which Roosevelt regarded as "ominous." He strenuously sought the middle road between unbridled individualism and paternalistic collectivism. His conservation crusade, which tried to mediate between the romantic wilderness-preservationists and the rapacious resource-predators, was probably his most typical and his most lasting achievement.

Several other contributions of Roosevelt lasted beyond his presidency. First, he greatly enlarged the power and prestige of the presidential office—and masterfully developed the technique of using the big stick of publicity as a political bludgeon. Second, he helped shape the progressive movement and beyond it the liberal reform campaigns later in the century. His Square Deal, in a sense, was the grandfather of the New Deal later launched by his fifth cousin, Franklin D. Roosevelt. Finally, to a greater degree than any of his predecessors, TR opened the eyes of Americans to the fact that they shared the world with other nations. As a great power they had fallen heir to great responsibilities—and had been seized by ambitions—from which there was no escaping.

Taft: A Round Peg in a Square Hole

William Howard Taft, with his ruddy complexion and upturned mustache, at first inspired widespread confidence. "Everybody loves a fat man," the saying goes, and the jovial Taft, with "mirthquakes" of laughter bubbling up from his abundant abdomen, was personally popular. He had graduated second in his class at Yale and had established an admirable reputation as a lawyer and judge, though widely regarded as hostile to labor unions. He had been a trusted administrator under Roosevelt—in the Philippines, at home, and in Cuba, where he had served capably as a troubleshooter.

But "good old Will" suffered from lethal political handicaps. Roosevelt had led the conflicting elements of the Republican party by the sheer force of his personality. Taft, in contrast, had none of the arts of a dashing political leader, and none of Roosevelt's zest for the fray. Recoiling from the clamor of controversy, he generally adopted an attitude of passivity toward Congress. He was a poor judge of public opinion, and his candor made him a chronic victim of "foot-in-mouth" disease.

"Peaceful Bill" was no doubt a mild progressive, but at heart he was more wedded to the status quo than to change. Significantly, his cabinet did not contain a single representative of the party's "insurgent" wing, which was on fire for reform of current abuses, especially the tariff.

The Dollar Goes Abroad as a Diplomat

Though ordinarily lethargic, Taft bestirred himself to use the lever of American investments to boost American political interests abroad. Washington warmly encouraged Wall Street bankers to sluice their surplus dollars into foreign areas of strategic concern to the United States, especially in East Asia and in the regions critical to the security of the Panama Canal. New York bankers would thus strengthen American defenses and foreign policies while bringing further prosperity to their homeland—and to themselves. The almighty dollar thereby supplanted the big stick.

China's Manchuria was the object of Taft's most spectacular effort to inject the reluctant dollar into the East Asian theater. Newly ambitious Japan and imperialistic Russia, recent foes, controlled the rail-roads of this strategic province. President Taft saw in the Manchurian railway monopoly a possible stran-gulation of Chinese economic interests and a conse-quent slamming of the Open Door in the faces of U.S. merchants. An American attempt to persuade foreign investors to invest in Manchurian railroads ran into stiff Japanese and Russian opposition.

Another dangerous new trouble spot was the revolution-riddled Caribbean—now virtually a Yan-kee lake. Hoping to head off trouble, Washington urged Wall Street bankers to pump dollars into the financial vacuums in Honduras and Haiti to keep out foreign funds. But dollar diplomacy did not bring an end to armed Caribbean intervention. Sporadic dis-orders in palm-fronded Cuba, Honduras, and the Dominican Republic brought American forces to these countries to restore order. A revolutionary upheaval in Nicaragua, perilously close to the nearly completed canal, resulted in the landing of twenty-five hundred U.S. Marines in 1912.

Taft the Trustbuster

Taft managed to gain some fame as a smasher of monopolies. The ironic truth is that the colorless Taft brought ninety suits against the trusts during his four years in office, compared with some forty-four for Roosevelt in seven and a half years.

By fateful happenstance the most sensational judicial actions during the Taft regime came in 1911. In that year the Supreme Court ordered dissolution of the mighty Standard Oil Company, which was judged to be a combination in restraint of trade in violation of the Sherman Anti-Trust Act of 1890. At the same time the Court handed down its famous "rule of rea-son." This doctrine held that only those combina-tions that "unreasonably" restrained trade were illegal. This fine-point proviso ripped a huge hole in the government's antitrust net.

Even more explosively, in 1911 Taft decided to press an antitrust suit against United States Steel Cor-poration. This initiative infuriated Roosevelt, who had personally been involved in one of the mergers that prompted the suit. Once Roosevelt's protégé, President Taft was increasingly taking on the role of his antagonist. The stage was being set for a bruising confrontation.

Taft Splits the Republican Party

Lowering the barriers of the high protective tariff—the "Mother of Trusts"—was high on the agenda of the progressive members of the Republican party, and they at first thought they had a friend and ally in Taft. When the president called Congress into special session in March 1909, the House passed a moder-ately reductive bill. But senatorial reactionaries, led by Senator Nelson Aldrich of Rhode Island, tacked on hundreds of upward tariff revisions. Only such items as hides, sea moss, and canary-bird seed were left on the duty-free list.

After much handwringing, Taft signed the Payne-Aldrich Bill, thus betraying his campaign promises and outraging the progressive wing of his party, heavily drawn from the Midwest. Taft rubbed salt in the wound by proclaiming it "the best bill that the Republican party ever passed."

Taft revealed a further knack for shooting him-self in the foot in his handling of conservation. The portly president was a dedicated conservationist, and his contributions actually equaled or surpassed those of Roosevelt. He set up the Bureau of Mines to control mineral resources, rescued millions of acres of west-ern coal lands from exploitation, and protected water-power sites from private development. But those praiseworthy accomplishments were largely erased in the public mind by the noisy Ballinger-Pinchot quarrel that erupted in 1910.

When Secretary of the Interior Ballinger opened public lands in Wyoming, Montana, and Alaska to corporate development, he was sharply criticized by Gifford Pinchot, chief of the Agriculture Department's Division of Forestry and a stalwart Rooseveltian. When Taft dismissed Pinchot on the narrow grounds of insubordination, a storm of protest arose from conservationists and from Roo-sevelt's friends, who were legion. The whole unsavory episode further widened the growing rift between the president and the former president, one-time close political partners.

The reformist wing of the Republican party was up in arms, while Taft was being pushed increasingly into the embrace of the standpat Old Guard. By the spring of 1910, the Grand Old Party was split wide open, owing largely to the clumsiness of Taft. A suspicious Roosevelt returned triumphantly to New York in June

1910 and shortly thereafter stirred up a tempest. In a flaming speech at Osawatamie, Kansas, he proclaimed a doctrine—popularly known as the "New Nationalism"—that urged the national government to increase its power to remedy economic and social abuses.

Weakened by these internal divisions, the Republicans lost badly in the congressional elections of 1910. The Democrats emerged from their landslide victory with 228 seats to only 161 for the once-dominant Republicans. In a further symptom of the reforming temper of the times, a Socialist representative, Austrian-born Victor L. Berger, was elected from Milwaukee.* The Republicans, by virtue of holdovers, retained the Senate, 51 to 41, but the insurgents in their midst were numerous enough to make that hold precarious.

The Taft-Roosevelt Rupture

The sputtering uprising in Republican ranks now blossomed into a full-fledged revolt. Early in 1911 the National Progressive Republican League was formed, with the fiery, white-maned Senator La Follette of Wisconsin its leading candidate for the Republican presidential nomination. The assumption was that Roosevelt would not permit himself to be "drafted."

But the restless Rough Rider began to change his views about third terms as he saw Taft, hand

---

* He was eventually denied his seat in 1919, during a wave of anti-red hysteria.

in glove with the hated Old Guard, discard "my policies." In February 1912 Roosevelt formally wrote to seven state governors that he was willing to accept the Republican nomination. His reasoning was that the third-term tradition applied to three *consecutive elective* terms. Exuberantly he cried, "My hat is in the ring!" and "The fight is on and I am stripped to the buff!"

Roosevelt forthwith seized the Progressive banner, while La Follette, who had served as a convenient pathbreaker, was protestingly elbowed aside. Girded for battle, the Rough Rider clattered into the presidential primaries then being held in many states. He shouted through half-clenched teeth that the president had fallen under the thumb of the reactionary bosses, and that although Taft "means well, he means well feebly." The once-genial Taft, now in a fighting mood, branded Roosevelt supporters as "emotionalists and neurotics."

A Taft-Roosevelt explosion was near in June 1912, when the Republican convention met in Chicago. The Rooseveltites, who were about 100 delegates short of winning the nomination, challenged the right of some 250 Taft delegates to be seated. Most of these contests were arbitrarily settled in favor of Taft, whose supporters held the throttle of the convention steamroller. The Roosevelt adherents, crying "fraud" and "naked theft," in the end refused to vote, and Taft triumphed.

Roosevelt, the supposedly good sportsman, refused to quit the game. Having tasted for once the bitter cup of defeat, he was now on fire to lead a third-party crusade.

Roosevelt the Take-Back Giver

Chronology

1901	Commission system established in Galveston, Texas.
	Progressive Robert La Follette elected governor of Wisconsin.
1902	Lincoln Steffens and Ida Tarbell publish muckraking exposés.
	Anthracite coal strike.
	Newlands Act.
1903	Department of Commerce and Labor established.
	Elkins Act.
1904	*Northern Securities* case.
	Roosevelt defeats Alton Parker for presidency.
1905	*Lochner* v. *New York*.
1906	Hepburn Act.
	Upton Sinclair publishes *The Jungle*.
	Meat Inspection Act.
	Pure Food and Drug Act.
1907	"Roosevelt panic."
1908	*Muller* v. *Oregon*.
	Taft defeats Bryan for presidency.
1909	Payne-Aldrich Tariff.
1910	Ballinger-Pinchot affair.
1911	Triangle Shirtwaist Company fire.
	Standard Oil antitrust case.
	U.S. Steel Corporation antitrust suit.
1912	Taft wins Republican nomination over Roosevelt.
1913	Seventeenth Amendment passed (direct election of U.S. senators).

SUGGESTED READINGS

Primary Source Documents

Lincoln Steffens, *The Shame of the Cities** (1904), is an exemplary muckraking document, as is Upton Sinclair's notorious novel *The Jungle* (1906). For a less-than-gracious assessment of the muckrakers see Theodore Roosevelt, "The Man with the Muckrake,"* *Putnam's Monthly and The Critic*, vol. I (October 1906), pp. 42–43. A revealing account of municipal politics is George Washington Plunkitt, *Plunkitt of Tammany Hall** (1905). See also the decision of the Supreme Court on state bakery regulations in *Lochner* v. *New York*, 198 U.S. 45 (1905). Oliver Wendell Holmes, Jr.'s thundering dissent in the *Lochner* case is reprinted in Richard Hofstadter, *Great Issues in American History* (1958).

Secondary Sources

A brief introduction is John W. Chambers, *The Tyranny of Change: America in the Progressive Era, 1900–1917* (1980). Perceptive interpretations are Samuel P. Hays, *The Response to Industrialism, 1885–1914* (1957); Robert H. Wiebe, *The Search for Order* (1967); and Richard Hofstadter, *The Age of Reform* (1955). Especially provocative are James Weinstein, *The Corporate Ideal in the Liberal State* (1968), and Gabriel Kolko, *The Triumph of Conservatism* (1963). Consult also Alfred D. Chandler, Jr., *The Visible Hand* (1977), and Morton Keller, *Regulating a New Economy: Public Policy and Economic Change in America, 1900–1933* (1990). On pure food and drugs see James Harvey Young, *Pure Food: Securing the Federal Food and Drugs Act of 1906* (1989). On progressive social work and social concerns consult Allen F. Davis, *Spearheads for Reform: The Social Settlements and the Progressive Movement, 1890–1914* (1967); Mina Carson, *Settlement Folk: Social Thought and the American Settlement Movement, 1885–1930* (1990); James Patterson, *America's Struggle Against Poverty, 1900–1980* (1981); David B. Tyack, *The One Best System: A History of American Urban Education* (1974); and Lynn Gordon, *Gender and Higher Education in the Progressive Era* (1990). On religion see Martin E. Marty, *Modern American Religion:*

The Irony of It All, 1893–1919 (1986); T. J. Jackson Lears takes a different perspective in *No Place of Grace: Antimodernism and the Transformation of American Culture* (1981). On conservation see Samuel P. Hays, *Conservation and the Gospel of Efficiency* (1959); Elmo Richardson, *The Politics of Conservation* (1962); and James Penick, Jr., *Progressive Politics and Conservation* (1968). Socialism is discussed in Nick Salvatore, *Eugene V. Debs: Citizen and Socialist* (1982); James Weinstein, *The Decline of Socialism in America, 1912–1925* (1967); and Mari Jo Buhle, W*omen and American Socialism, 1897–1920* (1981). Another perspective on women in this period is given in Rosalind Rosenberg, *Beyond Separate Spheres* (1982). Jacqueline Jones focuses on black women in *Labor of Love, Labor of Sorrow: Black Women, Work, and the Family from Slavery to the Present* (1985). The Taft era is summarized in Paolo Coletta, *The Presidency of William Howard Taft* (1973).

---

* An asterisk indicates that the document, or an excerpt from it, can be found in Thomas A. Bailey and David M. Kennedy, eds., *The American Spirit: United States History as Seen by Contemporaries*, 9th ed. (Boston: Houghton Mifflin, 1998).

30

★★★★★★★★★

Wilsonian Progressivism at Home and Abroad,

1912–1916

★★★★★★

This is not a day of triumph; it is a day of dedication. Here muster not the forces of party, but the forces of humanity. . . . I summon all honest men, all patriotic, all forward-looking men, to my side. God helping me, I will not fail them, if they will but counsel and sustain me!

★★★★★★

THOMAS WOODROW WILSON, INAUGURAL ADDRESS, 1913

The Emergence of Dr. Thomas Woodrow Wilson

Office-hungry Democrats—the "outs" since 1897—were jubilant over the disruptive Republican brawl at Chicago. If they could come up with an outstanding reformist leader, they had an excellent chance to win the White House. Such a leader appeared in Dr. Woodrow Wilson, once a mild conservative but now a militant progressive. Beginning professional life as a brilliant academic lecturer on government, he rose in 1902 to the presidency of Princeton University, where he achieved some sweeping educational reforms.

Wilson entered politics in 1910 when New Jersey bosses, needing a respectable "front" candidate for the governorship, offered him the nomination. They expected to lead the academic novice by the nose, but to their surprise, Wilson waged a passionate reform campaign in which he assailed the "predatory" trusts and promised to return state government to the people. Riding the crest of the progressive wave, the "Schoolmaster in Politics" was swept into office.

Once in the governor's chair, Wilson drove through the legislature a sheaf of forward-looking measures that made reactionary New Jersey one of the more liberal states. Filled with righteous indignation, Wilson revealed irresistible reforming zeal, burning eloquence, superb powers of leadership, and a refreshing habit of appealing over the heads of the scheming bosses to the sovereign people. Now a figure of national eminence, Wilson was being widely mentioned for the presidency.

When the Democrats met at Baltimore in 1912, Wilson was nominated on the forty-sixth ballot, aided by William Jennings Bryan's switch to his side. The Democrats gave Wilson a strong progressive platform to run on, including calls for antitrust legislation, banking reform, and tariff reductions.

The "Bull Moose" Campaign of 1912

Surging events had meanwhile been thrusting Roosevelt to the fore as a candidate for the presidency on a third-party Progressive ticket. The fighting ex-cowboy, angered by his recent rebuff, was eager to lead the charge. A pro-Roosevelt Progressive convention, with about two thousand delegates from forty states, assembled in Chicago during August 1912. Dramatically symbolizing the rising political status of women, as well as Progressive support for the cause of social justice, settlement-house pioneer Jane Addams placed Roosevelt's name in nomination for the presidency.

Fired-up Progressives entered the campaign with righteousness and enthusiasm. Roosevelt boasted that he felt "as strong as a bull moose," so the bull moose took its place with the donkey and the elephant in the American political zoo.

Roosevelt and Taft were bound to slit each other's political throats: by dividing the Republican vote they virtually guaranteed a Democratic victory. The two antagonists tore into each other as only former friends can. "Death alone can take me out now," cried the once-jovial Taft, as he branded Roosevelt a "dangerous egotist" and a "demagogue." Roosevelt, fighting mad, assailed Taft as a "fathead" with the brain of a "guinea pig."

Beyond the clashing personalities, the overshadowing question of the 1912 campaign was which of two varieties of progressivism would prevail—Roosevelt's New Nationalism or Wilson's New Freedom. Both men favored a more active government role in economic and social affairs, but they disagreed sharply over specific strategies. Roosevelt preached the theories spun out by the progressive thinker Herbert Croly in his book *The Promise of American Life* (1910). Croly and TR both favored continued consolidation of trusts and labor unions, paralleled by the growth of powerful regulatory agencies in Washington. Roosevelt and his "bull moosers" also campaigned for woman suffrage and a broad program of social welfare, including minimum-wage laws and social insurance. Clearly, the bull moose

GOP Divided by Bull Moose Equals Democratic Victory, 1912

Progressives looked forward to the kind of activist welfare state that Franklin Roosevelt's New Deal would one day make a reality.

Wilson's New Freedom, by contrast, favored small enterprise, entrepreneurship, and the free functioning of unregulated and unmonopolized markets. The Democrats shunned social welfare proposals and pinned their economic faith on competition—on the "man on the make," as Wilson put it. The keynote of Wilson's campaign was not regulation but fragmentation of the big industrial combines, chiefly by means of vigorous enforcement of the antitrust laws. The election of 1912 thus offered the voters a choice not merely of policies but of political and economic philosophies—a rarity in United States history.

The heat of the campaign cooled a bit when, in Milwaukee, Roosevelt was shot in the chest by a fanatic. The Rough Rider suspended active campaigning for more than two weeks after delivering, with bull moose gameness and a bloody shirt, his scheduled speech.

Woodrow Wilson: A Minority President

Former professor Wilson won handily, with 435 electoral votes and 6,296,547 popular votes, The "third-party" candidate, Roosevelt, finished second, with 88 electoral votes and 4,118,571 popular votes. Taft won only 8 electoral votes and 3,486,720 popular votes.

The election figures are fascinating. Wilson, with only 41 percent of the popular vote, was clearly a minority president, though his party won a majority in Congress. Wilson's popular total was actually smaller than Bryan's in any of his three defeats, despite the increase in population. Taft and Roosevelt together polled over a million and a quarter more votes than the Democrats. Progressivism rather than Wilson was the runaway winner. Although the Democratic total obviously included many conservatives in the solid South, the combined progressive vote for Wilson and Roosevelt still exceeded the tally of the more conservative Taft. To the progressive totals must be added some support for the Socialist candidate, persistent Eugene V. Debs, who rolled up 900,672 votes, or more than twice as many as he had netted four years earlier. Starry-eyed Socialists dreamed of being in the White House within eight years.

Roosevelt's lone-wolf course was tragic both for himself and for his former Republican associates. The Progressive party, which was primarily a one-man show, had no future because it had elected few candidates to state and local offices. Without patronage plums to hand out to the faithful workers, death by slow starvation was inevitable. Yet the Progressives made a tremendous showing for a hastily organized third party and helped spur the enactment of many of their pet reforms by the Wilsonian Democrats.

As for the Republicans, they were thrust into unaccustomed minority status in Congress for the next six years and were frozen out of the White House for eight years. Taft himself had a fruitful old age. He taught law for eight pleasant years at Yale University and in 1921 became chief justice of the Supreme Court—a job for which he was far more happily suited than the presidency.

The Presidential Vote, 1912

Candidate	Party	Electoral Vote	Popular Vote	Approximate Percentage
Woodrow Wilson	Democratic	435	6,296,547	41
Theodore Roosevelt	Progressive	88	4,118,571	27
William H. Taft	Republican	8	3,486,720	23
Eugene V. Debs	Socialist	—	900,672	6
E. W. Chafin	Prohibition	—	206,275	1
A. E. Reimer	Socialist-Labor	—	28,750	0.2

Wilson: The Idealist in Politics

(Thomas) Woodrow Wilson, the second Democratic president since 1861, looked like the ascetic intellectual he was, with clean-cut features, pinched-on eyeglasses, and trim figure (5 feet, 11 inches, and 179 pounds). Born in Virginia shortly before the Civil War and reared in Georgia and the Carolinas, the professor-politician was the first man from one of the seceded southern states to reach the White House since Zachary Taylor, sixty-four years earlier.

Son of a Presbyterian minister, Wilson was reared in an atmosphere of fervent piety. He later used the presidential pulpit to preach his inspirational political sermons. A moving orator, Wilson could rise on the wings of spiritual power to soaring eloquence. Skillfully using a persuasive voice, he relied not on arm waving but on sincerity and moral appeal. As a lifelong student of finely chiseled words, he turned out to be a "phraseocrat" who coined many noble epigrams. Someone remarked that he was born halfway between the Bible and the dictionary and never strayed far from either.

Splendid though Wilson's intellectual equipment was, he suffered from serious defects of personality. Though jovial and witty in private, he could be cold and standoffish in public. Incapable of unbending and acting the showman, like "Teddy" Roosevelt, he lacked the common touch. He loved humanity in the mass rather than the individual in person. His academic background caused him to feel most at home with scholars, although he had to work with politicians. An austere and somewhat arrogant intellectual, he looked down his nose through pince-nez glasses upon lesser minds, including journalists. He was especially intolerant of stupid senators, whose "bungalow" minds made him "sick."

Wilson's burning idealism—especially his desire to reform ever-present wickedness—drove him forward faster than lesser spirits were willing to go. His sense of moral righteousness was such that he often found compromise difficult: black was black, wrong was wrong, and one should never compromise with wrong. Wilson's Scottish Presbyterian ancestors had passed on to him an inflexible stubbornness. When convinced that he was right, he would break before he would bend, unlike the pragmatic Roosevelt.

Wilson Attacks the "Triple Wall of Privilege"

Few presidents have arrived at the White House with a clearer program than Wilson's or one destined to be so completely achieved. The new president called for an all-out assault on what he called the "triple wall of privilege": the tariff, the banks, and the trusts.

Wilson tackled the tariff first. In a precedent-shattering move, he appeared in person before a joint session of Congress in 1913 and presented his appeal with stunning eloquence and effectiveness. Moved by Wilson's aggressive leadership, the House swiftly passed the Underwood Tariff Bill, which provided for a substantial reduction of rates. It was also a landmark in tax legislation. Under authority granted by the recently ratified Sixteenth Amendment, Congress enacted a graduated income tax, beginning with a modest levy on incomes over $3,000 (then considerably higher than the average family's income). By 1917 revenue from the income tax shot ahead of receipts from the tariff. This gap has since been vastly widened.

A second bastion of the "triple wall of privilege" was the antiquated and inadequate banking and currency system, long since outgrown by the Republic's lusty economic expansion. The most serious shortcoming of the country's financial structure, as exposed by the panic of 1907, was the inelasticity of the currency. Banking reserves were heavily concentrated in New York and a handful of other large cities and could not be mobilized in times of financial stress into areas that were badly pinched.

In 1911 a special commission headed by ultra-conservative Republican Senator Nelson Aldrich recommended a gigantic bank with numerous branches—in effect, a third Bank of the United States. Democratic banking reformers preferred the findings of a House committee chaired by Congressman Arsene Pujo, which traced the tentacles of the "money monster" into the hidden vaults of American banking and business. President Wilson's confidant, progressive-minded Massachusetts attorney Louis D. Brandeis, further fanned the flames of reform with his incendiary though scholarly book *Other People's Money and How the Bankers Use It* (1914).

In June 1913, in a second dramatic personal appearance before Congress, the president ringingly endorsed sweeping Democratic proposals for a decentralized bank in government hands, as opposed to Republican demands for a huge private bank. Again appealing to the sovereign people, Wilson scored another triumph. In 1913 he signed the Federal Reserve Act, the most important piece of economic legislation between the Civil War and the New Deal.

The new Federal Reserve Board, appointed by the president, oversaw a nationwide system of twelve regional reserve districts, each with its own central bank. Although these regional banks were actually bankers' banks, owned by member financial institutions, the final authority of the Federal Reserve Board guaranteed a substantial measure of public control. The board was also empowered to issue paper money—"Federal Reserve notes"—backed by commercial paper, such as the promissory notes of businesspeople. Thus the amount of money in circulation could be swiftly increased as needed for the legitimate requirements of business.

The Federal Reserve Act was a red-letter achievement. It carried the nation with flying banners through the financial crises of the World War of 1914–1918. Without it, the Republic's progress toward the modern economic age would have been seriously retarded.

Without pausing for breath, Wilson pushed toward the last remaining rampart in the "triple wall of privilege"—the trusts. A third personal appearance before Congress in 1914 led to the Federal Trade Commission Act of 1914. The new law empowered a presidentially appointed commission to turn a searchlight on industries engaged in interstate commerce, such as the meatpackers. The commissioners were expected to crush monopoly in the cradle by rooting out unfair trade practices, including unlawful competition, false advertising, mislabeling, adulteration, and bribery.

The knot of monopoly was further cut by the Clayton Anti-Trust Act of 1914. It lengthened the shopworn Sherman Act's list of business practices that were deemed objectionable, including price discrimination and interlocking directorates (whereby the same individuals served as directors of supposedly competing firms).

The Clayton Act also conferred long-overdue benefits on labor. The law exempted labor and agricultural organizations from antitrust prosecutions under the Sherman Act, while explicitly legalizing strikes and peaceful picketing. Union leader Samuel Gompers hailed the act as the Magna Carta of labor because it legally lifted human labor out of the category of "a commodity or article of commerce." But the rejoicing was premature, as conservative judges in later years continued to clip the wings of the union movement.

Wilsonian Progressivism at High Tide

Energetically scaling the "triple wall of privilege," Woodrow Wilson had treated the nation to a dazzling demonstration of vigorous presidential leadership. He proved nearly irresistible in his first eighteen months in office. For once, a political creed was matched by deed as the progressive reformers racked up victory after victory.

Standing at the peak of his powers at the head of the progressive forces, Wilson pressed ahead with further reforms. The Federal Farm Loan Act of 1916 made credit available to farmers at low rates of interest—as long demanded by the Populists. Sweaty laborers also made gains as the progressive wave foamed forward. Sailors, treated brutally from cat-o'-nine-tails days onward, were given relief by the La Follette Seamen's Act of 1915. It required decent treatment and a living wage on American merchant ships.

Wilson further helped workers with the Workingmen's Compensation Act of 1916, granting assistance to federal civil-service employees during periods of disability. In the same year the president approved an act restricting child labor on products flowing into interstate commerce, though the standpat Supreme Court soon invalidated the law. The Adamson Act of 1916 established an eight-hour workday for all employees on trains in interstate commerce, with extra pay for overtime.

Wilson earned the enmity of businesspeople and bigots but endeared himself to progressives when in 1916 he nominated for the Supreme Court the prominent reformer Louis D. Brandeis—the first Jew to be called to the high bench. Yet even Wilson's progressivism had its limits, and it clearly stopped short of better treatment for blacks. The southern-bred Wilson actually presided over accelerated segregation in the federal bureaucracy. When a delegation of black leaders personally protested to him, the schoolmasterish president virtually froze them out of his office.

Despite these limitations, Wilson knew that to be reelected in 1916, he needed to identify himself clearly as the candidate of progressivism. Wilson's election in 1912 had been something of a fluke, owing largely to the Taft-Roosevelt split in the Republican ranks. To remain in the White House, the president would have to woo the bull moose voters into the Democratic fold.

·

New Directions in Foreign Policy

In one important area, Wilson chose not to answer the trumpet call of the bull moosers. In contrast to Roosevelt and even Taft, Wilson recoiled from an aggressive foreign policy. Hating imperialism, he was repelled by TR's big stickism. Suspicious of Wall Street, he detested the so-called dollar diplomacy of Taft.

In office only a week, Wilson declared war on dollar diplomacy. He proclaimed that the government would no longer offer special support to American investors in Latin America and China. Shivering from this Wilsonian bucket of cold water, American bankers pulled out of the Taft-engineered six-nation loan to China the next day. Wilson's anti-imperialism also produced the Jones Act of 1916, which granted territorial status and promised eventual independence for the Philippines.

Events in the Caribbean soon forced Wilson to eat some of his anti-imperialist words. In response to disorders in Haiti in 1914–1915, the president reluctantly dispatched marines to protect American lives and property. In 1916 he stole a page from the Roosevelt Corollary to the Monroe Doctrine and concluded a treaty with Haiti providing for U.S. supervision of finances and police. In the same year, Wilson sent the leathernecked marines to the riot-rocked Dominican Republic, which came under the shadow of the American eagle's wings. In 1917 Wilson purchased from Denmark the Virgin Islands in the West Indies. Increasingly the Caribbean Sea, with its vital approaches to the now-completed Panama Canal, was taking on the earmarks of a Yankee preserve.

Moralistic Diplomacy in Mexico

Rifle bullets whining across the southern border served as a constant reminder that all was not quiet in Mexico. For decades Mexico had been sorely exploited by foreign investors in oil, railroads, and mines. By 1913 American capitalists had sunk about a billion dollars into the underdeveloped but richly endowed country. But if Mexico was rich, the Mexicans were poor. Fed up with their miserable lot, they at last revolted.

Their revolution took an ugly turn in 1913, when a conscienceless clique murdered the popular new revolutionary president and installed General Victoriano Huerta in the president's chair. All this chaos accelerated a massive migration of Mexicans to the United States. More than a million Spanish-speaking newcomers tramped across the southern border in the first three decades of the twentieth century. Settling mostly in Texas, New Mexico, Arizona, and California, they helped to create a unique borderland culture that blended Mexican and American folkways. The revolutionary bloodshed also menaced American lives and property in Mexico. Cries for intervention burst from the lips of American jingoes like publisher William Randolph Hearst, owner of a Mexican ranch larger than Rhode Island.

Wilson stood firm against demands to step in. He also refused to recognize the murderous government of "that brute" Huerta. "I am going to teach the South American republics to elect good men," the former professor declared. He put his munitions where his mouth was in 1914, when he allowed American arms to flow to Huerta's principal rivals, white-bearded Venustiano Carranza and the firebrand Francisco ("Pancho") Villa.

The Mexican volcano erupted at the Atlantic seaport of Tampico in April 1914, when a small party of American sailors was arrested. The Mexicans promptly released the captives and apologized, but they refused the hotheaded American admiral's demand for a salute of twenty-one guns. Wilson then ordered the navy to seize the Mexican port of Vera Cruz. Huerta as well as Carranza hotly condemned this high-handed Yankee intervention.

Just as a full-dress shooting conflict seemed inevitable, Wilson was rescued by an offer of

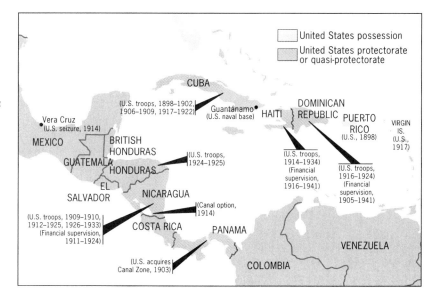

The United States in the Caribbean *This map explains why many Latin Americans accused the United States of turning the Caribbean Sea into a Yankee lake. It also suggests that Uncle Sam was much less "isolationist" in his own backyard than he was in faraway Europe or Asia.*

mediation from the ABC powers—Argentina, Brazil, and Chile. Huerta collapsed in July 1914 under pressure from within and without. He was succeeded by his archrival, Venustiano Carranza, still fiercely resentful of Wilson's military meddling. The whole sorry episode did not augur well for the future of United States–Mexican relations.

"Pancho" Villa, a combination of bandit and Robin Hood, had meanwhile emerged as the chief rival of President Carranza, whom Wilson reluctantly supported. Villa punished the "gringos" by killing sixteen young American mining engineers who were traveling through northern Mexico in January 1916. A month later Villa's men murdered nineteen more Americans during a raid across the border into Columbus, New Mexico.

General John J. ("Black Jack")* Pershing, a ramrod-erect veteran of the Cuban and Philippine campaigns, was ordered to break up the bandit band. His hastily organized force of several thousand mounted troops penetrated deep into rugged Mexico with surprising speed. They clashed with Carranza's forces and mauled the Villistas but missed capturing

---

* So called from his earlier service as an officer with the crack black Tenth Cavalry.

Villa himself. As the threat of war with Germany loomed larger, the invading army was withdrawn in January 1917.

A Precarious Neutrality

Europe's powder magazine, long smoldering, blew up in the summer of 1914, when the flaming pistol of a Serb patriot killed the heir to the throne of Austria-Hungary in Sarajevo. An outraged Vienna government, backed by Germany, forthwith presented a stern ultimatum to Serbia.

An explosive chain reaction followed. Russian mobilization in support of Serbia threatened Germany in the east, even as the tsar's ally, France, confronted Germany in the west. In alarm, the Germans struck suddenly at France through unoffending Belgium. Great Britain in turn was sucked into the conflagration on the side of France.

Almost overnight most of Europe was locked in a fight to the death. On one side were arrayed the Central Powers: Germany and Austria-Hungary, and later Turkey and Bulgaria. On the other side were the Allies, principally France, Britain, and Russia, and later Japan and Italy. Americans thanked God for the ocean moats and self-righteously congratulated themselves on having had ancestors wise enough to have abandoned the hell pits of Europe. Americans felt strong, snug, smug, and secure—but not for long.

President Wilson sorrowfully issued the routine neutrality proclamation and called on Americans to be neutral in thought as well as deed. But such scrupulous evenhandedness proved difficult. Both sides wooed the United States, the great neutral to the west. The British enjoyed the boon of close cultural, linguistic, and economic ties with America and had the added advantage of controlling most of the transatlantic cables. Their censors sheared away war stories harmful to the Allies and drenched the United States with tales of German bestiality.

Some German-American immigrants expressed noisy sympathy for the fatherland, but most Americans were anti-German from the outset. With his villainous upturned mustache, Kaiser Wilhelm II seemed the embodiment of arrogant autocracy, an impression strengthened by Germany's ruthless strike at neutral Belgium. Inept German plans for industrial sabotage in the United States further inflamed opinion against the kaiser and Germany. Yet the great majority of Americans earnestly hoped to stay out of the horrible war.

America Earns Blood Money

When Europe burst into flames in 1914, the United States was bogged down in a worrisome business recession. But as fate would have it, British and French war orders soon pulled American industry out of the morass of hard times and onto a peak of war-born prosperity. Part of this boom was financed by American bankers, notably the Wall Street firm of J. P. Morgan and Company, which eventually advanced to the Allies the enormous sum of $2.3 billion during the period of American neutrality. The Central Powers protested bitterly against the immense trade between America and the Allies, but this traffic did not in fact violate international neutrality laws. Germany was technically free to trade with the United States, but the tight British naval blockade prevented it from doing so.

Hard-pressed Germany did not tamely consent to being starved out. In retaliation for the British blockade, in February 1915 Berlin announced a submarine war area around the British Isles. The submarine was a weapon so new that existing international law could not be made to fit it. The old rule that a warship must stop and board a merchantman could hardly apply to submarines, which could easily be rammed or sunk if they surfaced.

The cigar-shaped marauders posed a dire threat to the United States—as long as Wilson insisted on maintaining America's neutral rights. Berlin officials declared that they would try not to sink *neutral* shipping, but they warned that mistakes would probably occur. Wilson now determined on a policy of calculated risk. He would continue to claim profitable neutral trading rights while hoping that no high-seas incident would force his hand to grasp the sword of war. He emphatically warned Germany that it would be held to "strict accountability" for any attacks on American vessels or citizens.

The German submarines meanwhile began their deadly work. In the first months of 1915, they sank about ninety ships in the war zone. Then the submarine issue became acute when the British passenger liner *Lusitania* was torpedoed and sank off the coast of Ireland on May 7, 1915, with the loss of 1,198 lives, including 128 Americans.

The *Lusitania* was carrying forty-two hundred cases of small-arms ammunition, a fact the Germans used to justify the sinking. But Americans were swept by a wave of shock and anger at this act of "mass murder" and "piracy." The eastern United States, closer to the war, seethed with talk of fighting, but the rest of the country showed a strong distaste for hostilities. The peace-loving Wilson had no stomach for leading a disunited nation into war, and instead relied on a series of increasingly strong notes to bring the German warlords sharply to book. "There is such a thing," he said, "as a man being too proud to fight."

Yet Wilson, sticking to his verbal guns, made some diplomatic progress. After another British liner, the *Arabic,* was sunk in August 1915, with the loss of two American lives, Berlin reluctantly agreed not to sink unarmed and unresisting passenger ships *without warning.*

This pledge appeared to be violated in March 1916, when the Germans torpedoed a French passenger steamer, the *Sussex.* The infuriated Wilson informed the Germans that unless they renounced the inhuman practice of sinking merchant ships

Advertisement from the New York *Herald,* May 1, 1915 *Six days later the* Lusitania *was sunk. Notice the German warning.*

without warning he would break diplomatic relations—an almost certain prelude to war.

Germany reluctantly knuckled under to President Wilson's *Sussex* ultimatum, agreeing not to sink passenger ships and merchant vessels without giving warning. But the Germans attached a long string to their *Sussex* pledge: the United States would have to persuade the Allies to modify what Berlin regarded as their illegal blockade. This, obviously, was something that Washington could not do. Wilson promptly accepted the German pledge, without accepting the "string." He thus won a temporary but precarious diplomatic victory—precarious because Germany could pull the string whenever it chose, and the president might suddenly find himself hauled over the cliff of war.

Wilson Wins Reelection in 1916

Against this ominous backdrop, the presidential campaign of 1916 gathered speed. Both the bull moose Progressives and the Republicans met in Chicago. The Progressives uproariously renominated Theodore Roosevelt, but the Rough Rider, who loathed Wilson and all his works, had no stomach for splitting the Republicans again and ensuring the reelection of his hated rival. In refusing to run, he sounded the death knell of the Progressive party.

Roosevelt's Republican admirers also clamored for "Teddy," but the Old Guard detested the renegade who had ruptured the party in 1912. Instead, they drafted Supreme Court Justice Charles Evans Hughes, a cold intellectual who had achieved a solid record as governor of New York. The Republican platform condemned the Democratic tariff, assaults on the trusts, and Wilson's wishy-washiness in dealing with both Mexico and Germany.

The thick-whiskered Hughes ("an animated feather duster") left the bench for the campaign stump, where he was not at home. In anti-German areas of the country, he assailed Wilson for not standing up to the kaiser, whereas in isolationist areas he took a softer line. This fence-straddling operation led to the jeer "Charles Evasive Hughes."

Hughes was further plagued by Roosevelt, who was delivering a series of skin-'em-alive speeches

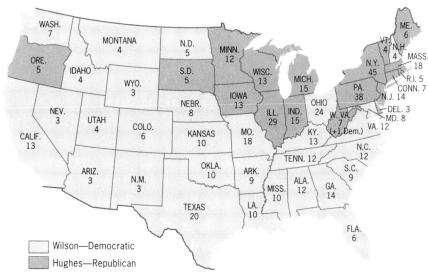

Presidential Election of 1916 (with electoral vote by state)   *Wilson was so worried about being a lame-duck president in a time of great international tensions that he drew up a plan whereby Hughes, if victorious, would be appointed secretary of state, Wilson and the vice president would resign, and Hughes would thus succeed immediately to the presidency.*

against "that damned Presbyterian hypocrite Wilson." Frothing for war, TR privately sneered at Hughes as a "whiskered Wilson." The only difference between the two, he said, was "a shave."

Wilson, nominated by acclamation at the Democratic convention in St. Louis, ignored Hughes on the theory that one should not try to murder a man who is committing suicide. His campaign was built on the slogan "He Kept Us Out of War." And Democratic orators warned that by electing Charles Evans Hughes, the nation would be electing a fight—with a certain frustrated Rough Rider leading the charge. A Democratic advertisement appealing to American workers read:

> You are Working;
>   —Not Fighting!
> Alive and Happy;
>   —Not Cannon Fodder!
> Wilson and Peace with Honor?
>   or
> Hughes with Roosevelt and War?

On election day, Hughes swept the East and looked like a surefire winner. Wilson went to bed that night prepared to accept defeat, while New York newspapers displayed huge portraits of "The President-Elect—Charles Evans Hughes." But the rest of the country turned the tide. Midwesterners and westerners, attracted by Wilson's progressive reforms and antiwar policies, flocked to the polls for the president. The final result, in doubt for several days, hinged on California, which Wilson carried by some 3,800 votes out of about a million cast.

Wilson barely squeaked through, with a final vote of 277 to 254 in the Electoral College and 9,127,695 to 8,533,507 in the popular column. The prolabor Wilson received strong support from the working class and from renegade bull moosers, whom Republicans failed to lure back into their camp. Wilson had not specifically promised to keep the country out of war, but probably enough voters relied on such implicit assurances to ensure his victory. Their hopeful expectations were soon rudely shattered.

AMERICA FIRST

Wilson, That's All !

HENRY ROBINSON CO. PUB. N. Y.

Wilson Campaign Poster, 1916   *This poster presents Wilson's campaign theme of patriotism.*

Chronology

1912	Wilson defeats Taft and Roosevelt for presidency.
1913	Underwood Tariff Act. Sixteenth Amendment passed (income tax). Federal Reserve Act. Huerta takes power in Mexico.
1914	Clayton Anti-Trust Act. Federal Trade Commission established. U.S. occupation of Vera Cruz, Mexico. World War I begins in Europe.
1915	La Follette Seamen's Act. *Lusitania* torpedoed and sunk by German U-boat. U.S. Marines sent to Haiti.
1916	*Sussex* ultimatum and pledge. Workingmen's Compensation Act. Federal Farm Loan Act. Adamson Act. Pancho Villa raids New Mexico. Brandeis appointed to Supreme Court. U.S. Marines sent to Dominican Republic. Wilson defeats Hughes for presidency.
1917	United States buys Virgin Islands from Denmark.

SUGGESTED READINGS

Primary Source Documents

Theodore Roosevelt's "Acceptance Speech"* at the Progressive convention of 1912, and Woodrow Wilson's collection of campaign speeches, *The New Freedom** (1913), give the substance and flavor of the critical 1912 campaign. Louis D. Brandeis, *Other People's Money and How the Bankers Use It** (1914), expresses the philosophy of a key Wilson adviser. On the *Lusitania* incident see *Foreign Relations of the United States*, 1915, Supplement, pp. 394–395, 420.

Secondary Sources

John M. Cooper, Jr., *The Warrior and the Priest* (1983), deftly contrasts Wilson and Theodore Roosevelt. Biographies of Wilson include August Heckscher's voluminous *Woodrow Wilson: A Biography* (1991), Arthur Link's five-volume *Wilson* (1947–1965), and John M. Blum's *Woodrow Wilson and the Politics of Morality* (1956). Particularly interesting is Alexander and Juliette George's psychological study, *Woodrow Wilson and Colonel House* (1956). For a sharply contrasting view see Edwin A. Weinstein, *Woodrow Wilson: A Medical and Psychologi-*

varying

viewpoints

Who Were the Progressives?

Debate about progressivism has revolved mainly around a question that is simple to ask but devilishly difficult to answer: who were the progressives? It was once taken for granted that progressive reformers were simply the heirs of the Jeffersonian-Jacksonian-Populist reform crusades; they were the oppressed and downtrodden common folk who finally erupted in wrath and demanded their due. But in his influential *Age of Reform* (1955), Richard Hofstadter astutely challenged that view.

Progressive leaders, Hofstadter argued, were not drawn from the ranks of society's poor and marginalized. Rather, they were middle-class people threatened from above by the emerging power of new corporate elites and from below by a restless working class. It was not economic deprivation, but "status anxiety," Hofstadter insisted, that prompted these people to become reformers. Their psychological motivation, he concluded, rendered many of their reform efforts quirky and ineffectual.

By contrast, New Left historians, notably Gabriel Kolko, argue that progressivism was dominated by established business leaders who successfully directed "reform" to their own conservative ends. In this view, government regulation (as embodied in new agencies like the Federal Reserve Board and the Federal Tariff Commission, and in legislation like the Meat Inspection Act) simply accomplished what two generations of private efforts had failed to accomplish: dampening cutthroat competition, stabilizing markets, and making America safe for monopoly capitalism.

Still other scholars, notably Robert H. Wiebe and Samuel P. Hays, argue that the progressives were neither the psychologically or economically disadvantaged, nor the old capitalist elite, but rather were members of a rapidly emerging, self-confident social class possessed of the new techniques of scientific management, technological expertise, and organizational know-how. This "organizational school" of historians does not see progressivism as a struggle of the "people" against the "interests," or as a confused and nostalgic campaign by status-threatened reformers, or as a conservative coup d'état. The progressive movement, in this view, was by and large an effort to rationalize and modernize many social institutions by introducing the wise and impartial hand of government regulation.

This view has much to recommend it. Yet despite its widespread acceptance among historians, it is an explanation that cannot adequately account for the titanic political struggles of the progressive era over the very reforms that the "organizational school" regards as simple adjustments to modernity. Recently, scholars such as Robyn Muncie, Linda Gordon, and Theda Skocpol have stressed the role of women in advocating progressive reforms. Building the American welfare state in the early twentieth century, they argue, was fundamentally a gendered activity inspired by a "female dominion" of social workers and "social feminists." Moreover, in contrast to many European countries where labor movements sought a welfare state to benefit the working class, American female reformers promoted welfare programs specifically to protect women and children.

cal Biography (1981). The road to World War I finds comprehensive treatment in Ernest May, *The World War and American Isolation, 1914–1917* (1959). Consult also Ross Gregory, *The Origins of American Intervention in the First World War* (1971), and Patrick Devlin, *Too Proud to Fight: Woodrow Wilson's Neutrality* (1975). Mira Wilkins traces *The History of Foreign Investment in the United States to 1914* (1989). Superb biographies of prominent intellectuals include David Levy, *Herbert Croly of the New Republic: The Life and Thought of an American Progressive* (1985); Edward A. Stettner, *Shaping Modern Liberalism: Herbert Croly and Progressive Thought* (1993); and Philippa Strum, *Brandeis: Justice for the People* (1984). On Wilson's struggle over freedom of the seas, special studies of value are Thomas A. Bailey and Paul Ryan, *The* Lusitania *Disaster* (1975), and Jeffrey J. Safford, *Wilsonian Maritime Diplomacy* (1978). Social and intellectual currents are described in Henry F. May, *The End of American Innocence: A Study of the First Years of Our Own Time, 1912–1917* (1959). Michael C. Adams, *The Great Adventure: Male Desire and the Coming of World War I* (1990), is a provocative work that tries to link Victorian gender ideology to the martial enthusiasms of the early twentieth century.

---

* An asterisk indicates that the document, or an excerpt from it, can be found in Thomas A. Bailey and David M. Kennedy, eds., *The American Spirit: United States History as Seen by Contemporaries*, 9th ed. (Boston: Houghton Mifflin, 1998).

31

★★★★★★★★★★

The War to End War,

1917–1918

★★★★★★

The world must be made safe for democracy. Its peace must be planted upon the tested foundations of political liberty. We have no selfish ends to serve. We desire no conquest, no dominion. We seek no indemnities for ourselves, no material compensation for the sacrifices we shall freely make.

★★★★★★

WOODROW WILSON, WAR MESSAGE, APRIL 2, 1917

War by Act of Germany

Destiny dealt cruelly with Woodrow Wilson. The lover of peace, as fate would have it, was forced to lead a hesitant and peace-loving nation into war. As the last days of 1916 slipped through the hourglass, the president made one final futile attempt to mediate between the embattled belligerents. On January 22, 1917, he delivered one of his most moving addresses, realistically declaring that only a negotiated "peace without victory" would prove durable.

Germany's warlords responded with a blow of the mailed fist. On January 31, 1917, they announced to an astonished world that they intended to wage *unlimited* submarine warfare, sinking *all* ships, including America's, in the war zone. The Germans thus jerked viciously on the string they had attached to their *Sussex* pledge in 1916.

Wilson, his bluff called, broke diplomatic relations but refused to move toward war unless the Germans undertook "overt" acts against American lives and property. To defend American interests short of war, the president asked Congress for authority to arm American merchant ships. When a band of midwestern senators launched a filibuster to block the measure, Wilson denounced them as a "little group of willful men" who were rendering a great nation "help-less and contemptible." But their obstructionism was a powerful reminder of the continuing strength of American isolationism.

Meanwhile, the sensational Zimmermann note was intercepted and published on March 1, 1917, infuriating Americans, especially westerners. German foreign secretary Zimmermann had secretly proposed a German-Mexican alliance, tempting anti-Yankee Mexico with thoughts of recovering Texas, New Mexico, and Arizona.

On the heels of this provocation came the long-dreaded "overt" acts in the Atlantic, where German U-boats sank four unarmed American merchant vessels in the first two weeks of March. As one Philadelphia newspaper observed, "the difference between war and what we have now is that now we aren't fighting back." Simultaneously came the rousing news that a revolution in Russia had toppled the cruel regime of the tsars. America could now fight foursquare for democracy on the side of the Allies without the black sheep of Russian despotism in the Allied fold.

Subdued and solemn, Wilson at last stood before a hushed joint session of Congress on the evening of April 2, 1917, and asked for a declaration of war. He had lost his gamble that America could pursue the profits of neutral trade without being sucked into the ghastly maelstrom. A myth developed in later years that America was dragged unwittingly into war by munitions makers and Wall Street bankers, desperate to protect their profits and loans. Yet the weapons merchants and financiers were already thriving, unhampered by wartime government restrictions and heavy taxation. Their slogan might well have been "Neutrality Forever." The simple truth is that British harassment of American commerce had been galling but endurable; Germany had resorted to the mass killing of civilians. President Wilson had drawn a clear, if risky, line against the depredations of the submarine. The German high command, in a last desperate throw of the dice, chose to cross it. In a figurative sense, America's war declaration of April 6, 1917, bore the unambiguous trademark "Made in Germany."

Wilsonian Idealism Enthroned

"It is a fearful thing to lead this great peaceful people into war," Wilson said in his war message. It was fearful indeed, not least of all because of the formidable challenge it posed to Wilson's leadership skills. Ironically, it fell to the scholarly Wilson, deeply respectful of American traditions, to shatter one of the most sacred of those traditions by entangling America in a distant European war.

How could the president arouse the American people to shoulder this unprecedented burden? Isolationism remained strong, and no fewer than six senators and fifty representatives (including the first congresswoman, Jeannette Rankin of Montana) had voted against the war resolution. Wilson could whip up no enthusiasm, especially in the landlocked Midwest, for fighting to make the world safe from the submarine. To galvanize the country, Wilson would have to proclaim more glorified aims.

Wilson's burning idealism led him instinctively to an inspired decision. Radiating the spiritual fervor of his Presbyterian ancestors, he declared the twin goals of "a war to end war" and a crusade "to make the world safe for democracy." Flourishing the sword of righteousness, Wilson virtually hypnotized the nation with his lofty ideals. He contrasted the selfish war aims of the other belligerents, Allied and enemy alike, with America's shining altruism. America, he preached, did not fight for the sake of riches or territorial conquest. The Republic sought only to shape an international order in which democracy could flourish without fear of power-crazed autocrats and militarists.

In Wilsonian idealism, the personality of the president and the necessities of history were perfectly matched. The high-minded Wilson genuinely believed in the principles he so eloquently intoned. And probably no other appeal could have successfully converted the American people from their historic hostility to involvement in European squabbles. Americans, it seemed, could be either isolationists or crusaders, but nothing in between.

Wilson's appeal worked—perhaps too well. Holding aloft the torch of idealism, the president fired up the public mind to a fever pitch. "Force, force to the utmost, force without stint or limit," he cried, while the country responded less elegantly with, "Hang the kaiser!" Lost on the gale was Wilson's earlier plea for "peace without victory."

Fourteen Potent Wilsonian Points

Wilson quickly came to be recognized as the moral leader of the Allied cause. He scaled a summit of inspiring oratory on January 8, 1918, when he delivered his famed Fourteen Points Address to an enthusiastic Congress. Though one of his primary purposes was to keep reeling Russia in the war, Wilson's eloquence inspired all the drooping Allies to make mightier efforts and demoralized the enemy governments by holding out alluring promises to their dissatisfied minorities.

The first five of the Fourteen Points were broad in scope: (1) A proposal to abolish secret treaties pleased liberals of all countries. (2) Freedom of the seas appealed to the Germans, as well as to Americans who distrusted British sea power. (3) A removal of economic barriers among nations was comforting to Germany, which feared postwar vengeance. (4) Reduction of armament burdens was gratifying to taxpayers everywhere. (5) An adjustment of colonial claims in the interests of both native peoples and the colonizers was reassuring to the anti-imperialists.

Other points among the fourteen proved to be no less seductive. They held out the promise of independence ("self-determination") to oppressed minority groups, such as the Poles, millions of whom lay under the heel of Germany and Austria-Hungary. The capstone point, number fourteen, foreshadowed the League of Nations—an international organization that Wilson dreamed would provide a system of collective security. Wilson earnestly prayed that this new scheme would effectively guarantee the political independence and territorial integrity of all countries, whether large or small.

Yet Wilson's appealing points, though raising hopes the world over, were not everywhere applauded. Certain leaders of the Allied nations, with an eye to territorial booty, were less than enthusiastic. Hard-nosed Republicans at home grumbled, and some of them openly mocked the "fourteen commandments" of "God Almighty Wilson."

Creel Manipulates Minds

Mobilizing the mind for war, both in America and abroad, was an urgent task facing the Washington authorities. For this purpose the Committee on Public Information was created. It was headed by a youngish journalist, George Creel, who, though

Anti-German Propaganda *The government relied extensively on emotional appeals and hate propaganda to rally support for the First World War, which most Americans regarded as a distant "European" affair.*

outspoken and tactless, was gifted with zeal and imagination. His job was to sell America on the war and sell the world on Wilsonian war aims. The Creel organization, employing 150,000 workers at home and overseas, proved that words were indeed weapons. It sent out an army of 75,000 "four-minute men"—often longer-winded than that—who delivered countless speeches full of "patriotic pep."

Creel's propaganda took varied forms. Posters were splashed on billboards in the "Battle of the Fences," as artists "rallied to the colors." Millions of leaflets and pamphlets, which contained the most pungent Wilsonisms, were showered like confetti upon the world. Propaganda booklets with red-white-and-blue covers were printed by the millions. Hang-the-kaiser movies, carrying such titles as *The Kaiser, the Beast of Berlin* and *To Hell with the Kaiser,* revealed the "Hun" at his bloodiest. Arm-waving conductors by the thousands led huge audiences in songs that poured scorn on the enemy and glorified the "boys" in uniform.

Creel typified American war mobilization, which relied more on aroused passion and voluntary compliance than on formal laws. But he oversold the ideals of Wilson and led the world to expect too much. When the president proved to be a mortal and not a god, the resulting disillusionment at home and abroad was disastrous.

Enforcing Loyalty and Stifling Dissent

German-Americans numbered over 8 million, counting those with at least one parent foreign-born, out of a total population of 100 million. As emotion mounted, hate hysteria against Germans and things Germanic swept the nation. Orchestras found it unsafe to present German-composed music, such as that of Wagner and Beethoven. The teaching of the German language was shortsightedly discontinued in many high schools and colleges. Sauerkraut was renamed "liberty cabbage" and hamburger became "liberty steak." A few German-Americans were tarred, feathered, and beaten; in one extreme case a German Socialist in Illinois was lynched by a drunken mob.

Both the Espionage Act of 1917 and the Sedition Act of 1918 reflected current fears about Germans and antiwar Americans. Especially visible among the nineteen hundred prosecutions undertaken under these laws were antiwar Socialists and members of the radical union Industrial Workers of the World (IWW). Kingpin Socialist Eugene V. Debs was convicted under the Espionage Act in 1918 and sentenced to ten years in a federal penitentiary. IWW leader William D. ("Big Bill") Haywood and ninety-nine associates were similarly convicted. There was also mild press censorship, and some leftist journals such as the *Masses* were denied mailing privileges.

Socialist Leader Eugene V. Debs Addresses an Antiwar Rally in Columbus, Ohio, 1918 *For his remarks in this speech, Debs was convicted under the Espionage Act of 1917 and sent to federal prison. He ran as a presidential candidate in 1920 while still incarcerated in his cell and received nearly a million votes.*

These prosecutions form an ugly chapter in the history of American civil liberty. With the dawn of peace, presidential pardons were rather freely granted, including President Harding's to Eugene Debs in 1921. Yet a few victims lingered behind bars into the 1930s.

The Nation's Factories Go to War

Victory was no foregone conclusion, especially since the Republic, despite ample warning, was caught flat-footedly unready for its leap into global war. Wilson had only belatedly backed some mild preparedness measures beginning in 1915, including a shipbuilding program and a civilian Council of National Defense to study problems of economic mobilization. It would take a herculean effort to mobilize America's daunting but disorganized resources and throw them into the field quickly enough to bolster the Allied war effort.

Towering obstacles confronted economic mobilizers. Sheer ignorance was among the biggest roadblocks. No one knew precisely how much steel or explosive powder the country was capable of producing. Old ideas also proved to be liabilities, as traditional fears of big government hamstrung efforts to orchestrate the economy from Washington.

Late in the war, and after some bruising political battles, Wilson succeeded in imposing some order on this economic confusion. In March 1918 he appointed lone-eagle stock speculator Bernard Baruch to head the War Industries Board. But the War Industries Board never had more than feeble formal powers. Even in a globe-girdling crisis, the American preference for laissez-faire and for a weak central government proved amazingly strong.

The War, Workers, and Women

Spurred by the slogan "Labor Will Win the War," American workers sweated their way to victory. In 1918 the War Department threatened to draft any unemployed male, but for the most part the government tried to treat labor fairly. The National War Labor Board, chaired by former president Taft, pressed employers to pay higher wages and adopt the eight-hour workday.

Samuel Gompers and his American Federation of Labor (AF of L) loyally supported the war, though some smaller and more radical labor organizations like the Industrial Workers of the World, who represented many poor, transient workers in the lumber and fruit industries, did not.

Mainstream labor's loyalty was rewarded with a doubling of membership to over 3 million and a 20 percent rise in real wages in the most heavily unionized industries.

Still, labor harbored grievances. The right to organize eluded labor's grasp. Strikes broke out during and after the war, culminating in the great steel strike of 1919. A quarter of a million workers walked off the job to demand the right to organize and bargain collectively. The strike was broken only after violent confrontations and the use of thirty thousand African-American strikebreakers.

Many thousands more southern blacks were drawn to the North by the magnet of war-industry employment. Their sudden appearance in previously all-white areas sometimes sparked interracial violence. An explosive riot in East St. Louis, Illinois, in July 1917 left nine whites and at least forty blacks dead. An equally gruesome riot ripped through Chicago in July 1919, fanned by tensions between white working-class neighborhoods and African-Americans who had found jobs as strikebreakers in meatpacking plants. Fifteen whites and twenty-three blacks were killed during nearly two weeks of terror.

Women also heeded the call of patriotism and opportunity. Thousands of female workers took jobs in factories and fields during the war, encouraging President Wilson to endorse woman suffrage as "a vitally necessary war measure." The Nineteenth Amendment was eventually passed in 1920 (for text, see the Appendix). Yet women's wartime economic gains proved fleeting, for most women workers gave up their jobs when hostilities ended. Meanwhile Congress affirmed its support for women in their traditional role as mothers by passing the Sheppard-Towner Maternity Act of 1921, providing federally financed instruction in maternal and infant health care. Postwar feminists continued to push for a day when women's wage labor and political power would reshape the American way of life.

Women Ordnance Plant Workers with Pneumatic Hammers, 1918
A minority of women had long been in the work force, but World War I drew more of them into heavy industrial labor.

Forging a War Economy

Mobilization relied more on the heated emotions of patriotism than on the cool majesty of the laws. The largely voluntary and somewhat haphazard character of economic war organization testified eloquently to ocean-insulated America's safe distance from the fighting—as well as to the still-modest scale of government power in the progressive-era Republic.

As the larder of democracy, America had to feed itself and its allies. By a happy inspiration, the man chosen to head the Food Administration was the Quaker humanitarian Herbert C. Hoover, already a hero for his successful charitable drive to feed the starving people of war-racked Belgium.

In common with other American war administrators, Hoover preferred to rely on voluntary compliance rather than on formal edicts. Instead of rationing food supplies, he waged a whirlwind propaganda campaign through posters, billboards, newspapers, pulpits, and movies. To save food for export, Hoover proclaimed wheatless Wednesdays and meatless Tuesdays—all on a voluntary basis. Even children, when eating apples, were urged to be "patriotic to the core."

The country soon broke out in a rash of backyard "victory gardens." Congress severely restricted the use of foodstuffs for manufacturing alcoholic beverages. The wartime drive against German-descended brewers aided in the passage of the Eighteenth Amendment in 1919, which—temporarily—prohibited all alcoholic drinks.

Thanks to the fervent patriotic wartime spirit, Hoover's voluntary approach worked. Farm production increased by one-fourth, and food exports to the Allies tripled in volume. Hoover's methods were widely imitated in other war agencies. The Fuel Administration exhorted Americans to save fuel with "heatless Mondays" and "gasless Sundays." The Treasury Department sponsored huge parades and invoked slogans such as "Halt the Hun" to promote four great Liberty Loan drives, followed by a Victory Loan campaign in 1919. Together, these efforts netted the then-fantastic sum of about $21 billion, or two-thirds of the cost of the war to the United States. The remainder was raised by increased taxes.

Despite the Wilson administration's preference for voluntary means of mobilizing the economy, the government on occasion reluctantly exercised its sovereign formal power, notably when it took over the nation's railroads following indescribable traffic snarls in late 1917. Washington also launched a gigantic shipbuilding program, though it was slow to get under way.

Making Plowboys into "Doughboys"

Most citizens, at the outset, did not dream of sending a mighty force to France. They expected America to use its navy to uphold freedom of the seas, ship war materials to the Allies, and supply them with loans. But in April and May of 1917, the European associates confessed that they were scraping the bottom not only of their money chests but, more ominously, of their manpower barrels. A huge American army would have to be raised, trained, and transported, or the whole western front would collapse.

Conscription was the only answer to the need for raising an immense army with all possible speed. Wilson disliked a draft, but he eventually accepted and eloquently supported conscription as a disagreeable and temporary necessity. After six weeks of criticism and debate, Congress grudgingly passed conscription.

The draft act required the registration of all males between the ages of eighteen and forty-five. The draft machinery, on the whole, worked effectively. No draftee could purchase an exemption or hire a substitute, as in the days of the Civil War. Within a few frantic months the army grew to over 4 million men. For the first time, women were admitted to the armed forces: some 11,000 to the navy and 269 to the marines.

Recruits were supposed to receive six months of training in America and two more months overseas. But so great was the urgency that many "doughboys" were swept swiftly into battle scarcely knowing how to handle a rifle, much less a bayonet.

America Helps Hammer the Hun

Russia's collapse underscored the need for haste. As the communistic Bolsheviks withdrew their beaten country from the war, Germany moved its forces to the western front in France. The Germans hoped to deliver the knockout blow to the Allies in about six months, long before American reinforcements could arrive.

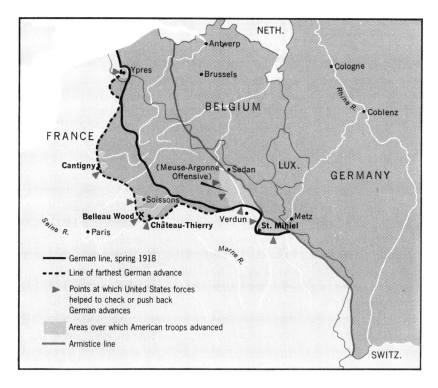

Major U.S. Operations in France, 1918   *One doughboy recorded in his diary his baptism of fire at St. Mihiel: "Hiked through dark woods. No lights allowed, guided by holding on the pack of the man ahead. Stumbled through underbrush for about half mile into an open field where we waited in soaking rain until about 10:00 P.M. We then started on our hike to the St. Mihiel front, arriving on the crest of a hill at 1:00 A.M. I saw a sight which I shall never forget. It was the zero hour and in one instant the entire front as far as the eye could reach in either direction was a sheet of flame, while the heavy artillery made the earth quake."*

Over There *American troops ("doughboys") man a machine gun in a bomb-blasted forest.*

Berlin's calculations as to American tardiness were surprisingly accurate. No really effective American fighting force reached France until about a year after Congress declared war. Nevertheless, France gradually began to bustle with American doughboys. The first trainees to reach the front were used as replacements in the Allied armies. The newcomers soon made friends with the French girls—or tried to—and one of the most sung-about women in history was the fabled "Mademoiselle from Armentières." One of the printable stanzas ran

> She was true to me, she was true to you,
> She was true to the whole damned army, too.

The dreaded German drive on the western front exploded in the spring of 1918. Spearheaded by about half a million troops, the enemy rolled forward with terrifying momentum. So dire was the peril that the Allies for the first time united under a supreme commander, the quiet Frenchman Marshal Ferdinand Foch.

At last the ill-trained "Yanks" were coming—and not a moment too soon. Late in May 1918, the forward-rolling Germans, smashing to within forty miles of Paris, threatened to knock out France. Newly arrived American troops, numbering fewer than thirty thousand, were thrown into the breach at Château-Thierry, right in the teeth of the German advance. This was a historic moment—the first significant engagement of American troops in a European war. With their arrival, it was clear that a new American giant had arisen in the West to replace the dying Russian titan in the East.

By July 1918 the awesome German drive had spent its force, and keyed-up American boys participated in a Foch counteroffensive in the Second Battle of the Marne. This engagement marked the beginning of a German withdrawal that was never effectively reversed. In September 1918 nine American divisions (about 243,000 men) joined four French divisions to push the Germans from the St. Mihiel salient, a German dagger in France's flank.

The Americans, dissatisfied with merely bolstering the British and French, demanded and got their own army under General John J. ("Black Jack") Pershing. Pershing was finally assigned a front stretching from the Swiss border to meet the French lines. As part of the last mighty Allied assault, involving several million men, Pershing's army undertook the Meuse-Argonne offensive, from September 26 to November 11, 1918. This battle, the most gargantuan thus far in American history, lasted forty-seven days and engaged 1.2 million American troops. With especially heavy fighting in the rugged Argonne Forest, the killed and wounded mounted to 120,000, or 10 percent of the Americans involved.

Victory was in sight—and fortunately so. The slowly advancing American armies in France were eating up their supplies so rapidly that they were in grave danger of running short. But the battered Germans were reeling under the sledgehammer blows of the Allies and suffering from critical food shortages caused by the British blockade. Propaganda leaflets containing seductive Wilsonian promises rained upon their crumbling lines from balloons, shells, and rockets.

Berlin was now ready to hoist the white flag. The Germans first sought a peace based on the Fourteen Points in October 1918. But a stern Wilson made it clear that the kaiser must be thrown overboard before an armistice could be negotiated. The war-weary Germans then forced the disgraced kaiser to flee to Holland.

The exhausted Germans laid down their arms at eleven o'clock on the eleventh day of the eleventh month of 1918, and an eerie, numbing silence fell over the western front. War-taut America burst into a delirium of around-the-clock rejoicing, as streets were jammed with laughing, whooping, milling, dancing masses. The war to end wars had ended.

The United States' main contribution to the ultimate victory had been foodstuffs, munitions, credits, oil, and manpower—but not battlefield victories. The Yanks fought only two major battles, at St. Mihiel and the Meuse-Argonne. It was the *prospect* of endless U.S. troop reserves, rather than America's actual military performance, that eventually demoralized the Germans.

Ironically enough, General Pershing in some ways depended more on the Allies than they depended on him. Most of his army's supplies and weapons were purchased from the British and French. The United States was no arsenal of democracy in this

Wilson in Dover, England, 1919 *Hailed by many Europeans in early 1919 as the savior of the Western world, Wilson was a fallen idol only a few months later, when his own countrymen repudiated the peace treaty he had helped to craft.*

war; that role awaited it in the next global conflict, two decades later.

Wilson Steps Down from Olympus

Woodrow Wilson had helped to win the war. What role would he now play in shaping the peace? Expectations ran extravagantly high. As the fighting in Europe crashed to a close, the American president towered at the peak of his popularity and power. No other man had ever occupied so dizzy a pinnacle as moral leader of the world. Wilson also had behind him the prestige of victory and the economic resources of the mightiest nation on earth. But at this fateful moment, his sureness of touch deserted him, and he began to make a series of tragic fumbles.

Under the slogan "Politics is adjourned," partisan political strife had been kept below the surface during the war crisis. Hoping to strengthen his hand at the Paris peace table, Wilson broke the truce by personally appealing for a Democratic victory in the congressional elections of November 1918. But the maneuver backfired when voters instead returned a narrow Republican majority to Congress. Having staked his reputation on the outcome, Wilson went to Paris as a diminished leader. Unlike all the parliamentary statesmen at the table, he did not command a legislative majority at home.

Wilson's decision to go in person to Paris to help make the peace infuriated Republicans, who saw it as flamboyant grandstanding. He further ruffled Republican feathers when he neglected to include a single Republican senator in his official peace delegation. The logical choice was the new chairman of the Senate Committee on Foreign Relations, slender and aristocratically bewhiskered Henry Cabot Lodge of Massachusetts, a Harvard Ph.D. But including Lodge would have been problematic for the president. The senator's mind, quipped one critic, was like the soil of his native New England: "naturally barren but highly cultivated." Wilson loathed him, and the feeling was hotly reciprocated. An accomplished author, Lodge had been known as "the scholar in politics" until Wilson came on the scene. The two men were at daggers drawn, personally and politically.

Hammering Out the Treaty

Woodrow Wilson, the great prophet arisen in the West, received tumultuous welcomes from the masses of France, England, and Italy late in 1918 and early in 1919. But the realistic statesmen of Italy and France were determined that Wilsonian idealism should not disrupt their fine-spun imperialistic plans.

The Paris Conference of great and small nations fell into the hands of an inner clique, known as the "Big Four." Wilson, representing the richest and freshest great power, more or less occupied the driver's seat. He was joined by Vittorio Orlando of Italy, David Lloyd George of Britain, and cynical, hard-bitten Georges Clemenceau of France, the seventy-eight-year-old "organizer of victory" known as "the Tiger."

Speed was urgent when the conference opened on January 18, 1919. Europe seemed to be slipping into anarchy; the red tide of communism was licking westward from V. I. Lenin's revolutionary Russia.

Wilson's ultimate goal was a world parliament to be known as the League of Nations, but he first bent his energies to preventing any cynical parceling out of the former colonies and protectorates of the vanquished powers. He forced through a compromise between naked imperialism and Wilsonian idealism, in which the victors received conquered territory only as trustees of the League of Nations. But in practice this half-loaf solution was little more than the old prewar colonialism, thinly disguised.

Wilson envisioned a League of Nations consisting of an assembly with seats for all nations and a council to be controlled by the great powers. He gained a signal victory over the skeptical Old World diplomats in February 1919, when they agreed to make the League Covenant, Wilson's brainchild, an integral part of the final peace treaty.

On a quick trip to America, Wilson discovered that certain Republican senators, led by Senator Lodge, were sharpening their knives. To them the League was either a useless "sewing circle" or an overpotent "super-state." Their hard core was composed of a dozen or so isolationists, led by Senators William Borah of Idaho and Hiram Johnson of California, who were known as the "irreconcilables" or "the battalion of death."

Thirty-nine Republican senators or senators-elect—enough to defeat the treaty—proclaimed that the Senate would not approve the League of Nations in its existing imperfect form. These difficulties delighted Wilson's Allied adversaries in Paris. They were now in a stronger bargaining position because Wilson would have to beg them for changes in the League Covenant that would safeguard the Monroe Doctrine and other U.S. interests dear to the senators.

As soon as Wilson was back in Paris, hard-headed Premier Clemenceau pressed French demands for the German-inhabited Rhineland and the Saar Valley, a rich coal area. Faced with fierce Wilsonian opposition to this violation of self-determination, France settled for a compromise whereby the Saar basin would remain under the League of Nations for fifteen years and then a popular vote would determine its fate.* In exchange for dropping its demands for the Rhineland, France got a security treaty in which both Britain and America pledged to come to its aid in the event of another German invasion. The French later felt betrayed when the pact was quickly pigeonholed by the U.S. Senate, which shied away from all entangling alliances.

Wilson's next battle was with Italy over Fiume, a valuable seaport inhabited by both Italians and Yugoslavs. When Italy demanded Fiume, Wilson insisted that the seaport go to Yugoslavia and appealed over the heads of Italy's leaders to the country's masses. The maneuver fell flat. The Italian delegates went home in a huff, and the Italian populace turned savagely against Wilson.

Another crucial struggle was with Japan over China's Shantung peninsula and the German islands in the Pacific, which the Japanese had seized during the war. Japan was conceded the strategic Pacific islands under a League of Nations mandate,† but Wil-

son fiercely opposed Japanese control of Shantung as a violation of self-determination for its 30 million Chinese residents. But when the Japanese threatened to walk out, Wilson reluctantly accepted a compromise whereby Japan kept Germany's economic holdings in Shantung and pledged to return the peninsula to China at a later date. The Chinese were outraged by this imperialistic solution, while Clemenceau jeered that Wilson "talked like Jesus Christ and acted like Lloyd George."

The Peace Treaty That Bred a New War

A completed Treaty of Versailles, after more weeks of wrangling, was handed to the Germans in June 1919—almost literally on the point of a bayonet. Loud and bitter cries of betrayal burst from their throats—charges that Adolf Hitler would soon reiterate during his meteoric rise to power in Germany.

Wilson, of course, was guilty of no conscious betrayal. But he had been forced to compromise away some of his less cherished Fourteen Points in order to salvage the more precious League of Nations. He was much more like a mother who had to throw her sickly younger children to the pursuing wolves to save her sturdy firstborn. Greeted a few months earlier with frenzied acclaim in Europe, Wilson was now a fallen idol, condemned alike by disillusioned liberals and frustrated imperialists. He was keenly aware of some of the injustices that had been forced into the treaty. But he was hoping that a potent League of Nations, led by America, would iron out the inequities.

The loudly condemned treaty had much to commend it. Not least among its merits was its liberation of millions of minority peoples, such as the Poles, from the yoke of an alien dynasty. Wilson's critics to the contrary, the settlement was almost certainly a fairer one because he had gone to Paris.

Wilson's Battle for the League

Returning to America, Wilson found the Treaty of Versailles and the League of Nations being showered

---

* The Saar population voted overwhelmingly to rejoin Germany in 1935.

† In due time the Japanese illegally fortified these islands—the Marshalls, Marianas, and Carolines—and used them as bases against the United States in World War II.

with abuse from all sides. Isolationists raised a whirlwind of protest against entanglement in a new-fangled "League of Notions." Rabid Hun-haters, regarding the pact as not harsh enough, voiced their discontent. Principled liberals, like the editors of the *Nation*, thought it too harsh—and a gross betrayal to boot. German-Americans, Italian-Americans, Irish-Americans, and other "hyphenated Americans" were aroused because the peace settlement was not sufficiently favorable to their native lands.

Despite mounting discontent, a strong majority of the people still seemed favorable to the treaty, with the "Wilson League" firmly riveted as Part I. At this time—early July 1919—Senator Lodge had no real hope of defeating the Treaty of Versailles. His strategy was merely to amend it in such a way as to "Americanize," "Republicanize," or "senatorialize" it.

Lodge effectively used delay to muddle and divide public opinion. He read the entire 264-page treaty aloud in the Senate Foreign Relations Committee and held protracted hearings in which people of various nationalities aired their grievances. With the treaty bogged down in the Senate, Wilson decided to go to the country in a spectacular speechmaking tour. Physicians and friends warned the increasingly frail president against making the strenuous trip. But he declared that he was willing to die, like the soldiers he had sent into battle, for the sake of the new world order.

The presidential tour, begun in September 1919, got off to a rather lame start in the Midwest, where German-American influence was strong and two hostile "irreconcilable" senators, Borah and Johnson, trailed Wilson and spoke against the treaty in the same cities a few days later. But the Rocky Mountain region and the Pacific Coast, areas that had elected Wilson in 1916, welcomed him with heartwarming outbursts. The high point—and the breaking point—of the return trip was at Pueblo, Colorado, September 25, 1919. Wilson, with tears coursing down his cheeks, pleaded for the League of Nations as the only real hope of preventing future wars. That night he collapsed from physical and nervous exhaustion.

Wilson was whisked back in the "funeral train" to Washington where several days later a stroke paralyzed one side of his body. During the next few weeks

he lay in a darkened room in the White House, as much a victim of the war as the unknown soldier buried at Arlington. For seven and a half months he did not meet with his cabinet.

Defeat Through Deadlock

Senator Lodge, coldly calculating, was now at the helm. After failing to amend the treaty outright, he came up with fourteen formal reservations to protect American sovereignty and guard Congress's war-declaring power against the League. Wilson, hating Lodge, saw red at the mere suggestion of the *Lodge* reservations, which he insisted "emasculated" the entire pact.

Although too feeble to lead, Wilson was still strong enough to obstruct. When the day finally came for voting in the Senate, he sent word to all true Democrats to vote *against* the treaty with the odious Lodge reservations attached. Loyal Democrats in the Senate, on November 19, 1919, blindly did Wilson's bidding. Combining with the "irreconcilables," mostly Republicans, they rejected the treaty with the Lodge reservations appended, 55 to 39.

So strong was public indignation at this outcome that the Senate was forced to vote a second time in March 1920. There was only one possible path to success. Unless the Senate approved the pact with the Lodge reservations, the entire document would be rejected. But the sickly Wilson signed the treaty's death warrant by again sending word to all loyal Democrats to vote down the treaty with the obnoxious Lodge reservations. On a fateful March 19, 1920, the treaty netted a simple majority but failed to get the necessary two-thirds majority by a count of 49 yeas to 35 nays.

Who defeated the treaty? The Lodge-Wilson personal feud, traditionalism, isolationism, disillusionment, and partisanship all contributed to the confused picture. But Wilson himself must bear a substantial share of the responsibility. He asked for all or nothing—and got nothing.

The "Solemn Referendum" of 1920

Wilson's own pet solution for the deadlock was to settle the treaty issue by appealing to the people for a "solemn referendum" in the presidential election of 1920. This was sheer folly, for a true mandate on the League in the noisy arena of politics was clearly an impossibility.

Gathering in Chicago in June 1920, jubilant Republicans devised a masterfully ambiguous platform that could appeal to both pro-League and anti-League sentiment in the party. As the leading presidential contestants jousted with one another, a group of Senate bosses, meeting rather casually in the historic "smoke-filled" Room 404 of the Blackstone Hotel, informally decided on affable, malleable Senator Warren G. Harding of Ohio as the candidate. To run with the "folksy," back-slapping former newspaper editor, the party nominated frugal, grim-faced Governor Calvin ("Silent Cal") Coolidge of Massachusetts.

Meeting in San Francisco, Democrats nominated earnest Governor James M. Cox of Ohio, who strongly supported the League. His running mate was assistant navy secretary Franklin D. Roosevelt, a young, handsome, vibrant New Yorker.

Democratic attempts to make the campaign a referendum on the League were thwarted by Senator Harding, who issued muddled and contradictory statements on the issue from his front porch. Pro-League and anti-League Republicans both claimed that Harding's election would advance their cause, while the candidate suggested that if elected he would work for a vague Association of Nations—*a* league but not *the* League.

With newly enfranchised women swelling the vote totals, Harding was swept into power with a prodigious plurality of over 7 million votes—16,143,407 to 9,130,328 for Cox. The electoral count was 404 to 127. Eugene V. Debs, federal prisoner number 9653 at the Atlanta Penitentiary, rolled up the largest vote ever for the left-wing Socialist party—919,799.

Public desire for a change found vent in a resounding repudiation of "high and mighty" Wilsonianism. People were tired of professional highbrowism, star-reaching idealism, bothersome do-goodism, moral overstrain, and constant self-sacrifice. Eager to lapse back into "normalcy," they were willing to accept a second-rate president—and they got a third-rate one.

Although the election could not be considered a true referendum, Republican isolationists successfully turned Harding's victory into a death sentence for the League. Politicians increasingly shunned the League as they would a leper. When the legendary Wilson died in 1924, admirers knelt in the snow outside his Washington home. His "great vision" of a league for peace had died long before.

The Betrayal of Great Expectations

America's spurning of the League was tragically shortsighted. The Republic had helped to win a costly war, but it foolishly kicked the fruits of victory under the table. Whether a strong international organization would have averted World War II in 1939 will always be a matter of dispute. But there can be no doubt that the orphaned League of Nations was undercut at the start by the refusal of the mightiest power on the globe to join it. The Allies themselves were largely to blame for the new world conflagration that flared up in 1939, but they found a convenient justification for their own shortcomings by pointing an accusing finger at Uncle Sam.

The ultimate collapse of the Treaty of Versailles must be laid, at least in some degree, at America's doorstep. This complicated pact, tied in with the four other peace treaties through the League Covenant, was a top-heavy structure designed to rest on a four-legged table. The fourth leg, the United States, was never put into place. This rickety structure teetered for over a decade and then crashed in ruins—a debacle that played into the hands of German demagogue Adolf Hitler.

The United States, as the tragic sequel proved, hurt its own cause when it buried its head in the sands. Granted that the conduct of its Allies had been disillusioning, it had its own ends to serve by carrying through the Wilsonian program. It would have been well advised if it had forthrightly assumed its war-born responsibilities and had resolutely played the role of global leader that had been thrust upon it. In the interests of its own security, if for no other reason, the United States should have used its enormous strength to shape world-shaking events. Instead, it permitted itself blithely to drift toward the abyss of a second and even more bloody international disaster.

varying

viewpoints

Woodrow Wilson: Realist or Idealist?

As the first president to take the United States into a foreign war, Woodrow Wilson was obliged to make a systematic case to the American people to justify his unprecedented European intervention. His ideas have largely defined the character of American foreign policy ever since—for better or worse.

"Wilsonianism" comprises three closely related principles: (1) The era of American isolation from world affairs has irretrievably ended. (2) The United States must infuse its own founding political and economic ideas—including democracy, the rule of law, free trade, and national self-determination (or anticolonialism)—into the international order. (3) American influence can eventually steer the world away from rivalry and warfare toward a cooperative and peaceful international system, maintained by the League of Nations or, later, the United Nations.

Whether that Wilsonian vision constitutes hard-nosed realism or starry-eyed idealism has excited scholarly debate for nearly a century. "Realists," such as George F. Kennan and Henry Kissinger, insist Wilson was anything but realistic. They criticize the president as a naive, impractical dreamer who failed to understand that the international order is, and always will be, an anarchic, unruly arena, outside the rule of law, where only military force can effectively protect the nation's security. In a sharp critique in his 1950 study, *American Diplomacy*, Kennan condemned Wilson's vision as "moralism-legalism." In this view, Wilson dangerously threatened to sacrifice American self-interests on the altar of his admirable but ultimately unworkable ideas.

Wilson's defenders, including conspicuously his principal biographer, Arthur S. Link, disagree with that assessment. They argue that Wilson's idealism was a kind of higher realism, recognizing that armed conflict on the scale of World War I could never again be tolerated, and that some framework of peaceful international relations simply had to be found.

Some leftist scholars, such as William Appleman Williams, argue that Wilson was a realist of another kind: a subtle and wily imperialist whose stirring rhetoric cloaked a grasping ambition to make the United States the world's dominant economic power. Sometimes called "the imperialism of free trade," this strategy allegedly sought to decolonialize the world and open up international commerce, not for the good of peoples elsewhere, but to create a system in which American economic might would prevail.

Still other scholars, especially John Milton Cooper, Jr., emphasize the absence of economic factors in shaping Wilson's diplomacy. Isolationism, so this argument goes, held such sway over American thinking precisely because the United States had such a puny financial stake abroad—no hard American economic interests were mortally threatened in 1917 or for a long time thereafter. In these circumstances, Wilson—and the Wilsonians who came after him, such as Franklin D. Roosevelt—had no choice but to appeal to abstract ideals and high principles. The "idealistic" Wilsonian strain in American diplomacy, in this view, may be an unavoidable heritage of America's historically isolated situation. If so, it was Wilson's genius to make practical use of those ideas in his bid for popular support of his diplomacy.

Chronology

1915	Council of National Defense established.
1917	Germany resumes unrestricted submarine warfare. Zimmermann note. United States enters World War I. Espionage Act of 1917.
1918	Wilson proposes the Fourteen Points. Sedition Act of 1918. Battle of Château-Thierry. Second Battle of the Marne. Meuse-Argonne offensive. Armistice ends World War I.
1919	Paris Conference and Treaty of Versailles. Wilson's pro-League tour and collapse. Eighteenth Amendment passed (prohibition of alcohol).
1920	Final Senate defeat of Versailles Treaty. Nineteenth Amendment passed (women's suffrage). Harding defeats Cox for presidency.

SUGGESTED READINGS

Primary Source Documents

John J. Pershing, *My Experiences in the World War** (1931), recounts American fighting tactics. Woodrow Wilson's "Fourteen Points Address" to Congress on January 8, 1918* (*Congressional Record*, 65th Congress, 2d Session, p. 691), defined the nation's war aims. William E. Borah, *"Speech on the League of Nations"* (1919), in Richard Hofstadter, *Great Issues in American History* (1958), reveals the isolationist position. Ernest Hemingway's *A Farewell to Arms* (1929) is an outstanding war novel.

Secondary Sources

The home front is emphasized in David M. Kennedy, *Over Here: The First World War and American Society* (1980). Economic mobilization is covered in Robert Cuff, *The War Industries Board* (1973), and Daniel R. Beaver, *Newton D. Baker and the American Financing of World War I* (1970). Politics is treated in Seward Livermore, *Politics Is Adjourned: Woodrow Wilson and the War Congress, 1916–1918* (1966). The abuse of civil liberties is luridly described in H. C. Peterson and Gilbert C. Fite, *Opponents of War, 1917–1918* (1957), and is more soberly analyzed in Harry N. Scheiber, *The Wilson Administration and Civil Liberties, 1917–1921* (1960), and Paul L. Murphy, *World War I and the Origin of Civil Liberties in the United States* (1979). Military matters are handled in Edward M. Coffman, *The War to End All Wars: The American Military Experience in World War I* (1968); Arthur E. Barbeau and Florette Henri, *Unknown Soldiers: Black American Troops in World War One* (1974); and John Whiteclay Chambers II, *To Raise an Army: The Draft Comes to Modern America* (1987). The war experiences of women are captured in Maurine W. Greenwald, *Women, War, and Work* (1980). Works of cultural history include Stanley Cooperman, *World War I and the American Novel* (1966); Stuart Rochester, *American Liberal Disillusionment in the Wake of World War I* (1977); and Paul Fussell, *The Great War and Modern Memory* (1975). On the peace see Arthur S. Link, *Woodrow Wilson: Revolution, War, and Peace* (1979), and two studies by Thomas A. Bailey, *Woodrow Wilson and the Lost Peace* (1944) and *Woodrow Wilson and the Great Betrayal* (1945). Consult also N. Gordon Levin, Jr., *Woodrow Wilson and World Politics* (1968); Arno J. Mayer, *Politics and Diplomacy of Peacemaking* (1967); Thomas J. Kuock, *To End All Wars: Woodrow Wilson and the Quest for a New World Order* (1992); Robert H. Ferrell, *Woodrow Wilson and World War I, 1917–1921* (1985); and Lloyd C. Gardner, *Safe for Democracy: The Anglo-American Response to Revolution, 1913–1923* (1984). On Wilson's archenemy see William C. Widenor, *Henry Cabot Lodge and the Search for an American Foreign Policy* (1980). The end of this troubled period is sketched in Burl Noggle, *Into the Twenties: The U.S. from Armistice to Normalcy* (1974).

---

* An asterisk indicates that the document, or an excerpt from it, can be found in Thomas A. Bailey and David M. Kennedy, eds., *The American Spirit: United States History as Seen By Contemporaries*, 9th ed. (Boston: Houghton Mifflin, 1998).

32

****

American Life in the "Roaring Twenties," 1919–1929

★★★★★★

America's present need is not heroics but healing; not nostrums but normalcy; not revolution but restoration; . . . not surgery but serenity.

★★★★★★

WARREN G. HARDING, 1920

Insulating America from the Radical Virus

Bloodied by the war and disillusioned by the peace, Americans turned inward in the 1920s. Shunning diplomatic commitments to foreign countries, they also denounced "radical" foreign ideas, condemned "un-American" lifestyles, and clanged shut the immigration gates against foreign peoples. They partly sealed off the domestic economy from the rest of the world and plunged headlong into a dizzying decade of homegrown prosperity.

Hysterical fears of red Russia continued to color American thinking for several years after the Bolshevik revolution of 1917, which spawned a tiny Communist party in America. Tensions were heightened by an epidemic of strikes that convulsed the Republic at war's end, many of them the result of high prices and frustrated union-organizing drives. Upstanding Americans jumped to the conclusion that labor troubles were fomented by bomb-and-whisker Bolsheviks. A general strike in Seattle in 1919, though modest in its demands and orderly in its methods, prompted a call from the mayor for federal troops to head off "the anarchy of Russia."

The big "red scare" of 1919–1920 resulted in a nationwide crusade against left-wingers whose Americanism was suspect. Attorney General A. Mitchell Palmer, who "saw red" too easily, earned the title "Fighting Quaker" for his excess of zeal in rounding up suspects. When a bomb shattered both Palmer's nerves and his Washington home in June 1919, the "Fighting Quaker" was dubbed the "Quaking Fighter." Late in December 1919, a shipload of 249 alleged alien radicals was deported on the *Buford* ("Soviet Ark") to the "workers' paradise" of Russia. Hysteria was revived in September 1920 when a still-unexplained bomb blast in Wall Street killed thirty-eight people and wounded several hundred others.

Various states joined the pack in the outcry against radicals. In 1919–1920 a number of legislatures passed criminal syndicalism laws. These anti-red statutes outlawed the mere *advocacy* of violence to secure social change. Critics protested that mere words were not criminal deeds, that there was a great gulf between throwing fits and throwing bombs, and that "free screech" was for the nasty as well as the nice. Violence was done to traditional American concepts of free speech as IWW members and other radicals were vigorously prosecuted. The hysteria went so far that in 1920 five members of the New York legislature, all lawfully elected, were denied their seats simply because they were Socialists.

The red scare was a godsend to conservative businesspeople, who used it to break the backs of the fledgling unions. Labor's call for the "closed," or all-union, shop was denounced as "Sovietism in disguise." Employers, in turn, hailed their own anti-union campaign for the "open" shop as "the American plan."

Anti-redism and antiforeignism were reflected in a notorious case regarded by liberals as a "judicial lynching." Nicola Sacco, a shoe-factory worker, and Bartolomeo Vanzetti, a fish peddler, were convicted in 1921 of the murder of a Massachusetts paymaster and his guard. The jury and judge were prejudiced in some degree against the defendants because they were Italians, atheists, anarchists, and draft dodgers.

Liberals and radicals the world over rallied to the defense of the two immigrants doomed to die. The case dragged on for six years until 1927, when the condemned men were electrocuted. Communists and other radicals were thus presented with two martyrs in the "class struggle," while many American liberals hung their heads.

Hooded Hoodlums of the KKK

A new Ku Klux Klan, spawned by the postwar reaction, mushroomed fearsomely in the early 1920s. Despite the familiar sheets and hoods, it more closely resembled the antiforeign "nativist" movements of the 1850s than the antiblack nightriders of the 1860s. It was antiforeign, anti-Catholic, antiblack, anti-Jewish, antipacifist, anticommunist, anti-internationalist, anti-evolutionist, anti-adultery, and anti–birth control. It was also pro–Anglo-Saxon, pro–"native" American, and pro-Protestant. In short, the besheeted Klan betokened an extremist, ultra-conservative uprising against many of the forces of diversity and modernity that were transforming American culture.

The reconstituted Klan spread with astonishing rapidity, especially in the Midwest and the "Bible Belt" South. At its peak in the mid-1920s, it enrolled about 5 million dues-paying members and wielded potent political influence. The Klan's most impressive displays were "konclaves" and huge flag-waving parades. The chief warning was the blazing cross. The principal weapon was the bloodied lash, supplemented by tar and feathers.

KKK Parade of Forty Thousand Men in Washington, 1925

This reign of hooded horror, so repulsive to the best American ideals, collapsed rather suddenly in the late 1920s. Decent people at last recoiled from the orgy of ribboned flesh and terrorism, and scandalous embezzling by Klan officials resulted in a congressional investigation. The bubble was punctured when the movement was exposed, not as a crusade, but as a vicious racket based on a $10 initiation fee. The KKK was an alarming manifestation of the intolerance and prejudice plaguing people anxious about the dizzying pace of social change in the 1920s.

Stemming the Foreign Flood

Isolationist America of the 1920s, ingrown and provincial, had little use for the immigrants who began to flood into the country again as peace settled soothingly on the war-torn world. Some 800,000 stepped ashore in 1920–1921, about two-thirds of them from southern and eastern Europe (see "Makers of America: The Poles," pp. 472–473). The "one hundred-percent Americans," recoiling at the sight of this resumed "New Immigration," once again cried that the famed poem at the base of the Statue of Liberty was all too literally true: they claimed that a sickly Europe was indeed vomiting on America "the wretched refuse of its teeming shore."

Congress temporarily plugged the breach with the Emergency Quota Act of 1921. This stopgap legislation was soon replaced by the Immigration Act of 1924. Quotas for foreigners were cut from 3 percent of persons of each nationality living in the United States to 2 percent. The national-origins base was shifted from the census of 1910 to that of 1890, when comparatively few southern Europeans had arrived.* The purpose was clearly to freeze America's existing ethnic composition, which was largely northern European. A flagrantly discriminatory section of the Immigration Act of 1924 slammed the door absolutely against Japanese immigrants. Exempt from the quota system were Canadians and Latin Americans.

The quota system effected a pivotal departure in American policy. Immigration henceforth dwindled to a mere trickle. Quotas thus caused America to sacrifice something of its tradition of freedom and opportunity, as well as its future ethnic diversity.

The Immigration Act of 1924 marked the end of an era—a period of virtually unrestricted immigra-

---

* Five years later the Immigration Act of 1929, using 1920 as the quota base, virtually cut immigration in half by limiting the total to 152,574 a year. In 1965 Congress abolished the national-origins quota system.

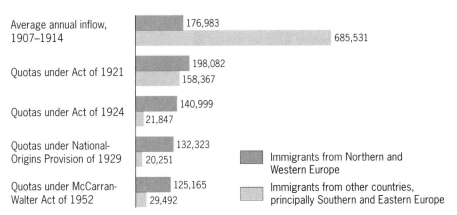

	Immigrants from Northern and Western Europe	Immigrants from other countries, principally Southern and Eastern Europe
Average annual inflow, 1907–1914	176,983	685,531
Quotas under Act of 1921	198,082	158,367
Quotas under Act of 1924	140,999	21,847
Quotas under National-Origins Provision of 1929	132,323	20,251
Quotas under McCarran-Walter Act of 1952	125,165	29,492

Annual Immigration and the Quota Laws   *The national-origins quota system was abolished in 1965. Legislation in that year capped the level of immigration at 170,000 per year but made exceptions for children, spouses, and parents of persons already arrived. It also restricted immigration from any single country to 20,000 people per year. The immigration laws were again significantly revised in 1986 (see p. 640).*

tion that in the previous century had brought some 35 million newcomers to the United States, mostly from Europe. The immigrant tide was now cut off, but it left on American shores by the 1920s a patchwork of ethnic communities separated from the larger society and from each other by language, religion, and customs. Many Italians, Jews, Poles, and others lived in isolated enclaves with their own houses of worship, newspapers, and theaters. Efforts to organize labor unions repeatedly foundered on the rocks of ethnic rivalries—often played upon by cynical employers. Ethnic variety thus undermined class and political solidarity in America.

The Prohibition Experiment

One of the last peculiar spasms of the progressive reform movement was prohibition, loudly supported by crusading churches and by many women. The arid new order was authorized in 1919 by the Eighteenth Amendment (for text, see the Appendix), as implemented by the Volstead Act passed by Congress later that year. Together these laws made the world "safe for hypocrisy."

The legal abolition of alcohol was fairly popular in the Midwest and especially so in the South. Southern whites were eager to keep stimulants out of the hands of blacks, lest they burst out of "their place." But despite the overwhelming ratification of the "dry" amendment, strong opposition persisted in the larger eastern cities. For many "wet" foreign-born people, sociability was built around drinking in beer gardens and corner taverns. Yet most Americans assumed that prohibition had come to stay.

But prohibitionists were naive in the extreme. They overlooked the tenacious American tradition of strong drink and of weak control by the central government, especially over private lives. They forgot that the federal authorities had never satisfactorily enforced a law that the majority of the people—or a strong minority—were hostile to. Lawmakers could not legislate away a thirst.

Prohibition simply did not prohibit. The old-time "men only" corner saloons were replaced by thousands of "speakeasies," each with its tiny grilled window through which the thirsty spoke softly before the barred door was opened. Hard liquor, especially

the cocktail, was drunk in staggering volume by both men and women. Largely because of the difficulties of transporting and concealing bottles, beverages of high alcoholic content were popular. Foreign rumrunners, often from the West Indies, had their inning, and countless cases of liquor leaked down from Canada. "Home brew" and "bathtub gin" became popular, as law-evading adults engaged in "alky cooking" with toy stills. The worst of the homemade "rotgut" produced blindness, even death.

Yet the "noble experiment" was not entirely a failure. Bank savings increased, and absenteeism in industry decreased, presumably because of the newly sober ways of formerly soused barflies. On the whole, probably less alcohol was consumed than in the days before prohibition, though strong drink continued to be available. As a legendary tippler remarked, prohibition was "a darn sight better than no liquor at all."

The Golden Age of Gangsterism

Prohibition spawned shocking crimes. The lush profits of illegal alcohol led to bribery of the police, many of whom were induced to see and smell no evil. Violent gang wars broke out in the big cities between rivals seeking to corner the rich market in booze. Rival triggermen used their sawed-off shotguns and chattering "typewriters" (machine guns) to "erase" bootlegging competitors who were trying to "muscle in" on their "racket." In the gang wars of the 1920s in Chicago, about five hundred low characters were murdered.

Chicago was by far the most spectacular example of lawlessness. In 1925 "Scarface" Al Capone, a grasping and murderous booze distributor, began six years of gang warfare that netted him millions of blood-spattered dollars. He zoomed through the streets in an armor-plated car with bulletproof windows.

Gangsters rapidly moved into other profitable and illicit activities: prostitution, gambling, and narcotics. Racketeers even invaded the ranks of local labor unions as organizers and promoters. Organized crime had come to be one of the nation's most gigantic businesses. By 1930 the annual "take" of the underworld was estimated to be from $12 billion to

The Poles

The Poles were among the largest immigrant groups to respond to industrializing America's call for badly needed labor after the Civil War. Between 1870 and World War I, some 2 million Polish-speaking peasants boarded steamships bound for the United States. By the 1920s, when antiforeign feeling led to restrictive legislation that choked the immigrant stream to a trickle, Polish immigrants and their American-born children began to develop new identities as Polish-Americans.

The first Poles to arrive in the New World had landed in Jamestown in 1608 and helped to develop that colony's timber industry. Over the ensuing two and a half centuries, scattered religious dissenters and revolutionary nationalists also made their way from Poland to America. During the Revolution about one hundred Poles, including two officers recruited by Benjamin Franklin, served in the Continental army.

Poland disappeared as an independent nation in the late 1700s, and many Polish patriots looked to America as a model of liberty. But the Polish hopefuls who poured into the United States in the late nineteenth century came primarily to stave off starvation and to earn money to buy land. Known in their homeland as *za chlebem* ("for bread") emigrants, they belonged to the mass of central and eastern European peasants who had been forced off their farms by growing competition from large-scale, mechanized agriculture. An exceptionally high birthrate among the Catholic Poles compounded this economic pres-sure, creating an army of the land-poor and landless. With wages in the United States more than eight times higher than in Poland, the American magnet was irresistible.

Many Polish immigrants were also lured by glowing letters from friends and relatives already

Polish Coal Miners, c. 1905   *It was common practice in American mines to segregate mining crews by ethnicity and race.*

living in the United States. The first wave of Polish immigrants had established a thriving network of self-help and fraternal associations, organized around Polish Catholic parishes. Often Polish-American entrepreneurs helped their European compatriots make travel arrangements or find jobs in the United States. One of the most successful of these, the energetic Chicago grocer Anton Schermann, is credited with "bringing over" a hundred thousand Poles and causing the Windy City to earn the nickname the "American Warsaw."

Most of the Poles arriving in the United States in the late nineteenth century headed for booming industrial cities such as Buffalo, Pittsburgh, Detroit, Milwaukee, and Chicago. In 1907, four-fifths of the men toiled as unskilled laborers in coal mines, meat-packing factories, textile and steel mills, oil refineries, and garment-making shops. Although married women usually stayed home and contributed to the family's earnings by taking in laundry and boarders, children and single girls often joined their fathers and brothers on the job.

When an independent Poland was created after World War I, few Poles chose to return to their Old World homeland. Instead, like other immigrant groups in the 1920s, they redoubled their efforts to integrate into American society. Polish institutions like churches and fraternal organizations, which had served to perpetuate a distinctive Polish culture in the New World, now facilitated the transformation of Poles into Polish-Americans. When Poland was absorbed into the Communist bloc after World War II, Polish-Americans clung still more tightly to their American identity, pushing for landmarks like Chicago's Pulaski Road to memorialize their culture in the New World.

$18 billion—several times the income of the Washington government.

Monkey Business in Tennessee

Education in the 1920s continued to make giant bootstrides. More and more states were requiring young people to remain in school until age sixteen or eighteen, or until graduation from high school. The proportion of seventeen-year-olds who finished high school almost doubled in the 1920s, to more than one in four.

The most revolutionary contribution to educational theory during these years was made by mild-mannered Professor John Dewey, who served on the faculty of Columbia University from 1904 to 1930. By common consent one of America's few front-rank philosophers, he set forth the principles of "learning by doing" that formed the foundation of so-called progressive education, with its greater "permissiveness." He believed that the workbench was as essential as the blackboard and that "education for life" should be a primary goal of the teacher.

Science also scored wondrous advances in these years. A massive public health program, launched by the Rockefeller Foundation in the South in 1909, had virtually wiped out the ancient affliction of hookworm by the 1920s. Better nutrition and health care helped to increase the life expectancy of a newborn infant from fifty years in 1901 to fifty-nine years in 1929.

Yet both science and progressive education in the 1920s were subjected to unfriendly fire from Fundamentalists. These old-time religionists charged that the teaching of Darwinian evolution was destroying faith in God and the Bible while contributing to the moral breakdown of youth in the jazz age. Numerous attempts were made to secure laws prohibiting the teaching of evolution, "the bestial hypothesis," in the public schools, and three southern states adopted such measures. The trio included Tennessee, in the heart of the so-called Bible Belt South, where evangelical religion was especially robust.

The stage was set for the memorable "Monkey Trial" at the hamlet of Dayton, Tennessee, in 1925. A

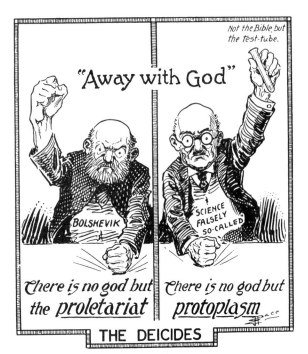

The Fundamentalist Outcry *Radicalism and science are both condemned.*

likable high school biology teacher, John T. Scopes, was indicted for teaching evolution. Batteries of newspaper reporters, armed with notebooks and cameras, descended on the quiet town to witness the spectacle. Scopes was defended by nationally known attorneys, while former presidential candidate William Jennings Bryan, an ardent Presbyterian Fundamentalist, joined the prosecution. Taking the stand as an expert on the Bible, Bryan was made to appear foolish by the famed criminal lawyer, Clarence Darrow. Five days after the trial was over, Bryan died of a stroke, no doubt brought on by the heat and strain.

This historic clash between theology and biology proved inconclusive. Scopes, the forgotten man of the drama, was found guilty and fined $100. But the supreme court of Tennessee, while upholding the law, set aside the fine on a technicality.* The Fundamentalists at best won only a hollow victory, for the

_____

* The Tennessee law was not formally repealed until 1967.

trial cast ridicule on their cause. Yet even though increasing numbers of Christians were coming to reconcile the revelations of religion with the findings of modern science, Fundamentalism, with its emphasis on literal reading of the Bible, remained a vibrant force in American spiritual life. It was especially strong in the Baptist church and in the rapidly growing Churches of Christ, organized in 1906.

The Mass-Consumption Economy

Prosperity—real, sustained, and widely shared—put much of the "roar" into the twenties. The economy kicked off its war harness in 1919, faltered a few steps in the recession of 1920–1921, and then sprinted forward for nearly seven years. Both the recent war and Treasury Secretary Andrew Mellon's tax policies favored the rapid expansion of capital investment. Ingenious machines, powered by relatively cheap energy from newly tapped oil fields, dramatically increased the productivity of the laborer. Assembly-line production was so advanced at Henry Ford's famed Rouge River plant near Detroit that a finished automobile emerged every ten seconds.

Great new industries suddenly sprouted forth. Supplying electrical power for the humming new machines became a giant business in the 1920s. Above all the automobile, once the horseless chariot of the rich, now became the carriage of the common citizen. By 1930 Americans owned almost 30 million cars. The nation's deepening "love affair" with the automobile headlined a momentous shift in the character of the economy. American manufacturers seemed to have mastered the problems of production; their worries now focused on consumption. Could they find the mass markets for the goods they had contrived to spew forth in such profusion?

Responding to this need, a new arm of American commerce came into being: advertising. By persuasion and ploy, allure and sexual suggestion, advertisers sought to make Americans chronically discontented with their paltry possessions and want more, more, more.

In this commercialized atmosphere, even sports were becoming a big business. Ballyhooed by the "image makers," home-run heroes like George H. ("Babe") Ruth were far better known than most statesmen. In 1921 a Jersey City crowd paid more than a million dollars to watch heavyweight champion Jack Dempsey knock out challenger George Carpentier—the first in a series of million-dollar "gates" in the golden 1920s.

Buying on credit was another innovative feature of the postwar economy. "Possess today and pay tomorrow" was the message directed at buyers. Once-frugal descendants of Puritans went ever deeper into debt to own all kinds of newfangled marvels—refrigerators, vacuum cleaners, and especially cars and radios—now. Prosperity thus accumulated an overhanging cloud of debt, and the economy became increasingly vulnerable to disruptions of the credit structure.

Putting America on Rubber Tires

A new industrial revolution slipped into high gear in America in the 1920s. Thrusting out steel tentacles, it changed the daily life of the people in unprecedented ways. Machinery was the new messiah—and the automobile was its principal prophet. Of all the inventions of the era, the automobile cut the deepest mark. It heralded an amazing new industrial system, based on assembly-line methods and mass-production techniques.

Americans adapted rather than invented the gasoline engine; Europeans can claim the original honor. By the 1890s a few daring American inventors and promoters, including Henry Ford and Ransom E. Olds (Oldsmobile), were developing the infant automotive industry. By 1910 sixty-nine car companies rolled out a total annual production of 181,000 units. Soon an enormous industry sprang into being, as Detroit became the motorcar capital of America.

Best known of the new crop of industrial wizards was Henry Ford, who, more than any other individual, put America on rubber tires. His high and hideous Model T ("Tin Lizzie") was cheap, rugged, and reasonably reliable, though rough and clattering. The parts of Ford's "flivver" were highly standardized, but the behavior of this "rattling good car" was so individualized that it became the butt of numberless jokes.

Lean and silent Henry Ford, who was said to have wheels in his head, erected an immense per-

sonal empire on the cornerstone of his mechanical genius. Ill-educated, this multimillionaire mechanic was socially and culturally narrow; "history is bunk," he once testified. But he devoted himself with one-track devotion to the gospel of standardization. After two early failures, he grasped and applied fully the techniques of assembly-line production—"Fordism."

The flood of Fords was phenomenal. In 1914 the "Automobile Wizard" turned out his five hundred thousandth Model T. By 1930 his total had risen to 20 million. By 1929, when the great bull market collapsed, 26 million motor vehicles were registered in the United States. This figure, averaging 1 for every 4.9 Americans, represented far more automobiles than existed in all the rest of the world.

The impact of the self-propelled carriage on various aspects of American life was tremendous. A gigantic new industry emerged, dependent on steel but displacing steel from its kingpin role. Employing directly or indirectly about 6 million people by 1930, it was a major prop of the nation's prosperity. Thousands of new jobs, moreover, were created by supporting industries. The lengthening list would include rubber, glass, and fabrics, to say nothing of thousands of service stations and garages. America's standard of living, responding to this infectious prosperity, rose to an enviable level.

Zooming motorcars were agents of social change. At first a luxury, they rapidly became a necessity. Essentially devices for needed transportation, they soon developed into a badge of freedom and equality—a necessary prop for self-respect. Women were further freed from their dependence on men. Isolation among the sections was broken down, and the less attractive states lost population at an alarming rate. Buses made possible the consolidation of schools and to some extent of churches. Virtuous home life partially broke down as joy-riders of all ages forsook the parlor for the highway. The morals of flaming youth sagged correspondingly—at least in the judgment of their elders.

Yet no sane American would plead for a return of the old horse and buggy, complete with fly-breeding manure. The automobile contributed notably to improved air and environmental quality, despite its later notoriety as a polluter. Life might be cut short on the highways, and smog might poison the air, but the automobile brought more convenience, pleasure, and excitement into people's lives than almost any other single invention.

Humans Develop Wings

Gasoline engines also provided the power that enabled humans to fulfill their age-old dream of sprouting wings. After near-successful experiments by others with heavier-than-air craft, the Wright brothers, Orville and Wilbur, performed "the miracle at Kitty Hawk," North Carolina. On a historic day—December 17, 1903—Orville Wright took aloft a feebly engined plane that stayed airborne for twelve seconds and 120 feet. Thus the air age was launched by two obscure bicycle repairmen.

Airplanes—once "flying coffins" for stuntmen—were first used with marked success for a serious purpose during the Great War of 1914–1918. Shortly thereafter private companies began to operate passenger lines with airmail contracts, which were in effect a subsidy from Washington. The first transcontinental airmail route was established from New York to San Francisco in 1920.

In 1927 modest and skillful Charles A. Lindbergh, the so-called Flyin' Fool, electrified the world with the first solo west-to-east conquest of the Atlantic. Seeking a prize of $25,000, the lanky stunt flier courageously piloted his single-engine plane, the *Spirit of St. Louis*, from New York to Paris in a grueling thirty-three hours and thirty-nine minutes.

Lindbergh's exploit swept Americans off their feet. Fed up with the cynicism and debunking of the jazz age, they found in this wholesome and handsome youth a genuine hero. "Lucky Lindy" received an uproarious welcome in the "hero canyon" of lower Broadway, as eighteen hundred tons of ticker tape and other improvised confetti showered upon him. His achievement—it was more than a "stunt"—did much to dramatize and popularize flying while giving a strong boost to the infant aviation industry.

The impact of the airplane was tremendous. The floundering railroads received another sharp setback through the loss of passengers and mail. A lethal new weapon was given to the gods of war with the coming of city-busting aerial bombs. The Atlantic Ocean was shriveling to about the size of the Aegean Sea in the days of Socrates, while isolation behind ocean moats was becoming a bygone dream.

The Radio and Film Revolutions

The speed of the airplane was far eclipsed by the speed of radio waves. Guglielmo Marconi, an Italian, invented wireless telegraphy in the 1890s, and his brainchild was used for long-range communication during World War I.

Next came the voice-carrying radio, a triumph of many minds. A red-letter day was posted in November 1920, when the Pittsburgh station KDKA broadcast the news of the Harding landslide.

The radio not only created a new industry but added richness to the fabric of American life. More joy was given to leisure hours, and the nation was better knit together. Advertising was further perfected as an art.

Crude filmmaking first developed in the 1890s. But the real birth of the movie came in 1903, when the first story sequence reached the screen. This breathless melodrama—The Great Train Robbery—was featured in the five-cent theaters, popularly called "nickelodeons." Spectacular among the first full-length classics was D. W. Griffith's The Birth of a Nation (1915), which glorified the Ku Klux Klan of Reconstruction days and defamed both blacks and northern carpetbaggers.

A fascinating industry was thus launched. Hollywood, California, quickly became the movie capital of the world, for it enjoyed a maximum of sunshine and other advantages. The motion picture really arrived during the World War of 1914–1918, when it was used as an engine of anti-German propaganda.

A new era began in 1927 with the success of the first "talkie"—The Jazz Singer, starring the white performer Al Jolson in blackface. The age of the "silents" was ushered out as theaters everywhere were wired for sound. About the same time, reasonably satisfactory color films were being produced.

Movies eclipsed all other new forms of amusement in the phenomenal growth of their popularity. Movie "stars" commanded much larger salaries than the president of the United States, in some cases as much as $100,000 for a single picture.

Critics bemoaned the vulgarization of popular taste wrought by the technologies of radio and movies, but the effects of the new mass media were not all negative. Much of the rich diversity of immigrant cultures was lost, as children, especially, turned away from Grandma's storytelling to the downtown movie theater or "Amos 'n' Andy." But the standardization of tastes and language hastened entry into the American mainstream—and set the stage for the emergence of a working-class political coalition that, for a time, would overcome the divisive ethnic differences of the past.

The Dynamic Decade

Far-reaching changes in lifestyles and values paralleled the dramatic upsurge of the economy. The census of 1920 revealed that for the first time most Americans no longer lived in the countryside but in urban areas. Women continued to find new opportunities for employment in the cities, though they tended to cluster in a few low-paying jobs (such as retail clerking and office typing) that quickly became classified as "women's work." An organized birth control movement, led by fiery feminist Margaret Sanger, openly championed the use of contraceptives. A National Women's party began in 1923 to campaign for an Equal Rights Amendment to the Constitution. To some defenders of traditional ways, it seemed that the world had suddenly gone mad.

Even before the war, one observer thought the chimes had "struck sex o'clock in America," and the 1920s witnessed what many old-timers thought was a veritable erotic eruption. Advertisers exploited sexual allure to sell everything from soap to car tires. Once-modest maidens now proclaimed their new freedom as "flappers" in bobbed tresses and dresses. Young women appeared with hemlines elevated, stockings rolled, breasts taped flat, cheeks rouged, and lips a "crimson gash" that held a dangling cigarette. Thus did the flapper symbolize a yearned-for and devil-may-care independence (some said wild abandon) in American women.

Justification for this new sexual frankness could be found in the recently translated writings of Dr. Sigmund Freud. This Viennese physician appeared to argue that sexual repression was responsible for a variety of nervous and emotional ills. Thus not pleasure alone, but health, demanded sexual gratification and liberation.

Many taboos flew out the window as sex-conscious Americans let themselves go. As unknowing Freudians, teenagers pioneered the sexual frontiers. Glued together in syncopated embrace, they danced to jazz music squeaking from phonographs. In an earlier day a kiss had been the equivalent of a proposal of marriage. But in the new era exploratory young folk sat in darkened movie houses or took to the highways and byways in automobiles—branded "houses of prostitution on wheels" by straitlaced elders. There the youthful "neckers" and "petters" poached upon the forbidden territory of each other's bodies.

If the flapper was the goddess of the "era of wonderful nonsense," jazz was its sacred music. With its virtuoso wanderings and tricky syncopation, jazz moved up from New Orleans along with migrating blacks during World War I. Tunes like W. C. Handy's "St. Louis Blues" became instant classics as the wailing saxophone became the trumpet of the new era. Blacks such as Handy, "Jelly Roll" Morton, and Joseph ("Joe") King Oliver gave birth to jazz, but the entertainment industry soon spawned all-white bands—notably Paul Whiteman's. Caucasian impresarios cornered the profits, though not the creative soul, of America's most native music.

A new racial pride also blossomed in the northern black communities that grew so rapidly during and after the war. Harlem in New York City, counting some 100,000 African-American residents in the 1920s, was one of the largest black communities in the world. Harlem sustained a vibrant, creative culture that nourished poets like Langston Hughes, whose first volume of verse, *Weary Blues*, appeared in 1926.

Harlem in the 1920s also spawned a charismatic leader, Marcus Garvey. Jamaican-born Garvey founded the United Negro Improvement Association (UNIA) to promote the resettlement of American blacks in Africa. His Black Star Steamship Company and other enterprises failed financially, and Garvey himself was convicted of fraud in 1927 and deported by a nervous United States government. But the race pride that Garvey inspired among his 4 million UNIA followers helped them gain self-confidence and self-reliance. His example proved important to the later founding of the Nation of Islam (Black Muslim) movement.

King Oliver's Creole Jazz Band, Early 1920s *Joseph ("Joe") King Oliver arrived in Chicago from New Orleans in 1918. His band became the first important black jazz ensemble and made Chicago's Royal Garden Cafe a magnet for jazz lovers. Left to right: Honoré Dutrey, trombone; Baby Dodds, drums; King Oliver, cornet; Lil Hardin, piano; Bill Johnson, banjo; and Johnny Dodds, clarinet. Kneeling in the foreground is the young Louis Armstrong, playing a trombone.*

Literary Liberation

Likewise in literature, an older era seemed to have ground to a halt with the recent war. By the dawn of the 1920s, most of the custodians of an aging genteel culture had died—Henry James in 1916, Henry Adams in 1918, and William Dean Howells (the "dean of American literature") in 1920. A few novelists who had been popular in the previous decades continued to thrive, notably the well-to-do, cosmopolitan New Yorker Edith Wharton and the Virginia-born Willa Cather, esteemed for her stark but sympathetic portrayals of pioneering on the prairies.

But in the decade after the war, a new generation of writers burst on the scene. Many of them hailed from ethnic and regional backgrounds different from that of the Protestant New Englanders who traditionally had dominated American cultural life. The newcomers exhibited the energy of youth, the ambition of excluded outsiders, and, in many cases, the smoldering resentment of ideals betrayed. They bestowed on American literature a new vitality, imaginativeness, and artistic quality.

A patron saint of many young authors was H. L. Mencken, the "Bad Boy of Baltimore," who admired their critical attitude toward American society. In the pages of his green-covered monthly *American Mercury*, Mencken assailed marriage, patriotism, democracy, prohibition, Rotarians, and the middle-class American "booboisie." The South he contemptuously dismissed as "the Sahara of the Bozart" (a bastardization of *beaux arts*, French for the "fine arts"), and he scathingly attacked do-gooders as "Puritans." Puritanism, he jibed, was "the haunting fear that someone, somewhere, might be happy."

The war had jolted many young writers out of their complacency about traditional values and literary standards. With their pens they probed for new codes of morals and understanding, as well as fresh forms of expression. F. Scott Fitzgerald, a handsome Minnesota-born Princetonian then only twenty-four years old, became an overnight celebrity when he published *This Side of Paradise* in 1920. The book became a kind of Bible for the young. It was eagerly devoured by aspiring flappers and their ardent wooers, many of whom affected an air of bewildered abandon toward life. Catching the spirit of the hour (often about 4 A.M.), Fitzgerald found "All gods dead, all wars fought, all faiths in man shaken." He followed this melancholy success with *The Great Gatsby*

(1925), a brilliant evocation of the glamour and cruelty of an achievement-oriented society. Theodore Dreiser's masterpiece of 1925 explored much the same theme: *An American Tragedy* dealt with the murder of a pregnant working girl by her socially ambitious young lover.

Ernest Hemingway, who had seen action on the Italian front in 1917, was among the writers most affected by the war. He responded to pernicious propaganda and the overblown appeal of patriotism by devising his own lean, word-sparing but word-perfect style. In *The Sun Also Rises* (1926) Hemingway told of disillusioned, spiritually numb American expatriates in Europe. In *A Farewell to Arms* (1929) he crafted one of the finest novels in any language about the war experience. A troubled soul, he finally blew out his brains with a shotgun blast in 1961.

Other writers turned to a critical probing of American small-town life. Sherwood Anderson dissected various fictional personalities in *Winesburg, Ohio* (1919), finding them all in some way warped by their cramped psychological surroundings. Sinclair Lewis, a hot-headed journalistic product of Sauk Centre, Minnesota, sprang into prominence in 1920 with *Main Street*, the story of one woman's unsuccessful war against provincialism. In *Babbitt* (1922) he affectionately pilloried George F. Babbitt, a prosperous, vulgar, middle-class real estate broker who slavishly conformed to the respectable materialism of his group. The word *Babbittry* was quickly coined to describe his all-too-familiar lifestyle.

William Faulkner, a dark-eyed, pensive Mississippian, penned a bitter war novel, *Soldier's Pay*, in 1926. He then turned his attention to a fictional chronicle of an imaginary, history-rich Deep South county. In powerful books like *The Sound and the Fury* (1929) and *As I Lay Dying* (1930), Faulkner peeled back layers of time and consciousness from the constricted souls of his ingrown southern characters.

Nowhere was innovation in the 1920s more obvious than in poetry. Ezra Pound, a brilliantly erratic Idahoan who deserted America for Europe, rejected what he called "an old bitch civilization, gone in the teeth," and proclaimed his doctrine: "make it new." Pound strongly influenced Missouri-born and Harvard-educated T. S. Eliot, who took up

F. Scott Fitzgerald and His Wife, Zelda   *They are shown here in the happy, early days of their stormy marriage.*

residence in England. In "The Waste Land" (1922) Eliot produced one of the most impenetrable but influential poems of the century. Robert Frost, a San Francisco–born poet, wrote hauntingly about his adopted New England.

On the stage, Eugene O'Neill, a New York dramatist and Princeton dropout of globe-trotting background, laid bare Freudian notions of sex in plays like *Strange Interlude* (1928). A prodigious playwright, he wrote more than a dozen productions in the 1920s and won the Nobel Prize in 1936.

O'Neill arose from New York's Greenwich Village, which before and after the war was a seething cauldron of writers, painters, musicians, actors, and other would-be artists. After the war, a black cultural renaissance also took root uptown in Harlem, led by such gifted writers as Claude McKay and Langston

Hughes, and by jazz artists like Louis Armstrong and Eubie Blake. They proudly exulted in their black culture and argued for a "New Negro" who was a full citizen and a "social equal" to whites.

Architecture also married itself to the new materialism and functionalism. Long-range city planning was being intelligently projected, and architects such as Frank Lloyd Wright were advancing the theory that buildings should grow from their sites and not slavishly imitate Greek and Roman importations. The machine age outdid itself in New York City in 1931 when it thrust upward the cloud-brushing Empire State Building, 102 stories high.

Wall Street's Big Bull Market

The boom of the golden twenties showered genuine benefits on Americans. Their incomes and living standards assuredly rose, but there always seemed to be something fantastic about it all. People sang, somewhat incredulously:

> My sister she works in the laundry,
>   My father sells bootlegger gin,
> My mother she takes in the washing,
>   My God! how the money rolls in!

Signals abounded that the economic joy ride might end in a crash; even in the best years of the 1920s several hundred banks failed annually. This something-for-nothing craze was well illustrated by real estate speculation, especially the fantastic Florida boom that culminated in 1925. Numerous underwater lots were sold to eager purchasers for preposterous sums. The whole wildcat scheme collapsed when the peninsula was devastated by a hurricane.

The stock exchange provided even greater sensations. Speculation ran wild, and an orgy of boom-or-bust trading pushed the bull market to dizzy peaks as Wall Street gamblers gored one another and fleeced greedy lambs. The stock market became a veritable gambling den.

As the 1920s lurched forward, everybody seemed to be buying stocks "on margin"—that is, with a small down payment. Barbers, stenographers, and elevator boys cashed in on "hot tips" picked up while on duty. One valet was reported to have par-

layed his wages into a quarter of a million dollars. Rags-to-riches Americans eagerly worshiped at the altar of the ticker-tape machine. So powerful was the intoxicant of quick profits that few heeded the voices raised in certain quarters to warn that this kind of tinsel prosperity could not last forever.

Little was done by Washington to curb money-mad speculators. In the wartime days of Wilson, the national debt had rocketed from the 1914 figure of $1,188,235,400 to the 1921 peak of $23,976,250,608. Conservative principles of money management pointed to a diversion of surplus funds to reduce this financial burden.

The burdensome taxes inherited from the war were especially distasteful to Secretary of the Treasury Mellon, as well as to his fellow millionaires. Their theory was that such high levies forced the rich to invest in tax-exempt securities rather than in factories that provided prosperous payrolls. The Mellonites also argued, with considerable persuasiveness, that high taxes not only discouraged business but also brought a smaller net return to the Treasury than moderate taxes.

Seeking to succor the "poor" rich people, Mellon helped engineer a series of tax reductions from 1921 to 1926. Congress followed his lead by repealing the excess-profits tax, abolishing the gift tax, and reducing excise taxes, the surtax, the income tax, and estate taxes. In 1921 a wealthy person with an income of $1 million had paid $663,000 in income taxes; in 1926 the same person paid about $200,000. Mellon's spare-the-rich policies thus shifted much of the tax burden from the wealthy to middle-income groups.

Mellon, lionized by conservatives as the "greatest secretary of the treasury since Hamilton," remains a controversial figure. True, he reduced the national debt by $10 billion—from about $26 billion to $16 billion. But foes of the emaciated multimillionaire charged that he should have bitten a larger chunk out of the debt, especially while the country was pulsating with prosperity. He was also accused of indirectly encouraging the bull market. If he had absorbed more of the national income in taxes, there would have been less money left for frenzied speculation. His refusal to do so typified the single-mindedly probusiness regime that dominated the political scene throughout the postwar decade.

Chronology

1903	Wright brothers fly the first airplane. First story-sequence motion picture.
1919	Eighteenth Amendment ratified (prohibition). Volstead Act. Seattle general strike. Anderson publishes *Winesburg, Ohio*.
1919– 1920	"Red scare."
1920	Radio broadcasting begins. Fitzgerald publishes *This Side of Paradise*. Lewis publishes *Main Street*.
1921	Sacco-Vanzetti trial. Emergency Quota Act of 1921.
1922	Lewis publishes *Babbitt*. Eliot publishes "The Waste Land."
1923	Equal Rights Amendment (ERA) proposed.
1924	Immigration Act of 1924.
1925	Scopes trial. Florida real estate boom. Fitzgerald publishes *The Great Gatsby*. Dreiser publishes *An American Tragedy*.
1926	Hughes publishes *Weary Blues*. Hemingway publishes *The Sun Also Rises*.
1927	Lindbergh flies the Atlantic solo. First talking motion pictures. Sacco and Vanzetti executed.
1929	Faulkner publishes *The Sound and the Fury*. Hemingway publishes *A Farewell to Arms*.

SUGGESTED READINGS

Primary Source Documents

For the fallout from the red scare see Walter Lippmann's eloquent plea for the lives of the Italian-American radicals Sacco and Vanzetti in the New York *World** (August 19, 1927). For caustic fictional versions of the decade's social conditions see the novels of Sinclair Lewis, *Main Street* (1920), *Babbitt* (1922), and *Arrowsmith* (1925).

Secondary Sources

The best introduction to the 1920s is William Leuchtenburg, *The Perils of Prosperity, 1914–1932* (1958). Also strong is Michael E. Parrish, *Anxious Decades: America in Prosperity and Depression, 1920–1941* (1992). Frederick Lewis Allen, *Only Yesterday* (1931), is an evocative recollection of the texture of life in the decade. Equally informative are Robert S. Lynd and Helen M. Lynd's classic sociological studies, *Middletown* (1929) and *Middletown in Transition* (1937). Robert K. Murray, *Red Scare* (1955), is authoritative. Immigration restriction is dealt with in John Higham, *Strangers in the Land* (1955). The standard work on the revived Klan is David M. Chalmers, *Hooded Americanism* (rev. ed., 1981). Also valuable is Kenneth T. Jackson, *The Ku Klux Klan in the City, 1915–1930* (1967), and Nancy MacLean, *Behind the Mask of Chivalry: The Making of the Second KKK* (1993). The changing experiences of women are discussed in Winnifred Wandersee, *Women's Work and Family Values, 1920–1940* (1981); Lois Scharf and Joan M. Jensen, eds., *Decades of Discontent: The Women's Movement, 1920–1940* (1983); Nancy F. Cott, *The Grounding of Modern Feminism* (1987); and Phyllis Palmer, *Domesticity and Dirt: Housewives and Domestic Servants in the United States, 1920–1945* (1990). On the Scopes trial see George Marsden, *Fundamentalism and American Culture* (1980). The "youth culture" is the subject of Paula Fass, *The Damned and the Beautiful: American Youth in the 1920s* (1977). Changing sexual attitudes are analyzed in David M. Kennedy, *Birth Control in America: The Career of Margaret Sanger* (1970), and Linda Gordon, *Woman's Body, Woman's Right: A Social History of Birth Control in America* (1976). See also Ellen Chesler, *Woman of Valor: Margaret Sanger and the Birth Control Movement in America* (1992). Gilbert Osofsky describes the background of the Harlem Renaissance in *Harlem: The Making of a Ghetto, 1890–1930* (1966). See also David Lewis, *When Harlem Was in Vogue* (1981). William M. Tuttle, *Race Riot: Chicago in the Red Summer of 1919* (1970), describes the violent side of race relations in the 1920s. The "Great Migration" of blacks to the North is described in James R. Grossman's *Land of Hope: Chicago, Black Southerners, and the Great Migration* (1989). Judith Stein, *The World of Marcus Garvey* (1986), discusses the most popular black leader of the period. Richard W. Fox and T. J. Jackson Lears have edited a fascinating collection of essays on American culture, *The Culture of Consumption: Critical Essays in American History, 1880–1980* (1983). Also see Warren I. Susman, *Culture as History: The Transformation of American Society in the Twentieth Century* (1984). David M. Kennedy, *Over Here: The First World War and American Society* (1980), pays special attention to the literature that emerged from the war experience.

---

* An asterisk indicates that the document, or an excerpt from it, can be found in Thomas A. Bailey and David M. Kennedy, eds., *The American Spirit: United States History as Seen by Contemporaries*, 9th ed. (Boston: Houghton Mifflin, 1998).

33

The Politics of Boom and Bust,

1920–1932

★★★★★★

We in America today are nearer to the final triumph over poverty than ever before in the history of any land. We have not yet reached the goal—but . . . we shall soon, with the help of God, be in sight of the day when poverty will be banished from this nation.

★★★★★★

HERBERT HOOVER, 1928

The Republican "Old Guard" Returns

Handsome President Harding—with erect figure (6 feet), broad shoulders, high forehead, bushy eyebrows, and graying hair—was one of the best-liked men of his generation. An easygoing, warm-handed first-namer, he exuded graciousness and love of people. Yet the amiable, smiling exterior concealed a weak, flabby interior. With a mediocre mind, Harding quickly found himself beyond his depths in the presidency.

Harding, like Grant, was unable to detect moral halitosis in his evil associates, and he was soon sur-rounded by his poker-playing, shirt-sleeved cronies of the "Ohio gang." He hated to hurt people's feelings, especially those of his friends, by saying "no"; and designing political leeches capitalized on this weak-ness. He "was not a bad man," said one Washington observer. "He was just a slob."

Well intentioned but weak willed, Harding was a perfect "front" for enterprising industrialists. A McKinley-style old order settled heavily back into place at war's end, crushing the reform seedlings that had sprouted in the progressive era. This new Old Guard hoped to improve on the old business doctrine of laissez-faire. Their plea was not simply for government to keep hands off business but for government to help guide business along the path to profits. They subtly and effectively achieved their ends by putting the courts and the administrative bureaus into the safekeeping of fellow standpatters.

The Supreme Court was a striking example of this trend. Harding lived less than three years as president, but he appointed four of the nine justices. In the first years of the 1920s, the Supreme Court axed progressive legislation. It killed a federal child-labor law, stripped away many of labor's hard-won gains, and rigidly restricted governmental intervention in the economy. In the landmark case of *Adkins* v. *Children's Hospital* (1923), the Court reversed its own reasoning in *Muller* v. *Oregon* (see p. 430) and invalidated a minimum-wage law for women. Its strained ruling was that because females now had the vote (Nineteenth Amendment), they could no longer be protected by special legislation. The contradictory premises of the *Muller* and *Adkins* cases framed a debate over gender differences that would continue for the rest of the century: were women sufficiently different from men that they merited special legal and social treatment, or were they effectively equal in the eyes of the law and therefore undeserving of special protection and preferences?

Corporations, under Harding, could once more relax and expand. Antitrust laws were often ignored, circumvented, or feebly enforced by friendly prosecutors in the attorney general's office. The Interstate Commerce Commission, to single out one agency, came to be dominated by members who were sympathetic to the managers of the railroads.

Big industrialists, striving to lessen competition, now had a free hand to set up trade associations. Cement manufacturers, for example, would use these agencies to agree upon standardization of product, publicity campaigns, and a united front in dealing with the railroads and labor. Although many of these associations ran counter to the spirit of existing antitrust legislation, their formation was encouraged by Secretary of Commerce Herbert Hoover. His sense of engineering efficiency was shocked by the waste resulting from cutthroat competition.

The Aftermath of War

Wartime government controls on the economy were swiftly dismantled. The War Industries Board disappeared with almost indecent haste. With its passing, progressive hopes for more government regulation of big business evaporated.

Washington likewise returned the railroads to private management in 1920. The Esch-Cummins Transportation Act of 1920 encouraged private consolidation of the railroads and obligated the federal Interstate Commerce Commission to guarantee their profitability.

Labor, suddenly deprived of its wartime crutch of friendly government support, limped along badly in the postwar decade. The Railway Labor Board, a successor body to the wartime labor boards, ordered a wage cut of 12 percent in 1922, provoking a two-month strike. It ended when Attorney General Harry Daugherty, who fully shared Harding's big-business bias, clamped on the strikers one of the most sweeping injunctions in American history. Unions wilted in this hostile political environment, and membership dropped by nearly 30 percent between 1920 and 1930.

Needy veterans were among the few nonbusiness groups to reap lasting gains from the war. In 1921 Congress created the Veterans' Bureau to operate hospitals and provide vocational rehabilitation for the disabled. The American Legion, founded in Paris in 1919 by Colonel Theodore Roosevelt, Jr., became known for its militant conservatism and aggressive lobbying for veterans' benefits. It pressed fervently for "adjusted compensation" to make up for the wages veterans had "lost" while in uniform. Harding vetoed one such bill in 1922, but in 1924 Congress passed the Adjusted Compensation Act over President Calvin Coolidge's veto. It gave every former soldier a paid-up insurance policy due in twenty years—adding about $3.5 billion to the total cost of the war.

Isolationism and the Washington Conference

Isolation was enthroned in Washington during the Harding administration. With the Senate "irreconcilables" holding a hatchet over its head, the U.S. government continued to regard the League of Nations as a thing unclean.

But disarmament was one international issue on which Harding set isolationism aside and seized the initiative. He was prodded by businesspeople unwilling to dig deeper into their pockets for money to finance the ambitious naval building program started during the war. A deadly contest was shaping up with Britain and Japan, which watched with alarm as the oceans filled with American vessels. Public agitation in America, fed by worries about British and Japanese cooperation in the Pacific, brought about the headline-making Washington Disarmament Conference in 1921–1922. The double agenda included naval disarmament and the situation in East Asia.

At the outset, Secretary of State Charles Evans Hughes dramatically proposed a ten-year "holiday" on construction of battleships, and even the scrapping of some of the huge dreadnoughts already built or being built. He suggested that the scaled-down navies of America and Britain should enjoy parity in battleships and aircraft carriers, with Japan on the small end of a 5-5-3 ratio.

Complex bargaining followed in the wake of Hughes's proposals. The Five-Power Naval Treaty of 1922 embodied Hughes's ideas on ship ratios, but only after face-saving compensation was offered to the Japanese. The British and the Americans both conceded that they would refrain from fortifying their East Asian possessions, including the Philippines. The Japanese were not subjected to such restraints in their possessions. In addition, a Four-Power Treaty bound Britain, Japan, France, and the United States to preserve the status quo in the Pacific—another concession to the Japanese. Finally, the Washington Conference gave chaotic China—"the sick man of East Asia"—a shot in the arm with the Nine-Power Treaty of 1922, whose signatories agreed to nail wide open the Open Door in China.

The Hardingites boasted of this globe-shaking achievement in disarmament, but their satisfaction was somewhat illusory. No restrictions had been placed on small warships, and the other powers churned ahead with the construction of cruisers, destroyers, and submarines, while penny-pinching Uncle Sam lagged dangerously behind. Ominously,

the American people seemed content to rely for their security on words and wishful thinking rather than weapons and hardheaded realism.

A similar sentimentalism welled up later in the decade, when Americans clamored for the "outlawry of war." The Kellogg-Briand Pact, declaring war illegal, was signed by Coolidge's secretary of state and the French foreign minister in 1928 and was ultimately ratified by sixty-two nations. It was delusory in the extreme. Lacking both muscles and teeth, it was a diplomatic derelict and virtually useless in a showdown. Yet it accurately—and dangerously—reflected the American mind in the 1920s, which was all too ready to be lulled into a false sense of security. This mood took even deeper hold in the ostrichlike neutralism of the 1930s.

Hiking the Tariff Higher

A comparable lack of realism afflicted foreign economic policy in the 1920s. Businesspeople, short-sightedly obsessed with the dazzling prospects in the prosperous home market, sought to keep that market to themselves by flinging up insurmountable tariff walls around the United States. Congress passed the Fordney-McCumber Tariff Law of 1922, which boosted schedules from the average of 27 percent under Wilson's Underwood Tariff of 1913 to an average of 38.5 percent.

The high-tariff course thus charted by the Republican regimes set off an ominous chain reaction. European producers felt the squeeze, for the American tariff walls prolonged the postwar chaos. Impoverished Europe needed to sell manufactured goods to the United States, particularly if it hoped to achieve economic recovery and to pay its huge war debt to Washington. America needed to give foreign nations a chance to make a profit so that they could buy U.S. manufactured articles and repay debts. International trade, Americans were slow to learn, is a two-way street.

Erecting tariff walls was also a game that two could play. The American example spurred European nations, throughout the feverish 1920s, to pile up higher barriers themselves. The whole vicious circle further deepened the international economic distress, providing one more rung on the ladder by which Adolf Hitler scrambled to power.

The Stench of Scandal

The loose morality and get-rich-quickism of the Harding era manifested themselves spectacularly in a series of scandals. Early in 1923 the head of the Veterans' Bureau, Colonel Charles R. Forbes, was caught with his hand in the till and later convicted of fraud. An appointee of the gullible Harding, he and his accomplices looted the government to the tune of about $200 million, chiefly in connection with the building of veterans' hospitals.

Most shocking of all was the Teapot Dome scandal, an affair that involved priceless naval oil reserves at Teapot Dome (Wyoming) and Elk Hills (California). In 1921 the slippery secretary of the interior, Albert B. Fall, induced his careless colleague, the secretary of the navy, to transfer these valuable properties to the Interior Department. Harding indiscreetly signed the secret order. Fall then quietly leased the lands to oilmen Harry F. Sinclair and Edward L. Doheny, but not until he had received a bribe ("loan") of $100,000 from Doheny and about three times that amount in all from Sinclair.

Teapot Dome, no tempest in a teapot, finally came to a whistling boil. Details of the crooked transaction leaked out in March 1923. Fall, Sinclair, and Doheny were indicted in 1924. Fall was found guilty of taking a bribe and sentenced to one year in jail. The two bribe givers were acquitted, though Sinclair served time in jail for "shadowing" jurors and for refusing to testify before a Senate committee.

Still more scandals erupted. Persistent reports about the underhanded doings of Attorney General Daugherty brought a Senate investigation in 1924 of the illegal sale of pardons and liquor permits. Forced to resign, the accused official was tried in 1927 but released after a jury twice failed to agree on a verdict. During the trial, Daugherty hid behind the trousers of the now-dead Harding by implying that persistent probing might uncover crookedness in the White House.

Harding was mercifully spared the full revelation of these iniquities. Just as the scandals were breaking, he died in San Francisco on August 2, 1923, of pneumonia and thrombosis.

The brutal fact is that Harding simply was not a strong enough man for the presidency—as he himself privately admitted. Such was his weakness that he tolerated people and conditions that subjected the Republic to its worst disgrace since the days of President Grant.

The Harding Scandals
This 1924 cartoon satirizing the misdemeanors of the Harding administration shows the sale of the Capitol, the White House, and even the Washington Monument.

Calvin Coolidge: A Yankee in the White House

News of Harding's death was sped to Vice President Coolidge, then visiting at his father's New England farmhouse. By the light of two kerosene lamps the elder Coolidge, a justice of the peace, used the old family Bible to administer the presidential oath to his son.

This homespun setting was symbolic of Coolidge. Quite unlike Harding, the stern-faced Vermonter, with his thin nose and tightly set lips, embodied the New England virtues of honesty, morality, industry, and frugality. His dour, serious visage prompted the acerbic observation that he had been "weaned on a pickle."

Coolidge seemed to be a crystallization of the commonplace. A painfully shy individual of average height (5 feet, 10 inches), he was blessed with only mediocre powers of leadership. He would occasionally display a dry wit in private; but his speeches, delivered in a nasal New England twang, were invariably boring. A staunch apostle of the status quo, he became the "high priest of the great god Business." He believed that "the man who builds a factory builds a temple" and that "the man who works there worships there." Coolidge "luck" held during his five and a half prosperity-blessed years.

Cash Register Chorus   *Business croons its appreciation of "Coolidge prosperity."*

Ever a profile in caution, Coolidge slowly gave the Harding regime a badly needed moral fumigation. Teapot Dome had scalded the Republican party badly, but so transparently honest was the vinegary Vermonter that the scandalous oil did not rub off on him.

Frustrated Farmers

Sun-bronzed farmers were squarely in a boom-or-bust cycle in the postwar decade. While the fighting had raged, they had raked in money, hand over gnarled fist; but peace ended high farm prices.

Machines also threatened to plow the farmer under an avalanche of his own overabundant crops. The gasoline-engine tractor was working a revolution on American farms. This steel mule was to cultivation and sowing what the McCormick reaper was to harvesting. Blue-denimed farmers could sit on their chugging mechanical chariots and harrow many acres in a single day. But such improved efficiency and expanded agricultural production helped to pile up more price-dampening surpluses. A withering depression swept through agricultural districts in the 1920s, when one farm in four was sold for debt or taxes.

Schemes abounded for bringing relief to the hard-pressed farmers. A bipartisan "farm bloc" from the agricultural states coalesced in Congress in 1921 and succeeded in driving through some helpful laws. Noteworthy was the Capper-Volstead Act, which exempted farmers' marketing cooperatives from antitrust prosecution. The farm bloc's favorite proposal was the McNary-Haugen Bill, pushed energetically from 1924 to 1928. It sought to keep agricultural prices high by authorizing the government to buy up surpluses and sell them abroad. Government losses were to be made up by a special tax on the farmers. Congress twice passed the bill, but frugal Coolidge twice vetoed it. Farm prices stayed down, and the farmers' political temperatures stayed high, reaching fever pitch in the election of 1924.

A Three-Way Race for the White House in 1924

Self-satisfied Republicans, chanting "Keep cool and keep Coolidge," nominated "Silent Cal" for the

Presidential Election of 1924 (showing popular vote by county) *Notice the concentration of La Follette's votes in the old Populist strongholds of the Midwest and the mountain states. His ticket did especially well in the grain-growing districts battered by the postwar slump in agricultural prices.*

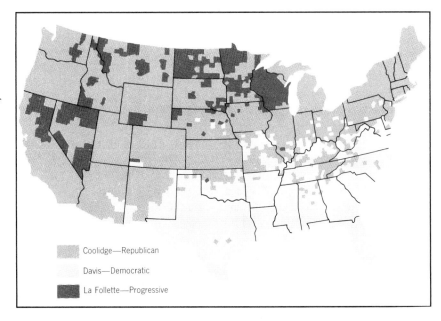

Coolidge—Republican

Davis—Democratic

La Follette—Progressive

presidency at their convention in Cleveland in the simmering summer of 1924. Squabbling Democrats had more difficulty choosing a candidate when they met in New York's sweltering Madison Square Garden. Reflecting many of the cultural tensions of the decade, the party was hopelessly split between "wets" and "drys," urbanites and farmers, Fundamentalists and Modernists, northern liberals and southern standpatters, immigrants and old-stock Americans. Deadlocked for an unprecedented 102 ballots, the convention at last turned wearily, sweatily, and unenthusiastically to John W. Davis. A wealthy Wall Street lawyer, the polished nominee was no less conservative than cautious Calvin Coolidge.

The field was now wide open for a liberal candidate, and white-pompadoured Senator Robert ("Fighting Bob") La Follette of Wisconsin sprang forward to lead a new Progressive grouping. He gained the endorsement of the American Federation of Labor and enjoyed the support of the Socialist party, but his major constituency was the price-pinched farmers. La Follette's new Progressive party, only a shadow of the robust progressive coalition of prewar days, called for government ownership of railroads and relief for farmers, lashed out at monopoly and antilabor injunctions, and urged a constitutional

amendment to limit the Supreme Court's power to invalidate laws passed by Congress.

La Follette turned in a respectable showing, polling nearly 5 million votes. But "Cautious Cal" and the oil-bespattered Republicans slipped easily back into office, overwhelming Davis, 15,718,211 votes to 8,385,283. The electoral count stood at 382 for Coolidge, 136 for Davis, and 13 for La Follette, all from his home state of Wisconsin.

Foreign-Policy Flounderings

Isolation continued to reign in the Coolidge era. Despite presidential proddings, the Senate proved unwilling to allow America to adhere to the World Court—the judicial arm of the still-suspect League of Nations. Coolidge only half-heartedly—and unsuccessfully—pursued further naval disarmament after the loudly trumpeted agreements worked out at the Washington Conference in 1922.

A glaring exception to the United States' inward-looking indifference to the outside world in the 1920s was the armed interventionism in the Caribbean and Central America. American troops were withdrawn (after an eight-year stay) from the Dominican Republic in 1924, but they remained in

Haiti from 1914 to 1934. President Coolidge in 1925 briefly removed American bayonets from troubled Nicaragua, where they had glinted intermittently since 1909, but in 1926 he sent them back, five thousand strong, and they stayed until 1933. American oil companies clamored for a military expedition to Mexico in 1926 when the Mexican government began to assert its sovereignty over oil resources. Coolidge kept cool and defused the Mexican crisis with some skillful diplomatic negotiating. But his mailed-fist tactics elsewhere bred sore resentments south of the Rio Grande, where angry critics loudly assailed "*yanqui* imperialism."

Overshadowing all other foreign-policy problems in the 1920s was the knotty issue of international debts, a complicated tangle of private loans, Allied war debts, and German reparations. The key knot in the debt tangle was the $10 billion that the U.S. Treasury had loaned to the Allies during and immediately after the war. Uncle Sam held their IOUs—and he wanted to be paid. The Allies, in turn, protested that they had held up a wall of flesh and bone against the common foe until America the Unready had entered the fray. America, they argued, should write off its loans as war costs, just as the Allies had been tragically forced to write off the lives of millions of young men. And the final straw, protested the Europeans, was that America's postwar tariff walls made it almost impossible for them to sell the goods to earn the dollars to pay their debts.

Unraveling the Debt Knot

America's tightfisted insistence on getting its money back helped to harden the hearts of the Allies against conquered Germany. The French and the British demanded that the Germans make enormous reparations payments, totaling some $32 billion, as compensation for war-inflicted damages. The Allies hoped to settle their debts to America with the money received from Germany. The French, seeking to extort lagging reparations payments, sent troops into Germany's industrialized Ruhr Valley in 1923. Berlin responded by permitting its currency to inflate astronomically. At one point in October 1923, a loaf of bread cost 480 million marks, or about $120 million in preinflation money. German society teetered on the brink of mad anarchy, and the whole international house of financial cards threatened to flutter down in colossal chaos.

The fact that the Allied debt was linked to reparations was partly recognized in the Dawes Plan of 1924. Negotiated largely by Charles Dawes, about to be Coolidge's running mate, it rescheduled German reparations payments and opened the way for further American private loans to Germany. The whole financial cycle became still more complicated as U.S. bankers loaned money to Germany, Germany paid reparations to France and Britain, and the former Allies paid war debts to the United States. Clearly the source of this monetary merry-go-round was the

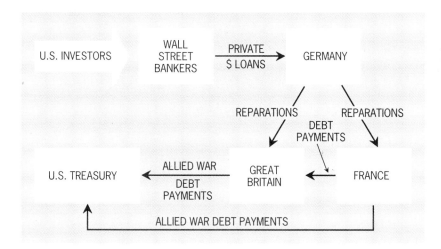

Aspects of the Financial Merry-Go-Round, 1921–1933 *Great Britain, with a debt of over $4 billion to the U.S. Treasury, had a huge stake in proposals for inter-Allied debt cancellation, but France's stake was even larger. Less prosperous than Britain in the 1920s, and more battered by the war, which had been fought on its soil, France owed nearly $3.5 billion to the United States and additional billions to Britain.*

flowing well of American credit. When that well dried up after the great crash in 1929, the tangled jungle of international finance quickly turned into a desert.

The United States never did get its money, but it harvested a bumper crop of ill will. Throughout Europe Uncle Sam was caricatured as Uncle Shylock, greedily whetting his knife for the last pound of Allied flesh. The bad taste left in American mouths by the whole sorry episode contributed powerfully to the storm-cellar neutrality legislation passed by Congress in the 1930s.

The Triumph of Herbert Hoover in 1928

Poker-faced Calvin Coolidge, the tight-lipped "Sphinx of the Potomac," bowed out of the 1928 presidential race when he announced, "I do not choose to run." His logical successor was super-Secretary (of Commerce) Herbert Hoover. He was nominated on a platform that clucked contentedly over both prosperity and prohibition.

Still-squabbling Democrats nominated Alfred E. Smith, the wisecracking, glad-handing governor of New York. "Al (cohol)" Smith was soaking wet on prohibition, abrasively urban, and Roman Catholic in an overwhelmingly Protestant—and unfortunately prejudiced—land. Many dry, rural, and Fundamentalist Democrats gagged on his candidacy, and they saddled Smith with a dry running mate and a dry platform.

Radio figured prominently in this campaign for the first time, and it helped Hoover more than Smith. The New Yorker had more personal sparkle, but he could not project it through the radio. Iowa-born Hoover, with his double-breasted dignity, came out of the microphone better than he went in.

Chubby-faced, ruddy-complexioned Herbert Hoover, with his painfully high starched collar, was a living example of the American success story, and an intriguing mixture of two centuries. As a poor orphan boy who had worked his way through Stanford University, he had absorbed the nineteenth-century copybook maxims of industry, thrift, and self-reliance. As a fabulously successful mining engineer and businessman, he had honed to a high degree the efficiency doctrines of the progressive era.

A small-town boy from Iowa and Oregon, he had traveled and worked abroad extensively. His experiences there had further strengthened his faith in American individualism, free enterprise, and small government.

As befitted America's newly mechanized civilization, Hoover was the ideal businessperson's candidate. A self-made millionaire, he recoiled from anything suggesting socialism, paternalism, or "planned economy." Yet as secretary of commerce, he had exhibited some progressive instincts. He endorsed labor unions and supported federal regulation of the new radio industry. He even flirted for a time with the idea of government-owned radio, similar to the British Broadcasting Corporation (BBC).

Despite the best efforts of Hoover and Smith, below-the-belt tactics were employed by their lower-level campaigners. Religious bigotry raised its hideous head over Smith's Catholicism. A whispering campaign claimed that "A vote for Al Smith is a vote for the Pope" and that the White House, under Smith, would become a branch of the Vatican.

Hoover triumphed in a landslide. He bagged 21,391,993 popular votes to 15,016,169 for his embittered opponent, while rolling up an electoral count of 444 to 87. A huge Republican majority was returned to the House of Representatives. Tens of thousands of dry southern Democrats—"Hoovercrats"—rebelled against Al Smith. Hoover carried all the Border States and five states of the former Confederacy, the first Republican candidate to disrupt the solid South.

President Hoover's First Moves

Prosperity in the late 1920s smiled broadly as the Hoover years began. Soaring stocks on the bull market continued to defy the laws of financial gravity. But two immense groups of citizens were not getting their share of the riches flowing from the national cornucopia: the unorganized wage earners and especially the disorganized farmers.

Hoover's administration, in line with its philosophy of promoting self-help, responded to the outcry of the farmers with the Agricultural Marketing Act. Passed by Congress in June 1929, it was designed to help the farmers help themselves, largely through producers' cooperatives. A Federal Farm Board also lent half a billion dollars to farm organizations seeking to buy, sell, and store agricultural surpluses.

Farmers also clutched at the tariff as a possible straw to keep their heads above the water of financial ruin. But the Hawley-Smoot Tariff of 1930, which started out as a modest measure to assist farmers, acquired more than a thousand amendments and turned into the highest protective tariff in the nation's peacetime history. The average duty was raised from 38.5 percent to nearly 60 percent. To angered foreigners, the Hawley-Smoot Tariff seemed like a declaration of economic warfare. It widened the yawning trade gaps and plunged both America and other nations deeper into the terrible depression that had already begun. It forced the United States further into the bog of economic isolationism, thus playing directly into the demagogic hands of Adolf Hitler.

The Great Crash Ends the Golden Twenties

When Herbert Hoover confidently took the presidential oath on March 4, 1929, America's productive colossus—stimulated by the automobile, radio, movie, and other new industries—was roaring along at a dizzy speed that suggested a permanent plateau of prosperity. Prices on the stock exchange continued to spiral upward and create a fool's paradise of paper profits. A few prophets of disaster sounded warnings, but they were drowned out by the mad chatter of the ticker-tape machine.

A catastrophic crash came on "Black Tuesday," October 29, 1929, when 16,410,030 shares of stock were sold in a save-who-may scramble. Wall Street became a wailing wall as gloom and doom replaced boom. Losses, even in blue-chip securities, were unbelievable. By the end of 1929—two months after the initial crash—stockholders had lost $40 billion in paper values, or more than the total cost of World War I to the United States.

The stock-market collapse heralded a business depression, at home and abroad, that was the most prolonged and withering in American or world experience. No other industrialized nation suffered so severe a setback. By the end of 1930, more than 4 million workers in the United States were jobless; two years later the figure had about tripled. Hungry and despairing workers pounded pavements in search of nonexistent jobs ("We're firing, not hiring"). When employees were not discharged, wages and salaries were often slashed.

The misery and gloom were incalculable, as forests of dead factory chimneys stood stark against the sky. Over five thousand banks collapsed in the

The Great Crash of 1929 *The stock-market collapse caused fear to run like wildfire through the financial world. These anxious depositors lined up outside a New York bank, clamoring to withdraw their deposits before the bank failed. Such "runs" on banks actually sped the downward economic spiral.*

Index of Common Stock Prices
(1926 = 100)

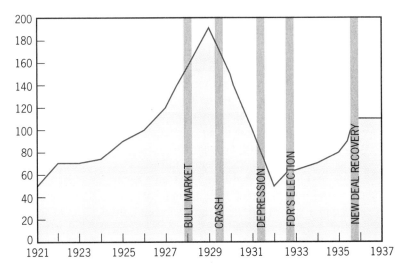

first three years of the depression, carrying down with them the life savings of tens of thousands of ordinary citizens. Countless thousands of honest, hardworking people lost their homes and farms to the forecloser's hammer. Bread lines formed, soup kitchens dispensed food, and apple sellers stood shivering on street corners trying to peddle their wares for five cents. Families felt the stress, as jobless fathers nursed their guilt and shame at not being able to provide for their households. Breadless breadwinners often blamed themselves for their plight, despite abundant evidence that the economic system, not individual initiative, had broken down. Mothers meanwhile nursed fewer babies as hard times reached even into the nation's bedrooms, precipitating a decade-long dearth of births. As cash registers gathered cobwebs, the song "My God, How the Money Rolls In" gave way to "Brother, Can You Spare a Dime?"

Hooked on the Horn of Plenty

What caused the Great Depression? One basic explanation was overproduction by both farm and factory. Ironically, the depression of the 1930s was one of abundance, not want. It was the "great glut" or the "plague of plenty."

The nation's ability to produce goods had clearly outrun its capacity to consume or pay for them. Too much money was going into the hands of a few wealthy people, who in turn invested it in factories and other agencies of production. Not enough was going into salaries and wages, where revitalizing purchasing power could be more quickly felt.

This already bleak picture was further darkened by economic anemia abroad. Britain and the European continent had never fully recovered from the upheaval of World War I. A drying up of international trade, moreover, had been hastened by the short-sighted Hawley-Smoot Tariff of 1930.

By 1930 the depression had become a national calamity. Through no fault of their own, a host of industrious citizens had lost everything. The insidious effect of all this dazed despair on the spirit was incalculable and long lasting. Hitherto the people had grappled with storms, trees, stones, and other physical obstacles. But the depression was a baffling wraith they could not grasp. Panhandlers begged for food or "charity soup." In extreme cases "ragged individualists" slept under "Hoover blankets" (old newspapers), fought over the contents of garbage cans, or cooked their findings in old oil drums in tin-and-paper shantytowns cynically named "Hoovervilles." The very foundations of America's social structure trembled.

Rugged Times for Rugged Individualists

Hoover's exalted reputation as a wonder worker and efficiency engineer crashed about as dismally as the stock market. The perplexed president was impaled on the horns of a cruel dilemma. As a deservedly famed humanitarian, he was profoundly distressed by the widespread misery about him. Yet as a "rugged individualist," deeply rooted in an earlier era of free enterprise, he shrank from the heresy of government handouts. Convinced that industry, thrift, and self-reliance were the virtues that had made America great, he feared that a government doling out doles would weaken, or perhaps destroy, the national fiber.

The president at last worked out a compromise between the old hands-off philosophy and the "soul-destroying" direct dole then being used in Britain. He would assist the hard-pressed railroads, banks, and rural credit corporations, in the hope that if financial health were restored at the top of the economic pyramid, unemployment would be relieved at the bottom on a trickle-down basis.

Early in 1932 Congress, responding to Hoover's belated appeal, established the Reconstruction Finance Corporation (RFC). With an initial working capital of half a billion dollars, this agency became a government lending bank. It was designed to provide indirect relief by assisting insurance companies, banks, agricultural organizations, railroads, and even hard-pressed state and local governments. But to preserve individualism and character, there would be no loans to individuals from this "billion-dollar soup kitchen."

"Pump-priming" loans by the RFC were no doubt of widespread benefit, though the organization was established many months too late for maximum

Home Relief Station, by Louis Ribak, 1935–1936   *Destitute and despairing, millions of hard-working Americans like these had to endure the degradation and humiliation of going on relief as the pall of depression descended over the land.*

usefulness. Projects that it supported were largely self-liquidating, and the government as a banker actually profited to the tune of many millions of dollars. Giant corporations so obviously benefited from this assistance that the RFC was dubbed—rather unfairly—"the millionaires' dole."

Hoover's administration also provided some indirect benefits for labor. After stormy debate, Congress passed the Norris–La Guardia Anti-Injunction Act in 1932, and Hoover signed it. The measure outlawed "yellow dog" (antiunion) contracts and forbade the federal courts to issue injunctions to restrain strikes, boycotts, and peaceful picketing.

The truth is that Herbert Hoover, despite criticism of his "heartlessness," did inaugurate a significant new policy. In previous panics the masses had been forced to "sweat it out." Slow though Hoover was to abandon this nineteenth-century bias, by the end of his term he had traveled a long way toward government assistance for needy citizens—a road that Franklin Roosevelt would travel much farther.

Routing the Bonus Army in Washington

Many veterans of World War I were numbered among the hard-hit victims of the depression. They began to agitate for the premature payment of the deferred "adjusted compensation" (see p. 484) voted by Congress in 1924 and payable in 1945. Thousands of impoverished veterans, both of war and of unemployment, prepared to move on Washington, there to demand of Congress the immediate payment of their *entire* bonus. The "Bonus Expeditionary Force," which mustered about twenty thousand men, converged on the capital in the summer of 1932. These supplicants promptly set up unsanitary public camps on vacant lots—a gigantic "Hooverville."

Following riots that cost two lives, Hoover ordered the army to evacuate the unwanted guests. The eviction was carried out by General Douglas MacArthur with bayonets and tear gas and with far more severity than Hoover had planned. A few of the former soldiers were injured as the torch was put to their pathetic shanties in the inglorious "Battle of Anacostia Flats." An eleven-month-old "bonus baby" allegedly died from exposure to tear gas.

This brutal episode brought down additional abuse on the once-popular Hoover, who by now was the most loudly booed man in the country. Cynics sneered that the "Great Engineer" had in a few months "ditched, drained, and damned the country." The existing panic was unfairly branded "the Hoover depression." In truth, Hoover had been oversold as a superman—and the public grumbled when his magician's wand failed to produce rabbits. The time was ripening for the Democratic party—and Franklin D. Roosevelt—to cash in on Hoover's calamities.

Japanese Aggressors and Latin American Good Neighbors

The Great Depression, which brewed enough distress at home, added immensely to difficulties abroad. Militaristic Japan stole the East Asian spotlight. In September 1931, the Japanese imperialists, noting that the Western world was badly mired down in depression, lunged into Manchuria. Alleging provocation, they rapidly overran the coveted Chinese province and proceeded to bolt shut the Open Door in the conquered area.

Peaceful peoples were stunned by this act of naked aggression. Numerous indignant Americans, though by no means a majority, urged strong measures, ranging from boycotts to blockades. Possibly a tight blockade by the League of Nations, backed by the United States, would have brought Japan sharply to book. But the League was handicapped in taking two-fisted action by the nonmembership of the United States. Washington flatly rebuffed initial attempts in 1931 to secure American cooperation in applying economic pressures.

Hoover and Secretary of State Henry L. Stimson decided in the end to fire only paper bullets at the Japanese aggressors. The so-called Stimson Doctrine, proclaimed in 1932, declared that the United States would not recognize any territorial acquisitions achieved by force. Righteous indignation would substitute for vigorous initiatives. But there was no real sentiment for stronger measures among a depression-ridden people who remained strongly isolationist during the 1930s.

Chronology

SUGGESTED READINGS

Primary Source Documents

Herbert Hoover, *American Individualism* (1922), contains the philosophy of the man and his times. See also Hoover's "Rugged Individualism" speech (1928), in Richard Hofstadter, *Great Issues in American History* (1958). As the Great Depression descended, Hoover fought to maintain his principles in a noteworthy speech at New York's Madison Square Garden.* (*New York Times,* November 1, 1932.) On foreign affairs see the "Stimson Doctrine" (1931), in Henry Steele Commager, ed., *Documents of American History* (1988).

Secondary Sources

A lively introduction to the postwar decade is Burl Noggle, *Into the Twenties: The United States from Armistice to Normalcy* (1974). On Harding see Robert K. Murray's balanced *The Harding Era* (1969) and his *Politics of Normalcy: Government Theory and Practice in the Harding-Coolidge Era* (1973). John D. Hicks presents the standard liberal interpretation of the decade in *Republican Ascendancy* (1960). Burl Noggle looks at the chief scandal of the period in *Teapot Dome* (1962). David M. Kennedy, *Over Here: The First World War and American Society* (1980), discusses postwar race relations and demobilization as well as the international economic aftermath of the war, a subject treated at greater length in Joan Hoff Wilson, *American Business and Foreign Policy, 1920–1933* (1971). Robert Cohen explores *When the Old Left Was Young: Student Radicals and America's First Mass Student Movement, 1929–1941* (1993). The complicated international financial tangle of the 1920s is deftly discussed in Herbert Feis, *The Diplomacy of the Dollar* (1950), and in the early chapters of Charles Kindleberger, *The World in Depression* (1973). The drama of the 1928 election is captured in Allan J. Lichtman, *Prejudice and the Old Politics: The Presidential Election of 1928* (1979), and in Oscar Handlin, *Al Smith and His America* (1958). The election is placed in a larger context in Samuel Lubell's classic *The Future of American Politics* (1952) and in Paul Kleppner's *Who Voted? The Dynamics of Electoral Turnout, 1870–1980* (1982). George H. Nash's multivolume biography, *The Life of Herbert Hoover* (1988), is detailed, while the best brief biography of Hoover is Joan Hoff Wilson, *Herbert Hoover, Forgotten Progressive* (1975). Brilliantly unsympathetic toward Hoover is Arthur M. Schlesinger, Jr., *The Crisis of the Old Order, 1919–1933* (1957). On the depression itself, consult John K. Galbraith's breezy *The Great Crash, 1929* (1955); Peter Temin's trenchant *Did Monetary Factors Cause the Great Depression?* (1976); Robert McElvaine, *The Great Depression* (1984); and Lester V. Chandler's comprehensive *America's Greatest Depression* (1970).

---

* An asterisk indicates that the document, or an excerpt from it, can be found in Thomas A. Bailey and David M. Kennedy, eds., *The American Spirit: United States History as Seen by Contemporaries,* 9th ed. (Boston: Houghton Mifflin, 1998).

34

****

The Great Depression and the New Deal,

1933–1938

******

The country needs and . . . demands bold, persistent experimentation. It is common sense to take a method and try it. If it fails, admit it frankly and try another. But above all, try something.

******

FRANKLIN D. ROOSEVELT, CAMPAIGN SPEECH, 1932

FDR: Politician in a Wheelchair

Voters were in an ugly mood as the presidential campaign of 1932 neared. Countless factory chimneys remained ominously cold, while more than 11 million unemployed workers and their families sank ever deeper into the pit of poverty.

Hoover, sick at heart, was renominated by the Republican convention in Chicago without great enthusiasm. The rising star in the Democratic firmament was Governor Franklin Delano Roosevelt of New York, a fifth cousin of Theodore Roosevelt. Like the Rough Rider, he was born to a wealthy New York

family, graduated from Harvard, was elected as a kid-gloved politician to the New York legislature, served as governor of the Empire State, was nominated for the vice presidency (though not elected), and served capably as assistant secretary of the navy.

Infantile paralysis, while putting steel braces on Franklin Roosevelt's legs, put additional steel into his soul. Until 1921, when the dread disease struck, young Roosevelt—tall (6 feet, 2 inches), athletic, classic featured, and handsome—impressed observers as charming and witty yet at times a superficial and arrogant "lightweight." But suffering humbled him; courageously fighting his way back from complete helplessness to a hobbling mobility, he schooled himself in patience, tolerance, compassion, and strength of will. He once remarked that after trying for two years to wiggle one big toe, all else seemed easy.

Another of Roosevelt's great personal and political assets was his wife, Eleanor. The niece of Theodore Roosevelt, she was Franklin Roosevelt's distant cousin as well as his spouse. Tall, ungainly, and toothy, she overcame the misery of an unhappy childhood and emerged as a champion of the dispossessed—and ultimately as the "conscience of the New Deal." She was to become the most active First Lady in history. Through her lobbying of her husband, her speeches, and her syndicated newspaper column, she powerfully influenced the policies of the national government. Always,

Eleanor Roosevelt (1884–1962) *America's most active First Lady, she commanded enormous popularity and influence during FDR's presidency. Here she emerges, miner's cap in hand, from an Ohio coal mine.*

she battled for the impoverished and the oppressed. At one meeting in Birmingham, Alabama, she confounded local authorities and flouted the segregation statutes by deliberately straddling the aisle separating the black and white seating sections. Sadly, her personal relationship with her husband was often rocky due to his occasional infidelity. Condemned by conservatives and loved by liberals, she was one of the most controversial—and consequential—public figures of the twentieth century.

Roosevelt's political appeal was amazing. His commanding presence and his golden speaking voice, despite a sophisticated accent, combined to make him the premier American orator of his generation. He could turn on charm in private conversations as one would turn on a faucet. As a popular depression governor of New York, he had sponsored heavy state spending to relieve human suffering. Though favoring frugality, he believed that money, rather than humanity, was expendable. He revealed a deep concern for the plight of the "forgotten man"—a phrase he used in a 1932 speech—although he was assailed by the rich as a "traitor to his class."

Exuberant Democrats met in Chicago in June 1932 and speedily nominated Roosevelt, who flew daringly through stormy weather to Chicago to accept the nomination in person. He electrified the delegates and the public with these words: "I pledge you, I pledge myself to a new deal for the American people."

Roosevelt Routs Hoover in 1932

In the campaign that followed, Roosevelt consistently preached a New Deal for the "forgotten man," but he was annoyingly vague and somewhat contradictory. Many of his speeches were ghost-written by the "Brains Trust" (popularly the "Brain Trust"), a small group of reform-minded intellectuals. They were predominantly youngish college professors who, as a kind of Andrew Jackson–style "Kitchen Cabinet," later authored much of the New Deal legislation. Roosevelt rashly promised a balanced budget and berated heavy Hooverian deficits. All this was to make ironic reading in later months.

Hoover had been swept into office on the rising tide of prosperity; he was swept out by the receding tide of depression. The flood of votes totaled

22,809,638 for Roosevelt and 15,758,901 for Hoover; the electoral count stood at 472 to 59. In all, the loser carried only six rock-ribbed Republican states.

One striking feature of the election was a distinct shift of blacks from the Republican party of Lincoln to the Roosevelt camp. Beginning with the election of 1932, they became, notably in the great urban centers of the North, a vital element in the Democratic party.

Defeated and repudiated, Hoover remained president during four long months, until March 4, 1933. But he was helpless to embark on any long-term policies without Roosevelt's cooperation. In two meetings with Roosevelt on the war-debt issue, Hoover tried to bind his successor to an anti-inflationary policy that would have made impossible many of the later New Deal experiments. But Roosevelt refused to assume responsibility without authority and airily remarked to the press, "It's not my baby."

With Washington deadlocked, the vast and vaunted American economic machine clanked to a virtual halt. One worker in four tramped the streets, feet weary and hands idle. Banks were locking their doors all over the nation as people nervously stuffed paper money under their mattresses.

FDR and the Three Rs: Relief, Recovery, and Reform

Great crises often call forth gifted leaders, and the hand of destiny tapped Roosevelt on the shoulder. On a dreary inauguration day, March 4, 1933, his vibrant voice provided the American people with inspirational new hope. He denounced the "money changers" who had brought on the calamity, and he declared that the government must wage war on the Great Depression as it would wage war on an armed foe. His clarion note was: "Let me assert my firm belief that the only thing we have to fear is fear itself."

Roosevelt moved decisively. Now that he had full responsibility, he boldly declared a nationwide bank holiday, March 6–10, as a prelude to opening the banks on a sounder basis. He then summoned the overwhelmingly Democratic Congress into special session to cope with the national emergency. For the so-called Hundred Days (March 9–June 16, 1933), members hastily ground out an unprecedented basketful of remedial legislation.

Roosevelt Speaks on Radio, 1932 *FDR's smooth, confident radio voice made him seem like an intimate friend to millions of distressed Americans during the Great Depression, especially when he delivered his "fireside chats."*

Roosevelt's New Deal program aimed at three Rs—relief, recovery, and reform. Short-range goals were relief and immediate recovery, especially in the first two years. Long-range goals were permanent recovery and reform of current abuses, particularly those that had produced the boom-and-bust catastrophe. The three-R objectives often overlapped and got in one another's way. But amid all the topsy-turvy haste, the gigantic New Deal program lurched forward.

Firmly ensconced in the driver's seat, President Roosevelt cracked the whip. A green Congress so fully shared the panicky feeling of the country that it was ready to rubber-stamp bills drafted by White House advisers. More than that, Congress gave the president extraordinary blank-check powers: some laws expressly delegated legislative authority to the chief executive.

Roosevelt was delighted to exert executive leadership. He was inclined to do things by intuition—off the cuff. He was like the quarterback, as he put it, whose next play depends on the outcome of the previous play. So desperate was the mood of an action-starved public that *any* movement, even in the wrong direction, seemed better than no movement at all.

The frantic Hundred Days Congress passed many essentials of the New Deal's three *R*s, though important long-range measures were added in later

Principal New Deal Acts During Hundred Days Congress, 1933
(Items in parentheses indicate secondary purposes.)

Recovery	*Relief*	*Reform*
FDR closes banks, March 6, 1933		
⚹ Emergency Banking Relief Act, March 9, 1933		
(Beer Act)	(Beer Act)	Beer and Wine Revenue Act, March 22, 1933
(CCC)	Unemployment Relief Act, March 13, 1933, creates Civilian Conservation Corps (CCC)	
FDR orders gold surrender, April 5, 1933		
FDR abandons gold standard, April 19, 1933		
(FERA)	Federal Emergency Relief Act, May 12, 1933, creates Federal Emergency Relief Administration (FERA)	
(AAA)	Agricultural Adjustment Act (AAA), May 12, 1933	
(TVA)	(TVA)	⚹ Tennessee Valley Authority Act (TVA), May 18, 1933
		Federal Securities Act, May 27, 1933
Gold-payment clause repealed, June 5, 1933		
(HOLC)	Home Owners' Refinancing Act, June 13, 1933, creates Home Owners' Loan Corporation (HOLC)	
National Industrial Recovery Act, June 16, 1933, creates National Recovery Administration (NRA), Public Works Administration (PWA)	(NRA; PWA)	(NRA)
⚹ (Glass-Steagall Act)	(Glass-Steagall Act)	⚹ Glass-Steagall Banking Reform Act, June 16, 1933, creates Federal Deposit Insurance Corporation

For later New Deal measures, see p. 507.

sessions. These reforms owed much to the legacy of the pre–World War I progressive movement. Many of them were long overdue, sidetracked by World War I and the Old Guard reaction of the 1920s. The New Dealers, sooner or later, embraced such progressive ideas as unemployment insurance, old-age insurance, minimum-wage regulations, conservation and development of natural resources, and restrictions on child labor. Many of these forward-looking measures had been adopted a generation or so earlier by the more advanced countries of western Europe. In the area of social welfare, the United States, in the eyes of many Europeans, remained a backward nation.

Roosevelt Tackles Money and Banking

Banking chaos cried aloud for immediate action. Congress pulled itself together and in an incredible eight hours had the Emergency Banking Relief Act of 1933 ready for Roosevelt's busy pen. The new law invested the president with power to regulate banking transactions and foreign exchange and to reopen solvent banks.

Roosevelt, the master showman, next turned to the radio to deliver the first of thirty "fireside chats." As some 35 million people hung on his soothing words, he gave assurances that it was now safer to keep money in a reopened bank than "under the mattress." Confidence returned with a gush, and the banks unlocked their doors.

The Hundred Days Congress also buttressed public reliance on the banking system by enacting the memorable Glass-Steagall Banking Reform Act. This measure provided for the Federal Deposit Insurance Corporation, which insured individual deposits up to $5,000 (later raised).

Roosevelt moved swiftly elsewhere on the financial front, seeking to protect the melting gold reserve and to prevent panicky hoarding. He ordered all private holdings of gold to be surrendered to the Treasury in exchange for paper currency and then took the nation off the gold standard.

The goal of Roosevelt's "managed currency" was inflation, which he believed would relieve debtors' burdens and stimulate new production. Roosevelt's principal instrument for achieving inflation was gold buying. He instructed the Treasury Department to purchase gold, ratcheting the dollar price of gold up from $21 an ounce in 1933 to $35 an ounce in 1934, a price that held for nearly four decades. This policy did increase the amount of dollars in circulation, as holders of gold cashed it in at the newly elevated prices, although "sound-money" critics gagged on the "baloney dollar." The gold-buying scheme came to an end in February 1934, when FDR returned the nation to a limited gold standard for the purposes of international trade only. Thereafter (until 1971), the United States pledged

itself to pay foreign bills, if requested, in gold at the rate of one ounce of gold for every $35 due.

Creating Jobs for the Jobless

Overwhelming unemployment clamored for prompt remedial action. One of every four workers was jobless when FDR took his inaugural oath—the highest level of unemployment in the nation's history. Roosevelt had no hesitancy about using federal money to assist the unemployed and at the same time to "prime the pump" of industrial recovery. (A farmer has to pour a little water into a dry pump to start the flow.)

The Hundred Days Congress responded to Roosevelt's spurs when it created the Civilian Conservation Corps (CCC). This agency provided employment in fresh-air government camps for about 3 million uniformed young men. Their useful work included reforestation, firefighting, flood control, and swamp drainage. The recruits were required to help their parents by sending home most of their pay. Both human resources and natural resources were thus conserved.

The first major effort of the new Congress to grapple with the millions of adult unemployed was the Federal Emergency Relief Act. Its chief aim was immediate relief rather than long-range recovery. The resulting Federal Emergency Relief Administration (FERA) was handed over to zealous Harry L. Hopkins, a painfully thin, shabbily dressed, chain-smoking New York social worker who had earlier won Roosevelt's friendship and who became one of his most influential advisers. Hopkins's agency finally granted about $3 billion to the states for direct dole payments or preferably for wages on work projects.

Immediate relief was also given to two large and hard-pressed special groups by the Hundred Days Congress. One section of the Agricultural Adjustment Act (AAA) made available many millions of dollars to help farmers meet their mortgages. Another law created the Home Owners' Loan Corporation (HOLC). Designed to refinance mortgages on nonfarm homes, it ultimately assisted about a million badly pinched households while simultaneously bailing out mortgage-holding banks.

Harassed by the continuing plague of unemployment, FDR himself established the Civil Works Administration (CWA) under Hopkins's direction late in 1933. Designed to provide temporary jobs during the cruel winter emergency, it employed tens of thousands of jobless people in leaf raking and other make-work tasks. The CWA served a useful purpose, although it was heavily criticized as "boondoggling."

Direct relief from Washington to needy families helped pull the nation through the ghastly winter of 1933–1934. But the disheartening persistence of unemployment and suffering demonstrated that emergency relief measures must be not only continued but supplemented. One danger signal was the appearance of various demagogues, notably a magnetic "microphone messiah," Father Charles Coughlin, a Catholic priest in Michigan who began broadcasting in 1930 with the slogan "Social Justice." His anti–New Deal harangues to some 40 million radio fans finally became so anti-Semitic, fascistic, and demagogic that he was silenced in 1942 by his ecclesiastical superiors.

Also notorious among the new brood of agitators were those who capitalized on popular discontent to make pie-in-the-sky promises. Most conspicuous of these individuals was Senator Huey P. ("Kingfish") Long of Louisiana, who used his abundant rabble-rousing talents to publicize his "Share Our Wealth" program, which promised to make "Every Man a King." Every family was to receive $5,000, supposedly at the expense of the prosperous. Fear of Long's becoming a fascist dictator ended when he was shot by an assassin in the Louisiana state capitol in 1935.

Another Pied Piper was gaunt Dr. Francis E. Townsend of California, a retired physician whose savings had recently been wiped out. He attracted the trusting support of perhaps 5 million "senior citizens" with his fantastic plan, which nonetheless spoke to earthly need. Each oldster sixty years of age or over was to receive $200 a month, provided that the money was spent within the month. One estimate had the scheme costing one-half of the national income.

Partly to quiet the groundswell of unrest produced by such crackbrained proposals, Congress authorized the Works Progress Administration (WPA) in 1935. The objective was employment on useful projects. Launched under the supervision of the ailing but energetic Hopkins, this remarkable agency ultimately spent about $11 billion on thousands of public buildings, bridges, and hard-surfaced roads. It also controlled crickets in Wyoming and built a monkey pen in Oklahoma City. Critics sneered that WPA meant "We Provide Alms." But the fact is that over a period of eight years nearly 9 million persons were given jobs, not handouts.

Agencies of the WPA also found part-time occupations for needy high school and college students and for such unemployed white-collar workers as actors, musicians, and writers. John Steinbeck, future Nobel Prize novelist, counted dogs in his California county. Cynical taxpayers condemned lessons in tap dancing, as well as the painting of scenes on post office walls. But much precious talent was nourished, self-respect was preserved, and more than a million pieces of art were created, many of them publicly displayed.

A Helping Hand for Industry and Labor

A daring attempt to stimulate a nationwide comeback was initiated when the Hundred Days Congress authorized the National Recovery Administration (NRA). This ingenious scheme was by far the most complex and far-reaching effort by the New Dealers to combine immediate relief with long-range recovery and reform. Triple-barreled, it was designed to assist industry, labor, and the unemployed.

Individual industries—over two hundred in all—were to work out codes of "fair competition," under which hours of labor would be reduced so that employment could be spread over more people. A ceiling was placed on the maximum hours of labor; a floor was placed under wages to establish minimum levels.

Labor, under the NRA, was granted additional benefits. Workers were formally guaranteed the right to organize and bargain collectively through representatives *of their own choosing*—not through hand-picked agents of the company's choosing. The hated "yellow dog," or antiunion, contract was expressly forbidden, and certain safeguarding restrictions were placed on the use of child labor.

Industrial recovery through the NRA fair competition codes would be at best painful, for these called for self-denial by both management and labor. Patriotism was aroused by mass meetings and huge parades, which included 200,000 marchers on New York City's Fifth Avenue. A handsome blue eagle was designed as the symbol of the NRA, and merchants subscribing to a code displayed it in their windows with the slogan "We Do Our Part." Such was the enthusiasm for the NRA that for a brief period there was a marked upswing of business activity.

But the high-flying eagle gradually fluttered to earth. Too much self-sacrifice was expected of labor, industry, and the public for such a scheme to work. Critics began to brand the NRA "Nuts Running America," symbolized by what Henry Ford called "that damn Roosevelt buzzard."

Complete collapse was imminent when, in 1935, the Supreme Court shot down the dying eagle in the *Schechter* "sick chicken" decision. The learned justices unanimously held that Congress could not "delegate legislative powers" to the executive. They further declared that congressional control of interstate commerce could not properly apply to a local fowl business, like that of the Schechter brothers in Brooklyn. Roosevelt was incensed by this "horse and buggy" interpretation of the Constitution, but actually the Court helped him out of a bad jam.

The same act of Congress that hatched the NRA eagle also authorized the Public Works Administration (PWA), likewise intended both for industrial recovery and for unemployment relief. The agency was headed by acid-tongued Harold L. Ickes, a former bull mooser. Long-range recovery was the primary purpose of the new agency, and in time over $4 billion was spent on some thirty-four thousand projects, which included public buildings, highways, and parkways. One spectacular achievement was the Grand Coulee Dam on the Columbia River—the largest structure erected by humans since the Great Wall of China.

Special stimulants aided the recovery of one segment of business—the liquor industry. The Hundred Days Congress legalized and taxed "light" wine and beer (3.2% alcohol), providing new employment and federal revenue. Prohibition was officially repealed by the Twenty-first Amendment late in 1933 (see the Appendix)—and the saloon doors swung open.

Paying Farmers Not to Farm

Ever since the war-boom days of 1918, farmers had suffered from low prices and overproduction, espe-

cially in grain. During the depression conditions became desperate as innumerable mortgages were foreclosed, as corn was burned for fuel, and as embattled farmers tried to prevent shipment of crops to glutted markets. In Iowa several volatile counties were placed under martial law.

A radical new approach to farm recovery was embraced when the Hundred Days Congress established the Agricultural Adjustment Administration (AAA). Through "artificial scarcity" this agency was to establish "parity prices" for basic commodities. "Parity" was the price set for a product that gave it the same real value, in purchasing power, that it had enjoyed during the period from 1909 to 1914. The AAA would eliminate price-depressing surpluses by paying growers to reduce their crop acreage.

Unhappily, the AAA got off to a wobbly start. It was begun after much of the cotton crop for 1933 had been planted, and balky mules, trained otherwise, were forced to plow under countless young plants. Several million squealing pigs were purchased and slaughtered. Much of their meat was distributed to persons on relief, but some of it was used for fertilizer. This "sinful" destruction of food, at a time when thousands of citizens were hungry, increased condemnation of the American economic system by many left-leaning voices. The much-criticized AAA was itself plowed under in 1936 by the Supreme Court, which declared its regulatory taxation provisions unconstitutional.

The New Deal recovered from this blow by passing the Soil Conservation and Domestic Allotment Act (1936), which paid subsidies to farmers if they planted soil-conserving crops, like soybeans, or let their land lie fallow. The Second Agricultural Adjustment Act (1938) permitted parity payments if farmers observed acreage restrictions on commodities such as cotton and wheat. Other provisions of the new AAA were designed to give farmers not only a fairer price but a more substantial share of the national income. Both goals were partially achieved.

Dust Bowls and Black Blizzards

Nature meanwhile had been providing some unplanned scarcity. Late in 1933 a prolonged drought struck the states of the trans-Mississippi Great Plains.

Rainless weeks were followed by furious, whining winds, while the sun was darkened by millions of tons of powdery topsoil torn from homesteads in Texas, Kansas, Colorado, Arkansas, and Oklahoma—an area soon dubbed the "Dust Bowl." Despondent citizens sat on front porches with protective masks on their faces, watching the farms swirl by. Some victims of the Dust Bowl disaster predicted the end of the world or the second coming of Christ.

Burned and blown out of the Dust Bowl, tens of thousands of refugees fled their ruined acres (see "Makers of America: The Dust Bowl Migrants," pp. 504–505). In five years about 350,000 Oklahomans and Arkansans—"Okies" and "Arkies"—trekked to southern California in "junkyards on wheels." The dismal story of these human tumbleweeds was realistically portrayed in John Steinbeck's best-selling novel *The Grapes of Wrath* (1939), which proved to be the *Uncle Tom's Cabin* of the Dust Bowl.

Zealous New Dealers, sympathetic toward these desperate soil-tillers, made various efforts to relieve their burdens. The Frazier-Lemke Farm Bankruptcy Act, passed in 1934, made possible a suspension of mortgage foreclosures for five years; a revised version was upheld by the Supreme Court. In 1935 the president set up the Resettlement Administration to help farmers move to better land. And more than 200 million young trees were successfully planted on the bare prairies as windbreaks by the young men of the Civilian Conservation Corps.

Native Americans also felt the far-reaching hand of New Deal reform. Commissioner of Indian Affairs John Collier ardently sought to reverse the forced-assimilation policies in place since the Dawes Act of 1887 (see p. 387). The Indian Reorganization Act of 1934 (the "Indian New Deal") encouraged tribes to establish local self-government, helped stop the loss of Indian lands, and revived tribes' interest in their identity and culture. Seventy-seven tribes refused to organize under its provisions, though nearly two hundred did establish tribal governments.

Battling Bankers and Big Business

Reformist New Dealers were determined from the outset to curb the "money changers" who had played fast and loose with gullible investors before the Wall Street crash of 1929. The Hundred Days Congress passed the "Truth in Securities Act" (Federal Securities Act), which required promoters to transmit to the investor sworn information regarding the soundness of their stocks and bonds. In 1934 Congress took further steps to protect the public against fraud, deception, and inside manipulation. It authorized the Securities and Exchange Commission (SEC), which was designed as a watchdog administrative agency. Stock markets henceforth were to operate more as trading marts and less as gambling casinos.

New Dealers likewise directed their fire at public utility holding companies, those super-corporations. When Chicagoan Samuel Insull's multibillion-dollar financial empire crashed in 1932, citizens rebelled against such pyramided layers of big business. The Public Utility Holding Company Act of 1935 delivered a "death sentence" to this type of bloated growth.

The TVA Harnesses the Tennessee River

Inevitably, the sprawling electric-power industry attracted the fire of New Deal reformers. Within a few decades it had risen from nothingness to a behemoth with an investment of $13 billion. As a public utility, it reached directly and regularly into the pocketbooks of millions of consumers for vitally needed services. Ardent New Dealers accused it of gouging the public with excessive rates, especially since it owed its success to having secured, often for a song, priceless water-power sites from the public domain.

The tempestuous Tennessee River provided New Dealers with a rare opportunity. With its tributaries, the river drained a badly eroded area about the size of England containing some 2.5 million of the most poverty-stricken people in America. The federal government already owned valuable properties at Muscle Shoals, where it had erected plants for needed nitrates in World War I. By developing the hydroelectric potential of the entire area, Washington could combine the immediate advantage of putting thousands of people to work with a long-term project for reforming the power monopoly.

An act creating the Tennessee Valley Authority (TVA) was passed in 1933 by the Hundred Days Congress. This far-ranging enterprise was largely a result of the steadfast vision and unflagging zeal of Senator

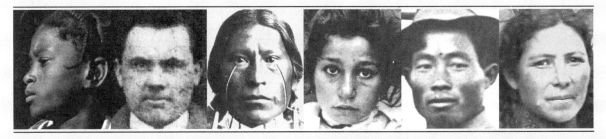

The Dust Bowl Migrants

Black dust clouds rolled across the southern Great Plains in the 1930s, darkening the skies above a landscape already desolated by the Great Depression. Its soil depleted by erosion, exhausted by overintensive farming, and parched by drought, the prairie of Oklahoma, Arkansas, and northern Texas became a dust bowl. The thirsty land offered up neither crops nor livelihood to the sturdy people whose forebears had staked out homesteads there. The desiccated earth exhaled only black dust and a dry wind that blew hundreds of thousands of people—the so-called Okies and Arkies—out of the Dust Bowl forever.

They headed mainly for California. Some piled aboard buses or hopped freight trains. But most journeyed in their own autos, cramming their meager possessions into old jalopies and sputtering down the highway. But unlike the aimless, isolated Joad family of John Steinbeck's classic novel *The Grapes of Wrath*, most Dust Bowl migrants knew where they were headed. Although many had lost everything in the depression, they had relatives or friends who had migrated to California before the crash and had sent back word about its abundant promise.

But when the Okies neared California, they were greeted with a billboard posted by the state of California proclaiming "NO JOBS in California . . . If YOU are looking for work—KEEP OUT." Still, they refused to believe that the depression could sully the Golden State's bright promise. Some went to California cities, but many of them favored the San Joaquin Valley, the southern part of central California's agricultural kingdom. The migrants chose it for its familiarity. The valley shared much in common with the southern plains—arid climate, cotton growing, newfound deposits of oil, and abundant land.

During the 1930s the San Joaquin Valley also proved all too familiar in its poverty. Food, shelter, and clothing were scarce; the winter months, without work and without heat, proved nearly unendurable for the migrants. John Steinbeck, writing in a San Francisco newspaper, exposed the tribulations of the Dust Bowl refugees: "First the gasoline gives out. And without gasoline a man cannot go to a job even if he

An Okie Family Hits the Road in the 1930s

could get one. Then the food goes. And then in the rains, with insufficient food, the children develop colds."

Eventually, the Farm Security Administration—a New Deal agency—set up camps to house the Okies. A fortunate few purchased land and erected makeshift homes, creating tiny "Okievilles" or "Little Oklahomas." Most Okies eventually escaped the uncertainty of seasonal farm labor, securing regular jobs in defense industries. But the "Okievilles" remained to form the bedrock of a still-thriving subculture in California—one that has brought the Dust Bowl's country and western music, pecan pie, and evangelical religion to the Far West.

George W. Norris of Nebraska, after whom one of the mighty dams was named. From the standpoint of "planned economy," the TVA was by far the most revolutionary of all New Deal schemes.

New Dealers pointed with pride at the amazing achievements of the TVA. The gigantic project brought to the area not only cheap power but full employment, low-cost housing, abundant cheap nitrates, restoration of eroded soil, reforestation, improved navigation, and flood control.

Exulting New Dealers agitated for parallel enterprises in the valleys of the Columbia, Colorado, and Missouri rivers. Hydroelectric power from federally built dams would drive the growth of the urban West, and the waters they diverted would nurture agriculture in the previously bone-dry western deserts. But conservative reaction against the "socialistic" New Deal confined the TVA's brand of federally guided resource management and comprehensive regional development to the Tennessee Valley.

Housing Reform and Social Security

The New Deal had meanwhile framed sturdy new policies for housing construction. To speed recovery and better homes, Roosevelt set up the Federal Housing Administration (FHA) as early as 1934. The building industry was to be stimulated by small loans to householders. So popular did the FHA prove to be that it was one of the few "alphabetical agencies" to outlast the age of Roosevelt.

Congress bolstered the program in 1937 by authorizing the United States Housing Authority (USHA)—an agency designed to lend money to states or communities for low-cost construction. Although units for about 650,000 low-income people were started, new building fell tragically short of needs. New Deal efforts to expand the project collided with brick-wall opposition from real estate promoters, builders, and landlords ("slumlords"), to say nothing of anti–New Dealers who attacked what they considered down-the-rathole spending. Nonetheless, for the first time in a century the slum areas in America ceased growing and even shrank.

Incomparably more important was the success of New Dealers in the field of unemployment insurance and old-age pensions. Their greatest victory was the Social Security Act of 1935—one of the most complicated and far-reaching laws ever to pass Congress. To cushion future depressions, the measure provided for federal-state unemployment insurance. To provide security for old age, specified categories of retired workers were to receive regular payments from Washington, ranging from $10 to $85 a month (later raised) and financed by a payroll tax on both employers and employees. Provision was also made for the blind, the physically handicapped, delinquent children, and other dependents.

Social Security was largely inspired by the example of some of the more highly industrialized nations of Europe. The United States government was finally recognizing its responsibility for the economic welfare of its citizens in an urban industrial economy. By 1939 over 45 million persons were eligible for Social Security benefits, and in subsequent years further categories of workers were added and the payments to them were periodically increased.

A New Deal for Unskilled Labor

The NRA blue eagles, with their call for collective bargaining, had been a godsend to organized labor. As

New Deal expenditures brought some slackening of unemployment, labor began to feel more secure and hence more self-assertive. A rash of walkouts occurred in the summer of 1934, including a paralyzing general strike in San Francisco that was broken only when outraged citizens resorted to vigilante tactics.

When the Supreme Court axed the blue eagle, a Congress sympathetic to labor unions undertook to fill the vacuum. The fruit of its deliberations was the Wagner, or National Labor Relations, Act of 1935. This trailblazing law created a powerful new National Labor Relations Board for administrative purposes and reasserted the right of labor to engage in self-organization and to bargain collectively through representatives of its own choice. The Wagner Act proved to be one of the real milestones on the rocky road of the U.S. labor movement.

Under the encouragement of a highly sympathetic National Labor Relations Board, a host of unskilled workers began to organize themselves into effective unions. The leader of this drive was beetle-browed, domineering, and melodramatic John L. Lewis, boss of the United Mine Workers. In 1935 he succeeded in forming the Committee for Industrial Organization (CIO) within the ranks of the skilled-craft American Federation of Labor. But skilled workers, ever since the days of the ill-fated Knights of Labor in the 1880s, had shown only lukewarm sympathy for the cause of unskilled labor, especially blacks. In 1936, following inevitable friction with the CIO, the older federation suspended the upstart unions associated with the newer organization.

Nothing daunted, the rebellious CIO moved on a concerted scale into the huge automobile industry. Late in 1936 the workers resorted to a revolutionary technique known as the sit-down strike: they refused to leave the factory buildings of General Motors at Flint, Michigan, and thus prevented the importation of strikebreakers. Conservative respecters of private property were scandalized. The CIO finally won a resounding victory when its union, after heated negotiations, was recognized by General Motors as the sole bargaining agency for its employees.

Roosevelt's "Coddling" of Labor

Unskilled workers now pressed their advantage. The United States Steel Corporation, previously an impossible nut for labor to crack, averted a costly strike when it voluntarily granted rights of unionization to its CIO-organized employees. But the "little steel" companies fought back savagely. Citizens were shocked in 1937 by the Memorial Day massacre at the plant of the Republic Steel Company in South Chicago, where police fire killed several picketers.

A better deal for labor continued when Congress, in 1938, passed the memorable Fair Labor Standards Act (Wages and Hours Bill). Industries involved in interstate commerce were to set up minimum-wage and maximum-hour levels. The eventual goals were forty cents an hour (later raised) and a forty-hour workweek. Labor by children under sixteen was forbidden; under eighteen, if the occupation was dangerous. These reforms were bitterly though futilely opposed by many industrialists, especially by those southern textile manufacturers who had profited from low-wage labor.

In later New Deal days, labor unionization flourished; "Roosevelt wants you to join a union" was the rallying cry of professional organizers. The president received valuable support at ballot-box time from labor leaders and many appreciative working men and women. One mill worker remarked that Roosevelt was "the only man we ever had in the White House who would know that my boss is an s.o.b."

The CIO surged forward, breaking completely with the AF of L in 1938. On that occasion the *Committee* for Industrial Organization was formally reconstituted as the *Congress* of Industrial Organizations (the new CIO), under the high-handed presidency of John L. Lewis. By 1940 the CIO could claim about 4 million members in its constituent unions, including some 200,000 blacks.

Landon Challenges "the Champ" in 1936

As the presidential campaign of 1936 neared, the New Dealers were on top of the world. They had achieved considerable progress, and millions of "reliefers" were grateful to their bountiful government. The exultant Democrats renominated Roosevelt on a platform squarely endorsing the New Deal.

To run against "the Champ" Roosevelt, the Republicans settled on the colorless, homespun governor of Kansas, Alfred M. Landon. Landon himself

Later Major New Deal Measures, 1933–1939
(Items in parentheses indicate secondary purposes.)

Recovery	Relief	Reform
(CWA)	FDR establishes Civil Works Administration (CWA), Nov. 9, 1933	
Gold Reserve Act, Jan. 30, 1934, authorizes FDR's devaluation, Jan. 31, 1934		
		Securities and Exchange Commission (SEC) authorized by Congress, June 6, 1934
(Reciprocal Trade Agreements)	(Reciprocal Trade Agreements)	Reciprocal Trade Agreements Act, June 12, 1934
(FHA)	National Housing Act, June 28, 1934, authorizes Federal Housing Administration (FHA)	(FHA)
(Frazier-Lemke Act)	Frazier-Lemke Farm Bankruptcy Act, June 28, 1934	
(Resettlement Administration)	FDR creates Resettlement Administration, April 30, 1935	
(WPA)	FDR creates Works Progress Administration (WPA), May 6, 1935, under act of April 8, 1935	
(Wagner Act)	(Wagner Act)	(Wagner) National Labor Relations Act, July 5, 1935
		Social Security Act, Aug. 14, 1935
		Public Utility Holding Co. Act, Aug. 26, 1935
(Soil Conservation Act)	Soil Conservation and Domestic Allotment Act, Feb. 29, 1936	
(USHA)	(USHA)	U.S. Housing Authority (USHA) established by Congress, Sept. 1, 1937
(Second AAA)	Second Agricultural Adjustment Act, Feb. 16, 1936	
(Fair Labor Standards)	(Fair Labor Standards)	Fair Labor Standards Act, June 25, 1938
		Reorganization Act, April 3, 1939
		Hatch Act, Aug. 2, 1939

was a moderate who accepted some New Deal reforms, although not Social Security. But the Republican platform vigorously condemned the New Deal for its radicalism, experimentation, confusion, and "frightful waste." Democrats denounced the GOP as the party of big moneyed interests and big depression. Backing Landon, ex-president Hoover called for a "holy crusade for liberty." The American Liberty League, a group of wealthy conservatives, organized to fight "socialistic" New Deal schemes and "that man" Roosevelt.

Such reactionary rhetoric provided a made-to-order target for FDR. Angry enough to stretch sheet iron, Roosevelt took to the stump to denounce "economic royalists" who "hide behind the flag and

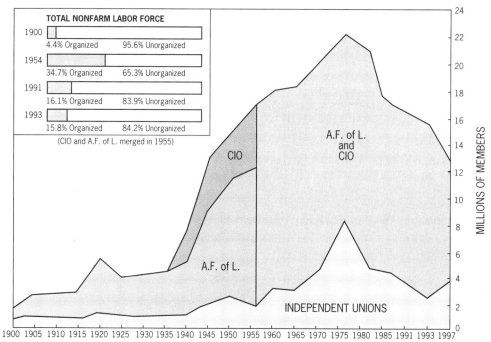

The Rise of Organized Labor, 1900–1997 *The percentage of the total labor force that was organized increased until 1954, and it has declined ever since.*

the Constitution." "I welcome their hatred," he proclaimed.

A landslide overwhelmed Landon as the demoralized Republicans carried only two states, Maine and Vermont. The popular vote was 27,752,869 to 16,674,665; the electoral count was 523 to 8—the most lopsided in 116 years. Democratic majorities were again returned to Congress. Jubilant Democrats could now claim more than two-thirds of the seats in the House and a like proportion in the Senate.

The battle of 1936, perhaps the most bitter since Bryan's in 1896, partially bore out Republican charges of class warfare. Even more than in 1932, the needy economic groups were lined up against the so-called greedy economic groups. CIO units contributed generously to FDR's campaign chest. Many left-wingers turned to Roosevelt as the customary third-party protest vote sharply declined. Blacks, several million of whom had also appreciated federal relief, had by now largely shaken off their traditional allegiance to the Republican party. To them, Lincoln was "finally dead."

FDR won primarily because he appealed to the "forgotten man," whom he never forgot. Roosevelt in fact had forged a powerful and enduring coalition of the South, blacks, urbanites, and the poor. He proved especially effective in marshaling the support of the multitudes of "New Immigrants"—mostly Catholics and Jews who had swarmed into the great cities since the turn of the century. These once-scorned newcomers, with their now-numerous sons and daughters, had at last come politically of age. In the 1920s, one out of every twenty-five federal judgeships went to a Catholic; Roosevelt appointed Catholics to one out of every four.

Conflict over the Court

Bowing his head to the sleety blasts, Roosevelt took the presidential oath on January 20, 1937, instead of the traditional March 4. The Twentieth Amendment to the Constitution had been ratified in 1933 (see the Appendix). It swept away the postelection lame duck session of Congress and shortened by six weeks the awkward period before inauguration.

Flushed with victory, Roosevelt interpreted his reelection as a mandate to continue New Deal reforms. But in his eyes the cloistered old men on the supreme bench, like fossilized stumbling blocks, stood stubbornly in the pathway of progress. In nine major cases involving the New Deal, the Roosevelt administration had been thwarted seven times. The Supreme Court was ultraconservative, and six of the nine oldsters in black were over seventy. As luck would have it, not a single member had been appointed by FDR in his first term.

Roosevelt—his "Dutch up"—viewed with mounting impatience what he regarded as the obstructive conservatism of the Court. Some of these Old Guard appointees were hanging on with a senile grip, partly because they felt it their patriotic duty to curb the "socialistic" tendencies of that radical in the White House.

To overcome such obstructionism, Roosevelt suddenly announced, early in 1937, a scheme to expand the Supreme Court. He bluntly asked Congress for legislation to add a new justice to the Supreme Court for every member over seventy who would not retire. The maximum membership could then be fifteen.

Congress and the nation were promptly convulsed over the scheme to "pack" the Supreme Court with a "dictator bill," which one critic called "too damned slick." Franklin "Double-crossing" Roosevelt was savagely condemned for attempting to break down the delicate checks and balances among the three branches of the government.

The Court had meanwhile seen the ax hanging over its head. Whatever his motives, Justice Owen J. Roberts, formerly regarded as a conservative, began to vote on the side of his liberal colleagues. "A switch in time saves nine" was the classic witticism inspired by this change. By a five-to-four decision, the Court, in March 1937, upheld the principle of a state minimum wage for women, thereby reversing its stand on a different case a year earlier. In succeeding decisions, the Court, more sympathetic to the New Deal, upheld the National Labor Relations Act (Wagner Act) and the Social Security Act.

With these changes under way, Congress refused to endorse the Court-packing scheme, and

Roosevelt suffered his first major legislative defeat at the hands of his own party. Yet in losing this battle, Roosevelt incidentally won his campaign. The Court, as he had hoped, became markedly more friendly to New Deal reforms. Furthermore, a succession of deaths and resignations enabled him to make nine appointments to the tribunal.

Yet in a sense FDR lost both the Court battle and the war. He so aroused conservatives of both parties in Congress that few New Deal reforms were passed after 1937, the year of the fight to "pack" the Supreme Court. With this catastrophic miscalculation, he squandered much of the political goodwill that had carried him to such a resounding victory in the 1936 election.

The Twilight of the New Deal

Roosevelt's first term, from 1933 to 1937, did not banish the depression from the land. Unemployment stubbornly persisted in 1936 at about 15 percent, down from the grim 25 percent of 1933 but still miserably high. Despite the inventiveness of New Deal programs and the billions of dollars in "pump-priming," recovery had been dishearteningly modest, though the country seemed to be inching its way back to economic health.

Then, in 1937 the economy took another sharp downturn, a surprisingly severe depression-within-a-depression that the president's critics quickly dubbed the "Roosevelt recession." In fact, government policies had caused the nosedive, as Social Security taxes began to bite into payrolls and as the administration cut back on spending out of continuing reverence for the orthodox economic doctrine of the balanced budget.

Only at this late date did Roosevelt at last frankly and deliberately embrace the recommendations of the British economist John Maynard Keynes. Now, in April 1937, FDR announced a bold program to stimulate the economy by planned deficit spending. Although the deficits were still relatively small, this abrupt policy reversal endorsing "Keynesianism" marked a turning point in the government's relation to the economy.

Facing an increasingly conservative Congress, Roosevelt successfully backed only a few reform measures like the 1939 Hatch Act prohibiting federal employees from active political campaigning. By

1939 the New Deal had clearly lost most of its early momentum. Magician Roosevelt could find few dazzling new reform rabbits to pull out of his tall silk hat. In the congressional elections of 1938 the Republicans, for the first time, cut heavily into the New Deal majorities in Congress, though failing to gain control of either house.

The international crisis that came to a boil in 1938–1939 shifted public attention away from domestic reform and no doubt helped save the political hide of the Roosevelt "spendocracy." The New Deal, for all practical purposes, had shot its bolt.

New Deal or Raw Deal?

Foes of the New Deal condemned its alleged radicalism, incompetence, confusion, and cross-purposes. New Dealers conceded some weaknesses but defended their record as a necessary and effective response to the depression.

To some conservatives, the New Deal was a radical attempt to make America over in a Bolshevik-Marxist image. They condemned "Rooseveltski" for bringing to Washington "crackpot" college professors, leftist "pinkos," and outright communists. The Hearst newspapers lambasted

The Red New Deal with a Soviet seal
Endorsed by a Moscow hand,
The strange result of an alien cult
In a liberty-loving land.

Other critics accused Roosevelt of bringing too many bright young Jewish leftists to Washington ("The Jew Deal"), or even asserted that Roosevelt himself was Jewish ("Rosenfeld").

More widespread was the charge that the New Deal brought bureaucracy, waste, and a welfare-state mentality that undermined the old American virtues of individualism, thrift, self-reliance, and limited government. The federal government, with its hundreds of thousands of employees, became incomparably the largest single business in the country, as the states faded farther into the background. Promises of budget balancing were forgotten as the national debt skyrocketed from $19,487,000,000 in 1932 to $40,440,000,000 by 1939. Critics charged that the lavish benefactions of the "handout state" were turning once-self-reliant Americans into relief-seeking loafers with wishbones larger than their backbones.

Hardheaded businesspeople, mostly Republicans, bitterly attacked what they saw as the New Deal's governmental oppression and regimentation, its class warfare, and Roosevelt's one-man rule. Private enterprise, they charged, was being stifled by a "planned economy" and "creeping socialism."

The most damning indictment of the New Deal was that it failed to cure the depression. Despite some $20 billion poured out in six years of deficit spending and lending, many economists believed that better results would have been achieved by much greater deficit spending. The New Deal, some believed, merely administered aspirin, sedatives, and

Unemployment, 1929–1942 *The cold figures can only begin to suggest the widespread human misery caused by mass unemployment. One man wrote to a newspaper in 1932: "I am forty-eight; married twenty-one years; four children, three in school. For the last eight years I was employed as a Pullman conductor. Since September, 1930, they have given me seven months of part-time work. Today I am an object of charity. . . . My small, weak, and frail wife and two small children are suffering and I have come to that terrible place where I could easily resort to violence in my desperation."*

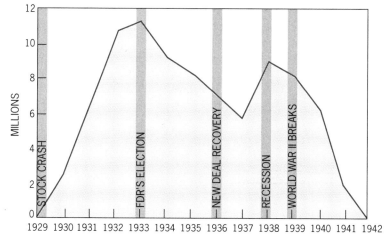

Band-Aids, with the result that in 1939 millions of dispirited men and women were still unemployed. Not until World War II increased the national debt from $40 billion in 1939 to $258 billion in 1945 was the unemployment headache solved.

New Dealers staunchly defended their record. Admitting that there was bureaucratic inefficiency and waste, they argued that it was trivial in view of the immense sums spent and the obvious need for haste. The New Deal, they insisted, relieved a crisis by demonstrating that the Washington regime was to be used, not feared. The collapse of America's economic system was averted; a fairer distribution of the national income was achieved; and the citizens were enabled to regain and retain their self-respect.

Though hated by business tycoons, FDR should have been their patron saint, so his admirers claimed. He deflected popular resentments against business and may have saved the American system of free enterprise. Roosevelt's quarrel was not with capitalism but with capitalists; he purged American capitalism of some of its worst abuses so that it might be saved from itself. He may even have headed off a more radical swing to the left by a mild dose of what

was mistakenly condemned as "socialism." The head of the American Socialist party, when once asked if the New Deal had carried out the Socialist program, reportedly replied that it had indeed—on a stretcher.

Roosevelt, like Jefferson, provided reform without a bloody revolution—at a time in history when some foreign nations were suffering armed uprisings and when many Europeans were predicting either communism or fascism for America. He was upbraided by the left-wing radicals for not going far enough and by the right-wing radicals for going too far. Choosing the middle road, he has been called the greatest American conservative since Hamilton. He was in fact Hamiltonian in his espousal of big government, but he was Jeffersonian in his concern for the "forgotten man." Demonstrating anew the value of powerful presidential leadership, he exercised that power to relieve the erosion of the nation's greatest physical resource—its people. He helped preserve democracy in America at a time when democracies abroad were disappearing down the sinkhole of dictatorship. And in playing this role he unwittingly girded the nation for its part in the gruesome war that loomed on the horizon—a war in which democracy the world over would be at stake.

Chronology

1932 Roosevelt defeats Hoover for presidency.

1933 Bank holiday.
Emergency Banking Relief Act.
Hundred Days Congress enacts HOLC, AAA, NRA, PWA, and TVA.
Federal Securities Act.
Glass-Steagall Banking Reform Act.
CWA established.
Twentieth Amendment (changed calendar of congressional sessions and date of presidential inauguration).
Twenty-first Amendment (prohibition repealed).

1934 Securities and Exchange Commission authorized.
Indian Reorganization Act.
FHA established.
Frazier-Lemke Farm Bankruptcy Act.

1935 WPA established.
Wagner Act.
Resettlement Administration.
Social Security Act.
Public Utility Holding Company Act.
Schechter "sick chicken" case.
CIO organized.

1936 Soil Conservation and Domestic Allotment Act.
Roosevelt defeats Landon for presidency.

1937 USHA established.
Roosevelt announces Court-packing plan.

1938 Second AAA.
Fair Labor Standards Act.

1939 Hatch Act.

varying

〜〜〜〜〜〜〜〜〜〜〜〜

viewpoints

How Radical Was the New Deal?

The Great Depression was both a great calamity and a great opportunity. How effectively Franklin Roosevelt responded to the calamity and what use he made of the opportunity are the two questions that have animated historical debate about the New Deal.

Some historians have denied that there was much of a connection between the depression and the New Deal. Arthur M. Schlesinger, Jr., for example, who believes in "cycles" of reform and reaction in American history, has written that "there would very likely have been some sort of New Deal in the 1930s even without the Depression." But most of the first generation of historians who wrote about the New Deal (in the 1940s, '50s, and early '60s) agreed with Carl Degler's judgment that the New Deal was "a revolutionary response to a revolutionary situation." In this view, though Roosevelt never found a means short of war to bring about economic recovery, he shrewdly utilized the stubborn economic crisis as a means to enact sweeping reforms.

Some leftist scholars writing in the 1960s, however, notably Barton J. Bernstein, charged that the New Deal did not reach far enough. This criticism echoed the socialist complaint in the 1930s that the depression represented the total collapse of American capitalism, and that the New Deal muffed the chance truly to remake American society. Roosevelt had the chance, these historians argue, to redistribute wealth, improve race relations, and bring the giant corporations to heel. Instead, say these critics, the New Deal simply represented a conservative holding action to shore up a sagging and corrupt capitalist order.

Those charges against the New Deal stimulated another generation of scholars in the 1970s, '80s, and '90s to look closely at the concrete institutional, attitudinal, and economic circumstances in which the New Deal unfolded. Historians including James Patterson, Alan Brinkley, Kenneth Jackson, Harvard Sitkoff, and Lizabeth Cohen— sometimes loosely referred to as the "constraints school"—conclude that the New Deal offered just about as much reform as circumstances allowed and as the majority of Americans wanted. The findings of these historians are impressive: the system of checks and balances limited presidential power; the disproportionate influence of southern Democrats in Congress stalled attempts to move toward racial justice; the federal system, in fact, inhibited all efforts to initiate change from Washington; and most important, a majority of the American people at the time wanted to reform capitalism, not overthrow it.

The best proof of the soundness of that conclusion is probably the durability of the political alliance that Roosevelt assembled. The great "New Deal coalition" that dominated American politics for nearly four decades after Roosevelt's election in 1932 represented a broad consensus in American society about the legitimate limits of government efforts to shape the social and economic order. William Leuchtenburg offered the most balanced historical assessment in his description of the New Deal as a "half-way revolution," neither radical nor conservative but accurately reflecting the American people's needs and desires in the 1930s—and for a long time thereafter.

SUGGESTED READINGS

Primary Source Documents

James Agee and Walker Evans, in *Let Us Now Praise Famous Men* (1940), brilliantly evoke the misery of the depression in words and photographs. Franklin D. Roosevelt's dramatic "First Inaugural Address" (1933), in Henry Steele Commager, ed., *Documents of American History* (1988), captured the imagination of the distressed nation. Less successful was Roosevelt's "Radio Address on Supreme Court Reform" (1937), in Richard Hofstadter, *Great Issues in American History* (1982). See also Dorothy Thompson's attack on the Court plan in the Washington *Star,* February 10, 1937.* Clifford Odets' play *Waiting for Lefty* (1935) and John Steinbeck's novel *The Grapes of Wrath* (1939) exemplify the literature stimulated by the Great Depression. Robert S. McElvaine has collected a compelling set of letters in *Down and Out in the Great Depression* (1983).

Secondary Sources

A masterly summation is William E. Leuchtenburg, *Franklin D. Roosevelt and the New Deal, 1932–1940* (1963). Briefer and more critical of the limitations of reform is Paul Conkin, *The New Deal* (rev. ed., 1975). A detailed biography is Frank Freidel, *Franklin D. Roosevelt* (4 vols., 1952–1973). Brilliantly pro-FDR are the three volumes of Arthur M. Schlesinger, Jr., *Age of Roosevelt: The Crisis of the Old Order* (1957), *The Coming of the New Deal* (1959), and *The Politics of Upheaval* (1960). A concise biography is Frank Freidel, *Franklin D. Roosevelt: Rendezvous with Destiny* (1990). The social impact of the depression is vividly etched in Studs Terkel, *Hard Times* (1970); Ann Banks, *First Person America* (1980); and James N. Gregory, *American Exodus: The Dust Bowl Migration and Okie Culture in California* (1989). Of special interest are Lois Scharf, *To Work and to Wed: Female Employment, Feminism, and the Great Depression* (1980), and *Eleanor Roosevelt: First Lady of American Liberalism* (1987). Also see Susan Ware, *Beyond Suffrage: Women in the New Deal* (1981), and Blanche Wiesen Cook, *Eleanor Roosevelt: A Life* (1992). Alan Brinkley brilliantly chronicles *Voices of Protest: Huey Long, Father Coughlin, and the Great Depression* (1982). See also his treatment of the later New Deal in *The End of Reform* (1995). Ellis Hawley, *The New Deal and the Problem of Monopoly* (1966), is a superb analysis of the conflicting currents of economic policy in the Roosevelt administration. A comprehensive assessment by several noted scholars is Harvard Sitkoff, ed., *Fifty Years Later: The New Deal Evaluated* (1985). Especially good on intellectual history are Richard H. Pells, *Radical Visions and American Dreams: Culture and Social Thought in the Depression Years* (1973), and Daniel Aaron, *Writers on the Left* (1961). A trenchant appraisal of the New Deal legacy is Steven Fraser and Gary Gerstle, eds., *The Rise and Fall of the New Deal Order* (1989).

---

* An asterisk indicates that the document, or an excerpt from it, can be found in Thomas A. Bailey and David M. Kennedy, eds., *The American Spirit: United States History as Seen by Contemporaries,* 9th ed. (Boston: Houghton Mifflin, 1998).

35

★★★★★★★★★

Franklin D. Roosevelt and the Shadow of War, 1933–1941

★★★★★★

The epidemic of world lawlessness is spreading. When an epidemic of physical disease starts to spread, the community approves and joins in a quarantine of the patients in order to protect the health of the community against the spread of the disease. . . . There must be positive endeavors to preserve peace.

★★★★★★

FRANKLIN D. ROOSEVELT, CHICAGO QUARANTINE SPEECH, 1937

FDR's Early Foreign Policy

Roosevelt's early foreign policy was intended to serve his schemes for domestic recovery. This was first demonstrated by his actions at the London Economic Conference in the summer of 1933. Sixty-six nations had gathered to attack the depression by stabilizing national currencies. But Roosevelt, unwilling to subordinate his gold-juggling policies to an international agreement that might tie his hands, torpedoed the conference with an explosive message that scolded the delegates for even trying to stabilize currencies. Whether the conference could have arrested the worldwide economic slide is debatable, but Roosevelt's every-man-for-himself attitude plunged the planet even deeper into economic crisis. Roosevelt also plunged the world deeper into narrow isolationism and extreme nationalism—a trend that played directly into the hands of power-mad dictators.

Roosevelt matched isolationism from Europe with withdrawal from Asia. With the descent into hard times, American taxpayers were eager to throw overboard their expensive tropical liability in the Philippines. Congress passed the Tydings-McGuffie Act in 1934, which provided for the independence of the Philippines in 1946 but threatened to leave the islands economically prostrate. American isolationists rejoiced once again, and Japanese militarists calculated that they had little to fear from inward-looking America.

Closer to home, Roosevelt inaugurated a refreshing new era in relations with Latin America. He proclaimed in his inaugural address: "I would dedicate this nation to the policy of the Good Neighbor." He renounced the policies of armed intervention that had accompanied the corollary to the Monroe Doctrine devised by his cousin Theodore Roosevelt. Accordingly, in 1934 the United States withdrew the last marines from Haiti, and in 1936 relaxed its grip on Panama. When the Mexican government seized Yankee oil properties in 1938, Roosevelt successfully resisted business pressure to intervene and eventually thrashed out a settlement in 1941. These earnest acts of friendliness paid rich dividends in goodwill among the peoples to the south and made Roosevelt a hero in Latin America.

Taken together, Roosevelt's noninvolvement in Europe and withdrawal from Asia, along with his brotherly embrace of his New World neighbors, suggested that the United States was giving up its ambition to be a world power and would content itself instead with being merely a regional power, its interests and activities confined exclusively to the Western Hemisphere.

Impulses Toward Isolationism

Post-1918 chaos in Europe, followed by the Great Depression, spawned the ominous spread of totalitarianism—the notion that the individual was nothing and the state was everything. The Communist Soviet Union led the way, with the crafty and ruthless Joseph Stalin finally emerging as dictator. Blustery Benito Mussolini, a swaggering Fascist, seized the reins of power in Italy during 1922. And Adolf Hitler, a fanatic with a toothbrush mustache, plotted and harangued his way into control of Germany in 1933 with liberal use of the "big lie."

Jut-jawed Mussolini, seeking both glory and empire in Africa, brutally attacked Ethiopia in 1935 with bombers and tanks. But Hitler was the most dangerous dictator because he combined tremendous power with impulsiveness. A frustrated Austrian painter, with hypnotic talents as an orator and leader, he led the Nazi party to power in Germany by making political capital of the Treaty of Versailles and the country's depression-spawned unemployment. In 1936 the Nazi Hitler and the Fascist Mussolini allied themselves in the Rome-Berlin Axis.

International gangsterism was likewise spreading in East Asia, where imperial Japan was on the make. Like Germany and Italy, Japan was a so-called have-not power. Like them, it resented the ungenerous Treaty of Versailles. Like them, it demanded additional space for its teeming millions, cooped up in their crowded island nation. Determined to find a place in the Asian sun, Tokyo terminated the Washington Naval Treaty in 1934 and in the following year accelerated Japan's construction of giant battleships.

Isolationism, long festering in America, received a strong boost from these alarms abroad. Though disapproving of the dictators, Americans still believed that their encircling seas conferred a kind of mystic immunity. They were continuing to suffer the disillusionment born of their participation in World War I, which they now regarded as a colossal blunder. They likewise nursed bitter memories of the ungrateful and defaulting debtors. As early as 1934 a spiteful Congress had passed the Johnson Debt Default Act, which prevented debt-dodging nations from borrowing further from the United States.

As the gloomy 1930s lengthened, an avalanche of lurid articles and books condemning the munitions manufacturers as war-fomenting "merchants of death" poured forth from American presses. A Senate committee headed by Senator Gerald Nye of North Dakota was appointed in 1934 to investigate the "blood business." By sensationalizing evidence regarding America's entry into World War I, the senatorial probers tended to shift the blame away from the German submarine onto the American bankers and arms manufacturers. Because the munitions makers had obviously made money out of the war, many a naive citizen leaped to the illogical conclusion that these scavengers had *caused* the war in order to make money. This kind of reasoning suggested that if the profits could only be removed from the arms traffic—"one hell of a business"—the country could steer clear of any future world conflict.

Responding to overwhelming popular pressure, Congress made haste to legislate the nation out of war. Action was spurred by the danger that Mussolini's Ethiopian assault would plunge the world into a new bloodbath. The Neutrality Acts of 1935, 1936, and 1937, taken together, stipulated that *when the president proclaimed* the existence of a foreign war, certain restrictions would automatically go into effect: no American could legally sail on a belligerent ship, sell or transport munitions to a belligerent, or make loans to a belligerent.

Such head-in-the-sand neutrality proved to be tragically shortsighted. Through its neutrality laws, America served notice that it would make no distinction between brutal aggressors and innocent victims. By striving to hold the scales even, it actually overbalanced them in favor of the dictators, who had armed themselves to the teeth. By declining to use its vast industrial strength to aid its democratic friends and defeat its totalitarian foes, America helped goad the aggressors along their blood-spattered path of conquest.

The Spanish Civil War of 1936–1939—a proving ground and dress rehearsal in miniature for World War II—was a painful object lesson in the folly of neutrality-by-legislation. Spanish rebels, who rose against the left-leaning republican government in Madrid, were headed by fascistic General Francisco Franco. Generously aided by his fellow conspirators Hitler and Mussolini, he undertook to overthrow the established Loyalist regime, which in turn was assisted on a smaller scale by the Soviet Union. This pipeline from communist Moscow offended many Americans, especially Roman Catholics.

In accordance with previous American practice, the Loyalist government should have been free to purchase desperately needed munitions from the United States. But Congress, with the encouragement of Roosevelt and with only one dissenting vote,

amended the existing neutrality legislation so as to apply an arms embargo to both Loyalists and rebels.

Uncle Sam thus sat on the sidelines while Franco, abundantly supplied with arms and men by his fellow dictators, strangled the republican government of Spain. The democracies, including the United States, were so determined to stay out of war that they helped to condemn a fellow democracy to death. In so doing they further encouraged the dictators to take the dangerous road that led over the precipice to World War II.

Appeasing Japan and Germany

Sulfurous war clouds had meanwhile been gathering in tension-taut East Asia. In 1937 the Japanese militarists, at the Marco Polo Bridge near Beijing (Peking), touched off the explosion that led to a full-dress invasion of China. In a sense this attack was the curtain raiser of World War II.

Roosevelt declined to invoke the recently passed neutrality legislation by refusing to call the so-called China incident an officially declared *war*. If he had put the existing restrictions into effect, he would have cut off the tiny trickle of munitions on which the Chinese were desperately dependent. The Japanese, of course, could continue to buy mountains of war supplies in the United States.

In Chicago—unofficial isolationist "capital" of America—President Roosevelt delivered his sensational "Quarantine Speech" in the autumn of 1937. Alarmed by the recent aggression of Italy and Japan, he called for "positive endeavors" to "quarantine" the aggressors—presumably by economic embargoes. The speech triggered a cyclone of protest from isolationists and other foes of involvement; they feared that a moral quarantine would lead to a shooting quarantine. Startled by this angry response, Roosevelt retreated and sought less direct means to curb the dictators.

America's isolationist mood intensified in December 1937 when Japanese aviators bombed and sank an American gunboat, the *Panay*, in Chinese waters. In the days of 1898, when the *Maine* went down, this outrage might have provoked war. But after Tokyo apologized and paid an indemnity, Americans breathed a sigh of relief.

What Next? *The western European democracies looked on helplessly as Nazi Germany swallowed up Austria and part of Czechoslovakia in 1938. Hitler's juggernaut seemed unstoppable.*

Adolf Hitler meanwhile grew louder and bolder in Europe. In 1935 he had openly flouted the Treaty of Versailles by introducing compulsory military service in Germany. The next year he boldly marched into the demilitarized German Rhineland, likewise contrary to the detested treaty, while France and Britain looked on in an agony of indecision. Lashing his following to a frenzy, Hitler undertook to persecute and then exterminate the Jewish population in the areas under his control. In the end, he wiped out about 6 million innocent victims, mostly in gas chambers (see "Makers of America: Refugees from the Holocaust," pp. 518–519). Calling upon his people to sacrifice butter for guns, he whipped the new German air force and mechanized ground divisions into the most devastating military machine the world had yet seen.

Suddenly, in March 1938, Hitler bloodlessly occupied German-speaking Austria, his birthplace. The democratic powers, wringing their hands in despair, prayed that this last grab would satisfy his passion for conquest. But like a drunken reveler calling for madder music and stronger wine, Hitler could

not stop. Intoxicated by his recent gains, he began to make bullying demands for the German-inhabited Sudetenland of neighboring Czechoslovakia.

British and French leaders, eager to appease Hitler, frantically arranged a conference with Hitler and Mussolini at Munich, Germany, in September 1938, where they consented to Hitler's demand. Europeans and Americans alike hoped that these concessions would bring "peace in our time." Indeed, Hitler publicly promised that the Sudetenland "is the last territorial claim I have to make in Europe."

"Appeasement" of the dictators, symbolized by the ugly word *Munich*, turned out to be merely surrender on the installment plan. It was like giving a cannibal a finger in the hope of saving an arm. In March 1939, scarcely six months later, Hitler suddenly erased the rest of Czechoslovakia from the map, contrary to his solemn vows. The democratic world was again stunned.

Hitler's Belligerency and U.S. Neutrality

Joseph Stalin, the sphinx of the Kremlin, was a key to the peace puzzle. When efforts to secure a mutual defense treaty with Britain and France fell through in the summer of 1939, the Soviet Union astounded the world by signing, on August 23, 1939, a nonaggression treaty with the German dictator. The notorious Hitler-Stalin pact meant that, contrary to hopes of wishful thinkers in western Europe, the two dictators would not bleed each other to death, but rather join hands to share the spoils.

With the signing of the Nazi-Soviet pact, World War II was only hours away. Hitler now demanded from neighboring Poland a return of the areas wrested from Germany after World War I. Failing to secure satisfaction, he sent his mechanized divisions crashing into Poland at dawn on September 1, 1939. Honoring their commitments, Britain and France promptly declared war. But they were powerless to aid Poland, which was quickly divided between Hitler and his partner in crime, Stalin. Long-dreaded World War II was now fully launched, and the long truce of 1919–1939 came to an end.

Americans were overwhelmingly anti-Nazi and anti-Hitler, but they were desperately determined to stay out of war; they were not going to be "suckers"

MAKERS OF AMERICA

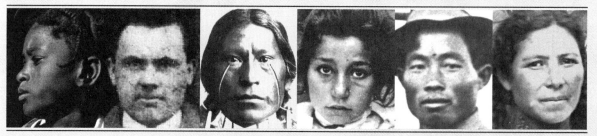

Refugees from the Holocaust

Fed by Adolf Hitler's genocidal delusions, anti-Semitism bared its fangs in the 1930s, spreading across Europe as Nazi Germany seized Austria and Czechoslovakia. Eluding the jackboots of Hitler's bloodthirsty SS (*Schutzstaffel*, an elite military and police force), Jews tried to flee from the Nazi juggernaut. Some succeeded, including the world's premier nuclear physicist, Albert Einstein, the Nobel laureate whose plea to Franklin Roosevelt helped initiate the top-secret atomic bomb project; the philosopher Hannah Arendt; the painter Marc Chagall; and the composer Kurt Weill. In all, some 150,000 Jews fled the Nazi "Third Reich" for America in the 1930s—a tiny fraction of the millions of Jews who eventually came under Hitler's heel. Why did America not make room for more?

For one thing, those exiled luminaries who managed to make it out of Germany found a divided Jewish community in America. On the one hand, prosperous German Jews who had established themselves in America in the nineteenth century had little in common with later-arriving Jews from eastern Europe and feared stirring an outburst of anti-Semitism if they advocated further immigration. On the other hand, less influential organizations of eastern European Jews struggled to pressure the Roosevelt administration to rescue Europe's Jews. This internal discord undermined the political effectiveness of the American Jewish community in the face of the refugee dilemma.

Other factors also kept America's doors shut against Jews seeking refuge in the United States. The restrictive American immigration law of 1924 set rigid national quotas and made no provisions for seekers of asylum from racial, religious, or political persecution. The Great Depression made it impossible to provide employment for workers already in the United States, much less make room in the job line for newcomers.

Hannah Arendt, 1933 *A brilliant political theorist, she fled the Nazis and continued her career in the United States.*

Many Jews and non-Jews alike, including Congressman Emmanuel Celler and Senator Robert Wagner, both of New York, lobbied Roosevelt's government to extend a welcoming hand to Jews seeking asylum—to no avail. In 1941 Congress rejected a Wagner bill to bring twenty thousand German-Jewish children to the United States outside the quota restrictions.

Once the United States entered the war, the State Department suppressed early reports of Hitler's plan to exterminate all European Jewry. After the Führer's sordid "final solution" became more widely known in America, the War Department rejected pleas to bomb rail lines leading to the gas chambers. Military officials maintained that a raid on death camps like Auschwitz would divert essential military resources and needlessly extend the war. Thus only a lucky few escaped the Nazi terror, while 6 million died in one of history's most ghastly testimonials to the human capacity for evil.

again. Neutrality promptly became a heated issue in the United States. Britain and France urgently needed American airplanes and weapons, but the Neutrality Act of 1937 raised a sternly forbidding hand. Roosevelt summoned Congress into special session, and after hectic debate it came up with the makeshift Neutrality Act of 1939. This law provided that henceforth the European democracies might buy American war materials, but only on a "cash-and-carry" basis—that is, they would have to pay for munitions in cash and transport them in their own ships.

Despite its defects, this unneutral neutrality law clearly favored the democracies against the dictators—and was so intended. Because the British and French navies controlled the Atlantic, the European aggressors could not send their ships to buy America's munitions. The United States not only improved its moral position but simultaneously helped its economic position. Overseas demand for war goods brought a sharp upswing from the recession of 1937–1938 and ultimately solved the decade-long unemployment crisis (see the chart on p. 510).

The Fall of France and the Destroyer Deal (1940)

The months following the collapse of Poland, while France and Britain marked time, were known as the "phony war." An ominous silence fell on Europe as Hitler shifted his victorious divisions from Poland for a knockout blow at France. Inaction during this anxious period was relieved by the Soviets, who wantonly attacked neighboring Finland in an effort to secure strategic buffer territory.

An abrupt end to the "phony war" came in April 1940 when Hitler, again without warning, overran his weaker neighbors, Denmark and Norway. Hardly pausing for breath, the next month he attacked the Netherlands and Belgium, then struck a paralyzing blow at France. By late June, France was forced to surrender, but not until Mussolini had pounced on its rear for a jackal's share of the loot. In a pell-mell but successful evacuation from the French port of Dunkirk, the British managed to salvage the bulk of their shattered army. The crisis providentially brought forth an inspired leader in Prime Minister Winston Churchill, the bulldog-jawed orator who nerved the English to fight off the fearful air bombings of their cities.

France's sudden collapse shocked Americans out of their daydreams. Stouthearted Britons, singing "There'll Always Be an England," were all that stood between Hitler and the death in Europe of constitutional government. If Britain went under, Hitler would have at his disposal the workshops, shipyards, and slave labor of western Europe. He might even have the powerful British fleet as well. This frightening possibility, which seemed to pose a dire threat to American security, steeled the American people to a tremendous effort.

Roosevelt moved with electrifying energy and dispatch. He called upon an already debt-burdened nation to build huge airfleets and a two-ocean navy, which could also check Japan. Congress, jarred out of its apathy toward preparedness, within a year appropriated the astounding sum of $37 billion, more than the total cost of fighting World War I. Congress also passed a conscription law on September 6, 1940, America's first peacetime draft.

Before the fall of France in June 1940, Washington had generally observed a technical neutrality. But now the wisdom of neutrality seemed increasingly questionable.

As the Battle of Britain raged in the air over the British Isles, debate intensified in the United States over what foreign policy to embrace. Supporters of aid to Britain formed propaganda groups, the most potent of which was the Committee to Defend America by Aiding the Allies. The isolationists, both numerous and sincere, were by no means silent. Determined to avoid bloodshed at all costs, they organized the America First Committee. Their basic philosophy was "the Yanks are not coming," and their most effective speechmaker was the famed aviator Colonel Charles A. Lindbergh, who, ironically, had narrowed the Atlantic in 1927.

Destroyer-Bases Deal

Britain was in critical need of destroyers, for German submarines were again threatening to starve it out with attacks on shipping. Roosevelt moved boldly when, on September 2, 1940, he agreed to transfer to Great Britain fifty old destroyers left over from World War I. In return, the British promised to hand over to the United States eight valuable defensive base sites, stretching from Newfoundland to South America. These strategically located outposts were to remain under the Stars and Stripes for ninety-nine years.

Shifting warships from a "neutral" United States to a belligerent Britain was, beyond question, a flagrant violation of neutral obligations. But public-opinion polls demonstrated that a majority of Americans were determined to provide the battered British with "all aid short of war."

FDR Shatters the Two-Term Tradition (1940)

In the midst of this crisis came the distracting presidential election of 1940. The Republican convention in Philadelphia was miraculously swept off its feet by Wendell L. Willkie, a colorful German-descended Indiana public utilities corporation executive who was a complete novice in politics. With the galleries in Philadelphia wildly chanting "We Want Willkie," the delegates finally accepted this magnetic political upstart as the only candidate who could possibly beat Roosevelt. The outspoken Willkie was opposed not so much to the New Deal as to its extravagances and inefficiencies. Democratic critics branded him "the rich man's Roosevelt" and "the simple barefoot Wall Street lawyer."

Roosevelt delayed to the last minute the announcement of his decision to challenge the sacred two-term tradition. Despite what he described as his personal yearning for retirement, he avowed that in so grave a crisis he owed his experienced hand to the service of his country and humanity.

With the country already badly split between interventionists and isolationists, Willkie might have widened the breach dangerously by a violent attack on Roosevelt's aid-to-Britain policies. But the Republican candidate refrained from assailing the president's interventionism and accepted the essential premises of an internationalist foreign policy. Willkie campaigned hard against Rooseveltian "dictatorship" and the third term. Roosevelt, busy at his desk with important problems, stayed close to the White House and generally ignored Willkie. But in a speech in Boston he emphatically declared, "Your boys are not going to be sent into any foreign wars"—a pledge that later came back to plague him.

Roosevelt triumphed, although Willkie ran a strong race. The electoral count was 449 to 82. The popular vote was much closer—27,307,819 to 22,321,018.

Congress Passes the Landmark Lend-Lease Law

By late 1940 embattled Britain was nearing the end of its financial tether; its credits in America were being rapidly consumed by insatiable war orders. But Roosevelt, who had bitter memories of the wrangling over the Allied debts of World War I, was determined, as he put it, to eliminate "the silly, foolish, old dollar sign." He finally hit on the scheme of lending or leasing American arms to the reeling democracies. When the shooting was over, to use his comparison, the guns and tanks could be returned, just as one's next-door neighbor would return a garden hose when a threatening fire was put out. But isolationist Senator Robert Taft retorted that lending arms was like lending chewing gum: "You don't want it back." Who wants a chewed-up tank?

The lend-lease bill, patriotically numbered 1776, was entitled "An Act Further to Promote the Defense of the United States." The underlying concept was "Send guns, not sons" or "Billions, not bodies." America, so President Roosevelt promised, would be the "arsenal of democracy." It would send a limitless supply of arms to the victims of aggression, who in turn would finish the job and keep the war on their side of the Atlantic. Isolationists assailed the lend-lease scheme as "the blank-check bill." Isolationist Senator Burton Wheeler called it "the new triple-A [Agricultural Adjustment Act] bill"—a measure designed to "plow under every fourth American boy." Nevertheless, lend-lease was finally approved in March 1941 by sweeping majorities in both houses of Congress.

Lend-lease was one of the most momentous laws ever to pass Congress; it was a challenge hurled squarely into the teeth of the Axis dictators. America eventually sent about $50 billion worth of arms and equipment—much more than the cost to the country of World War I—to those nations fighting aggressors. By its very nature, lend-lease marked the abandonment of any pretense of neutrality. It was no destroyer deal arranged privately by Roosevelt. The bill was universally debated, over drugstore counters and cracker barrels, from California to Maine; and the

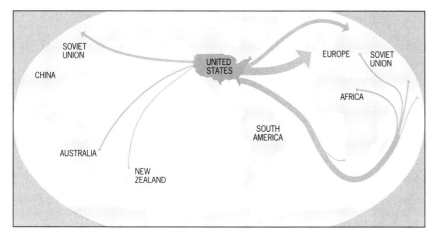

Main Flow of Lend-Lease Aid (width of arrows indicates relative amount) *The proud but desperate British prime minister, Winston Churchill, declared in early 1941: "Give us the tools and we will finish the job." Lend-lease eventually provided the British and other Allies with $50 billion worth of "tools."*

sovereign citizens at last spoke through convincing majorities in Congress. Lend-lease had the somewhat incidental result of gearing U.S. factories for all-out war production. The enormously increased capacity thus achieved helped to save America's own skin when, at long last, the shooting war burst around its head.

Hitler himself evidently recognized lend-lease as an unofficial declaration of war. Until then, Germany had avoided attacking U.S. ships; memories of America's decisive intervention in 1917–1918 were still fresh in German minds. But after the passing of lend-lease there was less point in trying to curry favor with the United States. On May 21, 1941, the *Robin Moor*, an unarmed American merchant ship, was torpedoed and destroyed by a German submarine in the South Atlantic, outside a war zone. The sinkings had started, but on a limited scale.

U.S. Destroyers and Hitler's U-Boats Clash

Lend-lease shipments of arms to Britain on British ships were bound to be sunk by German wolf-pack submarines. If the intent was to get the munitions to Britain, not to dump them into the ocean, the freighters would have to be escorted by U.S. warships. Britain simply did not have enough destroyers. The fateful decision to convoy was taken in July 1941. Roosevelt issued orders to the U.S. Navy to escort lend-lease shipments to Iceland. The British would then shepherd them the rest of the way.

Inevitable clashes with submarines ensued on the Iceland run, even though Hitler's orders were to strike American warships only in self-defense. In September 1941, the U.S. destroyer *Greer*, provocatively trailing a German U-boat, was attacked by the undersea craft, without damage to either vessel. Roosevelt then proclaimed a shoot-on-sight policy. On October 17 the escorting destroyer *Kearny*, while engaged in a battle with U-boats, lost eleven men when it was crippled but not sent to the bottom. Two weeks later the destroyer *Reuben James* was torpedoed and sunk off southwestern Iceland, with the loss of more than one hundred officers and men.

Neutrality was still inscribed on the statute books but not in American hearts. In August 1941, Roosevelt met secretly with Prime Minister Churchill on a warship off the foggy coast of Newfoundland. There they signed the Atlantic Charter, affirming the rights of peoples to choose their own form of government and proposing a "permanent system of general security" (a new League of Nations). Isolationists protested the Atlantic Charter between belligerent Britain and "neutral" America, but in fact the nation was no longer neutral. Hitler's invasion of the Soviet Union in June 1941 made the Nazi dictator's global ambitions even clearer. Congress, responding to public pressures and confronted with a shooting war in the North Atlantic, voted in mid-November 1941 to pull the teeth from the now-useless Neutrality Act of 1939. Merchant ships could henceforth be legally armed, and they could enter the combat zones with munitions for Britain. Americans braced themselves for wholesale attacks by Hitler's submarines.

The Surprise Assault at Pearl Harbor

The blowup came not in the Atlantic, but in the far-away Pacific. This explosion should have surprised no close observer, for Japan, since September 1940, had been a formal military ally of Nazi Germany—America's shooting foe in the North Atlantic.

Japan's position in East Asia had grown more perilous by the hour. It was still mired down in the costly and exhausting "China incident," from which it could extract neither honor nor victory. Its war machine was fatally dependent on immense shipments from the United States of steel, scrap iron, oil, and aviation gasoline. Such assistance to the Japanese aggressor was highly unpopular in America. But Roosevelt had resolutely held off an embargo, lest he goad the Tokyo warlords into a descent on the oil-rich but defense-poor Dutch East Indies (present-day Indonesia).

Washington, late in 1940, finally imposed the first of its embargoes on Japan-bound supplies. This blow was followed in mid-1941 by a freezing of Japanese assets in the United States and a cessation of all shipments of gasoline and other sinews of war. As the oil gauge dropped, the squeeze on Japan grew steadily more nerve-racking. Japanese leaders were faced with two painful alternatives. They could either knuckle under to the Americans or break out of the embargo ring by a desperate attack on the oil supplies and other riches of Southeast Asia.

The Battleship *West Virginia*, blown up at Pearl Harbor

Final tense negotiations with Japan took place in Washington during November and early December of 1941. The State Department insisted that the Japanese clear out of China, but to sweeten the pill offered to renew trade relations on a limited basis. Japanese imperialists, after waging a bitter war against the Chinese for more than four years, were unwilling to lose face by withdrawing at the behest of the United States. Faced with capitulation or continued conquest, they chose the sword.

Officials in Washington, having "cracked" the top-secret code of the Japanese, knew that Tokyo's decision was for war. But the United States, as a democracy committed to public debate and action by Congress, could not shoot first. Roosevelt, misled by Japanese ship movements in the western Pacific, evidently expected the blow to fall on British Malaya or on the Philippines. No one in high authority in Washington seems to have believed that the Japanese were either strong enough or foolhardy enough to strike Hawaii.

But the paralyzing blow struck Pearl Harbor, while Tokyo was deliberately prolonging negotiations in Washington. Japanese bombers, winging in from distant aircraft carriers, attacked without warning on the "Black Sunday" morning of December 7, 1941. It was a date, as Roosevelt told Congress, "which will live in infamy." About three thousand casualties were inflicted on American personnel; many aircraft were destroyed; the battleship fleet was virtually wiped out when all eight of the craft were sunk or otherwise immobilized; and numerous small vessels were damaged or destroyed. Fortunately for America, the three priceless aircraft carriers happened to be outside the harbor.

An angered Congress, the next day, officially recognized the war that had been "thrust" upon the United States. The roll call in the Senate and House fell only one vote short of unanimity. Germany and Italy, allies of Japan, spared Congress the indecision of debate by declaring war on December 11, 1941. This challenge was formally accepted on the same day by a unanimous vote of both the Senate and the House. The unofficial war was now official.

America's Transformation from Bystander to Belligerent

Japan's hara-kiri gamble in Hawaii paid off only in the short run. True, the U.S. Pacific fleet was largely destroyed or immobilized, but the sneak attack aroused and united America as almost nothing else could have done. To the very day of the blowup, a strong majority of Americans still wanted to keep out of war. But the bombs that pulverized Pearl Harbor blasted the isolationists into silence. The only thing left to do, growled isolationist Senator Wheeler, was "to lick hell out of them."

But Pearl Harbor was not the full answer to the question as to why the United States went to war. This treacherous attack was but the last explosion in a long chain reaction. After the fall of France, Americans were confronted with a devil's dilemma. They desired above all to stay out of the conflict, yet they did not want Britain to be knocked out. They wished to halt Japan's conquests in East Asia—conquests that menaced not only American trade and security but international peace as well. To keep Britain from collapsing, the Roosevelt administration felt compelled to extend the unneutral aid that invited attacks from German submarines. To keep Japan from expanding, Washington undertook to cut off vital Japanese supplies with embargoes that invited possible retaliation. Rather than let democracy die and dictatorship rule supreme, a strong majority of citizens were evidently determined to support a policy that might lead to war. It did.

Clear-headed Americans had come to the conclusion that no nation was safe in an era of international anarchy. Appeasement—the tactic of throwing the weaker persons out of the sleigh to the pursuing wolves—had been tried but had merely whetted dictatorial appetites. Power-drunk dictators had flouted international law and decency. Asserting the philosophy that might makes right, they had cynically negotiated nonaggression treaties with their intended targets, merely to lull them into a false sense of security. Most Americans were determined to stand firm—and let war come if it must—because they were convinced that with ruthless dictators on the loose, the world could not long remain half-enchained and half-free.

Chronology

1933	FDR torpedoes the London Economic Conference. FDR declares Good Neighbor policy toward Latin America.
1934	Tydings-McDuffie Act provides for Philippine independence. Reciprocal Trade Agreements Act.
1935	Mussolini invades Ethiopia. First U.S. Neutrality Act.
1936	Second U.S. Neutrality Act.
1936–1939	Spanish Civil War.
1937	U.S. Neutrality Act of 1937. *Panay* incident. Japan invades China.
1938	Hitler seizes Austria. Munich conference.
1939	Nazi-Soviet pact. Hitler seizes all of Czechoslovakia. World War II begins in Europe with Hitler's invasion of Poland. U.S. Neutrality Act of 1939.
1940	Hitler invades Denmark, Norway, the Netherlands, and Belgium. Fall of France. United States invokes first peacetime draft. Battle of Britain. Bases-for-destroyers deal with Britain. FDR defeats Willkie for presidency.
1941	Lend-Lease Act. Hitler attacks the Soviet Union. Atlantic Charter. Japan attacks Pearl Harbor. The United States declares war on Japan. Germany declares war on the United States.

SUGGESTED READINGS

Primary Source Documents

For background on the date that will live in infamy see *Pearl Harbor Attack: Hearings Before the Joint Committee on the Investigation of the Pearl Harbor Attack*, 79 Cong., 1 sess.* (1946). Franklin D. Roosevelt's "Quarantine the Aggressors" speech (1937), in Richard Hofstadter, *Great Issues in American History* (1958), revealed what would become the goal of the president's foreign policy in succeeding years. See also Roosevelt's "Press Conference on Lend-Lease" (1940), in *The Public Papers and Addresses of Franklin D. Roosevelt, 1940 Volume* (1941), pp. 606–608.* For opposition to lend-lease see the speech of January 12, 1941, by Montana senator Burton K. Wheeler, *Congressional Record*, 77 Cong., 1 sess., Appendix, pp. 178–179.* Charles A. Lindbergh elaborated the isolationist position in the *New York Times*, April 24, 1941, p. 12.* Warren F. Kimball, ed., *Churchill and Roosevelt: The Complete Correspondence* (1984), is enlightening on many topics.

Secondary Sources

Indispensable and comprehensive is Robert Dallek, *Franklin D. Roosevelt and American Foreign Policy, 1932–1945* (1979). Also strong is Kenneth S. Davis, *FDR: Into the Storm, 1937–1940; A History* (1993). A useful brief survey is John E. Wiltz, *From Isolation to War, 1931–1941* (1968). More specialized is Lloyd Gardner, *Economic Aspects of New Deal Diplomacy* (1964). Isolationism is ably handled in Manfred Jonas, *Isolationism in America, 1935–1941* (1966); Thomas Guinsburg, *The Pursuit of Iso-lationism in the United States Senate from Versailles to Pearl Harbor* (1982); and Robert A. Divine, *The Reluctant Belligerent* (1965). Sympathetic to the isolationists is Wayne S. Cole, *Roosevelt and the Isolationists, 1932–1945* (1983), and *Charles A. Lindbergh and the Battle Against American Intervention in World War II* (1974). On the Spanish Civil War see Douglas Little, *Malevolent Neutrality: The United States, Great Britain, and the Origins of the Spanish Civil War* (1985). On East Asia consult Dorothy Borg, *The United States and the Far Eastern Crisis of 1933–1938* (1964); P. W. Schroeder, *The Axis Alliance and Japanese-American Relations, 1941* (1958); and Akira Iriye and Warren Cohen, eds., *American, Chinese, and Japanese Perspectives on Wartime Asia, 1931–49* (1990). Warren F. Kimball analyzes *The Most Unsordid Act: Lend Lease, 1939–1941* (1969). David L. Porter examines *The Seventy-Sixth Congress and World War II, 1939–1940* (1979). The Japanese attack on Pearl Harbor is considered in Gordon W. Prange, *At Dawn We Slept* (1981), and Michael Slackman, *Target: Pearl Harbor* (1990). A provocative analysis of the reasons (or lack of them) for U.S. entry into the conflict is Bruce Russett, *No Clear and Present Danger* (1972). See also Donald Cameron Watt, *How War Came: The Immediate Origins of the Second World War, 1938–1939* (1989).

---

* An asterisk indicates that the document, or an excerpt from it, can be found in Thomas A. Bailey and David M. Kennedy, eds., *The American Spirit: United States History as Seen by Contemporaries*, 9th ed. (Boston: Houghton Mifflin, 1998).

36

****

America in World War II,

1941–1945

******

Never before have we had so little time in which to do so much.

******

Franklin D. Roosevelt, 1942

The Allies Trade Space for Time

The United States was plunged into the inferno of World War II with the most stupefying and humiliating military defeat in its history. In the dismal months that ensued, the democratic world teetered on the edge of disaster.

Japan's fanatics forgot that whoever stabs a king must stab to kill. A wounded but still potent American giant pulled itself out of the mud of Pearl Harbor, grimly determined to avenge the bloody treachery. "Get Japan first" was the cry that rose from millions of infuriated Americans, especially on the Pacific Coast. These outraged souls regarded America's share in the global conflict as a private war of vengeance in the Pacific, with the European front a kind of holding operation.

But Washington, in the so-called ABC-1 agreement with the British, had earlier and wisely adopted the grand strategy of "getting Germany first." If Amer-

ica diverted its main strength to the Pacific, Hitler might crush both the Soviet Union and Britain and then emerge unconquerable in Fortress Europe. But if Germany was knocked out first, the combined Allied forces could be concentrated on Japan, and its daring game of conquest would be up. Meanwhile, just enough American strength would be sent to the Pacific to prevent Japan from digging in too deeply.

The get-Germany-first strategy was the solid foundation on which all American military strategy was built. But it encountered much unwarranted criticism from two-fisted Americans who thirsted for revenge against Japan. Aggrieved protests were also registered by shorthanded American commanders in the Pacific and by Chinese and Australian allies. But President Roosevelt, a competent strategist in his own right, wisely resisted these pressures.

Given time, the Allies seemed bound to triumph. But would they be given time? True, they had on their side the great mass of the world's population, but the wolf is never intimidated by the number of the sheep.

Time, in a sense, was the most needed munition. Expense was no limitation. The overpowering problem confronting America was to retool itself for all-out war production, while praying that the dictators would not meanwhile crush the democracies. Haste was all the more imperative because the highly skilled German scientists might turn up with unbeatable secret weapons, including rocket bombs and perhaps even atomic arms.

America's task was far more complex and backbreaking than during World War I. It had to feed, clothe, and arm itself, as well as transport its forces to regions as far separated as Britain and Burma. More than that, it had to send a vast amount of food and munitions to its hard-pressed allies, who stretched all the way from the USSR to Australia. Could the American people, reputedly "gone soft," measure up to this herculean task? Was democracy "rotten" and "decadent," as the dictators sneeringly proclaimed?

The Shock of War

National unity was no worry, thanks to the electrifying blow by the Japanese at Pearl Harbor. Prewar controversies melted away, while millions of Italian-Americans and German-Americans loyally supported the nation's war program. In contrast to World War I, when the patriotism of millions of immigrants was hotly questioned, World War II actually speeded the assimilation of many ethnic groups into American society. Immigration had been choked off for almost two decades before 1941, and America's ethnic communities were now composed of well-settled members, whose votes were crucial to Franklin Roosevelt's Democratic party. Consequently, there was virtually no governmental witch-hunting of minority groups, as had happened in World War I.

A painful exception was the plight of some 110,000 Japanese-Americans, concentrated on the Pacific Coast (see "Makers of America: The Japanese," pp. 528–529). The Washington top command, fearing that they might act as saboteurs for Japan in case of invasion, forcibly herded them together in internment camps in 1942, though about two-thirds of them were American-born U.S. citizens. This brutal precaution was both unnecessary and unfair, as the loyalty and combat record of Japanese-Americans proved to be admirable. But a wave of post–Pearl Harbor hysteria, backed by the long historical swell of anti-Japanese prejudice on the West Coast, temporarily robbed many Americans of their good sense—and their sense of justice. The internment camps deprived these uprooted Americans of dignity and basic rights; the internees also lost hundreds of millions of dollars in property and forgone earnings. The wartime Supreme Court in 1944 upheld the constitutionality of the Japanese relocation in *Korematsu* v. *U.S.* But more than four decades later, in 1988, the U.S. government officially apologized for its actions and approved the payment of reparations of $20,000 to each camp survivor.

The war prompted other changes in the American mood. Many programs of the once-popular New Deal were wiped out by the conservative Congress elected in 1942, and even President Roosevelt declared in 1943 that "Dr. New Deal" was going into retirement, to be replaced by "Dr. Win-the-War." The era of New Deal reform was over.

World War II was no idealistic crusade, as World War I had been. The Washington government emphasized action rather than propaganda. According to opinion polls during the war, a majority or near-majority of citizens confessed to having "no clear idea what the war is about." All Americans knew was that they had a dirty job on their hands and that the only way out was forward. They went about their bloody task with astonishing efficiency.

Building the War Machine

The war crisis made the drooping American economy snap to attention. Massive military orders—over $100 billion in 1942 alone—almost instantly soaked up the idle industrial capacity of the still-lingering Great Depression. Orchestrated by the War Production Board, American factories poured forth an avalanche of weaponry: 40 billion bullets, 300,000 aircraft, 76,000 ships, 86,000 tanks, and 2.6 million machine guns.

MAKERS OF AMERICA

The Japanese

In 1853 the American commodore Matthew Perry sailed four gunboats into Japan's Uraga Bay and demanded that the nation open itself to diplomatic and commercial exchange with the United States. Within two decades of Perry's arrival, Japan's new "Meiji" government had launched the nation on an ambitious program of industrialization and militarization designed to make it the economic and political equal of the Western powers.

As Japan rapidly modernized, its citizens increasingly took ship for America. A steep land tax drove more than 300,000 Japanese farmers off their land. In 1884 the Meiji government permitted Hawaiian planters to recruit contract laborers from among this displaced population. By the 1890s many Japanese were sailing beyond Hawaii to the ports of Long Beach, San Francisco, and Seattle.

Between 1885 and 1924, roughly 200,000 Japanese migrated to Hawaii, and around 180,000 more ventured to the U.S. mainland. They were a select group: because the Meiji government saw overseas Japanese as representatives of their homeland, it strictly regulated emigration. Thus Japanese immigrants to America arrived with more money and better education than their European counterparts.

Women as well as men migrated. The Japanese government, wanting to avoid the problems of an itinerant bachelor society that it observed among the Chinese in the United States, actively promoted women's migration. Although most Japanese immigrants were young men in their twenties and thirties,

thousands of women also ventured to Hawaii and the mainland as contract laborers or "picture brides," so called because their courtship had consisted exclusively of an exchange of photographs with their prospective husbands.

In Hawaii most Japanese labored on the vast sugar cane plantations. On the mainland they initially found migratory work on the railroads or in fish, fruit, or vegetable canneries. A separate Japanese economy of restaurants, stores, and boardinghouses soon sprang up in cities to serve the immigrants' needs.

From such humble beginnings, many Japanese—particularly those on the Pacific Coast—quickly moved into farming. In the late nineteenth century, the spread of irrigation shifted California

Japanese-American Evacuees, 1942 *This farm family in Los Angeles County was "relocated" shortly after this photograph was taken.*

agriculture from grain to fruits and vegetables, and the invention of the refrigerated railcar opened hungry new markets in the East. The Japanese, with centuries of experience in intensive farming, arrived just in time to take advantage of these developments. By 1940 Japanese farmers produced most of the state's strawberries, beans, and tomatoes.

But the very success of the Japanese proved a lightning rod for trouble. On the West Coast, Japanese immigrants had long endured racist barbs and social segregation. Increasingly, white workers and farmers, jealous of Japanese success, pushed for immigration restrictions. Bowing to this pressure, President Theodore Roosevelt in 1908 negotiated the "Gentlemen's Agreement," under which the Japanese government voluntarily agreed to limit emigration. In 1913 the California legislature denied Japanese immigrants already living in the United States the right to own land.

Discriminated against in their adopted homeland, Japanese immigrants (the "Issei," from the Japanese word for *first*) became more determined than ever that their American-born children (the "Nissei," from the Japanese word for *second*) would succeed. Japanese parents encouraged their children to learn English, to excel in school, and to get a college education. Many Nissei grew up in two worlds, a fact they often recognized by Americanizing their Japanese names. Although education and acculturation did not protect the Nissei from the hysteria of World War II, those assets did give them a springboard to success in the postwar era.

Farmers, too, rolled up their sleeves and increased their output. The armed forces drained the farms of workers, but heavy new investment in agricultural machinery and improved fertilizers more than made up the difference. In 1944 and 1945, blue-jeaned farmers hauled in record-breaking billion-bushel wheat harvests.

These wonders of production also brought economic strains. Full employment and scarce consumer goods fueled a sharp inflationary surge in 1942. The Office of Price Administration eventually brought ascending prices under control with extensive regulations. Rationing held down the consumption of critical goods such as meat and butter, though some "black marketeers" and "meatleggers" cheated the system. The War Labor Board (WLB) imposed ceilings on wage increases.

Labor unions, whose memberships grew from about 10 million to more than 13 million workers during the war, fiercely resented the government-dictated wage ceilings. Despite the no-strike pledges of most major unions, a rash of labor walkouts plagued the war effort. Threats of lost production through strikes became so worrisome that Congress, in June 1943, passed the Smith-Connally Anti-Strike Act, which authorized the federal government to seize and operate tied-up industries. Under the Smith-Connally Act, Washington took over the coal mines and, for a brief period, the railroads. Yet work stoppages accounted for less than 1 percent of the total working hours of the United States' wartime laboring force.

Manpower and Womanpower

The armed services enlisted nearly 15 million men in World War II—and some 216,000 women, who were employed for noncombat duties. Best known of these "women in arms" were the WAACS (army), WAVES (navy), and SPARS (Coast Guard).

Despite draft exemptions for key categories of industrial and agricultural workers, military needs left the nation's farms and factories so drained of personnel that new workers had to be found. An agreement with Mexico in 1942 brought thousands of Mexican agricultural workers, called *braceros*, across the border to harvest the fruit and grain crops of the West. The *bracero* program outlived the war by some twenty years, becoming a fixed feature of the agricultural economy in many western states.

Even more dramatic was the march of women onto the factory floor. More than 6 million women

War Workers   *More than 6 million women—3 million of them homemakers who had never before worked for wages—entered the work force during World War II. In contrast to the experience of women workers in World War I, many of these newly employed women continued as wage workers after the war ended.*

took up jobs outside the home; over half of them had never before worked for wages. Many of them were mothers, and the government was obliged to set up some three thousand day-care centers to care for "Rosie the Riveter's" children while Rosie drilled the fuselage of a heavy bomber or joined the links of a tank track. When the war ended, Rosie and many of her sisters wanted to keep on working and often did. The war thus foreshadowed an eventual revolution in the roles of women in American society.

Yet the war's immediate impact on women's lives has frequently been exaggerated. The great majority of women—especially those with husbands present in the home or with small children to care for—did not work for wages in the wartime economy but continued in their traditional roles. In both Britain and the Soviet Union, a far greater percentage of women were pressed into industrial service as the gods of war laid a much heavier hand on those societies than they did on the United States. The main result of wartime experience for women appeared to be not economic liberation but the postwar rush into suburban domesticity and the mothering of the "baby boomers," who were born by the tens of millions in the decade and a half after 1945. America was destined to experience a revolution in women's status later in the postwar period, but that epochal change was only beginning to gather momentum in the war years.

The war also proved to be a demographic cauldron, churning and shifting the American population. Many of the 15 million men and women in uniform, having seen new sights and glimpsed new horizons, chose not to go home again at war's end. War industries sucked people into boomtowns like Los Angeles, Detroit, Seattle, and Baton Rouge. California's population grew by nearly 2 million. The South experienced especially dramatic changes. The states of the old Confederacy received a disproportionate share of defense contracts, including nearly $6 billion of federally financed industrial facilities. Here were the origins of the postwar blossoming of the "Sunbelt."

Despite this economic stimulus in the South, some 1.6 million blacks left the land of their past enslavement to seek jobs in the war plants of the West and North (see "Makers of America: The Great African-American Migration," pp. 532–533). Forever after, race relations constituted a national, not a regional, issue. Explosive tensions developed over employment, housing, and segregated facilities. Black leader A. Philip Randolph, head of the Brotherhood of Sleeping Car Porters, threatened a massive "Negro March on Washington" in 1941 to demand equal opportunities for blacks in war jobs and in the armed forces. Roosevelt's response was to issue an executive order forbidding discrimination in defense industries. In addition, the president established the Fair Employment Practices Commission (FEPC) to monitor compliance with his edict. Blacks were also drafted into the armed forces, though they were generally assigned to service groups rather than combat units.

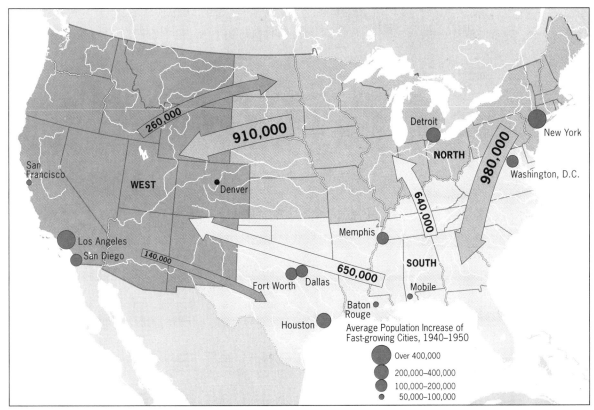

Internal Migration in the United States During World War II   *Few events in American history have moved the American people about so massively as World War II. The West and the South boomed, and several war-industry cities grew explosively. Some 1.3 million migrants from the South were blacks.*

But in general the war helped to embolden blacks in their long struggle for equality. Membership in the National Association for the Advancement of Colored People (NAACP) shot up almost to the half-million mark, and a new militant organization, the Congress of Racial Equality (CORE), was founded in 1942.

The northward migration of African-Americans accelerated after the war, thanks to the advent of the mechanical cotton picker—an invention whose impact rivaled that of Eli Whitney's cotton gin. Overnight, the Cotton South's historic need for cheap labor disappeared. Their muscle no longer required in Dixie, some 5 million black tenant farmers and sharecroppers headed north in the three decades after the war. Within a single generation, a near-majority of African-Americans gave up their historic homeland and their rural way of life. By 1970 half of

all blacks lived outside the South, and *urban* had become almost a synonym for *black*.

The war also prompted an exodus of Native Americans from the reservations. Thousands of Indian men and women found war work in the major cities, and thousands more answered Uncle Sam's call to arms. More than 90 percent of Indians resided on reservations in 1940; four decades later almost half lived in cities.

The sudden rubbing against one another of unfamiliar peoples produced some distressingly violent friction. In 1943 young "zoot-suit"–clad Mexicans and Mexican-Americans in Los Angeles were viciously attacked by Anglo sailors who cruised the streets in taxicabs, searching for victims. At almost the same time, an even more brutal race riot that killed twenty-five blacks and nine whites erupted in Detroit.

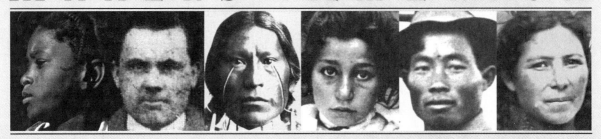

The Great African-American Migration

So many black southerners took to the roads during World War II that local officials could not keep track of the migrants passing through the towns. Black workers on the move—a vast population with no addresses and no telephone numbers—crowded into boardinghouses, camped out in cars, and clustered in the juke joints of roadside America en route to a new, uncertain future in northern and western cities.

Southern cotton fields and tobacco plantations had yielded but slender sustenance to African-American farmers, most of whom labored as tenants and sharecroppers. The Great Depression had been yet another setback, with many tenants evicted from their land as a result of New Deal farm programs that paid farmers to remove land from production. With few other opportunities in the depression-ravaged country, dispossessed former sharecroppers toiled as seasonal farm laborers or found themselves without work, without shelter, and without hope for the future.

The shiny new war plants and busy shipyards of the South offered little solace to African-Americans. In 1940 and 1941, the labor-hungry war machine soaked up white unemployment but commonly denied jobs to southerners with the "wrong" skin color. Fed up with such injustices, many African-Americans headed for shipyards, factories, foundries, and fields north of the Mason-Dixon line, where their willing hands found waiting work in abundance.

Angered by the racism that drove their people from the South, black leaders pressured President Roosevelt into declaring that "there shall be no discrimination in the employment of workers in defense industries or government because of race, creed, color, or national origin." This executive order was but a tenuous, rudimentary step; still, many African-Americans were heartened to see a presidential response to their protests. The war experience emboldened the civil rights movement, adding

Detroit Race Riot, 1943 *A black passenger is dragged from a streetcar.*

momentum and tactical knowledge to the cause. NAACP leader Walter White concluded that the war "immeasurably magnified the Negro's awareness of the disparity between the American profession and practice of democracy."

By war's end, many African-Americans made new homes in the North and Far West, shifting the heart of America's black community from southern plantations to northern cities. There they competed for scarce housing in overcrowded slums and paid outrageous rents to secure a foothold in the few neighborhoods of northern cities that would admit them.

The entire nation was now grappling with the evil of racism, as bloody World War II–era riots in Detroit, New York, and other cities tragically revealed. The trek to northern cities was an economic boon for most African-Americans, but it did not end the intractable national problem of black poverty. Black teenage unemployment, a scourge to this day, dates from World War II. Southern farms, though providing the barest subsistence, had been all too generous in dispensing work to all members of the family—work not so readily found by African-American youth in today's decaying northern cities.

Holding the Home Front

Despite these ugly episodes, Americans on the home front suffered little from the war, compared with the peoples of the other fighting nations. By war's end much of the planet was a smoking ruin. But in America the war invigorated the economy and lifted the country out of a decade-long depression. The gross national product vaulted from less than $100 billion in 1940 to more than $200 billion in 1945. Corporate profits approximately doubled during the war. Despite wage ceilings, overtime pay fattened pay envelopes. On December 7, 1944, the third anniversary of Pearl Harbor, Macy's department store rang up the biggest sales day in its history. Americans had never had it so good—and they wanted it a lot better.

The hand of government touched more American lives more intimately during the war than ever before. The war, perhaps even more than the New Deal, pointed the way to the post-1945 era of big-government interventionism. Millions of men and women worked for Uncle Sam in the armed forces or defense industries, and their personal needs were cared for by government-sponsored housing projects, day-care facilities, and health plans. The Office of Scientific Research and Development channeled hundreds of millions of dollars into university-based scientific research, establishing the partnership between the government and universities that underwrote America's technological and economic leadership in the postwar era.

The flood of war dollars—not the relatively modest rivulet of New Deal spending—at last swept the plague of unemployment from the land. War, not enlightened social policy, cured the depression. As the postwar economy continued to depend dangerously on military spending for its health, many observers looked back to the years 1941–1945 and saw the origins of a "warfare-welfare state."

The conflict was phenomenally expensive. The wartime bill amounted to more than $330 billion—ten times the direct cost of World War I and twice as much as *all* previous federal spending since 1776. Despite an expanded income tax and higher tax rates, only about two-fifths of the war costs were paid from current revenues. The remainder was borrowed. The national debt skyrocketed from $49 billion in 1941 to $259 billion in 1945.

The Rising Sun in the Pacific

Early successes of the efficient Japanese militarists were breathtaking: they realized that they would have to win quickly or lose slowly. Simultaneously with the assault on Pearl Harbor, the Japanese launched widespread and uniformly successful attacks on various bastions in the Pacific and East Asia. These included the American outposts of Guam, Wake, and the Philippines, as well as Hong Kong and British Malaya, with its critically important supplies of rubber and tin.

Nor did the Japanese stop there. The soldiers of the emperor, plunging into the snake-infested jungles of Burma, cut the famed Burma road. This was the route over which the United States had been trucking a trickle of munitions to the armies of Jiang Jieshi (Chiang Kai-shek), the Chinese generalissimo who was resisting the Japanese invader in China. Thereafter, intrepid American aviators were forced to fly a handful of war supplies to Jiang "over the hump" of the towering Himalaya Mountains from the India-Burma theater of operations. Meanwhile, the Japanese had lunged southward against the oil-rich Dutch East Indies, which speedily fell to the assailant.

In the Philippines, General Douglas MacArthur's resistance effectively slowed the Japanese advance for five months. Twenty thousand American troops and a larger force of Filipinos withdrew to a strong defensive position at Bataan, near Manila, where they held off violent Japanese attacks until April 9, 1942. The eloquent and egotistical MacArthur himself was ordered to depart secretly for Australia but proclaimed as he departed, "I shall return." The battered remnants of his army were treated with vicious cruelty in the infamous eighty-five-mile Bataan death march to prisoner-of-war camps. The island fortress of Corregidor, in Manila harbor, held out until May 6, 1942, when it surrendered and left Japanese forces in complete control of the Philippine archipelago.

Japan's High Tide at Midway

The aggressive warriors from Japan, making hay while the Rising Sun shone, pushed relentlessly southward. They invaded the turtle-shaped island of New Guinea, north of Australia, and landed on the Solomon Islands, from which they threatened Australia itself. Their onrush was finally checked by a crucial naval battle in the Coral Sea, in May 1942. An American carrier task force, with Australian support, inflicted heavy losses on the victory-flushed Japa-

United States Thrusts in the Pacific, 1942–1945 *American strategists had to choose among four proposed plans for waging the war against Japan:*
1. Defeating the Japanese in China by funneling supplies over the Himalayan "hump" from India
2. Carrying the war into Southeast Asia (a proposal much favored by the British, who could thus regain Singapore)
3. Heavy bombing of Japan from Chinese air bases
4. "Island-hopping" from the South Pacific to within striking distance of the Japanese home islands
The fourth strategy, favored by General Douglas MacArthur, was the one finally emphasized.

nese. For the first time in history, the fighting was all done by carrier-based aircraft.

Japan next undertook to seize Midway Island, more than a thousand miles northwest of Honolulu. From this strategic base, it could launch devastating assaults on Pearl Harbor and perhaps force the weakened American Pacific fleet into destructive combat. A critical naval battle was fought near Midway from June 3 to 6, 1942. Admiral Chester W. Nimitz, a high-grade naval strategist, directed a smaller but skillfully maneuvered carrier force against the powerful invading fleet. The fighting was all done by aircraft, and the Japanese broke off action after losing four vitally important carriers.

Midway was a pivotal victory. Combined with the Battle of Coral Sea, the U.S. success at Midway halted Japan's juggernaut. But the thrust of the Japanese into the eastern Pacific did net them America's fog-girt islands of Kiska and Attu in the Aleutian archipelago, off Alaska. This easy conquest aroused fear of an invasion of the United States from the northwest. Much American strength was consequently diverted to the defense of Alaska.

But the Japanese imperialists, overextended in 1942, suffered from "victory disease." Their appetites were bigger than their stomachs. If they had only dug in and consolidated their gains, they would have been much more difficult to dislodge.

American Leapfrogging Toward Tokyo

Following the heartening victory at Midway, the United States for the first time was able to seize the initiative in the Pacific. In August 1942 American ground forces gained a toehold on Guadalcanal Island, in the Solomons, in an effort to protect the lifeline from America to Australia through the Southwest Pacific. After several desperate sea battles for naval control of the area, the Japanese troops evacuated Guadalcanal in February 1943.

American and Australian forces, under General MacArthur, meanwhile had been hanging on grimly to the southeastern tip of New Guinea, the last buffer protecting Australia. Aided by American naval forces, MacArthur eventually fought his way westward through the tropical jungle hells and completed the conquest of New Guinea by August 1944.

The U.S. Navy, with marines and army divisions doing the meat-grinder fighting, had meanwhile been "leapfrogging" the Japanese islands in the Pacific. Rather than proceed on a broad front and reduce Japanese outposts on their flank, as old-fashioned strategy dictated, the new American strategy of island-hopping called for bypassing the most heavily fortified Japanese posts, capturing nearby islands and setting up airfields on them, and then neutralizing the enemy bases through heavy bombing. Deprived of essential supplies from the homeland, Japan's outposts would slowly wither on the vine—as they did.

With Admiral Nimitz skillfully coordinating the efforts of naval, air, and ground units, the American attacks achieved brilliant success. In May and August 1943, Attu and Kiska in the Aleutians were easily retaken. In November 1943 "Bloody Tarawa" and Makin in the Gilbert Islands fell after suicidal resistance, and key outposts in the Marshall Islands succumbed after savage fighting in January and February 1944. The conquest of Guam and other islands in the Marianas in July and August 1944 provided airfields for America's new B-29 superbombers to carry out round-trip bombing raids on Japan's home islands. With these unsinkable aircraft carriers now available, virtual round-the-clock bombing of Japan began in November 1944.

The Allied Halting of Hitler

Early setbacks for America in the Pacific were paralleled in the Atlantic. Hitler had entered the war with a formidable fleet of ultramodern submarines, which ultimately operated in "wolf packs" with frightful effect. During ten months of 1942 more than five hundred merchant ships were lost. Not until the spring of 1943 did the Allies clearly gain the upper hand against the U-boat.

The turning point of the land-air war against Hitler came late in 1942. The British, who had launched a thousand-plane raid on Cologne in May, were joined by the American air force in cascading bombs on German cities. The Germans under Marshal Erwin Rommel—the "Desert Fox"—had driven eastward across the hot sands of North Africa into Egypt, perilously close to the Suez Canal. A breakthrough would have spelled disaster for the Allies. But late in October 1942, British General Bernard Montgomery delivered a withering attack at El Alamein, west of Cairo. With the aid of several hundred hastily shipped American Sherman tanks, he speedily drove the enemy back to Tunisia, more than 1,000 miles away.

On the Soviet front, the unexpected successes of the red army gave a new lift to the Allied cause. In September 1942 the Russians halted the German steamroller at rubble-bestrewn Stalingrad, graveyard of Hitler's hopes. In November 1942 the resilient Russians unleashed a crushing counteroffensive, which was never seriously reversed. A year later, Stalin had regained about two-thirds of the blood-soaked Soviet Motherland wrested from him by the German invader.

North Africa and Italy

Soviet losses were already staggering in 1942. By war's end, the grave had closed over some 20 million Soviets, and their country had been laid waste. It is small wonder that the Kremlin leaders incessantly clamored for a second front. Many Americans, including FDR, were eager to begin a diversionary invasion of France in 1942 or 1943, because they feared that the

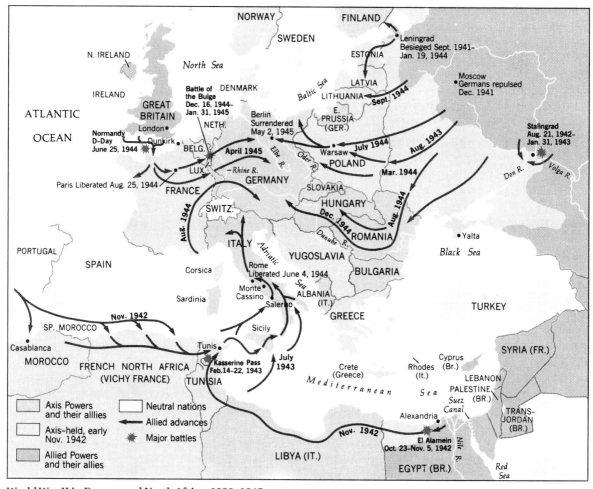

World War II in Europe and North Africa, 1939–1945

Allies Landing in Normandy, June 6, 1944 *Nine-foot ocean swells on invasion day made loading the assault landing craft, such as the one pictured here, treacherous business. Many men were injured or tossed into the sea as the bathtublike amphibious vessels bobbed wildly up and down alongside the troop transports. As the vulnerable boats churned toward the beach, some officers led their tense, grim-faced troops in prayer. One major, recalling the remarkable Battle of Agincourt in 1415, quoted from Shakespeare's* Henry V: *"He that outlives this day, and comes safe home / Will stand a tip-toe when this day is named."*

Soviets might make a separate peace with Hitler. But British military planners, remembering their appalling losses in 1914–1918, were not enthusiastic about a frontal assault on German-held France. It might end in complete disaster. They preferred to attack Hitler's Fortress Europe through the "soft underbelly" of the Mediterranean. Faced with British reluctance, the Americans reluctantly agreed to postpone a massive invasion of Europe.

An invasion of French-held North Africa was a compromise second front. The highly secret attack, launched in November 1942, was headed by a gifted and easy-smiling American general, Dwight D. ("Ike") Eisenhower. The surprise landing in North Africa was highly successful. After savage desert fighting, the remnants of the German-Italian army were finally trapped in Tunisia and surrendered in May 1943.

At Casablanca, in newly occupied French Morocco, President Roosevelt met with Winston Churchill in January 1943 to plan strategy. The "Big Two" agreed to step up the Pacific war, invade Sicily,

increase pressure on Italy, and insist on "unconditional surrender" by the enemy. Designed to reassure the ultrasuspicious Soviets, who professed to fear separate Allied peace negotiations, "unconditional surrender" proved to be one of the most controversial moves of the war. The main criticism was that it steeled the enemy to fight to a last-bunker resistance, and the harsh policy clearly complicated the problems of postwar reconstruction.

Following the Casablanca strategy, American, British, and Canadian forces captured Sicily in August 1943. In September 1943, while Allied troops were pouring onto the toe of the Italian boot, Mussolini was deposed and a new Rome government surrendered unconditionally.

But if Italy dropped out of the war, the Germans did not drop out of Italy. Hitler's well-trained troops resisted the Allied invaders in some of the filthiest, bloodiest, and most frustrating fighting of the war. After a touch-and-go assault on the Anzio beachhead, Rome was finally taken on June 4, 1944. But not until May 2, 1945, only five days before Germany's official surrender, did several hundred thousand Axis troops in Italy lay down their arms and become prisoners of war.

Eisenhower's D-Day Invasion of France

The Soviets never ceased to clamor for an all-out second front. Plans for a major Allied invasion were finally settled at a conference of Stalin, Churchill, and Roosevelt in Teheran, Iran, held from November 28 to December 1, 1943. The Soviets agreed to launch attacks on Germany from the east simultaneously with the prospective Allied assault from the west.

Preparations for the cross-channel invasion of France were gigantic. Britain's fast-anchored isle virtually groaned with munitions, supplies, and troops, as nearly 3 million fighting men were readied. Because the United States was to provide most of the Allied warriors, the overall command was entrusted to an American, General Eisenhower.

French Normandy, less heavily defended than other parts of the European coast, was pinpointed for the invasion assault. On D-Day, June 6, 1944, the enormous operation, which involved some forty-six hundred vessels, unwound. Stiff resistance was encountered from the Germans, who had been mis-led by a feint into expecting the blow to fall farther north.

The Allied beachhead, at first clung to with fingertips, was gradually enlarged, consolidated, and reinforced. After desperate fighting, the invaders finally broke out of the German iron ring that enclosed the Normandy landing zone. Most spectacular were the lunges across France by American armored divisions, brilliantly commanded by blustery and profane General George S. ("Blood 'n' Guts") Patton. The retreat of the German defenders was hastened when an American-French force landed in August 1944 on the southern coast of France and swept northward. With the assistance of the French "underground," Paris was liberated in August 1944.

Allied forces rolled irresistibly toward Germany. The first important German city (Aachen) fell to the Americans in October 1944, and the days of Hitler's "thousand-year Reich" were numbered.

FDR: The Fourth-Termite of 1944

The presidential campaign of 1944 came awkwardly as the awful conflict roared to its climax. Victory-starved Republicans nominated short, mustachioed, and dapper Thomas Dewey, the popular governor of New York. A former prosecutor, Dewey was only forty-two years old, causing one veteran New Dealer to sneer that the candidate had cast his diaper into the ring. To offset Dewey's mild internationalism, the convention nominated for the vice presidency a strong isolationist, Senator John Bricker of Ohio.

FDR, aging under the strain but still the "indispensable man," was nominated by acclamation for a fourth term. The scramble for the vice-presidential plum turned into a free-for-all. Roosevelt's third-term vice president, former agriculture secretary Henry A. Wallace, was a committed liberal who desired renomination. Conservative Democrats developed a "ditch Wallace" movement that gained tremendous momentum and finally won Roosevelt's blessing. The vice-presidential nomination then went to smiling and self-assured Senator Harry S Truman of Missouri, who had recently attained national visibility by conducting an investigation of wasteful war expenditures.

A dynamic Dewey took the offensive in the campaign, proclaiming in his beautiful baritone voice that it was "time for a change" after "twelve long years" of New Dealism. In the closing weeks of the campaign, Roosevelt left his desk for the stump. He was eager to show himself, even in chilling rains, to spike well-founded rumors of failing health.

Democrats relied heavily on the new Political Action Committee of the CIO, which provided union funds and campaign workers. Roosevelt, as customary, won a sweeping victory: 432 to 99 in the Electoral College, 25,606,585 to 22,014,745 in the popular totals. Elated, he quipped that "the first twelve years are the hardest."

The Last Days of Hitler

By mid-December 1944, the month after Roosevelt's fourth-term victory, Germany seemed to be wobbling on its last legs. The Soviet surge had penetrated eastern Germany. Allied aerial "blockbuster" bombs, making the "rubble bounce" with around-the-clock attacks, were falling like giant explosive hailstones on cities, factories, and transportation arteries. The German western front seemed about to buckle under the sledgehammer blows of the United States and its allies.

Hitler then staked everything on one last throw of his reserves. Secretly concentrating a powerful force, he hurled it, on December 16, 1944, against the thinly held American lines in the heavily befogged and snow-shrouded Ardennes Forest. Caught off guard, the outmanned Americans were driven back, creating a deep "bulge" in the Allied line. The ten-day penetration was finally halted after the 101st Airborne Division had stood firm at the vital bastion of Bastogne. The commander, Brigadier General A. C. McAuliffe, defiantly answered the German demand for surrender with one word: "Nuts." Reinforcements were rushed up, and the last-gasp Hitlerian offensive was at length bloodily stemmed in the Battle of the Bulge.

In March 1945, forward-driving American troops reached Germany's Rhine River, where, by incredibly good luck, they found one strategic bridge undemolished. Pressing their advantage, General Eisenhower's troops reached the Elbe River in April

1945. There, a short distance south of Berlin, American and Soviet advance guards dramatically clasped hands.

The conquering Americans were horrified to find blood-bespattered concentration camps, where the German Nazis had engaged in scientific mass murder of "undesirables," including an estimated 6 million Jews. The Washington government had long been informed about Hitler's campaign of genocide against the Jews and had been reprehensibly slow to take steps against it—such as bombing rail lines that carried the victims to the camps. But until the war's end, the full dimensions of the "Holocaust" were not known. When the details were revealed, the whole world was aghast.

The vengeful Soviets, clawing their way forward from the east, reached Berlin in April 1945. After desperate house-to-house fighting, followed by an orgy of pillage and rape, they captured the bomb-shattered city. Adolf Hitler, after a hasty marriage to his mistress, committed suicide in an underground bunker on April 30, 1945.

Tragedy had meanwhile struck the United States. President Roosevelt, while relaxing at Warm Springs, Georgia, suddenly died from a massive cerebral hemorrhage on April 12, 1945. Leaderless citizens discussed the future anxiously, as bewildered, unbriefed Vice President Truman took the helm.

On May 7, 1945, what was left of the German government surrendered unconditionally. May 8 was officially proclaimed V-E Day—Victory in Europe Day—and was greeted with frenzied rejoicing in the Allied countries.

Japan Dies Hard

Japan's rickety bamboo empire meanwhile was tottering to its fall. American submarines—"the silent service"—were sending the Japanese merchant marine to the bottom so fast they were running out of prey. All told, these underseas craft destroyed 1,042 ships, or about 50 percent of Japan's entire life-sustaining merchant fleet.

Giant bomber attacks were more spectacular. Launched from Saipan and other captured Marianas, they were reducing the enemy's fragile cities to cinders. The massive fire-bomb raid on Tokyo, March

9–10, 1945, was annihilating. It destroyed over 250,000 buildings, gutted a quarter of the city, and killed an estimated 83,000 persons—a loss comparable to that later inflicted by atomic bombs.

General MacArthur was also on the move. Completing the conquest of jungle-draped New Guinea, he headed northwest for the Philippines, en route to Japan, with six hundred ships and 250,000 men. In a scene well staged for the photographers, he splashed ashore at Leyte Island, on October 20, 1944. Manila was taken in March 1945, but the Philippines were not finally conquered until July, after bitter fighting against holed-in Japanese, who took a toll of over 60,000 American casualties.

Japan's navy—still menacing—was at last subdued in the gigantic clash at Leyte Gulf (October 23–26, 1944). Japan was through as a sea power. With American fleets now commanding the western Pacific, a steel vise was tightening mercilessly around Japan. In March 1945 the tiny, strategic island of Iwo Jima was captured in a desperate assault that cost over four thousand American dead. The island of Okinawa, well defended by Japanese soldiers fighting with incredible courage from caves, was finally taken in June 1945 after fifty thousand American casualties and far heavier Japanese losses. The American navy, which covered the invasion of Okinawa, sustained severe damage when Japanese suicide pilots began crashing their bomb-laden planes onto the decks of the invading fleet, sinking over thirty ships and damaging scores more.

Atomic Awfulness

Strategists in Washington were meanwhile planning an all-out invasion of the main islands of Japan—an invasion that presumably would cost hundreds of thousands of American (and even more Japanese) casualties. Tokyo, recognizing imminent defeat, had secretly sent peace feelers to Moscow, which had not yet entered the East Asian war. But bomb-scorched Japan still showed no outward willingness to surrender *unconditionally* to the Allies.

The Potsdam conference, held near Berlin in July 1945, sounded the death knell of the Japanese. There President Truman, new on the job, met in a seventeen-day parley with Joseph Stalin and the

British leaders. The conferees issued a stern ultimatum to Japan: surrender or be destroyed. American bombers showered the dire warning on Japan in tens of thousands of leaflets, but no encouraging response was forthcoming.

America had a fantastic ace up its sleeve. Early in 1940, after Hitler's wanton assault on Poland, Roosevelt was persuaded by American and exiled scientists, notably German-born Albert Einstein, to push ahead with preparations for unlocking the secret of an atomic bomb. Congress, at Roosevelt's blank-check request, blindly made available nearly $2 billion.

The huge atomic project was pushed feverishly forward, as American know-how and industrial power were combined with the most advanced scientific knowledge. Much technical skill was provided by British and refugee scientists, who had fled to America to escape the torture chambers of the dictators. Finally, in the desert near Alamogordo, New Mexico, on July 16, 1945, the experts detonated the first awesome and devastating atomic device.

With Japan still refusing to surrender, the Potsdam threat was fulfilled. On August 6, 1945, a lone American bomber dropped one atomic bomb on the military-base city of Hiroshima, Japan. In a blinding flash of death, followed by a mushroom-shaped cloud, about 180,000 persons were left killed, wounded, or missing. Some 70,000 of them died instantaneously. Sixty thousand more soon perished from burns and radiation disease.

Two days later, on August 8, Stalin entered the war against Japan, exactly on the deadline date previously agreed upon with his allies. Soviet armies speedily overran the depleted Japanese defenses in Manchuria and Korea in a six-day "victory parade" that involved several thousand Russian casualties. Stalin was evidently determined to be in on the kill, lest he lose a voice in the final division of Japan's holdings.

Fanatically resisting Japanese, though facing atomization, still did not surrender. American aviators, on August 9, dropped a second atomic bomb on the naval-base city of Nagasaki. The explosion took a horrible toll of about eighty thousand people killed or missing.

At last the Japanese nation could endure no more. On August 10, 1945, Tokyo sued for peace on one condition: that Hirohito, the bespectacled Son of Heaven, be allowed to remain on his throne as nominal emperor. Despite their "unconditional surrender" policy, the Allies accepted this condition on August 14, 1945. The formal surrender took place on the battleship *Missouri* on September 2, 1945.

The Allies Triumphant

World War II proved to be terribly costly. American forces suffered some 1 million casualties, about one-third of which were deaths. Compared with other wars, the proportion killed by wounds and disease was sharply reduced, owing in part to the use of blood plasma and "miracle" drugs, notably penicillin.

America was fortunate in emerging with its mainland virtually unscathed. Much of the rest of the world was utterly destroyed and destitute. America alone was untouched and healthy—oiled and muscled like a prize bull, standing astride the world's ruined landscape.

This complex conflict was the best-fought war in America's history. Though unprepared for it at the

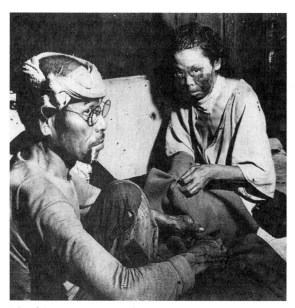

Hiroshima Atomic Bomb Survivors, 1945 *This Japanese man and woman suffered severe burns from the atomic bomb dropped on their city on August 6, 1945.*

outset, the nation was better prepared than for the others, partly because it had begun to buckle on its armor about a year and a half before the war officially began. In the end the United States showed itself to be resourceful, tough, adaptable—able to accommodate itself to the tactics of an enemy who was relentless and ruthless.

American military leadership proved to be of the highest order. A new crop of war heroes emerged in brilliant generals like Eisenhower, MacArthur, and George Marshall (chief of staff) and in imaginative admirals like Nimitz. President Roosevelt and Prime Minister Churchill, kindred spirits, collaborated closely in planning strategy. "It is fun to be in the same decade with you," FDR once cabled Churchill.

Industrial leaders were no less skilled, for marvels of production were performed almost daily. Assembly lines proved as important as battle lines; and victory went again to the side with the most smokestacks. The enemy was almost literally smoth-

ered by bayonets, bullets, bazookas, and bombs. Hitler and his Axis coconspirators had chosen to make war with machines, and the ingenious Yankees could ask for nothing better. They demonstrated again, as they had in World War I, that the American way of war was simply more—more men, more weapons, more machines, more technology, and more money than any enemy could hope to match. From 1940 to 1945, the output of American factories was simply phenomenal.

Hermann Goering, a Nazi leader, had sneered, "The Americans can't build planes—only electric iceboxes and razor blades." Democracy had given its answer, as the dictators, despite long preparation, were overthrown and discredited. It is true that an unusual amount of direct control was exercised over the individual by the Washington authorities during the war emergency. But the American people preserved their precious liberties without serious impairment.

Chronology

1941	Randolph plans black march on Washington. Fair Employment Practices Commission (FEPC) established. The United States declares war on Japan. Germany declares war on the United States.
1942	Japanese-Americans sent to internment camps. Japan conquers the Philippines. Battle of the Coral Sea. Battle of Midway. United States invades North Africa. Congress of Racial Equality (CORE) founded.
1943	Allies hold Casablanca conference. Japanese driven from Guadalcanal. Allies invade Italy. Smith-Connally Anti-Strike Act. "Zoot-suit" riots in Los Angeles. Race riot in Detroit. Teheran conference.
1944	*Korematsu* v. *U.S.* D-Day invasion of France. Battle of Marianas. Roosevelt defeats Dewey for presidency.
1944– 1945	Battle of the Bulge.
1945	Roosevelt dies; Truman assumes presidency. Germany surrenders. Battles of Iwo Jima and Okinawa. Potsdam conference. Atomic bombs dropped on Hiroshima and Nagasaki. Japan surrenders.

varying

viewpoints

World War II: Triumph or Tragedy?

After World War II ended in 1945, many historians were convinced that the tragedy could have been averted if the United States had awakened earlier from its isolationist illusions. These scholars condemned the policies and attitudes of the 1930s as a "retreat from responsibility." Much of the historical writing in the postwar period contained the strong flavor of medicine to ward off another infection by the isolationist virus.

This approach fell into disfavor during the Vietnam War in the 1960s, when many U.S. policymakers defended their actions in Southeast Asia by making dubious comparisons to the decade before World War II. Some scholars responded by arguing that the "lessons" of the 1930s—especially about the need to avoid "appeasement" and to take quick and decisive action against "aggressors"—could not properly be applied to any and all subsequent situations. Ho Chi Minh, they pointed out, was not Hitler, and Vietnam was not Nazi Germany.

Most recent writing has tended to avoid finding lessons for posterity in America's entry into World War II. Attention has focused instead on the wisdom or folly of specific policies, such as Washington's hard line toward Tokyo throughout 1941, when the possibility of a negotiated settlement with Japan perhaps existed. P. W. Schroeder's *The Axis Alliance and Japanese-American Relations, 1941* makes that point with particular force.

No decision of the war era has provoked sharper controversy than the atomic bombings of Japan in August 1945. Lingering moral questions about the nuclear incineration of Hiroshima and Nagasaki have long threatened to tarnish the crown of military victory. America is the only nation ever to use an atomic weapon in war; and some critics have claimed to find elements of racism in the fact that the bombs were dropped on people of a nonwhite race. The fact is, however, that Germany surrendered before the bombs were ready; if the war in Europe had lasted just a few months longer, some German city would probably have suffered the fate of Hiroshima.

Some scholars, notably Gar Alperovitz, have further charged that the atomic holocausts at Hiroshima and Nagasaki were not the last shots of World War II but the first salvos in the emerging Cold War. Alperovitz argues that the Japanese were already defeated in the summer of 1945 and were in fact attempting to arrange a *conditional* surrender. President Truman ignored those attempts and unleashed his horrible new weapons, so the argument goes, not simply to defeat Japan but to frighten the Soviets into submission to America's will and to keep them out of the final stages of the war—and postwar reconstruction—in Asia.

Could the use of the atomic bombs have been avoided? As Martin J. Sherwin's studies have shown, few policymakers at the time seriously asked that question. American leaders wanted to end the war as quickly as possible. Intimidating the Soviets might have been a "bonus" to using the bomb against Japan, but influencing Soviet behavior was never the *primary* reason for the fateful decision. American military strategists had always assumed the atomic bomb would be dropped as soon as it was available. That moment came on August 6, 1945. Yet misgivings and remorse about the atomic conclusion of World War II have plagued the American conscience ever since.

SUGGESTED READINGS

Primary Source Documents

Vivid portraits of the fighting are found in Ernie Pyle, *Here Is Your War* (1943) and *Brave Men* (1944). On the atomic bomb consult the reactions of the *Nippon Times** (August 10, 1945), *The Christian Century** (August 29, 1945), and President Truman's justification of the bombing in *Memoirs of Harry S Truman** (1955).

Secondary Sources

A scholarly discussion of the home front is John M. Blum, *V Was for Victory: Politics and American Culture During World War II* (1976). Consult also Doris Kearns Goodwin, *No Ordinary Time* (1994); William L. O'Neill, *A Democracy at War: America's Fight at Home and Abroad in World War II* (1993); Richard Polenberg, *War and Society: The United States, 1941–1945* (1972); and Harold G. Vatter, *The U.S. Economy in World War II* (1985). Studs Terkel compiled an interesting oral history of the war experience in *The Good War* (1984). On women see Susan M. Hartmann, *The Home Front and Beyond* (1982). On blacks see Neil A. Wynn, *The Afro-Americans and the Second World War* (1976), and Nicholas Lemann, *The Promised Land: The Great Black Migration and How It Changed America* (1991). The military history of the war is capably summarized in H. P. Willmott, *The Great Crusade: A New Complete History of the Second World War* (1990), and in Gerhard Weinberg's massively detailed *A World at Arms* (1994). A good introduction to wartime diplomacy is Gaddis Smith, *American Diplomacy During the Second World War* (1965). More detailed are Herbert Feis's three volumes: *Churchill, Roosevelt,* *Stalin* (2nd ed., 1967), *Between War and Peace: The Potsdam Conference* (1960), and *The Atomic Bomb and the End of World War II* (1966). See also John L. Gaddis, *The United States and the Origins of the Cold War, 1941–1947* (1972), and two "revisionist" studies that are highly critical of American policy: Gabriel Kolko, *The Politics of War: The World and United States Foreign Policy, 1943–1945* (1968), and Lloyd Gardner, *Architects of Illusion: Men and Ideas in American Foreign Policy, 1941–1949* (1970). The war in Asia is covered in Ronald H. Spector's gracefully written *Eagle Against the Sun: The American War with Japan* (1985). John W. Dower explores the racial ideas that underlay the war against Japan in *War Without Mercy: Race and Power in the Pacific War* (1986). Paul Fussell contrasts actual combat and wartime rhetoric in *Wartime: Understanding and Behavior in the Second World War* (1989). On the atomic bomb the most comprehensive account is Richard Rhodes, *The Making of the Atomic Bomb* (1986). Also see Richard G. Hewlett and Oscar E. Anderson, Jr., *The New World* (1962); Martin J. Sherwin, *A World Destroyed: The Atomic Bomb and the Grand Alliance* (1975); and Gar Alperovitz's questionable critique of American nuclear strategy, *Atomic Diplomacy* (rev. ed., 1985). Paul Boyer, *By the Bomb's Early Light* (1985), analyzes the bomb's impact on the American mind.

---

* An asterisk indicates that the document, or an excerpt from it, can be found in Thomas A. Bailey and David M. Kennedy, eds., *The American Spirit: United States History as Seen by Contemporaries*, 9th ed. (Boston: Houghton Mifflin, 1998).

PART SIX

****

Making Modern America

World War II broke the back of the Great Depression in the United States and also ended the century-and-a-half-old American tradition of isolationism in foreign affairs. Alone among the warring powers, the United States managed to emerge from the great conflict physically unscarred, economically healthy, and diplomatically strengthened. Yet if Americans faced a world full of promise at the war's end, it was also a world full of dangers, none more disconcerting than Soviet communism. These two themes of promise and menace mingled uneasily throughout the nearly five decades of the Cold War era, from the end of World War II in 1945 to the collapse of the Soviet Union in 1991.

At home, unprecedented prosperity in the postwar quarter-century nourished a robust sense of national self-confidence and fed a revolution of rising expectations. Invigorated by the prospect of endlessly spreading affluence, Americans in the 1940s, '50s, and '60s had record numbers of babies, aspired to ever-higher standards of living, generously expanded the welfare state (especially for the elderly), widened opportunities for women, welcomed immigrants, and even found the will to grapple at long last with the nation's grossest legacy of injustice, its treatment of African-Americans. With the exception of Dwight Eisenhower's presidency in the 1950s, Americans elected liberal Democratic presidents (Harry Truman in 1948, John F. Kennedy in 1960, and Lyndon Johnson in 1964). The Democratic party, the party of the liberal New Deal at home and of an activist foreign policy abroad, comfortably remained the nation's majority party. Americans trusted their government and had faith in the American dream that their children's lives would be richer than their own lives had been. Anything and everything seemed possible.

The rising curve of expectations, propelled by economic growth, ascended through the 1950s. It peaked in the 1960s, an exceptionally stormy decade during which faith in government, in the wisdom of American foreign policy, and in the American dream itself began to sour. Lyndon Johnson's "Great Society" reforms, billed as the completion of the unfinished work of the New Deal, foundered on the rocks of fiscal limitations and stubborn racial resentments.

Johnson, the most ambitious reformer in the White House since Franklin Roosevelt, eventually saw his presidency destroyed by the furies unleashed over the Vietnam War.

When economic growth flattened in the 1970s, the horizon of hopes for the future seemed to sink as well. The nation entered a frustrating period of stalled expectations, increasingly rancorous racial tensions, disillusion with government, and political stalemate. With the exceptions of Jimmy Carter in the 1970s and Bill Clinton in the 1990s, Americans after 1968 elected conservative Republicans to the White House (Richard Nixon in 1968 and 1972, Ronald Reagan in 1980 and 1984, George Bush in 1988), but they continued to elect Democratic congresses. Yet by the 1990s, a newly invigorated conservative Republican party was bidding to achieve long-term majority status.

Abroad, competition with the Soviet Union, and after 1949 with communist China as well, colored every aspect of America's foreign relations and shaped domestic American life too. Unreasoning fear of communists at home unleashed the destructive force of McCarthyism in the 1950s—a modern-day witch-hunt in which careers were capsized and lives ruined by reckless accusations of communist sympathizing. The FBI encroached on sacred American liberties in its zeal to uncover communist "subversives."

The Cold War remained cold, in the sense that no shooting conflict broke out between the great-power rivals. But the United States did fight two shooting wars, in Korea in the 1950s and in Vietnam in the 1960s. Vietnam, the only foreign war in which the United States was defeated, cruelly convulsed American society, ending not only Lyndon Johnson's presidency but the thirty-five-year era of the Democratic party's political dominance as well. Vietnam also touched off the most vicious inflationary cycle in American history, and it embittered and disillusioned an entire generation.

Uncle Sam in the Cold War era also built a fearsome arsenal of nuclear weapons, great air and missile fleets to deliver them, a two-ocean navy, and, for a time, a large army raised by conscription. Whether the huge expenditures necessary to maintain that gigantic defense establishment stimulated or distorted the economy was a question that remained controversial as the twentieth century came to an end.

37

★★★★★★★★★

The Cold War Begins,

1945–1952

★★★★★★

America stands at this moment at the summit of the world.

★★★★★★

Winston Churchill, 1945

Postwar Economic Anxieties

The American people, 140 million strong, cheered the blinding atomic climax of World War II in 1945. But when the shouting faded away, countless men and women began to worry about their future. Four fiery years of war had not entirely driven from their minds the painful memories of twelve desperate years of the Great Depression.

The decade of the 1930s had left deep scars. Joblessness and insecurity had dampened the marriage rate. Babies went unborn as pinched budgets and sagging self-esteem wrought a sexual depression in American bedrooms. The war had banished the blight of depression, but grim-faced observers warned that peace would bring the return of hard times.

The faltering economy in the initial postwar years threatened to confirm the worst predictions of the doomsayers who foresaw another Great Depression. Real gross national product (GNP) slumped sickeningly in 1946 and 1947 from its wartime peak. With the removal of price controls, prices giddily levitated by 33 percent in 1946–1947. An epidemic of strikes swept the country, as 4.6 million laborers conducted work stoppages during 1946 alone.

The growing muscle of organized labor deeply annoyed many conservatives. They had their revenge against labor's New Deal gains in 1947, when a Republican-controlled Congress (the first in fourteen years) passed the Taft-Hartley Act over President Truman's vigorous veto. Labor leaders condemned the Taft-Hartley Act as a "slave-labor law." It outlawed the "closed" (all-union) shop, made unions liable for damages resulting from jurisdictional disputes, and required union leaders to take a non-Communist oath.

The Democratic administration meanwhile took steps of its own to forestall an economic downturn. It sold war factories and other government

The GI Bill   *Financed by the federal government, thousands of World War II veterans crowded into college classrooms in the 1940s. Here a fresh crop of ex-soldier students lays in supplies for the new term.*

installations to private businesses at fire-sale prices. It secured passage in 1946 of the Employment Act, which created a three-member Council of Economic Advisers to provide the president with data and recommendations to "promote maximum employment, production, and purchasing power."

Most dramatic was the passage of the Serviceman's Readjustment Act of 1944—better known as the GI Bill of Rights, or the GI Bill. Enacted partly out of fear that the employment markets would never be able to absorb 15 million returning veterans at war's end, the GI Bill made generous provisions for sending the former soldiers to school. In the postwar decade, some 8 million veterans advanced their education at Uncle Sam's expense. The majority attended technical and vocational schools, but colleges and universities were crowded to the blackboards as more than 2 million ex-GIs stormed the halls of higher learning. The total eventually spent for education was some $14.5 billion in taxpayer dollars. The act also enabled the Veterans Administration (VA) to guarantee about $16 billion in loans for veterans to buy homes, farms, and small businesses. By raising educational levels and stimulating the construction industry, the GI Bill powerfully nurtured the robust and long-lived economic expansion that eventually took hold in the late 1940s—and that profoundly shaped the entire history of the postwar era.

The Long Economic Boom, 1950–1970

Gross national product began to climb haltingly in 1948. Then, beginning about 1950, the American economy surged onto a dazzling plateau of sustained growth that was to last virtually uninterrupted for two decades. America's economic performance became the envy of the world. National income nearly doubled in the 1950s and almost doubled again in the 1960s, shooting through the trillion-dollar mark in 1973. Americans, some 6 percent of the world's people, were enjoying about 40 percent of the planet's wealth.

As the gusher of prosperity poured forth its riches, Americans drank deeply from the gilded goblet. Millions of depression-pinched souls sought to make up for the sufferings of the 1930s. They determined to "get theirs" while the getting was good. A people who had once considered a chicken in every pot the standard of comfort and security now hungered for two cars in every garage, swimming pools in their backyards, vacation homes, and gas-guzzling recreational vehicles. The size of the "middle class," defined as households earning between $3,000 and $10,000 a year, doubled from pre–Great Depression days and included 60 percent of the American people by the mid-1950s. By the end of that decade, the vast majority of American families owned their own car and washing machine, and nearly 90 percent owned a television set—a gadget invented in the 1920s but virtually unknown until the late 1940s. In another revolution of sweeping consequences, almost 60 percent of American families owned their own homes by 1960, compared with less than 40 percent in the 1920s.

Of all the beneficiaries of postwar prosperity, none reaped greater rewards than women. More than ever, urban offices and shops provided them with a bonanza of employment as the service sector of the economy dramatically outgrew the old industrial and manufacturing sectors. Women accounted for one-quarter of the American work force at the end of World War II, and for nearly half the labor pool five decades later. Yet even as women continued their march into the workplace in the 1940s and 1950s, popular culture glorified the traditional feminine roles of homemaker and mother. The clash between the demands of suburban housewifery and the realities of employment eventually sparked a feminist revolt in the 1960s.

Nothing loomed larger in the history of the post–World War II era than this fantastic eruption of affluence. It did not enrich all Americans, and it did not touch all people evenly, but it transformed the lives of a majority of citizens and molded the agenda of politics and society for at least two generations. What propelled this unprecedented economic explosion?

The Second World War itself provided a powerful stimulus. While other countries had been ravaged by years of fighting, the United States had used the war crisis to fire up its smokeless factories and rebuild its depression-plagued economy. America had almost effortlessly come to dominate the ruined global landscape of the postwar period.

Ominously, much of the glittering prosperity of the 1950s and 1960s rested on the underpinnings of colossal military budgets, leading some critics to speak of a "permanent war economy." The economic upturn of 1950 was fueled by massive appropriations for the Korean War, and defense spending accounted for some 10 percent of the GNP throughout the ensuing decade. Pentagon dollars primed the pumps of high-technology industries such as aerospace, plastics, and electronics, and also financed much of the scientific research and development that spurred the economy.

Cheap energy also fed the economic boom. American and European companies that controlled

Agribusiness *Expensive machinery of the type shown here made most of American agriculture a capital-intensive, phenomenally productive big business by the 1990s—and sounded the death knell for many small-scale family farms.*

the flow of abundant petroleum from the Middle East kept their prices low, and Americans consequently doubled their consumption of the seemingly inexhaustible oil in the quarter-century after the war. Anticipating a limitless future of low-cost fuels, they flung out endless ribbons of highways, installed air conditioning in their homes, and spread electrical cables everywhere to activate the tools of workers on the factory floor.

With the forces of nature increasingly harnessed in their hands, workers chalked up spectacular gains in productivity—the amount of output per hour of work. In the two decades after the outbreak of the Korean War in 1950, productivity increased at an average rate of more than 3 percent per year. Gains in productivity were also enhanced by the rising educational level of the work force. By 1970 nearly 90 percent of the school-age population was enrolled in educational institutions—a dramatic contrast with the opening years of the century, when only half of this age group had attended school. Better educated and better equipped, American workers in 1970 could produce nearly twice as much in an hour's labor as they had done in 1950. Productivity was the key to prosperity. Rising productivity in the 1950s and 1960s virtually doubled the average American's standard of living in the postwar quarter-century.

The Smiling Sunbelt

The convulsive economic changes of the post-1945 period shook and shifted the American people, amplifying the population redistribution set in motion by World War II. As immigrants and westward-trekking pioneers, Americans had always been a people on the move, but they were astonishingly footloose in the postwar years. For some three decades after 1945, an average of 30 million persons changed residences every year. Families especially felt the strain, as distance divided parents from children, and brothers and sisters from one another. One sign of this kind of stress was the phenomenal popularity of advice books on child-rearing, especially Dr. Benjamin Spock's *The Common Sense Book of Baby and Child Care*. First published in 1945, it instructed millions of parents during the ensuing decades in the kind of homely wisdom that was once transmitted

naturally from grandparent to parent, and from parent to child.

Especially striking was the growth of the "Sunbelt"—a fifteen-state area stretching in a smiling crescent from Virginia through Florida and Texas to Arizona and California. This region increased its population at a rate nearly double that of the old industrial zones of the Northeast (the "Frostbelt"). A Niagara of federal dollars accounted for much of the Sunbelt region's new prosperity, even though southern and western politicians led the cry against government spending. By the 1990s the South and West were annually receiving some $125 billion more in federal funds than the Northeast and Midwest. Northeasterners and their allies from the hard-hit region of the Ohio Valley tried to rally political support with the sarcastic slogan "The North shall rise again."

These dramatic shifts of population and wealth further broke the historic grip of the North on the nation's political life. Every occupant of the White House elected from 1964 until the end of the century hailed from the Sunbelt, and the region's congressional representation rose as its population grew. With their devotion to unregulated economic growth, the Sunbelters were redrawing the Republic's political map.

The Rush to the Suburbs

In all regions, America's modern migrants—if they were white—fled from the cities to the burgeoning new suburbs. Government policies encouraged this momentous movement. Federal Housing Authority (FHA) and Veterans Administration (VA) home-loan guarantees made it more economically attractive to own a home in the suburbs than to rent an apartment in the city. Tax deductions for interest payments on home mortgages provided additional financial incentive. And government-built highways that sped commuters from suburban homes to city jobs further facilitated this mass migration. By 1960 one of every four Americans dwelt in suburbia, and the same leafy neighborhoods held more than half the nation's population as the century neared its end.

The construction industry boomed in the 1950s and 1960s to satisfy this demand. Pioneered by innovators such as the Levitt brothers, whose first "Levittown" sprouted on New York's Long Island in the

America on the Move, 1953   *Millions of Americans migrated to the suburbs and the Sunbelt in the years after World War II. Here a new housing development has just opened near Los Angeles.*

1940s, builders developed efficient new techniques for constructing mass-produced housing. Critics wailed about the esthetic monotony of the suburban "tract" developments, but eager home-buyers nevertheless moved into them by the millions.

"White flight" to the green suburbs left the inner cities—especially in the Northeast and Midwest—black, brown, and broke. Migrating blacks from the South filled up the urban neighborhoods abandoned by the departing white middle class. Taxpaying businesses fled with their affluent customers from downtown shops to suburban shopping malls.

The Postwar Baby Boom

Of all the upheavals in postwar America, none was more dramatic than the "baby boom"—the huge leap in the birthrate in the decade and a half after 1945. Confident young men and women tied the nuptial knot in record numbers at war's end and began immediately to fill the nation's empty cradles. They thus touched off a demographic explosion that added more than 50 million bawling babies to the nation's population by the end of the 1950s. The soaring birthrate finally crested in 1957 and was followed by a deepening birth dearth. By 1973 fertility rates had dropped below the point necessary to maintain existing population figures. If the trend persisted, only further immigration would lift the U.S. population above its 1998 level of some 268 million.

This boom-or-bust cycle of births begot a bulging wave along the American population curve. As the oversize postwar generation grew to maturity, it was destined—like the fabled pig passing through the python—to strain and distort many aspects of American life. Elementary-school enrollments, for example, swelled to nearly 34 million pupils in 1970. Then began a steady decline as the onward-marching age group left in its wake closed schools and unemployed teachers.

Truman: The "Gutty" Man from Missouri

Presiding over the opening of the postwar period was the "accidental president"—Harry S Truman. "The moon, the stars, and all the planets" had fallen on him, he remarked when he was called upon to shoulder Roosevelt's awesome burdens of leadership. Trim and owlishly bespectacled, with graying hair and a friendly, toothy grin, Truman was called "the average man's average man." The first president in many years without a college education, he had farmed, served as an artillery officer in France during World War I, and failed as a haberdasher. He then tried his hand at precinct-level Missouri politics, through which he rose from a judgeship to the U.S. Senate. Though a protégé of a notorious political machine in Kansas City, he had managed to keep his own hands clean.

The problems of the postwar period were staggering, and the firm-mouthed new president initially approached his tasks with becoming humility. Gradually gaining confidence to the point of cockiness, he evolved from a shrinking pipsqueak into a scrappy little cuss. A smallish man thrust suddenly into a giant job, Truman permitted designing old associates of the "Missouri gang" to gather around him and, like Grant, was stubbornly loyal to them when they were caught with cream on their whiskers. On occasion, he would send critics hot-tempered and profane "s.o.b." letters. Most troubling, in trying to demonstrate to a skeptical public his decisiveness and power of command, he was inclined to go off half-cocked or stick mulishly to a wrongheaded notion.

But if Truman was sometimes small in the small things, he was often big in the big things. He had down-home authenticity, few pretensions, rock-solid probity, and a lot of that old-fashioned character trait called moxie. Not one to dodge responsibility, he placed a sign on his White House desk that read, "The buck stops here." Among his favorite sayings was, "If you can't stand the heat, get out of the kitchen."

Yalta: Bargain or Betrayal?

Vast and silent, the Soviet Union continued to be the great enigma. The conference in Teheran in 1943,

What Next? 1946 *This cartoon expresses the feeling of many Americans that their new president was overwhelmed, even bamboozled, by his job.*

where Roosevelt had first met Stalin on a man-to-man basis, had done something to clear the air, but much had remained unresolved—especially questions about the postwar fates of Germany, Eastern Europe, and Asia.

A final fateful conference of the "Big Three" had taken place in February 1945 at Yalta. At this former tsarist resort on the relatively warm shores of the Black Sea, Stalin, Churchill, and the fast-failing Roosevelt reached momentous agreements. Stalin agreed that Poland, with revised boundaries, should have a representative government based on free elections—a pledge he soon broke. Bulgaria and Romania were likewise to have free elections—a promise also flouted. The Big Three further announced plans for fashioning a new international peacekeeping organization—the United Nations.

The most controversial decisions at Yalta concerned Moscow's entry into the war against Japan.

Uncertain of the untested atomic bomb, and expecting frightful American casualties in the projected assault on Japan, the Americans were willing to offer inducements to the Soviets to enter the Asian war and pin down Japanese troops in Manchuria and Korea.

Horse trader Stalin was in a position at Yalta to exact a high price. He agreed to attack Japan within three months after the collapse of Germany, and he later redeemed this pledge in full. In return, the Soviets were promised the southern half of Sakhalin Island, Japan's Kurile Islands, and railroad and industrial concessions in China's Manchuria.

As it turned out, Moscow's entry into the war was unnecessary to defeat Japan. Critics quickly charged that Roosevelt's concessions to Stalin at Yalta undermined Jiang Jieshi (Chiang Kai-shek) and contributed to his overthrow by the Chinese communists four years later. Roosevelt's defenders countered that Stalin's mighty red army could have secured much more of China and that the Yalta conference really set limits to his ambitions. Apologists for Roosevelt also noted that Soviet troops had already occupied much of Eastern Europe and a war to throw them out was unthinkable.

The fact is that the Big Three at Yalta were not drafting a comprehensive peace settlement; at most they were sketching general intentions and testing one another's reactions. In the case of Poland, Roosevelt admitted that the Yalta agreement was "so elastic that the Russians can stretch it all the way from Yalta to Washington without ever technically breaking it." More specific understandings among the wartime allies—especially the two emerging superpowers, the United States and the Soviet Union—awaited the arrival of peace.

The United States and the Soviet Union

History provided little hope that the United States and the Soviet Union would reach cordial understandings about the shape of the postwar world. Mutual suspicions were ancient, abundant, and deep. Communism and capitalism were historically hostile social philosophies. The United States had refused officially to recognize the Bolshevik revolutionary government in Moscow until 1933. America had also aroused Soviet suspicions by its delays in opening a second front against Germany, by freezing its ally out of the project to develop atomic weapons, and by abruptly terminating vital lend-lease aid in 1945 and spurning Moscow's plea for a $6 billion reconstruction loan.

Different visions of the postwar world also separated the two superpowers. Stalin aimed above all to guarantee the security of the Soviet Union by establishing friendly governments along its western border, especially in Poland. By maintaining an extensive Soviet sphere of influence in Eastern and Central Europe, the USSR could protect itself and consolidate its revolutionary base as the world's leading communist country.

To many Americans, that "sphere of influence" looked like an ill-gained "empire." They remembered the earlier Bolshevik call for world revolution and doubted whether Stalin's emphasis on "spheres" could be reconciled with Franklin Roosevelt's Wilsonian dream of a decolonized, demilitarized, and democratized world, with a strong international organization to oversee the global peace.

Even the ways in which the United States and the Soviet Union resembled each other were troublesome. Both countries had been largely isolated from world affairs before World War II. Both nations also had a history of conducting a kind of "missionary" diplomacy—of trying to export to all the world the political doctrines precipitated out of their respective revolutionary origins.

Unaccustomed to their great-power roles, America and the USSR suddenly found themselves staring eyeball-to-eyeball over the prostrate body of battered Europe—a Europe that had been the traditional center of international affairs. In these circumstances, some kind of confrontation was virtually unavoidable. In a fateful progression of events, marked often by misperceptions as well as by genuine conflicts of interest, the two powers provoked each other into a tense standoff known as the "Cold War." Enduring four and a half decades, the Cold War not only shaped Soviet-American relations, but overshadowed the entire postwar international order.

Shaping the Postwar World

Despite these obstacles, the United States did manage at war's end to erect some of the structures that would support Roosevelt's vision of an open world. Meeting at Bretton Woods, New Hampshire, in 1944, the Western Allies established the International Monetary Fund (IMF) to encourage world trade and the International Bank for Reconstruction and Development (World Bank) to promote economic growth in war-ravaged and underdeveloped areas. In contrast to its behavior after World War I, the United States took the lead in creating these important international bodies.

Meeting in San Francisco in April 1945, representatives from fifty nations at the United Nations Conference fashioned a charter that strongly resembled the old League of Nations Covenant. It featured a Security Council dominated by the "Big Five" powers (the United States, Britain, the USSR, France, and China), each of whom had the right of veto, and a General Assembly that could be controlled by smaller countries. The U.S. Senate overwhelmingly approved the document on July 28, 1945.

The United Nations had some gratifying initial successes. It helped preserve peace in Iran, Kashmir, and other trouble spots. It played a large role in creating the new Jewish state of Israel. The U.N. Trusteeship Council guided former colonies to independence. Through such arms as UNESCO (United Nations Educational, Scientific, and Cultural Organization), FAO (Food and Agricultural Organization), and WHO (World Health Organization), the U.N. brought benefits to peoples the world over. But it proved far less successful in controlling the fearsome new technology of the atom. The Soviets rejected an American proposal in 1946 for a U.N. agency to prevent the manufacture of nuclear weapons, and the atomic clock therefore ticked ominously on.

The Problem of Germany

Hitler's ruined Reich posed especially thorny problems for all the wartime Allies. They agreed only that the cancer of Nazism had to be cut out of the German body politic, which involved punishing Nazi leaders for war crimes. The Allies tried twenty-two top culprits at Nuremberg, Germany, during 1945–1946 for crimes against the laws of war and humanity. Justice, Nuremberg-style, was harsh. Twelve of the accused Nazis swung from the gallows, and seven were sentenced to long jail terms.

Witnesses for the Prosecution, 1945

Beyond punishing the top Nazis, the Allies could agree on little about postwar Germany. Some American Hitler-haters wanted to deindustrialize Germany, while the Soviets sought to extract enormous reparations from the Germans. Both these desires clashed headlong with the reality that an industrial, healthy German economy was indispensable to the recovery of Europe. The Americans soon came to appreciate that fact, but the fearful Soviets resisted all efforts to revitalize Germany.

Along with Austria, Germany had been divided at war's end into four military occupation zones, each assigned to one of the "Big Four" powers (France, Britain, America, and the USSR). Before long, it was apparent that Germany would remain indefinitely divided. West Germany eventually became an independent country, wedded to the West. East Germany, along with other Soviet-dominated East European countries, became nominally independent "satellite" states bound to the Soviet Union. East Europe virtually disappeared from Western sight behind the "iron curtain" of secrecy and isolation for more than four decades.

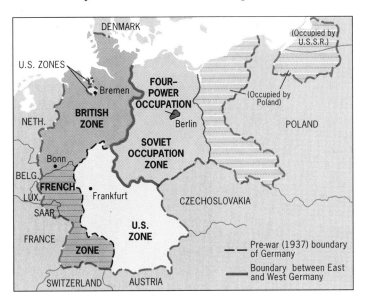

Postwar Partition of Germany

With Germany split in two, there remained the problem of the rubble heap known as Berlin. Lying deep within the Soviet zone (see map above), this beleaguered isle in a red sea had been broken, like Germany as a whole, into sectors occupied by troops of each of the four victorious powers. In 1948 the Soviets abruptly choked off all rail and highway access to Berlin, evidently reasoning that the Allies would be starved out.

Berlin became a hugely symbolic issue for both sides. The Americans organized a gigantic airlift in the midst of hair-trigger tension. For nearly a year American pilots ferried thousands of tons of supplies to the grateful Berliners. The Soviets, their bluff dramatically called, finally lifted their blockade in May 1949. In the same year the governments of the two Germanies, East and West, were formally established. The Cold War had icily congealed.

Crystallizing the Cold War

A crafty Stalin also probed the West's resolve at other sensitive points, including oil-rich Iran. In 1946 he broke an agreement to remove his troops from Iran's northernmost province. Truman sent off a stinging protest, and the Soviet dictator backed down.

Moscow's hard-line policies in Germany, Eastern Europe, and the Middle East wrought a psycho-logical Pearl Harbor. Any remaining goodwill from the period of comradeship-in-arms evaporated in a cloud of dark mistrust. "I'm tired of babying the Soviets," Truman remarked privately in 1946, as attitudes on both sides began to harden frostily.

Truman's piecemeal responses to various Soviet challenges took on intellectual coherence in 1947 with the formulation of the "containment doctrine." Crafted by a brilliant young diplomat and Soviet specialist, George F. Kennan, this concept held that Russia, whether tsarist or communist, was relentlessly expansionary. But the Kremlin was also cautious, Kennan argued, and the flow of Soviet power into "every nook and cranny available to it" could be stemmed by "firm and vigilant commitment."

Kennan's advice seemed to require a globe-girdling strategy of military and political preparedness. Truman embraced this advice when he formally and publicly adopted a "get-tough-with-Russia" policy in 1947. His first dramatic move was triggered by word that heavily burdened Britain could no longer bear the financial and military load of defending Greece against communist pressures. If Greece fell, Turkey would presumably collapse and the strategic eastern Mediterranean would pass into the Soviet orbit.

The president went before Congress on March 12, 1947, and requested support for what came to be known as the Truman Doctrine. Specifically, he asked for $400 million to bolster Greece and Turkey, which Congress quickly granted. More generally, he declared that "it must be the policy of the United States to support free peoples who are resisting attempted subjugation by armed minorities or outside pressures"—a sweeping and open-ended commitment of vast and worrisome proportions. Critics then and later charged that the Truman Doctrine committed the United States to back "anticommunist" despots, needlessly polarized the world into pro-Soviet and pro-American camps, and unwisely construed the Soviet threat as primarily military in nature. Apologists for Truman have explained that it was Truman's fear of a revised isolationism that led him to exaggerate the Soviet threat and to cast his message in the charged language of a holy global war against godless communism—a description of the Cold War that straitjacketed future policymakers who would seek to tone down Soviet-American competition and animosity.

A threat of a different sort loomed in Western Europe—especially France, Italy, and Germany. Still suffering from the hunger and economic chaos spawned by the war, these key nations were in grave danger of being taken over from the inside by Communist parties that could exploit these hardships. Truman responded boldly. On June 5, 1947, Secretary of State George C. Marshall offered American financial assistance for European economic recovery. The democratic nations of Europe enthusiastically accepted the so-called Marshall Plan at a Paris conference in July 1947.

The U.S. Congress at first balked at the Marshall Plan's proposal for spending $12.5 billion over four years in sixteen cooperating countries. But a Soviet-sponsored communist coup in Czechoslovakia finally awakened the legislators to reality, and they voted the initial appropriations in April 1948. Truman's Marshall Plan was a spectacular success. American dollars pumped reviving blood into the economic veins of the anemic Western European nations. Within a few years, an "economic miracle" drenched Europe in prosperity. The Communist parties in Italy and France lost ground, and these two keystone countries were saved from the westward thrust of communism.

A resolute Truman made another fateful decision in 1948. Access to Middle Eastern oil was crucial to European recovery and, increasingly, to the U.S.

economy. Yet the Arab oil countries adamantly opposed the creation of the Jewish state of Israel in the British mandate territory of Palestine. Defying Arab wrath and his own State and Defense departments, Truman officially recognized the state of Israel on May 14, 1948. Truman's policy of strong support for Israel would vastly complicate U.S. relations with the Arab world in the decades ahead.

America Begins to Rearm

The Cold War, the struggle to contain Soviet communism, was not war, yet it was not peace. The standoff with the Kremlin banished the dreams of tax-fatigued Americans that tanks could be beaten into automobiles.

The Soviet menace spurred the unification of the armed services as well as the creation of a huge new national security apparatus. Congress in 1947 passed the National Security Act, creating the Department of Defense. The uniformed heads of each service were brought together as the Joint Chiefs of Staff. The National Security Act also established the National Security Council (NSC) to advise the president on security matters, and the Central Intelligence Agency (CIA) to coordinate the government's foreign fact-gathering. In the same year, Congress resurrected the military draft, providing for the conscription of selected young men from nineteen to twenty-five years of age. The forbidding presence of the Selective Service System played a major role in shaping young people's educational, marital, and career plans in the following quarter-century. One shoe at a time, a war-weary America was reluctantly returning to a war footing.

The Soviet threat was also forcing the United States to join with the divided democracies of Western Europe in a defensive military alliance. On April 4, 1949, twelve nations signed the North Atlantic treaty, which pledged the signatories to regard an attack on one as an attack on all. Over last-ditch isolationist opposition, the U.S. Senate ratified the treaty on July 21, 1949, by a vote of eighty-two to thirteen.

The organization of the North Atlantic Treaty Organization (NATO) marked a dramatic departure from American diplomatic convention and a significant step in the militarization of the Cold War.

NATO became the cornerstone of all Cold War American policy toward Europe. With good reason, pundits summed up NATO's threefold purpose: "to keep the Russians out, the Germans down, and the Americans in."

Reconstruction and Revolution in Asia

Reconstruction in Japan was simpler than in Germany, primarily because it was largely a one-man show. The occupying American army, under General Douglas MacArthur as a kind of Yankee mikado, implemented his program for the democratization of Japan with stunning success. The Japanese saw that good behavior and the adoption of democracy would speed the end of occupation—and it did. A MacArthur-dictated constitution, adopted in 1946, paved the way for a phenomenal economic recovery that within a few decades made Japan one of the world's mightiest industrial powers.

If Japan was a success story for American policymakers, the opposite was true in China, where a bitter civil war had raged for years between Nationalists and Communists. Washington had halfheartedly supported the Nationalist government of Generalissimo Jiang Jieshi in his struggle with the Communists under Mao Zedong (Mao Tse-tung). But ineptitude and corruption within the generalissimo's regime eroded his people's confidence and enabled the Communist armies to sweep to victory late in 1949. Jiang was forced to flee with the remnants of his force to the island of Taiwan.

The collapse of Nationalist China was a depressing defeat for America and its allies in the Cold War. At one fell swoop nearly one-fourth of the world's population—some 500 million people—was swept into the communist camp. The Republicans charged that President Truman and his British-appearing secretary of state, Dean Acheson, had "lost China." Democrats heatedly replied that when a regime has forfeited the support of its people, no amount of outside help will save it. Truman, the argument ran, did not "lose" China because he never had China to lose.

More bad news came in September 1949, when President Truman shocked the nation by announcing that the Soviets had exploded an atomic bomb—approximately three years earlier than many experts had thought possible. To outpace the Soviets in nuclear weaponry, Truman ordered the development of the "H-bomb" (hydrogen bomb)—a city-smashing device many times more lethal than the atomic bomb. The United States exploded its first hydrogen device on a South Pacific atoll in 1952, despite warnings from some scientists that the H-bomb was so powerful that "it becomes a weapon which in practical effect is almost one of genocide." Not to be outdone, the Soviets exploded their first H-bomb in 1953, and the nuclear arms race entered a perilously competitive cycle. Nuclear "superiority" became a dangerous and elusive dream, as each side tried to outdo the other in the scramble to build more destructive weapons. But if the Cold War were to blaze into a hot war, there might be no world left for the communists to communize or the democracies to democratize: this chilling thought constrained both camps, and peace through mutual terror brought a shaky stability to the superpower standoff.

Ferreting Out Alleged Communists

One of the most active Cold War fronts was at home, where a new anti-red chase was in full cry. In 1947 Truman launched a massive "loyalty" program. A Loyalty Review Board investigated more than 3 million federal employees, some 3,000 of whom either resigned or were dismissed, none under formal indictment.

Individual states likewise became intensely security conscious. Loyalty oaths in increasing numbers were demanded of employees, especially teachers. The gnawing question for many earnest Americans was, Could the nation continue to enjoy traditional freedoms in a Cold War climate?

In 1949 eleven communists were convicted of advocating the overthrow of the American government under the Smith Act of 1940. In 1948 Congressman Richard M. Nixon, a member of the House Un-American Activities Committee (HUAC), led the chase after Alger Hiss, a prominent ex–New Dealer and a distinguished member of the "eastern establishment." Accused of being a communist agent in the 1930s, Hiss dramatically met his chief accuser before the committee and denied everything. But

Ethel and Julius Rosenberg Outside Court, 1951 *The Alger Hiss case and the Rosenberg case became highly emotional symbols of alleged communist subversion in America. Even some people who believed the Rosenbergs guilty of spying for the Soviet Union protested their death sentences, but to no avail.*

Hiss was caught in embarrassing falsehoods, convicted of perjury in 1950, and sentenced to five years in prison.

In February 1950 Senator Joseph R. McCarthy, a Wisconsin Republican, spectacularly charged that there were scores of known communists in the State Department. He proved utterly unable to substantiate his accusation, and many Americans, including President Truman, began to fear that the red-hunt was turning into a witch-hunt. In 1950 Congress passed, over Truman's veto, the McCarran Internal Security Bill, which authorized the president to arrest and detain suspicious persons during an "internal security emergency."

The stunning success of Soviet scientists in developing an atomic bomb was presumably due, at least in part, to the cleverness of communist spies in stealing American secrets. In 1951 two American citizens, Julius and Ethel Rosenberg, were convicted (many felt unfairly) of espionage. Their sensational trial and eventual electrocution in 1953, combined with sympathy for their two orphaned children, began to sour some sober citizens on the excesses of the red-hunters.

Democratic Divisions in 1948

Attacking high prices and "High-Tax Harry" Truman, the Republicans had won control of Congress in the congressional elections of 1946. Their prospects had seldom looked rosier as they gathered in Philadelphia to choose their 1948 presidential candidate. They noisily renominated warmed-over New York governor Thomas E. Dewey, still as debonair as if he had stepped out of a bandbox.

Also gathering in Philadelphia, Democratic politicos looked without enthusiasm on their hand-me-down president and sang "I'm Just Mild About Harry." But their "dump Truman" movement collapsed when war hero Dwight D. Eisenhower refused to be drafted. The peppery president, unwanted but undaunted, was then chosen in the face of vehement opposition by southern delegates. They were alienated by his strong stand in favor of civil rights for blacks, who now mustered many votes in the big-city ghettoes of the North.

Truman's nomination split the party wide open. Embittered southern Democrats from thirteen states, like their "fire-eating" forebears of 1860, met in their own convention, in Birmingham, Alabama, with Confederate flags brashly in evidence. Amid scenes of heated defiance, these "Dixiecrats" nominated Governor J. Strom Thurmond of South Carolina on a States' Rights party ticket.

To add to the confusion within Democratic ranks, former vice president Henry A. Wallace threw his hat into the ring. Having parted company with the administration over its get-tough-with-Russia policy, he was nominated at Philadelphia by the new Progressive party—a bizarre collection of disgruntled former New Dealers, starry-eyed pacifists, well-meaning liberals, and communist-fronters.

Wallace, a vigorous if misguided liberal, assailed Uncle Sam's "dollar imperialism" from the stump. This so-called Pied Piper of the Politburo took an apparently pro-Soviet line that earned him drenchings with rotten eggs in hostile cities. But to many Americans, Wallace raised the only hopeful voice in the deepening gloom of the Cold War.

With the Democrats deeply split three ways and the Republican congressional victory of 1946 just past, Dewey's victory seemed assured. Succumbing to overconfidence engendered by his massive lead in public-opinion polls, the cold, smug Dewey confined himself to dispensing soothing-syrup trivialities like "Our future lies before us."

The seemingly doomed Truman, with little money and few active supporters, had to rely on his "gut-fighter" instincts and folksy personality. Traveling the country by train to deliver some three hundred "give 'em hell" speeches, he lashed out at the Taft-Hartley "slave labor" law and the "do-nothing" Republican Congress while whipping up support for his program of civil rights, improved labor benefits, and health insurance. "Pour it on 'em, Harry!" cried increasingly large and enthusiastic crowds as the pugnacious president rained a barrage of verbal uppercuts on his opponent.

On election night the *Chicago Tribune* ran off an early edition with the headline "DEWEY DEFEATS TRUMAN." But in the morning it turned out that "President" Dewey had embarrassingly snatched defeat from the jaws of victory. Truman had swept to a stunning triumph, to the complete bewilderment of politicians, pollsters, prophets, and pundits. Even though Thurmond took away 39 electoral votes in the South, Truman won 303 electoral votes, primarily from the South, Midwest, and West. Dewey's 189 electoral votes came principally from the East. The popular vote was 24,179,345 for Truman, 21,991,291 for Dewey, 1,176,125 for Thurmond, and 1,157,326 for Wallace. To make the victory sweeter, the Democrats regained control of Congress as well.

Truman's victory rested on farmers, workers, and blacks, all of whom were Republican-wary. Republican overconfidence and Truman's lone-wolf, never-say-die campaign also won him the support of many Americans who admired his "guts." No one wanted him, someone remarked, except the people.

Smilingly confident, Truman sounded a clarion note, in the fourth point of his inaugural address, when he called for a "bold new program" ("Point Four"). The plan was to lend U.S. money and technical aid to underdeveloped lands to help them help themselves. Truman wanted to spend millions to keep underprivileged peoples from becoming communists rather than to spend billions to shoot them after they had become communists. This farseeing program was officially launched in 1950, and it brought badly needed assistance to impoverished countries, notably in Latin America, Africa, the Middle East, and East Asia.

At home, Truman outlined a sweeping "Fair Deal" program in his 1949 message to Congress. It called for badly needed housing, full employment, a higher minimum wage, better farm price supports, new TVAs, and an extension of Social Security. But most of the Fair Deal fell victim to congressional opposition from Republicans and southern Democrats. The only major successes came in raising the minimum wage, providing for public housing in the Housing Act of 1949, and extending old-age insurance to many more beneficiaries in the Social Security Act of 1950.

The Korean Volcano Erupts (1950)

Korea, "Land of the Morning Calm," heralded a new and more ominous phase of the Cold War—a shooting phase—in June 1950. When Japan collapsed in 1945, Soviet troops had accepted the Japanese surrender north of the thirty-eighth parallel on the Korean peninsula, and American troops had done likewise south of that line. Both superpowers professed to want reunification of Korea, but, as in Germany, each helped to set up rival regimes above and below the parallel. When the Soviets and Americans withdrew in 1949, the entire peninsula was a bristling armed camp.

Secretary of State Acheson seemed to wash his hands of the dispute early in 1950, when he declared that Korea was outside the essential United States defense perimeter in the Pacific. But when North Korean army columns rumbled across the thirty-eighth parallel on June 25, 1950, and shoved the South Koreans southward into a tiny defensive area around Pusan, President Truman sprang quickly into the breach. The invasion seemed to provide devastating proof of a fundamental premise in the "containment doctrine" that shaped Washington's foreign policy: that even a slight relaxation of America's guard was an invitation to communist aggression somewhere.

The Korean invasion also provided the occasion for a vast expansion of the American military. Truman's National Security Council had recommended in a document of 1950 (known as National Security Council Memorandum Number 68, or NSC-68) that the United States should quadruple defense spending. Buried at the time, NSC-68 was resurrected by the Korean crisis. Truman now ordered a massive military buildup, well beyond what was necessary for the immediate purposes of the Korean War. Soon the United States had 3.5 million men under arms and was spending $50 billion per year on the defense budget—some 13 percent of the GNP.

The Military Seesaw in Korea

Rather than fight his way out of the southern Pusan perimeter, MacArthur launched a daring amphibious landing behind the enemy's lines at Inchon. This bold gamble, on September 15, 1950, succeeded brilliantly; within two weeks the North Koreans had scrambled back behind the "sanctuary" of the thirty-eighth parallel. Truman's avowed intention was to restore South Korea to its former borders, but the pursuing South Koreans had already crossed the thirty-eighth parallel, and there seemed little point in permitting the North Koreans to regroup and come again. The U.N. Assembly tacitly authorized a crossing by MacArthur, whom President Truman ordered northward, provided that there was no intervention in force by the Chinese or Soviets.

The Americans thus raised the stakes in Korea, and in so doing they quickened the fears of another potential player in this dangerous game. The Chinese communists had publicly warned that they would not sit idly by and watch hostile troops approach the strategic Yalu River boundary between Korea and China. But MacArthur pooh-poohed all predictions of an effective intervention by the Chinese and reportedly boasted that he would "have the boys home by Christmas."

MacArthur erred badly. In November 1950 hordes of Chinese "volunteers" fell upon his rashly overextended lines and hurled the U.N. forces reeling back down the peninsula. The fighting then sank into

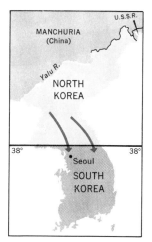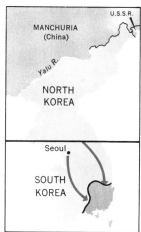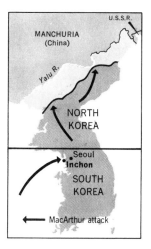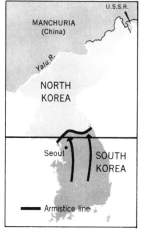

The Shifting Front in Korea

a frostbitten stalemate on the icy terrain near the thirty-eighth parallel.

An imperious MacArthur, humiliated by this rout, pressed for drastic retaliation. He favored a blockade of the China coast and bombardment of Chinese bases in Manchuria. But Washington policymakers, with anxious eyes on Moscow, refused to enlarge the already costly conflict. The chairman of the Joint Chiefs of Staff declared that a wider clash in Asia would be "the wrong war, at the wrong place, at the wrong time, and with the wrong enemy." Europe, not Asia, was the administration's first concern; and the USSR, not China, loomed as the more sinister foe.

Two-fisted General MacArthur felt that he was being asked to fight with one hand tied behind his back. He sneered at the concept of a "limited war" and insisted that "there is no substitute for victory." When the general began to take issue publicly with presidential policies, Truman had no choice but to remove the insubordinate MacArthur from command (April 11, 1951). The imperious war hero, a legend in his own mind, returned to the United States to an uproarious welcome, while Truman was condemned as a "pig," an "imbecile," a "Judas," and an appeaser of "Communist Russia and Communist China."

In July 1951 truce discussions began in a rude field tent near the firing line but were almost immediately snagged on the issue of prisoner exchange. Talks dragged on unproductively for nearly two years— while men continued to die.

Chronology

1944	Servicemen's Readjustment Act (GI Bill). Bretton Woods economic conference.
1945	Spock publishes *The Common Sense Book of Baby and Child Care*. Yalta conference. United Nations established.
1945– 1946	Nuremberg war crimes trials in Germany.
1946	Employment Act creates Council of Economic Advisers. Iran crisis.
1947	Truman Doctrine. Marshall Plan. Taft-Hartley Act. National Security Act creates Department of Defense, National Security Council (NSC), and Central Intelligence Agency (CIA).
1948	United States officially recognizes Israel. Hiss case begins. Truman defeats Dewey for presidency.
1948– 1949	Berlin crisis.
1949	NATO established. Communists defeat Nationalists in China.
1950	American economy begins postwar growth. McCarthy red-hunt begins. McCarran Internal Security Act passed by Congress over Truman's veto.
1950– 1953	Korean War.
1951	Truman fires MacArthur. Rosenbergs convicted of treason.
1952	United States explodes first hydrogen bomb.
1957	Postwar peak of U.S. birthrate.
1973	U.S. birthrate falls below replacement level.

varying

viewpoints

Who Was to Blame for the Cold War?

Whose fault was the Cold War? And, for that matter, who should get credit for ending it? For two decades after World War II, American historians generally agreed that the aggressive Soviets were solely responsible for causing the Cold War. This "orthodox" or "official" appraisal squared with the traditional view of the United States as a virtuous, innocent land with an idealistic foreign policy. This point of view also justified America's Cold War containment policy, which cast the Soviet Union as an aggressor that must be confined by the ever-vigilant United States. America supposedly had only defensive intentions and no expansionary ambitions of its own.

In the 1960s a vigorous revisionist interpretation flowered, powerfully influenced by disillusion over U.S. involvement in Vietnam. The revisionists stood the orthodox view on its head. The Soviets, they argued, had only defensive intentions at the end of World War II; it was the Americans who behaved provocatively by brandishing their new atomic weaponry. Some of these critics pointed an accusing finger at President Truman, alleging that he abandoned Roosevelt's conciliatory approach to the Soviets and adopted a bullying attitude, emboldened by the American atomic monopoly. More radical revisionists like Gabriel and Joyce Kolko even claimed to have found the roots of Truman's alleged belligerence in long-standing American policies of economic imperialism—policies that eventually resulted in the tragedy of Vietnam.

In the 1970s a "postrevisionist" interpretation emerged that is widely agreed upon today. Historians such as John Lewis Gaddis and Melvyn Leffler pooh-pooh the economic determinism of the revisionists while frankly acknowledging that the United States did have vital security interests at stake in the post–World War II era. The postrevisionists analyze the ways in which inherited ideas (like isolationism) and the contentious nature of post–World War II domestic politics, as well as miscalculations by American leaders, led a nation in search of security into seeking not simply a sufficiency but a "preponderance" of power. The American *overreaction* to its security needs, these scholars suggest, exacerbated U.S.-Soviet relations and precipitated the four-decade-long nuclear arms race that formed the centerpiece of the Cold War.

In the case of Vietnam, the postrevisionist historians focus not on economic necessity but on a failure of political intelligence, induced by the stressful conditions of the Cold War, that made the dubious domino theory seem plausible. Misunderstanding Vietnamese intentions, exaggerating Soviet ambitions, and fearing to appear "soft on communism" in the eyes of their domestic political rivals, American leaders plunged into Vietnam, sadly misguided by their own Cold War obsessions. Most postrevisionists, however, still lay the lion's share of the blame for the Cold War on the Soviet Union.

The great unknown, of course, is the precise nature of Soviet thinking in the Cold War years. Were Soviet aims predominantly defensive, or did the Kremlin incessantly plot world conquest? Was there an opportunity for reconciliation with the West following Stalin's death in 1953? Should Mikhail Gorbachev or Ronald Reagan be remembered as the leader who ended the Cold War? With the opening of Soviet archives, scholars are eagerly pursuing answers to such questions.

SUGGESTED READINGS

Primary Source Documents

George F. Kennan's "long telegram," *Foreign Relations of the United States, 1946* (vol. 6, 1969, pp. 696–709),* outlined the containment doctrine that would form the foundation of U.S. foreign policy in the Cold War era. Harry S Truman first applied the containment doctrine when he enunciated the Truman Doctrine, *Congressional Record*, 80 Cong., 1 sess., p. 1981* (1947). On the changing postwar family consult Dr. Benjamin Spock, *Baby and Child Care** (1957).

Secondary Sources

Lucid overviews of the postwar years can be found in James Patterson, *Grand Expectations* (1996); William H. Chafe, *The Unfinished Journey: America Since World War II* (1986); John Patrick Diggins, *The Proud Decades: America in War and Peace, 1941–1960* (1988); and William O'Neill, *American High: The Years of Confidence, 1945–1960* (1986). Harold G. Vatter gives a valuable account of *The United States Economy in the 1950s* (1963). Suburbia is the subject of Kenneth T. Jackson's sweeping synthesis, *Crabgrass Frontier* (1986). On the baby boom and its implications consult Richard A. Easterlin, *Birth and Fortune: The Impact of Numbers on Personal Welfare* (1980); Landon Y. Jones, *Great Expectations: America and the Baby Boom Generation* (1980); and Michael X. Delli Carpini, *Stability and Change in American Politics: The Coming of Age of the Generation of the 1960s* (1986). Mark Silk chronicles the role of organized religion in America since the 1940s in *Spiritual Politics: Religion and America Since World War II* (1988). On the Cold War consult John L. Gaddis, *Strategies of Containment* (1982). For an ambitious revisionist synthesis see Thomas J. McCormick, *America's Half-Century: U.S. Foreign Policy in the Cold War* (1989). Useful surveys of the diplomatic history of the period, all of them in varying degrees critical of American policy, are Stephen Ambrose, *Rise to Globalism: American Foreign Policy Since 1938* (rev. ed., 1983); Walter LaFeber, *America, Russia and the Cold War, 1945–1984* (5th ed., 1985); and Daniel Yergin, *Shattered Peace* (1977). Among the most comprehensive postrevisionist studies is Melvyn P. Leffler, *A Preponderance of Power: National Security, the Truman Administration, and the Cold War* (1992). Korea is discussed in Callum A. MacDonald, *Korea: The War Before Vietnam* (1986); Bruce Cumings, ed., *Child of Conflict: The Korean-American Relationship, 1943–1953* (1983); and Bruce Cumings and Jon Halliday, *Korea: The Unknown War* (1988). On the red scare at home see Richard M. Freeland, *The Truman Doctrine and the Origins of McCarthyism* (1971), as well as David M. Oshinsky, *A Conspiracy So Immense: The World of Joe McCarthy* (1983). Daniel Bell, ed., *The Radical Right* (1963), places McCarthyism in a larger context. Examinations of the impact of the Cold War on American culture include Nora Sayre, *Running Time: The Films of the Cold War* (1982); Nancy Schwartz, *The Hollywood Writers' Wars* (1982); Ellen Schrecker, *No Ivory Tower: McCarthyism and the Universities* (1986); and Richard H. Pells, *The Liberal Mind in a Conservative Age* (1985).

---

*An asterisk indicates that the document, or an excerpt from it, can be found in Thomas A. Bailey and David M. Kennedy, eds., *The American Spirit: United States History as Seen by Contemporaries*, 9th ed. (Boston: Houghton Mifflin, 1998).

38

★★★★★★★★★★

The Eisenhower Era,

1952–1960

★★★★★★

Every warship launched, every rocket fired signified . . . a theft from those who hunger and are not fed, those who are cold and are not clothed.

★★★★★★

Dwight D. Eisenhower, April 16, 1953

The Advent of Eisenhower

Democratic prospects in the presidential election of 1952 were blighted by the military deadlock in Korea, Truman's clash with MacArthur, war-bred inflation, and whiffs of scandal from the White House. Dispirited Democrats, convening in Chicago, nominated a reluctant Adlai E. Stevenson, the witty, eloquent, and idealistic governor of Illinois.

Republicans enthusiastically chose General Dwight D. Eisenhower on the first ballot. As "Ike's" running mate the convention selected California Senator Richard M. Nixon, who had distinguished himself as a relentless red-hunter.

Eisenhower was already the most popular American of his time, as "I Like Ike" buttons everywhere testified. Striking a grandfatherly, nonpartisan pose, Eisenhower left the rough campaigning to

Nixon, who relished pulling no punches. The vice-presidential candidate lambasted his opponents with charges that they had cultivated corruption, caved in on Korea, and coddled communists. He particularly blasted the intellectual ("egghead") Stevenson as "Adlai the appeaser," with a "Ph.D. from [Secretary of State] Dean Acheson's College of Cowardly Communist Containment."

The outcome of the presidential election of 1952 was never really in doubt. Given an extra prod by Eisenhower's last-minute pledge to go personally to Korea to end the war, the voters massively declared for "Ike." He garnered 33,963,234 votes to Stevenson's 27,314,992. He cracked the solid South wide open, ringing up 442 electoral votes to 89 for his opponent. "Ike" not only ran far ahead of his ticket but pulled enough Republicans into office on his military coat-tails to ensure GOP control of the new Congress by a paper-thin margin.

True to his campaign pledge, president-elect Eisenhower undertook a flying three-day visit to Korea in December 1952. But even the shrewd "Ike" could not immediately budge the peace negotiations off dead center. Seven long months later, after Eisenhower had threatened to use atomic weapons, an armistice was finally signed but was repeatedly violated in succeeding decades.

The brutal and futile fighting had lasted three years. About fifty-four thousand Americans lay dead, joined by more than a million Chinese, North Koreans, and South Koreans. Tens of billions of American dollars had been poured down the Asian sinkhole. Yet this terrible toll in blood and treasure bought only a return to the conditions of 1950; Korea remained divided at the thirty-eighth parallel. Americans took what little comfort they could from the fact that communism had been "contained" and that the bloodletting had been "limited" to something less than full-scale global war. The shooting had ended, but the Cold War remained frigidly frozen.

"Ike" Takes Command

In Dwight Eisenhower, the man and the hour apparently met. The nation sorely needed a respite from twenty years of depression and war. Yet the American people in the 1950s unexpectedly found themselves dug into the front lines of the Cold War abroad and dangerously divided at home over the issues of communist subversion and civil rights. They longed for reassuring leadership. "Ike" seemed ready to give it to them.

"Ike" seemed ideally suited to soothe the anxieties of troubled Americans, much as a distinguished and well-loved grandfather brings stability to his family. He played this role well as he presided over a decade of shaky peace and shining prosperity. Yet critics charged that he unwisely hoarded the "asset" of his immense popularity, rather than spend it for a good cause (especially civil rights), and that he cared much more for social harmony than for social justice.

One of the first problems with which Eisenhower had to contend was the swelling popularity and fearful power of Senator Joseph R. McCarthy, the anticommunist "crusader." McCarthy had crashed into the limelight in February 1950, when he charged in a public speech that Secretary of State Dean Acheson was knowingly employing 205 Communist party members in the State Department. Pressed to reveal the names, McCarthy at first conceded that there were only 57 genuine Communists and in the end failed to find even one. His Republican colleagues nevertheless realized the political usefulness of this kind of attack on the Democratic administration. Ohio Senator John Bricker reportedly said, "Joe, you're a dirty s.o.b., but there are times when you've got to have an s.o.b. around, and this is one of them."

Exposing "Reds" *Senator McCarthy makes a point at the army-McCarthy hearings in 1954 while army counsel Joseph Welch ponders a reply. McCarthy declared in a speech in 1951: "Let me assure you that regardless of how high-pitched becomes the squealing and screaming of those left-wing, bleeding-heart, phony liberals, this battle is going to go on."*

McCarthy flourished in the seething Cold War atmosphere of suspicion and fear. He was not the first or even the most effective anti-red, but he was surely the most ruthless, and he did the most damage to American traditions of fair play and free speech.

Politicians trembled in the face of the assaults of "low-blow Joe," especially when opinion polls showed that a majority of the American people approved of McCarthy. Eisenhower privately loathed McCarthy but publicly tried to stay out of his way. Trying to appease the brash demagogue from Wisconsin, Eisenhower allowed him, in effect, to control personnel policy at the State Department. One baleful result was severe damage to the morale and effectiveness of the professional foreign service. In particular, McCarthyite purges deprived the government of a number of Asian specialists who might have counseled a wiser course in Vietnam in the fateful decade that followed.

McCarthy finally bent the bow too far when he attacked the U.S. Army. The embattled military fought back in thirty-five days of televised hearings in the spring of 1954. The political power of the new medium of television was demonstrated as up to 20 million Americans watched in fascination as the boorish, surly McCarthy cut his own throat by parading his essential meanness and irresponsibility. A few months later the Senate condemned him for "conduct unbecoming a member." Three years later McCarthy died unwept and unsung. But "McCarthyism" passed into the English language as a label for the dangerous forces of unfairness and fear that a democratic society can unleash only at its peril.

Desegregating the South

America counted some 15 million black citizens in 1950, two-thirds of whom still made their homes in the South. There they lived bound by the iron folkways of a segregated society. A rigid set of antiquated rules known as "Jim Crow" laws governed all aspects of their existence, from the schoolroom to the restroom.

Blacks everywhere in the South not only attended segregated schools but were compelled to use separate public toilets, drinking fountains, restaurants, and waiting rooms. Trains and buses had "whites only" and "colored only" seating. Only about 20 percent of eligible southern blacks were registered to vote, and fewer than 5 percent in some Deep South states such as Mississippi and Alabama.

Where the law proved insufficient to enforce this regime, vigilante violence did the job. Six black war veterans, claiming the rights for which they had fought overseas, were murdered in the summer of 1946. A Mississippi mob lynched black fourteen-year-old Emmett Till in 1955 for allegedly leering at a white woman. It is small wonder that a black clergyman declared that "everywhere I go in the South the Negro is forced to choose between his hide and his soul."

In his notable book of 1944, *An American Dilemma*, Swedish scholar Gunnar Myrdal had exposed the contradiction between America's professed belief that all men are created equal and its

The Face of Segregation *These women in the segregated South of the 1950s were compelled to enter the movie theater through the "Colored Entrance." Once inside, they were restricted to a separate seating section, usually in the rear of the theater.*

sordid treatment of black citizens. There had been token progress in race relations since the war—Jack Roosevelt ("Jackie") Robinson, for example, had cracked the racial barrier in big-league baseball when the Brooklyn Dodgers signed him in 1947. But for the most part, the national conscience still slumbered, and blacks still suffered.

Increasingly, however, African-Americans refused to suffer in silence. The war had generated a new militancy and restlessness among many members of the black community. The National Association for the Advancement of Colored People (NAACP) had for years pushed doggedly to dismantle the legal underpinnings of segregation and now enjoyed some success. In 1944 the Supreme Court ruled the "white primary" unconstitutional, thereby undermining the status of the Democratic party in the South as a white persons' club. And in 1950, NAACP chief legal counsel Thurgood Marshall (himself later a Supreme Court justice) wrung from the high court a ruling that separate professional schools for blacks failed to meet the test of equality.

On a chilly day in December 1955, Rosa Parks, a college-educated black seamstress, made history in Montgomery, Alabama. She boarded a bus, took a seat in the "whites only" section, and refused to give it up. Her arrest for violating the city's Jim Crow statutes sparked a yearlong black boycott of the city buses and served notice throughout the South that blacks would no longer submit meekly to the absurdities and indignities of segregation.

The Montgomery bus boycott also catapulted to prominence a young pastor at Montgomery's Dexter Avenue Baptist Church, the Reverend Martin Luther King, Jr. Barely twenty-seven years old, King became a champion of the downtrodden and disfranchised. His oratorical skill, his passionate devotion to biblical and constitutional conceptions of justice, and his devotion to the nonviolent principles of India's Mohandas Gandhi thrust him to the forefront of the black revolution that soon pulsed across the South—and across the rest of the nation.

Seeds of the Civil Rights Revolution

In 1946 President Harry Truman commissioned a report on blacks entitled "To Secure These Rights."

Following the report's recommendations, Truman in 1948 ended segregation in federal civil service and ordered "equality of treatment and opportunity" in the armed forces. The military brass at first protested that "the army is not a sociological laboratory," but military manpower shortages in Korea forced the integration of combat units, without the predicted loss of effectiveness.

The judiciary assumed civil rights leadership when Chief Justice Earl Warren, former governor of California, shocked traditionalists with his active judicial intervention in previously taboo social issues. Publicly snubbed and privately criticized by President Dwight Eisenhower, Warren persisted in encouraging the Court to apply his straightforward populist principles to its interpretation of the Constitution: in short, legislation by the judiciary, in default of legislation by Congress.

The unanimous decision of the Warren Court in *Brown* v. *Board of Education of Topeka, Kansas,* in May 1954 was epochal. In a forceful opinion, the learned justices ruled that segregation in the public schools was "inherently unequal" and thus unconstitutional. The uncompromising sweep of the decision startled conservatives like an exploding time bomb, for it reversed the Court's earlier declaration of 1896 in *Plessy* v. *Ferguson* (see p. 338) that "separate but equal" facilities were allowable under the Constitution. That doctrine was now dead. Desegregation, the justices insisted, must go ahead with "all deliberate speed."

The Border States generally made reasonable efforts to comply with this ruling, but in the Deep South diehards organized massive resistance against the Court's attack on the sacred principle of "separate but equal." Several states diverted public funds to hastily created "private" schools, for there the integration order was more difficult to apply. Throughout the South, white citizens' councils, sometimes with fire and rope, thwarted attempts to make integration a reality. Ten years after the Court's momentous ruling, fewer than 2 percent of the eligible blacks in the Deep South states were sitting in classrooms with whites.

Crisis at Little Rock

President Eisenhower was little inclined toward promoting integration. He shied away from employing his vast popularity and the prestige of his office to educate white Americans about the need for racial justice. He had advised against integration of the armed forces in 1948 and criticized Truman's call for a permanent Fair Employment Practices Commission. He complained that the Supreme Court's decision in *Brown* v. *Board of Education* had upset "the customs and convictions of at least two generations of Americans," and he steadfastly refused to issue a public statement endorsing the Court's conclusions. "I do not believe," he explained, "that prejudices, even palpably unjustifiable prejudices, will succumb to compulsion."

But in September 1957 "Ike" was forced to act. Orval Faubus, governor of Arkansas, mobilized the National Guard to prevent nine black students from enrolling in Little Rock's Central High School. Confronted with a direct challenge to federal authority, Eisenhower sent troops to escort the children to their classes.

Blacks meanwhile continued to take the civil rights movement into their own hands. Martin Luther King, Jr., formed the Southern Christian Leadership Conference (SCLC) in 1957. It aimed to mobilize the vast power of black churches on behalf of black rights. The churches were the largest and best-organized black institutions that had been allowed to flourish in a segregated society.

More spontaneous was the "sit-in" movement launched on February 1, 1960, by four black college freshmen in Greensboro, North Carolina. Without a detailed plan or institutional support, they demanded service at a whites-only Woolworth's lunch counter. The following day, eighty-five students joined in; by the end of the week, a thousand. The sit-in movement rolled swiftly across the South, swelling into a wave of wade-ins, lie-ins, and pray-ins to compel equal treatment in restaurants, transportation, employment, housing, and voter registration. In April 1960, southern black students formed the Student Non-Violent Coordinating Committee (SNCC, pronounced "snick") to give more focus and force to these efforts. Young and impassioned, SNCC members would eventually lose patience with the more stately tactics of the SCLC and the even more deliberate legalisms of the NAACP.

Eisenhower Republicanism at Home

Balding, sixty-two-year-old General Eisenhower had entered the White House in 1953 pledging his administration to a philosophy of "dynamic conservatism." Above all, he strove to balance the federal budget and guard the Republic from what he called "creeping socialism." Eisenhower supported the transfer of control over offshore oil fields from the federal

Martin Luther King, Jr., and His Wife, Coretta, Arrested   *King and his wife were arrested for the first time in Montgomery, Alabama, in 1955 while organizing a bus boycott.*

government to the states. "Ike" also tried to curb the TVA by encouraging a private power company to build a generating plant to compete with the massive public utility spawned by the New Deal. His secretary of health, education, and welfare condemned free distribution of Salk antipolio vaccine as "socialized medicine."

Eisenhower responded to the Mexican government's worry that illegal Mexican immigration to the United States would undercut the *bracero* program of legally imported farmworkers inaugurated during World War II (see p. 529). In a massive roundup of illegal aliens, as many as a million Mexicans were apprehended and returned to Mexico in 1954.

In yet another of the rude and arbitrary reversals that have long afflicted the government's relations with Native Americans, Eisenhower sought to cancel the tribal preservation policies of the "Indian New Deal," in place since 1934 (see p. 387). He proposed to "terminate" the tribes as legal entities and to return to the assimilationist goals of the Dawes Severalty Act (see p. 387). But most Indians resisted termination, and the policy was abandoned in 1961.

Eisenhower Republicans obviously could not unscramble all the eggs that had been fried by New Dealers and Fair Dealers for twenty long years. Eisenhower pragmatically accepted and thereby legitimated many New Dealish programs. During his presidency, Social Security benefits were extended and the minimum wage was raised to a dollar an hour. In a public works project that dwarfed anything the New Deal had ever dreamed of, "Ike" backed a $27 billion plan to build forty-two thousand miles of sleek, fast, interstate highways. The construction of these modern, multilane roads created countless construction jobs and speeded the suburbanization of America.

A "New Look" in Foreign Policy

Mere "containment" of communism was condemned in the 1952 Republican platform as "negative, futile and immoral." Incoming Secretary of State John Foster Dulles promised not merely to stem the red tide but to "roll back" its gains and "liberate captive peoples." At the same time, the new administration promised to balance the budget by cutting military spending.

How were these two contradictory goals to be reached? Dulles answered with a "policy of boldness" in early 1954. Genial President Eisenhower would relegate the army and the navy to the back seat and build up an airfleet of superbombers with city-flattening nuclear bombs. These fearsome weapons would be equipped to inflict "massive retaliation" on the Soviets if they got out of hand.

In the end, the touted "new look" in foreign policy proved illusory. In 1956 the Hungarians rose up against their Soviet masters and appealed in vain to the United States for aid. To his dismay, Eisenhower also discovered that the aerial and atomic hardware necessary for "massive retaliation" was also staggeringly expensive. Military costs shot skyward. In 1960, as Eisenhower was about to leave office, he sagely but ironically warned against the dangerous growth of a "military-industrial complex" that his own policies had nurtured.

The Vietnam Nightmare

Europe, thanks to the Marshall Plan and NATO, seemed reasonably secure by the early 1950s, but East Asia was a different can of worms. Nationalist movements had sought for years to throw off the French colonial yoke in Indochina, inspired in part by Woodrow Wilson's doctrine of self-determination and by Franklin Roosevelt's anticolonialism.

Cold War events dampened the dreams of anticolonial Asian peoples. Their leaders—including Ho Chi Minh—became increasingly communist while the United States became increasingly anticommunist. By 1954, American taxpayers were financing nearly 80 percent of the costs of a bottomless French colonial war in Indochina. The United States' share amounted to about $1 billion a year.

Despite this massive aid, French forces continued to crumble under guerrilla insurgency. In March 1954 a key French garrison was trapped hopelessly in the fortress of Dienbienphu. The new "policy of boldness" was now put to the test. Secretary Dulles, Vice President Nixon, and the chairman of the Joint Chiefs of Staff favored intervention with American bombers to help bail out the beleaguered French. But Eisenhower, wary about another war in Asia soon after Korea, held back.

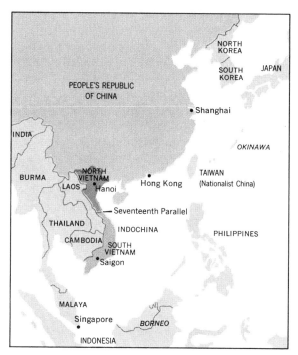

East Asia, 1955–1956

Dienbienphu fell, and a multination conference at Geneva roughly halved Vietnam at the seventeenth parallel, supposedly temporarily. The victorious Ho Chi Minh in the north consented to this arrangement on the assurance that Vietnam-wide elections would be held within two years. In the south a pro-Western government under Ngo Dinh Diem was soon entrenched in Saigon. The Vietnamese never held the promised elections, primarily because the communists seemed certain to win, and Vietnam remained a dangerously divided country.

Eisenhower promised economic and military aid to the conservative Diem regime, provided that it undertook certain social reforms. Change came at a snail's pace, but American aid continued as communist guerrillas heated up their campaign against Diem. The Americans had evidently backed a losing horse but could see no easy way to call off their bet.

Cold War Crises

The United States had initially backed the French in Indochina, in part to win French approval of a plan to rearm West Germany. Despite French fears, the Germans were finally welcomed into the NATO fold in 1955. In the same year, the East European countries and the Soviets signed the Warsaw Pact, creating a red military counterweight to the newly bolstered NATO forces in the West.

Despite these hardening military lines, the Cold War seemed to be thawing a bit in 1955. In May the Soviets rather surprisingly agreed to end their occupation of Austria. A summit conference in Geneva, Switzerland, in July produced little progress on the burning issues, but it bred a conciliatory "spirit of Geneva" that caused a modest blush of optimism to pass over the face of the Western world.

Violent events late in 1956 ended the post-Geneva lull. When the liberty-loving Hungarians struck for their freedom, they were ruthlessly overpowered by Soviet tanks while the Western world looked on in horror.

Fears of Soviet penetration in the Middle East also heightened Cold War tensions. The government of Iran, supposedly influenced by the Kremlin, began to resist the power of the gigantic Western companies that controlled Iranian petroleum. In response, the American Central Intelligence Agency (CIA) engineered a coup in 1953 that installed the youthful shah of Iran as a kind of dictator. Though successful in the short run in securing Iranian oil for the West, the American intervention left a bitter legacy of resentment among many Iranians. More than two decades later, they took their revenge on the shah and his American allies (see p. 609).

The Suez crisis proved far messier than the swift strike in Iran. President Nasser of Egypt, an ardent Arab nationalist, had obtained tentative offers of American and British aid to build a dam on the Nile, but when Nasser began to flirt openly with the communist camp, Secretary of State Dulles dramatically withdrew the dam offer. Nasser promptly regained face by nationalizing the Suez Canal, owned chiefly by British and French stockholders.

Nasser's action placed a razor's edge at the jugular vein of Western Europe's oil supply. America's apprehensive British and French allies, coordinating their blow with one from Israel, staged a joint assault on Egypt late in October 1956. But under sharp pressure from the United States, including a threat to withhold U.S. oil supplies, the allies resentfully withdrew their troops.

The Suez crisis marked the last time in history that the United States could brandish its oil weapon. As recently as 1940, the United States had produced two-thirds of the world's oil, but by 1948 America had become a net oil importer. Its days as an "oil power" clearly were numbered as the economic and strategic importance of the Middle East oil region grew dramatically.

The U.S. president and Congress proclaimed the Eisenhower Doctrine in 1957, pledging U.S. military and economic aid to Middle Eastern nations threatened by communist aggression. The real threat to U.S. interests in the Middle East, however, was not communism but nationalism. The Arab countries increasingly resolved to reap for themselves the lion's share of the enormous oil wealth that Western companies pumped out of the scorching Middle Eastern deserts. In a portentous move, Saudi Arabia, Kuwait, Iraq, and Iran joined with Venezuela to form the Organization of Petroleum Exporting Countries (OPEC). In the next two decades, OPEC's stranglehold on the Western economies would tighten.

Round Two for "Ike"

The election of 1956 was a replay of the 1952 contest, with President Eisenhower again pitted against Adlai Stevenson. Democrats were hard-pressed to find issues with which to attack the popular Eisenhower in a time of peace and general prosperity. The voters gave a resounding endorsement to Eisenhower. He piled up an enormous majority of 35,590,472 to Stevenson's 26,022,752; in the Electoral College the count was 457 to 73. But Eisenhower's victory was a distinctly personal one: he failed to win either house of Congress for his party.

In fragile health, Eisenhower began his second term as a part-time president. Critics charged that he had his hands on his golf clubs, fly rod, and shotgun more often than on the levers of power.

A key area in which the president bestirred himself was labor legislation. Congressional investigations revealed scandalous revelations of gangsterism in high unionist echelons, especially the Teamsters Union. The AFL-CIO had already expelled the Teamsters for choosing leaders like tough-fisted James R. Hoffa, who was later convicted for jury tampering, served part of his sentence, and disappeared—evidently the victim of the gangsters whom he had apparently crossed. Even labor's friends agreed that the house of labor needed a thorough cleaning. Eisenhower persuaded Congress in 1959 to pass the Landrum-Griffin Act, which forced financial reforms in union operations. Anti-laborites managed to make prohibitions against "secondary boycotts" a part of the law as well.

Soviet scientists astounded the world on October 4, 1957, by lofting into orbit around the globe a beep-beeping "baby moon" (*Sputnik I*), weighing 184 pounds. A month later they topped their own ace by sending aloft a larger satellite (*Sputnik II*), weighing 1,120 pounds and carrying a dog. This amazing scientific breakthrough shattered American self-confidence. America had seemingly taken a back seat in scientific achievement. Envious "backward" nations laughed at America's discomfiture, all the more so because the Soviets were occupying outer space while American troops were occupying the high school in Little Rock.

"Rocket fever" swept the nation. After humiliating and well-advertised failures (the Soviets concealed theirs), the Americans regained some prestige four months after the initial Soviet space triumph. They managed to put into orbit a grapefruit-size satellite weighing 2.5 pounds.

The *Sputnik* success led to a critical comparison of the American educational system, already under fire as too easygoing, with that of the Soviet Union. A strong move developed in the United States to replace "frills" with solid subjects—to substitute square roots for square dancing. Congress rejected demands for federal scholarships, but late in 1958 the National Defense and Education Act (NDEA) authorized $887 million for loans to needy college students and grants for the improvement of teaching the sciences and languages.

The Continuing Cold War

The fantastic race toward nuclear annihilation continued unabated. Humanity-minded scientists urged that nuclear tests be stopped before the atmosphere

What's So Funny? 1960   *Premier Khrushchev gloats over "Ike's" spying discomfiture.*

became so polluted as to produce generations of deformed mutants. The Soviets, after completing an intensive series of exceptionally "dirty" tests, proclaimed a suspension in March 1958 and urged the Western world to follow. Beginning in October 1958, Washington did halt both underground and atmospheric testing. But attempts to regularize such suspensions by proper inspection sank on the reef of mutual mistrust.

Thermonuclear suicide seemed nearer in July 1958, when both Egyptian and communist plottings threatened to engulf Western-oriented Lebanon. After its president had called for aid under the Eisenhower Doctrine, the United States boldly landed several thousand troops and helped restore order without taking a single life.

The burly Nikita Khrushchev, Stalin's successor, was eager to meet with Eisenhower and pave the way for a "summit conference" with Western leaders. Since November 1958, Khrushchev had been demanding that the Western powers pull their troops out of West

Berlin within six months. Despite grave misgivings as to any tangible results, the president invited the blustery Soviet leader to America in 1959. Arriving in New York, Khrushchev appeared before the U.N. General Assembly and dramatically resurrected the Soviet proposal of complete disarmament. But he offered no practical means of achieving this end.

A result of this tour was a meeting at Camp David, the presidential retreat in Maryland. Khrushchev emerged saying that his ultimatum for the evacuation of Berlin would be extended indefinitely. The relieved world gave prayerful but premature thanks for the "spirit of Camp David."

The Camp David spirit quickly evaporated when the follow-up Paris "summit conference," scheduled for May 1960, turned out to be a fiasco. Both Moscow and Washington had publicly taken a firm stand on the burning Berlin issue, and neither could risk a public backdown. Then, on the eve of the conference, an American U-2 spy plane was shot down deep in the heart of Russia. After bungling bureaucratic denials in Washington, "honest Ike" took the unprecedented step of assuming personal responsibility. Khrushchev stormed into Paris filling the air with invective, and the conference collapsed before it could get off the ground. The concord of Camp David was replaced with the grapes of wrath.

Cuba's Castroism Spells Communism

Latin Americans bitterly resented Uncle Sam's lavishing of billions of dollars on Europe while doling out only millions to the poor relations to the south. They also chafed at Washington's habit of intervening in Latin American affairs. For example, a CIA-directed coup ousted a leftist government in Guatemala in 1954, but Washington supported bloody dictators who claimed to be combating communists.

Most ominous to U.S. policymakers was the communist beachhead in Cuba. Iron-fisted Cuban dictator Fulgencio Batista had encouraged huge investments of American capital, and Washington had given him some support. But early in 1959 black-bearded Fidel Castro engineered a revolution ousting Batista, denounced the Yankee imperialists, and began to expropriate valuable American properties in pursuing a land-distribution program. Washington, finally losing patience, released Cuba from "imperialistic slavery" by cutting off the heavy U.S. imports of Cuban sugar. Castro retaliated with further wholesale confiscations of Yankee property and in effect made his left-wing dictatorship an economic and military satellite of Moscow. An exodus of anti-Castro Cubans headed for the United States, especially Florida. Nearly 750,000 arrived between 1960 and 1990. Washington broke diplomatic relations with Cuba early in 1961.

Americans talked seriously of invoking the Monroe Doctrine before the Soviets set up a communist base only ninety miles from their shores. Khrushchev angrily proclaimed that the Monroe Doctrine was dead and indicated that he would shower missiles on the United States if it attacked his good friend Castro.

Kennedy Challenges Nixon in 1960

Republicans approached the 1960 presidential campaign with Vice President Richard Nixon as their heir apparent. The "old" Nixon had been a no-holds-barred campaigner, especially in assailing Democrats and left-wingers. The "new" Nixon who appeared in 1960 was represented as a mature, seasoned statesman. Nixon gained stature with his global travels. He was nominated on the first ballot at the Republican

convention in Chicago; his running mate was the patrician Henry Cabot Lodge, Jr., of Massachusetts.

By contrast, the Democratic race for the presidential nomination started as a free-for-all. John F. Kennedy—a tall (6 feet), youthful, dark-haired, and tooth-flashing millionaire senator from Massachusetts—won impressive victories in the primaries. He then scored a first-ballot triumph in Los Angeles over his closest rival, Senator Lyndon B. Johnson, the Senate majority leader from Texas. A disappointed South was not completely appeased when Johnson accepted second place on the ticket.

The Presidential Election of 1960

Bigotry inevitably showed its snarling face. Senator Kennedy was a Roman Catholic, the first to be nominated since Al Smith's ill-starred campaign in 1928. Smear artists revived the ancient charges about the Pope's controlling the White House. Kennedy pointed to his fourteen years of service in Congress, denied that he would be swayed by Rome, and asked if some 40 million Catholic Americans were to be condemned to second-class citizenship from birth.

Kennedy's Catholicism aroused misgivings in the Protestant Bible Belt South, which was ordinarily

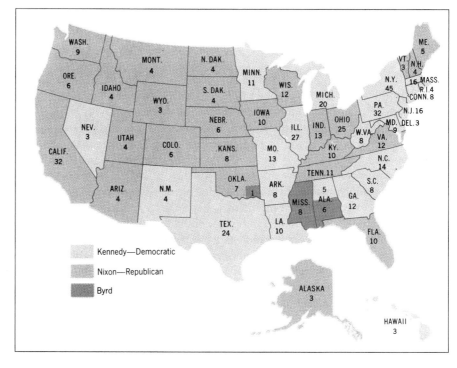

Presidential Election of 1960 (with electoral vote by state) *Kennedy owed his hairbreadth triumph to his victories in twenty-six of the forty largest cities—and to Lyndon Johnson's strenuous campaigning in the South, where Kennedy's Catholic religion may have been a hotter issue than his stand on civil rights.*

Democratic. "I fear Catholicism more than I fear communism," declaimed one Baptist minister in North Carolina. But the religious issue largely canceled itself out. If many southern Democrats stayed away from the polls because of Kennedy's Catholicism, northern Democrats in unusually large numbers supported Kennedy because of the bitter attacks on their Catholic faith.

Kennedy charged that the Soviets, with their nuclear bombs and circling *Sputnik*s, had gained on America in prestige and power. Nixon replied that the nation's prestige had not slipped, although Kennedy was causing it to do so by his unpatriotic talk. A series of television debates between the contestants may have tipped the scales. Many viewers found Kennedy's glamour and vitality far more appealing than Nixon's tired and pallid appearance.

Kennedy squeezed through by the electoral vote margin of 303 to 219, but with a breathtakingly close popular margin of only 118,574 votes out of over 68 million cast. Like Franklin Roosevelt, Kennedy ran well in the large industrial centers, where he had strong support from workers, Catholics, and African-Americans. (He had solicitously telephoned the pregnant Coretta King, whose husband, Martin Luther King, Jr., was then imprisoned in Georgia for participating in a sit-in.) Despite losing a few seats, the Democrats swept both houses of Congress by wide margins.

An Old General Fades Away

President Eisenhower, the aging "dynamic conservative," continued to enjoy extraordinary popularity to the final curtain. Despite Democratic gibes about "eight years of golfing and goofing," of "putting and puttering," Eisenhower was universally admired and respected for his dignity, decency, sincerity, goodwill, and moderation.

Pessimists had predicted that Eisenhower would be a seriously crippled lame duck during his second term, owing to the barrier against reelection erected by the Twenty-second Amendment, ratified in 1951 (see the Appendix). In truth, he displayed more vigor, more political know-how, and more aggressive leadership during his last two years as president than ever before.

America was fabulously prosperous in the Eisenhower years, despite pockets of poverty and unemployment, recurrent recessions, and perennial farm problems. To the north the vast St. Lawrence waterway project, constructed jointly with Canada and completed in 1959, had turned the cities of the Great Lakes into bustling ocean seaports.

"Old Glory" could now proudly display fifty stars. Alaska and Hawaii both attained statehood in 1959. Alaska, though gigantic, was thinly populated and economically underdeveloped, but these objections were overcome in a Democratic Congress that expected Alaska to vote Democratic. Hawaii had ample population (largely of Asian descent), advanced democratic institutions, and more acreage than Rhode Island, Delaware, or Connecticut. As the first noncontiguous states to join the Union, Alaska and Hawaii helped turn America's face toward the Pacific and East Asia.

Though a crusading general, Eisenhower as president mounted no moral crusade for civil rights. This was perhaps his greatest failing. Yet he had done far more than grin away problems and tread water. As a Republican president, he had further woven the reforms of the Democratic New Deal and Fair Deal into the fabric of national life. As a former general, he had exercised wise restraint in his use of military power and had soberly guided foreign policy away from countless threats to peace. He had ended one war and avoided all others. As the decades lengthened, appreciation of him grew.

Changing Economic Patterns

The continuing post–World War II economic boom wrought wondrous changes in American society in the 1950s. Prosperity triggered a fabulous surge in home construction: one of every four homes standing in America in 1960 had been built in the 1950s.

More than ever, science and technology drove economic growth. The invention of the transistor in 1948 sparked a revolution in electronics, especially in computers. The first electronic computers in the 1940s were massive machines, but eventually personal computers contained more computing power than room-size earlier models. Computer giant International Business Machines (IBM) became the prototype "high-tech" corporation in the dawning "information age."

The nature of the work force was also changing. A sort of quiet revolution was marked in 1956, when "white-collar" workers for the first time outnumbered "blue-collar" workers, signaling the passage from an industrial to a postindustrial era. Keeping pace with that fundamental transformation, organized labor withered as a percentage of the labor force, after peaking at about 35 percent in 1954.

The surge in white-collar employment opened special opportunities for women. Postwar culture developed a "cult of domesticity" celebrating the conventional female roles of wife and mother, portrayed on television programs like "Ozzie and Harriet" and "Leave It to Beaver." But it did so without irony. Much of middle-class America really did live in suburban households with a working husband and a wife who did not work outside the home.

But exploding employment opportunities in the 1950s, including 30 million new clerical and service jobs filled largely by women, unleashed a groundswell of social and psychological change that mounted to tidal-wave proportions in the decades that followed. Feminist Betty Friedan gave focus and fuel to women's feelings in 1963 when she published *The Feminine Mystique,* a runaway bestseller and a classic of the modern women's movement. Friedan spoke in rousing accents to millions of able, educated women who were already working for wages but also struggling against the guilt and frustration of trying to live up to the feminine "ideal" as defined by the postwar "cult of domesticity."

Consumer Culture in the Fifties

The 1950s witnessed a huge expansion of the middle class and the blossoming of a consumer culture. Diner's Club introduced the plastic credit card in 1950, and four years later the first McDonald's hamburger stand opened in San Bernardino, California. Also in 1955, Disneyland opened its doors in Anaheim, California. These innovations—easy credit, high-volume "fast-food" production, and new forms of recreation—were harbingers of an emerging new lifestyle of affluence that was in full flower by the decade's end.

Crucial to the development of that lifestyle was the rapid rise of the new technology of television. Only 6 TV stations were broadcasting in 1946; a decade later 442 stations were operating. TV sets were rich people's novelties in the 1940s, but 7 million sets were sold in 1951. By 1960 virtually every American home had one, in a stunning display of the speed with which new technologies can pervade and transform modern societies. By the mid-1950s advertisers

The King   *Rock superstar Elvis Presley greets a group of adoring fans in the 1950s.*

annually spent $10 billion to hawk their wares on television, while critics fumed that the wildly popular new mass medium was degrading the public's esthetic, moral, political, and educational standards.

Even religion capitalized on the powerful new electronic pulpit. "Televangelists" like the Baptist Billy Graham, the Pentecostal preacher Oral Roberts, and the Roman Catholic Fulton J. Sheen took to the airwaves to spread the Christian gospel. Television also catalyzed the commercialization of professional sports, as viewing audiences that once numbered in the stadium-capacity thousands could now be counted in the couch-potato millions.

Sports also reflected the shift in population toward the West and South. In 1958 baseball's New York Giants moved to San Francisco and the Brooklyn Dodgers abandoned Flatbush for Los Angeles. Those moves touched off a new westward movement—of sports franchises. Shifting population and spreading affluence led eventually to substantial expansion of the major baseball leagues and the principal football and basketball leagues as well.

Popular music was also dramatically transformed in the 1950s. The chief revolutionary was Elvis Presley, a white singer born in 1935 in Tupelo, Mississippi. Fusing black rhythm and blues with white bluegrass and country styles, he created a new musical idiom known forever after as rock 'n' roll. Rock was "crossover" music, carrying its heavy beat and driving rhythms across the cultural divide that separated black and white musical traditions. Listening and dancing to it quickly became a kind of religious rite for the millions of baby boomers coming of age in the 1950s.

Traditionalists were repelled by Presley, and they found much more to upset them in the affluent decade. Movie star Marilyn Monroe, with her ingenuous smile and mandolin-curved hips, helped to popularize—and commercialize—new standards of sensuous sexuality. So did *Playboy* magazine, first published in 1955. As the decade closed, Americans were well on their way to becoming free-spending consumers of mass-produced, standardized products advertised on the electronic medium of television and often sold for their alleged sexual allure.

Many critics lamented the implications of this new consumerist lifestyle. Harvard sociologist David Riesman criticized the postwar generation as conformists in *The Lonely Crowd* (1950), as did William H. Whyte, Jr., in *The Organization Man.* Novelist Sloan Wilson explored a similar theme in *The Man in the Gray Flannel Suit* (1955). Harvard economist John Kenneth Galbraith questioned the relation between private wealth and the public good in a series of books beginning with *The Affluent Society* (1958). The postwar explosion of prosperity, Galbraith claimed, had produced a troublesome combination of private opulence amid public squalor. Americans had televisions in their homes but garbage in their streets. They ate rich food but breathed foul air. Galbraith's call for social spending to match private purchasing proved highly influential in the 1960s.

Sociologist Daniel Bell, in *The Coming of Post-Industrial Society* (1973) and *The Cultural Contradictions of Capitalism* (1976), found even deeper paradoxes of prosperity. The hedonistic "consumer ethic" of modern capitalism, he argued, might undermine the older "work ethic" and thus destroy capitalism's very productive capacity. Collusion at the highest level of the military-industrial complex was the subject of *The Power Elite* (1956), an influential piece of modern muckraking by radical sociologist C. Wright Mills, who became a hero to New Left student activists in the 1960s.

The Life of the Mind in Postwar America

America's affluence in the heady post–World War II decades was matched by a mother lode of literary gems. In fiction writing some of the prewar realists continued to ply their trade, notably Ernest Hemingway in *The Old Man and the Sea* (1952). A Nobel laureate in 1954, Hemingway was dead by his own duck gun in 1961. John Steinbeck, another prewar writer who persisted in graphic portrayals of American society, such as *East of Eden* (1952) and *Travels with Charley* (1962), received the Nobel Prize for literature in 1962, the seventh American to be so honored.

Curiously, World War II did not inspire the same kind of literary outpouring as World War I had. Searing realism, the trademark style of war writers in the 1920s, characterized the earliest novels that portrayed soldierly life in World War II, such as Norman

Death of a Salesman   *First performed in 1949, Arthur Miller's play probed the psychic costs of failure in a society that held out the promise of "success" to all. The play especially resonated with audiences in the booming 1950s and quickly took its place as an American classic. This scene shows members of the original Broadway cast—Lee J. Cobb and Mildred Dunnock (seated), Arthur Kennedy (left), and Cameron Mitchell (right), above.*

Mailer's *The Naked and the Dead* (1948) and James Jones's *From Here to Eternity* (1951). But as time passed, realistic writing fell from favor. Authors tended increasingly to write about the war in fantastic and even psychedelic prose. Joseph Heller's *Catch-22* (1961) dealt with the improbable antics and anguish of American airmen in the wartime Mediterranean. A savage satire, it made readers hurt when they laughed.

The dilemmas created by the new mobility and affluence of American life were explored by Pennsylvania-born John Updike in books like *Rabbit, Run* (1960) and *Couples* (1968), and by Massachusetts-bred John Cheever in *The Wapshot Chronicle* (1957) and *The Wapshot Scandal* (1964).

Younger poets were also coming to the fore during the postwar period. Pacific Northwesterner Theodore Roethke wrote lyrically about the land until his death by drowning in Puget Sound in 1963. Robert Lowell, descended from a long line of patrician New Englanders, sought to apply the wisdom of the Puritan past to the perplexing present in allegorical poems like *For the Union Dead* (1964). Troubled Sylvia Plath crafted the moving verses of *Ariel* (published posthumously in 1966) and a disturbing novel, *The Bell-Jar* (1963), but her career was cut short when she took her own life in 1963. Anne Sexton produced brooding autobiographical poems until her death by apparent suicide in 1974. Another brilliant poet of the period, John Berryman, ended it all in 1972 by leaping from a Minneapolis bridge onto the frozen bank of the Mississippi River. Writing poetry seemed to be a dangerous pursuit in modern America. The life of the poet, it was said, began in sadness and ended in madness.

Playwrights were also active. Tennessee Williams wrote a series of searing dramas about psychological misfits struggling to hold themselves together amid the disintegrating forces of modern life. Noteworthy were *A Streetcar Named Desire* (1947) and *Cat on a Hot Tin Roof* (1955). Arthur Miller brought to the stage searching probes of American values, notably *Death of a Salesman* (1949) and *The Crucible* (1953), which treated the Salem witch trials as a dark parable warning against the dangers of McCarthyism. Lorraine Hansberry offered an affecting portrait of African-American life in *A Raisin in the Sun* (1959). In the 1960s Edward Albee exposed the rapacious underside of middle-class life in *Who's Afraid of Virginia Woolf?* (1962).

Books by black authors also made the best-seller lists, beginning with Richard Wright's chilling portrait of a black Chicago killer in *Native Son* (1940). Ralph Ellison depicted the black individual's quest for personal identity in *Invisible Man* (1952), one of the most haunting novels of the postwar era. James Baldwin won plaudits as a novelist and essayist, particularly for his sensitive reflections on the racial question in *The Fire Next Time* (1963). Black nationalist LeRoi Jones, who changed his name to Imamu Amiri Baraka, crafted powerful plays like *Dutchman* (1964).

Many southern writers grasped the torch after William Faulkner died in 1962. Robert Penn Warren immortalized Louisiana politico Huey Long in *All the King's Men* (1946). Flannery O'Connor wrote perceptively of her native Georgia, and Virginian William Styron confronted the harsh history of his home state in a controversial fictional representation of an 1831 slave rebellion, *The Confessions of Nat Turner* (1967).

Especially bountiful was the harvest of books by Jewish novelists. Some critics quipped that a knowledge of Yiddish was becoming necessary to understanding much of the dialogue presented in modern American novels. J. D. Salinger painted an unforgettable portrait of a sensitive, upper-class, Anglo-Saxon adolescent in *Catcher in the Rye* (1951), but other Jewish writers found their favorite subject matter in the experience of lower- and middle-class Jewish immigrants. Bernard Malamud rendered a touching portrait of a family of New York Jewish storekeepers in *The Assistant* (1957). Chicagoan Saul Bellow contributed masterful sketches of Jewish urban and literary life in *The Adventures of Augie March* (1953) and *Herzog* (1962). Bellow became the eighth American Nobel laureate for literature in 1977.

Chronology

1952	Eisenhower defeats Stevenson for presidency.
1953	CIA-engineered coup installs shah of Iran.
1954	French defeated in Vietnam. Army-McCarthy hearings. *Brown* v. *Board of Education*. CIA-sponsored coup in Guatemala.
1955	Montgomery bus boycott begins; emergence of Martin Luther King, Jr. Geneva summit meeting. Warsaw Pact signed. AF of L merges with CIO.
1956	Soviets crush Hungarian revolt. Suez crisis. Eisenhower defeats Stevenson for presidency.
1957	Little Rock school desegregation crisis. Southern Christian Leadership Conference (SCLC) formed. Eisenhower Doctrine. Soviet Union launches *Sputnik* satellite.
1958	U.S. troops sent to Lebanon. NDEA authorizes loans and grants for science and language education.
1958–1959	Berlin crisis.
1959	Castro leads Cuban revolution. Landrum-Griffin Act. Alaska and Hawaii attain statehood.
1960	Sit-in movement for civil rights begins. U-2 incident sabotages Paris summit. Kennedy defeats Nixon for presidency.

SUGGESTED READINGS

Primary Source Documents

Earl Warren's decision in *Brown* v. *Board of Education of Topeka*, 347 U.S. 492–495* (1954), altered the course of race relations in the United States. It also sparked the opposition of one hundred southern congressmen, *Congressional Record*, 84 Cong., 2 sess., pp. 4515–4516* (1956). Eisenhower's Farewell Address* (1961) warned of the dangers of the "military-industrial complex." John Kenneth Galbraith criticized the consumer culture in *The Affluent Society** (1958). Joe McCarthy's vitriol can be found in his *McCarthyism: The Fight for America** (1952).

Secondary Sources

The era is surveyed readably in several works, including those titles by James Patterson, William H. Chafe, John Patrick Diggins, and William O'Neill, cited in Chapter 37. Eisenhower is the subject of Stephen Ambrose's two-volume biography, *Eisenhower: Soldier, General of the Army, President-Elect, 1890–1952* (1983) and *Eisenhower: The President* (1984). See also Jeff Broadwater, *Eisenhower and the Anti-Communist Crusade* (1992). Various aspects of foreign policy are covered in Douglas Brinkley, *Dean Acheson: The Cold War Years* (1992). For background and consequences of the Supreme Court's 1954 desegregation decision see Richard Kluger, *Simple Justice: The History of Brown v. Board of Education* (1976);

Raymond Wolters, *The Burden of Brown: Thirty Years of School Desegregation* (1984); and Robert A. Margo, *Race and Schooling in the South, 1880–1950* (1990). Especially rich are Taylor Branch, *Parting the Waters: America in the King Years, 1954–1963* (1988), and David J. Garrow, *Bearing the Cross: Martin Luther King, Jr., and the Southern Christian Leadership Conference* (1986). The South before the civil rights movement is ably described in John Egerton, *Speak Now Against the Day: The Generation Before the Civil Rights Movement in the South* (1994). On the election of 1960 see Theodore H. White's colorful *The Making of the President, 1960* (1961). For more on cultural developments during the 1950s see Lary May, ed., *Recasting America: Culture and Politics in the Age of the Cold War* (1989); Elaine May, *Homeward Bound: American Families in the Cold War Era* (1988); Tino Balio, ed., *Hollywood in the Age of Television* (1990); David Halberstam, *The Fifties* (1993); Stephen J. Whitfield, *The Culture of the Cold War* (1991); Tom Engelhardt, *The End of Victory Culture* (1995); and Eugenia Kaledin, *Mothers and More: American Women in the 1950s* (1984).

---

*An asterisk indicates that the document, or an excerpt from it, can be found in Thomas A. Bailey and David M. Kennedy, eds., *The American Spirit: United States History as Seen by Contemporaries*, 9th ed. (Boston: Houghton Mifflin, 1998).

39

★★★★★★★★★

The Stormy Sixties,
1960–1968

★★★★★★

*In the final analysis it is their war. They are the ones who
have to win it or lose it . . . the people of Vietnam.*

★★★★★★

JOHN F. KENNEDY, SEPTEMBER 1963

Kennedy's New Frontier

Complacent and comfortable as the 1950s closed, Americans elected in 1960 a young, vigorous president who pledged "to get the country moving again." Neither the nation nor the new president had any inkling, as the new decade opened, of just how action packed it would be both at home and abroad. The 1960s would bring a sexual revolution, a civil rights revolution, the emergence of a youth culture, a devastating war in Vietnam, and the beginnings, at least, of a feminist revolution. By the end of the stormy sixties, many Americans would yearn nostalgically for the comparative calm of the fifties.

Hatless and topcoatless in the 22°F chill, John F. Kennedy delivered a stirring inaugural address on January 20, 1961. Tall, elegantly handsome, speaking crisply and with staccato finger jabs at the air, Kennedy personified the youth, glamour, and vitality of the new administration.

From the outset Kennedy inspired high expectations, especially among the young. His challenge of a "New Frontier" quickened patriotic pulses. He brought a warm heart to the Cold War when he proposed the Peace Corps, an army of idealistic and mostly youthful volunteers, to bring American skills to underdeveloped countries.

Kennedy came into office with fragile Democratic majorities in Congress. Southern Democrats threatened to team up with Republicans and ax New Frontier proposals such as medical assistance for the aged and increased federal aid to education.

Another vexing problem was the economy. Kennedy had campaigned on the theme of revitalizing the economy after the recessions of the Eisenhower years. His administration helped negotiate a noninflationary wage agreement in the steel industry in early 1962. The assumption was that the companies, for their part, would keep the lid on prices. But almost immediately, steel management announced significant price increases, thereby seemingly demonstrating bad faith. The president erupted in wrath, remarking that his father had once said that "all businessmen were sons of bitches." He called the "big steel" men onto the Oval Office carpet and unleashed his Irish temper. Overawed, the steel operators backed down.

The steel episode provoked fiery attacks by big business on the New Frontier, but Kennedy soon appealed to believers in free enterprise when he announced his support of a general tax-cut bill. He chose to stimulate the economy by slashing taxes and putting more money directly into private hands. When he announced his policy before a big-business group, one observer called it "the most Republican speech since McKinley."

Kennedy also promoted a multibillion-dollar project to land an American on the moon. When skeptics objected that the money could best be spent elsewhere, Kennedy "answered" them in a speech at Rice University in Texas: "But why, some say, the moon? . . . And they may well ask, why climb the highest mountain? Why, thirty-five years ago, fly the Atlantic? Why does Rice play Texas?" Twenty-four billion dollars later, in 1969, two American astronauts triumphantly planted human footprints on the moon's dusty surface.

Rumblings in Europe

A few months after settling into the White House, the new president met Premier Nikita Khrushchev at Vienna, in June 1961. The tough-talking Soviet leader adopted a belligerent attitude, threatening to cut off Western access to Berlin. Though visibly shaken, the president refused to be bullied. The Soviets backed off from their most bellicose threats but suddenly began to construct the Berlin Wall in August 1961. A barbed-wire-and-concrete barrier, the "Wall of Shame" looked to the free world like a gigantic enclosure around a concentration camp. The Wall stood for almost three decades as an ugly scar symbolizing the post–World War II division of Europe into two hostile camps.

Kennedy meanwhile turned his attention to Western Europe, now miraculously prospering after

the Marshall Plan and the growth of the Common Market, a trading union of six Western European nations formed in 1957. He finally secured passage of the Trade Expansion Act in 1962, authorizing tariff cuts of up to 50 percent to promote trade with the countries of the Common Market (later called the European Economic Community).

But not all of Kennedy's ambitious designs for Europe were realized. American policymakers were dedicated to an economically and militarily united "Atlantic Community," with the United States the dominant partner. But they found their way blocked by towering, stiff-backed Charles de Gaulle, president of France. De Gaulle deemed the Americans unreliable in a crisis, so he tried to preserve French freedom of action by developing his own small atomic force. Despite the perils of nuclear proliferation or Soviet domination, de Gaulle demanded an independent Europe, free of Yankee influence.

Foreign Flare-ups and "Flexible Response"

Special problems for U.S. foreign policy emerged from the worldwide decolonization of European overseas possessions after World War II. Many of the new nations emerging from once-colonial Asia and Africa were critical of U.S. foreign policy, while some became battlegrounds between the noncommunist and the communist worlds.

Sparsely populated Laos, freed of its French colonial overlords in 1954, was festering dangerously by the time Kennedy came into office. The Eisenhower administration had drenched this jungle kingdom with dollars but failed to cleanse the country of an aggressive communist element. A red Laos, many observers feared, would be a river on which the influence of communist China would flood into all of Southeast Asia.

As the Laotian civil war raged, Kennedy's military advisers seriously considered sending in American troops. But the president found that he had insufficient forces to put out the fire in Asia and still honor his commitments in Europe. Kennedy thus sought a diplomatic escape hatch in the fourteen-power Geneva conference, which imposed a shaky peace in Laos in 1962.

These "brushfire wars" intensified the pressure for a shift away from Secretary Dulles's dubious doctrine of "massive retaliation." Kennedy felt hamstrung by the knowledge that in a crisis he had the Devil's choice between humiliation or nuclear incineration. With Defense Secretary Robert McNamara, he pushed the strategy of "flexible response"—that is, developing an array of military "options" that could be precisely matched to the scope and importance of the crisis at hand. To this end, Kennedy increased spending on conventional military forces and bolstered the Special Forces ("Green Berets")—an elite anti-guerrilla outfit trained to survive on snake meat and to kill with scientific finesse.

Stepping into the Vietnam Quagmire

The doctrine of "flexible response" seemed sane enough, but it contained lethal logic. It potentially lowered the level at which diplomacy would give way to shooting. It also provided a mechanism for a progressive, and possibly endless, stepping-up of the use of force. Vietnam soon presented a grisly demonstration of these pitfalls.

Vietnam and Southeast Asia

The corrupt, right-wing Diem government in Saigon, despite a deluge of American dollars, had ruled shakily since the partition of Vietnam in 1954. Anti-Diem agitation, spearheaded by the local communist Viet Cong and encouraged by the red regime in the north, noisily threatened to topple the pro-American government from power. In a fateful decision late in 1961, Kennedy ordered a sharp increase in the number of "military advisers" (U.S. troops) in South Vietnam.

American forces allegedly entered Vietnam to foster political stability—to help protect Diem from the communists long enough to allow him to enact basic social reforms favored by the Americans. But the Kennedy administration eventually despaired of the reactionary Diem and encouraged a successful coup against him in November 1963. Ironically, the United States thus contributed to a long process of political disintegration that its original policy had meant to prevent. Kennedy still told the South Vietnamese that it was "their war," but he had made dangerously deep political commitments. By the time of his death, he had ordered more than fifteen thousand American men into the far-off Asian slaughterpen. A graceful pullout was becoming increasingly difficult.

"Backbone" *The United States supports South Vietnam.*

Cuban Confrontations

Although the United States regarded Latin America as its backyard, its southern neighbors feared and resented the powerful "Colossus of the North." In 1961 Kennedy extended the hand of friendship with the Alliance for Progress (*Alianza para el Progreso*), hailed as a Marshall Plan for Latin America. But results were disappointing; there was little alliance and even less progress. American handouts had little positive impact on Latin America's immense social problems.

President Kennedy also struck below the border with the mailed fist. He had inherited from the Eisenhower administration a CIA-backed scheme to topple Fidel Castro from power by invading Cuba with anticommunist exiles. On a fateful April 17, 1961, some twelve hundred exiles landed at Cuba's Bay of Pigs. When the invasion bogged down, the bullet-riddled band of anti-Castroites surrendered. President Kennedy assumed full responsibility for the failure, remarking that "victory has a hundred fathers, and defeat is an orphan."

The Bay of Pigs blunder, along with continuing American covert efforts to assassinate Castro and overthrow his government, naturally pushed the Cuban leader even further into the Soviet embrace. Wily Chairman Khrushchev lost little time taking full advantage of his Cuban comrade's position just ninety miles off Florida's coast. In October 1962 aerial photographs from American spy planes revealed that the Soviets were secretly and speedily installing nuclear-tipped missiles in Cuba.

Kennedy and Khrushchev now began a nerve-racking game of "nuclear chicken." The president, on October 22, 1962, ordered a naval "quarantine" of Cuba and demanded immediate removal of the threatening weaponry. He also served notice on Khrushchev that any attack on the United States from Cuba would be regarded as coming from the Soviet Union and would trigger nuclear retaliation against the Russian heartland. For an anxious week,

Americans waited while Soviet ships approached the patrol line established by the U.S. Navy off Cuba. The world teetered breathlessly on the brink of global atomization.

In this tense eyeball-to-eyeball confrontation, Khrushchev finally flinched. On October 28 he agreed to a partially face-saving compromise, by which he would pull the missiles out of Cuba. The United States in return agreed to end the quarantine and not invade the island.

Fallout from the Cuban missile crisis was considerable. A disgraced Khrushchev was ultimately hounded out of the Kremlin and became an "unperson." Kennedy, apparently sobered by the appalling risks he had just run, pushed harder for a nuclear test-ban treaty with the Soviet Union. After prolonged negotiations in Moscow, a pact prohibiting trial nuclear explosions in the atmosphere was signed in late 1963.

Most significant was Kennedy's speech at American University, Washington, D.C., in June 1963. The president urged Americans to abandon a view of the Soviet Union as a devil-ridden land filled with fanatics and instead to deal with the world "as it is, not as it might have been had the history of the last eighteen years been different." Kennedy thus tried to lay the foundations for a realistic policy of peaceful coexistence with the Soviet Union. Here were the modest origins of the policy that later came to be known as "détente" (French for "relaxation").

The Struggle for Civil Rights

Kennedy had campaigned with a strong appeal to black voters, but he proceeded gingerly to redeem his promises. Although he had pledged to eliminate racial discrimination in housing "with a stroke of the pen," it took him nearly two years to find the right pen. Civil rights groups meanwhile sent thousands of pens to the White House in an "Ink for Jack" protest against the president's slowness.

Political concerns stayed the president's hand on civil rights. Elected by a wafer-thin margin and with shaky control over Congress, Kennedy needed the support of southern legislators to pass his economic and social legislation, especially his medical and educational bills. But events soon scrambled these careful calculations.

Freedom Ride, 1961 *Rampaging whites near Anniston, Alabama, burned this bus carrying an interracial group of Freedom Riders on May 14, 1961.*

After the wave of sit-ins that surged across the South in 1960, groups of Freedom Riders fanned out to end segregation in facilities serving interstate bus passengers. A white mob torched a Freedom Ride bus near Anniston, Alabama, in May 1961, and Attorney General Robert Kennedy's personal representative was beaten unconscious in another anti–Freedom Ride riot in Montgomery. When southern officials proved unwilling or unable to stem the violence, Washington dispatched federal marshals to protect the Freedom Riders.

Reluctantly but fatefully, the Kennedy administration had now joined hands with the civil rights movement. For the most part, the relationship between Martin Luther King, Jr., and the Kennedys was a fruitful one. Encouraged by Robert Kennedy, SNCC and other civil rights groups inaugurated a Voter Education Project to register the South's historically disfranchised blacks.

Integrating southern universities threatened to provoke wholesale slaughter. Some desegregated painlessly, but the University of Mississippi ("Ole Miss") became a volcano. A twenty-nine-year-old air force veteran, James Meredith, encountered violent opposition when he attempted to register in October 1962. In the end President Kennedy was forced to send in four hundred federal marshals and three thousand troops to enroll Meredith in his first class— in colonial American history.

In the spring of 1963, Martin Luther King, Jr., launched a campaign against discrimination in Birmingham, Alabama, the most segregated big city in America. Although they constituted nearly half the city's population, blacks made up fewer than 15 percent of the city's voters. Previous attempts to crack rigid racial barriers had produced more than fifty cross burnings and eighteen bomb attacks since 1957. "Some of the people sitting here will not come back alive from this campaign," King advised his organizers. Events soon confirmed this grim prediction. Watching developments on television screens, a horrified world saw peaceful civil rights marchers repeatedly repelled by police with attack dogs and electric cattle prods. Most fearsome were the high-pressure water hoses directed at the civil rights demonstrators. They delivered water with enough force to knock bricks loose from buildings or strip bark from trees at a distance of one hundred feet. Water from the hoses bowled little children down the street like tumbleweed.

Jolted by these vicious confrontations, President Kennedy delivered a memorable televised speech to the nation on June 11, 1963. He called the situation a "moral crisis" and pleaded for new civil rights legislation to protect black citizens. On the very night of that stirring appeal a white gunman shot down Medgar Evers, a Mississippi civil rights worker. In August, Martin Luther King, Jr., led 200,000 black and white demonstrators on a peaceful "March on Washington" in support of the proposed civil rights legislation. Still the violence continued. In September 1963 an explosion blasted a Baptist church in Birmingham, killing four black girls who had just finished their Sunday school lesson called "The Love That Forgives."

The Killing of Kennedy

Violence haunted America in the mid-1960s and stalked onto center stage on November 22, 1963. While riding in an open limousine in downtown Dallas, Texas, President Kennedy was shot in the head by a concealed rifleman and died within seconds. As a stunned nation nursed its grief, the tragedy grew still more unbelievable. The alleged assassin, a furtive figure named Lee Harvey Oswald, was himself shot to death in front of the television cameras by a self-appointed avenger, Jack Ruby. So bizarre were the events surrounding the two murders that even an elaborate official investigation conducted by Chief Justice Warren could not quiet all doubts and theories about what had really happened. Vice President Johnson, sworn in as president on a waiting airplane in Dallas, managed a dignified and efficient transition, pledging continuity with his slain predecessor's policies.

For several days, the nation was steeped in sorrow. Not until then did many Americans realize how fully their young, vibrant president and his captivating wife had cast a spell over them. Chopped down in his prime after only slightly more than a thousand days in the White House, Kennedy was acclaimed more for the ideals he had enunciated and the spirit he had kindled than for the concrete goals he had achieved. He had laid one myth to rest forever—that a Catholic could not be trusted with the presidency of the United States.

In later years revelations about Kennedy's womanizing and allegations about his involvement with organized crime figures tarnished his reputation. But despite those accusations, his vigor, charisma, and idealism made him an inspirational figure for the generation of Americans who came of age in the 1960s—including Bill Clinton, who as a boy briefly met President Kennedy and was himself elected president in 1992.

The LBJ Brand on the Presidency

The torch passed to craggy-faced Lyndon Baines Johnson, a Texan who towered 6 feet, 3 inches. He could move political mountains or checkmate opponents as the occasion demanded, using what came to be known as the "Johnson treatment"—a flashing display of backslapping, flesh-pressing, and arm-twisting that overbore friend and foe alike.

As president, Johnson quickly shed the conservative coloration of his Senate years to reveal the latent liberal underneath. Seeking to carry on his predecessor's legacy, Johnson rammed Kennedy's stalled tax cut and civil rights bills through Congress and added proposals of his own for a billion-dollar "War on Poverty."

Johnson's nomination by the Democrats in 1964 was a foregone conclusion. He had dubbed his popular domestic program the "Great Society"—a sweeping set of New Dealish economic and welfare measures aimed at transforming the American way of life. Public support for LBJ's antipoverty war was aroused by Michael Harrington's *The Other America* (1962), which revealed that in affluent America 20 percent of the population—and over 40 percent of the black population—suffered in poverty.

The Republicans, convening in San Francisco, nominated box-jawed Senator Barry Goldwater of Arizona, a bronzed and bespectacled champion of rock-ribbed conservatism. The American stage was thus set for a historic clash of political principles.

Goldwater's forces had galloped out of the Southwest to ride roughshod over the moderate Republican "eastern establishment." Goldwater attacked the federal income tax, the Social Security system, the Tennessee Valley Authority, civil rights legislation, the nuclear test-ban treaty, and, most loudly, the Great Society. His fiercely dedicated fol-

lowers proclaimed, "In Your Heart You Know He's Right," which prompted the Democratic response, "In Your Guts You Know He's Nuts."

Johnson cultivated the contrasting image of a resolute statesman by seizing upon the Tonkin Gulf episode early in August 1964. Unbeknownst to the American public or Congress, U.S. Navy ships had been cooperating with South Vietnamese gunboats in provocative raids along the coast of North Vietnam. Two of these American destroyers were allegedly fired upon by the North Vietnamese on August 2 and 4, although exactly what happened remains unclear. Later investigations strongly suggested that the North Vietnamese fired in self-defense on August 2 and that the "attack" of August 4 never happened. Johnson later wisecracked, "For all I know, the Navy was shooting at whales out there."

Johnson nevertheless promptly called the attacks "unprovoked" and moved swiftly to make political hay out of this episode. He ordered a "limited" retaliatory air raid against the North Vietnamese bases, loudly proclaiming that he sought "no wider war"—thus implying that the truculent Goldwater did. Johnson also used the incident to spur congressional passage of the all-purpose Tonkin Gulf Resolution. With only two dissenting votes in both houses of Congress the lawmakers virtually abdicated their war-declaring powers and handed the president a blank check to use further force in Southeast Asia.

The towering Texan rode to a spectacular victory in November 1964. The voters were herded into Johnson's column by fondness for the Kennedy legacy, faith in Great Society promises, and fear of Goldwater. A stampede of 43,129,566 Johnson votes trampled the Republican ticket, with its 27,178,188 supporters. The tally in the Electoral College was 486 to 52. Goldwater carried only his native Arizona and five other states—all of them, significantly, in the racially restless South. Johnson's record-breaking 61 percent of the popular vote swept lopsided Democratic majorities into both houses of Congress.

The Great Society Congress

Johnson's huge victory temporarily smashed the conservative coalition of southern Democrats and northern Republicans. A wide-open legislative road stretched before the Great Society programs, as the president skillfully ringmastered his two-to-one Democratic majorities. Congress poured out a flood of legislation, comparable only to the output of the New Dealers in the Hundred Days Congress of 1933, as Johnson at last delivered on long-delayed Democratic promises of social reform.

Besides a greatly expanded "War on Poverty," other landmark laws flowed from Johnson's "hip-pocket Congress." Medicare for the elderly became a reality in 1965. Although it was a bitter pill for the American Medical Association to swallow, the system was welcomed by millions of older Americans who were being pushed into poverty by skyrocketing medical costs.

A tireless Johnson also prodded the Congress into creating two new cabinet offices: the Department of Transportation and the Department of Housing and Urban Development (HUD). He named the first black cabinet member in the nation's history, noted economist Robert C. Weaver, to be secretary of HUD.

Great Society programs came in for rancorous political attack in later years. Conservatives charged that poverty could not be papered over with greenbacks, yet the poverty rate did decline measurably in the ensuing decade. Medicare dramatically reduced poverty among America's elderly, and antipoverty programs like Project Head Start sharply improved the educational performance of underprivileged youth. Lyndon Johnson was not fully victorious in the war against poverty, but he did win several noteworthy battles.

The Black Revolution Explodes

In Johnson's native South, the walls of segregation were crumbling, but not fast enough for long-suffering African-Americans. The Civil Rights Act of 1964 gave the federal government more muscle to enforce school desegregation orders and to prohibit racial discrimination in all kinds of public accommodations and employment. But the problem of voting rights remained. In Mississippi, which had the largest black minority of any state, only about 5 percent of eligible blacks were registered to vote. The lopsided pattern was similar throughout the South. Ballot-denying devices like the poll tax, literacy tests, and

bare-faced intimidation still barred black people from the political process.

Beginning in 1964, opening up the polling booths became the chief goal of the black movement in the South. The Twenty-fourth Amendment, ratified in January 1964, abolished the poll tax in federal elections (see the Appendix). Blacks joined hands with white civil rights workers—many of them student volunteers from the North—in a massive voter-registration drive in Mississippi during the "Freedom Summer" of 1964. Singing "We Shall Overcome," they zealously set out to soothe generations of white anxieties and black fears.

But events soon blighted bright hopes. In late June 1964, one black and two white civil rights workers disappeared in Mississippi. Their badly beaten bodies were later found buried beneath an earthen dam. In August an integrated "Mississippi Freedom Democratic Party" delegation was denied its seat at the national Democratic convention.

Early in 1965 Martin Luther King, Jr., resumed the voter-registration campaign in Selma, Alabama. State troopers with tear gas and whips assaulted King's peaceful demonstrators. A Boston Unitarian minister was killed, and a few days later a white Detroit woman was shotgunned to death by Klansmen on the highway near Selma.

As the nation recoiled in horror before these violent scenes, President Johnson, speaking in soft southern accents, delivered a compelling address on television. What happened in Selma, he insisted, concerned all Americans, "who must overcome the crippling legacy of bigotry and injustice." Then, in a stirring adaptation of the anthem of the civil rights movement, the president concluded: "And we shall overcome." Following words with deeds, Johnson speedily shepherded through Congress the landmark Voting Rights Act of 1965, signed into law on August 6. It outlawed literacy tests and sent federal voter registrars into several southern states.

The passage of the Voting Rights Act, exactly one hundred years after the conclusion of the Civil War, climaxed a century of awful abuse and robust resurgence for African-Americans in the South. The act did not end discrimination and oppression overnight, but it placed an awesome lever for change in blacks' hands. Black southerners now had power and began to wield it without fear of reprisals. In the following decade, for the first time since emancipation, African-Americans began to migrate *into* the South.

Black Rage

The Voting Rights Act of 1965 marked the end of an era in the troubled history of the black movement—the era of civil rights campaigns, focused on the South, led by peaceable moderates such as Martin Luther King, Jr. Just five days after President Johnson signed the new voting law, a bloody riot erupted in Watts, a black ghetto in Los Angeles. The week-long violence left thirty-one blacks and three whites dead, more than a thousand people injured, and hundreds of buildings charred and gutted.

Increasingly, more militant voices began to be heard in the black movement. Deepening division among black leaders was highlighted by the career of Malcolm X, a brilliant Black Muslim preacher who trumpeted black separatism and inveighed against the "blue-eyed white devils." In early 1965, after he had begun to preach a more conciliatory message, he was cut down by black gunmen while speaking to a large crowd in New York City.

The moderation of Martin Luther King, Jr., came under heavy fire from younger black radicals, such as Trinidad-born Stokely Carmichael of the Student Non-Violent Coordinating Committee (SNCC). Carmichael urged the abandonment of peaceful demonstrations and instead promoted "Black Power."

The phrase "Black Power" unsettled many whites. Some Black Power advocates insisted that they simply intended the slogan to describe a broad-front effort to exercise the political and economic rights gained by the civil rights movement. But other African-Americans, recollecting previous black nationalist movements like that of Marcus Garvey earlier in the century (see p. 477), breathed a vibrant separatist meaning into the concept of Black Power. They emphasized African-American distinctiveness, shed their "white" names for new African identities, and demanded black studies programs in colleges and universities.

Shortly after the civil rights movement achieved its greatest successes, city-shaking riots erupted in the black ghettoes. A bloody outburst in Newark, New Jersey, in the summer of 1967, took twenty-five lives. In Detroit, Michigan, federal troops restored order after forty-three people died in the streets. Black rioters torched their own neighborhoods, attacking police officers, and even firefighters, who had to battle both flames and mobs chanting, "Burn, baby, burn."

These outbursts angered many white Americans, who threatened to retaliate with their own "backlash" against ghetto arsonists and killers. Inner-city anarchy baffled many northerners, who had considered racial problems a purely "southern" question. But black concerns had moved north—as had nearly half the nation's black people. In the North the Black Power movement now focused less on civil rights and more on economic demands. Black unemployment, for example, was nearly double that for whites. These oppressive problems seemed even less likely to be solved peaceably than the struggle for voting rights in the South.

Despair deepened when the magnetic and moderate voice of Martin Luther King, Jr., was forever silenced by a sniper's bullet in Memphis, Tennessee, on April 4, 1968. A martyr for justice, he had bled and died against the peculiarly American thorn of race. The killing of King cruelly robbed the American people of one of the most inspirational leaders in their history—at a time when they could least afford to lose him. This outrage triggered a nationwide orgy of ghetto-gutting and violence that cost over forty lives.

Rioters noisily made news, but thousands of other blacks quietly made history. Their voter registration had shot upward, and by the late 1960s there were several hundred black elected officials in the Old South. Cleveland, Ohio, and Gary, Indiana, had elected black mayors. By 1972 nearly half of southern black children sat in integrated classrooms. Actually, more schools in the South were integrated than in the North. About a third of black families had risen economically into the ranks of the middle class—though an equal proportion remained below the "poverty line." King left a shining legacy of racial progress, but he was cut down when the job was far from completed.

Combating Communism in Two Hemispheres

Violence at home eclipsed Johnson's legislative triumphs, whereas foreign flare-ups threatened his

The Agony of War, 1965   *A U.S. marine carries a South Vietnamese baby to safety. The child was wounded by American jets during the opening stages of a military operation at Cape Batangan, Vietnam.*

Cong guerrillas attacked an American air base at Pleiku, South Vietnam, in February 1965. The president immediately ordered retaliatory bombing raids against military installations in North Vietnam and for the first time ordered attacking U.S. troops to land. By the middle of March 1965, the Americans had "Operation Rolling Thunder" in full swing— regular full-scale bombing attacks against North Vietnam. Before 1965 ended, some 184,000 American troops were slogging through the jungles and rice paddies of South Vietnam searching for guerrillas.

Johnson had now taken the first fateful steps down a slippery path. He and his advisers believed that a fine-tuned, step-by-step escalation in American force would drive the enemy to defeat with a minimum loss of life. But the enemy matched every increase in American firepower with more men and more wiliness in the art of guerrilla warfare.

The South Vietnamese themselves were meanwhile becoming spectators in their own war, as the fighting became increasingly Americanized. Corrupt and collapsible governments succeeded each other in Saigon with bewildering rapidity. Yet American officials continued to talk of defending a faithful democratic ally. Washington spokespeople also defended the action as a test of Uncle Sam's "commitment" and of the reliability of his numerous treaty pledges to resist communist encroachment. Persuaded by such panicky thinking, Johnson steadily raised the military stakes in Vietnam. By 1968 he had poured more than half a million troops into Southeast Asia, and the annual bill for the war was exceeding $30 billion. Yet the end was nowhere in sight.

Vietnam Vexations

America could not defeat the enemy in Vietnam but seemed to be defeating itself. World opinion grew increasingly hostile; the blasting of an underdeveloped country by a mighty superpower struck many critics as obscene. Several nations expelled American Peace Corps volunteers. Haughty Charles de Gaulle, ever suspicious of American reliability, ordered NATO off French soil in 1966.

Overcommitment in Southeast Asia also tied America's hands elsewhere. Capitalizing on American distractions in Vietnam, the Soviet Union expanded

political life. Discontented Dominicans rose in revolt against their military government in April 1965. Johnson speedily announced that the Dominican Republic was the target of a Castrolike coup by "Communist conspirators," and he dispatched some twenty-five thousand American troops to restore order. But the evidence of a communist takeover was fragmentary at best. Johnson was widely condemned, at home and in Latin America, for his temporary reversion to the officially abandoned "gunboat diplomacy."

About the same time, Johnson was floundering deeper into the monsoon mud of Vietnam. Viet its influence in the Mediterranean area, especially in Egypt. Tiny Israel stunned the Soviet-backed Egyptians in a devastating Six-Day War in June 1967. The Middle East was becoming an ever more dangerously packed powder keg that the war-plagued United States was powerless to defuse.

Domestic discontent also festered as the Vietnamese entanglement dragged on. Antiwar demonstrations had begun on a small scale with campus "teach-ins" in 1965, and gradually these protests mounted to tidal-wave proportions. As the long arm of the military draft dragged more and more young men off to the Asian slaughterpen, resistance stiffened. Thousands of draft registrants fled to Canada; others publicly burned their draft cards. Hundreds of thousands of chanting marchers filled the streets of New York, San Francisco, and other cities. Many Americans felt pangs of conscience at the ghastly spectacle of their countrymen burning peasant huts and blistering civilians with ghastly napalm.

Opposition in Congress to the Vietnam involvement centered in the influential Senate Committee on Foreign Relations, headed by Senator J. William Fulbright of Arkansas. A constant thorn in the side of the president, he staged a series of widely viewed televised hearings in 1966 and 1967, during which prominent personages aired their views, largely antiwar. Gradually the public came to feel that it had been lied to about both the causes and the "winnability" of the war. A yawning "credibility gap" opened between the government and the people. New flocks of antiwar "doves" were hatching daily.

By early 1968 the brutal and futile struggle had become the longest and most unpopular foreign war in the nation's history. Casualties, killed and wounded, already exceeded 100,000. More bombs had been dropped on Vietnam than on all enemy territory in World War II. Evidence mounted that America had been entrapped in an Asian civil war, fighting against highly motivated rebels who were striving to overthrow an oppressive regime. Yet Johnson clung to his basic strategy of stepping up the pressure bit by bit. He stubbornly assured doubting Americans that he could see "the light at the end of the tunnel." But to growing numbers of Americans, it seemed that Johnson was bent on "saving" Vietnam by destroying it.

Vietnam Topples Johnson

Hawkish illusions that the struggle was about to be won were shattered by a blistering communist offensive launched in late January 1968, during Tet, the Vietnamese New Year. At a time when the Viet Cong were supposedly licking their wounds, they suddenly and simultaneously mounted savage attacks on twenty-seven key South Vietnamese cities, including the capital, Saigon. Although eventually beaten off with heavy losses, they demonstrated anew that victory could not be gained by Johnson's strategy of gradual escalation. With an increasingly insistent voice, American public opinion demanded a speedy end to the war. Opposition grew so vehement that President Johnson could feel the very foundations of government shaking under his feet.

American military leaders responded to the Tet attacks with a request for 200,000 more troops. The size of the request staggered many policymakers. Former secretary of state Dean Acheson advised Johnson that "the Joint Chiefs of Staff don't know what they're talking about."

Meanwhile, Senator Eugene J. McCarthy of Minnesota was sharply challenging the president from within his own party for the 1968 Democrat presidential nomination. McCarthy, a sometime poet and devout Catholic, gathered a small army of antiwar college students who helped him gain an incredible 42 percent of the Democratic vote in the New Hampshire presidential primary on March 12. Four days later, Senator Robert F. Kennedy of New York, the murdered president's younger brother and by now himself a "dove" on Vietnam, threw his hat into the ring. The charismatic Kennedy, heir to his fallen brother's mantle of leadership, stirred a passionate response among workers, African-Americans, Hispanics, and young people.

These startling events abroad and at home were not lost on LBJ. In a bombshell address on March 31, 1968, he announced that he would freeze American troop levels and scale down the bombing. He also startled his vast audience by firmly declaring that he would not be a candidate for the presidency in 1968.

Johnson's "abdication" had the effect of preserving the military status quo. The United States could thus maintain the maximum *acceptable* level of military activity in Vietnam with one hand, while trying to negotiate a settlement with the other. North Vietnam shortly agreed to negotiations in Paris, but progress was glacially slow, as prolonged bickering developed over the very shape of the conference table.

The Presidential Sweepstakes of 1968

Summer in 1968 was one of the hottest political seasons in the nation's history. Johnson's heir apparent for the Democratic nomination was Vice President Hubert Humphrey. Loyally supporting LBJ's Vietnam policies through thick and thin, he received the support of the White House–dominated party apparatus. Senators McCarthy and Kennedy meanwhile dueled in several state primaries, with Kennedy's bandwagon gathering ever-increasing speed. But on June 5, 1968, on the night of an exciting victory in the California primary, Kennedy was shot to death by a young Arab immigrant.

Antiwar forces, deprived by an assassin of their leading candidate, streamed into Chicago for the Democratic convention in August 1968. Mayor Richard Daley responded by arranging for barbed-wire barricades around the convention hall, as well as thousands of police and National Guard reinforcements. Some militant demonstrators baited the officers in blue as "pigs" and hurled bags of filth at police lines. As people the world over watched on television, the exasperated "peace officers" broke into a "police riot," clubbing and manhandling innocent and guilty alike. Acrid tear-gas fumes hung over the city even as Humphrey steamrollered to a first-ballot nomination. The Humphrey forces blocked the dovish McCarthyites' attempt to secure an antiwar platform plank and rammed through their own declaration that armed force would be relentlessly applied until the enemy showed more willingness to negotiate.

Scenting victory over the divided Democrats, the Republicans convened in plush Miami Beach, Florida, and nominated former vice president Richard Nixon, who arose from his political grave to win the nomination. As a "hawk" on Vietnam and a right-leaning middle-of-the-roader on domestic policy, Nixon pleased the Goldwater conservatives and was acceptable to party moderates. He appealed to

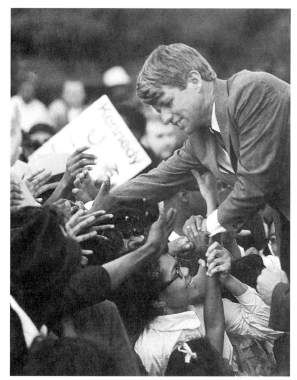

Robert F. Kennedy Campaigning for the Presidency, 1968 *Wrapped in the Kennedy family mystique and exuding his own boyish charm, Kennedy excited partisan crowds to wildly adulatory outpourings.*

southern whites and to the "law and order" element when he tapped as his running mate Maryland governor Spiro T. Agnew, noted for his tough stands against dissidents and black militants. The Republican platform called for victory in Vietnam and a strong anti-crime policy.

Adding color and confusion to the campaign was the third-party candidacy of former Alabama governor George C. Wallace. Wallace attacked "pointy-headed bureaucrats" and taunted hecklers as "bums" who needed a bath. He also called for prodding blacks back into their place. He and his running mate, former air force general Curtis LeMay, also proposed smashing the North Vietnamese to smithereens by "bombing them back to the Stone Age."

Between the positions of the Republicans and the Democrats on Vietnam, there was little choice.

Both candidates were committed to keeping on with the war until the enemy would settle for an "honorable peace," which seemed to mean an "American victory." The millions of "doves" had no place to roost, and many refused to vote at all. Humphrey, scorched by the LBJ brand, went down to defeat as a prisoner of his chief's policies.

Nixon, who had lost a cliff-hanger to Kennedy in 1960, won one in 1968. He garnered 301 electoral votes with 43.4 percent of the popular tally (31,785,480), as compared with 191 electoral votes and 42.7 percent of the popular votes (31,275,166) for Humphrey. Wallace won an impressive 9,906,473 popular votes and 46 electoral votes, all from five states of the Deep South, four of which the Republican Goldwater had carried in 1964.

The Obituary of Lyndon Johnson

Talented but tragedy-struck Lyndon Johnson returned to his Texas ranch in January 1969 and died there four years later. His party was defeated, and his "me-too" Hubert Humphrey was repudiated. Yet Johnson's legislative leadership for a time had been remarkable.

No president since Lincoln worked harder or did more for civil rights. None showed more compassion for the poor, blacks, and the ill educated. But by 1966 Johnson was already sinking into the Vietnam quicksands. Great Society programs began to wither on the vine as soaring war costs sucked tax dollars into the military machine. Johnson promised both guns and butter but could not keep that promise. Ever-creeping inflation blighted the prospects of prosperity, and the War on Poverty met resistance as stubborn as the Viet Cong and eventually went down to defeat. Great want persisted alongside great wealth.

The Southeast Asian quagmire engulfed Johnson's noblest intentions. Committed to some degree by his two predecessors, he chose to defend the American foothold and enlarge the conflict rather than be run out. He was evidently persuaded by his brightest advisers, both civilian and military, that a "cheap" victory was possible and would be achieved by massive aerial bombing and large, though limited,

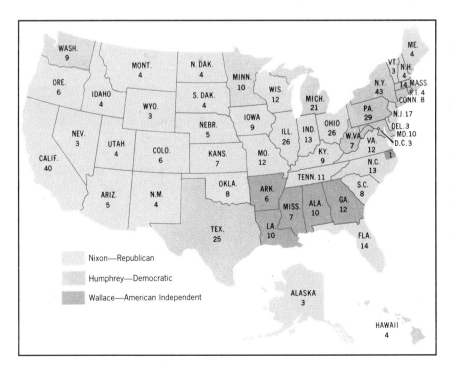

Presidential Election of 1968 (with electoral vote by state) *George Wallace won in five states and denied a clear majority to either of the two major-party candidates in twenty-five other states. A shift of some fifty thousand votes might have thrown the election into the House of Representatives, giving Wallace the strategic bargaining position that he sought.*

troop commitments. His decision not to escalate the fighting further offended the "hawks," and his refusal to back off altogether antagonized the "doves." Like the Calvinists of colonial days, luckless Lyndon Johnson was damned if he did and damned if he did not.

The Cultural Upheaval of the 1960s

The struggles of the 1960s against racism, poverty, and the war in Vietnam had momentous cultural consequences. The decade came to be seen as a watershed dividing two distinct eras in values, morals, and behavior.

Everywhere in 1960s America a negative attitude toward all kinds of authority began to take hold. Disillusioned by the discovery that American society was not free of racism, sexism, imperialism, and oppression, many young people lost their traditional moral rudders. Neither families nor churches nor schools seemed to be able to define values and shape behavior with the certainty of shared purpose that many people believed had once existed. This upheaval even churned the tradition-bound Roman Catholic church, among the world's oldest and most conservative institutions. Clerics abandoned their Roman collars and the Latin Mass; folk songs replaced Gregorian chants; and meatless Fridays became ancient history. No matter what the topic, conventional wisdom and inherited ideas came under fire. "Trust no one over thirty" was a popular sneer of rebellious youth.

Skepticism about authority had deep historical roots in American culture, and it had even bloomed in the supposedly complacent and conformist 1950s. "Beat" poets such as Allen Ginsberg and iconoclastic novelists like Jack Kerouac had voiced dark disillusion with the materialistic pursuits of "establishment" culture in the Eisenhower era. In movies like *Rebel Without a Cause* (1955), the attractive young actor James Dean expressed the restless frustration of many young people.

The disaffection of the young reached crisis proportions in the tumultuous 1960s. One of the first organized protests against established authority broke out at the University of California at Berkeley in 1964, in the so-called Free Speech Movement. Fired by seething resentment against the war in Vietnam, many sons and daughters of the middle class turned to mind-bending drugs, tuned in to "acid rock," and dropped out of "straight" society. Others "did their own thing" in communes or "alternative" institutions. "Patriotism" became a dirty word. Beflowered women in trousers and long-haired men with earrings heralded the rise of a self-conscious "counterculture" vehemently opposed to traditional American ways.

The 1960s also witnessed a "sexual revolution," though its novelty and scale are often exaggerated.

The "Free Speech Movement," Berkeley, California, December 4, 1964
Student leader Mario Savio addresses a crowd at the University of California at Berkeley. The Free Speech Movement marked the first of the large-scale student mobilizations that would rock campuses across the country throughout the rest of the 1960s.

Without doubt, the introduction of the birth-control pill in 1960 made unwanted pregnancies much easier to avoid and sexual appetites much easier to satisfy. By the 1960s, gay men and lesbians were also emerging from the closet and demanding sexual tolerance. A brutal attack on gay men by off-duty police officers at New York's Stonewall Inn in 1969 powerfully energized gay and lesbian militancy. Widening worries in the 1980s about sexually transmitted diseases like genital herpes and AIDS (acquired immunodeficiency syndrome) finally slowed, but did not reverse, the sexual revolution.

Launched in youthful idealism, many of the decade's reform movements sputtered out in violence and cynicism. Students for a Democratic Society (SDS), once at the forefront of the antipoverty and antiwar campaigns, had by decade's end spawned an underground terrorist group called the Weathermen. Peaceful civil rights demonstrations had given way to blockbusting urban riots. What started as apparently innocent experiments with drugs such as marijuana and LSD had fried many youthful brains and spawned a loathsome underworld of drug lords and addicts.

Strait-laced guardians of respectability denounced the self-indulgent romanticism of the "flower children" as the beginning of the end of modern civilization. Sympathetic observers hailed the "greening" of America—the replacement of materialism and imperialism by a new consciousness of human values. But the upheavals of the 1960s could be largely attributed to three *P*s: the youthful population bulge, protest against racism and the Vietnam War, and the apparent permanence of prosperity. As the decade flowed into the 1970s, the flower children grew older and had children of their own, the civil rights movement fell silent, the war ended, and economic stagnation blighted the bloom of prosperity. Young people in the 1970s seemed more concerned with finding jobs in the system than with tearing the system down. But if the "counterculture" had not managed fully to replace older values, it had weakened their grip, perhaps permanently.

Chronology

1961 Berlin crisis and construction of the Berlin Wall.
Bay of Pigs.
Alliance for Progress.
Kennedy sends "military advisers" to South Vietnam.

1962 Pressure from Kennedy results in a rollback of steel prices.
Laos neutralized.
Cuban missile crisis.

1963 Anti-Diem coup in South Vietnam.
Civil rights march in Washington, D.C.
Kennedy assassinated; Johnson assumes presidency.

1964 Twenty-fourth Amendment (abolishing poll tax in federal elections) ratified.
Tonkin Gulf Resolution.
Johnson defeats Goldwater for presidency.
"War on Poverty" begins.
Civil Rights Act.

1965 Great Society legislation.
Voting Rights Act.
U.S. troops occupy Dominican Republic.

1965–1968 Race riots in U.S. cities.
Escalation of the Vietnam War.

1967 Six-Day War between Israel and Egypt.

1968 Tet offensive in Vietnam.
Martin Luther King, Jr., and Robert Kennedy assassinated.
Nixon defeats Humphrey and Wallace for presidency.

1969 Astronauts land on moon.

varying

viewpoints

The Sixties: Constructive or Destructive?

The 1960s were convulsed by controversy, and they have remained controversial ever since. Conflicts raged in that turbulent decade between social classes, races, sexes, and generations. More than three decades later, conservative Republicans worked to repudiate the government activism of the sixties and uphold the "traditional values" that sixties culture supposedly trashed. Liberal Democrats, in contrast, continued to press such sixties causes as affirmative action for women and minorities, protection for the environment, an expanded welfare state, and sexual tolerance.

Four issues dominate historical discussion of the 1960s: the civil rights struggle; the Great Society's "War on Poverty"; the Vietnam War and the antiwar movement; and the emergence of the "counterculture." Most scholars praise the civil rights achievements of the 1960s, but they disagree over the mid-sixties turn away from nonviolence to separatism and Black Power. The Freedom Riders and Martin Luther King, Jr., find much more approval in most history books than do Malcolm X or the Black Panther party. But some scholars, notably William L. Van Deburg in *New Day in Babylon: The Black Power Movement and American Culture, 1965–1975* (1992), argue that the "flank effect" of radical Black Power advocates like Stokely Carmichael actually enhanced the bargaining position of moderates like Dr. King.

Johnson's War on Poverty has liberal defenders in scholars like Allen Matusow (*The Unraveling of America*, 1984) and John Schwarz (*America's Hidden Success*, 1988). Schwarz demonstrates, for example,

that Medicare and Social Security reforms virtually eliminated poverty among America's elderly. But the Great Society also provoked strong criticism from writers such as Charles Murray (*Losing Ground*, 1984) and Lawrence Meade (*Beyond Entitlements*, 1986). As those conservative critics see the poverty issue, to use a phrase popular in the 1960s, the Great Society was "part of the problem, not part of the solution." In their view, the War on Poverty did not simply fail to eradicate poverty among the so-called underclass; it actually deepened the dependency of the poor on the welfare state and even generated a multigenerational "cycle" of poverty.

For many young people of the 1960s, the antiwar movement protesting America's policy in Vietnam provided an initiation into politics and an introduction to "movement culture," with its sense of community and shared purpose. But scholars disagree over the movement's real effectiveness in checking the war. Writers like John Lewis Gaddis (*Strategies of Containment*, 1982) explain America's eventual withdrawal from Vietnam essentially without reference to the protesters in the streets. Others, like Todd Gitlin (*The Sixties: Years of Hope, Days of Rage*, 1987), insist that mass protest was the force that finally pressed the war to a conclusion.

Debate over the "counterculture" not only pits liberals against conservatives, but also pits liberals against radicals. A liberal historian like William O'Neill (*Coming Apart*, 1971) might sympathize with what he considers some of the worthy values pushed by student activists, such as racial justice, nonviolence, and the antiwar movement, but he also claims that much of the sixties "youth culture" degenerated into hedonism, arrogance, and social polarization. In contrast, younger historians such as David Farber, Michael Kazin, and Maurice Isserman argue that cultural radicalism and political radicalism were two sides of the same coin. Many young people in the sixties made little distinction between the personal and the political. As Sara Evans demonstrates in *Personal Politics* (1980), "the personal *was* the political" for many women.

Critics may argue over the "good" versus the "bad" sixties, but there is no denying the degree to which that tumultuous time, for better or worse, shaped the world in which we now live.

SUGGESTED READINGS

Primary Source Documents

Norman Mailer paints vivid portraits of the 1968 conventions in *Miami and the Siege of Chicago* (1968) and of the antiwar March on Washington in his *Armies of the Night* (1968). Martin Luther King, Jr.'s *Letter from Birmingham Jail** (1963) eloquently defends the civil rights movement. The progress of the war in Vietnam is chronicled in *The Pentagon Papers** (1971). Students for a Democratic Society (1962) and Young Americans for Freedom (1960) both issued manifestos* that suggest the political temper of the era. Stewart Alsop penned a notable editorial in *Newsweek** in 1970 that reflects "establishment" disgust with the cultural upheavals of the decade.

Secondary Sources

The tumultuous decade of the 1960s is treated in William L. O'Neill, *Coming Apart: An Informal History of America in the 1960s* (1971); in Allen Matusow, *The Unraveling of America* (1984); and in John Morton Blum, *Years of Discord* (1991). On Kennedy see Theodore C. Sorenson, *Kennedy* (1965), and Arthur M. Schlesinger, Jr., *A Thousand Days* (1965), both appreciative accounts by insiders. More critical is Henry Fairlie, *The Kennedy Promise* (1973). Michael Beschloss details *The Crisis Years: Kennedy and Khrushchev, 1960–1963* (1991). A splendid short biography is Bruce J. Schulman, *Lyndon B. Johnson and American Liberalism* (1994). Eric Goldman, *The Tragedy of Lyndon Johnson* (1969), is a sympathetic yet critical account of the Johnson presidency. In the same vein, with a psychoanalytic touch, is Doris Kearns, *Lyndon B. Johnson and the American Dream* (1976). Johnson's own memoir, *The Vantage Point* (1971), is marred by excessive self-justification. Equally unbalanced antidotes are Robert Caro, *The Years of Lyndon Johnson: The Path to Power* (1982) and *Means of Ascent* (1990). For a more complex portrait see Robert Dallek, *Lone Star Rising: Lyndon Johnson and His Times, 1908–1960* (1991). Two superb chronicles of the civil rights movement focusing on Martin Luther King, Jr., are the books by Taylor Branch and David J. Garrow cited in Chapter 38. The racial upheavals of the decade are discussed in Harvard Sitkoff, *The Struggle for Black Equality, 1954–1992* (1993); Clayborne Carson, *In Struggle: SNCC* [Student Non-Violent Coordinating Committee] *and the Black Awakening of the 1960s* (1981); and William H. Chafe, *Civilities and Civil Rights: Greensboro, North Carolina, and the Black Struggle for Freedom* (1980). On the New Left consult two volumes by Todd Gitlin, *The Sixties: Years of Hope, Days of Rage* (1987) and *The Whole World Is Watching: Mass Media in the Making and Unmaking of the New Left* (1980); James Miller, *"Democracy Is in the Streets": From Port Huron to the Sea of Chicago* (1987); Sara Evans, *Personal Politics* (1979); David Harris, *Dreams Die Hard* (1982); and Tom Hayden, *Reunion* (1988). On Vietnam consult Ronald Spector, *The United States Army in Vietnam* (1984); W. H. Brands, *Since Vietnam* (1996); and Stanley Karnow's encyclopedic *Vietnam: A History* (1983). Concise accounts are George Herring, *America's Longest War* (1986), and Marilyn B. Young, *The Vietnam Wars, 1945–1990* (1991). Robert S. McNamara, *In Retrospect: The Tragedy and Lessons of Vietnam* (1995), is the sorrowful apology of one of the war's principal architects for the "mistake" of Vietnam. Two works by John Lewis Gaddis shrewdly analyze the Cold War context of the Vietnam conflict: *The Long Peace* (1987) and *The United States and the End of the Cold War* (1992). In *American Genesis: A Century of Invention and Technological Enthusiasm* (1989), Thomas Hughes argues that the sixties marked the end of a century-long national love affair with technology. Also intriguing on the 1960s is Morris Dickstein, *The Gates of Eden: American Culture in the Sixties* (1977). A lucid survey of the intellectual history of the postwar era is Richard Pells, *The Liberal Mind in a Conservative Age* (1984). Changes in attitudes toward sex are scrutinized in Daniel Yankelovich, *The New Morality* (1974); Morton Hunt, *Sexual Behavior in the 1970s* (1974); and Paul Robinson, *The Modernization of Sex* (1976).

---

*An asterisk indicates that the document, or an excerpt from it, can be found in Thomas A. Bailey and David M. Kennedy, eds., *The American Spirit: United States History as Seen by Contemporaries*, 9th ed. (Boston: Houghton Mifflin, 1998).

40

★★★★★★★★★

The Stalemated Seventies,
1968–1980

★★★★★★

*In all my years of public life, I have never obstructed justice.
People have got to know whether or not their president is a
crook. Well, I'm not a crook; I earned everything I've got.*

★★★★★★

RICHARD NIXON, 1973

The Economy Stagnates in the 1970s

As the 1960s lurched to a close, the fantastic quarter-century economic boom of the post–World War II era also showed signs of petering out. By increasing their productivity, American workers had doubled their average standard of living in the twenty-five years since the end of World War II. Now, fatefully, productivity gains slowed to the vanishing point. The entire decade of the 1970s did not witness a productivity advance equivalent to even one year's progress in the preceding two decades. At the new rate, it would take five hundred more years to bring about another doubling of the average worker's standard of living. The rising baby-boom generation faced the depressing prospect of a living standard that would be lower than that of their parents.

What caused the sudden slump in productivity? Some observers cited the increasing presence in the work force of women and teenagers, who typically had fewer skills than male adult workers and were less likely to take the full-time, long-term jobs where skills might be developed. Other commentators blamed declining investment in new machinery, the heavy costs of compliance with government-imposed safety and health regulations, and the general shift of the economy from manufacturing to services, where productivity gains were allegedly more difficult to achieve.

The Vietnam War also precipitated painful economic distortions. The disastrous conflict in Southeast Asia drained tax dollars from needed

THE NIXON WAVE

The Nixon Wave *During Richard Nixon's presidency, Americans experienced the first serious inflation since the immediate post–World War II years. The inflationary surge grew to tidal-wave proportions by the late 1970s, when the consumer price index rose at annual rates of more than 10 percent.*

improvements in education, deflected scientific skill and manufacturing capacity from the civilian sector, and touched off a sickening spiral of inflation. Sharply rising oil prices in the 1970s also fed inflation, but its deepest roots lay in government policies of the 1960s—especially Lyndon Johnson's insistence on simultaneously fighting the war in Vietnam and funding the Great Society programs at home, all without a tax increase to finance the added expenditures. The cost of living more than tripled in the dozen years following Richard Nixon's inauguration, in the longest and steepest inflationary cycle in American history.

Other weaknesses in the nation's economy were also laid bare by the abrupt reversal of America's financial fortunes in the 1970s. The competitive advantage of many American businesses had been so enormous after World War II that they had small incentive to modernize plants and seek more efficient methods of production. The defeated German and Japanese people had meanwhile scratched their way out of the ruins of war and built wholly new factories with the most up-to-date technology and management techniques. By the 1970s their efforts paid handsome rewards, as they came to dominate industries like steel, automobiles, and consumer electronics—fields in which the United States had once been unchallengeable.

For all these reasons, the postwar wave of robust economic growth had clearly crested by the early 1970s. At home and abroad, the "can do" American spirit gave way to an unaccustomed sense of limits. This stifling realization hung over the 1970s like a pall. It frustrated both policymakers and citizens who keenly remembered the growth and optimism of the quarter-century after World War II. But now a stalemated, unpopular war and a stagnant, unresponsive economy heralded the end of the self-confident postwar era. With it ended the liberal dream, vivid since New Deal days, that an affluent society could spend its way to social justice.

Nixon "Vietnamizes" the War

Inaugurated on January 20, 1969, Richard Nixon urged the American people, torn with dissension over Vietnam and race relations, to "stop shouting at one another." Yet the new president seemed an unlikely conciliator of the clashing forces that appeared to be ripping apart American society. Solitary and suspicious by nature, Nixon could be brittle and testy in the face of opposition. He also harbored bitter resentments against the "liberal establishment" that had cast him into the political darkness for much of the preceding decade. Yet Nixon brought one hugely valuable asset with him to the White House—his broad knowledge and thoughtful expertise in foreign affairs.

The first burning need of American foreign policy was to quiet the public uproar over Vietnam. President Nixon's announced policy—called "Vietnamization"—was to withdraw the 540,000 U.S.

troops in South Vietnam over an extended period. The South Vietnamese—with American money, weapons, training, and advice—could then gradually take over the burden of fighting their own war. The so-called Nixon Doctrine thus evolved. It proclaimed that in the future, Asians and others would have to fight their own wars without the support of large bodies of American ground troops.

Nixon sought not to end the war but to win it by other means, without the further spilling of American blood. But even this much involvement was distasteful to the American "doves," many of whom demanded a withdrawal that was prompt, complete, unconditional, and irreversible. Antiwar protesters staged a massive national Vietnam moratorium in October 1969, as nearly 100,000 people jammed Boston Common and some 50,000 filed by the White House carrying lighted candles.

Undaunted, Nixon launched a counteroffensive by appealing to the "silent majority" who presumably supported the war. Though ostensibly conciliatory, Nixon's approach was in fact deeply divisive. His intentions soon became clear when he unleashed tough-talking Vice President Agnew to attack the "nattering nabobs of negativism" who demanded quick withdrawal from Vietnam. Nixon himself in 1970 sneered at the student antiwar demonstrators as "bums."

By January 1970 the Vietnam conflict had become the longest in American history and, with some 40,000 killed and over 250,000 wounded, the third most costly foreign war in the nation's experience. Especially in the war's early stages, African-Americans were disproportionately represented in the army and accounted for a disproportionately high share of combat casualties. Black and white soldiers alike floundered through booby-trapped swamps and steaming jungles, often unable to distinguish friend from foe among the black-clad peasants. Drug abuse, mutiny, and sabotage dulled the army's fighting edge. Domestic disgust with the war was further deepened in 1970 by revelations that in 1968 American troops had massacred innocent women and children in the village of My Lai. Increasingly desperate for a quick end to the demoralizing conflict, Nixon widened the war in 1970 by attacking Vietnam's neighbor, Cambodia.

"Cambodianizing" the Vietnam War

Without consulting Congress, Nixon suddenly ordered American forces on April 29, 1970, to invade Cambodia, which was officially neutral but had long been used as a staging area by the North Vietnamese and Viet Cong. Students nationwide responded to the Cambodian invasion with frustrations expressed every way from peaceful protests to more violent rock throwing and arson. Government efforts to contain the protests turned violent, too. During demonstrations at Kent State University in Ohio, National Guard troops opened fire and killed four students; at Jackson State College, in Mississippi, the highway patrol killed two students.

Nixon withdrew the American troops from Cambodia after only two months. Nevertheless, in America the invasion deepened the bitterness between "hawks" and "doves," as right-wing groups physically assaulted leftists. Disillusionment with "whitey's war" increased ominously among African-Americans in the armed forces. The Senate (though not the House) overwhelmingly repealed the Gulf of Tonkin blank check that Congress had given Johnson in 1964 and sought ways to restrain Nixon.

In the spring of 1971, mass rallies and marches once more erupted from coast to coast. New combustibles fueled the fires of antiwar discontent in June 1971, when the *New York Times* published a top-secret Pentagon study of America's involvement in the Vietnam War. These Pentagon Papers, "leaked" to the *Times* by former Pentagon official Daniel Ellsberg, laid bare the blunders and deceptions of the Kennedy and Johnson administrations, especially the provoking of the 1964 North Vietnamese attack in the Gulf of Tonkin.

Nixon in Beijing and Moscow

As the antiwar firestorm flared ever higher, Nixon daringly concluded that the road out of Vietnam ran through Beijing (Peking) and Moscow. He perceived that tensions between the Chinese and the Soviets afforded the United States an opportunity to play off one antagonist against the other—and to enlist the aid of both in pressuring North Vietnam into peace. Nixon's thinking was reinforced by his bespectacled and German-accented national security adviser,

LURIE'S OPINION

CHINESE SUMMIT

USSR SUMM

Balancing Act *Nixon treads delicately between the two communist superpowers in 1973, holding some of the wheat with which he enticed both into détente.*

Dr. Henry Kissinger, who in 1969 began negotiating secretly with North Vietnamese officials in Paris while preparing the president's path to Beijing and Moscow.

Nixon, heretofore an uncompromising anticommunist, startled the nation with his historic journey to China in February 1972, which paved the way for improved relations between Washington and Beijing. Nixon next traveled to Moscow in May 1972 to play his "China card" in a game of high-stakes diplomacy in the Kremlin. The Soviets, hungry for American foodstuffs and alarmed over the possibility of intensified rivalry with an American-backed China, were ready to deal.

Nixon's visits ushered in an era of détente, or relaxed tensions, and produced several significant agreements. First was the great grain deal of 1972, by which the food-rich United States agreed to sell the Soviets at least $750 million worth of wheat, corn, and other grain. More importantly, the two superpowers

agreed to an antiballistic missile (ABM) treaty, which limited each nation to two clusters of defensive missiles. Another significant pact was a SALT (for Strategic Arms Limitations Talks) agreement to freeze the numbers of long-range nuclear missiles for five years.

These accords, both ratified in 1972, constituted a long-overdue first step toward slowing the arms race. Yet even though the ABM treaty forbade elaborate defensive systems, the United States forged ahead with the development of "MIRVs" (Multiple Independently Targeted Reentry Vehicles), designed to overcome any defense by "saturating" it with large numbers of warheads, several to a rocket. Predictably, the Soviets proceeded to "MIRV" their own missiles, and the arms race ratcheted up to a still more perilous plateau, with over sixteen thousand nuclear warheads deployed by both sides in the 1980s.

Nixon's détente diplomacy did, to some extent, de-ice the Cold War. Moreover, by checkmating and co-opting the two great communist powers, the president had cleverly set the stage for America's exit from Vietnam. But the concluding act in that wrenching tragedy still remained to be played.

Nixon on the Home Front

Nixon had lashed out during the campaign at the "permissiveness" and "judicial activism" of the Supreme Court presided over by Chief Justice Earl Warren. Following his appointment in 1953, Warren had led the Court into a series of decisions that drastically affected sexual freedom, civil rights, criminal law, the practice of religion, and the structure of political representation. In *Griswold* v. *Connecticut* (1965), the Court struck down a state law that prohibited the use of contraceptives. The Court proclaimed (critics said "invented") a "right of privacy" that soon provided the intellectual foundation for Court decisions on abortion. Other controversial decisions were the case of *Miranda* (1966), which gave accused criminals the right to remain silent, and a set of decisions in 1962 and 1963 prohibiting required prayers and Bible readings in public schools on the basis of the First Amendment separation of church and state. Because these divisive decisions affected stubborn social problems, the Court came under relentless criticism, the bitterest since New Deal days.

Fulfilling campaign promises, President Nixon undertook to change the Court's philosophical complexion. Taking advantage of several vacancies, he sought appointees who would strictly interpret the Constitution, cease "meddling" in social and political questions, and not coddle radicals or criminals. The Senate in 1969 speedily confirmed his nomination of white-maned Warren E. Burger of Minnesota to succeed the retiring Earl Warren as chief justice. Before the end of 1971 the Court counted four conservative Nixon appointments out of nine members.

Yet Nixon was to learn the ironic lesson that many presidents have learned about their Supreme Court appointees: once seated on the high bench, the justices are fully free to think and decide according to their own beliefs, not according to the president's expectations. The Burger Court that Nixon shaped proved reluctant to dismantle the "liberal" rulings of the Warren Court; it even produced the most controversial judicial opinion of modern times, the *Roe* v. *Wade* decision in 1973, which legalized abortion (see p. 619).

Surprisingly, Nixon presided over significant expansion of the welfare programs that conservative Republicans routinely denounced. He approved increased funds for entitlements like Food Stamps, Medicaid, and Aid to Families with Dependent Children (AFDC), and he added a generous new program, Supplemental Security Income (SSI), to aid the indigent, blind, and disabled. Nixon also signed legislation in 1972 guaranteeing automatic Social Security cost-of-living increases to protect the elderly against the ravages of inflation. Ironically, this "indexing" actually helped to fuel the inflationary fires.

Amid much controversy, Nixon inaugurated his so-called Philadelphia Plan in 1969 to compel construction trade unions to hire more African-Americans. Soon extended to all federal contracts, the Philadelphia Plan required employers to meet hiring quotas or to establish "set-asides" for minority contractors. Nixon's policy went beyond earlier definitions of "affirmative action" to confer privileges on certain *groups*. While opening broad employment and educational opportunities for minorities and women, this approach opened a Pandora's box of protest from critics who assailed "reverse discrimination" created by executive orders and unelected courts.

Among other legacies of the Nixon years was the creation in 1970 of the Environmental Protection Agency (EPA) and a companion body, the Occupational Safety and Health Administration (OSHA). Their births climaxed two decades of mounting concern for the environment. Inspired in part by author Rachel Carson's enormously effective *Silent Spring* (1962), the environmental movement pushed through the Clean Air Act of 1970, the Endangered Species Act of 1973, and similar laws. As a result, the ensuing decades saw notable progress in cleaning up befouled air, water, and waste sites. Congress also stopped funding any more of the huge irrigation projects that had damaged much of the arid West over the preceding half-century.

Elected as a minority president, with only 43 percent of the vote in 1968, Nixon devised a clever but cynical plan—called the "southern strategy"—to achieve a solid majority in 1972. Appointing conservative Supreme Court justices, soft-pedaling civil rights, and opposing school busing to achieve racial balance were all part of the strategy.

The Nixon Landslide of 1972

As fate would have it, the war in Vietnam, not domestic issues, dominated the presidential campaign of 1972. Nearly four years had passed since Nixon had promised, as a presidential candidate, to end the war and "win" the peace. Yet in the spring of 1972 the fighting escalated anew to alarming levels when the North Vietnamese, heavily equipped with foreign tanks, burst through the demilitarized zone separating the two Vietnams. Nixon reacted promptly by launching massive bombing attacks on strategic centers in North Vietnam, including Hanoi, the capital. Gambling heavily on Soviet and Chinese forbearance, he also ordered the dropping of contact mines to blockade the principal harbors of North Vietnam.

The continuing Vietnam conflict spurred the rise of South Dakota senator George McGovern to the 1972 Democratic nomination. McGovern's promise to pull the remaining American troops out of Vietnam in ninety days earned him the backing of the large antiwar element in the party. But his appeal to racial minorities, feminists, leftists, and youth alienated the traditional working-class backbone of his party.

Moreover, the discovery, shortly after the convention, that McGovern's running mate, Missouri senator Thomas Eagleton, had undergone psychiatric care forced Eagleton's removal from the ticket and virtually doomed McGovern's candidacy.

Nixon's campaign emphasized that he had wound down the "Democratic war" in Vietnam from some 540,000 troops to about 30,000. His candidacy received an added boost just twelve days before the election when the high-flying Dr. Kissinger announced that "peace is at hand" in Vietnam and that an agreement would be settled in a few days.

Nixon won the election in a landslide. His lopsided victory encompassed every state except Massachusetts and the nonstate District of Columbia. He piled up 520 electoral votes to 17 and a popular majority of 47,169,911 votes to 29,170,383. Nixon's claim that the election gave him an unprecedented mandate for his policies was weakened by Republican election losses in both House and Senate.

The dove of peace, "at hand" in Vietnam just before the balloting, took flight after the election. After the fighting on both sides had again escalated, Nixon launched a furious two-week bombing of North Vietnam. This merciless pounding resulted in substantial losses of America's big B-52 bombers, but it drove North Vietnamese negotiators to agree to cease-fire arrangements on January 23, 1973, nearly three months after peace was prematurely proclaimed.

Nixon hailed the face-saving agreement as "peace with honor," but the boast rang hollow. The United States was to withdraw its remaining 27,000 or so troops and could reclaim some 560 American prisoners of war. The North Vietnamese were allowed to keep some 145,000 troops in South Vietnam, where they still occupied about 30 percent of the country. This shaky "peace" was in reality little more than a thinly disguised American retreat.

Watergate Woes

Nixon's electoral triumph was soon sullied by the so-called Watergate scandals. On June 17, 1972, some two months before his renomination, a bungled burglary had occurred in the Democratic headquarters, located in the Watergate apartment-office complex in Washington. Five men were arrested inside the building with electronic "bugging" equipment in their possession. They were working for the Republican Committee for the Re-election of the President—popularly known as CREEP—which had managed to raise tens of millions of dollars, often by secretive, unethical, or unlawful means. CREEP had also engaged in a "dirty tricks" campaign of espionage and sabotage, including faked documents, directed against Democratic candidates in the campaign of 1972.

The Watergate break-in was only the tip of an iceberg in a slimy sea of corruption that made the Grant and Harding scandals look almost respectable. The scandal in Washington also provoked the improper or illegal use of the Federal Bureau of Investigation and the Central Intelligence Agency. Even the Internal Revenue Service was called upon by Nixon's aides to audit or otherwise harass political opponents and others who had fallen into disfavor. A White

Nixon, the Law-and-Order Man

House "enemies list" turned up that included innocent citizens who were to be hounded or prosecuted in various ways. In the name of national security, Nixon's aides had authorized a burglary of the files of Dr. Daniel Ellsberg's psychiatrist, so great was the determination to convict the man who had "leaked" the Pentagon Papers. This was the most notorious exploit of the White House "plumbers unit," created to plug up leaks of confidential information.

A select Senate committee, headed by the aging Senator Sam Ervin of North Carolina, conducted a prolonged and widely televised series of hearings in 1973–1974. John Dean III, a former White House lawyer with a remarkable memory, testified glibly and at great length as to the involvement of the top echelons in the White House, including the president, in the cover-up of the Watergate break-in. Dean in effect accused Nixon of the crime of obstructing justice. But the committee then had only the unsupported word of Dean against weighty White House protestations of innocence.

The Great Tape Controversy

A bombshell exploded before Senator Ervin's committee in July 1973 when a former presidential aide reported the presence in the White House of bugging equipment, installed under the president's authority. President Nixon's conversations, in person or on the telephone, had been recorded on tape without notifying the other parties that electronic eavesdropping was taking place.

Nixon had emphatically denied prior knowledge of the Watergate burglary or involvement in the cover-up. Now Dean's sensational testimony could be checked against the White House tapes, and the Senate committee could better determine who was telling the truth. But for months Nixon flatly refused to produce the taped evidence. He took refuge behind various principles, including separation of powers and executive privilege.

The anxieties of the White House deepened when Vice President Spiro Agnew was forced to resign in October 1973 for taking bribes or "kickbacks" from Maryland contractors. President Nixon himself was now in danger of being removed by the impeachment route, so Congress invoked the Twenty-fifth Amendment (see the Appendix) to replace Agnew with a twelve-term congressman from Michigan, Gerald ("Jerry") Ford.

Ten days after Agnew's resignation came the "Saturday night massacre" (October 20, 1973). Archibald Cox, a Harvard law professor appointed as a "special prosecutor" by Nixon in May, issued a subpoena for relevant tapes and other documents from the White House. Nixon thereupon ordered the firing of Cox and then accepted the resignations of the attorney general and the deputy attorney general because they refused to fire him.

The Secret Bombing of Cambodia and the War Powers Act

As if Watergate were not enough, the constitutionality of Nixon's continued aerial battering of Cambodia came under increasing fire. In July 1973 America was shocked to learn that the U.S. Air Force had already secretly conducted some thirty-five hundred bombing raids against North Vietnamese positions in Cambodia. They had begun in March 1969 and continued for some fourteen months prior to the open American incursion in May 1970. The most disturbing feature of these sky forays was that, while they were going on, American officials, including the president, were avowing that Cambodian neutrality was being respected. Countless Americans began to wonder what kind of representative government they had if they were fighting a war they knew nothing about.

Defiance followed secretiveness. After the Vietnam cease-fire in January 1973, Nixon openly carried on his large-scale bombing of communist forces in order to help the rightist Cambodian government. This stretching of presidential war-making powers met furious opposition from the public and from a clear majority of both houses of Congress, which repeatedly tried to stop the bombing by cutting off appropriations. But Nixon's vetoes of such legislation were always sustained by at least one-third plus one vote in the House. Finally, with appropriations running short, Nixon agreed to a compromise in June 1973 whereby he would end the Cambodian bombing six weeks later and seek congressional approval of any future action in that bomb-blasted country.

Congressional opposition to the expansion of presidential war-making powers by Johnson and Nixon led to the War Powers Act in November 1973. Passed over Nixon's veto, it required the president to report to Congress within forty-eight hours after committing troops to a foreign conflict or "substantially" enlarging American combat units in a foreign country. Such a limited authorization would have to end within sixty days unless Congress extended it for thirty more days.

Compelling Nixon to end the bombing of Cambodia in August 1973 was but one manifestation of what came to be called the "New Isolationism." The draft had ended in January 1973, although it was retained on a standby basis. Future members of the armed forces were to be well-paid volunteers—a change that greatly eased tensions among youth.

The Arab Oil Embargo and the Energy Crisis

Adding to Nixon's problems, the long-rumbling Middle East erupted anew in October 1973, when the rearmed Syrians and Egyptians unleashed surprise attacks on Israel. Kissinger, who had become secretary of state in September, hastily flew to Moscow in an effort to restrain the Soviets, who were supplying the attackers. Believing that the Kremlin was poised to fly combat troops to the Suez area, Nixon placed America's nuclear forces on alert and ordered a gigantic airlift of nearly $2 billion in war materials to the Israelis. This assistance helped save the day, as the Israelis brilliantly turned the tide and threatened Cairo until American diplomacy brought about an uneasy cease-fire.

America's policy of backing Israel against its oil-rich neighbors exacted a heavy penalty. Late in October 1973, the Arab nations suddenly clamped an embargo on oil for the United States and other countries supporting Israel. Americans had to suffer through a long, cold winter of lowered thermostats and speedometers. Lines of automobiles at service stations lengthened as tempers shortened and a business recession deepened.

The "energy crisis" suddenly energized a number of long-deferred projects. Congress approved a costly Alaska oil pipeline and a national speed limit of 55 miles per hour in order to save fuel. Agitation mounted for heavier use of coal and nuclear power, despite the environmental threat posed by these energy sources.

The five months of the Arab "blackmail" embargo in 1974 clearly signaled the end of an era—a period of cheap and abundant energy. American oil production peaked in 1970 and then began an irreversible decline. Blissfully unaware of their dependence on foreign suppliers, Americans, like revelers on a binge, had more than tripled their oil consumption since the end of World War II. The number of automobiles increased two and a half times between 1949 and 1972.

By 1974 America was addicted to oil and extremely vulnerable to any interruption in supplies. That stark fact colored the diplomatic and economic history of the 1980s and 1990s. The Middle East loomed ever larger on the map of America's strategic interests, until the United States in 1990 at last found itself pulled into a shooting war with Iraq to protect its oil supplies (see page 622).

The Middle Eastern sheiks had approximately quadrupled their price for crude oil after lifting the embargo in 1974. Huge new oil bills wildly disrupted the U.S. balance of international trade and added fuel to the raging fires of inflation. Various sectors of the economy, including Detroit's carmakers, began their slow, grudging adjustment to the rudely dawning age of energy dependency. But full reconciliation to that uncomfortable reality was a long time coming.

The Unmaking of a President

Political tribulations added to the nation's cup of woe in 1974. The continuing impeachment inquiry cast damning doubts on Nixon's integrity. Responding at last to the House Judiciary Committee's demand for the Watergate tapes, Nixon agreed in the spring of 1974 to the publication of "relevant" portions of the tapes, declaring that these would vindicate him. But substantial sections of the wanted tapes were missing, and Nixon's frequent obscenities were excised with the phrase "expletive deleted."

Confronted with demands for the rest of the material, Nixon flatly refused. On July 24, 1974, the president suffered a disastrous setback when the

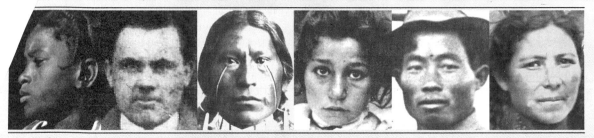
The Vietnamese

At first glance, the towns of Westminster and Fountain Valley, California, seem to resemble other California communities nearby. Tract homes line residential streets; shopping centers flank the busy thoroughfares. But these are no ordinary American suburbs. Instead, they make up "Little Saigons," vibrant outposts of Vietnamese culture in the contemporary United States.

Before South Vietnam fell in 1975, few Vietnamese ventured across the Pacific. Only in 1966 did U.S. immigration authorities even designate "Vietnamese" as a separate category of newcomers, and most early immigrants were the wives and children of U.S. servicemen. But as the communists closed in on Saigon, many Vietnamese, particularly those who had worked closely with American or South Vietnamese authorities, feared for their future. Gathering together as many of their extended-family members as they could assemble, thousands of Vietnamese fled for their lives. In a few hectic days in 1975, some 140,000 escaped before the approaching gunfire, a few dramatically clinging to the bottoms of departing helicopters. Another 60,000 less fortunate refugees escaped at the same time over land and sea to Hong Kong and Thailand, where they waited nervously for permission to move on.

Preserving the Past *A Vietnamese-American boy learns classical calligraphy from his grandfather.*

To accommodate the refugees, the U.S. government set up camps across the nation. Arrivals were crowded into army barracks affording little room and less privacy. These were boot camps not for military service but for assimilation into American society. A rigorous program trained the Vietnamese in English, forbade children from speaking their native language in the classroom, and even immersed them in American slang. Many resented this attempt to mold them and strip them of their culture.

Their discontent boiled over when authorities prepared to release the refugees from camps and board them with families around the nation. The resettlement officials had decided to find a sponsor for each Vietnamese family—an American family that would provide food, shelter, and assistance for the refugees until they could fend for themselves. But the Vietnamese people cherish their traditional extended families—grandparents, uncles, aunts, and cousins living communally with parents and children. The refugees were dispersed to Iowa, Illinois, Pennsylvania, New York, Washington, and California. But as soon as they could, they relocated, hastening to established Vietnamese enclaves around San Francisco, Los Angeles, and Dallas.

Soon a second throng of Vietnamese immigrants pushed into these Little Saigons. Fleeing from the ravages of poverty and from the oppressive communist government, these stragglers had crammed themselves and their few possessions into little boats, hoping to reach Hong Kong or get picked up by friendly ships. Eventually, many of these "boat people" reached the United States. Usually less educated than the first arrivals and receiving far less resettlement aid from the U.S. government, they were, however, more willing to start at the bottom. Today these two groups total more than half a million people. Differing in experience and expectations, the Vietnamese share a new home in a strange land. Their uprooting is an immense, unreckoned consequence of America's longest war.

Supreme Court unanimously ruled that "executive privilege" gave him no right to withhold from the special prosecutor portions of tapes relevant to criminal activity. Skating on thin ice over hot water, Nixon reluctantly complied.

The House Judiciary Committee pressed ahead with its articles of impeachment. The key vote came late in July 1974, when the committee adopted the first article, which charged obstruction of "the administration of justice," including Watergate-related crimes. Two other articles were later approved by the committee, accusing Nixon of abusing the powers of his office and showing contempt of Congress by ignoring lawful subpoenas for relevant tapes and other evidence.

On August 5, 1974, Nixon finally made public three subpoenaed tapes of conversations with his chief aide on June 23, 1972. One of them had him giving orders, six days after the Watergate break-in, to use the CIA to hold back an inquiry by the FBI. Now Nixon's own tape-recorded words convicted him of having been an active party to the attempted cover-up, in itself the crime of obstructing justice. More than that, he had solemnly told the American people on television that he had known nothing of the Watergate cover-up until about nine months later.

The public backlash proved to be overwhelming. Republican leaders in Congress concluded that the guilty and unpredictable Nixon was a loose cannon on the deck of the ship of state. They frankly informed the president that his impeachment by the full House and removal by the Senate were foregone conclusions and that he would do best to resign.

Left with no better choice, Nixon choked back his tears and announced his resignation in a dramatic television appearance on August 8, 1974. In his Farewell Address, Nixon admitted having made some "judgments" that "were wrong" but insisted that he had always acted "in what I believed at the time to be the best interests of the nation." Unconvinced, countless Americans would change the song "Hail to the Chief" to "Jail to the Chief."

The nation had survived a wrenching constitutional crisis, which proved that the impeachment

...nery forged by the Founding Fathers could when public opinion overwhelmingly de-...ided that it be implemented. The principles that person is above the law and that presidents must ...e held to strict accountability for their acts were strengthened. The United States of America, on the eve of its two-hundredth birthday as a republic, had given an impressive demonstration of self-discipline and self-government to the rest of the world.

The First Unelected President

Gerald Rudolph Ford, the first man to be made president solely by a vote of Congress, entered the besmirched White House, in August 1974, with serious handicaps. He was widely—and unfairly—suspected of being little more than a dim-witted former college football player. President Johnson had sneered that "Jerry" was so lacking in brainpower that he could not walk and chew gum at the same time. Worse, Ford had been selected, not elected, vice president, following Spiro Agnew's resignation in disgrace. The sour odor of illegitimacy hung about this president without precedent.

Then, out of a clear sky, Ford granted a complete pardon to Nixon for any crimes he may have committed as president, discovered or undiscovered. Democrats were outraged, and lingering suspicions about the pardon cast a dark shadow over Ford's prospects of being elected president in his own right in 1976.

Ford at first sought to enhance the so-called détente with the Soviet Union that Nixon had crafted. In July 1975 President Ford joined leaders from thirty-four other nations in Helsinki, Finland, to sign several sets of historic accords. One group of agreements officially wrote an end to World War II by finally legitimizing the Soviet-dictated boundaries of Poland and other East European countries. In return, the Soviets signed a "third basket" of agreements, guaranteeing more liberal exchanges of people and information between East and West and protecting certain basic "human rights." The Helsinki accords kindled small dissident movements in Eastern Europe and even in the USSR itself, but the Soviets soon poured ice water on these sputtering flames of freedom. Moscow's restrictions on Jewish emigration had already, in December 1974, prompted Congress to add punitive restrictions to a U.S.-Soviet trade bill.

West Europeans, especially the West Germans, cheered the Helsinki conference as a milestone of détente. But in the United States critics increasingly charged that détente was proving to be a one-way street, with American grain and technology flowing across the Atlantic to the USSR and little of comparable importance flowing back.

Despite these difficulties, Ford at first clung stubbornly to détente. But the American public's fury over Moscow's double-dealing so steadily mounted that by the end of his term the president was refusing even to pronounce the word *détente* in public. The thaw in the Cold War was threatening to prove chillingly brief.

Victory for North Vietnam

Early in 1975 the North Vietnamese gave full throttle to their long-expected drive southward. President Ford urged Congress to vote still more weapons for Vietnam. But his plea was in vain, and without the crutch of massive American aid, the South Vietnamese quickly and ingloriously collapsed.

The dam burst so rapidly that the remaining Americans had to be frantically evacuated by helicopter, the last of them on April 29, 1975. Also rescued were about 140,000 South Vietnamese, most of them so dangerously identified with the Americans that they feared a bloodbath by the victorious communists. Ford compassionately admitted these people to the United States, adding further seasoning to the melting pot. Eventually some 500,000 arrived (see "Makers of America: The Vietnamese," pp. 604–605).

America's longest, most frustrating war thus ended, not with a bang but a whimper. In a technical sense the Americans had not lost the war; their client nation had. The United States had fought the North Vietnamese to a standstill and had then withdrawn its troops in 1973, leaving the Vietnamese to fight their own war, with generous shipments of costly American aircraft, tanks, and other munitions. The estimated cost to America was $118 billion in current outlays, along with some 56,000 dead and 300,000 wounded. The people of the United States had in fact

Passing the Buck   *A satirical view of where responsibility for the Vietnam debacle should be laid.*

provided just about everything, except the will to win—and that could not be injected by outsiders.

Technicalities aside, America had in fact lost the war and more. It had lost face in the eyes of foreigners, lost its own self-esteem, lost confidence in its military prowess—and lost much of the economic muscle that had made possible its global leadership since World War II. Americans reluctantly came to realize that their power, as well as their pride, had been deeply wounded in Vietnam and that recovery would be slow and painful.

The Bicentennial Campaign and the Carter Victory

America's two-hundredth birthday, in 1976, fell during a presidential election year—a fitting coincidence for a proud democracy. Gerald Ford energetically sought nomination for the presidency in his own right and won the Republican nod at the Kansas City convention.

The Democratic standard-bearer was fifty-one-year-old James Earl Carter, Jr., a dark-horse candidate who galloped out of obscurity during the long primary-elections season. A former Georgia governor

who insisted on humble "Jimmy" as his first name, this born-again Baptist touched many people with his down-home sincerity. Untainted by ties with a corrupt and cynical Washington, Carter ran against the memory of Nixon and Watergate as much as he ran against Ford. His most effective campaign pitch was his promise that "I'll never lie to you."

Carter squeezed out a narrow victory on election day, with 51 percent of the popular vote. The electoral count stood at 297 to 240. The winner swept every state except Virginia in his native South. Especially important were the votes of African-Americans, 97 percent of whom cast their ballots for Carter.

Carter enjoyed hefty Democratic majorities in both houses of Congress. Hopes ran high that the stalemate of the Nixon-Ford years between a Republican White House and a Democratic Capitol Hill would now be ended. At first, Carter enjoyed notable political success, as Congress granted his requests to create a new cabinet-level Department of Energy and to cut taxes by some $18 billion in 1978. But Carter's honeymoon did not last long. An inexperienced outsider, he had campaigned against the Washington "establishment," and he never quite made the transition to being an insider himself. He repeatedly

d congressional fur the wrong way, and critics
ged that he isolated himself in a shallow pool of
ow Georgians.

Carter's Humanitarian Diplomacy

As a committed Christian, President Carter displayed from the outset an overriding concern for "human rights" as the guiding principle of his foreign policy. In the African nations of Rhodesia (later Zimbabwe) and South Africa, Carter and his eloquent United Nations ambassador, Andrew Young, championed the oppressed black majority.

The president's most spectacular foreign policy achievement came in September 1978 when he invited President Anwar Sadat of Egypt and Prime Minister Menachem Begin of Israel to the presidential retreat at Camp David, Maryland, in an attempt to prevent another blowup in the misery-drenched Middle East. Skillfully serving as go-between, Carter persuaded the two visitors to sign an accord (September 17, 1978) that held considerable promise of peace. Israel agreed in principle to withdraw from territory conquered in the 1967 war, and Egypt in return promised to respect Israel's borders. Both parties pledged themselves to sign a formal peace treaty within three months.

Carter achieved further diplomatic success by resuming full diplomatic relations with China in 1979. He also concluded two treaties designed to turn over complete ownership and control of the Panama Canal to Panamanians by the year 2000.

Despite these dramatic accomplishments, trouble stalked Carter's foreign policy. Overshadowing all international issues was the ominous reheating of the Cold War with the USSR. Détente fell into disrepute as thousands of Cuban troops, assisted by Soviet advisers, appeared in Angola, Ethiopia, and elsewhere in Africa to support revolutionary factions. Arms-control negotiations with Moscow stalled in the face of this Soviet military meddling.

Carter's Economic and Energy Woes

Adding to Carter's mushrooming troubles was the failing health of the economy. A stinging recession during Gerald Ford's presidency had temporarily slowed inflation, but virtually from the moment of Carter's inauguration, prices resumed their dizzying ascent, driving the inflation rate well above 13 percent by 1979. The soaring bill for imported oil pushed America's balance of payments deeply into the red (an unprecedented $40 billion in 1978).

The "oil shocks" of the 1970s taught Americans a painful but necessary lesson: they could never again seriously consider a policy of economic isolation, as they had tried to do between the two world wars. For most of American history, foreign trade had accounted for no more than 10 percent of gross national product (GNP), but the huge foreign-oil bills began a trend that, by century's end, left some 27 percent of GNP dependent on foreign trade. Unable to dominate international trade and finance as they once had, Americans would now have to master foreign languages and study foreign cultures if they wanted to prosper in the rapidly globalizing economy.

Yawning deficits in the federal budget, reaching nearly $60 billion in 1980, further aggravated the U.S. economy's inflationary ailments. The elderly and other Americans living on fixed incomes suffered from the shrinking dollar. People with money to lend pushed interest rates ever higher, hoping to protect themselves from being repaid in badly depreciated dollars. The "prime rate" (the rate of interest that banks charged their very best customers) vaulted to an unheard-of 20 percent in early 1980. The high cost of borrowing money shoved small businesses to the wall and strangled the construction industry.

Carter diagnosed America's economic disease as stemming primarily from the nation's costly dependence on foreign oil. Unfortunately, his legislative proposals in April 1977 for energy conservation ignited a blaze of indifference among the American people, who had already forgotten the long gasoline lines of 1973.

Events in Iran jolted Americans out of their complacency about energy supplies in 1979. The imperious Mohammed Reza Pahlevi, installed as shah of Iran with help from America's CIA in 1953, had long ruled his oil-rich land with a will of steel. His repressive regime was finally overthrown in January 1979 in a violent revolution spearheaded by Muslim fundamentalists. The crippling upheavals of the revolution soon spread to Iran's oil fields. As Iranian oil supplies stopped flowing, shortages appeared, petroleum prices rose steeply, and Americans once more found themselves waiting impatiently in long lines at gas stations or buying gasoline only on specified days.

As the oil crisis deepened, President Carter sensed the rising temperature of popular discontent. In July 1979 he retreated to Camp David, where he remained largely out of public view for ten days. Like a royal potentate of old summoning the wise men of the realm for their counsel in a time of crisis, Carter called in over one hundred leaders from all walks of life to give him their views. The nation anxiously awaited the results of these extraordinary deliberations.

When he finally came down from the mountaintop on July 15, 1979, Carter stunned and perplexed the nation by chiding his fellow citizens for falling into "moral and spiritual crisis" and for being too concerned with "material goods." A few days later, the president let drop another shoe when he fired four cabinet secretaries and circled the wagons of his Georgian advisers more tightly about the White House. Critics began to wonder aloud whether Carter, the professed man of the people, was losing touch with the popular mood of the country.

Foreign Affairs and the Iranian Imbroglio

Hopes for a less dangerous world rose slightly in June 1979, when President Carter met with Soviet leader Leonid Brezhnev in Vienna to sign the long-stalled SALT II agreements, limiting the levels of lethal strategic weapons in the Soviet and American arsenals. But conservative critics of the president's defense policies, deeply suspicious of the Soviet Union, unsheathed their long knives to carve up the SALT treaty when it came to the Senate for debate in the summer of 1979.

Political earthquakes in the petroleum-rich Persian Gulf region finally buried all hopes of ratifying the treaty. On November 4, 1979, a howling mob of rabidly anti-American Muslim militants stormed the United States embassy in Teheran, Iran, and took all of its occupants hostage. World opinion hotly condemned the diplomatic felony in Iran, while Americans agonized over both the fate of the hostages and the stability of the entire Persian Gulf region. The Soviet army then aroused the West's worst fears on December 27, 1979, when it blitzed into the mountainous nation of Afghanistan, next door to Iran, and appeared to be poised for a thrust at the oil-jugular of the gulf.

President Carter reacted vigorously to these alarming events. He slapped an embargo on the export of grain and high-technology machinery to the USSR, called for a boycott of the upcoming Olympic Games in Moscow, and requested that young people (including women) be made to register for a possible military draft. Proclaiming that the United States would "use any means necessary, including force," to protect the Persian Gulf against Soviet incursions, Carter grimly conceded that he had misjudged the Soviets. The SALT treaty became a dead letter in the Senate. Meanwhile, the Soviet army met unexpectedly stiff resistance in Afghanistan and became bogged down in a nasty guerrilla war that came to be called "Russia's Vietnam."

The Iranian hostage crisis was Carter's—and America's—bed of nails. The captured Americans languished in cruel captivity, while the nightly news broadcasts showed humiliating scenes of Iranian mobs burning the American flag and spitting on effigies of Uncle Sam.

Carter at first tried to apply economic sanctions and the pressure of world opinion against the Iranians. But the president's frustration grew as the political upheaval in Iran rumbled on. Carter at last ordered a daring rescue mission. A highly trained commando team penetrated deep into Iran's sandy interior, but when equipment failures prevented some members of the team from reaching their destination, the mission had to be scrapped. As the commandos withdrew, two of their aircraft collided, killing eight of the would-be rescuers.

The disastrous failure of the rescue raid proved anguishing for Americans. The episode seemed to underscore the nation's helplessness and even incompetence in the face of a mortifying insult to the national honor. The stalemate with Iran dragged on throughout the rest of Carter's term, providing an embarrassing backdrop to the embattled president's struggle for reelection.

˩ronology

1968	My Lai massacre.
1969	Antiwar demonstrations.
	Nixon's Philadelphia Plan.
1970	Nixon orders invasion of Cambodia.
	Kent State and Jackson State incidents.
	Environmental Protection Agency (EPA) created.
	Clean Air Act.
1971	Pentagon Papers published.
1972	Nixon visits China and the Soviet Union.
	ABM and SALT I treaties ratified.
	Nixon defeats McGovern for presidency.
1973	Vietnam cease-fire and U.S. withdrawal.
	Agnew resigns; Ford appointed vice president.
	War Powers Act.
	Arab-Israeli war and Arab oil embargo.
	Endangered Species Act.
1973–1974	Watergate hearings and investigations.
1974	Nixon resigns; Ford assumes presidency.
	First OPEC oil-price increase.
1975	Helsinki accords.
	South Vietnam falls to communists.
1976	Carter defeats Ford for presidency.
1978	Egyptian-Israeli Camp David agreement.
1979	Iranian revolution and oil crisis.
	SALT II agreements signed (never ratified by Senate).
	Soviet Union invades Afghanistan.
1979–1981	Iranian hostage crisis.

SUGGESTED READINGS

Primary Source Documents

Richard Nixon's vision of the international order is delineated in his *RN: The Memoirs of Richard Nixon** (1978). The articles of impeachment reported against Nixon can be found in *House of Representatives Report No. 93-1305*, 93 Cong., 2 sess., pp. 1–2* (1974). Opposing opinions on the Panama Canal treaty were voiced by Cyrus Vance and Ronald Reagan, *Hearings Before the Committee on Foreign Relations*, United States Senate, 95 Cong., 1 sess., pp. 10–15, 96–103 (1977).

Secondary Sources

The most comprehensive account of Nixon's early career is Stephen E. Ambrose, *Nixon: The Education of a Politician, 1913–1962* (1987). See also his *Nixon: The Triumph of a Politician, 1962–1972* (1989). Nixon's intriguing personality is examined in Gary Wills, *Nixon Agonistes: The Crisis of the Self-Made Man* (1970). A wide-ranging discussion of the home front is in Kim McQuaid, *The Anxious Years: America in the Vietnam-Watergate Era* (1989). Valuable background on U.S. foreign policy in the Nixon years can be found in David P. Calleo and Benjamin Rowland, *America and the World Political Economy* (1973). A good biography of Nixon's secretary of state is Robert D. Schulzinger, *Henry Kissinger: Doctor of Diplomacy* (1989). The background to the oil crisis is charted in Michael B. Stoff, *Oil, War and American Security* (1980). Arthur M. Schlesinger, Jr., traces the growth of *The Imperial Presidency* (1973). The Watergate crisis is vividly described in two books by Carl Bernstein and Robert Woodward, *All the President's Men* (1974) and *The Final Days* (1976), and in Stanley I. Kutler, *The Wars of Watergate* (1990). Jonathan Schell, *The Time of Illusion* (1976), assesses the impact of the crisis on the nation's spirit and institutions. Robert Greene describes the Nixon and Ford administrations in *The Limits of Power* (1992). "Jerry" Ford, the first appointed president, is analyzed by his former press secretary in J. F. ter Horst, *Gerald Ford and the Future of the Presidency* (1974). For a sharply critical view see Clark Mollenhoff, *The Man Who Pardoned Nixon* (1976). On Jimmy Carter consult David Kucharsky, *The Man from Plains* (1976), and Betty Glad, *Jimmy Carter: In Search of the Great White House* (1980).

---

*An asterisk indicates that the document, or an excerpt from it, can be found in Thomas A. Bailey and David M. Kennedy, eds., *The American Spirit: United States History as Seen by Contemporaries*, 9th ed. (Boston: Houghton Mifflin, 1998).

41

****

The Resurgence of Conservatism,

1980–1999

******

It will be my intention to curb the size and influence of the federal establishment and to demand recognition of the distinction between the powers granted to the federal government and those reserved to the states or to the people.

******

RONALD REAGAN, INAUGURAL ADDRESS, 1981

The Triumph of Conservatism

Bedeviled abroad and becalmed at home, Carter's administration struck many Americans as bungling and befuddled. Carter's inability to control double-digit inflation was especially damaging.

Disaffection with Carter's apparent ineptitude ran deep even in his own Democratic party, where an "ABC" (Anybody But Carter) movement gathered steam, especially among liberal inheritors of the New Deal tradition. They found their champion in Senator Edward Kennedy of Massachusetts, who in late 1979 declared his intention to contest Carter's renomina-

tion. Carter finally emerged the winner after a series of bruising primary elections, but the Democratic party was left divided and in disarray.

Meanwhile, delighted Republicans decorously proceeded to select their presidential nominee. Ronald Reagan, perennial darling of the right wing, easily outdistanced his rivals and secured the nomination he had sought for a decade.

The hour of the conservative right seemed at last to have arrived. Census figures confirmed that the average American was older than in the stormy and much more likely to live in the South [and West], the traditional bastions of the "old right." [The] conservative cause drew added strength from [the] emergence of a "new right" movement. Spearheading the new right were evangelical Christian groups such as the Moral Majority, who enjoyed startling success as political fund-raisers and organizers. Many new-right activists were especially agitated about cultural and social issues like abortion, the Equal Rights Amendment, pornography, homosexuality, feminism, and especially affirmative action. They championed prayer in the schools and tougher penalties for criminals. Together, the old and new right added up to a powerful political combination.

Of all the social issues, those involving race were among the most politically explosive. The Supreme Court in *Milliken* v. *Bradley* (1974) had effectively exempted suburban school districts from responsibility for desegregating inner-city schools, thereby reinforcing "white flight" from cities to suburbs. The problems of desegregation therefore fell to the least prosperous urban districts, often pitting disadvantaged white and black communities against one another. Boston and other cities were shaken to their foundations by attempts to implement school-desegregation plans.

Affirmative action programs also remained highly controversial. White workers denied advancement and white students refused college admission continued to cry "reverse discrimination." One white Californian, Alan Bakke, won a narrow five-to-four Supreme Court decision in 1978 when he claimed that his medical school application had been turned down because of an admission program that favored minority applicants. In a tortured decision that reflected the moral and political complexities of the issue, the Court ordered the University of California to admit Bakke and declared that automatic preference in admissions could not be given on the basis of racial or ethnic identity alone. Yet at the same time the justices ruled that racial factors might be taken into account in a school's overall admissions policy.

The Election of Ronald Reagan, 1980

Ronald Reagan was well suited to lead the gathering conservative crusade. Reared in a generation whose values were formed well before the upheavals of the 1960s, he naturally sided with the new right on social issues. In economic and social matters alike, he denounced the activist government and failed "social engineering" of the 1960s. As his early political hero

The Abortion Wars
Pro-choice and pro-life demonstrators brandish their beliefs. By the end of the twentieth century, the debate over abortion had become the most morally charged and divisive issue in American society since the struggle over slavery in the nineteenth century.

Franklin Roosevelt had championed the "forgotten man" against big business, the Republican Reagan championed the "common man" against big government. He aimed especially to win over from the Democratic column working-class and lower-middle-class white voters by implying that the Democratic party had become the exclusive tool of its minority constituents.

Although Reagan was no intellectual, he drew on the ideas of a small but influential group of thinkers known as "neoconservatives." Reacting against what they saw as the excesses of 1960s liberalism, the neoconservatives championed free-market capitalism liberated from government restraints, and they took tough, harshly anti-Soviet positions in foreign policy. They also questioned liberal welfare programs and affirmative-action policies and called for reassertion of traditional values of individualism and the centrality of the family.

An actor turned politician, Reagan enjoyed enormous popularity with his crooked grin and "aw-shucks" manner. Facing a badly battered Jimmy Carter, the Republican candidate proved to be a formidable campaigner. Reagan attacked the incumbent's fumbling performance in foreign policy and blasted the "big-government" philosophy of the Democratic party (a philosophy that Carter did not fully share).

Carter's spotty record in office was no defense against Reagan's popular appeal. On election day the Republican rang up a spectacular victory, bagging over 51 percent of the popular vote, while 41 percent went to Carter and 7 percent to independent candidate John Anderson. The electoral count stood at 489 for Reagan and 49 for Carter. Equally startling, the Republicans gained control of the Senate for the first time in twenty-five years. Democratic liberals who had been "targeted" for defeat by well-heeled new-right groups went down like dead timber in the conservative windstorm that swept the country.

Carter showed dignity in defeat. An unusually intelligent, articulate, and well-meaning president, he had been hampered by his lack of managerial talent and had been badly buffeted by events beyond his control, such as the soaring price of oil, runaway inflation, and the galling insult of the continuing hostage crisis in Iran. If Carter was correct in believ-

The New Right Wing *Republican conservatives scored a double victory in 1980, winning control of both the White House and the Senate. Aided by conservative Democratic "boll weevils," they also dominated the House of Representatives, and a new era of conservatism dawned in the nation's capital.*

ing that the country was suffering from a terrible "malaise," he never found the right medicine to cure the disease.

The Reagan Revolution

Reagan's arrival in Washington was triumphal. The Iranians contributed to the festive mood by releasing the hostages on Reagan's inauguration day, January 20, 1981, after 444 days of captivity. The new president, a hale and hearty sixty-nine-year-old, was devoted to fiscal fitness. A major goal of Reagan's political career was to reduce the size of the government by shrinking the federal budget and slashing taxes. Years of New Deal–style tax-and-spend programs, Reagan jested, had created a federal government that reminded him of the definition of a baby as a creature who was all appetite at one end, with no sense of responsibility at the other.

By the early 1980s, this antigovernment message was finding a receptive audience. In the two decades since 1960, federal spending had risen from about 18 percent of gross national product to nearly 23 percent. After four decades of advancing New Deal and Great Society programs, a strong countercurrent took hold. Californians staged a "tax revolt" in 1978 (known by its official ballot title of "Proposition 13") that slashed property taxes and forced painful cuts in government services. The California "tax quake" jolted other state capitals and rocked even Washington, D.C. Ronald Reagan rode this political shock wave to presidential victory in 1980 and proceeded to rattle the "welfare state" to its very foundation.

With near-religious zeal, Reagan set out to persuade Congress to legislate his smaller-government policies into law. He proposed a new federal budget that necessitated cuts of some $35 billion, mostly in social programs like Food Stamps and federally funded job-training centers. Reagan worked naturally in harness with the Republican majority in the Senate, while in the Democratic House he enterprisingly wooed a group of mostly southern conservative Democrats (dubbed "boll weevils"), who abandoned their own party's leadership to follow the president.

Then on March 20, 1981, a deranged gunman shot the president as he was leaving a Washington hotel. A .22-caliber bullet penetrated beneath Reagan's left arm and collapsed his left lung. With admirable courage and grace, and with impressive physical resilience for a man his age, Reagan recovered rapidly from his violent ordeal. Twelve days after the attack, he walked out of the hospital and returned to work. When he appeared a few days later on national television to address the Congress and the public on his budget, the outpouring of sympathy and support was enormous.

The Battle of the Budget

Swept along on a tide of presidential popularity, Congress swallowed Reagan's budget proposals, approving expenditures of some $695 billion. To hit those financial targets, drastic surgery was required, and Congress plunged its scalpel deeply into Great Society–spawned social programs. Reagan's triumph amazed political observers, especially defeated Democrats. The new president had descended on Washington like an avenging angel of conservatism. He sought nothing less than the dismantling of the welfare state and the reversal of the political evolution of the preceding half-century. Reagan's impressive performance demonstrated the power of the presidency with a skill not seen since Lyndon Johnson's day.

Reagan hardly rested to savor the sweetness of his victory. The second part of his economic program called for deep tax cuts, amounting to 25 percent across-the-board reductions over a period of three years. Thanks largely to Reagan's skill as a television performer and the continued defection of the "boll weevils" from the Democratic camp, the president again had his way. In August 1981 Congress approved a set of far-reaching tax reforms that lowered individual tax rates, virtually eliminated federal estate taxes, and created new tax-free savings plans for small investors. Reagan's "supply-side" economic advisers assured him that the combination of budgetary discipline and tax reduction would stimulate new investment, boost productivity, and foster dramatic economic growth.

But at first "supply-side" economics seemed to be a beautiful theory mugged by a gang of brutal facts, as the economy slid into its deepest recession since the 1930s. Unemployment reached nearly 11 percent in 1982, businesses folded, and several bank failures jolted the nation's entire financial system. The automobile industry, once the brightest jewel in America's industrial crown, reported losses in the hundreds of millions of dollars.

Ignoring the yawping pack of Democratic critics who charged that the president's budget cuts favored only the well-to-do, Reagan and his economic advisers serenely waited for their supply-side economic policies ("Reaganomics") to produce the promised results. The supply-siders seemed to be vindicated when a healthy economic recovery finally got under way in 1983. Yet the economy of the 1980s was not uniformly sound. For the first time in the twentieth century, income gaps widened between the richest and the poorest Americans. The poor got poorer and the very rich grew fabulously richer, while middle-class incomes largely stagnated. Symbolic of the new income stratification was the emergence of "yuppies," or young urban professionals, who sported Rolex watches and BMW sports cars. Though numbering only about 1.5 million people, yuppies showcased the values of materialism and the pursuit of wealth that came to symbolize the high-rolling 1980s.

Some economists located the sources of the economic upturn neither in the president's budget cuts and tax reforms nor in the go-get-'em avarice of the yuppies, but in his massive expenditures for the military. Reagan cascaded a budget of nearly $2 trillion onto the Pentagon in the 1980s, asserting the need to close the "window of vulnerability" in the armaments race with the Soviet Union. Ironically, this conservative president thereby plunged the government into a red-ink bath of deficit spending that made the New Deal look downright stingy. Federal budget deficits topped $100 billion in 1982, and the government's books were nearly $200 billion out of balance in every subsequent year of the 1980s. Massive government borrowing to cover these deficits kept interest rates high, and high interest rates in turn elevated the value of the dollar to record altitudes in international money markets. The soaring dollar dealt crippling blows to American exporters as the American international trade deficit reached a record $152 billion in 1987. The masters of international commerce and finance for a generation after World War II, Americans suddenly became the world's heaviest borrowers in the global economy of the 1980s.

Reagan Renews the Cold War

Hard as nails toward the Soviet Union in his campaign speeches, Reagan saw no reason to soften up after he checked in at the White House. He immediately warned that the Soviets were "prepared to commit any crime, to lie, to cheat" in pursuit of their goals of world conquest. In a later speech he characterized the Soviet empire as "the focus of evil in the modern world."

Reagan believed in negotiating with the Soviets—but only from a position of overwhelming strength. Accordingly, his strategy for dealing with Moscow was simple: by enormously expanding U.S. military capabilities, he could threaten the Soviet leaders with a fantastically expensive new round in the arms race. Desperate to avoid economic ruin, Kremlin leaders would come to the bargaining table and sing Reagan's tune.

This strategy resembled a riverboat gambler's ploy. It wagered the enormous sum of Reagan's defense budgets on the hope that the other side would not call Washington's bluff and initiate a new cycle of arms competition. Reagan played his trump card in this risky game in March 1983 when he announced his intention to pursue a high-technology missile defense system called the Strategic Defense Initiative (SDI), popularly known as "Star Wars." The plan called for orbiting battle stations in space that could fire laser beams or other forms of concentrated energy to vaporize intercontinental missiles on lift-off. Most scientists considered this an impossible goal, but the deeper logic of SDI lay in its fit with Reagan's overall Soviet strategy. By pitching the arms contest onto a stratospherically high plane of technology and astronomical expense, it would further force the Kremlin's hand.

Relations with the Soviets nose-dived in late 1981 when the government of Poland, needled by a popular union movement called "Solidarity," clamped martial law on the troubled country. Seeing the heavy fist of the Kremlin inside this Polish iron glove, Reagan imposed economic sanctions on Poland and the USSR alike.

Dealing with the Soviet Union was additionally complicated by the inertia and ill health of the aging oligarchs in the Kremlin, three of whom died between late 1982 and early 1985. Relations grew even more tense when the Soviets, in September 1983, blasted from the skies a Korean airliner, plummeting hundreds of civilians, including many Americans, to their deaths in the frigid Sea of Okhotsk. By the end of 1983, all arms-control negotiations with the Soviets were broken off. The deepening chill in the Cold War was further felt in 1984, when USSR and Soviet-bloc athletes boycotted the Olympic Games in Los Angeles.

Troubles Abroad

The volatile Middle Eastern pot continued to boil ominously. Israel badly strained its bonds of friendship with the United States by continuing to allow new settlements to be established in the occupied territory of the Jordan River's West Bank. Israel further raised the stakes in the Middle East in June 1982 when it invaded neighboring Lebanon, seeking to suppress once and for all the guerrilla bases from which Palestinian fighters harassed beleaguered Israel. The Palestinians were bloodily subdued, but Lebanon, already pulverized by years of episodic civil war, was plunged into armed chaos.

President Reagan was obliged to send American troops to Lebanon in 1983 as part of an inter-

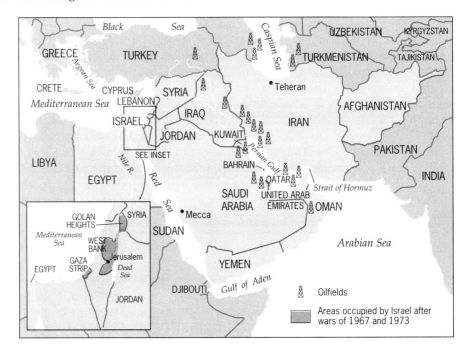

The Middle East *A combination of political instability and precious petroleum resources has made the region from Egypt to Afghanistan an "arc of crisis."*

national peacekeeping force, but their presence did not bring peace. A suicidal bomber crashed an explosives-laden truck into U.S. Marine Corps barracks on October 23, 1983, killing more than two hundred marines. President Reagan soon thereafter withdrew the remaining American troops, miraculously suffering no political damage from this horrifying and humiliating attack. His mystified Democratic opponents began to call him a "Teflon president," to whom nothing hurtful could stick.

Central America, in the United States' own backyard, also rumbled menacingly. A leftist revolution had deposed the long-time dictator of Nicaragua in 1979. President Carter had tried to ignore the anti-American rhetoric of the revolutionaries, known as "Sandinistas," and to establish good diplomatic relations with them. But Reagan took their words at face value and hurled back at them some hot language of his own.

He accused the Sandinistas of turning their country into a forward base for Soviet and Cuban military penetration of all of Central America. Brandishing photographs taken from high-flying spy planes, administration spokespeople claimed that

Nicaraguan leftists were shipping weapons to revolutionary forces in tiny El Salvador, torn by violence since a coup in 1979. Reagan sent military "advisers" to prop up the pro-American government of El Salvador. He also provided covert aid, including the CIA-engineered mining of harbors, to the "contra" rebels opposing the anti-American Sandinista government of Nicaragua.

Reagan also flexed his military muscles elsewhere in the turbulent Caribbean. In a dramatic display of American might, in October 1983 he dispatched a heavy-firepower invasion force to the island of Grenada, where a military coup had killed the prime minister and brought Marxists to power. Swiftly overrunning the tiny island, American troops vividly demonstrated Reagan's determination to assert the dominance of the United States in the Caribbean, just as Theodore Roosevelt had done.

Round Two for Reagan

A confident Ronald Reagan, bolstered by a buoyant economy at home and by the popularity of his muscular posture abroad, handily won the Republican nomination in 1984 for a second White House term. His opponent was Democrat Walter Mondale, who made history by naming as his vice-presidential running mate Congresswoman Geraldine Ferraro of New York. She was the first woman ever to appear on a major party presidential ticket. But even this dramatic gesture could not salvage Mondale's candidacy. On election day Reagan walked away with 525 electoral votes to Mondale's 13, winning everywhere except in Mondale's home state of Minnesota and the District of Columbia. Reagan also overwhelmed Mondale in the popular vote—52,609,797 to 36,450,613.

Shrinking the federal government and reducing taxes had been the main objectives of Reagan's first term; foreign-policy issues dominated the news in his second term. The president soon found himself contending for the world's attention with a charismatic new Soviet leader, Mikhail Gorbachev, installed as chairman of the Soviet Communist party in March 1985.

Gorbachev was personable, energetic, imaginative, and committed to radical reforms in the Soviet Union. He announced two policies with remarkable, even revolutionary, implications. *Glasnost*, or "openness," aimed to ventilate the secretive, repressive stuffiness of Soviet society by introducing free speech and a measure of political liberty. *Perestroika*, or "restructuring," was intended to revive the moribund Soviet economy by adopting many of the free-market practices—such as the profit motive and an end to subsidized prices—of the capitalist West.

Both *glasnost* and *perestroika* required that the Soviet Union shrink the size of its enormous military machine and redirect its energies to the civilian economy. That requirement, in turn, necessitated an end to the Cold War. Gorbachev accordingly made warm overtures to the West, including an announcement in April 1985 that the Soviet Union would cease to deploy intermediate-range nuclear forces (INF) targeted on Western Europe, pending an agreement on their complete elimination. He pushed this goal when he met with Ronald Reagan at their first of four summit meetings, in Geneva in November 1985. A second summit meeting in Reykjavik, Iceland, in October 1986 broke down in stalemate, but at a third summit in Washington, D.C., in December 1987, the two leaders at last signed the INF Treaty, banning all intermediate-range nuclear missiles from Europe.

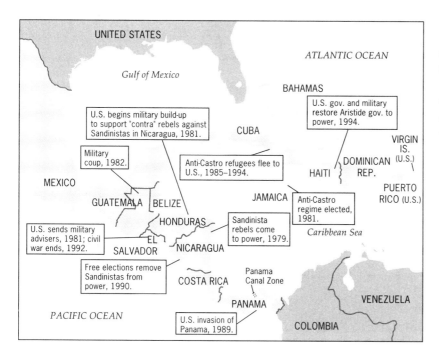

Central America and the Caribbean   *This region of historic importance to the United States experienced dramatic political upheavals in the 1970s, 1980s, and 1990s.*

Reagan and Gorbachev capped their new friendship in May 1988 at a final summit in Moscow. There President Reagan, who had entered office condemning the "evil empire" of Soviet communism, warmly praised Gorbachev. Reagan, the consummate cold warrior, had been flexible and savvy enough to seize a historic opportunity to join with the Soviet chief to bring the Cold War to a kind of conclusion. For this, history would give both leaders high marks.

The Iran-Contra Imbroglio

Two foreign-policy problems seemed insoluble to Reagan: the continuing captivity of a number of American hostages seized by Muslim extremist groups in bleeding, battered Lebanon; and the continuing grip on power of the left-wing Sandinista government in Nicaragua. The president repeatedly requested that Congress provide military aid to the contra rebels fighting against the Sandinista regime. Congress repeatedly refused, and the administration grew increasingly frustrated, even obsessed, in its search for a means to help the contras.

Unbeknownst to the American public, some Washington officials saw a possible linkage between the two thorny problems of the Middle Eastern hostages and the Central American Sandinistas. In 1985 American diplomats secretly arranged arms sales to the embattled Iranians in return for Iranian aid in obtaining the release of American hostages held by Middle Eastern terrorists. At least one hostage was eventually set free. Meanwhile, money from the payment for the arms was diverted to the contras. These actions brazenly violated a congressional ban on military aid to the Nicaraguan rebels—not to mention Reagan's repeated vow that he would never negotiate with terrorists.

News of these secret dealings broke in November 1986 and ignited a firestorm of controversy. President Reagan claimed he was innocent of wrongdoing and ignorant about the activities of his subordinates, but a congressional committee condemned the "secrecy, deception, and disdain for the law" displayed by administration officials and concluded that "if the president did not know what his national security advisers were doing, he should have."

The Iran-contra affair cast a dark shadow over Reagan's record in foreign policy, tending to obscure the president's achievement in establishing a new relationship with the Soviets. Although the several Iran-contra investigations presented damaging revelations of Reagan's weaknesses and laziness as a chief executive, he remained among the most popular and beloved presidents in modern American history.

Reagan's Economic Legacy

Ronald Reagan had taken office vowing to invigorate the American economy by rolling back government regulations, lowering taxes, and balancing the budget. He did ease many regulatory rules, and he pushed major tax-reform bills through Congress in 1981 and 1986. But a balanced budget remained grotesquely out of reach. The combination of tax reduction and huge increases in military spending opened a vast "revenue hole" of $200 billion in annual deficits. In his eight years in office, President Reagan added nearly $2 trillion to the national debt—more than all his predecessors combined.

The staggering deficits of the Reagan years assuredly constituted a great economic failure. And because foreign lenders, especially the Japanese, financed so much of the Reagan-era debt, the deficits virtually guaranteed that future generations of Americans would have to either work harder than their parents or lower their standard of living, or both, to pay their foreign creditors.

But if the deficits represented an economic failure, they also constituted, strangely enough, a kind of political triumph. By making new social spending both practically and politically impossible, the deficits achieved one of Reagan's paramount goals: slowing the growth of government and blocking or even repealing the social programs launched in the era of Lyndon Johnson's Great Society. They achieved, in short, Reagan's highest political objective: the containment of the welfare state. Ronald Reagan thus ensured the long-term perpetuation of his values to a degree that few presidents have managed to achieve. For better or worse, the consequences of "Reaganomics" would be large and durable.

Culture Wars

Reagan's legacy also was likely to be lasting with respect to the social issues that first helped get him elected president in 1980. The courts became his principal instrument in his battles against affirmative action and abortion, the two great icons of the liberal political culture that Reaganism repudiated. By the time he left office, Reagan had appointed a near-majority of all sitting federal judges. Equally important, he had named three conservative-minded justices to the Supreme Court. They included Sandra Day O'Connor, a brilliant Stanford Law School graduate who was sworn in on September 25, 1981, as the first woman justice in the Court's nearly two-hundred-year history.

The Court showed its newly conservative coloration in 1984, when it decreed, in a case involving Memphis firefighters, that union rules about job seniority could outweigh affirmative-action concerns in guiding promotion policies in the city's fire department. In two cases in 1989 (*Ward's Cove Packing* v. *Antonia* and *Martin* v. *Wilks*), the Court made it more difficult to prove that an employer practiced racial discrimination in hiring, and made it easier for white males to argue that they were the victims of reverse discrimination. Congress passed legislation in 1991 that partially reversed the effects of these decisions.

The vexed issue of abortion also reached the Court in 1989. In the case of *Roe* v. *Wade* in 1973, the Supreme Court had prohibited states from making laws that interfered with a woman's right to an abortion during the early months of pregnancy. For nearly two decades, that decision had been the bedrock principle on which "pro-choice" advocates built their case for abortion rights. It had also provoked bitter criticism from Roman Catholics and various "right-to-life" groups who wanted a virtually absolute ban on all abortions. In *Webster* v. *Reproductive Health Services*, the Court in July 1989 did not entirely overturn *Roe*, but it seriously compromised *Roe*'s protection of abortion rights. By approving a Missouri law that imposed certain restrictions on abortion, the Court signaled that it was inviting the states to legislate in an area from which *Roe* had previously forbidden them to legislate.

Right-to-life advocates were at first delighted by the *Webster* decision. But the Court's ruling also jolted pro-choice organizations into a new militancy. Bruising, divisive battles loomed as state legislatures across the land confronted abortion. This painful cultural conflict over the unborn was also part of the Reagan era's bequest to the future.

Referendum on Reaganism in 1988

Republicans lost control of the Senate in the off-year elections of November 1986. Hopes rose among Democrats that the "Reagan revolution" might be showing signs of political vulnerability at last. The newly Democratic majority in the Senate flexed its political muscle in 1987 when it rejected Robert Bork, the president's ultraconservative nominee for a Supreme Court vacancy. Democrats also relished the prospect of making political hay out of both the Iran-contra scandal and the allegedly unethical behavior that tainted an unusually large number of Reagan's "official family."

Disquieting signs of economic trouble also seemed to open political opportunities for Democrats. The "twin towers" of deficits—the federal budget deficit and international trade deficit—continued to mount ominously. Falling oil prices blighted the economy of the Southwest, slashing real estate values and undermining hundreds of savings and loan (S&L) institutions. The damage to the S&Ls was so massive that a federal rescue operation was eventually estimated to carry a price tag of well over $500 billion. A wave of mergers, acquisitions, and leveraged buyouts washed over Wall Street, leaving many brokers and traders mega-rich and many companies saddled with mega-debt. A cold spasm of fear struck the money markets on "Black Monday," October 19, 1987, when the leading stock-market index plunged 508 points—the largest one-day decline in history. This crash, said *Newsweek* magazine, heralded "the final collapse of the money culture . . . , the death knell of the 1980s." But as Mark Twain famously commented about his own obituary, this announcement proved premature.

Hoping to cash in on these ethical and economic anxieties, a pack of Democrats—dubbed the "Seven Dwarfs" by derisive Republicans—chased after their party's 1988 presidential nomination. Black candidate Jesse Jackson, a rousing speechmaker who hoped to forge a "rainbow coalition" of minorities and the disadvantaged, campaigned energetically. But the Democratic nomination in the end went to the coolly cerebral governor of Massachusetts, Michael Dukakis. Republicans nominated Reagan's vice president, George Bush, who ran largely on the Reagan record of tax cuts, strong defense policies, toughness on crime, opposition to abortion, and a long-running if hardly robust economic expansion. Dukakis made little headway exploiting the ethical and economic sorespots and came across to television viewers as almost supernaturally devoid of passion. On election day the voters gave him just 40,797,905 votes to 47,645,225 for Bush. The Electoral College count was 112 to 426.

George Bush and the End of the Cold War

George Herbert Walker Bush was born with a silver spoon in his mouth. His father had served as a U.S. senator from Connecticut, and young George enjoyed a first-rate education at Yale. After service in World War II, he amassed a modest fortune in the oil business in Texas. His deepest commitment, however, was to public service; he left the business world to serve briefly as a congressman and then held various posts in several Republican administrations, including emissary to China, ambassador to the United Nations, director of the Central Intelligence Agency, and vice president. He capped this long political career when he was inaugurated as president of the United States in January 1989, promising to work for "a kinder, gentler America."

In the first months of the Bush administration, the communist world commanded the planet's fascinated attention. Everywhere in the communist bloc it seemed, astoundingly, that the season of democracy had arrived.

In China hundreds of thousands of prodemocracy demonstrators thronged Beijing's Tiananmen Square in the spring of 1989. But in June of that year, China's aging and autocratic rulers brutally crushed the prodemocracy movement. Tanks rolled over the crowds, and machine-gunners killed hundreds of protesters. World opinion roundly condemned the bloody suppression of the Chinese prodemocracy demonstrators. President Bush joined in the criticism. Yet despite angry demands in Congress for punitive restrictions on trade with China, the president insisted on maintaining normal relations with Beijing.

Stunning changes also shook Eastern Europe. Long oppressed by puppet regimes propped up by Soviet guns, the region was revolutionized in just a few startling months in 1989. The Solidarity movement in Poland led the way when it toppled Poland's communist government in August. With dizzying speed, communist regimes collapsed in Hungary, Czechoslovakia, East Germany, and even hyperrepressive Romania. In December 1989, jubilant Germans danced atop the hated Berlin Wall, symbol of the division of Germany and all of Europe into two armed and hostile camps. The Wall itself soon came down, heralding the imminent end of the forty-five-year-long Cold War. With the approval of the victorious Allied powers of World War II, the two Germanies, divided since 1945, were at last reunited in October 1990.

Most startling of all were the changes that swept the heartland of world communism, the Soviet Union. Mikhail Gorbachev's policies of *glasnost* and *perestroika* had set in motion a groundswell that surged out of his control. Old-guard hard-liners, in a last-gasp effort to preserve the tottering communist system, attempted to dislodge Gorbachev with a military coup in August 1991. With the support of Boris Yeltsin, president of the Russian Republic (one of several republics that composed the Union of Soviet Socialist Republics), Gorbachev foiled the plotters. But in December 1991 Gorbachev resigned as president, and the Soviet Union dissolved into fifteen sovereign republics, with Russia the most powerful state and Yeltsin the dominant leader. To varying degrees, all the new governments in the former Soviet republics repudiated communism and embraced democratic reforms and free-market economies.

The demise of the Soviet Union wrote a definitive finish to the Cold War era. More than four decades of nail-biting tension between the two nuclear superpowers, the Soviet Union and the United States, evaporated when the USSR dismantled

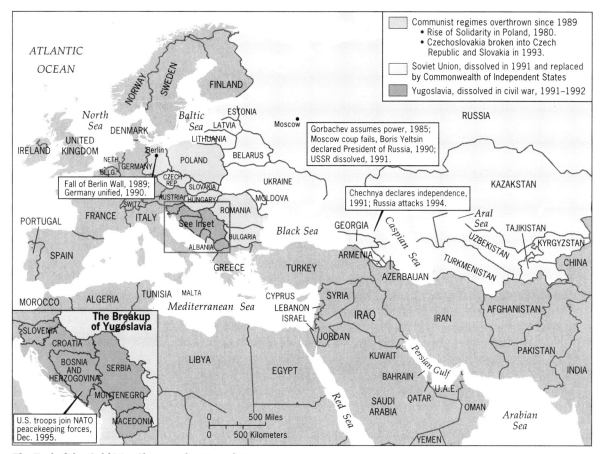

The End of the Cold War Changes the Map of Europe

itself. With the Soviet Union swept into the dustbin of history and communism all but extinct, Bush spoke hopefully of a "new world order" where democracy would reign and diplomacy would take the place of weaponry. But the disintegration of the Soviet Union posed new questions. Who would control the formidable Soviet nuclear arsenal and enforce arms-control agreements with the United States?

Throughout the former Soviet empire, waves of nationalistic fervor and long-suppressed ethnic and racial hatred rolled across the vast land as communism's roots were wrenched out. A particularly nasty conflict erupted in 1991, when the Chechnyan minority tried to declare their independence from Russia. Ethnic warfare flared in other former communist countries as well, notably in misery-drenched

former Yugoslavia, racked by vicious "ethnic cleansing" against minorities. The cruel and paradoxical truth stood revealed that the calcified communist regimes of Eastern Europe, whatever their sins, had at least bottled up the ancient ethnic antagonisms that were the region's peculiar curse and that now erupted in all their historical fury.

Refugees from the strife-torn regions flooded into Western Europe. The sturdy German economy, the foundation of European prosperity, wobbled under the awesome burden of absorbing technologically backward, physically decrepit East Germany. The Western democracies, which for more than four decades had feared the military strength of the Eastern bloc, now saw their well-being threatened by the social and economic weakness of the former communist lands.

"Operation Desert Storm": The Ground War

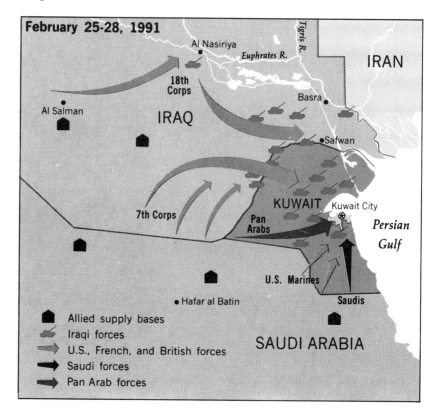

The end of the Cold War also proved a mixed blessing for the United States. With the Soviet threat canceled, Americans might resort to their traditional isolationism. The Soviet-American rivalry, with its demands for high levels of military preparedness, had also sustained huge sectors of the American economy such as aerospace. The Pentagon in 1991 closed thirty-four military bases and canceled a $52 billion order for a navy attack plane, and more cancellations followed. Unemployment soared in southern California and other areas that had been deluged with Pentagon dollars. The problems of weaning the U.S. economy from its decades of dependence on defense spending tempered the euphoria of Americans as they welcomed the Cold War's long-awaited finale.

The Persian Gulf War

Sadly, the end of the Cold War did not mean the end of all wars. President Bush flexed the United States' still-intimidating military muscle in tiny Panama in December 1989, when he sent airborne troops to capture dictator and drug lord Manuel Noriega.

Still more ominous events in the summer of 1990 severely tested Bush's dream of a democratic and peaceful new world order. On August 2, Saddam Hussein, the brutal and ambitious ruler of Iraq, sent his armies to overrun Kuwait, a tiny, oil-rich desert sheikdom on Iraq's southern frontier. Oil fueled his aggression. Financially exhausted by its eight-year war with Iran that had ended in stalemate in 1988, Iraq needed Kuwait's oil to pay its huge war bills. Saddam's larger design was iron-fisted control over the entire Persian Gulf region. With his hand thus firmly clutching the world's economic jugular vein, he dreamed of dictating the terms of oil supplies to the industrial nations, and perhaps of totally extinguishing the Arabs' enemy, Israel.

On August 2, 1990, Iraq's formidable invading army of some 100,000 men roared into Kuwait. The swiftness and audacity of the Iraqi invasion were stunning, but the world responded just as swiftly. The

U.N. Security Council unanimously condemned the invasion on August 3, 1990, and demanded the immediate and unconditional withdrawal of Iraq's troops. In November, the Security Council delivered an ultimatum to Iraq: leave Kuwait by January 15, 1991, or U.N. forces would "use all necessary means" to expel the Iraqi army.

In a logistical operation of astonishing complexity, meanwhile, the United States spearheaded a massive international military deployment on the sandy Arabian peninsula. As the January 15 deadline approached, some 539,000 U.S. soldiers, sailors, and pilots—many of them women and all of them members of the new, post-Vietnam, all-volunteer American military—had swarmed into the Persian Gulf region. They were joined by nearly 270,000 troops, pilots, and sailors from twenty-eight other countries in the coalition opposed to Iraq. When all diplomatic efforts to resolve the crisis failed, the U.S. Congress voted on January 12, 1991, to approve the use of force.

On January 16, 1991, the United States and its U.N. allies unleashed a hellish air war against Iraq. For thirty-seven days, warplanes pummeled targets in occupied Kuwait and in Iraq itself. Iraq responded to this pounding by launching several dozen "Scud" short-range ballistic missiles against military and civilian targets in Saudi Arabia and Israel. These missile attacks claimed several lives but did no significant military damage.

Yet if Iraq made but a feeble military response to the air campaign, the allied commander, the beefy and blunt American general Norman ("Stormin' Norman") Schwarzkopf, took nothing for granted. Saddam, who had threatened to wage "the mother of all battles," had the capacity to inflict awful damage. Iraq had stockpiled tons of chemical and biological weapons, including poison gas and the means to spread epidemics of anthrax, and Iraq might use them at any minute.

Saddam's tactics also included ecological warfare, as he released a gigantic oil slick into the Persian Gulf to forestall amphibious assault and ignited hundreds of oil-well fires whose smoky plumes shrouded the ground from aerial view. Faced with these horrifying tactics, Schwarzkopf's strategy was starkly simple: soften the Iraqis with relentless bombing, then suffocate them on the ground with a tidal-wave rush of troops and armor.

On February 23 the dreaded and long-awaited land war began. Dubbed "Operation Desert Storm," it lasted only four days—the "hundred-hour war." With the Iraqi air force grounded or destroyed,

The Hundred-Hour War   *In what some have called a lightning victory, the U.N. allies' fighting men and women reduced Saddam's military machine, the fourth-largest army in the world, to wreckage and rubble.*

Schwarzkopf had secretly moved a huge army far across the desert to the extreme western end of the Iraqi fortifications. With lightning speed it penetrated deep into Iraq, outflanking the occupying forces in Kuwait and blocking the enemy's ability either to retreat or to reinforce. Allied casualties were amazingly light whereas much of Iraq's remaining fighting force was quickly destroyed or captured. On February 27 Saddam accepted a cease-fire, and Kuwait was liberated.

Most Americans cheered the war's rapid and enormously successful conclusion. The war had nevertheless failed to dislodge Saddam Hussein from power. When the smoke cleared, he had survived to menace the world another day. The perpetually troubled Middle East knew scarcely less trouble after "Desert Storm" had ceased to thunder, and the United States, for better or worse, found itself more deeply ensnared in the region's web of mortal hatreds and intractable conflicts.

Bush on the Home Front

In his inaugural address, George Bush pledged that he would work for a "kinder, gentler America." He redeemed that promise in part when he signed the Americans with Disabilities Act (ADA) in 1990, a landmark law prohibiting discrimination against the 43 million U.S. citizens with physical or mental disabilities. The president also signed a major water projects bill in 1992 that put the interests of the environment ahead of agriculture, especially in California's heavily irrigated Central Valley.

The new president continued to aggravate the explosive "social issues" that had so divided Americans throughout the 1980s, especially the nettlesome questions of affirmative action and abortion. Bush challenged the legality of college scholarships targeted for racial minorities, and he only grudgingly approved a watered-down civil rights bill in 1991 that was designed to make it easier for employees to prove discrimination in hiring and promotion.

Most provocatively, in 1991 Bush nominated for the Supreme Court the conservative African-American jurist Clarence Thomas, a stern critic of affirmative-action policies. Thomas's nomination was loudly opposed by labor, civil rights, and women's organizations. Reflecting irreconcilable divisions over affirmative action and abortion, the Senate Judiciary Committee concluded its hearings with a divided 7-to-7 vote and forwarded the matter to the Senate without a recommendation.

Then, just days before the Senate was scheduled to vote in early October 1991, a press leak revealed that a University of Oklahoma law professor, Anita Hill, had accused Thomas of sexual harassment. The Senate Judiciary Committee was forced to reopen its hearings. For days, a prurient American public sat glued to their television sets as Hill graphically detailed her charges of sexual improprieties and Thomas angrily responded. In the end, by a 52-to-48 vote, the Senate narrowly confirmed Thomas as the second African-American ever to sit on the supreme bench (Thurgood Marshall was the first). While many Americans hailed Hill as a heroine for her role in raising the issue of sexual harassment, Thomas maintained that her unproved allegations amounted to "a high-tech lynching for uppity blacks who in any way deign to think for themselves, to do for themselves."

The furor over Clarence Thomas's confirmation suggested that the social issues that had helped produce three Republican presidential victories in the 1980s were losing some of their electoral appeal. Many women, enraged by the all-male judiciary committee's behavior in the Clarence Thomas hearings, grew increasingly critical of the president's uncompromising stand on abortion. A "gender gap" opened between the two political parties, as pro-choice women grew increasingly cool toward the strong anti-abortion stand of the Republicans.

Still more damaging to President Bush's political health, the economy sputtered and stalled almost at the outset of his administration. By 1992 the unemployment rate exceeded 7 percent, while the federal budget deficit continued to mushroom, topping $250 billion in each year of Bush's presidency. In a desperate attempt to stop the hemorrhage of red ink, Bush and Congress agreed in 1990 to a budget that included $133 billion in new taxes.

Bush's 1990 tax and budget package added up to a political catastrophe. In his 1988 presidential campaign, Bush had belligerently declared, "Read my lips—no new taxes." Now he had flagrantly broken that campaign promise.

The intractable budgetary crisis and the stagnant economy congealed into a lump of disgust with all political incumbents. Disillusion thickened in 1991 when it was revealed that many members of the House of Representatives had written thousands of bad checks from their accounts in a private House "bank." Unprecedented numbers of officeholders declined to seek reelection, and a movement to impose term limits on elected officials gained strength in many states.

Bill Clinton: The First Baby-Boomer President

The slumbering economy, the widening gender gap, and the rising anti-incumbent spirit spelled opportunity for Democrats, frozen out of the White House for all but four years since 1968. In a bruising round of primary elections, Governor William Jefferson Clinton of Arkansas weathered blistering accusations of womanizing and draft evasion to emerge as his party's standard-bearer, with Senator Albert Gore of Tennessee as his vice-presidential running mate.

Clinton claimed to be a "new" Democrat, chastened by his party's long exile in the political wilderness. Clinton and other centrist Democrats attempted to point their party away from its traditional antibusiness, dovish, champion-of-the-underdog orientation. Clinton campaigned especially vigorously on promises to stimulate the economy, reform the welfare system, and overhaul the nation's scandalously expensive and inefficient health-care apparatus.

Trying to wring one more win out of the social issues that had underwritten the presidential victories of Reagan and Bush, the Republican convention in Houston dwelled stridently on "family values" as it renominated George Bush and Vice President J. Danforth Quayle for a second term. A tired Bush attacked Clinton's character and tried to take credit for the end of the Cold War. But fear for the economic problems of the future swayed more voters than pride in the foreign policies of the past. The purchasing power of the average worker's paycheck had actually declined during Bush's presidency.

Reflecting pervasive economic unease and the virulence of the throw-the-bums-out national

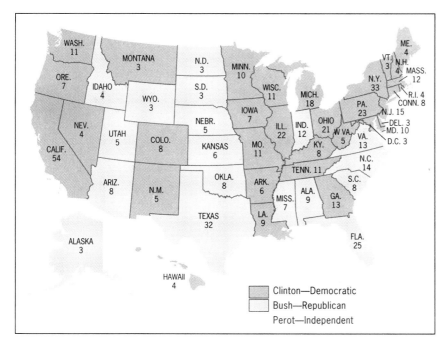

Presidential Election of 1992 (with electoral vote by state)

mood, nearly 20 percent of voters cast their ballots for independent presidential candidate H. Ross Perot, a bantam-weight, jug-eared Texas billionaire who made a boast of the fact that he had never held any public office. With a record turnout of voters on election day, the final tallies gave Clinton 43,728,275 popular votes and 370 in the Electoral College. Bush polled 38,167,416 popular and 168 electoral votes. Perot won no electoral votes but did gather 19,237,247 in the popular count—the strongest showing for an independent or third-party candidate since Theodore Roosevelt ran on the Bull Moose ticket in 1912. Democrats also racked up clear majorities in both houses of Congress, which seated near-record numbers of new members, including thirty-nine African-Americans, nineteen Hispanic-Americans,

seven Asian-Americans, one Native American, and forty-eight women. In Illinois Carol Moseley Braun became the first African-American woman elected to the U.S. Senate, where she joined five other women in the largest female contingent ever in the upper chamber.

Women also figured prominently in President Clinton's cabinet, including the first female attorney general, Janet Reno, and former Wisconsin University president Donna Shalala, who became secretary of health and human services. Vowing to shape a government that "looked like America," Clinton appointed several ethnic and racial minority members to his cabinet contingent, including former San Antonio mayor Henry Cisneros at Housing and Urban Development and an African-American, Ron Brown, as secretary of commerce. Clinton also seized the opportunity in 1993 to nominate Ruth Bader Ginsburg to the Supreme Court, where she joined Sandra Day O'Connor to make a pair of women justices.

Clinton's Ups and Downs

Badly overestimating his electoral mandate for liberal reform, the young president made a series of costly blunders upon entering the White House. He first stirred controversy by advocating an end to the ban on gays and lesbians in the armed forces. Faced with ferocious opposition, he had to settle for a "don't ask, don't tell" policy that meant no official acknowledgment of gay and lesbian soldiers and sailors.

Even more damaging to Clinton's political standing was the fiasco of his attempt to reform the nation's health-care system. In a dramatic innovation, the president put his wife, Hillary Rodham Clinton, in charge of a task force to redesign the medical-service industry. The committee unveiled its stupefyingly complicated plan in October 1993. It was virtually dead on arrival in Congress, and as its principal architect, the First Lady was doused with a torrent of abuse. Having entered the White House as a full political partner with her husband, she subsequently maintained a less visible though still active public profile.

Clinton had better luck with a deficit-reduction bill in 1993, which combined with an increasingly

The Ghosts of Presidents Past, 1993 *In this fanciful portrait of President Bill Clinton's inauguration, past presidents listen attentively as the new chief executive gives his inaugural address.*

buoyant economy to shrink the federal deficit to its lowest level in more than a decade. By 1998 Clinton's economic policymakers had ceased to fret about the rapacious deficit monster, and Congress had begun to argue over how to spend projected federal budget surpluses.

Clinton induced the Congress in 1993 to pass a gun-control law, the "Brady Bill," named for presidential aide James Brady, severely wounded in the assassination attempt on President Ronald Reagan in 1981. In 1994 Clinton also pushed through a $30 billion anticrime bill that included a ban on many assault weapons.

With these measures the government struggled to hold the line against an epidemic of violence that rocked American society in the 1990s. The World Trade Center in New York City was bombed in 1993. That same year federal agents stormed the Waco, Texas, compound of the fundamentalist Branch Davidians, resulting in many deaths, including women and children. On the second anniversary of the Waco assault, a bomb destroyed a federal office building in Oklahoma City, taking 169 lives. In July 1998 a lone gunman killed two policemen inside the U.S. Capitol building itself. These episodes brought to light a secretive underground of paramilitary private "militias" and fervent antigovernment activists often armed to the teeth.

Even many law-abiding citizens shared to some degree in the antigovernment attitudes that drove a few people to murderous extremes. Thanks largely to the disillusionment spawned by Vietnam and Watergate, the confidence in government that came naturally to the World War II generation was in short supply at century's end. Reflecting that pervasive disenchantment with politics, some twenty-four states had imposed term-limit restrictions on elected officials by the late 1990s, though the Supreme Court ruled in 1995 that such laws could not apply to federal officeholders.

Clinton's failed initiatives and widespread antigovernment sentiment offered conservative Republicans a golden opportunity in 1994, and they seized it aggressively. Led by outspoken Georgia representative Newt Gingrich, conservatives offered voters a "Contract with America" that promised an all-out assault on budget deficits and radical reduc-

tions in welfare programs. Their campaign succeeded fabulously, as Republicans picked up eleven governorships, eight Senate seats, and fifty-three seats in the House, giving them control of both chambers of Congress for the first time in forty years.

The Republican majority did achieve a few of its conservative goals. It restricted "unfunded mandates"—federal laws that imposed new obligations on state and local governments without providing new revenues. In 1996 it compelled a reluctant Clinton to sign a welfare-reform law that made deep cuts in welfare grants and restricted welfare benefits for legal and illegal immigrants alike.

Although the boisterous Republicans had apparently seized the initiative from a stunned President Clinton, they proceeded to overplay their mandate for conservative retrenchment. Elected House Speaker, Gingrich advocated provocative ideas, like sending the children of welfare families to orphanages, that seemed to bend the conservative bow too far. A tense congressional budget confrontation with Clinton actually forced the federal government to shut down for eleven days at the end of 1995. Such outrageously partisan antics bred a backlash that helped President Clinton rebound from his condition as a political dead duck.

As the Republicans slugged it out in a noisy round of presidential primaries, Clinton's reelection campaign raised spectacular sums of money—some of it, investigations later revealed, from questionable sources. The eventual Republican standard-bearer was Kansas senator Robert Dole, a decorated World War II veteran who ran a listless campaign. Clinton, buoyed by a healthy economy and by his artful trimming to the conservative wind, breezed to an easy victory with 45,628,667 popular votes to Dole's 37,869,435. The Reform party's egomaniacal leader, Ross Perot, ran a sorry third, picking up less than half the votes he had garnered in 1992. Clinton's electoral-vote count was 379 to 159 for Dole.

Clinton Again

As Clinton began his second term—the first Democrat since Franklin Delano Roosevelt to be reelected—he again composed a diversified cabinet, but the heady promises of far-reaching reform with which he had entered the White House four years earlier were no longer heard. Facing a skeptical electorate and Republican majorities in both houses of Congress, he proposed only modest legislative goals—even though soaring tax revenues generated by the prosperous economy produced a balanced federal budget for the first time in three decades in 1999.

Clinton managed to put Republicans on the defensive by claiming the political middle ground on contentious welfare and affirmative-action issues. The landmark Welfare Reform Act, passed in August 1996, was designed to require welfare recipients to pursue jobs or education as a condition of further assistance. Clinton claimed success for the plan, as worker-hungry businesses and governments hired the most employable former recipients, thereby shrinking welfare rolls by nearly 2 million persons in the first two years under the new program. Despite these developments, the states struggled to meet federal goals for helping less employable Americans find jobs that paid enough to offset transportation and child-care costs. Skeptics worried what would happen if the economy ever went into recession.

Juggling the political hot potato of affirmative action, Clinton pledged to "mend it, not end it." When voters in California in 1996 approved Proposition 208, prohibiting affirmative-action preferences in government and higher education, the number of minority students in the state's public universities dropped precipitously. A federal appeals court decision, *Hopwood* v. *Texas*, had similar effects on Texas universities. Clinton criticized these broad assaults on affirmative action in education and employment but stopped short of endorsing federal government intervention to reverse them. Trying to reduce polarization over the issue, Clinton proposed a "national dialogue on race." In 1997 he appointed a national commission that generated much talk but few concrete proposals. In California and elsewhere, Clinton-style Democrats increasingly sought ways to aid the economically disadvantaged, including minorities, without pushing the hot button of racial preferences.

Clinton's major political advantage continued to be the soaring economy, which by 1999 had sustained the longest period of growth in forty years. While unemployment crept down to 4 percent, and businesses scrambled for workers, inflationary pres-

sure remained remarkably low. An economic crisis in late 1997 plunged Southeast Asia, South Korea, and even once-mighty Japan into financial turmoil, arousing fears of a global economic meltdown. But though the U.S. stock market shuddered and sputtered during 1998, it recovered and even surged ahead, fueled by new Internet businesses and other high-tech and media companies. The economic "Asian flu" had apparently caused only a few sniffles for the robust American economy.

Overseas Struggles

The end of the Cold War robbed the United States of the basic principles on which it had conducted foreign policy for nearly half a century, and the Clinton administration groped for a diplomatic formula to replace anticommunism as the guiding mechanism in America's foreign affairs. The Cold War's finale also shook a number of skeletons loose from several government closets. Sensational revelations that Central Intelligence Agency double agents had sold secrets to the Soviets during the Cold War years, causing the execution of American agents abroad, demonstrated that the ghost of Cold War past still cast its frosty shadow over official Washington.

The international environment that the United States confronted in the 1990s was not the long-familiar one of great-power confrontation, but of numerous global hot spots that periodically threatened to boil over into major regional conflagrations. The Clinton administration generally tried to persuade international agencies, especially the United Nations and NATO, to support "multilateral" peace-keeping efforts—but often it was the United States that had to try to keep the lid on.

The Middle East remained a major source of trouble. The United States struggled to keep the Israeli-Palestinian peace process on track, with mixed success. In November 1998 Clinton brokered a new set of agreements between the two sides in marathon meetings at Wye River, Maryland, but prospects for implementation remained uncertain. In August 1998, terrorists killed over two hundred people by bombing the U.S. embassies in Kenya and Tanzania. In retaliation, the United States conducted missile attacks against alleged terrorist sites in Sudan and

Afghanistan. In Iraq, Saddam Hussein continued his game of hide-and-seek with United Nations weapons inspectors monitoring the Iraqi weapons program. In November 1997 Iraq expelled American members of the inspection team, setting off a yearlong series of mutual threats and postponed deadlines for Iraqi cooperation. In December 1998 the chief U.N. inspector reported that Iraq was out of compliance, and America and Britain then undertook repeated air strikes against Iraqi weapons factories and warehouses.

The Balkans also continued to command the Clinton administration's attention. Deadlines for removing American peacekeeping troops in Bosnia were postponed and then finally abandoned altogether as it became clear that they were the only force capable of preventing new hostilities. The planned expansion of NATO in 1999 to include Poland, Hungary, and the Czech Republic increased incentives to prevent more fighting and to keep refugees from spreading into Eastern Europe. But a rebellion in the province of Kosovo in February 1998 brought a harsh military crackdown from Serbia, setting off a new wave of massacres and "ethnic cleansing" in the region. After failed attempts at a negotiated political settlement, U.S.-led NATO forces launched air attacks against Serbia in March 1999.

Scandal and Impeachment

Scandal and even alleged criminal activity dogged Bill Clinton from the beginning of his presidency. Allegations of flagrant wrongdoing, reaching back to his prepresidential days in Arkansas, included a failed real estate investment known as the Whitewater Land Corporation. The Clintons' role in that deal prompted the appointment of a federal special prosecutor (Independent Counsel) to investigate. Suspicions were especially aroused by the death from apparent suicide in 1993 of White House counsel and close Clinton associate Vincent W. Foster, Jr., who had handled the Clintons' legal and financial affairs. The president's loose ethics and womanizing even found fictional expression in a runaway 1996 best-selling book, *Primary Colors*.

The 1996 election returns had hardly been counted before further allegations rocked the Clinton administration. Republicans charged that the Democratic campaign had been floated on a sea of dollars raised from corrupt and illegal sources. Congressional investigators revealed that the Clinton campaign had milked numerous questionable sources for funds, including contributors who paid to stay overnight in the White House and foreigners who were legally prohibited from giving to American campaigns.

But all the previous scandals were overshadowed when allegations broke in January 1998 that Clinton had engaged in a sexual affair with a young White House intern, Monica Lewinsky, and then lied about it when he testified under oath in a civil law suit. The law suit had been brought by an Arkansas woman, Paula Jones, who charged that then-Governor Clinton had sexually harassed her when she was a state employee. The Supreme Court had permitted the case to go forward in May 1997, ruling that being sued in a civil case would not "significantly distract" the president from his duties.

The accusation that Clinton had lied under oath in the Jones case about his sexual affair with Lewinsky presented a stunning windfall to the special prosecutor, Kenneth Starr, originally appointed to investigate the Whitewater deal. Like Captain Ahab pursuing the whale Moby Dick, Starr had relentlessly tracked Clinton's steps for years, spending $40 million but never succeeding in finding evidence against the president himself. Clinton, now suddenly caught in a legal and political trap, delivered vehement public denials that he had engaged in "sexual relations" with Lewinsky. After maintaining his complete innocence for eight months, Clinton was finally forced to acknowledge an "inappropriate relationship." Starr in September 1998 presented a stinging report to the House of Representatives that charged Clinton with eleven possible grounds for impeachment, all related to the Lewinsky matter.

Led by its fiercely anti-Clinton Republican majority, the House quickly cranked up the rusty machinery of impeachment. After a nasty partisan debate, the House Republicans eventually passed in December 1998 two articles of impeachment against the president: perjury before a grand jury and obstruction of justice. Crying foul, the Democratic minority charged that, however deplorable Clinton's personal misconduct, sexual transgressions did not

Impeachment Hearings   *The House Judiciary Committee, led by its chairman, Illinois congressman Henry Hyde (in the center), conducted the hearings that led to the impeachment of President Clinton in December 1998. Hyde later led the team of House Republican managers (prosecutors) who presented the unsuccessful case against the president in the Senate trial held in January and February 1999.*

rise to the level of "high crimes and misdemeanors" prescribed in the Constitution. (See Art. II, Sec. IV in the Appendix.) The House Republican managers (prosecutors) of impeachment, led by Illinois congressman and House Judiciary Committee chairman Henry Hyde, claimed that perjury and obstruction were grave public issues and that nothing less than "the rule of law" was at stake.

As cries of "honor the Constitution" and "sexual McCarthyism" filled the air, the nation debated whether the president's peccadillos amounted to high crimes or low follies. Most Americans tended toward the latter conclusion. In the 1998 mid-term elections, voters reduced the House Republicans' majority, causing fiery House Speaker Newt Gingrich to resign his post. Incredibly, Clinton's job approval

rating remained high and even rose throughout the long impeachment ordeal. Though Americans held a low opinion of Clinton's slipshod personal morals, most liked the president's political and economic policies and wanted him to stay in office.

In January and February 1999, for the first time in one hundred and thirty years the nation witnessed an impeachment trial in the U.S. Senate. Dusting off ancient precedents from Andrew Johnson's impeachment, the one hundred solemn senators heard arguments and evidence in the case, with Chief Justice William Rehnquist presiding. With the facts widely known and the two parties' political positions firmly locked in, the trial's outcome was a foregone conclusion. On the key obstruction of justice charge, five northeastern Republicans joined all forty-five Democratic senators in voting not guilty. The fifty Republican votes for conviction thus fell far short of the constitutionally required two-thirds majority. The vote on the perjury charge was forty-five guilty, fifty-five not guilty.

With the impeachment trial over, a weary nation yearned for Washington to move on to other business. What would be the long-term consequences of the trial, and of Bill Clinton's presidency, was yet to be determined. But it was likely that such an event, coming a generation after Vietnam and Watergate had first seriously disillusioned Americans about their political leaders, would only deepen disengagement and cynicism regarding public affairs. In a stunning commentary on the demythologizing of the American presidency, many Americans expressed the hope that their children would *not* grow up to be president. If distrust is fatal to the fragile tissue of democracy, these disturbing symptoms pointed to a seriously unhealthy Republic.

Chronology

1980 Reagan defeats Carter for presidency.

1981 Iran releases American hostages.
"Reaganomics" spending and tax cuts passed.
Solidarity movement in Poland.
O'Connor appointed to Supreme Court (first woman justice).

1981–1991 United States aids antileftist forces in Central America.

1982 Recession hits U.S. economy.

1983 Reagan announces SDI plan ("Star Wars").
U.S. marines killed in Lebanon.
U.S. invasion of Grenada.

1984 Reagan defeats Mondale for presidency.

1985 Gorbachev comes to power in Soviet Union.
First Reagan-Gorbachev summit meeting, in Geneva.

1986 Iran-contra scandal revealed.
Second Reagan-Gorbachev summit meeting, in Reykjavik, Iceland.

1987 508-point stock-market plunge.
Third Reagan-Gorbachev summit meeting, in Washington, D.C.; INF Treaty signed.

1988 Fourth Reagan-Gorbachev summit meeting, in Moscow.
Bush defeats Dukakis for presidency.

1989 Chinese government suppresses prodemocracy demonstrators.
Eastern Europe throws off communist regimes.
Berlin Wall torn down.

1990 Iraq invades Kuwait.
East and West Germany reunite.

1991 Persian Gulf War.
Thomas appointed to Supreme Court.
Gorbachev resigns as Soviet president.
Soviet Union dissolves; republics form Commonwealth of Independent States.

1992 Clinton defeats Bush and Perot for presidency.

1994 Republicans win majorities in both houses of Congress.

1996 Welfare reform bill becomes law.
Clinton defeats Dole for presidency.

1998 Lewinsky scandal.
U.S. military confrontation with Iraq.
House of Representatives impeaches Clinton.

1999 Senate acquits Clinton on impeachment charges.
Kosovo crisis; NATO warfare with Serbia.

varying

viewpoints

Where Did Modern Conservatism Come From?

Ronald Reagan's elections surprised many historians. Reflecting a liberal political outlook that is common among academic scholars, they were long accustomed to understanding American history as an inexorable unfolding of liberal principles, including the quests for economic equality, social justice, and active government. In progressive histories of the early twentieth century like those of Charles and Mary Beard, conservatives were portrayed as rich, privileged elites bent on preserving their wealth and power.

Even the "New Left" revisionists of the 1960s, while critical of the celebratory tone of their progressive forebears, were convinced that the deep currents of American history flowed leftward. But whether they were liberal or revisionist, most scholars writing in the first three post–World War II decades dismissed conservatives as fringe wackos—paranoid McCarthyites or racist demagogues who, in the words of liberal critic Lionel Trilling, trafficked only in "irritable mental gestures which seem to resemble ideas." Such an outlook is conspicuous in books like Daniel Bell, ed., *The Radical Right* (1963), and Richard Hofstadter, *The Paranoid Style in American Politics* (1965).

But what flowed out of the turbulent decade of the 1960s was not a strengthened liberalism but a revived conservatism. Reagan's success compelled a reexamination of the tradition of American conservatism and the sources of its resurgence.

Historians including Leo Ribuffo and Alan Brinkley have argued that characters once dismissed as irrational crackpots or colorful irrele-

vancies—including religious fundamentalists and depression-era figures like Huey Long and Father Charles Coughlin—articulated values deeply rooted and widely shared in American culture. These conservative spokespersons, whatever their peculiarities, offered a vision of free individuals, minimal government, and autonomous local communities that harkened back to the "civic republicanism" in the era of young nationhood.

Modern conservatism is also a product of the recent historical past. Scholars like Thomas Sugrue have shown that economic stagnation from the 1970s into the 1990s made Americans insecure about their future and receptive to new political doctrines. At the same time, as commentator Kevin Phillips has stressed, "social issues" like sexual liberation, abortion on demand, women's rights, and race relations sharply challenged traditional beliefs. Finally, the failure of government policies in Vietnam, runaway inflation in the 1970s, as well as the disillusioning Watergate episode, cast doubt on the legitimacy and even the morality of "big government."

Many modern conservatives, including pundit George Will, stress the deep historical roots of American conservatism. In their view, as Will once put it, it took sixteen years to count the ballots from the 1964 (Goldwater versus Johnson) election, and Goldwater won after all. But that argument is surely overstated. Goldwater ran against the legacy of the New Deal and was overwhelmingly defeated. Reagan ran against the consequences of the Great Society and won decisively. Many conservatives, in short, apparently acknowledge the legitimacy of the New Deal and the stake that many middle-class Americans feel they have in its programs of Social Security, home mortgage subsidies, farm price supports, and similar policies. But they reject the philosophy of the Great Society with its more focused attack on urban poverty and its vigorous support for affirmative action. Modern conservatism springs less from a repudiation of government per se and more from a disapproval of the particular priorities and strategies of the Great Society. The different historical fates of the New Deal and the Great Society suggest the key to the rise of modern conservatism.

SUGGESTED READINGS

Primary Source Documents

The debate over "Reaganomics" can be followed in Reagan's nationally televised address of July 27, 1981, *Weekly Compilation of Presidential Documents*, Vol. 17, no. 31,* and in the critical response of the *New York Times*, August 2, 1981.* See also the comments of Budget Director David Stockman, in William Greider, *The Education of David Stockman and Other Americans* (1982). On arms control see the pastoral letter of the National Council of Catholic Bishops and the reply of Albert Wohlstetter in Charles Kegley and Eugene Wittkopf, eds., *The Nuclear Reader* (1985). On Central American policy see Reagan's remarkable speech of March 16, 1986.* The inside workings of the Iran-contra scandal can be studied in *The Tower Commission Report* (1987).

Secondary Sources

Ronald Reagan is portrayed in Lou Cannon, *Reagan* (1982) and *President Reagan: The Role of a Lifetime* (1992); Laurence Barrett, *Gambling with History* (1984); Fred Greenstein, *The Reagan Presidency* (1983); and Michael Schaller, *Reckoning with Reagan* (1992). Reagan's economic policies are discussed in Paul C. Roberts, *The Supply-Side Revolution* (1984), and are sharply criticized in David A. Stockman, *The Triumph of Politics: Why the Reagan Revolution Failed* (1986). The neoconservative movement is best elucidated by the writings of its leaders. See Norman Podhoretz, *Breaking Ranks* (1979), and Irving Kristol, *Reflections of a Neoconservative* (1983). For a critical view consult Peter Steinfels, *The Neoconservatives* (1979). Issues of special concern to the neoconservatives are treated by Charles Murray, *Losing Ground* (1984), an indictment of federal government social programs. Its conclusions are sharply contested by John E. Schwartz, *America's Hidden Success* (rev. ed., 1988). Two studies of affirmative action are Allan P. Sindler, *Bakke, DeFinis and Minority Admissions* (1978), and J. Harvie Wilkinson, *From Brown to Bakke* (1979). For more on conservatism in the last decades of the twentieth century see William C. Berman, *America's Right Turn: From Nixon to Bush* (1994). Kevin P. Phillips is also insightful about the implications of the conservative revival in *Post-Conservative America* (1982). Eugene Genovese explores *The Southern Tradition: The Achievement and Limitations of an American Conservatism* (1994). Useful books on the role of religion in modern politics include Robert Booth Fowler, *A New Engagement: Evangelical Political Thought, 1966–1976* (1982); Robert Wuthrow, *The New Christian Right* (1983); and Richard John Neuhaus, *The Naked Public Square: Religion and Democracy in America* (1984). On the Supreme Court see Richard L. Pacelle, Jr., *The Transformation of the Supreme Court's Agenda: From the New Deal to the Reagan Administration* (1991). Critical of Reagan are William Leuchtenburg, *In the Shadow of FDR: From Harry Truman to Ronald Reagan* (1983); Paul D. Erickson, *Reagan Speaks: The Making of an American Myth* (1985); Garry Wills, *Reagan's America: Innocents at Home* (1987); Ronnie Duggar, *On Reagan* (1983); June Mayer and Doyle McManus, *Landslide: The Unmaking of the President, 1984–88* (1988); and Richard Reeves, *The Reagan Detour* (1985). More balanced are two books by John L. Palmer, *The Reagan Record* (co-edited with Isabel V. Sawhill, 1984) and *Perspectives on the Reagan Years* (1986). Important topics in foreign policy are covered in John Ehrman, *The Rise of Neoconservatism: Intellectuals and Foreign Affairs, 1945–1994* (1995); Walter LaFeber, *Inevitable Revolutions* (2nd ed., 1984), which discusses Central America; Robert Pastor's more probing study, *Condemned to Repetition: The United States and Nicaragua* (1987); and Bob Woodward, *Veil: The Secret Wars of the CIA* (1987). Theodore Draper details the Iran-contra affair in *A Very Thin Line* (1991). In *The Devil We Knew: Americans and the Cold War* (1993), H. W. Brands attempts to calculate how much it cost the United States to win the Cold War. Bob Woodward, in *The Agenda* (1994) and *The Choice* (1996), provides inside glimpses of politics in the Clinton years. On the precedent-shattering First Lady, see David Brock, *The Seduction of Hillary Rodham* (1996). James B. Stewart, *Blood Sport* (1996), is especially good on Clinton's complex relationship with the media.

---

* An asterisk indicates that the document, or an excerpt from it, can be found in Thomas A. Bailey and David M. Kennedy, eds., *The American Spirit: United States History as Seen by Contemporaries*, 9th ed. (Boston: Houghton Mifflin, 1998).

42

★★★★★★★★★

The American People Face a New Century

★★★★★★

*As our case is new, so we must think anew
and act anew. We must disenthrall ourselves,
and then we shall save our country.*

★★★★★★

Abraham Lincoln, 1862

The Weight of History

More than two hundred years old as the twentieth century drew to a close, the United States was both an old and a new nation. It boasted one of the longest uninterrupted traditions of democratic government of any country on earth. Indeed, it had pioneered the techniques of mass democracy and was, in that sense, the oldest modern polity. As one of the earliest countries to industrialize, America had also dwelled in the modern economic era longer than most nations.

But the Republic was in many ways still youthful as well. American society continued to be rejuvenated by fresh waves of immigrants, full of energy and ambition. The U.S. economy, despite problems, was generating new jobs at a rate of some 2 million per year. The whole world seemed to worship the icons of American culture—downing soft drinks and donning blue jeans, listening to rock or country music, even adopting indigenous American sports such as baseball and basketball. In the realm of consumerism, American products appeared to have Coca-Colonized the globe.

The history of American society also seemed to have increased global significance as the third millennium of the Christian era opened. Americans were a pluralistic people who had struggled for centuries to achieve tolerance and justice for many different religious, ethnic, and racial groups. Their historical experience could offer valuable lessons to the rapidly internationalizing planetary society that was emerging at the dawn of the twenty-first century.

In politics, economics, and culture, the great social experiment of American democracy was far from completed as the United States faced its future. Much history remained to be made as the country entered its third century of nationhood. But men and women make history only within the framework bequeathed to them by earlier generations. For better or worse, they march forward along time's path bearing the burdens of the past. Knowing when they have come to a truly new turn in the road, when they can lay part of their burden down, and when they cannot, or should not—all this constitutes the kind of wisdom that only historical study can engender.

Economic Revolutions

When the twentieth century opened, United States Steel Corporation was the flagship business of America's industrial revolution. A generation later, General Motors, annually producing millions of automobiles, became the characteristic American corporation, signaling the historic shift to a mass consumer economy that began in the 1920s and flowered fully in the 1950s.

The post–World War II era inaugurated the fast-paced "information age," when the storing, organizing, and processing of data became an industry in its own right. By century's end, the rapid emergence of Microsoft Corporation and the phenomenal growth of the Internet heralded an explosive communications revolution. Americans now rocketed down the "information superhighway" toward the uncharted terrain of an electronic global village.

The communications revolution was full of both promise and peril. Ordinary citizens could gain access to information once available only to privileged elites. Businesspeople instantaneously girdled the planet with transactions of prodigious scope and serpentine complexity. But the very speed and efficiency of the new communications tools threatened to wipe out entire occupational categories. Postal delivery people, travel agents, booksellers, bank tellers, stock brokers, and other kinds of workers whose business it was to mediate between product and client worried that they might find themselves rendered obsolete in the era of the Internet. As the computer made possible "classrooms without walls," even teachers, whose job was essentially to mediate between students and various bodies of knowledge, wondered whether they might end up as road-kill on the information superhighway.

Increasingly, scientific research was the engine that drove the economy, and new scientific knowledge posed new social and moral dilemmas. Early genetic discoveries, for instance, had yielded new strains of high-yield, pest-resistant crops, but also threatened the fragile ecological balance of the wondrous biosphere. As technical mastery of biological and medical techniques advanced, unprecedented ethical questions clamored for resolution. Should the human gene pool itself be "engineered"? What principles should govern the allocation of human organs for lifesaving transplants? What rules should guide efforts to clone human beings—or should such efforts not even be attempted?

Affluence and Inequality

Americans were still an affluent people as the twenty-first century opened. Median household income declined somewhat in the early 1990s then rebounded slightly by the late 1990s to about $35,000. But Americans were no longer the world's wealthiest people at century's end, as they had been in the quarter-century after World War II. In another unsettling reversal of long-term trends in American society, during the last two decades of the twentieth century the rich were getting richer and the poor were getting poorer at accelerating rates. In a development that first appeared in the 1980s, the richest 20 percent of Americans by the 1990s raked in nearly half the nation's income, whereas the poorest 20 percent received less than 4 percent.

Widening inequality could be measured in other ways as well. Chief executives in the 1970s typically earned 41 times the income of the average worker in their corporations; by the 1990s, they earned 225 times as much. At the same time some 36 million people, 13.8 percent of all Americans

Two Nations?   *While decaying neighborhoods and the sad legions of the homeless blighted American urban life in the closing decades of the twentieth century, affluent Americans took refuge in gated communities like this one in the Brentwood section of Los Angeles.*

(about 12 percent of whites, 29.3 percent of African-Americans, and just over 30 percent of Hispanics), remained mired in poverty—a depressing indictment of the inequities afflicting an affluent and allegedly egalitarian republic.

What caused the widening income gap? Some critics pointed to the tax and fiscal policies of the Reagan and Bush years, which favored the wealthy and penalized the poor. But deeper-running historical currents probably played a more important role. Among the most conspicuous causes were intensifying global competition; the shrinkage in high-paying manufacturing jobs for semiskilled and unskilled workers; the greater economic rewards commanded by educated workers in high-tech industries; the decline of unions; the rising tide of relatively low-skill immigrants; and the increasing tendency of educated men and women to marry one another, creating households with very high incomes.

The Feminist Revolution

All Americans were caught up in the great economic changes of the late twentieth century, but no group was more profoundly affected than women. When the twentieth century opened, women made up about 20 percent of all workers. Over the next five decades they increased their presence in the labor force at a fairly steady rate, except for a temporary spurt during World War II. Then, beginning in the 1950s, women's entry into the workplace accelerated dramatically. By the 1990s nearly half of all workers were women, and the majority of working-age women held jobs outside the home. Most astonishing was the upsurge in employment of mothers. In 1950, 90 percent of mothers with children under the age of six did not work for pay. But by the 1990s, a majority of women with children as young as one year old were wage earners. Women brought home the bacon and cooked it, too.

Beginning in the 1960s, many all-male strongholds—including Yale, Princeton, West Point, and even, belatedly, southern military academies like the Citadel and Virginia Military Institute—opened their doors to women. Women in the 1990s were piloting commercial airliners, orbiting outer space, governing states and cities, and writing Supreme Court decisions. Yet despite those gains, many feminists remained frustrated.

Women continued to receive lower wages than men in corresponding jobs, and they tended to concentrate in a few low-prestige, low-paying occupations (the "pink-collar ghetto"). Although they made up more than half the population, women in the 1990s accounted for only 25 percent of lawyers and judges (up from 5 percent in 1970) and 22 percent of physicians (up from 10 percent in 1970). Overt sexual discrimination explained some of this occupational segregation, but most of it seemed attributable to the greater burdens of parenthood on women than on men. Women were far more likely than men to interrupt their careers to bear and raise children, and even to choose less demanding career paths to allow for fulfilling those traditional roles.

As the revolution in women's status rolled on in the 1990s, men's lives changed as well. Some employers provided paternity leave in addition to maternity leave, in recognition of the shared burdens of the

Women's World: Something Old, Something New   *By the 1990s revolutionary changes in the economy and in social values had opened new career possibilities to women, while not fully relieving them of their traditional duties as mothers and homemakers. Dramatic changes in race relations and the redefinition of gender roles at the end of the twentieth century transformed even tradition-bound institutions like the U.S. Military Academy at West Point, New York, as this gathering of cadets suggests. Women's athletics came into their own in the wake of the feminist revolution. Here the U.S. Women's Basketball Team is on its way to a gold medal in the 1996 Olympic Games.*

two-worker household. Traditional female responsibilities such as cooking, laundry, and child care spilled over to men. Recognizing the new realities of the modern American household, Congress passed a Family Leave Bill in 1993, mandating job protection for working fathers as well as mothers who needed to take time off work for family-related reasons.

Fading Families and Aging Citizens

The nuclear family, once prized as the foundation of society and the nursery of the Republic, suffered heavy blows in postwar America. By the 1990s one out of every two marriages ended in divorce. Seven times more children were affected by divorce than at the turn of the century, and kids who commuted between separated parents were becoming commonplace.

Traditional families were not only falling apart at an alarming rate but also increasingly slow to form in the first place. The proportion of adults living alone tripled in the four decades after 1950, and by the 1990s nearly one-third of women age twenty-five to twenty-nine had never been married. In the 1960s, 5 percent of all births were to unmarried women, but three decades later one out of four white babies, one out of three Hispanic babies, and two out of three African-American babies were born to single mothers. Every fourth child in America was growing up in a household that lacked two parents. The collapse of the traditional family contributed heavily to the pauperization of many women and children, as single parents (usually mothers) struggled to keep their households economically afloat.

Child-rearing, the family's foremost function, was being increasingly assigned to "parent-substitutes" at day-care centers or schools—or to television, the modern age's "electronic babysitter." Estimates were that the average child by age sixteen had watched up to fifteen thousand hours of TV—more time than was spent in the classroom.

Born and raised without the family support enjoyed by their forebears, Americans were also increasingly likely to be lonely in their later years. Most elderly people in the 1990s depended on pension plans and government Social Security payments,

The Modern Family Tree *High divorce rates and the increasing numbers of "blended families" in modern American society could often be confusing.*

not on their loved ones, for their daily bread. The great majority of them drew their last breaths not in their own homes but in hospitals and nursing facilities. From youth to old age, the role of the family was dwindling.

Americans were living longer than ever before. A person born at the dawn of the century could expect to survive less than fifty years, but a white male born in the 1990s could anticipate a life span of more than seventy-six years. His white female counterpart would probably outlive him by seven years. (The figures were slightly lower for nonwhites, reflecting differences in living standards, especially diet and health care.) The census of 1950 recorded that women for the first time made up a majority of Americans, thanks largely to greater female longevity. Miraculous medical advances lengthened and strengthened lives. Noteworthy were the development of antibiotics after 1940 and Dr. Jonas Salk's discovery in 1953 of a vaccine against a dreaded crippler, polio.

Longer lives spelled more older people. One American in eight was over sixty-five years of age in the 1990s, and projections were that one of every five would be in the "sunset years" by 2050, as the median age rose toward forty. This aging of the population raised a host of political, social, and economic questions. Elderly people formed a potent electoral bloc that aggressively lobbied for government favors and achieved real gains for senior citizens. Poverty declined dramatically among those over sixty-five, even as the percentage of children in poverty rose to 20 percent in the 1990s.

These triumphs for senior citizens also brought fiscal strains, especially in the Social Security system, established in 1935 to provide income for retired workers. When Social Security began, most workers continued to toil after age sixty-five. By century's end only a small minority did (about 15 percent of men and 8 percent of women), and a majority of the elderly population relied primarily on Social Security checks for their living expenses. Contrary to popular mythology, Social Security payments to retirees did not simply represent reimbursement for contributions that the elderly had made during their working lives. In fact, the payments of current workers into the Social Security system funded the benefits of the current generation of retirees. By the 1990s those

Senior Power   *Living longer and living healthier, older Americans coalesced into one of America's most politically powerful interest groups as the twentieth century drew to a close.*

benefits had risen so high, and the ratio of active workers to retirees had dropped so low, that drastic adjustments were necessary.

At the beginning of the new century, as the huge wave of post–World War II baby boomers approached retirement age, it seemed that the "unfunded liability"—the difference between what the government promised to pay to the elderly and the taxes it expected to take in—might eventually rise above $7 trillion, a sum that threatened to bankrupt the Republic unless drastic reforms were adopted. Yet because of the electoral power of older Americans, Social Security reform remained the "third rail" of American politics, which public figures dared not touch. A war between the generations loomed in the twenty-first century as payments to the nonworking elderly threatened to soak up fully half the working population's income by about 2040.

The New Immigration

Newcomers flooded into modern America. They washed ashore in waves that numbered nearly a million persons per year in the 1980s and 1990s—the heaviest inflow of immigrants in America's experience. In striking contrast to the historic pattern of immigration, Europe contributed far fewer people than did the countries of Asia and Latin America.

What prompted this new migration to America? The truth is that the newest immigrants came for many of the same reasons as the old. They typically left countries where populations were growing rapidly and where agricultural and industrial revolutions were shaking people loose from old habits of life—conditions almost identical to those in nineteenth-century Europe. They came to America, as previous immigrants had done, in search of jobs and economic opportunity.

The Southwest, from Texas to California, felt the immigrant impact especially sharply, as Mexican migrants concentrated heavily in that region. By the turn of the century, Latinos made up nearly one-third of the population in Texas, Arizona, and California and almost 40 percent in New Mexico—amounting to a demographic *reconquista* of the lands lost by Mexico in the war of 1846.

The size and geographic concentration of the Hispanic population in the Southwest had few precedents in the history of American immigration. Most previous groups had been so thinly scattered across the land that they had little choice but to learn English and make their way in the larger U.S. society, however much they might have longed to preserve their native language and customs. But it seemed possible that Mexican-Americans might succeed in creating a truly bicultural zone in the booming southwestern states.

Some old-stock Americans worried about the capacity of the modern United States to absorb these new immigrants. The Immigration Reform and Control Act of 1986 attempted to choke off illegal entry by penalizing employers of undocumented aliens and by granting amnesty to many of those already here. Anti-immigrant sentiment flared especially sharply in California in the wake of an economic recession in the early 1990s. California voters approved a ballot initiative that attempted to deny benefits, including education, to illegal immigrants, and in 1998 passed another measure to end bilingual education in Cali-

fornia schools. Congress in 1996 had already restricted access to welfare even for *legal* immigrants.

Yet the fact was that foreign-born people accounted for less than 9 percent of the American population in the 1990s—a far smaller proportion than the historical high point of nearly 15 percent recorded in the census of 1910—and a number that suggested the society's ability to take in newcomers was far from exhausted. Somewhat inconsistently, critics charged both that immigrants robbed citizens of jobs and that they dumped themselves on the welfare rolls at the taxpayers' expense. But studies showed that immigrants took jobs scorned by Americans and that they paid more dollars in taxes (withholding and Social Security taxes, as well as sales taxes) than they claimed in welfare payments. A more urgent worry was that unscrupulous employers might take cruel advantage of immigrant workers, who often had scant knowledge of their legal rights.

Ethnic Pride

Thanks both to continued immigration and to their own high birthrate, Hispanic-Americans were becoming an increasingly important minority (see "Makers of America: The Latinos," pp. 642–643). The United States by the 1990s was home to about 27 million Hispanics. They included some 17 million Chicanos, or Mexican-Americans, mostly in the Southwest, as well as nearly 3 million Puerto Ricans, chiefly in the Northeast, and about 1 million Cubans in Florida.

Flexing their political muscles, Latinos elected mayors of Miami, Denver, and San Antonio. After years of struggle, the United Farmworkers Organizing Committee (UFWOC), headed by soft-spoken and charismatic César Chávez, succeeded in improving working conditions for the mostly Chicano "stoop laborers" who followed the cycle of planting and harvesting across the American West. Hispanic influence seemed likely to grow, as suggested by the increasing presence of Spanish-language ballots and television broadcasts. If current population and immigration trends continue, Hispanics will become the nation's largest ethnic minority sometime before the year 2025.

Asian-Americans also made giant strides. By the 1980s they were America's fastest-growing minority. Their numbers nearly doubled in that decade alone, thanks to heavy immigration, and continued to swell in the 1990s. Once feared and hated as the "yellow peril" and consigned to the most menial and degrading jobs, citizens of Asian ancestry were now counted among the most prosperous of Americans. The typical Asian-American household enjoyed an income nearly 20 percent greater than that of the typical white household.

Indians, the original Americans, shared in the general awakening of "cultural nationalism." The 1990 census counted some 1.5 million Native Americans, half of whom had left their reservations to live in cities. Meanwhile, unemployment and alcoholism had blighted reservation life.

Cities and Suburbs

America's "alabaster cities" of song and story grew more sooty and less safe in the closing years of the century. Crime was the great scourge of urban life. The rate of violent crimes committed in cities reached an all-time high in the drug-infested 1980s, then leveled off in the early 1990s. The number of violent crimes even began to decline substantially in many areas after 1995. Nevertheless, murders, robberies, and rapes remained shockingly common not only in cities but in suburbs and rural areas as well. America imprisoned a larger fraction of its citizens than almost any other country in the world, and some desperate citizens resorted to armed vigilante tactics to protect themselves.

The migration from cities to the suburbs was so swift and massive that by the mid-1990s a majority of Americans made such communities their home. With the ending of the nation's brief "urban age" that had begun in the 1920s, many observers saw a new fragmentation and isolation developing in suburbanized American life. Entire neighborhoods, usually containing economically and racially homogeneous populations, tried to insulate themselves from social problems by setting up "gated communities." In these safe but segregated enclaves, the sense of a larger and inclusive national community might prove hard to sustain.

Minority America

Racial and ethnic tensions exacerbated the problems of American cities. These stresses were especially evident in Los Angeles, which, like New York a century earlier, was a magnet for minorities, especially immigrants from Asia and Latin America. When in 1992 a mostly white jury exonerated white Los Angeles police officers who had been videotaped ferociously beating a black suspect, the minority neighborhoods in South Central Los Angeles erupted in rage. Arson and looting laid waste entire city blocks, and scores of people were killed. Some black rioters vented their anger against white police by attacking Asian shopkeepers, who in turn formed armed patrols to protect their property.

The Los Angeles riots vividly testified to black skepticism about the American system of justice. Just three years later, again in Los Angeles, the televised spectacle of former football star O. J. Simpson's murder trial fed white disillusionment with the state of race relations. After months of testimony that seemed to many to point to Simpson's guilt, the jury acquitted Simpson, presumably because certain Los Angeles police officers involved in the case had been shown to harbor racist sentiments. In a later civil trial, another jury unanimously found Simpson liable for the "wrongful deaths" of his former wife and another victim. The reaction to the Simpson verdicts revealed the yawning chasm that separated white and black America, as most whites continued to believe Simpson guilty, while a majority of African-Americans told pollsters that the original not-guilty verdict was justified.

American cities have always held an astonishing variety of ethnic and racial groups, but in the late twentieth century, minorities made up a majority of the population of many American cities, as whites fled to the suburbs. More than three-quarters of African-Americans lived in cities by the 1990s, whereas only about one-quarter of whites did. The most desperate black ghettos, housing a hapless "underclass" in the inner core of the old industrial cities, were especially problematic. Successful blacks who had benefited from the civil rights revolution of the 1950s and 1960s followed whites to the suburbs, leaving in the old ghetto a residue of the poorest

The Latinos

Today Mexican food is handed through fast-food drive-up windows in all fifty states, Spanish-language broadcasts fill the airwaves, and the Latino community has its own telephone book, the *Spanish Yellow Pages*. Latinos send representatives to Congress and mayors to city hall, record hit songs, paint murals, and teach history. Hispanic-Americans, among the fastest-growing segments of the U.S. population, include Puerto Ricans, frequent voyagers between their native island and northeastern cities; Cubans, many of them refugees from the communist dictatorship of Fidel Castro, concentrated in Miami and southern Florida; and Central Americans, fleeing the ravages of civil war in Nicaragua and El Salvador.

But the most populous group of Latinos derives from Mexico. The first significant numbers of Mexicans began heading for *El Norte* ("the North") around 1910, when the upheavals of the Mexican Revolution stirred and shuffled the Mexican population into more or less constant flux. Their northward passage was briefly interrupted during the Great Depression, when thousands of Mexican nationals were deported. But immigration resumed during World War II, and since then a steady flow of legal immigrants has passed through border checkpoints, joined by countless millions of their undocumented countrymen and countrywomen stealing across the frontier on moonless nights.

For the most part, these Mexicans came to work in the fields, following the ripening crops northward to Canada through the summer and autumn.

Others gathered in the cities of the Southwest—El Paso, Los Angeles, Houston, and San Bernardino. There they found regular work, even if racial discrimination often confined them to manual labor. Houses may have been shabby in the barrios, but these Mexican neighborhoods provided a sense of togetherness, a place to raise a family, and the chance to join a mutual aid society. Such societies, or *mutu-*

Chicana Pride   *A Mexican-American girl celebrates her cultural heritage at the Texas Folklife Festival in San Antonio.*

alistas, sponsored baseball leagues, helped the sick and disabled, and defended their members against discrimination.

Mexican immigrants lived so close to the border that their native country acted like a powerful magnet, drawing them back time and time again. Mexicans frequently returned to see relatives, and relatively few became U.S. citizens. In addition, the Mexican government sometimes intervened to discourage Mexicans from becoming citizens of their adopted country by promoting Mexicanization pro-

grams among the immigrants, including parades to observe *Cinco de Mayo* ("Fifth of May"), celebrating Mexico's defeat of a French army in 1862. Since World War II, the American-born generation has carried on the fight for political representation, economic opportunity, and cultural preservation.

Fresh arrivals from Mexico and from other Latin American nations daily swell the Hispanic communities across America. As the United States entered the twenty-first century, it was taking on a pronounced Spanish accent.

poor. Without a middle class to sustain community institutions like schools and small businesses, the inner cities, plagued by unemployment and drug addiction, seemed bereft of leadership, cohesion, resources, and hope.

The abandoned underclass, heavily composed of blacks and other minorities, represented a social failure that eluded any known remedy. But other segments of the African-American community had clearly prospered in the wake of the civil rights gains of the 1950s and 1960s, although they still had a long hill to climb before reaching full equality. By the 1990s about 40 percent of blacks were counted in the middle class (defined as enjoying family income greater than $25,000 per year). The number of black elected officials had risen above seven thousand, including more than a thousand in the Old South, some two dozen members of Congress, and the mayors of several large cities. Voting tallies demonstrated that successful black politicians were moving beyond isolated racial constituencies and into the political mainstream by appealing to a wide variety of voters. In 1989 Virginians, only 15 percent of whom were black, elected L. Douglas Wilder as the first African-American state governor. In 1994 voters in Illinois made Carol Mosely Braun the first African-American woman elected to the U.S. Senate.

Single women headed over half of black families, almost three times the rate for whites. Many of those African-American women, husbandless and jobless, necessarily depended on welfare to feed their

children. Congress, responding to persistent national exasperation with the welfare system, legislated a major overhaul of welfare programs in 1996. The new law restricted access to social services and required able-bodied welfare recipients to find work within two years. The 1996 welfare reform bill was a bold stroke but also something of a shot in the dark. Many critics warned that the proposed changes threatened to replace "welfare as we know it" with "welfare as we don't know it."

In the state of California, meanwhile, voters in 1996 approved Proposition 209, the "California Civil Rights Initiative," which required an end to all affirmative-action programs in the state. This ringing victory for the foes of affirmative action reflected smoldering resentment against liberal "social engineering" programs and mounting impatience with American society's apparent inability to resolve its racial problems. The action in California, so often a bellwether state, instigated a growing national effort to repeal the affirmative-action programs that had done so much since the 1960s to accelerate the growth of the black middle class and to advance the status of women.

The Life of the Mind

Despite the mind-sapping chatter of the "boob tube," Americans in the late twentieth century read more, listened to more music, and were better educated than ever before. By the 1990s colleges were awarding nearly a million degrees a year. The expanding ranks of educated people lifted the economy to more advanced levels while creating consumers of "high culture." Americans annually made some 300 million visits to museums in the 1990s and patronized about a thousand opera companies and fifteen hundred symphony orchestras—as well as countless popular music groups.

What Americans read said much about the state of American society at century's end. Among the most striking developments in American letters was the rise of authors from once-marginal regions and ethnic groups coming into their own. Reflecting the general population shift westward, the West became the subject of a particularly rich literary outpouring. Larry McMurtry lovingly recollected the end of the cattle-drive era in *Lonesome Dove* (1985). Raymond Carver penned understated and powerful stories about working-class life in the Pacific Northwest, and Annie Dillard re-created the gritty frontier history of that same region. David Guterson penned a moving tale of interracial anxiety and affection in the World War II–era Pacific Northwest in *Snow Falling on Cedars* (1994). Norman MacLean, a former English professor, left two unforgettable accounts of his boyhood in Montana: *A River Runs Through It* (1976) and *Young Men and Fire* (1992).

African-American authors and artists also increasingly made their mark. Playwright August Wilson retold the history of black Americans in the twentieth century, with special emphasis on the psychic costs of the northward migration, in *Fences* (1986) and *Joe Turner's Come and Gone* (1988). Alice Walker gave fictional voice to the experiences of black women in her hugely popular *The Color Purple* (1982). Toni Morrison wove a bewitching portrait of maternal affection in *Beloved* (1987) and in 1993 became the first African-American woman to win the Nobel Prize for literature. Native American authors like Kiowa N. Scott Momaday (*House Made of Dawn*, 1968) and Blackfoot James Welch (*Fools Crow*, 1986) also achieved literary recognition.

Asian-American authors, too, flourished. Maxine Hong Kingston imaginatively reconstructed the lives of the earliest Chinese immigrants in *The Woman Warrior* (1976) and *China Men* (1980). Amy Tan's *The Joy Luck Club* (1989) explored the some-times painful relationship between immigrant Chinese parents and their Asian-American children.

Women writers and women's themes forged to the fictional forefront as the feminist movement advanced. Jane Smiley modeled her touching narrative of a midwestern farm family on Shakespeare's *King Lear* in *A Thousand Acres* (1991) and followed up with a hilarious spoof on university life in *Moo* (1995). E. Annie Proulx won widespread acclaim with her comic yet tender portrayal of a struggling family in *The Shipping News* (1993). The rising interest in feminist and African-American themes revived the popularity of the 1930s writer Zora Neale Hurston, especially her naturalist novel *Their Eyes Were Watching God*, first published in 1937.

New York City became the art capital of the world after World War II, as well-heeled Americans supported a large number of painters and sculptors. The open and tradition-free American environment seemed especially congenial to the experimental mood of much modern art. Jackson Pollock pioneered abstract expressionism in the 1940s and 1950s, flinging paint on huge canvas flats stretched on his studio floor. Realistic representation went out the window as artists like Pollock and Willem de Kooning strove to create "action paintings" that made the viewer a creative participant in defining the painting's meaning. Pop artists in the 1960s, notably Andy Warhol, canonized on canvas everyday items of consumer culture, such as soup cans. Sculptors like Robert Rauschenberg and Claes Oldenburg also incorporated into their work objects like cardboard boxes and giant, pillow-soft telephones.

On the stage, playwright David Mamet analyzed the barbarity of American capitalism in plays like *Glengarry Glen Ross* and *American Buffalo*, in which he crafted a kind of poetry from the sludge of American slang. Mamet also made savage sport of feminism and "political correctness" in *Oleanna*, a biting satire about a woman student and her professor. The AIDS epidemic inspired Tony Kushner's sensationally inventive *Angels in America*, a broad-ranging commentary, alternately hilarious and touching, about the condition of American life at century's end. Film, the most characteristic American art form, continued to flourish, especially as a wave of younger film-makers like George Lucas, Steven

Spielberg, Spike Lee, and the Coen brothers, as well as the innovative documentary artist, Ken Burns, made their influence felt.

Architecture also benefited from the building boom of the postwar era. Old master Frank Lloyd Wright produced strikingly original designs, as in the round-walled Guggenheim Museum in New York. Louis Kahn employed stark geometric forms and basic building materials like brick and concrete to make beautiful, simple buildings. Eero Saarinen, the son of a Finnish immigrant, contributed a number of imaginative structures, including two Yale University residential colleges that evoked the atmosphere of an Italian hill town. Chinese-born I. M. Pei designed numerous graceful buildings on several college campuses, as well as the John F. Kennedy Library in Boston.

The American Prospect

The American spirit pulsed with vitality as the nation headed into the twenty-first century, but grave problems continued to plague the Republic. Women still fell short of first-class economic citizenship, and American society groped for ways to adapt the traditional family to the new realities of women's work outside the home. A whole generation after the civil rights triumphs of the 1960s, full equality remained an elusive dream for countless Americans of color. The scourge of drug abuse afflicted all sectors of U.S. society but wreaked its cruelest damage in the tortured underclass neighborhoods of the inner city.

Powerful foreign competitors challenged America's premier economic status. The alarming redistribution of wealth and income threatened to turn

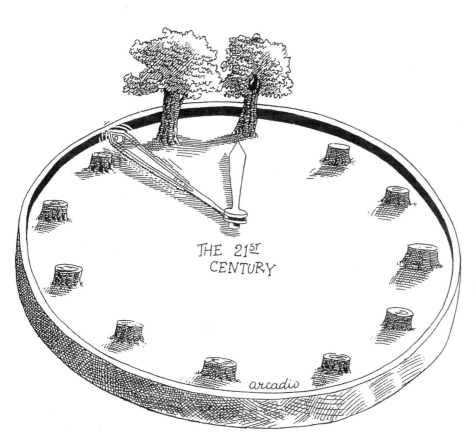

Time for Action   *As Americans closed the twentieth century and entered the twenty-first, the movement to save precious environmental resources rose higher on the national and international agenda. This cartoon highlights the urgency of stopping the often heedless exploitation of trees and forests, and the need to secure nature's bounty for future generations.*

America into a society of haves and have-nots, mocking the ideals of democracy and breeding seething resentments along the economic frontier that divided rich from poor.

Environmental worries clouded the country's future. Coal-fired electrical generating plants helped form acid rain and probably contributed to the greenhouse effect, an ominous warming in the planet's temperature. The unsolved problem of radioactive waste disposal hampered the development of nuclear power plants. The planet was being drained of oil, and disastrous accidents like the grounding and subsequent oil spill of the giant tanker *Exxon Valdez* in 1989 in Alaska's pristine Prince William Sound demonstrated the ecological risks of oil exploration and transportation at sea.

Some Americans, soured on the false satisfactions of wealth and anxious to set the globe on the path to ecological stability, welcomed the prospect of a "no-growth" economy. But enlarging the economic pie had historically been the American way of satisfying the appetites of virtually all people for a richer life.

Born as a revolutionary force in a world of conservatism, for much of the twentieth century America stood as a conservative force in a world of revolutionism. It held aloft the banner of liberal democracy in a world buffeted by revolutions of left and right, including communism, Nazism, and fascism. But much that is revolutionary remains in America's liberal democratic legacy, and its people have pioneered in the revolutions against colonialism, racism, sexism, ignorance, and poverty that roiled the planet in the twentieth century.

As the human family grows at an alarming rate on a shrinking globe, America's revolutionary heritage does not lack for new challenges. The task of cleansing Spaceship Earth of its abundant pollutants—including nuclear weapons—is one urgent mission confronting the American people in the opening years of the twenty-first century. Another is seeking ways to resolve the ethnic and cultural conflicts that erupted with renewed virulence around the globe in the wake of the Cold War's end. At the same time, new opportunities beckon in outer space and on inner-city streets, at the artist's easel and in the concert hall, at the inventor's bench and in the scientist's laboratory, and in the unending quest for social justice, individual fulfillment, and international peace. The challenges facing Americans, at home and abroad, are formidable, but so is the Republic. As a new century and a new millennium dawned, the people of the United States still aspired to live up to Lincoln's conviction that they and their heritage represent "the last best hope of earth."

SUGGESTED READINGS

Primary Source Documents

Up-to-date data on income and poverty can be found at the Census Bureau's web site, http://www.census.gov/hhes/income. The classic book that launched the modern women's movement is Betty Friedan, *The Feminine Mystique** (1963). For the views of a Christian conservative on the abortion issue see Ralph Reed, "We Stand at a Crossroads," *Newsweek*, May 13, 1996, p. 28.* *Statistical Abstract of the United States* is an annual government publication with a wealth of information on a variety of topics, including immigration, Social Security funding, and the social and economic condition of minorities.

Secondary Sources

A useful overview of recent history is Paul Boyer, *Promises to Keep: The United States Since World War II* (1995). Growing income inequality is discussed in Barbara Ehrenreich, *Fear of Falling: The Inner Life of the Middle Class* (1989), and in Kevin P. Phillips, *The Politics of Rich and Poor: Wealth and the American Electorate in the Reagan Aftermath* (1990). The evolving social participation of women, and the dilemmas thereby created, are clearly spelled out in Rosalind Rosenberg, *Divided Lives* (1992), and in William H. Chafe, *The Paradox of Change: American Women in the 20th Century* (1991). See also Betty Friedan, *The Second Stage* (1981); Sylvia Ann Hewlett, *A Lesser Life: The Myth of Women's Liberation in America* (1986); Susanne M. Bianchi, *American Women in Transition* (1987); Marion Faux, *Roe vs. Wade* (1988); Jean E. Friedman et al., eds., *Our American Sisters* (1987); and Susan Faludi's provocative bestseller, *Backlash: The Undeclared War Against American Women* (1991). On the looming problems in the Social Security system see Peter G. Peterson, *Will America Grow Up Before It Grows Old?* (1996); for a provocative analysis of the leading senior citizens' lobby, the American Association of Retired Persons, consult Charles R. Morris, *The AARP: America's Most Powerful Lobby and the Clash of Generations*

(1996). George J. Borjas turns an economist's critical eye on recent immigration in *Friends or Strangers* (1990). America's newest immigrants are the subjects of David M. Reimers, *Still the Golden Door: The Third World Comes to America* (1986). On Mexican-Americans see Carlos Munoz, Jr., *Youth, Identity, Power: The Chicano Movement* (1989); George J. Sanchez, *Becoming Mexican American* (1989); and Richard Rodriguez's poignant memoir, *Hunger of Memory* (1982). Asian-Americans are discussed in Bill Ong Hing, *Making and Remaking Asian America Through Immigration Policy* (1993), and in Ronald Takaki, *Strangers from a Different Shore* (1989). On blacks see Harvard Sitkoff, *The Struggle for Black Equality, 1954–1992* (rev. ed., 1993); Andrew Hacker, *Two Nations: Black and White, Separate, Hostile, Unequal* (1992); and Gerald David Jaynes and Robin M. Williams, Jr., *A Common Destiny: Blacks and American Society* (1989). The problems of the cities are examined in Jon C. Teaford, *The Rough Road to Renaissance: Urban Revitalization in America, 1940–1985* (1990), and Larry Bennett, *Fragments of Cities: The New American Downtowns and Neighborhoods* (1990). Suburbs are the subject of Paul G. Lewis's *Shaping Suburbia* (1996). For penetrating analyses of the problems of the inner cities consult three studies by William J. Wilson: *The Truly Disadvantaged: The Inner City, the Underclass, and Public Policy* (1987); *Poverty, Inequality, and the Future of Social Policy* (1995); and *When Work Disappears* (1996). Welfare reform is the subject of Mary Jo Bane, *Welfare Realities* (1994). Nicholas Lemann, *The Promised Land* (1991), provides a vivid account of the welfare system and the failed promises of Lyndon Johnson's "War on Poverty." The political implications of the debates over race and welfare policies are spelled out in Thomas Byrne Edsall and Mary D. Edsall, *Chain Reaction: The Impact of Race, Rights, and Taxes on American Politics* (1991). The broader cultural controversies of the era are examined in Arthur M. Schlesinger, Jr., *The Disuniting of America* (1992); Robert Hughes, *Culture of Complaint: The Fraying of America* (1993); and Henry Louis Gates, Jr., *Loose Canons: Notes on the Culture Wars* (1993). A sensitive and intriguing study of the values of modern Americans is Robert N. Bellah, *Habits of the Heart: Individualism and Commitment in American Life* (1985). See also Allan Bloom's conservative critique of modern higher education, *The Closing of the American Mind* (1987), and the rejoinder by Lawrence Levine, *The Opening of the American Mind* (1996).

---

* An asterisk indicates that the document, or an excerpt from it, can be found in Thomas A. Bailey and David M. Kennedy, eds., *The American Spirit: United States History as Seen by Contemporaries*, 9th ed. (Boston: Houghton Mifflin, 1998).

APPENDIX

✶✶✶✶✶✶✶✶✶

Declaration of Independence
In Congress, July 4, 1776
The Unanimous Declaration of the Thirteen United States of America

[Bracketed material in color has been inserted by the authors. For adoption background, see pp. 96–97.]

When, in the course of human events, it becomes necessary for one people to dissolve the political bands which have connected them with another, and to assume, among the powers of the earth, the separate and equal station to which the laws of nature and of nature's God entitle them, a decent respect to the opinions of mankind requires that they should declare the causes which impel them to the separation.

We hold these truths to be self-evident: That all men are created equal; that they are endowed by their Creator with certain unalienable rights; that among these are life, liberty, and the pursuit of happiness; that, to secure these rights, governments are instituted among men, deriving their just powers from the consent of the governed; that whenever any form of government becomes destructive of these ends, it is the right of the people to alter or to abolish it, and to institute new government, laying its foundation on such principles, and organizing its powers in such form, as to them shall seem most likely to effect their safety and happiness. Prudence, indeed, will dictate that governments long established should not be changed for light and transient causes; and accordingly all experience hath shown that mankind are more disposed to suffer, while evils are sufferable, than to right themselves by abolishing the forms to which they are accustomed. But when a long train of abuses and usurpations, pursuing invariably the same object, evinces a design to reduce them under absolute despotism, it is their right, it is their duty, to throw off such government, and to provide new guards for their future security. Such has been the patient sufferance of these colonies; and such is now the necessity which constrains them to alter their former systems of government. The history of the present King of Great Britain is a history of repeated injuries and usurpations, all having in direct object the establishment of an absolute tyranny over these states. To prove this, let facts be submitted to a candid world.

He has refused his assent to laws, the most wholesome and necessary for the public good. [See royal veto, p. 82.]

He has forbidden his governors to pass laws of immediate and pressing importance, unless suspended in their operation till his assent should be obtained; and, when so suspended, he has utterly neglected to attend to them.

He has refused to pass other laws for the accommodation of large districts of people [by establishing new counties], unless those people would relinquish the right of representation in the legislature, a right inestimable to them, and formidable to tyrants only.

He has called together legislative bodies at places unusual, uncomfortable, and distant from the depository of their public records, for the sole purpose of fatiguing them into compliance with his measures. [e.g., removal of Massachusetts Assembly to Salem, 1774]

He has dissolved representative houses repeatedly, for opposing, with manly firmness, his invasions on the rights of the people. [e.g., Virginia Assembly, 1765]

He has refused for a long time, after such dissolutions, to cause others to be elected; whereby the legislative powers, incapable of annihilation, have returned to the people at large for their exercise; the state remaining, in the mean time, exposed to all the dangers of invasions from without and convulsions within.

He has endeavored to prevent the population [populating] of these states; for that purpose obstructing the laws for naturalization of foreigners; refusing to pass others to encourage their migration hither, and raising the conditions of new appropriations of lands. [e.g., Proclamation of 1763, p. 78]

He has obstructed the administration of justice, by refusing his assent to laws for establishing judiciary powers.

He has made judges dependent on his will alone, for the tenure of their offices, and the amount and payment of their salaries. [See Townshend Acts, p. 85.]

He has erected a multitude of new offices, and sent hither swarms of officers to harass our people and eat out their substance. [See enforcement of Navigation Laws, pp. 81–82.]

He has kept among us, in times of peace, standing armies, without the consent of our legislatures. [See pp. 83–84.]

He has affected to render the military independent of, and superior to, the civil power.

He has combined with others to subject us to a jurisdiction foreign to our constitution, and unacknowledged by our laws, giving his assent to their acts of pretended legislation:

> For quartering large bodies of armed troops among us [see Boston Massacre, p. 85];
>
> For protecting them, by a mock trial, from punishment for any murders which they should commit on the inhabitants of these states [see 1774 Act, p. 87];
>
> For cutting off our trade with all parts of the world [see Boston Port Act, p. 87];
>
> For imposing taxes on us without our consent [see Stamp Act, p. 84];
>
> For depriving us, in many cases, of the benefits of trial by jury;
>
> For transporting us beyond seas, to be tried for pretended offenses;
>
> For abolishing the free system of English laws in a neighboring province [Quebec], establishing therein an arbitrary government, and enlarging its boundaries, so as to render it at once an example and fit instrument for introducing the same absolute rule into these colonies [Quebec Act, p. 87];
>
> For taking away our charters, abolishing our most valuable laws, and altering fundamentally the forms of our governments [e.g., in Massachusetts, p. 87];
>
> For suspending our own legislatures, and declaring themselves invested with power to legislate for us in all cases whatsoever [see Stamp Act repeal, p. 84].

He has abdicated government here, by declaring us out of his protection and waging war against us [Proclamation, p. 94].

He has plundered our seas, ravaged our coasts, burned our towns, and destroyed the lives of our people [e.g., the burning of Falmouth (Portland), p. 95].

He is at this time transporting large armies of foreign mercenaries [Hessians, p. 94] to complete the works of death, desolation, and tyranny already begun with circumstances of cruelty and perfidy scarcely paralleled in the most barbarous ages, and totally unworthy of the head of a civilized nation.

He has constrained our fellow-citizens, taken captive on the high seas [by impressment], to bear arms against their country, to become the executioners of their friends and brethren, or to fall themselves by their hands.

He has excited domestic insurrection among us [i.e., among slaves], and has endeavored to bring on the inhabitants of our frontiers the merciless Indian savages, whose known rule of warfare is an undistinguished destruction of all ages, sexes, and conditions.

In every stage of these oppressions we have petitioned for redress in the most humble terms; our repeated petitions have been answered only by repeated injury [e.g., pp. 93–94]. A prince, whose character is thus marked by every act which may define a tyrant, is unfit to be the ruler of a free people.

Nor have we been wanting in our attentions to our British brethren. We have warned them, from time to time, of attempts by their legislature to extend an unwarrantable jurisdiction over us. We have reminded them of the circumstances of our emigration and settlement here. We have appealed to their native justice and magnanimity; and we have conjured them, by the ties of our common kindred, to disavow these usurpations, which would inevitably interrupt our connections and correspondence. They, too, have been deaf to the voice of justice and of consanguinity [blood relationship]. We must, therefore, acquiesce in the necessity which denounces [announces] our separation, and hold them, as we hold the rest of mankind, enemies in war, in peace friends.

We, therefore, the representatives of the United States of America, in General Congress assembled, appealing to the Supreme Judge of the world for the rectitude of our intentions, do, in the name and by the authority of the good people of these colonies, solemnly publish and declare, That these United Colonies are, and of right ought to be, FREE AND INDEPENDENT STATES; that they are absolved from all allegiance to the British crown, and that all political connection between them and the state of Great Britain is, and ought to be, totally dissolved; and that, as free and independent states, they have full power to levy war, conclude peace, contract alliances, establish commerce, and do all other acts and things which independent states may of right do. And for the support of this declaration, with a firm reliance on the protection of Divine Providence, we mutually pledge to each other our lives, our fortunes, and our sacred honor.

[Signed by]

JOHN HANCOCK [President]
[and fifty-five others]

Constitution of the
United States of America

[Boldface headings and bracketed explanatory matter and marginal comments (both in color) have been inserted for the reader's convenience. Passages that are no longer operative are printed in italic type.]

PREAMBLE

On "We the people,"
see p. 180n.
We the people of the United States, in order to form a more perfect union, establish justice, insure domestic tranquillity, provide for the common defense, promote the general welfare, and secure the blessings of liberty to ourselves and our posterity, do ordain and establish this CONSTITUTION for the United States of America.

Article I.   Legislative Department

Section I.   Congress

Legislative power vested in a two-House Congress. All legislative powers herein granted shall be vested in a Congress of the United States, which shall consist of a Senate and a House of Representatives.

Section II.   House of Representatives

1. The people elect representatives biennially. The House of Representatives shall be composed of members chosen every second year by the people of the several States, and the electors [voters] in each State shall have the qualifications requisite for electors of the most numerous branch of the State Legislature.

2. Who may be representatives. No person shall be a Representative who shall not have attained to the age of twenty-five years, and been seven years a citizen of the United States, and who shall not, when elected, be an inhabitant of that State in which he shall be chosen.

3. Representation in the House based on population; census. Representatives and direct taxes[1] shall be apportioned among the several States which may be included within this Union, according to their respective numbers, *which shall be determined by adding to the whole number of free persons, including those bound to service for a term of years* [apprentices and indentured servants], *and excluding Indians not taxed, three-fifths of all other persons* [slaves].[2] The actual enumeration [census] shall be made within three years after the first meeting of the Congress of the United States, and within every subsequent term of ten years, in such manner as they shall by law direct. The number of Representatives shall not exceed one for every thirty

*See 1787
compromise,
pp. 115–117.*

*See 1787
compromise,
p. 116.*

---

[1] Modified in 1913 by the 16th Amendment re income taxes.

[2] The word *slave* appears nowhere in the Constitution; *slavery* appears in the 13th Amendment. The three-fifths rule ceased to be in force when the 13th Amendment was adopted in 1865 (see p. 49 and text of Amendments following).

thousand, but each State shall have at least one Representative; *and until such enumeration shall be made, the State of New Hampshire shall be entitled to choose three, Massachusetts eight, Rhode Island and Providence Plantations one, Connecticut five, New York six, New Jersey four, Pennsylvania eight, Delaware one, Maryland six, Virginia ten, North Carolina five, South Carolina five, and Georgia three.*

4. Vacancies in the House are filled by election. When vacancies happen in the representation from any State, the Executive authority [governor] thereof shall issue writs of election [call a special election] to fill such vacancies.

See Johnson trial, pp. 324–325; Nixon trial preliminaries, pp. 603, 605–606.

5. The House selects its Speaker; has sole power to vote impeachment charges (i.e., indictments). The House of Representatives shall choose their Speaker and other officers; and shall have the sole power of impeachment.

Section III. Senate

1. Senators represent the states. The Senate of the United States shall be composed of two Senators from each State, *chosen by the legislature thereof,*[1] for six years; and each Senator shall have one vote.

2. One-third of Senators chosen every two years; vacancies. *Immediately after they shall be assembled in consequence of the first election, they shall be divided as equally as may be into three classes. The seats of the Senators of the first class shall be vacated at the expiration of the second year, of the second class at the expiration of the fourth year, and of the third class at the expiration of the sixth year,* so that one-third may be chosen every second year; *and if vacancies happen by resignation or otherwise, during the recess of the legislature of any State, the Executive* [governor] *thereof may make temporary appointments until the next meeting of the legislature, which shall fill such vacancies.*[2]

3. Who may be Senators. No person shall be a Senator who shall not have attained to the age of thirty years, and been nine years a citizen of the United States, and who shall not, when elected, be an inhabitant of that State for which he shall be chosen.

4. The Vice-President presides over the Senate. The Vice-President of the United States shall be President of the Senate, but shall have no vote, unless they be equally divided [tied].

5. The Senate chooses its other officers. The Senate shall choose their other officers, and also a President *pro tempore*, in the absence of the Vice-President, or when he shall exercise the office of President of the United States.

See Johnson trial, pp. 324–325.

6. The Senate has sole power to try impeachments. The Senate shall have the sole power to try all impeachments. When sitting for that purpose, they shall be on oath or affirmation. When the President of the United States is tried, the Chief Justice shall preside:[3] and no person shall be convicted without the concurrence of two-thirds of the members present.

7. Penalties for impeachment conviction. Judgment in cases of impeachment shall not extend further than to removal from office, and disqualification to hold and enjoy any office of honor, trust or profit under the United States: but the party con-

---

[1] Repealed in favor of popular election in 1913 by the 17th Amendment.

[2] Changed in 1913 by the 17th Amendment.

[3] The vice president, as next in line, would be an interested party.

victed shall nevertheless be liable and subject to indictment, trial, judgment and punishment, according to law.

Section IV. Election and Meetings of Congress

1. Regulation of elections. The times, places and manner of holding elections for Senators and Representatives shall be prescribed in each State by the legislature thereof; but the Congress may at any time by law make or alter such regulations, except as to the places of choosing Senators.

2. Congress must meet once a year. The Congress shall assemble at least once in every year, and such meeting *shall be on the first Monday in December, unless they shall by law appoint a different day.*[1]

Section V. Organization and Rules of the Houses

1. Each house may reject members; quorums. Each house shall be the judge of the elections, returns and qualifications of its own members, and a majority of each shall constitute a quorum to do business; but a smaller number may adjourn from day to day, and may be authorized to compel the attendance of absent members, in such manner, and under such penalties, as each house may provide.

See "Bully" Brooks case, p. 278.

2. Each House makes its own rules. Each house may determine the rules of its proceedings, punish its members for disorderly behavior, and with the concurrence of two-thirds, expel a member.

3. Each House must keep and publish a record of its proceedings. Each house shall keep a journal of its proceedings, and from time to time publish the same, excepting such parts as may in their judgment require secrecy; and the yeas and nays of the members of either house on any question shall, at the desire of one-fifth of those present, be entered on the journal.

4. Both Houses must agree on adjournment. Neither house, during the session of congress, shall, without the consent of the other, adjourn for more than three days, nor to any other place than that in which the two houses shall be sitting.

Section VI. Privileges of and Prohibitions upon Congressmen

1. Congressional salaries; immunities. The Senators and Representatives shall receive a compensation for their services, to be ascertained by law and paid out of the treasury of the United States. They shall in all cases except treason, felony and breach of the peace, be privileged from arrest during their attendance at the session of their respective houses, and in going to and returning from the same; and for any speech or debate in either house, they shall not be questioned in any other place [i.e., they shall be immune from libel suits].

2. A Congressman may not hold any other federal civil office. No Senator or Representative shall, during the time for which he was elected, be appointed to any civil office under the authority of the United States, which shall have been created, or the emoluments whereof shall have been increased, during such time; and no person holding any office under the United States shall be a member of either house during his continuance in office.

---

[1] Changed in 1933 to January 3 by the 20th Amendment (see p. 508 and text of Amendments).

Section VII. Method of Making Laws

See 1787 compromise, p. 116.

1. Money bills must originate in the House. All bills for raising revenue shall originate in the House of Representatives; but the Senate may propose or concur with amendments as on other bills.

President Nixon, more than any predecessors, "impounded" billions of dollars voted by Congress for specific purposes, because he disapproved of them. The courts generally failed to sustain him, and his impeachment foes regarded wholesale impoundment as a violation of his oath to "faithfully execute" the laws.

2. The President's veto power; Congress may override. Every bill which shall have passed the House of Representatives and the Senate, shall, before it become a law, be presented to the President of the United States; if he approve he shall sign it, but if not he shall return it with his objections to that house in which it shall have originated, who shall enter the objections at large on their journal, and proceed to reconsider it. If after such reconsideration two-thirds of that house shall agree to pass the bill, it shall be sent, together with the objections, to the other house, by which it shall likewise be reconsidered, and if, approved by two-thirds of that house, it shall become a law. But in all such cases the votes of both houses shall be determined by yeas and nays, and the names of the persons voting for and against the bill shall be entered on the journal of each house respectively. If any bill shall not be returned by the President within ten days (Sundays excepted) after it shall have been presented to him, the same shall be a law, in like manner as if he had signed it, unless the Congress by their adjournment prevent its return, in which case it shall not be a law [this is the so-called pocket veto].

3. All measures requiring the agreement of both Houses go to President for approval. Every order, resolution, or vote to which the concurrence of the Senate and House of Representatives may be necessary (except on a question of adjournment) shall be presented to the President of the United States; and before the same shall take effect, shall be approved by him, or being disapproved by him, shall be repassed by two-thirds of the Senate and House of Representatives, according to the rules and limitations prescribed in the case of a bill.

Section VIII. Powers Granted to Congress

Congress has certain enumerated powers:

1. It may lay and collect taxes. The Congress shall have power to lay and collect taxes, duties, imposts, and excises, to pay the debts and provide for the common defense and general welfare of the United States; but all duties, imposts and excises shall be uniform throughout the United States;

2. It may borrow money. To borrow money on the credit of the United States;

3. It may regulate foreign and interstate trade. To regulate commerce with foreign nations, and among the several States, and with the Indian tribes;

For 1798 naturalization, see pp. 135–136.

4. It may pass naturalization and bankruptcy laws. To establish an uniform rule of naturalization, and uniform laws on the subject of bankruptcies throughout the United States;

5. It may coin money. To coin money, regulate the value thereof, and of foreign coin, and fix the standard of weights and measures;

6. It may punish counterfeiters. To provide for the punishment of counterfeiting the securities and current coin of the United States;

7. It may establish a postal service. To establish post offices and post roads;

8. It may issue patents and copyrights. To promote the progress of science and useful arts by securing for limited times to authors and inventors the exclusive right to their respective writings and discoveries;

See *Judiciary Act of 1789, p. 127.*

9. It may establish inferior courts. To constitute tribunals inferior to the Supreme Court;

10. It may punish crimes committed on the high seas. To define and punish piracies and felonies committed on the high seas [i.e., outside the three-mile limit] and offenses against the law of nations [international law];

11. It may declare war; authorize privateers. To declare war,[1] grant letters of marque and reprisal,[2] and make rules concerning captures on land and water;

12. It may maintain an army. To raise and support armies, but no appropriation of money to that use shall be for a longer term than two years;[3]

13. It may maintain a navy. To provide and maintain a navy;

14. It may regulate the army and navy. To make rules for the government and regulation of the land and naval forces;

See *Whiskey Rebellion, p. 130.*

15. It may call out the state militia. To provide for calling forth the militia to execute the laws of the union, suppress insurrections, and repel invasions.

16. It shares with the states control of militia. To provide for organizing, arming, and disciplining the militia, and for governing such part of them as may be employed in the service of the United States, reserving to the States respectively the appointment of the officers, and the authority of training the militia according to the discipline prescribed by Congress;

17. It makes laws for the District of Columbia and other federal areas. To exercise exclusive legislation in all cases whatsoever, over such district (not exceeding ten miles square) as may, by cession of particular States, and the acceptance of Congress, become the seat of government of the United States,[4] and to exercise like authority over all places purchased by the consent of the legislature of the State, in which the same shall be, for the erection of forts, magazines, arsenals, dock-yards, and other needful buildings;—and

Congress has certain implied powers:

This is the famous "Elastic Clause"; see p. 129.

18. It may make laws necessary for carrying out the enumerated powers. To make all laws which shall be necessary and proper for carrying into execution the foregoing powers, and all other powers vested by this Constitution in the government of the United States, or in any department or officer thereof.

Section IX.   Powers Denied to the Federal Government

See *1787 slave compromise, p. 116.*

1. Congressional control of slave trade postponed until 1808. *The migration or importation of such persons as any of the States now existing shall think proper to admit shall not be prohibited by the Congress prior to the year 1808; but a tax or duty may be imposed on such importation, not exceeding $10 for each person.*

---

[1] Note that the president, though he can provoke war (see the case of Polk, pp. 255–256) or wage it after it is declared, cannot declare it.

[2] Papers issued private citizens in wartime authorizing them to capture enemy ships.

[3] A reflection of fear of standing armies earlier expressed in the Declaration of Independence.

[4] The District of Columbia, ten miles square, was established in 1791 with a cession from Virginia (see p. 128).

2. The writ of habeas corpus[1] may be suspended only in case of rebellion or invasion. The privilege of the writ of habeas corpus shall not be suspended, unless when in cases of rebellion or invasion the public safety may require it.

3. Attainders[2] and ex post facto laws[3] forbidden. No bill of attainder or ex post facto law shall be passed.

4. Direct taxes must be apportioned according to population. No capitation [head or poll tax], or other direct, tax shall be laid, unless in proportion to the census or enumeration herein before directed to be taken.[4]

5. Export taxes forbidden. No tax or duty shall be laid on articles exported from any State.

6. Congress must not discriminate among states in regulating commerce. No preference shall be given by any regulation of commerce or revenue to the ports of one State over those of another; nor shall vessels bound to, or from, one State, be obliged to enter, clear, or pay duties in another.

7. Public money may not be spent without congressional appropriation; accounting. No money shall be drawn from the treasury, but in consequence of appropriations made by law; and a regular statement and account of the receipts and expenditures of all public money shall be published from time to time.

8. Titles of nobility prohibited; foreign gifts. No title of nobility shall be granted by the United States: and no person holding any office of profit or trust under them, shall, without the consent of the Congress, accept of any present, emolument, office, or title, of any kind whatever, from any king, prince, or foreign state.

Section X.   Powers Denied to the States

Absolute prohibitions on the states:

1. The states are forbidden to do certain things. No State shall enter into any treaty, alliance, or confederation; grant letters of marque and reprisal [i.e., authorize privateers]; coin money; emit bills of credit [issue paper money]; make anything but gold and silver coin a [legal] tender in payment of debts; pass any bill of attainder, ex post facto,[5] or law impairing the obligation of contracts, or grant any title of nobility.

On contracts, see Fletcher v. Peck, p. 164.

Conditional prohibitions on the states:

2. The states may not levy duties without the consent of Congress. No State shall, without the consent of the Congress, lay any imposts or duties on imports or exports, except what may be absolutely necessary for executing its inspection laws: and the net produce of all duties and imposts, laid by any State on imports or exports, shall be for the use of the treasury of the United States; and all such laws shall be subject to the revision and control of the Congress.

Cf. Confederation chaos, p. 112.

---

[1] A writ of habeas corpus is a document that enables a person under arrest to obtain an immediate examination in court to ascertain whether he is being legally held.

[2] A bill of attainder is a special legislative act condemning and punishing an individual without a judicial trial.

[3] An ex post facto law is one that fixes punishments for acts committed before the law was passed.

[4] Modified in 1913 by the 16th Amendment (see text of following Amendments).

[5] For definitions, see footnotes 2 and 3.

3. Certain other federal powers are forbidden the states except with the consent of Congress. No State shall, without the consent of Congress, lay any duty of tonnage [i.e., duty on ship tonnage], keep [non-militia] troops or ships of war in time of peace, enter into any agreement or compact with another State, or with a foreign power, or engage in war, unless actually invaded, or in such imminent danger as will not admit of delay.

Article II.   Executive Department

Section I.   President and Vice-President

1. The President the chief executive; his term. The executive power shall be vested in a President of the United States of America. He shall hold his office during the term of four years,[1] and, together with the Vice-President, chosen for the same term, be elected as follows:

See 1787 compromise, pp. 115–117.

2. The President is chosen by electors. Each State shall appoint, in such manner as the legislature thereof may direct, a number of electors, equal to the whole number of Senators and Representatives to which the State may be entitled in the Congress; but no Senator or Representative, or person holding an office of trust or profit under the United States, shall be appointed an elector.

A majority of the electoral votes needed to elect a President. *The electors shall meet in their respective States, and vote by ballot for two persons, of whom one at least shall not be an inhabitant of the same State with themselves. And they shall make a list of all the persons voted for, and of the number of votes for each; which list they shall sign and certify, and transmit sealed to the seat of government of the United States, directed to the President of the Senate. The President of the Senate shall, in the presence of the Senate and House of Representatives, open all certificates, and the votes shall then be*

See Burr-Jefferson disputed election of 1800, p. 141.

counted. The person having the greatest number of votes shall be the President, if such number be a majority of the whole number of electors appointed; and if there be more than one who have such majority, and have an equal number of votes, then the House of Representatives shall immediately choose by ballot one of them for President; and if no person have a majority, then from the five highest on the list the said house shall in like manner choose the President. But in choosing the President the votes shall be taken by States, the representation from each State having one vote; a quorum for this purpose shall consist of a member or members from two-thirds of the States, and a majority of all the States shall be necessary to a choice. In every case, after the choice of

See Jefferson as vice president in 1796, p. 133.

the President, the person having the greatest number of votes of the electors shall be the Vice-President. But if there should remain two or more who have equal votes, the Senate shall choose from them by ballot the Vice-President.[2]

3. Congress decides time of meeting of Electoral College. The Congress may determine the time of choosing the electors and the day on which they shall give their votes; which day shall be the same throughout the United States.

---

[1] No reference to reelection; for anti–third term 22nd Amendment, see text of Amendments following.

[2] Repealed in 1804 by the 12th Amendment (see text of Amendments following).

U.S. Constitution, Article II **A11**

To provide for foreign-born like Alexander Hamilton, born in the British West Indies.

4. Who may be President. No person except a natural-born citizen, *or a citizen of the United States at the time of the adoption of this Constitution,* shall be eligible to the office of President; neither shall any person be eligible to that office who shall not have attained to the age of thirty-five years, and been fourteen years a resident within the United States [i.e., a legal resident].

Modified by Amendments XX and XXV.

5. Replacements for President. In case of the removal of the President from office or of his death, resignation, or inability to discharge the powers and duties of the said office, the same shall devolve on the Vice-President, and the Congress may by law provide for the case of removal, death, resignation, or inability, both of the President and Vice-President, declaring what officer shall then act as President, and such officer shall act accordingly, until the disability be removed, or a President shall be elected.

6. The President's salary. The President shall, at stated times, receive for his services a compensation, which shall neither be increased nor diminished during the period for which he shall have been elected, and he shall not receive within that period any other emolument from the United States, or any of them.

7. The President's oath of office. Before he enter on the execution of his office, he shall take the following oath or affirmation;—"I do solemnly swear (or affirm) that I will faithfully execute the office of the President of the United States, and will to the best of my ability preserve, protect and defend the Constitution of the United States."

Section II.　Powers of the President

1. The President has important military and civil powers. The President shall be commander in chief of the army and navy of the United States, and of the militia of the several States, when called into the actual service of the United States; he may require the opinion, in writing, of the principal officer in each of the executive departments, upon any subject relating to the duties of their respective offices, and he shall have power to grant reprieves and pardon for offenses against the United States, except in cases of impeachment.[1]

See cabinet evolution, p. 127.

2. The President may negotiate treaties and nominate federal officials. He shall have power, by and with the advice and consent of the Senate, to make treaties, provided two-thirds of the Senators present concur; and he shall nominate, and by and with the advice and consent of the Senate, shall appoint ambassadors, other public ministers and consuls, judges of the Supreme Court, and all other officers of the United States, whose appointments are not herein otherwise provided for, and which shall be established by law: but the Congress may by law vest the appointment of such inferior officers, as they think proper, in the President alone, in the courts of law, or in the heads of departments.

For president's removal power, see pp. 324–325.

3. The President may fill vacancies during Senate recess. The President shall have power to fill up all vacancies that may happen during the recess of the Senate, by granting commissions which shall expire at the end of their next session.

---

[1] To prevent the president's pardoning himself or his close associates, as was feared in the case of Richard Nixon. See page 605.

Section III.   Other Powers and Duties of the President

*For president's
personal
appearances, see
pp. 443–444.*

Messages; extra sessions; receiving ambassadors; execution of the laws. He shall from time to time give to the Congress information of the state of the Union, and recommend to their consideration such measures as he shall judge necessary and expedient; he may, on extraordinary occasions, convene both houses, or either of them, and in case of disagreement between them, with respect to the time of adjournment, he may adjourn them to such time as he shall think proper; he shall receive ambassadors and other public ministers; he shall take care that the laws be faithfully executed, and shall commission all the officers of the United States.

Section IV.   Impeachment

*See Johnson's acquittal, pp. 324–325;
also Nixon's near
impeachment,
pp. 603, 605–606.*

Civil officers may be removed by impeachment. The President, Vice-President and all civil officers[1] of the United States shall be removed from office on impeachment for, and on conviction of, treason, bribery, or other high crimes and misdemeanors.

Article III.   Judicial Department

Section I.   The Federal Courts

The judicial power belongs to the federal courts. The judicial power of the United States shall be vested in one Supreme Court, and in such inferior courts as the Congress may from time to time ordain and establish. The judges, both of the Supreme and inferior courts, shall hold their offices during good behavior, and shall, at stated times, receive for their services a compensation which shall not be diminished[2] during their continuance in office.

*See Judiciary Act of
1789, p. 127.*

Section II.   Jurisdiction of Federal Courts

1. Kinds of cases that may be heard. The judicial power shall extend to all cases, in law and equity, arising under this Constitution, the laws of the United States, and treaties made, or which shall be made, under their authority;—to all cases affecting ambassadors, other public ministers and consuls;—to all cases of admiralty and maritime jurisdiction;—to controversies to which the United States shall be a party;—to controversies between two or more States;—*between a State and citizens of another State*,[3]—between citizens of different States;—between citizens of the same State claiming lands under grants of different States, and between a State, or the citizens thereof, and foreign states, citizens or subjects.

2. Jurisdiction of the Supreme Court. In all cases affecting ambassadors, other public ministers and consuls, and those in which a State shall be party, the Supreme Court shall have original jurisdiction.[4] In all the other cases before mentioned, the

---

[1] I.e., all federal executive and judicial officers, but not members of Congress or military personnel.

[2] In 1978, in a case involving federal judges, the Supreme Court ruled that diminution of salaries by inflation was irrelevant.

[3] The 11th Amendment (see text of Amendments following) restricts this to suits by a state against citizens of another state.

[4] I.e., such cases must originate in the Supreme Court.

Supreme Court shall have appellate jurisdiction,[1] both as to law and fact, with such exceptions, and under such regulations, as the Congress shall make.

3. Trial for federal crime is by jury. The trial of all crimes, except in cases of impeachment, shall be by jury; and such trial shall be held in the State where the said crimes shall have been committed; but when not committed within any State, the trial shall be at such place or places as the Congress may by law have directed.

Section III.   Treason

See Burr trial, p. 147.

1. Treason defined. Treason against the United States shall consist only in levying war against them, or in adhering to their enemies, giving them aid and comfort. No person shall be convicted of treason unless on the testimony of two witnesses to the same overt act, or on confession in open court.

2. Congress fixes punishment for treason. The Congress shall have power to declare the punishment of treason, but no attainder of treason shall work corruption of blood, or forfeiture except during the life of the person attainted.[2]

Article IV.   Relations of the States to One Another

Section I.   Credit to Acts, Records and Court Proceedings

Each state must respect the public acts of the others. Full faith and credit shall be given in each State to the public acts, records, and judicial proceedings of every other State.[3] And the Congress may by general laws prescribe the manner in which such acts, records, and proceedings shall be proved [attested], and the effect thereof.

Section II.   Duties of States to States

1. Citizenship in one state is valid in all. The citizens of each State shall be entitled to all privileges and immunities of citizens in the several States.

This stipulation is sometimes openly flouted. In 1978 Governor Jerry Brown of California, acting on humanitarian grounds, refused to surrender to South Dakota an American Indian, Dennis Banks, who was charged with murder in an armed uprising.

2. Fugitives from justice must be surrendered by the state to which they have fled. A person charged in any State with treason, felony, or other crime, who shall flee from justice, and be found in another State, shall on demand of the executive authority [governor] of the State from which he fled, be delivered up, to be removed to the State having jurisdiction of the crime.

Basis of fugitive slave laws; see pp. 263–264.

3. Slaves and apprentices must be returned. *No person held to service or labor in one State, under the laws thereof, escaping into another, shall, in consequence of any law or regulation therein, be discharged from such service or labor, but shall be delivered up on claim of the party to whom such service or labor may be due.*[4]

---

[1] I.e., it hears other cases only when they are appealed to it from a lower federal court or a state court.

[2] I.e., punishment only for the offender; none for his heirs.

[3] E.g., a marriage valid in one is valid in all.

[4] Invalidated in 1865 by the 13th Amendment (see text of Amendments following).

Section III.   New States and Territories

E.g., Maine (1820);
see p. 163.

1. Congress may admit new states. New States may be admitted by the Congress into this Union; but no new State shall be formed or erected within the jurisdiction of any other State; nor any State be formed by the junction of two or more States, or parts of States, without the consent of the legislatures of the States concerned as well as of the Congress.[1]

2. Congress regulates federal territory and property. The Congress shall have power to dispose of and make all needful rules and regulations respecting the territory or other property belonging to the United States; and nothing in this Constitution shall be so construed as to prejudice any claims of the United States, or of any particular State.

Section IV.   Protection to the States

United States guarantees to states representative government and protection against invasion and rebellion. The United States shall guarantee to every State in this Union a republican form of government, and shall protect each of them against invasion; and on application of the legislature, or of the executive [governor] (when the legislature cannot be convened), against domestic violence.

See Cleveland and
the Pullman strike,
pp. 396–397.

Article V.   The Process of Amendment

The Constitution may be amended in four ways. The Congress, whenever two-thirds of both houses shall deem it necessary, shall propose amendments to this Constitution, or, on the application of the legislatures of two-thirds of the several States, shall call a convention for proposing amendments, which, in either case, shall be valid to all intents and purposes, as part of this Constitution, when ratified by the legislatures of three-fourths of the several States, or by conventions in three-fourths thereof, as the one or the other mode of ratification may be proposed by the Congress; provided *that no amendments which may be made prior to the year one thousand eight hundred and eight shall in any manner affect the first and fourth clauses in the ninth section of the first article,*[2] and that no State, without its consent, shall be deprived of its equal suffrage in the Senate.

Article VI.   General Provisions

This pledge honored
by Hamilton,
pp. 127–128.

1. The debts of the Confederation are taken over. All debts contracted and engagements entered into, before the adoption of this Constitution, shall be as valid against the United States under this Constitution, as under the Confederation.

2. The Constitution, federal laws, and treaties are the supreme law of the land. This Constitution, and the laws of the United States which shall be made in pursuance thereof; and all treaties made, or which shall be made, under the authority of the United States, shall be the supreme law of the land; and the judges in every State shall be bound thereby, anything in the Constitution or laws of any State to the contrary notwithstanding.

---

[1] Loyal West Virginia was formed by Lincoln in 1862 from seceded Virginia. This act was of dubious constitutionality and was justified in part by the wartime powers of the president. See p. 289.

[2] This clause, re slave trade and direct taxes, became inoperative in 1808.

3. Federal and state officers bound by oath to support the Constitution. The Senators and Representatives before mentioned, and the members of the several State legislatures, and all executive and judicial officers, both of the United States and of the several States, shall be bound by oath or affirmation to support this Constitution; but no religious test shall ever be required as a qualification to any office or public trust under the United States.

Article VII.   Ratification of the Constitution

See 1787 irregularity, pp. 116–117.   **The Constitution effective when ratified by conventions in nine states.** The ratification of the conventions of nine States shall be sufficient for the establishment of this Constitution between the States so ratifying the same.

Done in Convention by the unanimous consent of the States present, the seventeenth day of September in the year of our Lord one thousand seven hundred and eighty-seven and of the Independence of the United States of America the twelfth. In witness whereof we have hereunto subscribed our names.

[Signed by]

G⁰ WASHINGTON
Presidt and Deputy from Virginia
[and thirty-eight others]

AMENDMENTS TO THE CONSTITUTION

Amendment I.   Religious and Political Freedom

For background of Bill of Rights, see pp. 126–127.   **Congress must not interfere with freedom of religion, speech or press, assembly, and petition.** Congress shall make no law respecting an establishment of religion,[1] or prohibiting the free exercise thereof; or abridging the freedom of speech, or of the press; or the right of the people peaceably to assemble, and to petition the government for a redress of grievances.

Amendment II.   Right to Bear Arms

The people may bear arms. A well-regulated militia being necessary to the security of a free State, the right of the people to keep and bear arms [i.e., for military purposes] shall not be infringed.[2]

Amendment III.   Quartering of Troops

See Declaration of Independence and British quartering above.   **Soldiers may not be arbitrarily quartered on the people.** No soldier shall, in time of peace, be quartered in any house without the consent of the owner, nor in time of war, but in a manner to be prescribed by law.

---

[1] In 1787 "an establishment of religion" referred to an "established church," or one supported by all taxpayers, whether members or not. But the courts have often acted under this article to keep religion, including prayers, out of the public schools.

[2] The courts, with "militia" in mind, have consistently held that the "right" to bear arms is a limited one.

Amendment IV.   Searches and Seizures

A reflection of colonial grievances against the Crown.

Unreasonable searches are forbidden. The right of the people to be secure in their persons, houses, papers, and effects, against unreasonable searches and seizures, shall not be violated, and no [search] warrants shall issue but upon probable cause, supported by oath or affirmation, and particularly describing the place to be searched, and the persons or things to be seized.

Amendment V.   Right to Life, Liberty, and Property

When witnesses refuse to answer questions in court, they routinely "take the Fifth Amendment."

The individual is guaranteed certain rights when on trial and the right to life, liberty, and property. No person shall be held to answer for a capital, or otherwise infamous crime, unless on a presentment [formal charge] or indictment of a grand jury, except in cases arising in the land or naval forces, or in the militia, when in actual service in time of war or public danger; nor shall any person be subject for the same offense to be twice put in jeopardy of life or limb; nor shall be compelled in any criminal case to be a witness against himself, nor be deprived of life, liberty, or property, without due process of law; nor shall private property be taken for public use [i.e., by eminent domain] without just compensation.

Amendment VI.   Protection in Criminal Trials

See Declaration of Independence above.

An accused person has important rights. In all criminal prosecutions, the accused shall enjoy the right to a speedy and public trial, by an impartial jury of the State and district wherein the crime shall have been committed, which district shall have been previously ascertained by law, and to be informed of the nature and cause of the accusation; to be confronted with the witnesses against him; to have compulsory process [subpoena] for obtaining witnesses in his favor, and to have the assistance of counsel for his defense.

Amendment VII.   Suits at Common Law

The rules of common law are recognized. In suits at common law, where the value in controversy shall exceed twenty dollars, the right of trial by jury shall be preserved, and no fact tried by a jury shall be otherwise re-examined in any court of the United States, than according to the rules of the common law.

Amendment VIII.   Bail and Punishments

Excessive fines and unusual punishments are forbidden. Excessive bail shall not be required, nor excessive fines imposed, nor cruel and unusual punishments inflicted.

Amendment IX.   Concerning Rights Not Enumerated

Amendments IX and X were bulwarks of southern states' rights before the Civil War.

The people retain rights not here enumerated. The enumeration in the Constitution, of certain rights, shall not be construed to deny or disparage others retained by the people.

Amendment X.   Powers Reserved to the States and to the People

A concession to states' rights, p. 129.   **Powers not delegated to the federal government are reserved to the states and the people.** The powers not delegated to the United States by the Constitution, nor prohibited by it to the States, are reserved to the States respectively, or to the people.

Amendment XI.   Suits Against a State

The federal courts have no authority in suits by citizens against a state. The judicial power of the United States shall not be construed to extend to any suit in law or equity, commenced or prosecuted against one of the United States by citizens of another state, or by citizens or subjects of any foreign state. [Adopted 1798.]

Amendment XII.   Election of President and Vice-President

1. Changes in manner of electing President and Vice-President; procedure when no presidential candidate receives electoral majority. The electors shall meet in their respective States, and vote by ballot for President and Vice-President, one of whom, at least, shall not be an inhabitant of the same State with themselves; they *Forestalls repetition of 1800 electoral dispute, p. 141.* shall name in their ballots the person voted for as President, and in distinct ballots the person voted for as Vice-President, and they shall make distinct lists of all persons voted for as President, and of all persons voted for as Vice-President, and of the number of votes for each, which lists they shall sign and certify, and transmit sealed *See 1876 disputed election, p. 337.* to the seat of government of the United States, directed to the President of the Senate;—the President of the Senate shall, in the presence of the Senate and House of Representatives, open all the certificates and the votes shall then be counted;—the person having the greatest number of votes for President shall be the President, if such number be a majority of the whole number of electors appointed; and if no person have such majority, then from the persons having the highest numbers not exceeding three on the list of those voted for as President, the House of Representa- *See 1824 election, p. 172.* tives shall choose immediately, by ballot, the President. But in choosing the President, the votes shall be taken by States, the representation from each State having one vote; a quorum for this purpose shall consist of a member or members from two-thirds of the States, and a majority of all the States shall be necessary to a choice. And if the House of Representatives shall not choose a President whenever the right of choice shall devolve upon them, before *the fourth day of March*[1] next following, then the Vice-President shall act as President, as in the case of death or other constitutional disability of the President.

2. Procedure when no vice-presidential candidate receives electoral majority. The person having the greatest number of votes as Vice-President shall be the Vice-President, if such number be a majority of the whole number of electors appointed; and if no person have a majority, then from the two highest numbers on the list the Senate shall choose the Vice-President; a quorum for the purpose shall consist of two-thirds of the whole number of Senators, and a majority of the whole number shall be necessary to a choice. But no person constitutionally ineligible to the office

---

[1] Changed to January 20 by the 20th Amendment (see text of Amendment following).

of President shall be eligible to that of Vice-President of the United States. [Adopted 1804.]

Amendment XIII.   Slavery Prohibited

For background, see p. 303.

Slavery forbidden. 1. Neither slavery[1] nor involuntary servitude, except as a punishment for crime whereof the party shall have been duly convicted, shall exist within the United States, or any place subject to their jurisdiction.

2. Congress shall have power to enforce this article by appropriate legislation. [Adopted 1865.]

Amendment XIV.   Civil Rights for Ex-slaves,[2] etc.

For background, see pp. 316–319.

For corporations as "persons," see p. 357.

1. Ex-slaves made citizens; U.S. citizenship primary. All persons born or naturalized in the United States, and subject to the jurisdiction thereof, are citizens of the United States and of the State wherein they reside. No State shall make or enforce any law which shall abridge the privileges or immunities of citizens of the United States; nor shall any State deprive any person of life, liberty, or property, without due process of law; nor deny to any person within its jurisdiction the equal protection of the laws.

Abolishes three-fifths rule for slaves, Art. I, Sec. II, para. 3.

2. When a state denies citizens the vote, its representation shall be reduced. Representatives shall be apportioned among the several States according to their respective numbers, counting the whole number of persons in each State, excluding Indians not taxed. But when the right to vote at any election for the choice of Electors for President and Vice-President of the United States, Representatives in Congress, the executive and judicial officers of a State, or the members of the legislature thereof, is denied to any of the male inhabitants of such State, being twenty-one years of age and citizens of the United States, or in any way abridged, except for participation in rebellion, or other crime, the basis of representation therein shall be reduced in the proportion which the number of such male citizens shall bear to the whole number of male citizens twenty-one years of age in such State.

Leading ex-Confederates denied office. See p. 320.

3. Certain persons who have been in rebellion are ineligible for federal and state office. No person shall be a Senator or Representative in Congress, or Elector of President and Vice-President, or hold any office, civil or military, under the United States, or under any State, who, having previously taken an oath, as a member of Congress, or as an officer of the United States, or as a member of any State legislature, or as an executive or judicial officer of any State, to support the Constitution of the United States, shall have engaged in insurrection or rebellion against the same, or given aid or comfort to the enemies thereof. But Congress may, by a vote of two-thirds of each house, remove such disability.

The ex-Confederates were thus forced to repudiate their debts and pay pensions to their own veterans, plus taxes for the pensions of Union veterans, their conquerors.

4. Debts incurred in aid of rebellion are void. The validity of the public debt of the United States, authorized by law, including debts incurred for payment of pensions and bounties for services in suppressing insurrection or rebellion, shall not be ques-

---

[1] The only explicit mention of slavery in the Constitution.

[2] Occasionally an offender is prosecuted under the 13th Amendment for keeping an employee or other person under conditions approximating slavery.

tioned. But neither the United States nor any State shall assume or pay any debt or obligation incurred in aid of insurrection or rebellion against the United States, or any claim for the loss or emancipation of any slave; but all such debts, obligations, and claims shall be held illegal and void.

5. Enforcement. The Congress shall have power to enforce, by appropriate legislation, the provisions of this article. [Adopted 1868.]

Amendment XV. Suffrage for Blacks

For background, see pp. 316–319.

Black males are made voters. 1. The right of citizens of the United States to vote shall not be denied or abridged by the United States or by any State on account of race, color, or previous condition of servitude.

2. The Congress shall have power to enforce this article by appropriate legislation. [Adopted 1870.]

Amendment XVI. Income Taxes

Congress has power to lay and collect income taxes. The Congress shall have power to lay and collect taxes on incomes, from whatever source derived, without apportionment among the several States, and without regard to any census or enumeration. [Adopted 1913.]

Amendment XVII. Direct Election of Senators

Senators shall be elected by popular vote. 1. The Senate of the United States shall be composed of two Senators from each State, elected by the people thereof, for six years; and each Senator shall have one vote. The electors in each State shall have the qualifications requisite for electors of [voters for] the most numerous branch of the State legislatures.

2. When vacancies happen in the representation of any State in the Senate, the executive authority of such State shall issue writs of election to fill such vacancies: Provided, that the Legislature of any State may empower the executive thereof to make temporary appointments until the people fill the vacancies by election as the Legislature may direct.

3. This amendment shall not be so construed as to affect the election or term of any Senator chosen before it becomes valid as part of the Constitution. [Adopted 1913.]

Amendment XVIII. National Prohibition

For background, see p. 471.

The sale or manufacture of intoxicating liquors is forbidden. 1. *After one year from the ratification of this article the manufacture, sale, or transportation of intoxicating liquors within, the importation thereof into, or the exportation thereof from the United States and all territory subject to the jurisdiction thereof, for beverage purposes, is hereby prohibited.*

2. *The Congress and the several States shall have concurrent power to enforce this article by appropriate legislation.*

3. *This article shall be inoperative unless it shall have been ratified as an amendment to the Constitution by the legislatures of the several States, as provided by the Constitu-*

tion, within seven years from the date of the submission thereof to the States by the Congress. [Adopted 1919; repealed 1933 by 21st Amendment.]

Amendment XIX.

For background, see pp. 226, 379, 429, 457.

Woman Suffrage

Women guaranteed the right to vote. 1. The right of citizens of the United States to vote shall not be denied or abridged by the United States or by any State on account of sex.

2. The Congress shall have power to enforce this article by appropriate legislation. [Adopted 1920.]

Amendment XX.

Shortens lame-duck periods by modifying Art. I, Sec. IV, para. 2.

Presidential and Congressional Terms

1. Presidential, vice-presidential, and congressional terms of office begin in January. The terms of the President and Vice-President shall end at noon on the 20th day of January, and the terms of Senators and Representatives at noon on the 3d day of January, of the years in which such terms would have ended if this article had not been ratified; and the terms of their successors shall then begin.

2. New meeting date for Congress. The Congress shall assemble at least once in every year, and such meeting shall begin at noon on the 3d day of January, unless they shall by law appoint a different day.

3. Emergency presidential and vice-presidential succession. If, at the time fixed for the beginning of the term of the President, the President-elect shall have died, the Vice-President-elect shall become President. If a President shall not have been chosen before the time fixed for the beginning of his term, or if the President-elect shall have failed to qualify, then the Vice-President-elect shall act as President until a President shall have qualified; and the Congress may by law provide for the case wherein neither a President-elect nor a Vice-President-elect shall have qualified, declaring who shall then act as President, or the manner in which one who is to act shall be selected, and such persons shall act accordingly until a President or Vice-President shall have qualified.

4. The Congress may by law provide for the case of the death of any of the persons from whom the House of Representatives may choose a President whenever the right of choice shall have devolved upon them, and for the case of the death of any of the persons from whom the Senate may choose a Vice-President whenever the right of choice shall have devolved upon them.

5. Sections 1 and 2 shall take effect on the 15th day of October following the ratification of this article.

6. This article shall be inoperative unless it shall have been ratified as an amendment to the Constitution by the Legislatures of three-fourths of the several States within seven years from the date of its submission. [Adopted 1933.]

Amendment XXI.

For background, see p. 502.

Prohibition Repealed

1. 18th Amendment repealed. The eighteenth article of amendment to the Constitution of the United States is hereby repealed.

2. Local laws honored. The transportation or importation into any State, Territory, or Possession of the United States for delivery or use therein of intoxicating liquors, in violation of the laws thereof, is hereby prohibited.

3. This article shall be inoperative unless it shall have been ratified as an amendment to the Constitution by conventions in the several States, as provided in the Constitution, within seven years from the date of the submission thereof to the States by the Congress. [Adopted 1933.]

Amendment XXII.   Anti–Third Term Amendment

Sometimes referred to as the anti–Franklin Roosevelt amendment.

Presidential term is limited. 1. No person shall be elected to the office of President more than twice, and no person who has held the office of President, or acted as President, for more than two years of a term to which some other person was elected President shall be elected to the office of President more than once. But this article shall not apply to any person holding the office of President when this article was proposed by the Congress [i.e., Truman], and shall not prevent any person who may be holding the office of President, or acting as President, during the term within which this article becomes operative [i.e., Truman] from holding the office of President or acting as President during the remainder of such term.

2. This article shall be inoperative unless it shall have been ratified as an amendment to the Constitution by the legislatures of three-fourths of the several States within seven years from the date of its submission to the States by the Congress. [Adopted 1951.]

Amendment XXIII.   District of Columbia Vote

Designed to give the District of Columbia three electoral votes and to quiet the century-old cry of "No taxation without representation." Yet the District of Columbia still has only one non-voting member of Congress.

1. Presidential electors for the District of Columbia. The District constituting the seat of Government of the United States shall appoint in such manner as the Congress may direct:

A number of electors of President and Vice-President equal to the whole number of Senators and Representatives in Congress to which the District would be entitled if it were a State, but in no event more than the least populous State; they shall be in addition to those appointed by the States, but they shall be considered for the purposes of the election of President and Vice-President, to be electors appointed by a State; and they shall meet in the District and perform such duties as provided by the twelfth article of amendment.

2. Enforcement. The Congress shall have the power to enforce this article by appropriate legislation. [Adopted 1961.]

Amendment XXIV.   Poll Tax

Designed to end discrimination against blacks and other poor folk. An aspect of the civil rights crusade under President Lyndon Johnson. See p. 586.

1. Payment of poll tax or other taxes not to be prerequisite for voting in federal elections. The right of citizens of the United States to vote in any primary or other election for President or Vice-President, for electors for President or Vice-President, or for Senator or Representative in Congress, shall not be denied or abridged by the United States or any State by reason of failure to pay any poll tax or other tax.

2. Enforcement. The Congress shall have the power to enforce this article by appropriate legislation. [Adopted 1964.]

Amendment XXV.   Presidential Succession and Disability[1]

1. Vice-President to become President. In case of the removal of the President from office or of his death or resignation, the Vice-President shall become President.[2]

2. Successor to Vice-President provided. Whenever there is a vacancy in the office of the Vice-President, the President shall nominate a Vice-President who shall take office upon confirmation by a majority vote of both Houses of Congress.

Gerald Ford was the first "appointed President." See pp. 602, 606.

3. Vice-President to serve for disabled President. Whenever the President transmits to the President pro tempore of the Senate and the Speaker of the House of Representatives his written declaration that he is unable to discharge the powers and duties of his office, and until he transmits to them a written declaration to the contrary, such powers and duties shall be discharged by the Vice-President as Acting President.

4. Procedure for disqualifying or requalifying President. Whenever the Vice-President and a majority of either the principal officers of the executive departments or of such other body as Congress may by law provide, transmit to the President pro tempore of the Senate and the Speaker of the House of Representatives their written declaration that the President is unable to discharge the powers and duties of his office, the Vice-President shall immediately assume the powers and duties of the office as Acting President.

Thereafter, when the President transmits to the President pro tempore of the Senate and the Speaker of the House of Representatives his written declaration that no inability exists, he shall resume the powers and duties of his office unless the Vice-President and a majority of either the principal officers of the executive department[s] or of such other body as Congress may by law provide, transmit within four days to the President pro tempore of the Senate and the Speaker of the House of Representatives their written declaration that the President is unable to discharge the powers and duties of his office. Thereupon Congress shall decide the issue, assembling within forty-eight hours for that purpose if not in session. If the Congress, within twenty-one days after receipt of the latter written declaration, or, if Congress is not in session, within twenty-one days after Congress is required to assemble, determines by two-thirds vote of both Houses that the President is unable to discharge the powers and duties of his office, the Vice-President shall continue to discharge the same as Acting President; otherwise, the President shall resume the powers and duties of his office. [Adopted 1967.]

Amendment XXVI.   Lowering Voting Age

A response to the current revolt of youth. See p. 598.

1. Ballot for eighteen-year-olds. The right of citizens of the United States, who are eighteen years of age or older, to vote shall not be denied or abridged by the United States or by any State on account of age.

2. Enforcement. The Congress shall have power to enforce this article by appropriate legislation. [Adopted 1971.]

---

[1] Passed by a two-thirds vote of both Houses of Congress in July 1965; ratified by the requisite three-fourths of the state legislatures, February 1967, or well within the seven-year limit.

[2] The original Constitution (Art. II, Sec. I, para. 5) was vague on this point, stipulating that "the powers and duties" of the president, but not necessarily the title, should "devolve" on the vice president. President Tyler, the first "accidental president," assumed not only the powers and duties but the title as well.

An American Profile: The United States and Its People

Growth of U.S. Population and Area

| Census | Population of United States | Increase over the Preceding Census | | Land Area (Sq. Mi.) | Pop. per Sq. Mi. | Percent of Pop. in Urban and Rural Territory | |
		Number	Percent			Urban	Rural
1790	3,929,214			867,980	4.5	5.1	94.9
1800	5,308,483	1,379,269	35.1	867,980	6.1	6.1	93.9
1810	7,239,881	1,931,398	36.4	1,685,865	4.3	7.2	92.8
1820	9,638,453	2,398,472	33.1	1,753,588	5.5	7.2	92.8
1830	12,866,020	3,227,567	33.5	1,753,588	7.3	8.8	91.2
1840	17,069,453	4,203,433	32.7	1,753,588	9.7	10.8	89.2
1850	23,191,876	6,122,423	35.9	2,944,337	7.9	15.3	84.7
1860	31,433,321	8,251,445	35.6	2,973,965	10.6	19.8	80.2
1870	39,818,449	8,375,128	26.6	2,973,965	13.4	24.9	75.1
1880	50,155,783	10,337,334	26.0	2,973,965	16.9	28.2	71.8
1890	62,947,714	12,791,931	25.5	2,973,965	21.2	35.1	64.9
1900	75,994,575	13,046,861	20.7	2,974,159	25.6	39.7	60.3
1910	91,972,266	15,997,691	21.0	2,973,890	30.9	45.7	54.3
1920	105,710,620	13,738,354	14.9	2,973,776	35.5	51.2	48.8
1930	122,775,046	17,064,426	16.1	2,977,128	41.2	56.2	43.8
1940	131,669,275	8,894,229	7.2	2,977,128	44.2	56.5	43.5
1950	150,697,361	19,028,086	14.5	2,974,726*	50.7	64.0	36.0
1960†	179,323,175	28,625,814	19.0	3,540,911	50.6	69.9	30.1
1970	203,235,298	23,912,123	13.3	3,536,855	57.5	73.5	26.5
1980	226,504,825	23,269,527	11.4	3,536,855	64.0	73.7	26.3
1990	248,709,873	22,164,068	9.8	3,536,855	70.3	74.1	25.9

* As remeasured in 1940; shrinkage offset by increase in water area.

† First year for which figures include Alaska and Hawaii.

Source: Census Bureau, *Historical Statistics of the United States*, updated by relevant *Statistical Abstract of the United States*.

Changing Characteristics of the U.S. Population

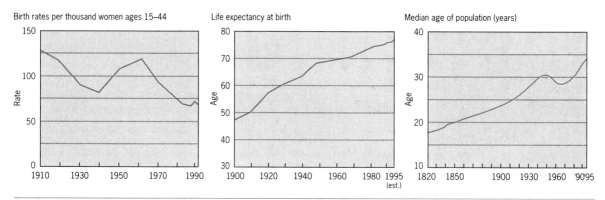

Sources: *Historical Statistics of the United States* and *Statistical Abstract of the United States,* relevant years.

Changing Lifestyles in the Twentieth Century

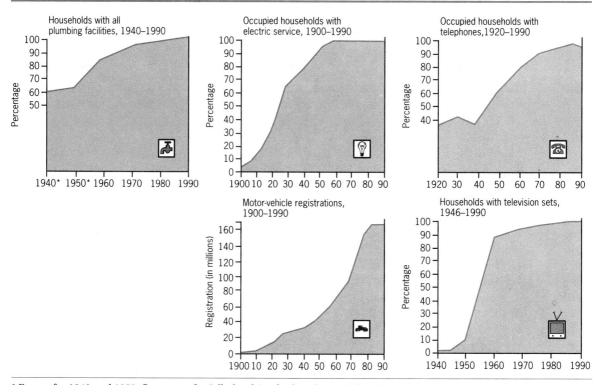

* Except for 1940 and 1950, figures are for "all plumbing facilities" (not defined in source). For 1940, figure is for flush toilet, inside structure, private use (64.7 percent had flush toilet, and private and/or shared inside structure, and 60.9 percent had installed bath or shower). For 1950, figure designates units with private toilet and bath, and hot running water (flush toilet, private or shared inside structure, is 74.3 percent; installed bathtub or shower, 72.9 percent).

Sources: *Historical Statistics of the United States* and *Statistical Abstract of the United States,* relevant years.

Characteristics of the U.S. Labor Force

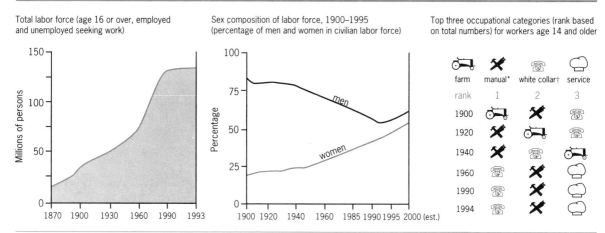

Total labor force (age 16 or over, employed and unemployed seeking work)

Sex composition of labor force, 1900–1995 (percentage of men and women in civilian labor force)

Top three occupational categories (rank based on total numbers) for workers age 14 and older

* Manual workers = operators, fabricators, and laborers plus precision production, craft, and repair.

† White-collar workers = managerial and professional plus technical, sales, and administrative support.

Sources: *Historical Statistics of the United States* and *Statistical Abstract of the United States,* relevant years, and Department of Labor Statistics, *Handbook of Labor Statistics,* relevant years.

Leading Economic Sectors (Various Years)

Percentage of value added contributed

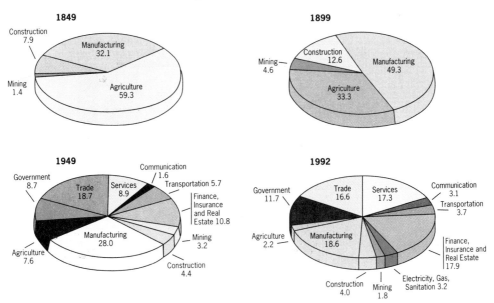

Sources: *Historical Statistics of the United States* and *Statistical Abstract of the United States,* relevant years.

Per-Capita Disposable Personal Income in Constant (1987) Dollars, 1940–1994

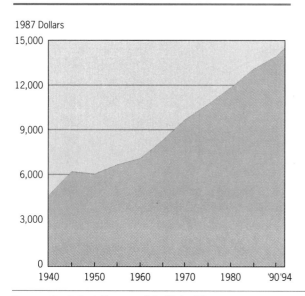

Source: *Statistical Abstract of the United States.*

Comparative Tax Burdens (Percentage of Gross Domestic Product paid as taxes in major industrial countries, 1994)

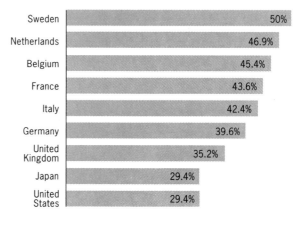

Value of Imports and Exports by Selected Place of Origin and Destination (Millions of Dollars)

Year	Canada		United Kingdom		Japan	
	Imports from	Exports to	Imports from	Exports to	Imports from	Exports to
1900	39	95	160	534	33	29
1910	95	216	271	506	66	22
1920	612	972	514	1,825	415	378
1930	402	659	210	678	279	165
1940	424	713	155	1,011	158	227
1950	1,960	2,039	335	548	182	418
1960	2,901	3,810	993	1,487	1,149	1,447
1970	11,092	9,079	2,194	2,536	5,875	4,652
1980	41,459	35,395	9,842	12,694	30,714	20,792
1990	91,372	82,697	20,288	23,484	89,655	48,585
1994	128,947	114,255	25,063	26,833	119,149	53,481

Sources: *Historical Statistics of the United States* and *Statistical Abstract of the United States,* relevant years.

Value of Exports and Imports and Status of the Balance of Trade

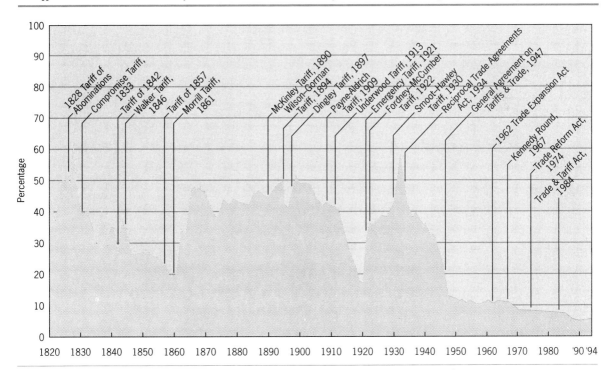

Sources: *Historical Statistics of the United States* and *Statistical Abstract of the United States,* relevant years.

Tariff Levies on Dutiable Imports, 1821–1994 (Ratio of Duties to Value of Dutiable Imports)

Sources: *Historical Statistics of the United States* and *Statistical Abstract of the United States,* relevant years.

Gross National Product in Current and Constant 1995 Dollars*

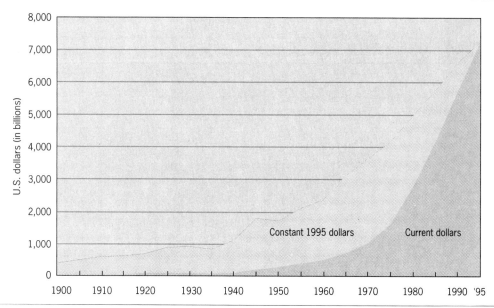

* Gross *national* product before 1960. Gross national product includes income from overseas investment, and excludes profits generated in the United States but accruing to foreign accounts. Gross *domestic* product excludes overseas profits owed to American accounts, but includes the value of all items originating in the United States, regardless of the ultimate destination of the profits. Until recent years, those factors made for negligible differences in the calculation of *national* and *domestic* product, but most economists now prefer the latter methodology.

Presidential Elections*

Election	Candidates	Parties	Popular Vote	Electoral Vote
1789	GEORGE WASHINGTON	No party designations		69
	John Adams			34
	Minor Candidates			35
1792	GEORGE WASHINGTON	No party designations		132
	John Adams			77
	George Clinton			50
	Minor Candidates			5
1796	JOHN ADAMS	Federalist		71
	Thomas Jefferson	Democratic-Republican		68
	Thomas Pinckney	Federalist		59
	Aaron Burr	Democratic-Republican		30
	Minor Candidates			48
1800	THOMAS JEFFERSON	Democratic-Republican		73
	Aaron Burr	Democratic-Republican		73
	John Adams	Federalist		65
	Charles C. Pinckney	Federalist		64
	John Jay	Federalist		1
1804	THOMAS JEFFERSON	Democratic-Republican		162
	Charles C. Pinckney	Federalist		14
1808	JAMES MADISON	Democratic-Republican		122
	Charles C. Pinckney	Federalist		47
	George Clinton	Democratic-Republican		6
1812	JAMES MADISON	Democratic-Republican		128
	DeWitt Clinton	Federalist		89
1816	JAMES MONROE	Democratic-Republican		183
	Rufus King	Federalist		34
1820	JAMES MONROE	Democratic-Republican		231
	John Q. Adams	Independent Republican		1
1824	JOHN Q. ADAMS (Min.)[†]	Democratic-Republican	108,740	84
	Andrew Jackson	Democratic-Republican	153,544	99
	William H. Crawford	Democratic-Republican	46,618	41
	Henry Clay	Democratic-Republican	47,136	37
1828	ANDREW JACKSON	Democratic	647,286	178
	John Q. Adams	National Republican	508,064	83
1832	ANDREW JACKSON	Democratic	687,502	219
	Henry Clay	National Republican	530,189	49
	William Wirt	Anti-Masonic ⎫	33,108	7
	John Floyd	National Republican ⎭		11
1836	MARTIN VAN BUREN	Democratic	765,483	170
	William H. Harrison	Whig ⎫		73
	Hugh L. White	Whig ⎬		26
	Daniel Webster	Whig ⎪	739,795	14
	W. P. Mangum	Whig ⎭		11

* Candidates receiving less than 1 percent of the popular vote are omitted. Before the 12th Amendment (1804), the Electoral College voted for two presidential candidates, and the runner-up became vice president. Basic figures are taken primarily from *Historical Statistics of the United States, 1789–1945* (1949), pp. 288–290; *Historical Statistics of the United States, Colonial Times to 1957* (1960), pp. 682–683; and *Statistical Abstract of the United States, 1969* (1969), pp. 355–357.

† "Min." indicates minority president—one receiving less than 50 percent of all popular votes.

Presidential Elections (Continued)

Election	Candidates	Parties	Popular Vote	Electoral Vote
1840	WILLIAM H. HARRISON	Whig	1,274,624	234
	Martin Van Buren	Democratic	1,127,781	60
1844	JAMES K. POLK (Min.)*	Democratic	1,338,464	170
	Henry Clay	Whig	1,300,097	105
	James G. Birney	Liberty	62,300	
1848	ZACHARY TAYLOR	Whig	1,360,967	163
	Lewis Cass	Democratic	1,222,342	127
	Martin Van Buren	Free Soil	291,263	
1852	FRANKLIN PIERCE	Democratic	1,601,117	254
	Winfield Scott	Whig	1,385,453	42
	John P. Hale	Free Soil	155,825	
1856	JAMES BUCHANAN (Min.)*	Democratic	1,832,955	174
	John C. Frémont	Republican	1,339,932	114
	Millard Fillmore	American	871,731	8
1860	ABRAHAM LINCOLN (Min.)*	Republican	1,865,593	180
	Stephen A. Douglas	Democratic	1,382,713	12
	John C. Breckinridge	Democratic	848,356	72
	John Bell	Constitutional Union	592,906	39
1864	ABRAHAM LINCOLN	Union	2,206,938	212
	George B. McClellan	Democratic	1,803,787	21
1868	ULYSSES S. GRANT	Republican	3,013,421	214
	Horatio Seymour	Democratic	2,706,829	80
1872	ULYSSES S. GRANT	Republican	3,596,745	286
	Horace Greeley	Democratic and Liberal Republican	2,843,446	66
1876	RUTHERFORD B. HAYES (Min.)*	Republican	4,036,572	185
	Samuel J. Tilden	Democratic	4,284,020	184
1880	JAMES A. GARFIELD (Min.)*	Republican	4,453,295	214
	Winfield S. Hancock	Democratic	4,414,082	155
	James B. Weaver	Greenback-Labor	308,578	
1884	GROVER CLEVELAND (Min.)*	Democratic	4,879,507	219
	James G. Blaine	Republican	4,850,293	182
	Benjamin F. Butler	Greenback-Labor	175,370	
	John P. St. John	Prohibition	150,369	
1888	BENJAMIN HARRISON (Min.)*	Republican	5,447,129	233
	Grover Cleveland	Democratic	5,537,857	168
	Clinton B. Fisk	Prohibition	249,506	
	Anson J. Streeter	Union Labor	146,935	
1892	GROVER CLEVELAND (Min.)*	Democratic	5,555,426	277
	Benjamin Harrison	Republican	5,182,690	145
	James B. Weaver	People's	1,029,846	22
	John Bidwell	Prohibition	264,133	
1896	WILLIAM MCKINLEY	Republican	7,102,246	271
	William J. Bryan	Democratic	6,492,559	176
1900	WILLIAM MCKINLEY	Republican	7,218,491	292
	William J. Bryan	Democratic; Populist	6,356,734	155
	John C. Woolley	Prohibition	208,914	

* "Min." indicates minority president—one receiving less than 50 percent of all popular votes.

Presidential Elections (Continued)

Election	Candidates	Parties	Popular Vote	Electoral Vote
1904	THEODORE ROOSEVELT	Republican	7,628,461	336
	Alton B. Parker	Democratic	5,084,223	140
	Eugene V. Debs	Socialist	402,283	
	Silas C. Swallow	Prohibition	258,536	
1908	WILLIAM H. TAFT	Republican	7,675,320	321
	William J. Bryan	Democratic	6,412,294	162
	Eugene V. Debs	Socialist	420,793	
	Eugene W. Chafin	Prohibition	253,840	
1912	WOODROW WILSON (Min.)*	Democratic	6,296,547	435
	Theodore Roosevelt	Progressive	4,118,571	88
	William H. Taft	Republican	3,486,720	8
	Eugene V. Debs	Socialist	900,672	
	Eugene W. Chafin	Prohibition	206,275	
1916	WOODROW WILSON (Min.)*	Democratic	9,127,695	277
	Charles E. Hughes	Republican	8,533,507	254
	A. L. Benson	Socialist	585,113	
	J. F. Hanley	Prohibition	220,506	
1920	WARREN G. HARDING	Republican	16,143,407	404
	James M. Cox	Democratic	9,130,328	127
	Eugene V. Debs	Socialist	919,799	
	P. P. Christensen	Farmer-Labor	265,411	
1924	CALVIN COOLIDGE	Republican	15,718,211	382
	John W. Davis	Democratic	8,385,283	136
	Robert M. La Follette	Progressive	4,831,289	13
1928	HERBERT C. HOOVER	Republican	21,391,993	444
	Alfred E. Smith	Democratic	15,016,169	87
1932	FRANKLIN D. ROOSEVELT	Democratic	22,809,638	472
	Herbert C. Hoover	Republican	15,758,901	59
	Norman Thomas	Socialist	881,951	
1936	FRANKLIN D. ROOSEVELT	Democratic	27,752,869	523
	Alfred M. Landon	Republican	16,674,665	8
	William Lemke	Union, etc.	882,479	
1940	FRANKLIN D. ROOSEVELT	Democratic	27,307,819	449
	Wendell L. Willkie	Republican	22,321,018	82
1944	FRANKLIN D. ROOSEVELT	Democratic	25,606,585	432
	Thomas E. Dewey	Republican	22,014,745	99
1948	HARRY S TRUMAN (Min.)*	Democratic	24,179,345	303
	Thomas E. Dewey	Republican	21,991,291	189
	J. Strom Thurmond	States' Rights Democratic	1,176,125	39
	Henry A. Wallace	Progressive	1,157,326	
1952	DWIGHT D. EISENHOWER	Republican	33,936,234	442
	Adlai E. Stevenson	Democratic	27,314,992	89
1956	DWIGHT D. EISENHOWER	Republican	35,590,472	457
	Adlai E. Stevenson	Democratic	26,022,752	73
1960	JOHN F. KENNEDY (Min.)*	Democratic	34,226,731	303
	Richard M. Nixon	Republican	34,108,157	219

* "Min." indicates minority president—one receiving less than 50 percent of all popular votes.

Election	Candidates	Parties	Popular Vote	Electoral Vote
1964	LYNDON B. JOHNSON	Democratic	43,129,566	486
	Barry M. Goldwater	Republican	27,178,188	52
1968	RICHARD M. NIXON (Min.)*	Republican	31,785,480	301
	Hubert H. Humphrey, Jr.	Democratic	31,275,166	191
	George C. Wallace	American Independent	9,906,473	46
1972	RICHARD M. NIXON	Republican	47,169,911	520
	George S. McGovern	Democratic	29,170,383	17
1976	JIMMY CARTER	Democratic	40,828,657	297
	Gerald R. Ford	Republican	39,145,520	240
1980	RONALD W. REAGAN	Republican	43,899,248	489
	Jimmy Carter	Democratic	35,481,435	49
	John B. Anderson	Independent	5,719,437	
1984	RONALD W. REAGAN	Republican	52,609,797	525
	Walter Mondale	Democratic	36,450,613	13
1988	GEORGE BUSH	Republican	47,946,000	426
	Michael Dukakis	Democratic	41,016,000	112
1992	WILLIAM CLINTON (Min.)*	Democratic	43,738,275	370
	George Bush	Republican	38,167,416	168
	H. Ross Perot	Independent	19,237,247	
1996	WILLIAM CLINTON	Democratic	45,628,667	379
	Robert Dole	Republican	37,869,435	159
	H. Ross Perot	Reform	7,874,283	

* "Min." indicates minority president—one receiving less than 50 percent of all popular votes.

Presidents and Vice Presidents

Term	President	Vice President
1789–1793	George Washington	John Adams
1793–1797	George Washington	John Adams
1797–1801	John Adams	Thomas Jefferson
1801–1805	Thomas Jefferson	Aaron Burr
1805–1809	Thomas Jefferson	George Clinton
1809–1813	James Madison	George Clinton (d. 1812)
1813–1817	James Madison	Elbridge Gerry (d. 1814)
1817–1821	James Monroe	Daniel D. Tompkins
1821–1825	James Monroe	Daniel D. Tompkins
1825–1829	John Quincy Adams	John C. Calhoun
1829–1833	Andrew Jackson	John C. Calhoun (resigned 1832)
1833–1837	Andrew Jackson	Martin Van Buren
1837–1841	Martin Van Buren	Richard M. Johnson
1841–1845	William H. Harrison (d. 1841) John Tyler	John Tyler
1845–1849	James K. Polk	George M. Dallas
1849–1853	Zachary Taylor (d. 1850) Millard Fillmore	Millard Fillmore

Term	President	Vice President
1853–1857	Franklin Pierce	William R. D. King (d. 1853)
1857–1861	James Buchanan	John C. Breckinridge
1861–1865	Abraham Lincoln	Hannibal Hamlin
1865–1869	Abraham Lincoln (d. 1865) Andrew Johnson	Andrew Johnson
1869–1873	Ulysses S. Grant	Schuyler Colfax
1873–1877	Ulysses S. Grant	Henry Wilson (d. 1875)
1877–1881	Rutherford B. Hayes	William A. Wheeler
1881–1885	James A. Garfield (d. 1881) Chester A. Arthur	Chester A. Arthur
1885–1889	Grover Cleveland	Thomas A. Hendricks (d. 1885)
1889–1893	Benjamin Harrison	Levi P. Morton
1893–1897	Grover Cleveland	Adlai E. Stevenson
1897–1901	William McKinley	Garret A. Hobart (d. 1899)
1901–1905	William McKinley (d. 1901) Theodore Roosevelt	Theodore Roosevelt
1905–1909	Theodore Roosevelt	Charles W. Fairbanks
1909–1913	William H. Taft	James S. Sherman (d. 1912)
1913–1917	Woodrow Wilson	Thomas R. Marshall
1917–1921	Woodrow Wilson	Thomas R. Marshall
1921–1925	Warren G. Harding (d. 1923) Calvin Coolidge	Calvin Coolidge
1925–1929	Calvin Coolidge	Charles G. Dawes
1929–1933	Herbert C. Hoover	Charles Curtis
1933–1937	Franklin D. Roosevelt	John N. Garner
1937–1941	Franklin D. Roosevelt	John N. Garner
1941–1945	Franklin D. Roosevelt	Henry A. Wallace
1945–1949	Franklin D. Roosevelt (d. 1945) Harry S Truman	Harry S Truman
1949–1953	Harry S Truman	Alben W. Barkley
1953–1957	Dwight D. Eisenhower	Richard M. Nixon
1957–1961	Dwight D. Eisenhower	Richard M. Nixon
1961–1965	John F. Kennedy (d. 1963) Lyndon B. Johnson	Lyndon B. Johnson
1965–1969	Lyndon B. Johnson	Hubert H. Humphrey, Jr.
1969–1973	Richard M. Nixon	Spiro T. Agnew
1973–1977	Richard M. Nixon (resigned 1974) Gerald R. Ford	Spiro T. Agnew (resigned 1973); Gerald R. Ford Nelson Rockefeller
1977–1981	Jimmy Carter	Walter F. Mondale
1981–1985	Ronald Reagan	George Bush
1985–1989	Ronald Reagan	George Bush
1989–1993	George Bush	J. Danforth Quayle III
1993–1997	William Clinton	Albert Gore, Jr.
1997–	William Clinton	Albert Gore, Jr.

Ratification of the Constitution   *Admission of States to the Union*

State	Date	Order of Admission	State	Date of Admission	Order of Admission	State	Date of Admission
1 Delaware	Dec. 7, 1787	14	Vermont	March 4, 1791	33	Oregon	Feb. 14, 1859
2 Pennsylvania	Dec. 12, 1787	15	Kentucky	June 1, 1792	34	Kansas	Jan. 29, 1861
3 New Jersey	Dec. 18, 1787	16	Tennessee	June 1, 1796	35	West Virginia	June 20, 1863
4 Georgia	Jan. 2, 1788	17	Ohio	March 1, 1803	36	Nevada	Oct. 31, 1864
5 Connecticut	Jan. 9, 1788	18	Louisiana	April 30, 1812	37	Nebraska	March 1, 1867
6 Massachusetts	Feb. 7, 1788	19	Indiana	Dec. 11, 1816	38	Colorado	Aug. 1, 1876
(inc. Maine)		20	Mississippi	Dec. 10, 1817	39	North Dakota	Nov. 2, 1889
7 Maryland	Apr. 28, 1788	21	Illinois	Dec. 3, 1818	40	South Dakota	Nov. 2, 1889
8 South Carolina	May 23, 1788	22	Alabama	Dec. 14, 1819	41	Montana	Nov. 8, 1889
9 New Hampshire	June 21, 1788	23	Maine	March 15, 1820	42	Washington	Nov. 11, 1889
10 Virginia	June 26, 1788	24	Missouri	Aug. 10, 1821	43	Idaho	July 3, 1890
11 New York	July 26, 1788	25	Arkansas	June 15, 1836	44	Wyoming	July 10, 1890
12 North Carolina	Nov. 21, 1789	26	Michigan	Jan. 26, 1837	45	Utah	Jan. 4, 1896
13 Rhode Island	May 29, 1790	27	Florida	March 3, 1845	46	Oklahoma	Nov. 16, 1907
		28	Texas	Dec. 29, 1845	47	New Mexico	Jan. 6, 1912
		29	Iowa	Dec. 28, 1846	48	Arizona	Feb. 14, 1912
		30	Wisconsin	May 29, 1848	49	Alaska	Jan. 3, 1959
		31	California	Sept. 9, 1850	50	Hawaii	Aug. 21, 1959
		32	Minnesota	May 11, 1858			

Estimates of Total Costs and Number of Battle Deaths of Major U.S. Wars*

	Total Costs** (Millions of Dollars)	Original Costs	Number of Battle Deaths
Vietnam Conflict	352,000	140,600	47,355[†]
Korean Conflict	164,000	54,000	33,629
World War II	664,000	288,000	291,557
World War I	112,000	26,000	53,402
Spanish-American War	6,460	400	385
Civil War { Union only	12,952	3,200	140,414
Civil War { Confederacy (est.)	N.A.	1,000	94,000
Mexican War	147	73	1,733
War of 1812	158	93	2,260
American Revolution	190	100	6,824

* Deaths from disease and other causes are not shown. In earlier wars especially, owing to poor medical and sanitary practices, non-battle deaths substantially exceeded combat casualties.

** The difference between total costs and original costs is attributable to continuing postwar payments for such items as veterans' benefits, interest on war debts, etc.

[†] 1959–1990

Sources: *Historical Statistics of the United States, Statistical Abstract of the United States,* relevant years, and *The World Almanac and Book of Facts, 1986.*

Photograph Credits

Index